Government Publications

A Guide to Bibliographic Tools

4th Edition

Prepared by
Vladimir M. Palic
Specialist in Government Document Bibliography
Serial Division

LIBRARY OF CONGRESS   WASHINGTON   1975

Library of Congress Cataloging in Publication Data

Palic, Vladimir M
  Government publications: a guide to bibliographic tools.

  Editions of 1927 and 1930, by J. B. Childs, published under title: An account of government document bibliography in the United States and elsewhere. Third ed., by J. B. Childs, published in 1942 under title: Government document bibliography in the United States and elsewhere.
  1. United States—Government publications—Bibliography. 2. Government publications—Bibliography. I. Childs, James Bennett, 1896–   . An account of government document bibliography in the United States and elsewhere. II. United States. Library of Congress. Serial Division. III. Title.

Z7164.G7C5   1975   016.01573   74–34440
ISBN 0–8444–0154–4

For sale by the Superintendent of Documents, U.S. Government Printing Office
Washington, D.C. 20402 - Price $6.70
Stock Number 030-001-00059-1

Foreword

The expansion of government at all levels—international, national, provincial or state, and local—has resulted in increasing government influence on the life of each citizen. Concomitant with this development is the proliferation of published directives, regulations, reports, technical studies, and other informational issuances in such volume that no one engaged in a business or profession, no financial tycoon, educator, researcher, farmer, housewife, welfare recipient, or unemployed person can function without some reference to government publications. Yet, in few areas of recorded human knowledge have control and bibliographic aids been so little systematized.

Librarians and others, both inside and outside government, who are the middlemen between the user and the producer have long recognized the problem and have made monumental efforts to provide guides to the materials. Such works as they have produced, however, are also in need of bibliographic control. The Library of Congress has been among the institutions that have attempted to do something about the situation, and one of its efforts, James B. Childs' *Government Document Bibliography in the United States and Elsewhere,* first published in 1927 when the problem was simpler, has become a classic in the library world.

The present work, designed to provide the prospective user as well as the trained researcher and librarian with a guide to the maze, is a direct descendant of the Childs essay. The extent to which the mass of published material has grown is underscored by the contrasting physical size of the two publications; Childs' was a 78-page pamphlet containing approximately 400 entries whereas this book of over 400 pages cites more than 3,000 titles.

It is our hope that many bewildered seekers after knowledge will find this a useful bibliographic tool.

S. BRANSON MARLEY, JR.
Chief, Serial Division

Preface

Bibliographic control of official publications in the beginning of this century was far from satisfactory. There seemed to be a lack of awareness of the importance of bibliographic tools for research in government publications. The United States was for a long time a pioneer in this field. The Printing Act of January 12, 1895 (28 Stat. 601–624), not only established centralized printing and distribution of federal documents but also instructed the Superintendent of Documents to provide appropriate tools for the bibliographic control of the documents published. Even before the enactment of the Printing Act, Benjamin Perley Poore compiled by order of Congress *A Descriptive Catalogue of the Government Publications of the United States*, covering the period September 5, 1774, to March 4, 1881 (Washington, Govt. Print. Off., 1885. 1392 p.), and John H. Hickox published his unofficial *United States Government Publications; a Monthly Catalogue*, from 1885 to 1894 (Washington, 1885–96).

Abroad, the bibliographic activities in the field of government publications had a much slower start, with a few exceptions. Great Britain is one of the outstanding exceptions. Catalogs of parliamentary papers were printed as early as 1807 and 1836. Other countries, such as Italy, Germany, the Netherlands, Sweden, Japan, and Australia, began publication of separate government document bibliographies mainly in the 1920's and 1930's. Official publications were often included in existing national bibliographies.

The impact of the Second World War and the increased interest in the authoritative information on all aspects of life contained in official documents brought an extraordinary impetus to governmental publication activities everywhere. James B. Childs wrote in 1942, "More and more the importance of government documentation is being recognized, despite the refractory nature of much of the material" (*Government Document Bibliography in the United States and Elsewhere*, 3d ed. Washington, Govt. Print. Off., 1942, Introduction). At the same time, the constantly increasing number of national governments and the proliferation of official and semiofficial agencies, bureaus, commissions, and services, as well as a substantially increasing number of international governmental organizations, contributed much to a government publication explosion. It became obvious that, without systematic bibliographical controls, the situation would get out of hand; valuable reports or documents would "disappear in the wings of oblivion," [1] and the increasing quantity of official publications would make the task of bibliographers and compilers of catalogs or lists of official documents more and more difficult. The problem was well defined in the introductory notes to a recent list of New York state official publications:

With an ever increasing number of official documents being issued by the units of New York State Government, the task of assuring their bibliographic control becomes, from year to year, more difficult. The quantity of ephemera and the proliferation of quasi-official agencies and their publications, adds to the complexity of the task. Finally, the many production forms, from letterpress through multilith to photocopy, that a publication may take, can cause the less persistent bibliographer to throw up his hands in despair. [2]

If we multiply this situation in the state of New York by the number of states, countries, international governmental organizations, and their component elements, and take into account the changes occurring at frequent intervals, the complexity of bibliographic control emerges in its true proportions.

This guide outlines bibliographic aids in the field of official publications issued by the United States, foreign countries, and international governmental organizations. It is intended to be a practical guide directing the researcher, the student, and, last but not least, the reference librarian to bibliographic tools which may help him to identify or locate the materials needed. Generally, current tools, wherever available, are cited first. Retrospective and secondary sources, as well as certain specialized bibliographies which list or include official publications, are also cited. Throughout the guide, the Library of Congress catalog entries and call numbers are provided.

Entries marked DLC (i.e., Library of Congress) either have not been cataloged at the time of the preparation of the *Guide* or are kept in the Library on a "current issues only" basis. Entries marked DLC LL are in the custody of the Law Library. Those without any indication of classification or location could not be identified in the Library of Congress.

The material is arranged by geographic areas, with U.S. federal, state, and local government publications listed separately. Foreign countries are grouped in five geographic areas: Western Hemisphere (including Canada, the Caribbean area, and Central and South America), Europe, Africa, Near East, and Asia and the Pacific area. International governmental organizations are the subject of a separate section.

A short history of each U.S. government agency is included, indicating also principal changes in name. Similar brief notes are included for U.S. states. Information on a foreign country includes a brief note on its more recent history, or at least the date of independence. For interna-

---

[1] A phrase coined by George B. Galloway in his *History of the United States House of Representatives* (Washington, U.S. Govt. Print. Off., 1962) p. 8.

[2] *Official Publications of the State of New York* (Albany, New York State Library, 1969) Introduction.

tional governmental organizations the date of establishment and the abbreviation of the English name is given.

The terms "government publications," official publications," "government documents," official documents," "public documents," etc., are used in the guide in these varied forms. For a detailed explanation of the term, see "Government Publications (Documents)" in the *Encyclopedia of Library and Information Science* (New York, M. Dekker 1968+) v. 10, p. 38.

The bibliographic material itself is not limited to government publication bibliographies alone, since relatively little of such material exists for many of the countries and areas. References have therefore been made to catalogs, checklists, pricelists, indexes, accessions lists, selected general bibliographies containing substantial information on government publications, and other indirect aids. Many of these tools are far from ideal sources of bibliographic information; their use requires time and patience, and they are not always readily available, but often these are the only means to identify a document or a report from years ago. Annotations of the bibliographical entries, kept as brief as possible, outline the scope and the period covered, if this is not evident from the entry itself. Quotations from the introduction or other prefatory notes are used in some annotations. Translation of foreign-language titles, if not included in the entry proper, is generally given in the annotation.

It also should be noted that general bibliographies which include listings of publications relating to a number of government agencies, countries or other territorial jurisdictions, or international organizations are included here only under an appropriate general heading. The citation is not repeated under the individual agencies, countries, etc., unless a substantial part of such a bibliographic tool is devoted to a specific area.

The index to the guide includes selected personal and corporate authors, titles of works, names of geographical areas, countries, provinces, states, etc., and names of international governmental organizations

Most of the bibliographic material included in the guide is found in the collections of the Library of Congress. In some instances (e.g., U.S. states), however, inquiries were sent to area libraries soliciting help in identifying additional bibliographic aids. Extensive use was made of the retrospective material contained in James B. Childs' *Government Document Bibliography in the United States and Elsewhere,* which in fact served as the basis for the present guide. Special gratitude is expressed here to Mr. Childs, honorary consultant in government document bibliography to the Library of Congress, whose assistance and advice in the compilation of the guide were invaluable. To many staff members of the Library of Congress, mainly in the Serial Division, the Orientalia Division, and the African Section of the General Reference and Bibliography Division, goes sincere appreciation for their help.

There is no doubt that many important bibliographic tools were over-looked, particularly in the field of foreign official publications. Also, some recent works may have been omitted. Generally December 31, 1971, was the closing date for inclusion in the guide, but a number of works published later came to our attention and have been included. The compilation of a guide of this nature and scope necessarily entails errors and omissions. The wide range of entries in foreign languages contributed much to the complexity of problems encountered during the compilation. Any corrections and suggestions of additional sources of information will therefore be most welcome.

VLADIMIR M. PALIC

Contents

Government Publications
in General

James B. Childs' *Government Document Bibliography in the United States and Elsewhere*, 3d ed. (Washington, Govt. Print. Off., 1942. xviii, 78 p. Z7164.G7C5) may be considered a pioneer work in the broad field of guides to bibliographies of official publications. It was first published in 1927 under the title *An Account of Government Document Bibliography in the United States and Elsewhere.* The introduction to the third edition gives an overall picture of bibliographic activities concerning government publications in the pre-World War II period. In the main body of the publication, divided into five sections (United States, Confederate States of America, states, foreign countries, and League of Nations), there are approximately 400 entries for bibliographies, catalogs, lists, etc., of official publications.

There are two other retrospective manuals dealing exclusively with government publications. Everett Somerville Brown's *Manual of Government Publications, United States and Foreign* (New York, Appleton-Century-Crofts, 1950. 121 p. Z7164.G7B85) is a description of basic bibliographic tools, concerning mainly publications of U.S. federal and state governments, Great Britain, Austria, France, Germany, Ireland, Italy, Soviet Russia, Latin America, Near and Far East, and three international organizations (the League of Nations, the Permanent Court of International Justice and its successor, the International Court of Justice, and the United Nations).

UNESCO's *Étude des bibliographies courantes des publications officielles nationales; A Study of Current Bibliographies of National Official Publications*, compiled by the International Committee for Social Sciences Documentation and edited by Jean Meyriat (Paris, 1958. 260 p. Z7164.G7I5), is a bilingual manual which resulted from a survey, conducted in 1954-55, of bibliographical services in various countries. In the summary guide and the inventory by countries, the manual gives first a comprehensive picture of various types of government publications and their bibliographic control in general and then describes printing and distribution, lists, catalogs and bibliographies, and principal official publications in individual countries. Countries are arranged by geographic areas, in French alphabetical order: Afrique, Amérique du Nord, Amérique du Sud, Asie et Pacifique-Sud, Europe, Moyen-Orient, and Union des républiques soviétiques socialistes.

3

An overall picture of post-World War II developments in the bibliographic control of official publications in some 50 countries is presented
in the article "Government Publications," by James B. Childs in *Library
Trends* (v. 15, Jan. 1967: 378–397). Another article by the same author
entitled "Current Bibliographies of National Official Publications," in
the *Herald of Library Science* (Varanasi, India; v. 5, Jan. 1966: 19–27),
also deals with various problems concerning the official publications of
national governments.

The most recent contribution of James B. Childs to the bibliographic
control of government documents in general is the section "Government
Publications (Documents)" appearing in the 10th volume of the *Encyclopedia of Library and Information Science* (New York, M. Dekker,
1968+ Z1006.E57). It is a survey of the history, printing, and bibliographic control of official publications in some 70 countries.

Following are guides and general or specialized bibliographies, as well
as leading library catalogs which include government publications:

Avicenne, Paul.   Bibliographical services throughout the world 1965–69. Paris, Unesco,
1972.303 p. (Documentation, libraries, and archives. Bibliographies and reference
works, no. 1)   Z1008.A95
    Previously published, since 1951, as "Unesco bibliographical handbooks," no.
    4, 9, and 11. Kept up to date by Unesco's bimonthly *Bibliography, Documenta-
    tion, Terminology* (Z1007.B5775).

Besterman, Theodore.   A world bibliography of bibliographies and of bibliographical
catalogues, calendars, abstracts, digests, indexes, and the like. 4th ed., rev. and
greatly enl. throughout. Lausanne, Societas Bibliographica [1965–66] 5 v.
                                                                             Z1002.B5685

Bibliographical services throughout the world; annual report. 1st/2d+ 1951/53+ Paris,
UNESCO.   Z1008.U54
    Compilers: 1951/53, L. N. Malclès (Unesco bibliographical handbooks, 4);
    1950/59, R. L. Collison (Unesco bibliographical handbooks, 9) ; 1960/64, P.
    Avicenne (Unesco bibliographical handbooks, 11).
    Continued for 1965/69 as Unesco's "Documentation, libraries, and archives.
    Bibliographies and reference works, no. 1," compiled by Paul Avicenne (see above).

Documents to the people. v. 1+ Sept. 1972+ Springfield, Ill., [Printed by the Illinois
State Library]   Z688.G6D6
    Issued by American Library Association's Government Documents Round
    Table. Includes information mainly on U.S. federal, state, and local government
    publications. Occasionally it includes information and bibliographic notes on
    international organization and foreign government documentation.

Goris, Hendrika.   List of national development plans. 2d ed. [Washington] International Bank for Reconstruction and Development, Development Services Dept.,
1968. 129 1.   Z7164.E15G6 1968

Government publications review; an international journal.   v. 1, no. 1+ Fall 1973+
Elmsford, N.Y., SEBD Publications, Inc.   DLC
    Reports on "government documents production, distribution, library handling
    and use of documents at all levels of government: federal, state and municipal,
    UN and international agencies and all countries."

Malclès, Louise N. Manuel de bibliographie. 2. éd. entièrement refondue et mise à jour. Paris, Presses universitaires de France, 1969 [ᶜ1963] 366 p.   Z1002.M28 1969
Lists general and specialized bibliographies, including bibliographies of government publications and other reference materials.

——— Les sources du travail bibliographique. Préf. de Julien Cain. Genève, E. Droz, 1950–58. 3 v. in 4.   Z1002.M4
Contents: t. 1. Bibliographies générales.—t. 2. Bibliographies spécialisées; sciences humaines. 2 v.—t. 3. Bibliographies spécialisées; sciences exactes et techniques.
Bibliographies of official publications are listed mainly in v. 2, p. 201–221 and p. 553–632.

Marshallsay, Diana. Official publications: survey of the current situation. [Southampton] University of Southampton, 1972. 31 p. (Southampton University Library. Occasional paper no. 3)   Z674.S63 no. 3
A discussion of official publications, mainly British, but also those of international governmental organizations and foreign governments.

Mason, John Brown. Research resources; annotated guide to the social sciences. Santa Barbara, Calif., ABC–Clio, 1968–71. 2 v.   Z7161.M36
Partial contents: v. 2. Official publications: U.S. government, United Nations, international organizations, and statistical sources.

Public Affairs Information Service. Bulletin. Annual cumulation. 1st+ 1915+ New York.   Z7163.P9
The *Bulletin* is issued weekly except for the last two weeks of each quarter and cumulated five times a year, the last being the annual. It is described as "a selective subject list of the latest books, pamphlets, government publications, reports of public and private agencies and periodical articles, relating to economic and social conditions, public administration and international relations, published in English throughout the world."

The Statesman's year-book; statistical and historical annual of the states of the world. Rev. after official returns. 1st+ 1864+ New York, St. Martin's Press.   JA51.S7
From 1866 includes lists of selected official and nonofficial publications for each country. From 1949 includes international governmental organizations and their publications.

Thiele, Walter. Official map publications: a historical sketch, and a bibliographical handbook of current maps and mapping services in the United States, Canada, Latin America, France, Great Britain, Germany, and certain other countries. Chicago, American Library Association, 1938. xvi, 356 p.   Z6021.T43

Totok, Wilhelm, Rolf Weitzel, *and* Karl-Heinz Weimann. Handbuch der bibliographischen Nachschlagewerke. 3 erw., völlig neu bearb. Aufl., Frankfurt a. M., V. Klostermann [1966] xxiv, 362 p.   Z1002.T68 1966
Lists of government publications appear on p. 100–106.

United Nations Educational, Scientific and Cultural Organization. Manuel des échanges internationaux de publications, préparé avec le concours de J. L. Dargent. Handbook on the international exchange of publications, prepared in collaboration with J. L. Dargent. [Paris] 1950. 369 p. (*Its* Publication 617)   Z690.U45
Lists bibliographies, catalogs, checklists, etc., of official publications (p. 138–164). Most of these were omitted from later editions.

U.S. *Library of Congress. General Reference and Bibliography Division.* Current national bibliographies. Washington, 1955. 132 p.   Z1002.A2U52
A reprint by Greenwood Press, New York, was published in 1968.

Walford, Albert J., *ed.* Guide to reference material. 2d ed. London, Library Association, 1966–70. 3 v.   Z1035.W252
    Lists of government publications appear in v. 2, which covers classes 1, 2, 3,
and 9 of the Universal Decimal Classification, and in v. 3, p. 156–164.

Wilcox, Jerome K. Bibliography of new guides and aides to public documents use,
1953–1956. New York, Special Libraries Association, 1957. 16 p. (SLA bibliography
no. 2)   Z7164.G7W5
    Covers general and special guides, bibliographies and indexes to publications
of U.S. and foreign governments and international organizations.

Winchell, Constance M. Guide to reference books. 8th ed. Chicago, American Library
Association, 1967. xx, 741 p.   Z1035.W79 1967
    Section AH (p. 155–163) lists government publication bibliographies.
—— —— Supplement. 1st+ 1965/66+ Chicago, American Library Association.
                                                                      Z1035.W79 Suppl.

Printed catalogs of large national libraries represent another source
of bibliographic information on official publications of individual countries and of international governmental organizations.

British Museum. *Dept. of Printed Books.* General catalogue of printed books. London,
W. Cloves, 1931–54. 51 v.   Z921.B868
—— —— Volumes I–III Supplement. London, W. Cloves, 1932. 38 p.
                                                                      Z921.B868 Suppl.

—— General catalogue of printed books. Photolithographic edition to 1955. London,
Trustees of the British Museum, 1959–66 [v. 1, 1965] 263 v.   Z921.B87
—— —— Additions. 1963+ London, Trustees of the British Museum. annual.
                                                                          Z921.B8702
—— —— Ten-year supplement, 1956–1965. London, Trustees of the British
Museum, 1968+   Z921.B8703

Paris. Bibliothèque nationale. Catalogue général des livres imprimés: auteurs, collectivités-auteurs, anonymes, 1960–1964. Paris, 1965+   Z927.P1957
    Official publications are listed under corporate entries (collectivités-auteurs)
and "anonymes." The previous *Catalogue général . . . Auteurs* (Paris, Imprimerie
nationale, 1897+ Z927.P2) does not include collectivités-auteurs and anonymes.,
thus excluding a great majority of government publications.

Holdings of the Library of Congress and other American libraries are
covered by the following catalogs:

The National union catalog; a cumulative author list representing Library of Congress
printed cards and titles reported by other American libraries. 1956+ Washington.
                                                                          Z881.A1U372
    Printed in nine monthly issues, three quarterly cumulations, annual cumula-
tions for four years and a quinquennial in the fifth.
    First quinquennial cumulation covers 1958–62; the entries for 1956–57 were
combined with the 1953–55 annual volumes of the *Library of Congress Catalog
. . . Books: Authors,* in a cumulation published in 1958 by J. W. Edwards, Ann
Arbor, Mich.
    Supersedes *Library of Congress Catalog . . . Books: Authors.*

—— Register of additional locations. June 1965+ Washington, Library of Congress.
                                                                          Z881.A1U3722

———— LC card number index. Jan. 1969+ Marblehead, Mass.   Z881.A1U3723
   Issues for Jan. 1969–Nov. 1969 published by American Indexing Co.; Feb.
   1970+ by Library & Information Services Co.

The National union catalog, pre-1956 imprints; a cumulative author list representing
   Library of Congress printed cards and titles reported by other American libraries.
   Compiled and edited with the cooperation of the Library of Congress and the
   National Union Catalog Subcommittee of the Resources Committee of the Re-
   sources and Technical Services Division, American Library Association. London,
   Mansell, 1968+   Z881.A1U518
       When completed, the catalog will consist of some 600 volumes and will su-
   persede all previous author catalogs of the Library of Congress.

Following are present catalogs of the holdings of the Library of
Congress:

A Catalog of books represented by Library of Congress printed cards issued to July 31,
   1942. Ann Arbor, Mich., Edwards Bros., 1942–46. 167 v.   Z881.A1C3
   ———— Supplement: cards issued August 1, 1942–December 31, 1947. Ann Arbor,
   J. W. Edwards, 1948. 42 v.   Z881.A1C312
       Reprinted by Pageant Books, *New York, and Paterson, N.J.*, 1958–60.

Library of Congress and National union catalog author lists, 1942–1962: a master
   cumulation. Compiled by the editorial staff of the Gale Research Company. Detroit,
   Gale Research Co., 1969–71. 152 v.   Z881.A1L63
       "Comprising a cumulation of entries appearing in the following:
   Catalog of books represented by Library of Congress printed cards—Supplement,
   1942–1947; The Library of Congress author catalog, 1948–1952; The National
   union catalog: a cumulative author list, 1953–1957 [and] 1958–1962."

U.S. *Library of Congress.*   Library of Congress catalog; a cumulative list of works rep-
   resented by Library of Congress printed cards. Books: authors. Jan. 1947–1955.
   Washington. 46 v.   Z881.A1U37
       Annual vol. for 1947 not issued as all the cards for that year appeared in the
   Supplement to the *Catalog of Books Represented by Library of Congress Printed
   Cards.* Title varies. Cumulative vols. for 1948–52 published in Ann Arbor, Mich.,
   by J. W. Edwards. Superseded by the *National Union Catalog; a Cumulative
   Author List.*

   ———— Library of Congress catalog—Books: subjects; a cumulative list of works represented by Library of Congress printed cards. Jan./Mar. 1950+ Washington.
                                                                Z881.A1U375
       Printed in three quarterly issues, an annual cumulation for four years, and
   a quinquennial in the fifth. Title varies.

PART I

United States of America

FEDERAL GOVERNMENT

Laurence F. Schmeckebier has pointed out that:

> In number and variety the publications of the government of the United States probably exceed those of any other government or of any commercial publisher. In size they range from pamphlets to ponderous volumes, and in content they vary from articles with a popular appeal to technical treatises of value mostly to the trained scientist. Taken as a whole, they constitute a great library covering almost every field of human knowledge and endeavor.[1]

In quantity and quality, the bibliographical literature on U.S. federal publications is extensive. No attempt will be made here to describe these bibliographic tools in great detail; but the reader will be referred to sources which do. Emphasis here will be placed on projecting a publication's usefulness to the researcher in terms of period and subject coverage. Significant works are presented in this chapter under the following major categories: guides and general bibliographies, Congress, federal agencies, and specialized bibliographies.

GUIDES AND GENERAL BIBLIOGRAPHIES

The basic guide to U.S. government publications is still Laurence F. Schmeckebier's *Government Publications and Their Use*, revised and updated by Roy B. Eastin, 2d rev. ed. (Washington, Brookings Institution, 1969. 502 p. Z1223.Z7S3 1969). Although a guide for rather advanced students, it will provide a quick reference answer for even the casual researcher. Its scope is defined in the foreword:

> The purpose of this volume is to describe the basic guides to government publications, to indicate the uses and limitations of available indexes, catalogs and bibliographies, to explain the systems of numbering and methods of titling, to call attention to certain outstanding compilations or series of publications, and to indicate how the publications may be obtained. It is thus a guide to the acquisition and use of government publications and not—even though it cites many publications by title—a catalog, a bibliography, or a checklist.

[1] Laurence F. Schmeckebier, *Government Publications and Their Use* (Washington: Brookings Institution, 1936), p. 1.   Z1223.Z7S3

Another comprehensive guide, although outdated to a certain extent, is Anne Morris Boyd and Ray Elizabeth Rips' *United States Government Publications*, 3d ed., reprinted with corrections (New York, Wilson Co., 1949 [i.e., 1952] xx, 627 p. Z1223.Z7B7 1952). According to the preface: "Although still primarily a textbook for library school students, the practicing librarian confronted with the necessity of providing and using a collection of United States government publications has been given increased consideration." Publications of executive agencies existing at the time (1948) and publications of certain agencies no longer in existence, including many World War II agencies, are treated extensively. It also outlines the history, organization, and duties of agencies.

U.S. federal publications are extensively treated also in three bibliographies mentioned in the preceding chapter, i.e., James B. Childs' *Government Document Bibliography in the United States and Elsewhere*, Everett Somerville Brown's *Manual of Government Publications, United States and Foreign*, and John Brown Mason's *Research Resources, Annotated Guide to the Social Sciences*, vol. 2.

Listed below are guides and other publications which will help the researcher to understand the complicated nature of U.S. official documents and furnish an insight into the past and present organizational structure of the U.S. government.

Andriot, John L. Guide to popular U.S. government publications. [Arlington, Va.] Documents Index, 1960. 125 p.   Z1223.Z7A545
    In two parts, arranged respectively by issuing agency and by subject.

——— Guide to U.S. government serials & periodicals, 1969+ ed. McLean, Va., Documents Index.   Z1223.Z7A574
    "Basic volumes published in March and a supplement, which updates the information through June 30 of each year, issued in September."
    Earlier editions published 1962–67 (pilot edition, 1959). Arrangement is alphabetical by branch of government, department, agency, and subagency. Subordinate field agency publications follow those of the Washington office.

Body, Alexander C. Annotated bibliography of bibliographies on selected government publications and supplementary guides to the Superintendent of Documents classification system. [Kalamazoo] Western Michigan University, 1967. 181 p. Z1223.Z7B65
    ——— ——— Supplement. 1st+ [Kalamazoo] Western Michigan University, 1968–
                                                                            Z1223.Z7B652
    Includes bibliographies, catalogs, and lists of publications issued by federal agencies, a list of abbreviations and symbols, and a list of government authors arranged according to the Superintendent of Documents classification system.

Clarke, Edith E. Guide to the use of United States government publications. Boston, Boston Book Co., 1918. 308 p. (Useful reference series, no. 20)   Z1223.Z7C6
    "... the work is not intended only as a manual for instruction in library training schools; nor for depository libraries only.... in different sections the work addresses itself to very different classes of readers."

Everhart, Elfrida. A handbook of United States public documents. Minneapolis, H. W. Wilson Co., 1910. 320 p.   Z1223.Z7E9
    "The effort has been made, first, to outline for the average inquirer the field

covered by the publishing divisions; and, second, to direct the student to matter necessary in his researches."
Describes and lists early serials and congressional and departmental publications.

Government reference books. 1st+ ed.; 1968–69+ [Littleton, Colo.] Libraries Unlimited.
"A biennial guide to U.S. Government publications."
Compiler: 1968/69– S. Wynkoop.
Arranged by broad subject, it lists bibliographies, directories, indexes, dictionaries, statistical works, handbooks, guides, catalogs, etc., published by government agencies.

Hirschberg, Herbert S., and Carl H. Melinat. Subject guide to United States government publications. Chicago, American Library Assn., 1947. 228 p.   Z1223.Z7H57
"The Guide represents the selection of those books and pamphlets, most of them published during the last twenty years, believed to be the most generally useful in libraries."

Jackson, Ellen P. Subject guide to major United States government publications. Chicago, American Library Association, 1968. 175 p.   Z1223.Z7J32
Originally planned as a revision of *Subject Guide to United States Government Publications*, by H. S. Hirschberg and C. H. Melinat. "... an essentially new work though retaining the arrangement of the earlier book was ... developed."
A bibliography of guides, catalogs, and indexes, compiled by W. A. Katz, is included (p. 159–175).

Leidy, William P. A popular guide to government publications. 3d ed. New York, Columbia University Press, 1968. xvii, 365 p.   Z1223.Z7L4 1968
Titles are arranged under detailed subject headings; the index is only to topic. Titles listed were published mainly between 1961 and mid–1966. Includes publications of the Pan American Union. Earlier editions, published in 1953 and 1963, covered publications issued from 1940 to 1950 and from 1951 to 1960.

Mechanic, Sylvia. Annotated list of selected United States government publications available to depository libraries. Compiled for the University of the State of New York, the New York State Library. New York, H. W. Wilson Co., 1971. 407 p.
Z1223.Z7M3
A list of some 500 basic titles for depository, public, and college libraries. "Catalogs, indexes and guides to United States Government publications," p. 391–395.

Merritt, Leroy C. The United States government as publisher. Chicago, Ill., University of Chicago Press [1943] xv, 179 p. (University of Chicago studies in library science)
Z1223.Z7M35
"It is the objective of the present study to discover the scope of the subject content of the present output of the publishing offices of the United States government and to trace the trend of subject emphasis in government publication since the turn of the century."

Miller, Kathryn N. The selection of United States serial documents for liberal arts colleges. New York, H. W. Wilson Co., 1937. 364 p.   Z1223.Z7M4
"The report attempts to show what place our federal documents should have in the college library. ..."

Powell, John H. The books of a new nation; United States government publications, 1774–1814. Philadelphia, University of Pennsylvania Press [1957] 170 p.
Z1223.Z7P65
"The A. S. W. Rosenbach fellowship in bibliography."
An essay on the most important printed documents of the earliest years of the United States.

Shaw, Thomas S., *ed.*   Federal, state and local government publications. Library trends,
   v. 15, July 1966: 3–194.   Z671.L6173, v. 15
      A survey of the trends in publication, distribution, bibliographic control, and
   cataloging.

Swanton, Walter I.   Guide to United States government publications. Washington,
   Govt. Print. Off., 1918. 206 p. ([U.S.] Office of Education. Bulletin, 1918. no. 2)
                                                                   L111.A6 1918, no. 2
                                                                   Z1223.Z7S9
      The guide lists for each department and agency principal administrative offi-
   cials, general information and duties, and publications.

Tompkins, Dorothy L. C. C.   Materials for the study of federal government. Chicago,
   Public Administration Service, 1948. 338 p.   Z7165.U5T6
      Issued by the Bureau of Public Administration, University of California.
      "It is the purpose of this volume to provide a guide to materials for the study
   of selected, domestic aspects of the federal government.... emphasis has been
   placed on the period 1940–1947."

U.S. *Congress. Senate. Committee on Government Operations.*   Organization of federal
   executive departments and agencies; report. Dec. 31, 1946+ [Washington, U.S.
   Govt. Print. Off.]   JK646.A3
      Issued semiannually from Dec. 31, 1946, to July 1, 1950, and annually from
   Jan. 1, 1951. Changes occurring during the year are listed by departments, agencies, and offices. From 1968, only a chart issued.

U.S. *Library of Congress. National Referral Center for Science and Technology.*   A
   directory of information resources in the United States: federal government, with
   a supplement of government-sponsored information resources. Washington, Library
   of Congress, 1967. 411 p.   AG521.U55
      Lists government agencies in alphabetical order, giving information on their
   areas of interest, holdings of "raw or analyzed data, library materials, specimens
   and museum collections," publications, and information services.

U.S. *Library of Congress. Serial Division.*   Popular names of U.S. government reports;
   a catalog. Rev. and enl. Compiled by Bernard A. Bernier, Jr., and Charlotte M.
   David. Washington, Library of Congress, 1970. 43 p.   Z1223.A199A5 1970
      Earlier edition (1966) compiled by Donald F. Wisdom and William P. Kilroy.
   Citations to reports are arranged alphabetically by popular name. The third
   edition is scheduled for publication in 1975.

U.S. government organization manual. 1935+ Washington, U.S. Govt. Print. Off.
                                                                          JK421.A3
      Published annually by the Office of the Federal Register, National Archives
   and Records Service, with occasional supplements.
      "Representative publications of departments and agencies of the Federal
   Government" were listed in Appendix B from 1940 to 1970/71.

White, Alex S.   Thirty million books in stock. [1961?+] Central Valley, N.Y., Aurea
   Publications.   Z1223.Z9W5
      "Everyone's guide to U.S. Government publications."
      Selected publications are listed under broad subjects.

Wilcox, Jerome K., *comp.*   United States reference publications; a guide to the current reference publications of the federal government. Boston, F. W. Faxon Co.,
   1931. 96 p. (Useful reference series, no. 43)   Z1223.Z7W65
      "This bibliography attempts to bring together into one list the most important
   reference compilations, handbooks, directories, etc., recently or currently issued
   by the federal government."
      Arranged alphabetically by agencies.

―――― ―――― 1932+ supplement. Boston, F. W. Faxon Co. (Useful reference series,
no. 47+) annual.   Z1223.Z7W65 Suppl.

Wyer, James I.   U.S. government documents, federal, state and city. Revised. Chicago,
     American Library Association, 1933. 56 p.   Z1223.W93   1933
          A consolidation, rewritten and revised, of the author's *U.S. Government Docu-
     ments in Small Libraries*, 3d and 4th ed., issued in 1910 and 1914 by the Ameri-
     can Library Association as *Library Handbook* no. 7, with *Government Docu-
     ments (State and City)* issued in 1915 and again in 1922 as chapter 23 of the
     A.L.A. Manual of Library Economy.

Wynkoop, Sally, *and* David W. Parish.   Directories of government agencies. Rochester,
     N.Y., Libraries Unlimited, 1969. 242 p.   Z7165.U5W9
          "The scope of this bibliography includes all directories and sources with im-
     portant directory-type information prepared by branches and departments of
     federal government, federal commissions and authorities, and directories pre-
     pared under contract with a federal agency."

Wynkoop, Sally.   Subject guide to government reference books. Littleton, Colo., Li-
     braries Unlimited, 1972. 276 p.   Z1223.Z7W95
          ". . . essentially a general orientation guide to the most important reference
     books published by the Government Printing Office and government agencies."

Since 1895, the basic and most comprehensive current bibliography of
U.S. government publications has been the *Monthly Catalog of United
States Government Publications*, issued by the U.S. Superintendent of
Documents (Z1223.A18). The title of the *Monthly Catalog* has varied
as follows: January-March 1895, *Catalogue of Publications Issued by the
Government of the United States*; April 1895-June 1907, *Catalogue of
United States Public Documents*; July 1907-June 1933, *Monthly Cata-
logue, United States Public Documents*; July 1933-December 1939,
Monthly Catalog, United States Public Documents; January 1940-Decem-
ber 1950, *United States Government Publications: Monthly Catalog*;
January 1951+ , *Monthly Catalog of United States Government Publications*. Entries in the *Monthly Catalog* are arranged alphabetically by
issuing bodies, using the keyword system (Agriculture Department,
Census Bureau, Education Office, etc.). Before September 1947, it was
arranged by agencies, with bureaus and subordinate units classed under
them. In the 1907/8 catalog, an attempt was made to list publications
by subject, but the 1908/9 catalog reverted to the government-as-author
system. From July 1907 to June 1934 the catalog consisted of 12 numbered volumes and was issued by fiscal rather than calendar years.

A monthly index was first included with the December 1897 issue.
The first annual index appears in the catalog for 1900, continuing from
1908/9 to 1933/34 by fiscal year and from 1935 to date by calendar year.
The original monthly index was changed to a progressively cumulative
monthly to quarterly, semiannual, and annual indexes in 1900. This
practice was discontinued in June 1913, leaving only the annual index
until July 1945, when the monthly index was reintroduced. Decennial
cumulative indexes were compiled for 1941–50 and 1951–60. Currently

a "Directory of United States Government Periodical and Subscription Publications" is included in the February issue of the *Monthly Catalog*, and a "List of Depository Libraries" in the September issue.

Entries in the *Monthly Catalog* have a classification number used in the library of the Division of Public Documents, Superintendent of Documents, which is also used as a catalog number for the sales stock. Symbols after entries show whether the publication is sold by the Superintendent of Documents or by the National Technical Information Service, Springfield, Va. (formerly Clearinghouse for Federal Scientific and Technical Information), and whether distribution is made by issuing office, or publication is for official use only, and which publications are sent to depository libraries.

Indexing of personal authors began with the January 1963 issue of the *Monthly Catalog*. A *Decennial Cumulative Personal Author Index* for the periods 1941–50, 1951–60, and a *Quinquennial Cumulative Personal Author Index* for 1961–65, was published by the Pierian Press, Ann Arbor, Mich., in 1971, edited by Edward Przebienda, lead programmer at the Center for Urban Studies of the University of Michigan.

In addition to the *Monthly Catalog*, the Superintendent of Documents issued from 1928 to 1971 a biweekly *Selected United States Government Publications* (Z1223.A193), which was superseded in 1972 by *Selected U.S. Government Publications*, also a biweekly, listing the most recent publications of general interest. An annual cumulation of the biweekly list has been compiled since 1968 by John L. Andriot and published under the same title (McLean, Va., Documents Index, Z1223.Z9S4).

Since 1898, the Superintendent of Documents has issued from time to time separate lists of public documents for sale, which later developed into numbered price lists, each covering a subject field. At present there are 48 price lists in print, issued in more or less frequently revised editions. Some 40 lists were discontinued, superseded, or merged with others. Many of the older lists may still be useful as reference sources for subjects and periods covered.

The first nine are mostly comprehensive lists of public documents and form a special group:

U.S. *Superintendent of Documents.*   Price list of U.S. public documents for sale by the
Superintendent. Washington, Govt. Print. Off. [1898–1905]   Z1223.A19
   1.   List of U.S. public documents for sale. 1898. 35 p.
   2.   —— 2d ed. 1899. 116 p.
   3.   Price list of U.S. public documents. 3d ed. 1900. 142 p.
   4.   —— Suppl. to 3d ed. 1901. 20 p.
   5.   List of government publications on irrigation for sale 1902. 10 p.
   6.   List of government publications on labor, industries, trusts, and immigration,
         and reports of Industrial Commission for sale. 1902. 9 p.
   7.   List of government publications on inter-oceanic canals, ship subsidy, com-
         merce and transportation, Pacific railroads, and statistics for sale. 1902. 12 p.
   8.   Price list of U.S. public documents for sale. 1903. 127 p.
   9.   Price list of U.S. public documents for sale. 1905. 156 p.

Following is a complete numerical list of the regular series. Asterisks denote price lists currently published; titles vary considerably. Generally, the title of the latest edition is used, often abbreviated.

U.S. *Superintendent of Documents.* [Price list] ... Washington, Govt. Print. Off. [1907+]   Z1223.A191

*10. Laws, rules and regulations. 1907+
10A. Decisions of courts, boards and commissions. 1949–51.
*11. Home economics, foods and cooking. 1907+
12. Water pollution, water purification. 1907–9. Superseded by no. 51.
13. Americana. 1907–8. Superseded by no. 50.
14. Medical research. 1907–8. Superseded by no. 51.
*15. Geology. 1907+
16. Farmers' bulletins. 1907–29.
17. Poultry. 1907–9. Superseded by no. 52.
18. Engineering and surveying. 1908–52. Merged with no. 53.
*19. Army; field manuals and technical manuals. 1908+
19A. List of army regulations. 1950–55?
19B. List of field manuals and technical manuals. 1951–54?
20. Public domain. 1908–47.
*21. Fish and wildlife. 1908+
22. Bird life. 1908. Superseded by no. 52.
23. Dairy industry. 1909. Superseded by no. 38.
24. Indians. 1910–45. Merged with no. 55.
*25. Transportation, highways, roads, and postal service. 1910+
26. Sociology. 1908, 1910. Merged with no. 54.
27. Ethnology. 1908, 1909. Merged with no. 55.
*28. Finance; national economy, accounting, insurance, securities. 1908+
29. Economics. 1910. Merged with no. 28.
30. Natural wonders. 1909. Superseded by no. 35.
*31. Education. 1910+
32. Insular possessions. 1910–45. Merged with no. 60.
*33. Labor. 1909+
*33A. Occupations, professions and job descriptions. 1948+
34. Library of Congress. 1909. (See also no. 83)
*35. National parks, historic sites, national monuments. 1911+
*36. Government periodicals and subscription services. 1910+
*37. Tariff and taxation. 1909+
*38. Animal industry, farm animals, poultry and dairying. 1910+
39. Birds and wild animals. 1909–39. Merged with no. 21.
40. Agricultural chemistry. 1909–28. Merged with no. 46.
*41. Insects, worms, and insects harmful to man, animals and plants. 1909+
*42. Irrigation, drainage and water power. 1909+
*43. Forestry; managing and using forest and range land, including timber and lumber, ranges and grazing, American woods. 1909+
*44. Plants, culture, grading, marketing, and storage of fruits, vegetables, grass, and grain. 1910+
45. Roads. 1909–48. Merged with no. 25.
*46. Soils and fertilizers, soil surveys, erosion, conservation. 1909+
47. Statistics bureau, Agriculture Dept., crop statistics. 1910–14.
*48. Weather, astronomy and meteorology. 1909+
49. Proceedings of Congress. 1909–46.
*50. American history. 1910+ Superseded no. 13.
*51. Health and medical services. 1910+ Superseded no. 12 and no. 14.
*51A. Diseases and physical conditions. 1949+
52. Poultry, birds. 1910–11. Superseded no. 17 and no. 22. Merged with no. 38.
*53. Maps; engineering, surveying. [1911+] Absorbed no. 18.
*54. Political science, government, crime, District of Columbia. 1911+ Superseded no. 26.

*55. Smithsonian Institution, National Museum and Indians. 1911+ Absorbed no. 24, 27, and 56.
 56. Indians, Smithsonian Institution, fine arts. 1911–14. Merged with no. 55.
 57. Astronomy (Astronomical papers). 1912–17. Merged with no. 48.
*58. Mines, explosives, fuel, gasoline, gas, petroleum, minerals. 1913+
*59. Interstate commerce. 1914+
 60. Territories and insular possessions. 1914–60. See also no. 32 and 87.
 61. Panama Canal. 1914–21. See also no. 32, 60, and 87.
*62. Commerce, business, patents, trademarks and foreign trade. 1914+
62A. Foreign trade. 1949–54. Merged with no. 62.
*63. Navy, Marine Corps and Coast Guard. 1914+
*64. Scientific tests, standards, mathematics, physics. 1914+
64A. Masonry. 1948–55.
*65. Foreign relations of the United States. Publications relating to foreign countries. 1915+
 66. Bee culture investigations. 1915.
*67. Immigration, naturalization and citizenship. 1916+
*68. Farm management, foreign agriculture, rural electrification, agricultural marketing. 1916+
 69. Pacific states. 1918–45.
*70. Census publications. 1920+
*71. Child development and other publications relating to children and youth. 1922+
*72. Homes; construction, maintenance, community development. 1924+
 73. Handy books. 1926–42.
 74. A bibliography for debaters. 1929.
 75. Federal specifications. 1934–47.
 76. Government publications of use to consumers. 1934–35.
 77. World War II. National defense, postwar planning. 1944–45.
*78. Social services; aging, family planning, handicapped . . . 1949+
*79. Air force, aviation, civil aviation, naval aviation, Federal Aviation Administration. 1949+
*79A. Space, missiles, the moon, NASA, and satellites; space education, exploration, research, and technology. 1967+
 80. Government forms. 1950–52.
*81. Posters and charts. 1951+
*82. Radio and electricity; electronics, radar and communications. 1951+
*83. Library of Congress. 1951+
*84. Atomic energy and civil defense. 1955+
*85. Defense, veterans' affairs. 1955+
*86. Consumer information; family finances, appliances, recreation, gardening, health and safety, food, house and home, child care, clothing and fabrics. 1964+
*87. States and territories of the United States and their resources. 1967+
*88. Ecology. 1972+

Among retrospective bibliographies, catalogs, checklists, and indexes, mention should be made first of the three basic tools that were compiled and printed in accordance with the Printing Act of Jan. 12, 1895 (28 Stat. 601–624).

The *Monthly Catalog* (1895+), a basic tool for both retrospective and current materials, was described in the preceding paragraphs. The *Document Index*, covering exclusively congressional documents from the 54th Congress, first session, to the 72d Congress, second session (Dec. 2, 1895–Mar. 4, 1933), will be described in the chapter dealing with bibliographic tools to congressional documents and proceedings. The biennial

Document Catalog, covering both congressional and departmental documents from March 1893 to December 1940, will be described below with similar tools dealing with both congressional and departmental publications:

Poore, Benjamin Perley. A descriptive catalogue of the government publications of the United States, September 5, 1774—March 4, 1881. Washington, Govt. Print. Off., 1885. 1392 p. (48th Cong., 2d sess. Senate. Misc. doc. no. 67)   Z1223.A 1885c
  Includes congressional, departmental, and judicial publications, arranged in chronological order, with general index. Reprinted by J. W. Edwards in 1953, and by Johnson Reprint Corporation in 1962.

U.S. *Dept. of the Interior. Division of Documents.* Comprehensive index of the publications of the United States government, 1889–93, by John G. Ames, Superintendent of Documents, Dept. of the Interior. Washington, Govt. Print. Off., 1894. 480 p. (52d Cong., 2d sess. House of Representatives. Misc. doc. no. 95)   Z1223.A13

—— Comprehensive index to the publications of the United States government, 1881–1893, by John G. Ames, Chief of the Document Division, Dept. of the Interior. Washington, Govt. Print. Off., 1905. 1590 p. (58th Cong., 2d sess. House of Representatives. Misc. doc. no. 754)   Z1223.A 1905
  Reprinted by J. W. Edwards, Ann Arbor, Mich., in 1953, and by Johnson Reprint Corp., New York, in 1970.
  A subject index, "compiled in compliance with the provisions of a joint resolution approved March 3, 1897, which directs the preparation of an index to all publications of the government from 1881, the date at which the *Descriptive Catalogue of the Government Publications* by Benj. Perley Poore terminates, to 1893, the date at which the index by the Superintendent of Documents begins . . ."

U.S. *Superintendent of Documents.* Catalog of the public documents of the Congress and of all departments of the government of the United States; the comprehensive index provided for by the Act of Jan. 12, 1895. no. [1]–25: Mar. 4, 1893/June 30, 1895–Jan. 1, 1939/Dec. 31, 1940. Washington, U.S. Govt. Print. Off. 25 no. biennial.
                                                                           Z1223.A13
  Generally known as *Document Catalog,* this is a dictionary catalog, with both congressional and departmental publications listed under corporate and personal author, subject, and distinctive title. Discontinued by resolution of the Joint Committee on Printing, Mar. 24, 1947.

—— Checklist of United States public documents 1789–1909, congressional: to close of Sixtieth Congress; departmental: to end of calendar year 1909. 3d ed., rev. and enl. Comp. under direction of the Superintendent of Documents. Washington, Govt. Print. Off., 1911. 1 v.   Z1223.A113
  Contents: v. 1. Lists of congressional and departmental publications. The proposed v. 2 (index) was never published. Reprinted by J. W. Edwards, Ann Arbor, Mich., in 1953.
  The first edition (1892), prepared by John G. Ames, Superintendent of Documents, was published under the title *List of Congressional Documents from the Fifteenth to the Fifty-first Congress, and of Government Publications Containing Debates and Proceedings of Congress from the First to the Fifty-first Congress, Together with Miscellaneous Lists of Public Documents, with Historical and Bibliographical Notes* (Z1223.A11 1892). The second edition, issued in 1895 by F. A. Crandall, Superintendent of Documents, has the title *Checklist of Public Documents Containing Debates and Proceedings of Congress from the First to the Fifty-third Congress, Together with Miscellaneous Lists of Documents, and Historical and Bibliographical Notes* (Z1223.A11 1895). Between the second and the third edition of the *Checklist,* the Superintendent of Documents in

1902 issued *Tables of and Annotated Index to the Congressional Series of United States Public Documents* (Z1223.A 1902). This was published in two parts: the *Tables*, listing publications from the 15th to 52d Congresses, and the annotated *Index*. This publication forms an integral part of the first two editions of the *Checklist* and has not been entirely superseded, since the index volume to the third edition has never been published.

United States government publications; a monthly catalogue. v. 1–10; Jan. 1885–Dec. 1894. Washington, D.C., J. H. Hickox, 1885–91; W. H. Loudermilk, 1892–[96] 10 v.
Z1223.Z7H5
A forerunner of the *Monthly Catalog*, which was issued from 1895 by the Superintendent of Documents, this is said to include entries for many publications not listed elsewhere.

A comprehensive bibliographic tool which appeared in 1971 on microfilm is the *Checklist of United States Public Documents, 1789–1970.* Prepared by the United States Historical Documents Institute, Washington, D.C., it lists all titles which appear in the shelflists of the Public Documents Library of the Government Printing Office, covering the period 1861 through October 1970. It also includes publications listed in the *Checklist of United States Public Documents, 1789–1909*, the *Monthly Catalog*, and Mary Elizabeth Poole's *Documents Office Classification to 1966.*

The following indexes to the *Checklist* on microfilm were published in 1972:

Lester, Daniel W., *and* Marilyn A. Lester. Checklist of United States public documents, 1789–1970: indexes. Washington, United States Historical Documents Institute, 1972. 5 v.
Z1223.Z7L45
Vol. 4 compiled by the staff of the United States Historical Documents Institute. Contents: v. 1. Superintendent of Documents classification number index of U.S. government author-organizations. Table of contents of microfilm reels.— v. 2. U.S. government author-organization index.—v. 3. Departmental keyword indexes to U.S. government author–organizations.—v. 4. U.S. government serial titles, 1789–1970.—v. 5. Master keyword index to the publication-issuing offices of the U.S. government, 1789–1970.

For the earliest period of U.S. publishing, Charles Evans' *American Bibliography; a Chronological Dictionary of all Books, Pamphlets, and Periodical Publications Printed in the United States of America from the Genesis of Printing in 1639 Down to and Including the Year 1820* (Chicago, Blakely Press, 1903–59. 14 v. Z1215.E92) should also be of assistance to researchers, as well as the following general bibliographies:

Cooper, Gayle. A checklist of American imprints for 1830+ Metuchen, N.J., Scarecrow Press, 1972+
Z1215.C66
Continues the work of Richard H. Shoemaker, *A Checklist of American Imprints for 1820–1829* (see below).

Shaw, Ralph R., *and* Richard H. Shoemaker. American bibliography, a preliminary checklist for 1801–1819. New York, Scarecrow Press, 1958–66. 22 v.   Z1215.S48

Shoemaker, Richard H.   A checklist of American imprints for 1820–1829. New York,
    Scarecrow Press, 1964–71. 10 v.   Z1215.S5
—— —— Title index, compiled by M. Frances Cooper. Metuchen, N.J., Scarecrow
    Press, 1972. 556 p.   Z1215.S5 Suppl.

Tanselle, George T.   Guide to the study of United States imprints. Cambridge, Mass.,
    Belknap Press of Harvard University Press, 1971. 2 v. (lxiv, 1050 p.)   Z1215.A2T35
    "Government documents [B370]," p. 86–108.

There are in the Library of Congress catalog some 800 entries for
bibliographies, catalogs, checklists, indexes, lists, and similar publications under the subject heading "U.S.—Government publications:
—Bibliographies; —Indexes; —Periodicals-Bibliographies; —(Counties)-
Bibliographies; —(Municipal governments)-Bibliographies; —(State governments)-Bibliographies." Many of these bibliographic tools are devoted to specialized subjects, to individual agencies, and to agencies no
longer existing. Some of these tools are not of sufficient value to be
included in bibliographic guides. Researchers probing deeper into the
maze of U.S. government documents, however, would be well advised
not to overlook this important source.

CONGRESS

There are few shortcuts in the search for a congressional document and
no simple guideline to tracing legislation on a given subject. Yet, scores
of reference librarians are faced daily with such problems, as well as
countless researchers, students, and other interested persons who need
to locate a document or a congressional resolution, or learn about a bill.
Outlined here are a few basic steps and indications of some basic tools
essential for locating the information or the desired document. For more
detailed information on congressional procedures, refer to Schmeckebier
and Eastin's *Government Publications and Their Use* (chapter 6), Boyd
and Rips' *United States Government Publications* (chapter 4), John
Brown Mason's *Research Resources* (vol. 2, *Official Publications*, chapter
3), and other sources.

CURRENT LEGISLATION

Legislation can be initiated in the House of Representatives or in the
Senate by the introduction of a bill or a joint resolution. If the number
of the bill or joint resolution is known, the legislative history can be
traced by consulting the section of the biweekly index to the *Congressional Record* entitled "History of Bills and Resolutions," which fur-
nishes information on the author or authors, committee to which the bill
was referred, report number, etc. If the number is not known, the index

must be searched for subject, title, or author. New bills and resolutions
are first listed in the daily issues of the *Congressional Record* and in the
biweekly index of the appropriate period, in numerical order. Otherwise, biweekly indexes list only those bills or resolutions, introduced
earlier, which have been acted upon during the preceding two weeks.

The history of a bill or a resolution can also be traced through the
following sources:

U.S. *Congress. House.* Calendars of the United States House of Representatives and
history of legislation. Washington, U.S. Govt. Print. Off.   J47.A3
The calendar gives information on bills which have been acted upon in either
house of Congress. The final edition, published after the close of each session of
of Congress, lists separately bills which have become law, those that failed to
become law by reason of Presidential veto, and a numerical list of all bills which
have been acted upon.

U.S. *Congress. Senate.* Calendar of business. Washington, U.S. Govt. Print. Off. J37.A3
The calendar gives only the daily order of business.

U.S. *Library of Congress. Legislative Reference Service.* Digest of public general bills
and selected resolutions with index. 74th+ Congress; 1936+ Washington, U.S. Govt.
Print. Off.   DLC LL
Published in five or more cumulative issues during a session of Congress, with
biweekly supplements and a final edition. In seven parts, it includes 1. Status
of measures receiving action; 2. Public laws (enacted during current session) ;
3. Digests of all public bills and resolutions, in numerical order, introduced during current session; 4. Author (sponsor) index; 5. Subject matter index; 6. Specific title index; 7. Identical bill index.

Tracing the history of legislation in past sessions of Congress is some-
what simpler, since all bills and joint resolutions introduced during the
session are listed in numerical order in a single final index to bound
volumes of the *Congressional Record.* The index specifically for the
second session of Congress, however, lists only those bills introduced
during that session and those bills introduced in the first session which
were acted upon during the second session. It should be noted that the
index to bound volumes cannot be used with the daily edition of the
Congressional Record and, vice-versa, the biweekly indexes cannot be
used with the bound volumes, because of the different pagination. An
overall "History of Bills Enacted into Public Law," in numerical order
of laws, is contained in the last "Daily Digest" of the *Congressional
Record* of each session. A list of "Bills Enacted into Public Law," in
numerical order of bills and joint resolutions, is also included in the
final "Daily Digest."

The history of bills and resolutions can also be traced through the
indexes to the Senate and House *Journals,* but these are published only
after the close of the session and do not include information on the
debates.

The following studies give detailed descriptions of legislative procedures:

Thaxter, John H. Printing of Congressional bills. Library resources & technical services. Richmond. v. 7, no. 3, summer 1963: 237–243.   Z671.L7154 vol. 7, no. 3

U.S. Congress. Senate. Enactment of a law; procedural steps in the legislative process, prepared by Floyd M. Riddick, parliamentarian of the Senate. Document no. 35) Govt. Print. Off., 1967. 29 p. (90th Congress, 1st session. Senate. Document no. 35)
KF4945.A35

Zinn, Charles J. How our laws are made. Washington, U.S. Govt. Print. Off., 1969. 57 p. (91st Congress, 1st session. House of Representatives. Document no. 91–127)
KF4945.Z9Z5 1969

Legislative procedures generate directly or indirectly a great number of publications. Bills, resolutions, joint resolutions, and concurrent resolutions form a substantial part of the printed congressional publications and are the starting point of legislative actions which, in turn, generate reports, documents, records of hearings, etc. The great majority of reports deal with proposed legislation, while documents cover an extremely varied field of topics and include many annual or other reports of executive agencies, ordered printed by one or the other house of Congress. Other categories of congressional publications include *Executive Documents* (communications to Congress from the executive branch) and a variety of publications issued by individual congressional committees (e. g., committee prints).

The House and Senate documents and reports are collected into bound volumes to form the Congressional Serial Set. The volumes have been numbered consecutively, beginning with the 15th Congress (1817). Individual documents and reports are numbered separately for each of the four series (currently: Senate reports, House reports, Senate documents, House documents). Numbers run consecutively throughout the two sessions of Congress.

Documents and reports are first listed in the Superintendent of Documents' *Monthly Catalog* and soon after the end of each session in:

U.S. *Superintendent of Documents.* Numerical lists and schedule of volumes of the reports and documents of the 73d+ Congress . . . 1933/34+ Washington [U.S. Govt. Print. Off.] 1934+   Z1223.A15
  Previously included in the *Checklist of United States Public Documents 1789–1909,* and in the *Index to the Reports and Documents of the 54th Congress, 1st Session-72d Congress, 2d Session, Dec. 2, 1895-March 4, 1933 with Numerical Lists and Schedule of Volumes,* also known as *Document Index* (see p. 28).

Hearings are an important part of legislative procedures. The history of a major bill would be incomplete without a close study of any hearings held on it. Indexes to the history of legislation do not refer to hearings, so information on them must be sought in the "Daily Digest" of the

Congressional Record, in the *Monthly Catalog,* in the reports on the bill, or in legislative calendars.

When a law is enacted, it is first published in the form generally called a "slip law," an unbound pamphlet issued separately for each law. After each session of Congress, the laws are published in permanent form in the *Statutes at Large.*

Besides bibliographic tools listed previously, a number of privately published indexes and other publications report currently on legislative activities of the U.S. Congress and on various publications of Congressional committees, including hearings. Following are a few examples:

Checklist of congressional hearings & reports. 1958+ Washington, Bernan Associates.
DLC LL

Congressional Information Service. CIS annual. 1970+ Washington.   KF49.C62
    Covers congressional hearings, reports, committee prints, and other congressional publications. In two parts: pt. 1, Abstracts; pt. 2, Index. Annual cumulation of the monthly and quarterly editions.

Congressional quarterly almanac. v. 1+ Jan./Mar. 1945+ Washington, Congressional Quarterly, Inc.   JK1.C66
    Published quarterly from 1945 to 1947, annually from 1948. Under broad subjects, it analyzes major legislation during the year.

CQ weekly report. [1945+] Washington, Congressional Quarterly, Inc.   JK1.C15
    Reports on major legislation, including committee hearings.

RETROSPECTIVE LEGISLATION

The debates and proceedings of U.S. Congresses have been reported and indexed in the following publications, listed here in chronological order:

1774–89

U.S. *Continental Congress.* Journals of the Continental Congress, 1774–1789. Edited from the original records in the Library of Congress. Washington, U.S. Govt. Print. Off., 1904–37. 34 v.   J10.A5
    Edited in the Division of Manuscripts, Library of Congress: v. 1–15, by Worthington Chauncey Ford; v. 16–27, by Gaillard Hunt; v. 28–31, by John C. Fitzpatrick; v. 32–34, by Roscoe R. Hill.
    Includes, at the end of the journal for each year, bibliographical notes based on Paul Leicester Ford's *Some Materials for a Bibliography of the Official Publications of the Continental Congress, 1774–1789,* (Boston, Public Library, 1890. Z1238.F71). It also includes the *Secret Journals of Acts and Proceedings of Congress.* There is an index for each year. Poore's *Descriptive Catalogue,* mentioned earlier, may also be used with the *Journals.*

1789–1824

U.S. *Congress.* The debates and proceedings in the Congress of the United States; with an appendix, containing important state papers and public documents, and all the laws of a public nature; with a copious index ... [First to] Eighteenth Congress, first session; comprising the period from [March 3, 1789] to May 27, 1824, inclusive. Washington, Gales and Seaton, 1834–56. 42 v.   J11.A4

Generally known as *Annals of Congress,* it was compiled from newspaper and other records of proceedings in the Congress. The indexes, which are separate for the Senate and the House proceedings, each cover one session. The *General Indexes to the Journals of Congress,* compiled by Albert Ordway (see Legislative journals, below) can also be used with the *Annals.*

1824–37

—— Register of debates in Congress, comprising the leading debates and incidents of the second session of the Eighteenth Congress: [Dec. 6, 1824 to the first session of the Twenty-fifth Congress. Oct. 16, 1837] together with an appendix, containing the most important state papers and public documents to which the session has given birth: to which are added the laws enacted during the session, with a copious index to the whole. Washington, Gales & Seaton, 1825–37. 14 v. in 29.   J11.D5

Although published contemporaneously, it is not a verbatim record of the proceedings. Indexes each cover a single session, like the indexes of the *Annals,* and are separate for the Senate and the House proceedings. The 23d, 24th, and the 1st session of the 25th Congresses are covered both by the *Register* and the following *Congressional Globe.*

1833–73

—— The Congressional globe ... [23d Congress to the 42d Congress, Dec. 2, 1833 to March 3. 1873] Washington, Printed at the Globe Office for the editors, 1834–73. 46 v.   J11.G5

Indexes are still separate for the Senate and the House proceedings and are included in the last volume for the session. Index for the 42d Congress, second session, was published as a separate volume. Appendixes to the close of the 39th Congress include messages of the President and reports of cabinet officers. Each appendix has its own index. From 1852, the *Congressional Globe* can generally be considered as a verbatim record of proceedings. Beginning with the 40th Congress (1867), the *Congressional Globe* includes "History of bills and resolutions."

1873–

—— Congressional record; proceedings and debates of the Congress. 43d+ (v. 1+); Mar. 4–26, 1873+ Washington, U.S. Govt. Print. Off.   J11.R5

Issued in three editions: a daily edition, which is reissued in biweekly (green paperbound) edition with index, and a permanent edition, issued at the end of the session, with the text revised and rearranged from the daily edition. It includes an index for the session and the "History of bills and resolutions." During the 43d to 46th Congresses, the *Record* continued the separate indexes for Senate and House proceedings. From the 47th Congress (1882), there is a unified index for both houses of Congress. The "Daily Digest" appeared with the *Record* of the 80th Congress (1947). From January 1968 (90th Congress, 2d session) a new heading, "Extension of Remarks," is used in lieu of "Appendix." Still another heading appeared in February 1970 (91st Congress, 2d session), entitled "Additional remarks (statements) of Senators," where statements, not made orally during the legislative sessions, are inserted in the *Record.*

A microfilm edition of the *Annals of Congress, Register of Debates, Congressional Globe* and the *Congressional Record* (up to and including 1964), was prepared in 1971 by the United States Historical Documents Institute, Washington, D.C., under the title *Proceedings of the U.S. Congress, 1789–1964.* Indexes to the *Proceedings* were published in book form in 101 volumes.

LEGISLATIVE JOURNALS

U.S. *Congress. House.* Journal of the House of Representatives of the United States. [1st to 14th Congress; 1789–1817] New York, Richmond, Philadelphia, Washington.
J24

—— Journal. [15th+ Congress; 1817+] Washington.   J45

U.S. *Congress. Senate.* Journal of the Senate of the United States of America. [1st to 14th Congress; 1789–1817] New York, Philadelphia, Washington.   J21

—— Journal. [15th+ Congress; 1817+] Washington.   J35

—— Journal of the executive proceedings of the Senate of the United States...
Printed by order of the Senate. Washington, 1828+   JK1251.A3
Journal for 1789–Feb. 23, 1829, printed by D. Green; March 4, 1829+ by the Government Printing Office.

Journals are indexed separately in each volume, and a section, "History of bills and resolutions," is also included. For the first 16 Congresses there are the following general indexes to the *Journals*:

Ordway, Albert. General index of the Journals of Congress, from the First to Tenth Congress inclusive. Being a synoptical subject–index of the proceedings of Congress on all public business from 1789 to 1809, with references to the debates, documents, and statutes connected therewith. Washington, Govt. Print. Off., 1880. 151 p. ([U.S.] 46th Cong., 2d sess. House. Report no. 1776)   Z1223.A 1880

—— General index of the Journals of Congress, from the Eleventh to Sixteenth Congress inclusive. Being a synoptical subject-index of the proceedings of Congress on all public business from 1809 to 1821, with references to the debates, documents, and statutes connected therewith. Washington, Govt. Print. Off., 1883. 118 p. ([U.S.] 47th Cong., 1st sess. House. Report no. 1559)   Z1223.A 1883

—— General personal index of the Journals of Congress, from the First to Eighth Congress inclusive. Being an index of the personal record of members of Congress from 1789 to 1805. Washington, Govt. Print. Off., 1885. 134 p. ([U.S.] 48th Cong., 2d sess. House. Rept. 2692)   Z1223.A 1885a

—— General personal index of the Journals of Congress, from the Ninth to the Sixteenth Congress inclusive. Being an index of the personal record of members of Congress from 1805 to 1821. Washington, Govt. Print. Off., 1887. 191 p. ([U.S.] 49th Cong., 1st sess. House. Rept. 3475) Serial no. 2446.   J66 no. 2446

DOCUMENTS, REPORTS, HEARINGS: INDEXES, LISTS

In addition to the bibliographic tools dealing with both Congressional and departmental publications mentioned in the preceding chapter (Guides and general bibliographies), the following lists and indexes will be helpful in identifying retrospective Congressional publications:

Greely, Adolphus W. Public documents of the first fourteen Congresses, 1789–1817. Papers relating to early congressional documents. Washington, Govt. Print. Off., 1900. 903 p. (U.S. 56th Cong., 1st sess., Senate. Doc. no. 428)   Z1223.A 1900

———— ———— [Supplement] Washington, Govt. Print. Off., 1904. Cover title, p. 343–406. Reprinted from the Annual report of the American Historical Association, 1903, v. 1: 343–406.   Z1223.A 1904

Thomen, Harold O.   Checklist of hearings before congressional committees through the Sixty-seventh Congress. Washington, Library of Congress, 1957–59 [pt. 1–3, 1959] 9 pts. in 1 v.   Z1223.Z7T5
    Parts 1–7 are House committee hearings; parts 8–9, Senate committee hearings.

U.S. *Congress. House.*   Index to documents and reports, House of Representatives U.S., 1789–1839 . . . [Washington, 1839?] 2 p. l., 3–247, 129, 152, 380 p.   Z1223.A4   1839a
    Consists of four separately printed indexes, each with its own title page: 1. Index to the executive communications . . . from the commencement of the present form of government until the end of the Fourteenth Congress . . . also an index to all the printed committee reports. 1824. —2. Index to the executive communications and reports of committees . . . from December 3d, 1817, to March 3d, 1823, 15th, 16th & 17th Congress. 1823. —3. A digested index to the executive documents and reports of the committees . . . from the Eighteenth to the Twenty-first Congress, both included. 1832. —4. Index to the executive documents and reports of committees . . . from the Twenty-second to the Twenty-fifth Congress, both included, commencing December 1831, and ending March 1839. [1839]
    Continued in the so-called McPherson's consolidated indexes, i.e.: *Consolidated Index of the Reports of the Committees of the House of Representatives from the Twenty-Sixth to the Fortieth Congress Inclusive* (Washington, Govt. Print. Off., 1869. 158 p.) , and *Consolidated Index of the Executive Documents of the House of Representatives from the Twenty-Sixth to the Fortieth Congress Inclusive* (Washington, Govt. Print. Off., 1870. 393 p.) .| Issued as Miscellaneous documents of the House of Representatives, they are included in the Congressional Serial Set as no. 1386 and no. 1387 (J66) .

———— Index to reports of committees of the House of Representatives, compiled under the direction of the Joint Committee on Printing, by T. H. McKee. Washington, Govt. Print. Off., 1887. 58 v. in 1.   Z1223.A4   1887
    The index covers the 14th to 49th Congresses inclusive. Classified by committees.

U.S. *Congress. House. Library.*   Index to congressional committee hearings in the Library of the United States House of Representatives. Jan. 5, 1937+ Washington, U.S. Govt. Print. Off.   Z1223.A1A3
    Latest edition issued in 1954 includes hearings held before Jan. 1, 1951. A supplement, issued in 1956, lists hearings from Jan. 3, 1949, to Jan. 3, 1955.

U.S. *Congress. Senate.*   [Index to reports of committees of the Senate, compiled under the direction of the Joint Committee on Printing, by T. H. McKee. Washington, Govt. Print. Off., 1887] 36 v. in 1.   Z1223.A3   1887
    The index covers the 14th to 49th Congress inclusive. Classified by committees.

U.S. *Congress. Senate. Library.*   Cumulative index of congressional committee hearings (not confidential in character) from Seventy-fourth Congress (January 3, 1935) through Eighty-fifth Congress (January 3, 1959) in the United States Senate Library. Washington, U.S. Govt. Print. Off., 1959. 823 p.   KF40.H8
———— ———— Quadrennial supplement. From Eighty-sixth Congress (January 7, 1959) through Eighty-seventh Congress (January 3, 1963) Washington, U.S. Govt. Print. Off., 1963. 762 p.   KF40.H8 Suppl.
———— ———— Second quadrennial supplement. From the Eighty-eighth Congress (January 3, 1963) through Eighty-ninth Congress (January 3, 1967) , together with selected committee prints in the United States Senate Library. Washington, U.S. Govt. Print. Off., 1967. 664 p.   KF40.H8 Suppl. 2

———— ———— Third quadrennial supplement. From the Ninetieth Congress (January 10, 1967) through Ninety-first Congress (January 2, 1971), together with selected committee prints in the United States Senate Library. Washington, U.S. Govt. Print. Off., 1971. 695 p.   KF40.H8 Suppl. 3

———— Important serial documents published by the government and how to find them. 1896. Washington, Govt. Print. Off., 1897. 91 p. (U.S. 54th Cong., 2d sess. Senate doc. no. 103)   Z1223.A 1897
   "Its sole purpose is to assist those who desire quick and ready reference to the principal documents published by order of Congress." The 1901 edition has title: *Finding List to Important Serial Documents ... in the Library of the United States Senate.*

———— Index of congressional committee hearings (not confidential in character) prior to January 3, 1935, in the United States Senate Library. Washington, U.S. Govt. Print. Off., 1935. 1056 p.   Z1223.A 1935

U.S. *Superintendent of Documents.* Index to the reports and documents of the 54th Congress, 1st session—72d Congress, 2d session, Dec. 2, 1895—March 4, 1933 with numerical lists and schedule of volumes. Being no. [1]–43 of the "Consolidated index" provided for by the act of January 12, 1895. Washington [Govt. Print. Off.] 1897–1933. 43 v.   Z1223.A14
   Generally known as the *Document Index,* it was issued both in the congressional series and separately, ordinarily after the close of each regular session. Title varies: nos. [1]–13, *Index to the Subjects of the Documents and Reports, and to the Committees, Senators and Representatives Presenting Them.* Discontinued with the 72d Congress, the *Numerical Lists and Schedule of Volumes* alone being issued, beginning with the 73d Congress.

In 1960–61, the Senate Committee on Government Operations initiated a project to compile a list of Senate and House reports, documents, committee prints, and staff studies that were considered to be of general interest. Most of the House and Senate committees cooperated in this project and the result was the following publication:

U.S. *Congress. Senate. Committee on Government Operations.* Select list of publications issued by Senate and House Committees; committee prints, staff studies, reports, and documents, 80th–86th Congress, 1947–1960, inclusive. Washington, U.S. Govt. Print. Off., 1961. 427 p.   Z1223.A3 1961

Individual congressional committees occasionally issue lists of their own publications, mostly as committee prints. The following are a few examples:

U.S. *Congress. Joint Committee on Atomic Energy.* Membership, publications, and other pertinent information. [Feb. 1956+ Washington, U.S. Govt. Print. Off.] annual   Z5160.U554
   From 1969, entitled *Current Membership of Joint Committee on Atomic Energy, Membership, Publications, and Other Pertinent Information.*

U.S. *Congress. Joint Economic Committee.* Committee publications and policies governing their distribution, 80th to 90th Congresses, 1947–68. Washington, U.S. Govt. Print. Off., 1968. 38 p.   Z7165.U5A47 1968

U.S. *Congress. House. Committee on Banking and Currency.* List of publications issued by Committee on Banking and Currency: hearings, reports, and committee prints, 39th-91st Congresses (1865–1970) . 91st Congress, 2d session. Washington, U.S. Govt. Print. Off., 1970. 151 p.   KF966.B32

U.S. *Congress. House. Committee on Science and Astronautics.* Publications of the Committee on Science and Astronautics, U.S. House of Representatives, from February 1959–December 1970. Washington, U.S. Govt. Print. Off., 1970. 15 p.
KF27.S3 1970

U.S. *Congress. House. Committee on the Judiciary. Subcommittee no. 5.* Index of Antitrust Subcommittee publications, 81st Congress (January 1949) through 91st Congress, 2d session (December 1970) ; a staff report. Washington, U.S. Govt. Print. Off., 1971. 81 p.   KF27.J8666 1971c

U.S. *Congress. House. Committee on Un-American Activities.* Cumulative index to publications of the Committee on Un-American Activities. 1939–41+ Washington, U.S. Govt. Print. Off.   E743.5.A28
Kept up to date by supplements.

U.S. *Congress. House. Select Committee on Small Business.* List of publications and committee membership of the Select Committee on Small Business, U.S. House of Representatives. 77th–91st Congresses (1941–70) . Washington, U.S. Govt. Print. Off., 1971. 41 p.   KF4997.S6A25 1971

U.S. *Congress. Senate. Committee on Banking and Currency.* Publications. Washington, U.S. Govt. Print. Off.   Z7164.E2U544

U.S. *Congress. Senate. Committee on Small Business.* List of publications. Washington, U.S. Govt. Print. Off.   Z7164.C81U458

U.S. *Congress. Senate. Committee on the Judiciary.* Index to hearings and reports of the Committee on the Judiciary, United States Senate, for the period 66th-91st Congresses (1921–1970) [Prepared by Richard F. Wambach] Washington, U.S. Govt. Print. Off., 1970. 66 p.   KF26.J8 1970z Index

U.S. *Congress. Senate. Committee on the Judiciary. Subcommittee to Investigate the Administration of the Internal Security Act and Other Internal Security Laws.* 21-year index; combined cumulative index, 1951–1971 to published hearings, studies and reports. Washington, U.S. Govt. Print. Off., 1972. 2 v. (1685 p.)
KF4987.J8A25 1972

U.S. *Congress. Senate. Special Committee on Aging.* Publications list: 87th to 91st Congresses, 1961–1970. Washington, U.S. Govt. Print. Off., 1971. 8 p.
KF390.A4A35 1971

The following publications on Presidential vetoes will also be of assistance in the study of the history of legislation.

Jackson, Carlton. Presidential vetoes, 1792–1945. Athens, University of Georgia Press [1967] 254 p.   JK586.J3

U.S. *Congress. Senate.* Presidential vetoes. 1935+ Washington, U.S. Govt. Print. Off.
J81.C35
Vols. for 1935–56 are cumulative from 1889 (51st Cong.) ; 1961+ cumulative from 1789 (1st Cong.)
Record of Presidential vetoes before 1889 may be found also in Senate Mis- cellaneous document 53, Forty-ninth Congress, second session; and House Document 493, Seventieth Congress, second session.

A privately published catalog of maps included in congressional publications appeared in 1941:

Claussen, Martin P., *and* Herman R. Friis. Descriptive catalog of maps published
    by Congress, 1817–1843. Washington, D.C., 1941. 104 p.   Z6027.U5C6
      A new revised and enlarged edition is in preparation by the authors, to be
    entitled *American and Foreign Maps Published by the U.S. Congress, 1789–1861*:
    Historical Catalog and Index. The work is "a combined descriptive catalog and
    analytical subject index, covering all of the some 3500 printed maps which ap-
    peared as illustrations in Congressional publications." To be published by Pied-
    mont Press, Washington, D.C., "the index will completely supersede the original
    Descriptive Catalog of Maps...." (publisher's announcement, May 8, 1970.)

FEDERAL AGENCIES

Publications of the federal departments and agencies are listed, as a rule, in the *Monthly Catalog* of the Superintendent of Documents. Also, many agencies publish regular or occasional catalogs or lists of their own publications. It has been estimated that only about half of all government publications are printed in the Government Printing Office, the balance being produced by departments and agencies in their own facilities.[2] Unfortunately, a considerable number of these agency-produced publications fail to be listed in the *Monthly Catalog* and escape bibliographic control.

To remedy this situation, and generally to improve the bibliographic control and the distribution of government publications, a survey was made among depository libraries and other institutions during the 85th Congress (1957–58) by the Subcommittee to Study Federal Printing and Paperwork, of the Committee on House Administration, and legislation was introduced which resulted in the Depository Library Act of 1962 (PL 87–579, 76 Stat. 352). The act contains the following provision concerning publications of federal agencies:

"Each component of the Government shall furnish the Superintendent of Documents a list of publications, except those required for official use only or those required
for strictly administrative or operational purposes which have no public interest or
educational value and publications classified for reasons of national security, which it
issued during the previous month that were obtained from sources other than the
Government Printing Office."

The Printing Act of 1968 (PL 90–620, 82 Stat. 1238) reiterated this provision and amplified on the distribution of agency publications to depository libraries. As a result of these two laws, the situation improved

---

[2] Jennings Wood, preface, *United States Government Publications; a Partial List of Non-GPO Imprints* (Chicago, American Library Association, 1964) .

to a certain degree, but there are still numerous agency publications which remain unrecorded in the *Monthly Catalog.*

The Library of Congress and other American libraries have long been concerned about the problem of non-GPO government publications, printed or otherwise reproduced. In 1946, the Documents Expediting Project was organized at the Library of Congress, sponsored by the Joint Committee on Government Publications of the Association of Research Libraries, the American Library Association, the American Association of Law Libraries, and the Special Libraries Association. Its purpose was to assist American libraries in obtaining government publications not readily available through regular channels. Non-GPO publications figure prominently in this program.

In 1951, the Documents Expediting Project issued the following list to assist its member libraries:

Documents Expediting Project. Classified checklist of U.S. government processed publications. Prelim. ed. Washington, 1951. 86 1.   Z1223.Z7D6
——— ——— Supplement A. Aug. 1, 1951/Mar. 1, 1952. Washington.   Z1223.Z7D62
   Entries are arranged by issuing agencies and mainly list processed publications, although "some printed publications, field publications, etc., which are not distributed by the Superintendent of Documents to depository libraries" are also included. The checklist also covers a few congressional committee prints. Unfortunately, the publication of supplements seems to have been abandoned very early. Short lists of publications distributed by the Documents Expediting Project have been included later in its *Bulletin* (Z689.D6) .

The enactment of the Depository Library Act of 1962, which authorized the Superintendent of Documents to make depository distribution of non-GPO publications, again made apparent the need to identify the titles. In 1964 the American Library Association, in cooperation with the Library of Congress, published the following list:

Wood, Jennings. United States government publications; a partial list of non-GPO imprints. Prepared under the direction of the Interdivisional Committee on Public Documents of the American Library Association. Chicago, American Library Association, 1964. 86 p.   Z1223.Z7W75
   Arranged by agencies, the list covers approximately the period 1961–64.

Since 1967, the Library of Congress has been making special efforts to acquire U.S. government publications printed outside the Government Printing Office. The following two lists have been published to date:

U.S. *Library of Congress. Exchange and Gift Division.* Non-GPO imprints received in the Library of Congress, July 1967 through December 1969; a selective checklist. Washington, Library of Congress, 1970. 73 p.   Z1223.A12A5

——— Non-GPO imprints received in the Library of Congress in 1970; a selective checklist. Washington, Library of Congress, 1971. 25 p.   Z1223.A12A52
   The checklist is divided into two sections; the first lists monographs and monographs in series, the second, periodicals.

CATALOGS, LISTS, INDEXES

Guides and general bibliographies of U.S. federal publications, listed previously, remain the basic tools for retrospective research in federal agencies' publications. Boyd and Rips' *United States Government Publications* (3d ed., 1949) gives a short history and organization of individual agencies, their most important publications, and catalogs or lists of their publications. Schmeckebier and Eastin's *Government Publications and Their Use* (2d rev. ed., 1969) has an extensive list of bibliographies, catalogs, indexes, and lists of publications of individual agencies. John Brown Mason's *Research Resources* (v. 2, 1971) lists selected agency publications, mainly annual reports, and a number of catalogs and lists.

Most federal agencies issue more or less extensive catalogs or lists of their publications. Many lists include only publications available at the time of their issuance, and some feature only a selection.

In the following list agencies are arranged according to their official name, as given in the *United States Government Organization Manual* and the Library of Congress catalogs. Generally, current lists and the more comprehensive retrospective catalogs or lists are included. Year of establishment of the agency and dates of major organizational changes are also indicated.

Administration on Aging
Established in 1965 within the Department of Health, Education and Welfare. It absorbed the Office of Aging, created in 1955.

U.S. *Administration on Aging.* AOA publications. [Washington, 1968] 12 p. (AOA publication 261)   DLC
  An annotated price list, occasionally updated.

U.S. *Office of Aging.* Office of Aging and the many faces of age [with list of publications] Washington, 1963. 6 p. (OA publication 215)   DLC

U.S. *Superintendent of Documents.* Social services; aging, family planning, handicapped ... Washington (*Its* Price list 78)   Z1223.A191 no. 78

Advisory Commission on Intergovernmental Relations
Established in 1959. See also Commission on Intergovernmental Relations.

U.S. *Advisory Commission on Intergovernmental Relations.* ACIR publications list. Washington, 1969. 6 p.   DLC
  An annotated list, occasionally updated.

——— Report. 1st+ 1960+ Washington, 1961+ annual.   JK325.A2
  Includes a list of publications issued during the year, as well as publications issued in previous years, currently available.

Aeronautical Chart and Information Center, St. Louis
Established in 1952.

U.S. *Aeronautical Chart and Information Center, St. Louis.* Catalog of publications, exclusive of charts, flight information publications and related specifications. [2d ed.] St. Louis [1962]   Z5064.N3U5

—— DOD catalog of aeronautical charts and flight information publications. St. Louis [1968+] 1 v. (looseleaf)   Z6026.A2U45
"Prepared for the Defense Intelligence Agency."

Agency for International Development
Established in 1961 within the Department of State. Predecessor agencies: Economic Cooperation Administration (1948–51); Mutual Security Agency (1951–53); Foreign Operations Administration (1953–55); International Cooperation Administration (1955–61).

U.S. *Agency for International Development.* Publications and films list. Washington [1969. 5 p.]   DLC
Except for occasional sales lists, the Agency for International Development and its predecessor agencies have not published comprehensive catalogs of their publications. Most publications are, however, listed in the *Monthly Catalog* of the U.S. Superintendent of Documents.

Agricultural Research Service
Established in 1953, superseding Agricultural Research Administration (1942–53). Its publications are listed in the catalogs of the U.S. Dept. of Agriculture. Special lists:

U.S. *Agricultural Research Service. Eastern Utilization Research and Development Division.* Publications and patents. Philadelphia. semiannual.   DLC
Specializes mainly in animal products and some plant products.

U.S. *Agricultural Research Service. Northern Utilization Research and Development Division.* Publications and patents. Peoria, Ill. semiannual.   DLC
Specializes mainly in cereal grains and oilseeds.

U.S. *Agricultural Research Service. Southern Utilization Research and Development Division.* Publications and patents. New Orleans. semiannual.   DLC
Specializes mainly in cotton and cottonseed, Southern fruits and vegetables, pine gum, sugar cane, rice.

U.S. *Agricultural Research Service. Western Utilization Research and Development Division.* List of publications and patents with abstracts. Albany, Calif. semiannual.   Z5073.U52
Specializes in western fruits, nuts, vegetables and rice, poultry products, forage crops, etc.

Note: In 1970, the names of regional research divisions were changed to: Eastern Marketing and Nutrition Research Division, Northern Marketing and Nutrition Research Division, Southern Marketing and Nutrition Research Division, and Western Marketing and Nutrition Research Division.

Arms Control and Disarmament Agency
Established in 1961 within the Department of State. Superseded the
United States Disarmament Administration.

Arms control and disarmament. v. 1+ winter 1964/65+ [Washington, U.S. Govt. Print.
Off.] quarterly.   JX1974.A1A7
    Compiled by Arms Control and Disarmament Bibliography Section, Library
    of Congress.

U.S. *Arms Control and Disarmament Agency.* A brief bibliography, arms control &
disarmament. [Washington, 1964] 33 p. *(Its* Publication 22)   JX1974.A1U52 no. 22
    Supplements and updates *A Basic Bibliography; Disarmament, Arms Control
    & National Security,* published by the U.S. Disarmament Administration in
    1961 (see below).

U.S. *Disarmament Administration.* A basic bibliography: disarmament, arms control
& national security. [Washington, U.S. Govt. Print. Off., 1961] 29 p. (Department
of State publication 7193. Disarmament series, 1)   JX1974.A1U538 no. 1

Atomic Energy Commission
Established in 1946.

U.S. *Atomic Energy Commission.* Bibliographies of interest to the atomic energy pro-
gram. [Compiled by Hugh E. Voress and Naomi K. Smelcer] Rev. 1. [Oak Ridge,
Tenn.] USAEC Technical Information Service [1958] 149 p.   Z5160.U487
    "TID–3043"
—— —— Supplement 1+ Nov. 1959+ [Oak Ridge, Tenn.] United States Atomic
Energy Commission, Technical Information Service.   Z5160.U4872

U.S. *Atomic Energy Commission.* A bibliography of selected AEC reports of interest
to industry. [Oak Ridge, Tenn.] Technical Information Service, U.S.A.E.C., 1953–
54. 9 pts. in 7. *(Its* TID–3050)   QC770.U63 TID–3050
    Contents: pt. 1. Metallurgy and ceramics. —pt. 2. Chemistry and chemical
    engineering. —pt. 3. Nuclear technology.—pt. 4. Electronics and electrical en-
    gineering.—pt. 5. Mechanics and mechanical engineering.—pt. 6. Construction
    and civil engineering.—pt. 7. Mining and geology.—pt. 8. Industrial manage-
    ment.—pt. 9. Health and safety.

—— Cumulated numerical list of available unclassified U.S. Atomic Energy Commission reports. 2d ed. Oak Ridge, Tenn., Technical Information Service Extension, 1956. 244. p.   Z1223.A76 1956
    First edition published in 1955 under the same title. Other editions published
    under the following titles:
        ——Availability listing of USAEC reports. 3d ed., Oak Ridge, Tenn., 1958.
    462 p.   Z1223.A75 1958
    "TID–4000"
        —— Availability listing of reports abstracted in Nuclear science abstracts.
    4th ed. Oak Ridge, Tenn., 1959. 487 p. "TID–4000"   Z1223.A74 1959
        —— Public availability of reports abstracted in Nuclear science abstracts.
    5th ed. Oak Ridge, Tenn., 1960. 2 v. (618 p.) "TID–4000" Z1223.A76 1960

—— Guide to AEC reports for the depository libraries, prepared by Technical Information Service. Oak Ridge, Tenn. [1954?] 21 p.   Z1223.A8

—— Guide to atomic energy literature for the civilian application program. [Washington] U.S. Atomic Energy Commission, Technical Information Service, 1957. 74 p.   Z5160. U49
"TID–4575"

—— Index to the Understanding the atom series. [Oak Ridge, Tenn.] U.S. Atomic Energy Commission, Division of Technical Information [1970] 33 p. (*Its* Understanding the atom series)   Z5160.U4915   1970

—— Nuclear Science abstracts. v. 1+ July 15, 1948+ Oak Ridge, Tenn., Technical Information Service Extension. semimonthly.   QC70.U64
Superseded the commission's *Abstracts of Declassified Documents* and *Guide to Published Research on Atomic Energy.* There are author, subject, and report number indexes, annual and cumulative.

—— Technical books and monographs sponsored by the U.S. Atomic Energy Commission. 1st+ ed.; Apr. 1959+ [Oak Ridge, Tenn.?]   Z7141.U53
Title varies slightly. Published by the commission's Division of Technical Information Service. Each issue covers publications from 1947.

—— What's available in the unclassified atomic energy literature. [1st]+ 1951+ Oak Ridge, Tenn., Technical Information Service Extension.   Z5160.U483
"TID–4550."
Title varies: 1951–54, *Availability of* usaec *Research and Development Reports.* 12th rev. (1959?) published under title: *Science Information Available from the Atomic Energy Commission.*

U.S. *Atomic Energy Commission. Laboratory, Ames, Iowa.* List of publications. 1960/ 61+ Ames. annual.   Z5160.U55
Superseded a publication with the same title, issued by Iowa State University of Science and Technology, Ames, Institute for Atomic Research, from 1942/55 to 1955/60 (Z5160.I55) .

U.S. *Scientific Laboratory, Los Alamos, N.M.* Publications of LASL research. Los Alamos.   Z7405.R4U56
Began in 1957 under title: *Selected Bibliography of Publications of* LASL *research.*

U.S. *Superintendent of Documents.* Atomic energy and civil defense. 1st+ ed.; Dec. 1955+ Washington. (*Its* Price list 84)   Z1223.A191 no. 84

Board of Governors of the Federal Reserve System
Established in 1913 as Federal Reserve Board. Name changed in 1935.

U.S. *Board of Governors of the Federal Reserve System.* Federal Reserve Board publications. [1966+] Washington. semiannual.   DLC
List of Federal Reserve Board publications is also included in the *Federal Reserve Bulletin* (HG2401.A5) .

U.S. *Board of Governors of the Federal Reserve System. Library.* Congressional testimony of board members and staff of the Federal Reserve System, 1913–1958; index compiled from material in the Library of the Board of Governors of the Federal Reserve System. [Washington? 1959?] [51] p.   Z7164.F5U456

Board on Geographic Names

Established in 1947. Previously: Geographic Board (1890–1934), Board on Geographical Names (1934–47).

U.S. *Board on Geographic Names.* Catalog of publications. Washington, 1949. 11 p.
                                                                      Z6824.U5   1949

—— Catalog of publications and indexes to decisions. Washington, Dept. of the Interior, 1953. 20 p.   Z6824.U5   1953

Bureau of American Ethnology

Established in 1879 within the Smithsonian Institution. Abolished in 1964.

U.S. *Bureau of American Ethnology.* Annual report. 1st–48th; 1879/80–1930/31. Washington, U.S. Govt. Print. Off., 1881–1933. 48 v.   E51.U55
                                                                        GN2.U5
Vol. 48, 1930/31 includes "General index, annual reports of the Bureau of American Ethnology, v. 1–48 (1879–1931)," p. 25–1220.

—— List of publications of the Bureau of American Ethnology, with index to authors and titles. 1894–[1961?] Washington, U.S. Govt. Print. Off.   Z5114.U58

U.S. *Superintendent of Documents.* Ethnology... [1908–9] Washington. (*Its* Price list 27)   Z1223.A191 no. 27
For later listing, see also price lists no. 24 (Indians), no. 55 (Smithsonian Institution...) and no. 56 (Indians, Smithsonian Institution).

Bureau of Chemistry and Soils

Established in 1927, absorbing Bureau of Chemistry and Bureau of Soils. In 1938 merged with Bureau of Agricultural Engineering to form Bureau of Agricultural Chemistry and Engineering.

U.S. *Bureau of Chemistry and Soils.* Index of publications of the Bureau of Chemistry and Soils, originally the Bureau of Chemistry and the Bureau of Soils. 75 years—1862–1937. [Washington] 1937 [i.e. 1939] 1 v.   Z5521.U5   1937

Bureau of Commercial Fisheries

Established in 1959 under United States Fish and Wildlife Service in the Department of the Interior, abolished in 1970.

U.S. *Bureau of Commercial Fisheries.* Monthly list of new publications. [1966–70] Washington.   DLC
In the series of *Fishery Leaflet,* the Bureau of Commercial Fisheries occasionally listed various series of its publications. *Fishery Leaflet* is currently published by the National Marine Fisheries Service (SH11.A4468).

Bureau of Employment Security

Established in 1939 within the Federal Security Agency, transferred to the Department of Labor in 1949, abolished in 1969.

U.S. *Bureau of Employment Security.* Publications. 1954– ? Washington.   Z1223.E52
   Title varies: 1954–56, *Employment Security Publications.* Volumes for 1954–
   56 issued in separate parts: pt. 1. *U.S. Employment Service;* pt. 2. *Unemployment Insurance Publications.* Superseded *Publications, 1949–1953,* issued by
   U.S. Employment Service (Z1223.E5) .

Bureau of Fisheries
Established in 1871 as U.S. Fish Commission, it became a bureau in the
Department of Commerce and Labor in 1903, transferred to the Depart-
ment of the Interior in 1939 and merged into U.S. Fish and Wildlife
Service in 1940.

Aller, Barbara B.   Publications of the United States Bureau of Fisheries, 1871–1940.
   Washington, U.S. Dept. of the Interior, Fish and Wildlife Service, 1958. 202 p.
   (U.S. Fish and Wildlife Service. Special scientific report: fisheries, no. 284)
                                                                   SH11.A335 no. 284

MacDonald, Rose M. E.   An analytical subject bibliography of the publications of the
   Bureau of Fisheries, 1871–1920. Washington, U.S. Govt. Print. Off., 1921. 306 p.
   (U.S. Bureau of Fisheries. Document 899. Report of the Commissioner, 1919/20.
   Appendix 5)   SH11.A15   1919/20   App. 5

Bureau of Foreign and Domestic Commerce
Established in 1912, its functions were reassigned in 1953 to other
offices of the Department of Commerce.

U.S. *Bureau of Foreign and Domestic Commerce.*   List of publications for sale by the
   Superintendent of Documents, Government Printing Office, Washington, and by
   district and cooperative offices of the Bureau of Foreign and Domestic Commerce.
   Washington, U.S. Govt. Print. Off. [1915–24?]   Z1223.C92

——— List of selected publications . . . Nov. 1, 1932–[1946?] Washington, U.S. Govt.
   Print. Off. irregular.   Z1223.C815

——— Publications . . . Washington, U.S. Govt. Print. Off., 1915–31.   Z1223.C91
      Title varies: 1915–22. *Catalogue of Bureau Publications;* 1925–27, *Catalogue
   of Publications of the Bureau of Foreign and Domestic Commerce;* 1928–31,
   Publications . . .

Bureau of Foreign Commerce
Established in 1953 within the Department of Commerce. Abolished
in 1961 and its functions vested in two new bureaus: Bureau of International Programs and Bureau of International Business Operations.
These two bureaus were abolished in 1963 and the Bureau of International Commerce established.

U.S. *Bureau of Foreign Commerce.*   Checklist of BFC publications. [1957–61] Washington.
      Revised twice a year, it appeared in the *Foreign Commerce Weekly*
   (HC1.R1987) and also as a separate publication.

—— Checklist of World trade information service reports, and other current publications. [Washington], 1958. 18 p.   Z7164.C8U4
    Lists of these reports were also occasionally published in the *Foreign Commerce
Weekly* (HC1.R1987) .

Bureau of International Commerce

Established in 1963, it superseded the Bureau of International Programs
and the Bureau of International Business Operations, which had been
established in the Department of Commerce after the Bureau of Foreign
Commerce was abolished in 1961.

U.S. *Bureau of International Commerce.* Semiannual checklist; international business
    publications. [1964+] Washington   DLC
        Continues previous checklists published by its predecessor bureaus.
        Publications of the Bureau of International Commerce and its predecessors
    are also listed in the catalog of the Department of Commerce publications, issued
    by its library.

Bureau of Labor Standards

Established in 1934 as Division of Labor Standards in the Department
of Labor. Name changed to Bureau of Labor Standards in 1948. Functions absorbed by the Occupational Safety and Health Administration
in May 1971.

U.S. *Bureau of Labor Standards.* Selected publications. [1944–70?] [Washington]
    irregular.   Z1223.L17

Bureau of Labor Statistics

Established in 1913 in the Department of Labor, which had succeeded
the Bureau of Labor, created in 1884 in the Department of the Interior.

U.S. *Bureau of Labor Statistics.* Catalog of publications: bulletins, reports and re-
    leases, periodicals. Jan. 1946/Apr. 1947+ [Washington] semiannual.   Z1223.L175
        From the July-December 1969 issue, the title has been *Publications of the
    Bureau of Labor Statistics.*

—— Publications of the Bureau of Labor Statistics, 1886–1967; numerical listings,
    annotations, subject index. Washington, U.S. Govt. Print. Off. [1968] 156 p.
    (*Its* Bulletin 1567)   HD8051.A62 no. 1567
                                                                       Z1223.L1835

The following retrospective catalogs and indexes of the publications
of the Bureau of Labor (1884–1918) and the Bureau of Labor Statistics
may be of assistance:

U.S. *Bureau of Labor.* Index of all reports issued by bureaus of labor statistics in
    the United States prior to March 1, 1902. Prepared under the direction of Carroll
    D. Wright for the use of the United States Department of Labor. With a new in-

troduction by Herbert G. Gutman. New York, Johnson Reprint Corp., 1970. 287 p.
(History of American Economy)   Z7164.L1U6   1970
Reprint of the 1902 ed. with Gutman's introduction added.

—— Publications of the U.S. Bureau of Labor prior to July 1, 1912. Washington,
Govt. Print. Off., 1912. 13 p.   Z7164.L1U65

U.S. *Bureau of Labor Statistics.* Checklist of regular Bureau of Labor Statistics series
for states and areas, 1955. [Washington, U.S. Govt. Print. Off.] 1956, 129 p.
                                                                      Z7164.L1U6605

—— Foreign labor publications of the Bureau of Labor Statistics, 1945–June 30,
1962. Washington, U.S. Dept. of Labor, 1962. 29 l.   Z7164.L1U6628

—— Publications of the U.S. Bureau of Labor Statistics up to March 1, 1914. Washington, Govt. Print. Off., 1914. 15 p.   Z7164.L1U65   1914
                                                                      Z1223.L18   1914

—— Subject index of bulletins published by the Bureau of Labor Statistics, 1915–59;
[prepared by M. Frances Marshall and Gladys B. Wash. Washington, U.S. Govt.
Print. Off., 1960] 102 p. (*Its* Bulletin no. 1281)   HD8051.A62 no. 1281
                                                                      Z1223.L1837

—— Subject index of the publications of the United States Bureau of Labor Statistics
up to May 1, 1915. September 1915. Washington, Govt. Print. Off., 1915. 233 p. (*Its*
Bulletin no. 174. Misc. series no. 11)   HD8051.A62 no. 174

Bureau of Land Management

Established in 1946 within the Department of the Interior. It succeeded
the General Land Office, created in 1812.

U.S. *Bureau of Land Management.* Public lands bibliography. Washington, U.S. Govt.
Print. Off., 1962. 106 p.   Z7164.L3U39
—— —— Supplement 1+ [Washington] U.S. Dept. of the Interior, Bureau of
Land Management [1964+]   Z7164.L3U39 Suppl.

U.S. *General Land Office.* Circulars and regulations of the General Land Office with
reference tables and index. Comp. by C. G. Fisher of the General Land Office.
January 1930. Washington, U.S. Govt. Print. Off., 1930. 1696 p.   HD181.G5   1930

—— Index to circulars and publications of the General Land Office ... Comp. in
the General Land Office. August 1928. Washington, U.S. Govt. Print. Off., 1928. 48 p.
                                                                      HD181.G5   1928

—— Index to circulars and regulations of the General Land Office issued since January 1930. Comp. by C. G. Fisher of the General Land Office. May 1932. Washington, U.S. Govt. Print. Off., 1932. 13 p.   HD181.G5   1932

U.S. *National Archives.* List of cartographic records of the General Land Office (Record group 49) . Comp. by Laura E. Kelsay. Washington, 1964. 202 p. (*Its* Publication no. 64–9. Special list no. 19)   CD3035.G4A5

U.S. *Superintendent of Documents.* Maps; engineering, surveying. [1911]+ Washington. (*Its* Price list 53)   Z1223.A191 no. 53

—— Public domain ... [1908–1947?] Washington. (*Its* Price list 20) Z1223.A191 no. 20

Bureau of Mines

Established in 1910 in the Department of the Interior. From 1925 to 1934, it was in the Department of Commerce and was transferred back to the Department of the Interior in 1934.

U.S. *Bureau of Mines.* List of Bureau of Mines publications and articles, with subject and author index. 1960+ Washington, U.S. Govt. Print Off. (*Its* Special publication)   Z6736.U759
> Supersedes the bureau's *List of Publications* (1910–60, Z6736.U75) and *List of Journal Articles by Bureau of Mines Authors* (Z6736.U758) .

—— List of journal articles by Bureau of Mines authors, with subject index. July 1910–Dec. 1930—July 1910–Jan. 1, 1960. Washington, U.S. Govt. Print. Off.
                                                                          Z6736.U758
> Volume for July 1910–Jan. 1, 1960, issued as the Bureau's Special publication. Title varies: July 1910–Dec. 1930—1934–37, *Index of Bureau of Mines Papers Published in the Technical Press;* 1938–46. *Bureau of Mines Papers Published in the Technical Press.* Superseded by the Bureau's *List of Bureau of Mines Publications and Articles* (1960+, Z6736.U759) .

—— List of publications [issued by the Bureau of Mines from July 1, 1910, to January 1, 1960, with subject and author index. By Hazel J. Stratton.] Washington, U.S. Govt. Print. Off. [1960. 826 p.]   Z6736.U75
> "This volume contains more than 7,500 listings of virtually all scientific and technical publications issued by the Bureau of Mines during the half-century of the Bureau's existence. Superseding all previous indexes of the Bureau's own publications, it also supplements the 'List of Journal Articles by Bureau of Mines Authors. Published July 1, 1910, to January 1, 1960.' " (Foreword)

—— New publications. 1911+ Washington.   DLC
> A monthly list of new publications, cumulated in annual and other lists.

Bureau of Plant Industry, Soils and Agricultural Engineering

Established as Bureau of Plant Industry in 1902 in the Department of Agriculture, absorbed other services in 1936, 1938, and 1942. Functions transferred to Agricultural Research Service in 1953.

U.S. *Bureau of Plant Industry. Library.* Check list of publications issued by the Bureau of Plant Industry, United States Department of Agriculture, 1901–1920 and by the divisions and offices which combined to form this bureau 1862–1901. Washington, 1921. 124 p. (U.S. Dept. of Agriculture. Library. Bibliographical contributions, no. 3)   Z5073.U57 no. 3

U.S. *Superintendent of Documents.* Plants, culture, grading, marketing . . . Washington [1910+] (*Its* Price list 44)   Z1223.A191 no. 44
> Title varies.

Bureau of Public Roads

Established in 1894 in the Department of Agriculture as Office of Road Inquiry. Known as Office of Public Roads and Rural Engineering from 1916 to 1918, and from 1918 as Bureau of Public Roads. In 1939 transferred from Dept. of Agriculture to Federal Works Agency and name changed to Public Roads Administration. In 1949, after three months under the General Services Administration, it was transferred to the Department of Commerce and name changed again to Bureau of Public Roads. In 1966, transferred to the Department of Transportation and its functions assigned to Federal Highway Administration.

Publications of the Bureau of Public Roads were listed, as a rule, in the catalogs of the Department of Agriculture and the Department of Commerce for the respective periods. The periodical *Public Roads* (May 1918+ TE23.P86) listed new and available publications.

U.S. *Bureau of Public Roads.* Publications of the Office of Public Road Inquiries. Washington, U.S. Govt. Print. Off., 1903. 10 p.   Z7295.U522

U.S. *Superintendent of Documents.* Roads. [1909–Mar. 1948] Washington. (*Its* Price list 45)   Z1223.A191 no. 45

——— Transportation, highways, roads and postal service. 1910+ Washington. (*Its* Price list 25)   Z1223.A191 no. 25

Bureau of Reclamation

Established in 1902 as Reclamation Service, part of the Geological Survey in the Department of the Interior. In 1923 the name was changed to Bureau of Reclamation.

U.S. *Bureau of Reclamation.* Engineering articles relating to the work of the Reclamation Service. List no. 1–[4?] Washington, 1911–[14?]   Z5853.H9U7
Reprinted from the *Reclamation Record* (TC823.6.A3) .

——— List of engineering articles... with index. no. 1–[8?] Washington, U.S. Govt. Print. Off. 1915–[34?]   Z5853.U705
Reprinted from the *Annual Report of the U.S. Reclamation Service* (TC823.6.A2) .

——— Price list of publications of the Reclamation Service, United States Reclamation Service... [Washington, Govt. Print. Off., 1920] 32 p.   Z5853.H9U72

——— Publications for sale. [1952+] Denver, Office of Chief Engineer.   DLC

——— Publications of the Bureau of Reclamation. Price list no. [1–11?] Washington [1912–37?]   Z5853.H9U71
Unnumbered lists published 1939–43, then 1950 and 1951.

Bureau of Sport Fisheries and Wildlife

Established in 1956 within the United States Fish and Wildlife Service, in the Department of the Interior.

U.S. *Bureau of Sport Fisheries and Wildlife.* Publications in the calendar year... [1966–67] Washington.   DLC
Only two issues, for 1966 and 1967, published. A monthly list published from 1967.

Bureau of the Census

Established in 1902 in the Department of the Interior, transferred to the new Department of Commerce and Labor in 1903, and to the Department of Commerce in 1913.

U.S. *Bureau of the Census.* Catalog of United States census publications. 1946+
   Washington, U.S. Govt. Print. Off.   Z7554.U5U32
      Issued quarterly with monthly supplement and annual cumulation.

——— Census Bureau programs and publications; area and subject guide. [Washington, U.S. Govt. Print Off., 1968] 146 p.   HA37.U52   1968

U.S. *Library of Congress. Census Library Project.* Catalog of United States census publications, 1790–1945. Prepared by Henry J. Dubester. New York, Greenwood Press [1968] 320 p.   Z7554.U5U62
      "A comprehensive listing of all materials issued by the Bureau of the Census and its predecessor organizations."
      A reprint of the 1950 ed.

U.S. *Superintendent of Documents.* Census publications. Washington, 1920+ (*Its* Price list 70)   Z1223.A191 no. 70

Bureau of Yards and Docks

Established in 1842 in the Department of the Navy. Abolished in 1966 and functions transferred to Naval Facilities Engineering Command.

U.S. *Bureau of Yards and Docks.* Index of Bureau of Yards and Docks publications. Washington [1963–66]   Z6834.C5U52
      "NAVDOCKS P–349." Cumulative.

Business and Defense Services Administration

Established in 1953 in the Department of Commerce. Abolished in 1970 and functions transferred to the Bureau of Domestic Commerce.

U.S. *Business and Defense Services Administration.* BDSA publications list. [1954–69] Washington.
      Title varies slightly. Publications are listed by categories.

U.S. *Business and Defense Services Administration. Office of Distribution.* Department of Commerce publications for use in marketing and distribution. 1955–[60?] Washington.   Z7164.C8U43

Children's Bureau

Established in 1912 in the Department of Labor. Transferred to Federal Security Agency in 1946 and to Department of Health, Education, and Welfare in 1953. Renamed Office of Child Development in 1969.

U.S. *Children's Bureau.* Children's Bureau publications. 1912/May 1964+ [Washington]   Z1223.C5U45
      "An index to publications by number, title, author and subject." A cumulative list published irregularly.

—— Publications of the Children's Bureau. 1960+ [Washington] U.S. Govt. Print. Off. annual.   Z7164.C5U557

—— Selected list of publications. Washington, U.S. Govt. Print. Off., 1920–[45]
    Z1223.C5U5
    Z7164.C5U56

U.S. *Superintendent of Documents.* Child development and other publications relating to children and youth. Washington, 1922+ (*Its* Price list 71)   Z1223.A191 no. 71

Civil Aeronautics Board
Established in 1938.

U.S. *Civil Aeronautics Board.* Cumulative index-digest: Economic cases. Aug. 1938–May 1955+ Washington, U.S. Govt. Print. Off.   TL521.A37452

—— List of publications. Washington.   DLC
Issued in mimeographed or printed form since 1938, irregularly.

—— Research and reference directory. Washington, 1969. 22 [21] p.   Z5065.U5A5
Divided into a subject index and a numbered list of source materials, the directory is a guide to materials available in the Public Reference Room of the Civil Aeronautics Board.

Civil Service Commission
Established in 1883.

U.S. *Civil Service Commission.* List of publications. [1923–30. Washington, U.S. Govt. Print. Off.]   Z1223.C58U5

U.S. *Civil Service Commission. Library.* A bibliography of public personnel administration literature. Washington, 1949. 1 v. (various pagings)   Z7164.C81U456

—— Congressional documents relating to civil service; 19th to 84th Congress, 1826–1956. Washington, 1959. 2 v. (253 p.)   Z7164.C6U52
In two parts: pt. 1. Hearings.—pt. 2. Reports and documents. Several supplements published (Z7164.C6U522).

U.S. *Superintendent of Documents.* Political science, government, crime, District of Columbia. Washington, 1911+ (*Its* Price list 54)   Z1223.A191 no. 54

Coast and Geodetic Survey
Established in 1807 as Coast Survey in the Treasury Department. Name changed to Coast and Geodetic Survey in 1878. Transferred to Department of Commerce and Labor in 1903 and to Department of Commerce in 1913. Transferred to Environmental Science Services Administration in 1965, and in 1970 it was consolidated with elements of the U.S. Lake Survey from the Army Corps of Engineers, under the name of National Ocean Survey, within the National Oceanic and Atmospheric Administration.

U.S. *Coast and Geodetic Survey.*   Aeronautical chart catalog. [Washington] 1947. 33 p.
TL587.U62   1947

────── Aeronautical chart catalog. [Washington] 1949. 53 p.   Z5064.C5U5   1949

────── Bibliography. Descriptive catalogue of publications relating to the U.S. Coast
and Geodetic Survey, 1807–1896, and to U.S. standard weights and measures,
1790–1896. Washington, Govt. Print. Off., 1898. 118 p. (*Its* Special publication no 2)
Z6000.U57   1898

────── Catalog of nautical charts and related publications. Washington [1866+]
Z6026.H9U5

────── Catalogue of maps of the United States and territories, coast survey, and northern and northwestern lakes, 1862. Washington, Printed by H. Polkinhorn, 1862.
74 l.   Z6026.H9U5   1862

────── The Coast and Geodetic Survey; its products and services. Washington, U.S.
Govt. Print. Off., 1966. 80 p. (*Its* Publication 10–2)   QB296.U847   1966
Other editions, describing the work and the publications of the Coast and
Geodetic Survey from 1816, published since 1834.

────── General index of professional and scientific papers contained in the United
States Coast Survey reports from 1851 to 1870. [Washington, 1874?] 17 p.
Z6000.U57   1874

────── Important publications of the United States Coast and Geodetic Survey appearing since January 1, 1914. Washington, Govt. Print. Off., 1919. 6 p. Z6000.U58   1919

────── List of publications of the Coast and Geodetic Survey available for distribution.
May 1, 1908. Washington, Govt. Print. Off., 1908. 25 p.   Z6000.U58   1908

────── List of publications of the Coast and Geodetic Survey, by Emily A. Baldwin,
Librarian. Provisional. [Washington] 1947. 44 p.   Z6000.U58   1947

────── ────── 4th ed. [Washington] 1951. 43 p.   Z6000.U58   1951

────── Publications of the Coast and Geodetic Survey. 5th ed. [Washington] 1955. 42 p.
Z6000.U58   1955

U.S. *Coast and Geodetic Survey. Library.*   List and catalogue of the publications issued
by the U.S. Coast and Geodetic Survey 1816–1902. By E. L. Burchard, librarian.
Reprint with Supplement, 1903–1908. Washington, Govt. Print. Off., 1908. 237,
44, [1] p.   Z6000.U57   1908

U.S. *Superintendent of Documents.*   Engineering and surveying. [1908–52] Washington.
(*Its* Price list 18)   Z1223.A191 no. 18

────── Maps; engineering, surveying. 1911+ Washington. (*Its* Price list 53)
Z1223.A191 no. 53

Coast Guard
Established in 1915 in the Treasury Department. Transferred in 1941
to the Department of the Navy, but returned in 1946 to the Treasury
Department. In 1966 transferred to the Department of Transportation.

U.S. *Coast Guard.* Directives, publications and reports index. [Washington, U.S. Govt.
Print. Off. 1954–61?]   HJ6645.A347

—— United States Coast Guard bibliography. Washington, Public Information Division [1950] 29 p.   HJ6645.A313 no. 230
Cover title.
"CG–230."

U.S. *Library of Congress. Division of Bibliography.* United States Coast Guard: a list
of books and pamphlets. Florence S. Hellman, Chief Bibliographer ... [Washington] 1943. 4 numb. l.   Z6725.U5U43

U.S. *Superintendent of Documents.* Navy, Marine Corps and Coast Guard. 1914+
Washington. (*Its* Price list 63)   Z1223.A191 no. 63

Commission on Civil Rights
Established in 1957.

U.S. *Commission on Civil Rights.* Catalog of publications. Washington.   DLC
Issued in 1966 and 1969. Includes publications available and out of print
since the commission's establishment.

Commission on Intergovernmental Relations
Established in 1953, terminated in 1955.

U.S. *Commission on Intergovernmental Relations.* Intergovernmental relations in the
United States: a selected bibliography on interlevel and interjurisdictional relations, prepared [by W. Brooke Graves] for the Commission on Intergovernmental
Relations. [Washington] 1955. 207 p.   Z7165.U5U483
An expansion of *Intergovernmental Relations in the United States,* published
in 1953 by the U.S. Library of Congress, Legislative Reference Service. (Z7165.U5
U62)

U.S. *Library of Congress. Legislative Reference Service.* Index to the reports of the
Commission on Intergovernmental Relations, including the Commission's report,
various study committees, staff and survey reports and supporting documents.
Prepared at request of the Senate Committee on Government Operations. [Washington, U.S. Govt. Print. Off., 1956] 143 p. (84th Cong. 2d sess. Senate. Document
no. 111)   Z7165.U5U617

Consumer and Marketing Service
Established in 1940 as Agricultural Marketing Service in the Department
of Agriculture. Merged into Agricultural Marketing Administration in
1942. Name changed to Consumer and Marketing Service in 1965.
Renamed again Agricultural Marketing Service in 1972.

U.S. *Agricultural Marketing Service.* Checklist of reports and charts issued by the
Agricultural Marketing Service [1953–64] Washington.

—— Periodic reports. Washington [1955–63?] (*Its* AMS–48)   HD1751.A9184 no. 48

—— Reports and publications of USDA's Agricultural Marketing Service (except market news reports) 1964. Washington. (*Its* AMS–523)   HD1751.A9184 no. 523
Supersedes in part the service's *Periodic Reports,* issued as AMS–48.

U.S. *Consumer and Marketing Service.* Available publications of USDA's Consumer and Marketing Service (except market news reports) Revised March 1968. Washington, 1968. 20 p. (*Its* C&MS 53)   HD1751.A91845 no. 53
Supersedes its AMS–523 (*Reports and Publications*) .

Cooperative State Research Service

Established in 1888 in the Department of Agriculture as Office of Experiment Stations. It became the Experiment Stations Division in 1953, in the Agricultural Research Service, was renamed Cooperative State Experiment Station Service in 1961 and then Cooperative State Research Service in 1964.

U.S. *Dept. of Agriculture. Office of Experiment Stations.* List of publications of the Office of Experiment Stations on agricultural education. [Washington, Govt. Print. Off., 1905–9]   Z5814.A3U5

U.S. National Agricultural Library. List of bulletins of the agricultural experiment stations. 1920—1941–42. Washington, U.S. Govt. Print. Off. 12 v. biennial.
        Z5075.U5U7
Issued 1920–26 as Dept. of Agriculture *Department Bulletin* no. 1199 and its supplements no. 1–3 (S21.A7); 1927–28 to 1939–40, as Dept. of Agriculture *Miscellaneous Publication* no. 65, 123, 181, 232, 294, 362, 459 (S21.A46); 1941–42, as Dept. of Agriculture *Bibliographical Bulletin* no. 4 (Z1009.U57) . Issued from 1920 to 1939–40 by Office of Experiment Stations, and in 1941/42 by the library under its earlier name, Dept. of Agriculture Library.

U.S. *Office of Experiment Stations.* Experiment station record. v. 1–[95] Sept. 1889–[Dec. 1946] Washington, Govt. Print. Off., 1890-[1946] monthly.   S21.E75 [1946]
—— —— General index to Experiment station record, vols. i-xii, 1889–1901 and to Experiment station bulletin no. 2 [the latter a digest of the annual reports of the experiment stations for 1888] Washington, Govt. Print. Off., 1903. 671 p.
Similar indexes compiled for vol. 13–25, 1901–11 (1913, 1159 p.) ; vol. 26–40, 1912–19 (1926, 640 p.) ; vol. 41–50, 1919–24 (1931, 709 p.) ; vol. 51–60, 1924–29 (1932, 677 p.); vol. 61–70, 1929–34 (1937, 752 p.); vol. 71–80, 1934–39 (1949, 832 p.)

—— List of agricultural experiment station publications received by the office. Nov. 1903–May 1943. Washington, 1904–43. 454 nos.   Z5075.U5U69

U.S. *Superintendent of Documents.* Irrigation, drainage and water power; list of publications relating to above subjects. Washington. 1909+ (*Its* Price list 42)
        Z1223.A191 no. 42
Title varies: 1st–3d ed., 1909–11, *Experiment Stations Office; Bulletins, Circulars;* 4th ed., 1913, *Agricultural Experiment Stations;* 5th ed., 1914, *Agricultural Experimentation;* 6th to 8th ed., 1915–17, *Agricultural Experiment Stations, Irrigation, Drainage;* 9th+ ed., 1918+ *Irrigation, Drainage and Water Power.*

Copyright Office

Established in 1897 in the Library of Congress. Formerly, from 1790 to 1859, copyright law had been administered by the Department of State;

from 1859 to 1870, by the Department of the Interior; and from 1870 to 1897 by the Librarian of Congress, when the Copyright Department (now Copyright Office) under a Register of Copyrights was created.

U.S. *Copyright Office.* Annual report. Washington, U.S. Govt. Print Off., 1910+
                                                  Z642.U59R
    Includes a list of publications issued during the year.

———— Publications of the Copyright Office. Washington, Library of Congress. (*Its*
    Circular)   DLC LL

Department of Agriculture
Established in 1862.

Currently, Office of Information of the Department of Agriculture issues a *Bimonthly List of Publications and Motion Pictures* (Z5075.-U5U58), which continues the *Monthly List of Publications*, issued from 1896 to February 1964 The following is a classified list by subject matter, issued irregularly:

U.S. *Dept. of Agriculture. Division of Publications.* List of available publications of the United States Dept. of Agriculture. June 1, 1929+ Washington, U.S. Govt. Print Off.   Z5075.U572
    Issued from June 1929 to July 1951 as Miscellaneous publication no. 60, with occasional revisions, and from February 1958 as List no. 11.

For retrospective research, the following indexes and lists will be of assistance:

Handy, Robert B., *and* Minna A. Cannon. List by titles of publications of the United States Department of Agriculture from 1840 to June 1901, inclusive. Washington, Govt. Print. Off., 1902. 216 p. (U.S. Dept. of Agriculture. Division of Publications. Bulletin 6)   S21.P9 no. 6
                                            Z5075.U5U56 1902

U.S. Dept. of Agriculture. Department bulletin no. 1–1500. Washington, U.S. Govt. Print. Off. 1913–29.   S21.A7
    Continued by the *Technical Bulletin.*
    ———— Index to department bulletins, nos. 1–1500, by Mabel G. Hunt. Washington, U.S. Govt. Print. Off., 1936. 384 p.   S21.A7 Index

———— Farmers' bulletins. no. 1+ Washington, Govt. Print. Off., 1889+   S21.A6
    Indexes to *Farmers' Bulletins* were issued for nos. 1–250, 1–500, 1–1000, 1001–1500, etc.

———— Technical bulletin. no. 1+ Washington, U.S. Govt. Print. Off., 1927+   S21.A72
    Supersedes its *Department Bulletin.*
    Indexes to *Technical Bulletin* were issued for nos. 1–500 and 501–750.

U.S. *Dept. of Agriculture. Division of Publications.* Index to authors with titles of their publications appearing in the documents of the U.S. Department of Agriculture, 1841 to 1897. By Geo. F. Thompson. Washington, Govt. Print. Off., 1898. 303 p. (*Its* Bulletin no. 4)   S21.P9 no. 4
                                            Z5075.U5U53

—— Index to publications of the United States Department of Agriculture. Washington, U.S. Govt. Print. Off.   Z5075.U5U533
    Four volumes published: 1901–25 (1932, 2689 p.) ; 1926–30 (1935, 694 p.) ; 1931–35 (1937, 518 p.) ; 1936–40 (1943, 763 p.) .

—— Index to the annual reports of the U.S. Department of Agriculture for the years 1837 to 1893, inclusive. Washington, Govt. Print. Off., 1896. 252 p. (*Its* Bulletin no. 1)   S21.P9 no. 1

—— List of publications of the United States Department of Agriculture, compiled by comparison with the originals. 1901–25+ Washington, U.S. Govt. Print. Off. quinquennial. (U.S. Dept. of Agriculture. Miscellaneous publication) Z5075.U5U57
    Miscellaneous publication for:
    1901–25, no. 9
    1926–30, no. 153
    1931–35, no. 252
    1936–40, no. 443
    1941–45, no. 611

U.S. *Dept. of Agriculture. Library.* List of publications of the United States Department of Agriculture from 1841 to June 30, 1895, inclusive. Comp. by Adelaide R. Hasse. Washington, Govt. Print. Off., 1896. 76 p. (*Its* Bulletin no. 9)
                                                                        Z5075.U5U56
                                                                        Z5076.U58 no. 9

U.S. *National Agricultural Library.* Bibliographical contributions. no. 1–35; June 1919—Sept. 1939. Washington.   Z5073.U57
    Issued by the library under its earlier name: U.S. Dept. of Agriculture. Library. Some numbers issued in revised editions. Contains specialized bibliographies.

U.S. *Superintendent of Documents.* List of publications of the Agriculture Department, 1862–1902, with analytical index. Prepared in the Office of the Superintendent of Documents, Government Printing Office. Washington, Govt. Print. Off., 1904. 623 p. (Bibliography of U.S. public documents. Department list no. 1)
                                                                        Z1223.A12
                                                                        Z5075.U5U573

Zimmerman, Fred L. Numerical list of current publications of the United States Department of Agriculture, compiled by comparison with the originals. Washington, U.S. Govt. Print. Off., 1941. 929 p. (U.S. Dept. of Agriculture. Miscellaneous publication no. 450)   Z1223.A7Z5
                                                                        S21.A46 no. 450
    "Under each number will be found the series (on left margin) , title, author, issuing bureau, and date of issuance of each current publication of the Department of Agriculture that bears a numerical designation."

Department of Commerce
Established in 1903 as Department of Commerce and Labor and as a separate department in 1913.

U.S. *Dept. of Commerce. Library.* United States Department of Commerce publications, compiled under the direction of Wanda Mae Johnson, librarian. Washington, U.S. Govt. Print. Off., 1952. 795 p.   Z1223.C75
    Covers publications from 1790 to October 1950.

—— —— Supplement. 1951/52+ Washington, U.S. Govt. Print. Off. annual.
                                                                        Z1223.C75 Suppl.
    Cumulations of the *Business Service Check List,* 1946+ (Z7913.U45)

Department of Defense

Established in 1949, as successor to the National Military Establishment, created in 1947. It includes the Department of the Air Force, Department of the Army, and the Department of the Navy, which are also listed separately in this guide.

U.S. *Dept. of Defense.* Catalog of armed forces informational material. Washington, 1950. 42 p.   Z6725.U5U422
    Other editions published in 1954, 1955, 1957, etc.

U.S. *Research and Development Board. Special Committee on Technical Information.* Inventory of technical information activities of the Department of Defense. Washington [1952] 36 p.   U393.A58
    "TI 202/6. 15 September 1951. Supersedes TI 17/2"

U.S. *Superintendent of Documents.* Defense, veterans' affairs. 1955+ Washington. (*Its* Price list 85)   Z1223.A191 no. 85

Department of Health, Education, and Welfare

Established in 1953, taking over all functions of the Federal Security Agency, created in 1939.

U.S. *Dept. of Health, Education, and Welfare. Office of Public Affairs.* Catalog, U.S. Department of Health, Education, and Welfare publications, July 1970/June 1971+ Washington, 1971+   DLC
    From July/Sept. 1971 issued quarterly, the last quarterly issue being cumulative for the fiscal year.

Publications are also listed in catalogs of its component agencies, as well as in:

U.S. *Superintendent of Documents.* Health and medical services...1910+ Washington. (*Its* Price list 51)   Z1223.A191 no. 51

—— Diseases and physical conditions. 1949+ Washington. (*Its* Price list 51A)
                                                        Z1223.A191 no. 51A

—— Social services; aging, family planning, handicapped...1949+ Washington (*Its* Price list 78)   Z1223.A191 no. 78

Department of Housing and Urban Development

Established in 1965.

U.S. *Dept. of Housing and Urban Development.* Publications. Washington, 1967. 20 p. (*Its* HUD MP no. 36)   DLC

U.S. *Superintendent of Documents.* Homes; construction, maintenance, community development. 1924+ Washington. (*Its* Price list 72)   Z1223.A191 no. 72

Department of Justice
Established in 1870.

U.S. *Dept. of Justice.* Letter from the Attorney General of the United States, transmitting a list embracing all the publications of that department in compliance
with Senate resolution of March 24, 1881. [Washington, Govt. Print. Off., 1882]
12 p. (47th Cong., 1st sess. Senate. Ex. doc. no. 109)   Z6456.U55
    Covers publications for the period 1789–1881.

U.S. *Superintendent of Documents.* Political science, government, crime, District of
Columbia. 1911+ Washington. (*Its* Price list 54)   Z1223.A191 no. 54

Department of Labor
Established in 1913, when the Department of Commerce and Labor was split into two departments.

U.S. *Dept. of Labor.* Publications of the Department of Labor available for distribution. Washington, Govt. Print. Off., 1913–?   Z1223.L2
    Occasional supplements published.

———— Publications of the U.S. Department of Labor, subject listing. 1948–1955+
[Washington]   Z7164.L1U672
    "...intended as a simplified guide for people interested in labor problems.
It is not intended as a library guide."
    Published annually either with supplements, or in five-year cumulations
(from 1958).

U.S. *Dept. of Labor. Manpower Administration.* Index to publications of the Manpower Administration, Jan. 1969 through June 1971. [Washington] 1971. 26 p.
                                                                     Z7164.L1U6865
    A supplement was issued for July–Dec. 1971 and cumulative indexes Jan.
1969 through June 1972, and Jan. 1969 through June 1973.

U.S. *Dept. of Labor. Office of Information, Publications and Reports.* New publications. [Washington, 1965+] monthly.   DLC

U.S. *Superintendent of Documents.* Labor. 1909+ Washington. (*Its* Price list 33)
                                                                     Z1223.A191 no. 33

———— Occupations, professions and job descriptions. 1984+ Washington. (*Its* Price
list 33A)   Z1223.A191 no. 33A

Department of State
Established in 1789.

U.S. *Dept. of State.* Publications of the Department of State. 1929–50—[1958–60]
Washington, U.S. Govt. Print. Off. (*Its* Publication)   Z1223.S775
    Each volume in three parts: subject list; periodicals; index by series. Pub-
lished irregularly and in various cumulations. The entire period from Oct. 1,
1929, to Dec. 1960 is covered in the following three volumes: 1929–53 (Publication no. 5059) ; 1953–57 (Publication no. 6591) ; 1958–60 (Publication no. 7219) .

U.S. *Dept. of State. Division of Publications.* Publications of the Department of State. [List of numbered publications] April 1, 1930–[1958?] Washington, U.S. Govt. Print. Off. ([U.S.] Dept. of State. Publication) Z1223.S78
Frequency varies.

Comprehensive lists ceased publication after 1960. Currently selected publications are listed in the department's *Selected Publications and Audio-Visual Materials,* issued quarterly.

For retrospective listing, the following publications will be of assistance:

Hasse, Adelaide R. Index to United States documents relating to foreign affairs, 1828–1861. Washington, Carnegie Institution of Washington, 1914. New York, Kraus Reprint Corp., 1965. 3 v. (Carnegie Institution of Washington publication no. 185, pt. 1–3) Z1223.Z7H22

U.S. *Dept. of State.* Foreign relations of the United States. Diplomatic papers. [1861]+ Washington, U.S. Govt. Print. Off. annual. JX233.A3
Indexes issued for 1861–99 and 1900–18. Title varies: 1861–1931, *Papers Relating to the Foreign Relations of the United States* (varies) .

—— List of treaties submitted to the Senate. 1789–1934. Washington, U.S. Govt. Print. Off., 1935. 138 p. (Publication no. 765) JX236 1934b

—— Publications on [miscellaneous subjects; lists of selected publications of] the Department of State. Washington, U.S. Govt. Print. Off., 1949–? Z1223.S782
An unnumbered series of folders each with "Department of State publication" series number. Only a few issues published.

—— Subject index of the Treaty series and the Executive agreement series. July 1, 1931. Washington, U.S. Govt. Print. Off., 1932. 214 p. (Publication no. 291)
JX235.9.A3 Index 1931

—— Treaties submitted to the Senate, 1935–[1944] Procedure on certain treaties submitted to the Senate, 1923–1934–[1944] Washington, U.S. Govt. Print. Off., 1936–[1945] (*Its* Publication no. 817, 966, 1126, 1424, 1516, 1620, 1751, 1894, 2311)
JX236 1935
Issued to supplement the *List of Treaties Submitted to the Senate, 1789–1934* (Publication 765) . The 1945 issue covers 1935–44 (Publication 2311) .

U.S. *Dept. of State. Division of Research and Publication.* Department of State publications, by Cyril Wynne. Washington, U.S. Govt. Print. Off., 1935. 14 p. ([U.S.] Dept. of State. Publication no. 724) Z1223.S77

U.S. *Dept. of State. Historical Office.* Department of State publications on diplomatic history, international law, and the conduct of foreign relations. Washington, U.S. Govt. Print. Off., 1961. 17 p. ([U.S.] Dept. of State. Publication 7320. General foreign policy series 177) Z6465.U5A55

—— Major publications of the Department of State; an annotated bibliography. [Rev. Washington] 1966 [i.e. 1967] 17 p. ([U.S.] Dept. of State. Publication 7843. General foreign policy series 200) Z1223.S7825 1967
A revised edition published in 1969.

U.S. *Dept. of State. Office of Media Services.* Department of State public information materials. Washington [U.S. Govt. Print. Off., 1966] 16 p. ([U.S.] Dept. of State Publication 8088. General foreign policy series 213) E183.7.U64

U.S. *Dept. of State. Office of the Legal Adviser.* Treaties in force; a list of treaties and other international agreements of the United States. [Washington, U.S. Govt. Print. Off.] ([U.S.] Dept. of State. Publication)   JX236   1929c
Began publication with 1929 issue.

U.S. *Superintendent of Documents.* Foreign relations of the United States. Publications relating to foreign countries. 1915+ Washington. (*Its* Price list 65)
Z1223.A191 no. 65

Department of the Air Force
Established in 1947 as part of the National Military Establishment; in 1949 it was redesignated the Department of Defense, with the Department of the Air Force as a military department within the Department of Defense, operating under the authority of the Secretary of Defense.

Air Force research résumés. [1959+] Washington. [U.S. Air Force. Office of Aerospace Research] OAR)   UG633.A153   Subser.

U.S. *Air Force. Cambridge Research Laboratories.* Bibliography of AFCRL in-house technical reports. Bedford, 1967. (*Its* Special report 61)   DLC
From July 1, 1967, quarterly supplements issued under the title *Bibliography of AFCRL Publications.* (Special reports 73, 74, 76, 77 . . .)

U.S. *Air Force. Office of Aerospace Research.* OAR cumulative index of research results. 1959–62+ [Washington]   UG633.A153   Subser.
Issued quarterly from 1964, with the last issue of each year being an annual cumulation. Quarterly issues have title: OAR *Quarterly Index of Current Research Results.*

U.S. *Air Force. Operational Applications Office.* Bibliography of technical publications, November 1949–31 August 1960. Bedford, Mass. 1961. 1 v. (unpaged)
Z6260.U5

———— ———— Supplement. no. 1+ Bedford, Mass., 1961+   Z6260.U512

U.S. *Air Force. Research and Technology Division.* Bibliography of technical presentations and publications. [1964/65] Washington.   Z5066.U53
Publications selected from papers produced in the Air Force Laboratories and the Systems Engineering Group.

U.S. *Air Force. USAF Historical Division.* Studies and histories prepared by the USAF Historical Division, Research Studies Institute, Air University, as of 1 September 1956. [Maxwell Air Force Base, Ala., 1956] 11 1.   Z6724.A3U42

U.S. *Dept. of the Air Force.* Publications bulletin. [1960?+] Washington.   DLC

U.S. *Library of Congress. Science and Technology Division.* Air Force scientific research bibliography. Washington, U.S. Govt. Print. Off. [1961–69]   Z7401.U373
This eight-volume bibliography covers the period 1950–65. Discontinued with vol. 8, since ". . . the Defense Documentation Center system, in conjunction with the Clearinghouse for Federal Scientific and Technical Information, has broadened its services . . . and is in a position to assume many of the functions of this series" (Foreword to vol. 8) .

———— Materials research abstracts, a review of the Air Force materials research and development. Edited by Charles D. Thibault. [Washington] Published for Directorate of Materials and Processes. Aeronautical Systems Division, Wright-Patterson Air Force Base. Ohio. 1962. 534 p.   TA403.U5825

U.S. *Superintendent of Documents.* Air Force ... [1949+] Washington. (*Its* Price list 79) Z1223.A191 no. 79

Department of the Army

Established in 1789 as the Department of War. It was renamed in 1947 the Department of the Army within the National Military Establishment, which in 1949 was redesignated as Department of Defense. The Department of the Army is a military department within the Department of Defense, operating under the authority of the Secretary of Defense.

A great number of lists and indexes have been issued by the Department of the Army and its predecessor, the Department of War. Currently, the *Monthly Catalog* of the U.S. Superintendent of Documents is the most comprehensive source of information concerning the publications of the department. Following are examples of some current and retrospective lists of the Department and its various services.

U.S. *Army Material Command.* Military publications; index of AMC publications and blank forms. [Washington] (*Its* AMC pamphlet, AMCP 310–1) Z6724.S9U433

U.S. *Army Supply and Maintenance Command.* Register of approved recurring reports. December 1965. [Washington, U.S. Govt. Print. Off., 1966] 200 p. (SMC pamphlet 335–1) Z6725.U5A554

U.S. *Dept. of the Army.* Military publications; index of administrative publications: Army regulations, Special regulations, Department of the Army pamphlets, Commercial traffic bulletins, General orders, Bulletins, Circulars, and Army procurement circulars. [Washington] (Pamphlet no. 310–1) Z6725.U5A4225

—— Military publications; index of graphic training aids and devices. [Current as of 30 June 1955. Washington] 1956. 232 p. (*Its* Pamphlet no. 310–5) U15.U64 no. 310–5

—— Military publications: index of supply catalogs and supply manuals (excluding types 7, 8 and 9) [Washington] 1966. 128 p. "Department of the Army pamphlet no. 310–6." UC263.A5168 1966

—— Military publications; index of supply manuals, Corps of Engineers. [Washington, U.S. Govt. Print. Off. 1956] "Department of the Army pamphlet." Z6724.S9U46

—— Military publications; index of training publications. [Washington] "Department of the Army pamphlet no. 310–3." U15.U64 Subser.

U.S. *Dept. of the Army. Office of Military History.* Publications of the Office, Chief of Military History, United States Army. Washington, 1969. 23 p. Z6725.U5A58

U.S. *Superintendent of Documents.* Army; field manuals and technical manuals. [1908]+ Washington. (*Its* Price list 19) Z1223.A191 no. 19

—— List of army regulations. Special regulations. [1950–55?] Washington. (*Its* Price list 19A) Z1223.A191 no. 19A

U.S. *War Dept.*   Index to general orders, bulletins, and numbered circulars, War Department, 1920–1942, both years inclusive. Washington, U.S. Govt. Print. Off., 1943. 195 p.   UB502   1920–42   Index

—— Letter from the Secretary of War, transmitting, in response to Senate resolution of March 24, 1881, reports of the publications, etc. of the respective bureaus

of the War Department from March 4, 1789, to March 4, 1881 ... [Washington, Govt. Print. Off., 1882] 19 p. (47th Cong., 1st sess. Senate. Ex. doc. 47) "Serial no. 1987."   Z6725.U5U5

—— List and index of War Department publications ... Washington, U.S. Govt. Print Off. (*Its* [Training publications] FM21–6)   U408.3.A13   FM21–6

—— Subject index of the General orders of the War Department, from January 1, 1809 to December 31, 1860. Washington, Govt. Print. Off., 1886. 192 p.
                                                        UB502   1809–1860   Index

—— Subject index of the General orders of the War Department, from January 1, 1861, to December 31, 1880. Washington, Govt. Print. Off., 1882. 506 p.
                                                        UB502   1861–1880   Index

—— Subject index to the General orders and Circulars of the War Department and the Headquarters of the Army, Adjutant General's Office. From January 1, 1881, to December 31, 1911 ... Washington, Govt. Print. Off., 1912. 650 p. [War Dept. Doc. 417]   UB502   1881–1911   Index

Department of the Interior
Established in 1849.

U.S. *Dept. of the Interior.*   Letter from the Secretary of the Interor, transmitting, in response to Senate resolution of March 24, 1881, a list of all books, reports, documents, and pamphlets printed or published by this department from 1879 to 1881. [Washington, Govt. Print. Off., 1882] 76 p. (47th Cong., 1st sess. Senate. Ex. doc. no. 182) "Serial no. 1991."   Z1223.I5   1882

U.S. *Dept. of the Interior. Division of Documents.*   Report of the clerk in charge of documents to the Secretary of the Interior for the fiscal year ended June 30 [1883]–1907. Washington, Govt. Print. Off., 1886–1907. 21 v.   Z1223.I5
    1896–1907 relate only to the output of certain documents from the Department of the Interior.

U.S. *Dept. of the Interior. Library.*   List of accessions. Washington [1953?+] frequency varies.   Z881.U466
    Annual supplements listing Department of the Interior publications are also issued. A cumulation for 1966–68 issued in 1968.

U.S. *Dept. of the Interior. Office of Information.*   U.S. Department of the Interior publications. Washington, U.S. Govt. Print. Off., 1964. 28 p.   DLC
    Those departmental publications most in demand, listed by title, with a short annotation.

Department of the Navy
Established in 1789. In 1947 incorporated in the National Military Establishment, which in 1949 was redesignated as Department of Defense. The Department of the Navy is a military department within the Depart-

ment of Defense, operating under the authority of the Secretary of Defense.

U.S. *Navy Dept.* Letter from the Secretary of the Navy, transmitting, in compliance with Senate resolution of March 24, 1881, a complete list of all books, reports, documents, and pamphlets issued, printed or published by the Navy Department [1789–1881] Washington, Govt. Print. Off., 1882. 15 p. (47th Cong., 1st sess., Senate. Ex. doc. 37) "Serial no. 1987."   Z6833.U58

U.S. *Superintendent of Documents.* Navy, Marine Corps and Coast Guard. 1914+ Washington. (*Its* Price list 63)   Z1223.A191 no. 63

Department of the Treasury
Established in 1789.

The Department of the Treasury occasionally issued lists of its publications. Currently, besides the *Monthly Catalog* of the U.S. Superintendent of Documents, they are also listed in its price lists, mainly no. 28 (*Finance; National Economy, Accounting, Insurance, Securities* 1908+), and no. 37 (*Tariff and Taxation* 1909+).

Following are a few retrospective lists:

Ford, Paul L. A list of Treasury reports and circulars issued by Alexander Hamilton, 1789–1795. Brooklyn, N.Y., 1886. 47 p.   Z8384.F75

U.S. *Treasury Dept.* List of publications (classified according to subjects) July 1, 1947. Washington, 1947. 19 l. (Processed)

—— Periodical publications of the Treasury Department, rev. to February 1, 1928, and summary of tabular material in the annual reports of the Secretary of the Treasury from 1914 to 1927. Washington, U.S. Govt. Print. Off., 1928. 20 p.
Z1223.T78 1928

—— Publications of the Treasury Department as of July 1, 1940. [Washington, 1940] (Reproduced from typewritten copy)   Z1223.T78 1940

Department of Transportation
Established in 1966.

U.S. *Superintendent of Documents.* Transportation, highways, roads, and postal service. 1910+ Washington. (*Its* Price list 25)   Z1223.A191 no. 25

Federal Aviation Administration
Established originally as Civil Aeronautics Authority, an independent agency, in 1938. Certain administrative functions transferred in 1940 to the Department of Commerce and designated as Civil Aeronautics Administration. In 1958 functions transferred to Federal Aviation Agency, and in 1966, as Federal Aviation Administration, to the Department of Transportation.

Lists of Civil Aeronautics Administration publications have been issued irregularly, but at least once a year from 1942 (title varies) and continued by *FAA Publications* from 1959. The catalog of the U.S. Department of Commerce publications lists CAA publications until 1958. Other bibliographic sources are the following:

Briddon, Arnold E. Federal Aviation Agency historical fact book; a chronology, 1926–1963. Washington, Office of Management Services, Federal Aviation Agency. U.S. Govt. Print. Off., 1966. 130 p.   TL521.B72
    Bibliography, p. 107–109, includes official publications.

Herner and Company, *Washington, D.C.* FAA headquarters library list of unpublished research reports; listed by AD number, cataloged by author, title series and corporate entry. Washington, Federal Aviation Agency, 1961. 155 p.   Z881.U595

—— —— Subject guide. Washington, Federal Aviation Agency, 1962. 48 p.   Z881.U595 Guide

—— List of FAA and CAA technical development reports and CAA research reports, with list of the subject headings used for indexing the reports. Washington, Federal Aviation Agency, 1961. 37 p.   Z5063.H4

U.S. *Federal Aviation Agency. Library Services Division.* Bibliographies of technical reports. Washington, 1962. 45 p. (*Its* Information retrieval list no. 1) Z7911.A1U6

U.S. *Federal Aviation Agency. Library Services Division. Information Retrieval Branch.* Title listing of CAA publications. Washington, 1964. 85 p. (*Its* Information retrieval list no. 2)   Z5063.U5945

U.S. *Superintendent of Documents.* Air Force, aviation, civil aviation, naval aviation, Federal Aviation Administration. 1949+ Washington. (*Its* Price list 79)   Z1223.A191 no. 79
    Before 1949, publications listed in price list 25 (*Transportation ...*) .

Federal Communications Commission
Established in 1934.

The commission has occasionally issued lists of its publications: from 1957, ADM *Bulletin*, no. 1, currently *ED Bulletin*, no. 1. The commission's publications are also listed in:

U.S. *Superintendent of Documents.* Radio and electricity; electronics, radar, and communications. 1951+ Washington. (*Its* Price list 82)   Z1223.A191 no. 82
    Before 1951, its publications were included in price lists no. 25 (*Transportation*) and no. 59 (*Interstate Commerce*) .

Federal Highway Administration
Established in 1966 in the Department of Transportation, absorbing the Bureau of Public Roads.

U.S. *Federal Highway Administration.* Publications. 1967+ Washington.   DLC

U.S. *Superintendent of Documents.* Transportation, highways, roads, and postal service. 1910+ Washington. (*Its* Price list 25)   Z1223.A191 no. 25

Federal Power Commission
Established in 1920.

U.S. *Federal Power Commission.* Publications list. 1961+ Washington. semiannual?
DLC

———— Reports. Opinions, decisions and orders. v. 1+ Jan. 1931/June 1939+ Washington, U.S. Govt. Print. Off. KF2120.A553
———— Cumulative index-digest to the opinions, decisions and orders. v. A+
1931/57+ KF2120.A5532

U.S. *Superintendent of Documents.* Irrigation, drainage and water power. 1909+
Washington. (*Its* Price list 42) Z1223.A191 no. 42

Federal Trade Commission
Established in 1915.

U.S. *Federal Trade Commission.* Digest of decisions of the Federal Trade Commission.
From 1915 to June 1, 1938. Washington, U.S. Govt. Print. Off., 1940. 60 p.
HD2775.F7 Digest

———— Digest of Federal Trade Commission decisions. 1 FTC decisions to 45 FTC decisions, incl. Washington [1949?] 2 v. DLC LL
"Digest of all the Commission cases where complaints were issued for violation
of sections 5 and 12 of the Federal Trade Commission Act and the Wool products
labeling act." Vol. 2, Index.

———— Federal trade commission decisions. Washington, U.S. Govt. Print. Off., 1920+
HD2775.F7

———— Index-digest of vols. I, II, and III of Decisions of the Federal Trade Commission with annotations of federal cases. March 16, 1915 to June 30, 1921. Washington, Govt. Print. Off., 1922. 233 p. HD2775.F7 Index

———— List of publications. [1941?+] Washington. Z1223.F4

Fish and Wildlife Service
Established originally in 1940 in the Department of the Interior, absorbing the Bureau of Fisheries, which had been transferred from the Department of Commerce in 1939. The service was reorganized in 1956 and in 1970.

U.S. *Dept. of the Interior. Library.* Fishery publication index, 1920–54; publications
of the Bureau of Fisheries and fishery publications of the Fish and Wildlife Service
by series, authors, and subjects. [A joint undertaking of the Dept. of the Interior
Library and the Fish and Wildlife Service. Washington, U.S. Govt. Print. Off.,
1956] 254 p. (U.S. Fish and Wildlife Service. Circular 36) SK361.A29 no. 36
Continued for 1955–64 in the Fish and Wildlife Service Circular 296, compiled
by George Washington University, Washington, D.C., 240 p. SK361.A29 no. 296.

U.S. *Fish and Wildlife Service.* Monthly list of printed and duplicated material.
Washington, [1953?–65] DLC

From 1966 issued as separate lists by the service's Bureau of Commercial
Fisheries (1966–70) and Bureau of Sport Fisheries and Wildlife.

—— New publications, Fish and Wildlife Service. List 1, July 1939–Apr. 1942.
[Washington] U.S. Govt. Print. Off., 1942. 6 p.   Z7999.U6

U.S. *Superintendent of Documents.* Fish and wildlife. 1908+ Washington. (*Its* Price
list 21)   Z1223.A191 no. 21

U.S. *Wildlife Research Laboratory, Denver.* Publications, 1941–1950. [Denver, U.S.
Dept of the Interior, Fish and Wildlife Service, Branch of Wildlife Research,
1952] 13 p.   Z7999.U63

Foreign Agricultural Service

Established in 1930 in the Department of Agriculture. In 1939 certain
functions were transferred to the Department of State, and the remaining
functions went to the newly created Office of Foreign Agricultural Relations in the Department of Agriculture. In 1953, the Foreign Agricultural Service was reestablished.

U.S. *Foreign Agricultural Service.* Foreign Agricultural Service special reports [list]
Washington. 1964?+
      Revised semiannually.

—— List of maps and charts published by the Foreign Agricultural Service. Washington, 1955. 42 p.   Z6028.U48
      "Supersedes the *Index to Maps and Charts* and *Supplements* nos. 1, 2, and 3,
      published by the Foreign Agricultural Service (formerly Office of Foreign Agri-
      cultural Relations) , July 1950, 1951, 1952, 1953."
      —— —— Supplement. Nov. 1, 1955/June 1, 1956+ Washington. Z6028.U482

—— Published information on agriculture in foreign countries, January 1937–December 1953. Washington, 1954. 65 p.   Z5071.U52

Forest Service

Established in 1905 in the Department of Agriculture. Previously, Division of Forestry (1881–1901) and Bureau of Forestry (1901–5).

U.S. *Forest Service.* Classified list of publications. [1905–13] Washington, U.S. Dept.
of Agriculture.   Z5991.U45
      Title varies.

—— List of Forest Service publications; title, series, author. July 1970. Washington.
164 p. (*Its* FS-51)   DLC
      "For internal use."

—— List of publications by subject. Washington, 1970. 85 p.   DLC

U.S. *Superintendent of Documents.* Forestry. 1909+ Washington. (*Its* Price list 43)
                                                                          Z1223.A191 no. 43

Forest Experiment Stations

First Forest Experiment Stations were established in 1908, and regional stations were started in 1922. Publications are listed in their respective annual reports and also in more or less regularly issued lists. Following is a list of existing stations, with indication of changes, and lists of their publications:

Institute of Northern Forestry, Juneau, Alaska

Previously Alaska Forest Research Center, established in 1948, and Northern Forest Experiment Station (1961–65?).

Institute of Northern Forestry, *Juneau, Alaska.* List of publications, 1970. 13 p.

Intermountain Forest and Range Experiment Station, Ogden, Utah

Absorbed Northern Rocky Mountain Forest and Range Experiment Station, Missoula, Mont., in 1954.

Israelson, Marguerite A. Publications of the Intermountain Forest and Range Experiment Station, 1912 through 1952. Ogden, Utah [1952] 45 p. (U.S. Forest Service. Intermountain Forest and Range Experiment Station. Research paper no. 29)
SD11.A455452 no. 29
Two supplements, published in 1956 and 1961 respectively, extend coverage from 1953 to 1960.

U.S. *Intermountain Forest and Range Experiment Station, Ogden, Utah.* Publications. 1961?+ Ogden, Utah. annual. DLC

—— Recent reports. 1967+ Ogden, Utah. bimonthly. DLC

U.S. *Northern Rocky Mountain Forest and Range Experiment Station, Missoula, Mont.* List of publications available for distribution or loan, 1910–1947. Missoula, Mont., 1948. 11, 26 l. (*Its* Station paper no. 14) SD11.A4555 no. 14

—— Publications. 1912–1950. Missoula, Mont., 1951. 69 p. (*Its* Station paper no. 31)
SD11.A4555 no. 31

North Central Forest Experiment Station, St. Paul, Minn.

Formerly, Lake States Forest Experiment Station, St. Paul, Minn.; name changed to North Central Forest Experiment Station, merged with Central States Forest Experiment Station, Columbus, Ohio, in 1965–66.

Schober, Helen C. List of publications. Written wholly or in part by members of the Central States Forest Experiment Station staff from the time the Station was established in 1927 to January 1955. Rev. Columbus, Ohio, U.S. Dept. of Agriculture, Forest Service, 1955. 52 p. ([U.S.] Central States Forest Experiment Station, Columbus, Ohio. Miscellaneous release no. 6) SD11.U5 no. 6
Revised and updated to January 1960 by Dorothy E. Bennett (1960. 68 p.) .

U.S. *Central States Forest Experiment Station, Columbus, Ohio.* Publications.. [1960–Mar. 1966] annual.

U.S. *Lake States Forest Experiment Station, St. Paul, Minn.* Publications of Lake States Forest Experiment Station, 1923–55; assembled by L. P. Olsen and H. A.

Woodworth. St. Paul, Minn., 1956. 130 p. (*Its* Station paper no. 39)
SD11.A45547 no. 39
Supplements: 1956–60 (1961. 67 p.) and 1961–65 (1966. 57 p.)

U.S. *North Central Forest Experiment Station, St. Paul, Minn.* List of publications; annotated. [1966+] St. Paul, Minn.   DLC

Northeastern Forest Experiment Station. Upper Darby, Pa.
First established in Amherst, Mass. (1923); merged with Allegheny Forest Experiment Station, Philadelphia, Pa. (1942).

Horowitz, Sylvia. Publications of the Northeastern Forest Experiment Station 1950–1965. Upper Darby, Pa., Northeastern Forest Experiment Station, Forest Service, U.S. Dept. of Agriculture, 1967. 134 p. (U.S. Forest Service research paper NE–62)
SD11.A455493 no. 62
Updates earlier bibliography issued as Station paper no. 33 by the Northeastern Forest Experiment Station

U.S. *Northeastern Forest Experiment Station, Upper Darby, Pa.* New publications available. 1968?+ Upper Darby, Pa.

Pacific Northwest Forest and Range Experiment Station, Portland, Or.
Established in 1924 as Pacific Northwest Forest Experiment Station; name changed to Pacific Northwest Forest and Range Experiment Station, in 1938.

U.S. *Pacific Northwest Forest and Range Experiment Station, Portland. Or.* Annotated list of publications . . . for the year [1966?+] Portland, Or. annual.   DLC

—— List of available publications. 1965?+ Portland, Or.   DLC

—— Lists of publications for the years 1938 thru 1952. Portland, Or., 1953. 26 p.
Z5991.U445

—— Publications of the Pacific Northwest Forest and Range Experiment Station, compiled by Mildred Hoyt and Edith P. Tomkins. Portland, Or., 1965. 67 p.
Z5991.U566
Covers period 1928–64. Author index 1938–64 only.

Pacific Southwest Forest and Range Experiment Station, Berkeley, Calif.
Formerly, California Forest and Range Experiment Station. Name changed in 1958.

U.S. *Pacific Southwest Forest and Range Experiment Station, Berkeley, Calif.* List of available publications. Apr. 1967+ Berkeley, quarterly.   DLC

—— Publications. [1966?+] Berkeley, Calif. annual.   Z5991.U568

—— Staff publications. [1916–?] Berkeley.   Z5991.U57

Rocky Mountain Forest and Range Experiment Station. Fort Collins, Colo.

Merged with Southwestern Forest and Range Experiment Station, Tucson, Ariz., in 1954.

U.S. *Rocky Mountain Forest and Range Experiment Station, Fort Collins, Colo.* List of publications. June 1963+ Fort Collins. quarterly.								DLC

—— Publications. [1969?+] Fort Collins. annual.								DLC

Southeastern Forest Experiment Station. Asheville, N.C.

Name changed from Appalachian Forest Experiment Station in 1946.

U.S. *Southeastern Forest Experiment Station, Asheville, N.C.* Publications. [1953?–65?] Asheville.											Z5991.U58
    Title varies: 1953–57, *Bibliography.*

—— Research information digest; recent publications of the Southeastern Forest Experiment Station. [1966?+] Asheville. semiannual.					DLC

—— Station paper. no. 1+ May 15, 1949+ Asheville.						SD11.A4575
    No. 117: *Publications of Southeastern Forest Experiment Station, 1921–1958;* comp. by Hilda J. Brown (1960. 115 p.)
    No. 117, Suppl.: *Publications of Southeastern Forest Experiment Station, 1959–1963;* comp. by Hilda J. Brown (1965. 71 p.) .

Southern Forest Experiment Station. New Orleans, La.

U.S. *Southern Forest Experiment Station, New Orleans.* Publications. [1963?+] New Orleans. annual.										DLC
    Also, two or three times a year, *Recent Publications.*

—— Occasional paper. New Orleans.							SD11.A4579
    No. 108 rev.: *Publications of Southern Forest Experiment Station, July 1921– Dec. 1954.* New Orleans. 1955. 128 p.
    No. 108, Suppl. 1: *Publications of Southern Forest Experiment Station, 1955– 1961; with Lists of Serial publications,* by Louis E. Punch. New Orleans, 1962. 57 p.

The Forest Products Laboratory in Madison, Wis., issues a semiannual *List of Publications* and specialized subject lists.

General Accounting Office

Established in 1921.

U.S. *General Accounting Office.* List of GAO publications. v. [1] no. 1+ June 1967+ [Washington] semiannual.									DLC

Geological Survey

Established in 1879 in the Department of the Interior.

U.S. *Geological Survey.* Publications of the Geological Survey, 1879–1961. [Washington, U.S. Govt. Print. Off., 1964] 457 p.   Z6034.U49U53
  "This catalog is a new and complete list through December 1961 of Geological Survey books, maps and charts. It should be retained for permanent use, as updating and revision of the catalog are not intended. Newly issued publications will continue to be reported monthly in 'New Publications of the Geological Survey,' and supplements to this permanent catalog will be published from time to time."

—— Publications of the Geological Survey. 1893– [1958] Washington, U.S. Govt. Print. Off.   Z6034.U49U5
  Title varies. Published irregularly. Supplements accompany some editions.

U.S. *Superintendent of Documents.* Geology. 1907+ Washington. (*Its* Price list 15)
                                  Z1223.A191 no. 15

Interstate Commerce Commission
Established in 1887.

U.S. *Interstate Commerce Commission.* Interstate Commerce Commission reports. Decisions. v. 1+ Apr. 5, 1887–Apr. 5, 1888+ Washington, U.S. Govt. Print. Off.
                                  DLC LL
  Indexes which cover five volumes each, beginning with v. 300 and excluding financial volumes, are available: *Consolidated Index-Digest of Reports of the Interstate Commerce Commission Involving Rates and Practices.*

—— Interstate Commerce Commission reports: Motor carrier cases. Decisions. v. 1+ June 1936–May 1937+ Washington, U.S. Govt. Print. Off.   HE5623.A25
  Indexes which cover five volumes each, beginning with v. 71 and excluding financial volumes, are available: *Consolidated Index-Digest of Reports of the Interstate Commerce Commission Involving Motor Carrier Operating Rights.*

In addition, the following two indexes and the Superintendent of Documents' price list cover the commission's reports:

U.S. *Interstate Commerce Commission.* Consolidated index-digest of reports of the Interstate Commerce Commission involving finance. Dec. 1957–Apr. 1962+ Washington, U.S. Govt. Print. Off.   HE2708.I8512
  Covers finance volumes of the commission's reports, beginning with v. 307, and its reports on motor carrier cases, beginning with v. 75.

—— Interstate Commerce Commission reports. Decisions. (*Indexes*) Consolidated current index to I.C.C. decisions. 1955 ed. Washington, Association of Interstate Commerce Commission Practitioners, 1955. 862 p.
  "A compilation of the Index to I.C.C. decisions which appeared monthly in the I.C.C. practitioners' journal from January 1951 through January 1955."

U.S. *Superintendent of Documents.* Interstate commerce. 1914+ Washington. (*Its* Price list 59)   Z1223.A191 no. 59

Joint Publications Research Service
Established in 1957.

Bibliography-index to current U.S. JPRS translations: China & Asia exclusive of Near

East. v. 1+ July/Sept. 1962+ [New York] Research & Microfilm Publications, CCM
Information Corp. monthly. AS36.U572
Absorbed *Asian Developments: a Bibliography*, in 1964.

Bibliography-index to current U.S. JPRS translations: East Europe; Albania, Bulgaria,
Czechoslovakia, East Germany, Hungary, Poland, Rumania, Yugoslavia. v. 1+
July/Sept. 1962+ [New York] Research & Microfilm Publications, CCM Informa-
tion Corp. monthly. Z2483.B52

Bibliography-index to current U.S. JPRS translations: International developments,
Africa, Latin America, Near East, international communist developments. no. 1+
July/Sept. 1962+ [New York] Research & Microfilm Publications, CCM Informa-
tion Corp. monthly. Z3501.B53

Bibliography-index to current U.S. JPRS translations: Soviet Union. v. 1+ July/Sept.
1962+ [New York] Research & Microfilm Publications, CCM Information Corp.
monthly. Z2491.B52

Catalog cards in book form for United States Joint Publications Research Service
translations. New York, CCM Information Corp. semiannual. Z1223.Z9K9
Began with volume for 1957/61. Superseded from 1971 by *Transdex* (see
below).

Poole, Mary E. Index to Readex microprint edition of JPRS reports. New York,
Readex Microprint Corp. [1964] 137 l. AS36.U5612
An index correlating the JPRS report numbers, Oct. 1958-Dec. 1963, with the
entry numbers of the *Monthly Catalog of United States Government Publications*, by which the microprint ed. is arranged.

Transdex; bibliography and index to the United States Joint Publications Research
Service (JPRS) translations. New York, CCM Information Corp. [1971+] monthly,
with semiannual cumulation. AS36.U574
Supersedes *Bibliography-Index to Current U.S. JPRS Translations*, beginning
with vol. 9 (1970/71), and *Catalog Cards in Book Form for United States Joint
Publications Research Service Translations* (see above).

White, Thomas N. Guide to United States J.P.R.S. research translations, 1957–1966:
China, U.S.S.R., Asia, East Europe, Africa, Near East, Latin America, West Europe.
Washington, Research & Microfilm Publications [1966] 67 p. Z1223.Z7W55
"Prepared for the 1966 annual meeting of the American Political Science
Association."

JPRS translations have been listed since 1958 in the *Monthly Catalog
of United States Government Publications*. Other bibliographies, covering mainly the period 1957–61/62, are:

Kyriak, Theodore E. China, 1957-July 1960; bibliography of United States Joint Publications Research Service translations on microfilm. Annapolis, Research & Microfilm Publications [1962?] 59 p. on [37] l. [Z3106.K9]

—— Indonesia, 1957–1961; a bibliography and guide to contents of a collection of
United States Joint Publications Research Service translations on microfilm.
Annapolis, Research & Microfilm Publications [1962?] 34 p. on [21] l. [Z3271.K9]

—— International communist developments, 1957–1961; an index and guide to a
collection of U.S. JPRS translations emanating from Africa, Latin America and

Western Europe. Annapolis, Research Microfilms [1962] 54 l.   Z7164.S67K9
Issued also for 1962 (Jan.–June) 32 p. on [17] l. [Z7164.S67K92]

——— Mongolia, 1957–1961; a bibliography and guide to contents of a collection of
United States Joint Publications Research Service translations on microfilm. Annapolis, Research & Microfilm Publications [1962?] 10 p. on [8] l.   [Z3107.M7K9]

——— North Korea, 1957–1961; a bibliography and guide to contents of a collection
of United States Joint Publications Research Service translations on microfilm.
Annapolis, Research & Microfilm Publications [1966?] 29 p. on [17] l.
[Z7165.K62K9]

——— North Vietnam, 1957–1961; a bibliography and guide to contents of a collection of United States Joint Publications Research Service translations on microfilm. Annapolis, Research & Microfilm Publications [1966?] 62 p. on [34] l.
[Z3228.V52K9]
Issued also for Jan.-June 1962.

——— Subject index to United States Joint Publications Research Service translations.
[Jan./June 1966–July/Dec. 1968?] Annapolis, Research & Microfilm Publications
[New York, CCM Information Corp.] semiannual.   DLC

Lake Survey
Established in 1841 in the War Department. Lake Survey Office was in
Buffalo 1841–45, and from 1845 on in Detroit. In 1970 it combined with
the Coast and Geodetic Survey under the name of National Ocean Survey, within the National Oceanic and Atmospheric Administration.

U.S. *Lake Survey.* Catalog of Charts of the Great Lakes and connecting waters, also
Lake Champlain, New York canals, Minnesota-Ontario border lakes. Detroit
[1904?+]   Z6026.H9U63

——— Catalog of charts of the Great Lakes and outflow rivers, also Lake Champlain,
New York State barge canal system, Minnesota-Ontario border lakes. Detroit
[1964] 23 p.   Z6026.H9U65

Library of Congress
Established in 1800.

U.S. *Library of Congress.* Publications in print. May 6, 1901+ Washington. annual.
Z733.U57B15
Title varies slightly. Supplements accompany some issues. Issue of May 1935
called *Publications Issued by the Library since 1897.* Issue of 1947 called *Publications 1936–46.*

——— Report of the Librarian of Congress. 1865/66+ Washington, U.S. Govt. Print.
Off. annual.   Z733.U57A
From 1902, the report includes a list of publications issued during the year.
The 1901 report includes "List of publications of the Library of Congress,
1800–1901."

U.S. *Superintendent of Documents.* Library of Congress. June 1951+ Washington.
(*Its* Price list 83)   Z1223.A191 no. 83
See also Price list no. 34 (1909) .

Marine Corps
Established in 1798, within the Navy Department.

Dollen, Charles. Bibliography of the United States Marine Corps. New York, Scarecrow Press, 1963. 115 p. Z6725.U5D6

Donnelly, Ralph W. An annotated bibliography of United States Marine Corps artillery. Washington, Historical Division, Headquarters, U.S. Marine Corps, 1970. 68 p. (Marine Corps Historical bibliography) Z6724.A8D6

U.S. *Superintendent of Documents.* Navy, Marine Corps and Coast Guard. 1914+ Washington. (*Its* Price list 63) Z1223.A191 no. 63

Maritime Administration
Established in 1950 in the Department of Commerce, where, together with the Federal Maritime Board, it succeeded the United States Maritime Commission.

The Maritime Administration issues occasionally a list of its current publications. Its publications are also listed in the catalog of the Department of Commerce. Regulations are indexed in:

U.S. *Maritime Administration. Office of General Counsel.* Index of current regulations of the Federal Maritime Board, Maritime Administration [and] National Shipping Authority. [1959?+ Washington] DLC LL

National Advisory Committee for Aeronautics
Established in 1915; abolished in 1958 and functions transferred to National Aeronautics and Space Administration.

Niewald, Roy J. Bibliography of NACA reports related to aircraft control and guidance systems. Jan. 1949-April 1954. Washington, National Advisory Committee for Aeronautics, 1954. 55 p. (NACA research memorandum RM, 54F01) Z5064.D4N5

U.S. *National Advisory Committee for Aeronautics.* Index of NACA technical publications. 1947–1957/58. Washington. 9 v. Z5063.U634
　　　Issues for 1947–49 cumulative from 1915. Issued 1957/58 by the National Aeronautics and Space Administration. Superseded by U.S. National Aeronautics and Space Administration's *Index of NASA Technical Publications.*

—— List of NACA wartime reports. [Washington, 1948] 1 v. (various pagings) Z5063.U5953

—— List of reports with prices. [1926–45] Washington. irregular. Z5063.U64

U.S. *Superintendent of Documents.* Army; field manuals and technical manuals. 1908+ Washington. (*Its* Price list 19) Z1223.A191 no. 19
　　　After 1949, listed in Price list 79 (*Air Force, Aviation ...*)

National Aeronautics and Space Administration
Established in 1958; succeeded National Advisory Committee for Aeronautics.

Aeronautical engineering; a special bibliography. 1970+ Washington, Scientific and Technical Information Office, National Aeronautics and Space Administration [available from the National Technical Information Service, Springfield, Va.] (NASA SP–7037)   Z5063.A2A28
"A selection of annotated references to unclassified reports and journal articles that were introduced into the NASA scientific and technical information system and announced . . . in *Scientific and Technical Aerospace Reports; International Aerospace Abstracts.*" Supplements 1+ published January 1971+

Scientific and technical aerospace reports. v. 1+ Jan. 8, 1963+ [Washington] semimonthly.   TL500.S35
Indexes to individual issues are cumulated semiannually and annually, including subject index, personal author index, corporate source index, contract number index, report/accession number index and accession number/report index. See also the *Guide to the Subject Indexes* for these, below.

U.S. *Library of Congress. Science and Technology Division.* List of selected references on NASA programs. Prepared for the National Aeronautics and Space Administration. 1962. 236 p. (NASA SP–3)   TL521.A333 no. 3

U.S. *National Aeronautics and Space Administration.* Guide to the subject indexes for Scientific and technical aerospace reports. Issue no. 1+ Apr. 1964+ [Washington]   Z695.1.A25U57
"It supersedes the *Guide to the Subject Index for Technical Publications Announcements,* published December 31, 1962."

———— Index of NASA technical publications. Oct. 1958/June 1959+ Washington.
Z5063.U6342
Supersedes National Advisory Committee for Aeronautics' *Index of NACA Technical Publications.*

———— NASA educational publications. 1962+ Washington.   DLC

———— NASA special publications [catalog] 1966+ Washington.   DLC
Four to six pages of every issue are devoted to listing bibliographies and other reference works published by NASA.

———— Technical publications announcements. v. 1–2, Nov. 14, 1958-Dec. 20, 1962. Washington.   TL501.U5895
Title varies: Nov. 14, 1958-June 30, 1959, *Publications Announcements.* Superseded from Jan. 1963 by *Scientific and Technical Aerospace Reports.*

U.S. *National Aeronautics and Space Administration. Scientific and Technical Information Division.* NASA publications manual. Washington, U.S. Govt. Print. Off., 1964. 74 p. (NASA SP–7013)   TL521.312.A58

———— A selected listing of NASA scientific and technical reports. 1963+ Washington. (NASA SP)   TL501.U5894

U.S. *Superintendent of Documents.* Space, missiles, the moon, NASA, and satellites. 1967+ Washington. (*Its* Price list 79A)   Z1223,A191 no. 79A

National Archives and Records Service

Established originally in 1934 as National Archives Establishment, it became National Archives and Records Service in 1949 and was placed within the General Services Administration.

Colket, Meredith B. Guide to genealogical records in the National Archives. Washington, National Archives and Records Service, General Services Administration
...1964. 145 p. (National Archives publication no. 64–8) CS15.C6

U.S. *National Archives.* Federal population censuses 1790–1890: a price list of microfilm copies of the schedules. Washington, 1969. 186 p. *(Its* Publication no. 69–3) HA37.U547 1969

—— Guide to the records in the National Archives. Washington, U.S. Govt. Print. Off., 1948. 684 p. *(Its* Publication no. 49–13) CD3023.A46 1948

—— List of National Archives microfilm publications. 1947+ Washington. *(Its* Publication) CD3027.M514

—— Publications of the National Archives. [1942?+] Washington. Z1223.N25

National Bureau of Standards
Established in 1901.

U.S. *National Bureau of Standards.* Publications. Nov. 1907+ Washington. U.S. Govt. Print. Off. Z1223.S75
   Issued 1910–25 as its Circular 24 (1st to 7th ed.) with supplements for July 1, 1925–Dec. 1931 and for Jan. 1932–Dec. 1941; then appeared as Circular 460, entitled *Publications of the National Bureau of Standards 1901 to June 30, 1947,* including subject and author indexes. Brief abstracts are also included for the period Jan. 1941 to June 30, 1947, only. The period since July 1947 *to date* is covered by the following lists: Supplement to Circular 460 (July 1, 1947–June 30, 1957) ; Miscellaneous publication 240 (July 1, 1957–June 30, 1960) , including titles of papers published in outside journals, 1950–59; Supplement to Miscellaneous publication 240 (July 1960–June 1966) , including titles of papers published in outside journals from 1960 to 1965; Special publication 305 (July 1966–Dec. 1967) , with key-word and author indexes; Supplement 1 to Special publication 305 (1968–69) , "a compilation of abstracts and key-word and author indexes." From 1970, supplements published annually.
   Currently, publications of the National Bureau of Standards are announced in *Publication Announcements* (TRA series) , issued irregularly, and in *NBS Publications Newsletter,* issued quarterly since Nov. 1963.

In 1968, the National Bureau of Standards initiated the publication of a new series to implement the provisions of Public Law 89–306, concerning the establishment of a Federal Information Processing Standards Register:

Federal information processing standards publication. FIPS PUB. 0+ [Washington] U.S. National Bureau of Standards [U.S. Govt. Print. Off.] 1968+ JK468.A8A3
   Includes publications announcing newly approved federal information processing standards and maintaining established standards. Also, a complete index of relevant standards publications is issued through the series.

National Guard Bureau
Established in 1908 as Division of Militia Affairs in the War Department, its name was changed to Militia Bureau in 1916, and to National Guard Bureau in 1933.

U.S. *National Guard Bureau.* Publications, National Guard Bureau; National Guard
regulations and NGB pamphlets. Washington. annual. (*Its* NGB pamphlet)
Z6725.U5A26
Latest issued in 1970 as *Publications, Index of National Guard Bureau Publications* (NGB pamphlet 310–1).

National Institute of Mental Health
Established in 1946.

U.S. *National Institute of Mental Health.* Catalog: mental health pamphlets and re-
prints available for distribution. 1949+ Washington.   Z6673.U5
Issues for 1950+ published as Public Health Service publication, and as
Public health bibliography series, no. 2 (Z6673.U515).

Related bibliographies have been published by the National Clearinghouse for Mental Health Information:

U.S. *National Clearinghouse for Mental Health Information.* Bibliography of informational publications issued by state mental health agencies. [Washington] National Institute of Mental Health [1964] 66 p.   Z6673.U47

―――― Bibliography on drug dependence and abuse, 1928–1966. [Chevy Chase, Md.,
1969] 258 p.   Z7164.N17U56

―――― Publications resulting from National Institute of Mental Health research
grants, 1947–1961. [Washington, U.S. Govt. Print. Off., 1968] 599 p. (Public Health
Service publication no. 1647)   Z6664.N5U55

National Institutes of Health
Established in 1930 as National Institute of Health, within the Public
Health Service; in 1947 the Institute was renamed National Institutes
of Health.

U.S. *National Institutes of Health.* NIH publications list. July 1969+ [Washington] DLC

―――― Scientific directory and annual bibliography. 1956+ [Washington, U.S. Govt.
Print. Off.] (Public Health Services publication. Public health bibliography series)
Z6673.U515 subser.
Title varies: 1956–57, *Published Scientific Papers of the National Institutes
of Health.*

National Labor Relations Board
Established in 1935.

U.S. *National Labor Relations Board.* Decisions and orders. v. 1+ Dec. 7, 1935/July 1.
1936+ Washington, U.S. Govt. Print. Off.   DLC LL
Indexes: v. 1–150, Dec. 7, 1935–Feb. 12, 1965 (3 v.)

―――― Digest and index of decisions. v. [1]–6, [1935/42]–1953/56. Washington, U.S.
Govt. Print. Off.   DLC LL
Vols. for 1935/42–1946/47 called v. 1/45–71/74 in agreement with the num-

bering of the Board's *Decisions and Orders.* Title varies: 1935/42, *Digest of Decisions.* Kept up to date by annual supplements and from 1967 also by bimonthly *Digest of Decisions of National Labor Relations Board* (CS–series) .

National Museum

Established originally in the Patent Office in 1842, it became part of the Smithsonian Institution in 1846.

Smithsonian Institution. A list and index of the publications of the United States National Museum, 1875–1946. Washington, U.S. Govt. Print. Off., 1947. 306 p. (U.S. National Museum, Bulletin 193) Q11.U6 no. 193
Z7403.U547

——— ——— Supplement 1+ Jan. 1947/June 1958+ Washington.

U.S. National Museum. Publications of the United States National Museum (1947–1970) . Washington, Smithsonian Institution Press, 1971. 77 p. (*Its* Bulletin 298) Q11.U6 no. 298
Z7401.U3795

U.S. *Superintendent of Documents.* Smithsonian Institution, National Museum and Indians. Oct. 1911+ Washington. (*Its* Price list 55) Z1223.A191 no. 55
For the period 1911–14, also Price list 56. (*Indians, Smithsonian Institution, Fine Arts*)

National Ocean Survey

Established in 1970 in the Department of Commerce, within the National Oceanic and Atmospheric Administration. At that time it absorbed the former Coast and Geodetic Survey, from Environmental Science Services Administration, and parts of the United States Lake Survey.

National Ocean Survey. Catalog of aeronautical charts and related publications. Jan. 1971+ Washington. DLC Map

——— Nautical chart catalog. 1+ Jan. 1971+ Washington. DLC Map

National Oceanic and Atmospheric Administration

Established in 1970 in the Department of Commerce, replacing the Environmental Science Services Administration, created in 1965, and elements of a number of other organizations.

U.S. *National Oceanic and Atmospheric Administration.* NOAA publications announcement no. 71–1+ Feb. 1971+ Washington.

National Park Service

Established in 1916 in the Department of the Interior.

U.S. *Superintendent of Documents.* Checklist, National Park Service publications and other publications relating to national parks. Washington [1950–55?] DLC

—— National parks, historic sites, national monuments. 1911+ Washington. (*Its*
Price list 35)   Z1223.A191 no. 35

National Science Foundation
Established in 1950.

U.S. *National Science Foundation.* Publications . . . [1959+] Washington.   DLC
    Lists of publications issued during the year included also in the *Annual Report*
    (Q11.U82) .

—— Publications resulting from National Science Foundation research grants through
    fiscal year ending June 20, 1956. Comp. by Virginia Boteler, Washington, U.S.
    Govt. Print Off. [1957] 38 p.   Z7401.U38

National Transportation Safety Board
Established in 1966 in the Department of Transportation, with an autonomous status.

U.S. *National Transportation Safety Board.* Publications. Washington [1969?+] an-
    nual.   DLC

Naval Facilities Engineering Command
Established in 1966 in the Department of the Navy, it absorbed the
functions of the Bureau of Yards and Docks.

U.S. *Naval Facilities Engineering Command.* Index of Naval Facilities Engineering
    Command publications. [1966?+] Washington. "NAVFAC P-349"

—— Key word subject index (KWOC) , NAVFAC publications. Washington. "NAVFAC
    P-349.1"

Naval Observatory
Established in 1830 in the Navy Department under the name of Depot
of Charts and Instruments; from 1844 to 1866, the names National
Observatory, Naval Observatory, and Naval Observatory and Hydrographic Office were used; since 1866, Naval Observatory.

Holden, Edward S. A subject-index to the publications of the United States Naval
    Observatory, 1845–1875. Washington, Govt. Print. Off., 1879. 74 p. (U.S. Naval
    Observatory Washington astronomical observations for 1876. Appendix 1)
                                                              Z5156.U6 1879

U.S. *Naval Observatory. Library.* List of publications issued by the United States Naval
    Observatory, 1845–1908. By Wm. D. Horigan, Librarian. Washington, Govt. Print.
    Off., 1911. 36 p.   Z5156.U6 1911
        "Reprint of Publications of the U.S. Naval Observatory, Second series, volume
    VI—appendix III." Pages designated D1–D36.

Naval Oceanographic Office

Established in 1962 in the Department of the Navy, absorbing the functions of the Hydrographic Office, created in 1866.

U.S. *Hydrographic Office.* General catalog of mariners' and aviators' charts and books. Washington, U.S. Govt. Print. Off., 1871–?   Z6026.H9U6
> Title varies: 1871–1907, *Catalogue of Charts*...; 1910–29, *General Catalogue of Mariners' Charts and Books*...; 1931–41?, *General Catalogue of Mariners' and Aviators' Charts and Books.*...Divided up after 1941: *Catalog of Aeronautical Charts and Publications*... (*Its* H.O. pub. no. 1–V, Z5063.U5946) ; *Catalog of Loran Charts and Service Areas* (*Its* H.O. pub. no. 1–L, Z5066.U56) ; *Index-Catalog of Nautical Charts and Publications* (*Its* H.O. pub. no. 1–N, Z6026.H9U615)

U.S. *Naval Oceanographic Office.* Catalog of informal reports. Washington, Aug. 1, 1968 104 p. (*Its* Publication 1–IR)   DLC
> Covers *Informal Oceanographic Manuscripts* (IOM) , *Informal Manuscript Reports* (IMR) , *Informal Manuscripts* (IM) , and *Informal Reports* (IR) , for years 1960–68.

———— Catalog of nautical charts and publications. Washington, 1962+ (*Its* H.O. pub. no. 1–N)   Z6026.H9U59
> "Replaces the ...*Index-Catalog of Nautical Charts and Publications,* and has been completely reorganized for issue as a sectional publication."

———— Catalog of Oceanographic Office technical reports and special publications. [Feb. 1967+] Washington [U.S. Govt. Print. Off.] (*Its* H.O. pub. 1–TR)
Z6004.P6U44

————Catalog of publications. 1968+ [Washington, U.S. Govt. Print. Off.] (*Its* H.O. pub. 1–P)   GC1.U45

———— Monthly information bulletin. Washington.   DLC
> Contains lists of new charts and publications, new editions, cancellations, and various other notices of importance to navigators.

Office of Civil Defense

Established in 1961 in the Defense Department; previously, Federal Civil Defense Administration (1950–58) and Office of Civil and Defense Mobilization (1958–61).

U.S. *Office of Civil Defense.* Publications index. [Washington]   Z6724.C6U535
> Title varies: 1952–58, *Index to Federal Civil Defense Administration Publications* (Z6724.C6U455) ; 1958–60, *Index to Publications* (varies slightly) .

Office of Education

Established in 1867. From 1869, part of the Department of the Interior; name changed to Bureau of Education, 1870–1929. Transferred to Federal Security Agency in 1939, and to Department of Health, Education, and Welfare in 1953.

U.S. *Office of Education.* Bibliography of publications of the United States Office of Education, 1867–1959. With an introductory note by Francesco Cordasco. Totowa, N.J., Rowman and Littlefield, 1971. 57, 158, 157 p. (*Its* Bulletin, 1910, no. 3; 1937, no. 22; 1960, no. 3)   Z5815.U5U5354
  Reprint of three publications, originally issued as *Bulletin* of the Office of Education (L111.A6) under the following titles: *List of Publications of the United States Bureau of Education, 1867–1910; List of Publications of the Office of Education, 1910–1936, Including Those of the Former Federal Board of Vocational Education for 1917–1933;* and *Publications, Office of Education, 1937–1959.*

—— Publications of the Office of Education. 1959+ [Washington, U.S. Govt. Print. Off. annual (irregular). (*Its* Bulletin)   L111.A6
  Issued as publication OE–11000 in 1959, Bulletin no. 25; OE–11000A in 1961, Bulletin no. 7; OE–11000B in 1962, Bulletin no. 1; OE–11000C in 1963, Bulletin no. 29; OE–11000D in 1966, (without Bulletin number); OE–11000E in 1967; OE–11000F in 1968. From 1969, OE–11000–69 . . .

U.S. *Superintendent of Documents.* Education. 1910+ Washington. (*Its* Price list 31)
                                                                          Z1223.A191 no. 31

Following publications relate to Office of Education's educational research program and the information center (ERIC):

Complete guide and index to ERIC reports: thru December 1969. Compiled by the Prentice-Hall editorial staff. Englewood Cliffs, N.J., Prentice-Hall [1970] 1338 p.
                                                                          Z5814.R4C6

Prentice-Hall, Inc. Educator's complete ERIC handbook, compiled by the Prentice-Hall editorial staff. Englewood Cliffs, N.J. [1968, c1967] 862 p.   Z5814.C52P7
  "A complete guide to Phase One, the first Educational Research Information Center (ERIC) of the U.S. Office of Education program for the dissemination of information to the nation's educational community."

U.S. *Educational Research Information Center.* Office of Education research reports, 1956–65, ED 002 747–ED 003 960. [Washington, U.S. Govt. Print. Off. 1967] 2 v.
                                                                          Z5814.R4U5
  OE–12028–29

Office of Naval Research
Established in 1946 in the Department of the Navy.

U.S. *Naval Research Laboratory, Washington, D.C. Engineering Psychology Branch.* Engineering Psychology Branch bibliography. July 1957+ Washington, U.S. Naval Research Laboratory.   Z6834.E7U55
  Includes publications from 1945.

U.S. *Office of Naval Research.* Bibliography of unclassified research reports. Washington [1956?+]   Z7914.A2U615
  Issued by the office's Personnel and Training Branch, Psychological Sciences Division.

Office of Price Administration
Established in 1941; made part of Office of Temporary Controls in 1946. Distribution of all functions to other agencies, 1947.

Wilson, William J. OPA bibliography, 1940–1947 . . . Publications of the Office of Price Administration and its predecessor agencies . . . Washington, Office of Temporary Controls, Off. of Price Administration [1948] 441 p. (Historical reports on War Administration)   Z1223.O37
     Issued as miscellaneous publication no. 3, of the Office of Temporary Controls, Office of Price Administration.

Patent Office

The Superintendent of Patents was established in 1802 in the State Department; reorganized as Patent Office in 1836. From 1849 to 1925, the Office was in the Department of the Interior; from 1925, in the Department of Commerce.

U.S. *Patent Office.* Index of patents issued from the United States Patent Office. 1920+ Washington, U.S. Govt. Print. Off., 1921+   T223.D3

——— Index of trade-marks issued from the United States Patent Office. Washington, U.S. Govt. Print. Off., 1928+   T223.V4A2

U.S. *Superintendent of Documents.* Commerce, business, patents, trademarks and foreign trade. 1914+ Washington. (*Its* Price list 62)   Z1223.A191 no. 62

Peace Corps

Established in 1961.

U.S. *Peace Corps. Division of Public Information.* The Peace Corps bibliography, March 1961–March 1965. [Washington, 1965] 39 p.   Z7164.P3U5

Postal Service

Created originally in 1775 as the Postal Service, it was changed to an executive department (Post Office Department) in 1872, although the Postmaster General had been a member of the President's cabinet since 1829. The present United States Postal Service was established in 1970.

U.S. *Superintendent of Documents.* Transportation, highways, roads and postal service. 1910+ Washington. (*Its* Price list 25)   Z1223.A191 no. 25
     The Superintendent of Documents also issued occasionally a separate list called *Post Office Department Publications for Sale by Superintendent of Documents.*

Public Health Service

Established originally in 1789, the service was under the Department of the Treasury until 1939, when it was transferred to the new Federal Security Agency, and in 1953 to the Department of Health, Education, and Welfare.

U.S. *Public Health Service.* Public health bibliography series. no. 1+ Washington, U.S. Govt. Print. Off. 1951+ (*Its* Publication)   Z6673.U515

Mostly specialized bibliographies. No. 55 is *Public Health Service Numbered Publications, a Catalog, 1950–1962*, which includes a complete list of bibliography series.

────── Public Health Service numbered publications, a catalog, 1950–1962. Washington, U.S. Dept. of Health, Education, and Welfare, Public Health Service, Office of the Information and Publications. U.S. Govt. Print. Off. [1964] (Public Health Service publication no. 1112. Public Health Service bibliography series no. 55)
Z6673.U515 no. 55
────── ────── Supplement no. 1+ 1963–1964+ Washington. Z6673.U515 no. 55 Suppl.

────── Public Health Service publications. A list of publications issued during the period [October 1922 to 1939?] Washington, U.S. Govt. Print. Off.   Z6673.U555
Reprints no. 838, 880, 923, 1003, 1055, 1072, 1179, 1238, 1321, 1408, 1446, 1491, 1526, 1552, 1578, 1595, 1625, 1641, 1672, 1699, 1741, 1771, 1811, 1849, 1927, 1966, 2036, 2092, from the *Public Health Reports*. From 1939 lists continued to be published in the *Public Health Reports* (RA11.B17).

────── Publications. Washington, U.S. Govt. Print. Off., 1908–27.   Z6673.U55
Issued as Miscellaneous publication no. 12, 1910–27. Title, 1908–12, *Publications of the United States Public Health and Marine Hospital Service*.

────── Publications issued by the Public Health Service. 1952+ Washington.
Z6673.U517
Title varies: July 1966–June 1968, *List of Publications Issued;* July 1968+ *Public Health Service Numbered Publications*. Issued annually, 1952–65, semi-annually, 1966+.

In January 1971, the following catalog was also issued:

U.S. *Health Services and Mental Health Administration*. Publications of the Health Services and Mental Health Administration. [Washington] 1971. 158 p. (PHS publication no. 2156)   Z6672.A1U53

Public Works Administration

Established in 1933 as Federal Emergency Administration of Public Works. Name changed in 1939 to Public Works Administration. Functions transferred to Federal Works Administrator in 1943.

U.S. *Public Works Administration*. Bibliography of PWA publications and official documents pertaining to PWA. [Washington, 1938]   Z7164.P97U5

Securities and Exchange Commission
Established in 1934.

U.S. *Securities and Exchange Commission*. The work of the Securities and Exchange Commission. [1940?+] Washington.   HG4556.U5A365
Each issue includes a description of its publications and a list of periodicals. Title varies: 1964, 1965, *United States Securities and Exchange Commission: Its Functions and Activities*.

Small Business Administration
Established in 1953.

U.S. *Small Business Administration.* Publications. [1958?+] Washington. annual. (SBA
115A, B, etc.) DLC
From 1961 published with various subtitles: *Free Publications* ... (SBA 115A),
For Sale Booklets (SBA 115B), *Classification of Management Publications* (SBA
115E).

—— Small business bibliography. no. 1+ Washington. Z7164.C81U718
Title varies: 1958-62, *Small Business Bulletin.*
Specialized bibliographies concerning various categories of small business.

—— A survey of federal government publications of interest to small business. Compiled by Elizabeth G. Janezeck. 3d ed. Washington [U.S. Govt. Print. Off.] 1969.
85 p. Z7164.C81U719 1969

Smithsonian Institution
Established in 1846.

Smithsonian Institution. Annual report. 1846-1963/64. Washington, U.S. Govt. Print.
Off., 119 v. Q11.S66
Superseded in 1964/65 by *Smithsonian Year.* Includes lists of publications
issued during the year.

—— Annual report. (*Indexes*) Author-subject index to articles in Smithsonian annual reports, 1849-1961. Compiled by Ruth M. Stemple and the Editorial and
Publications Division, Smithsonian Institution. Washington, 1963. 200 p. (Smithsonian Institution. Publication 4503) Q11.S6612
In 1971 the Carrollton Press, Inc., of Washington, D.C., published a facsimile
reprint edition entitled *Annual Reports and General Appendices of the Smithsonian Institution, 1846-1932,* and the *Author-Subject Index to Articles in the
Annual Reports, 1849-1961.*

—— Classified list of Smithsonian publications available for distribution. April
1904+ Washington, Smithsonian Institution. Z5055.U4S61

—— List of publications of the Smithsonian Institution 1846-1903, by William Jones
Rhees. Washington City, 1903. 99 p. (Smithsonian miscellaneous collections [vol.
xliv, art. III]) Publication 1376. Z5055.U4S6

—— List of Smithsonian miscellaneous collections and special publications issued
between May 1, 1952 and June 30, 1960. [Washington, 1961] 8 p. Z5055.U4S615

—— Smithsonan year. 1964/65+ Washington. annual. Q11.S672
Includes lists of publications issued during the year.
Supersedes three publications of the Smithsonian Institution: *Report of the
Secretary and the Financial Report of the Executive Committee of the Board
of Regents; Annual Report of the Board of Regents; Annual Report* of the
National Museum.

U.S. *Superintendent of Documents.* Smithsonian Institution, National Museum and
Indians. 1911+ Washington. (*Its* Price list 55) Z1223.A191 no. 55
See also price lists no. 24 (*Indians,* 1910-45), no. 27 (*Ethnology,* 1908-9),
and no. 56 (*Indians, Smithsonian Institution, Fine Arts,* 1911-14).

Social Security Administration

Established originally as Social Security Board in 1935, which became part of the Federal Security Agency in 1939. Abolished in 1946 and functions transferred to Social Security Administration under Federal Security Agency. From 1953, under Department of Health, Education, and Welfare.

U.S. *Dept. of Health, Education and Welfare. Library.*   Basic readings in social security.
1936+ [Washington, U.S. Govt. Print. Off.]   Z7164.L1U6687
> Beginning in Oct. 1937, this was issued as Social Security Administration Publication no. 28 (HD7123.A3) . Title varies: 1936–46, *Some Basic Readings in Social Security.* A special edition for the 25th anniversary of the Social Security Act was published in 1960 (below) .

—— Basic readings in social security; 25th anniversary of the social security act, 1935–1960. New York, Greenwood Press [1968] 221 p.   Z7164.L1U6688
> Reprint of the 1960 issue of *Basic Readings in Social Security.* "Compiled as a guide to the significant books, pamphlets, articles and periodical sources on the Social Security Act and the programs administered under the Act, the bibliography also includes references to programs closely related to social security" (preface to the 1960 ed.) .

U.S. *Superintendent of Documents.* Social services, aging, family planning, handicapped, medicare, nursing homes, pensions and retirement, poverty, social security and social welfare. 1949+ Washington. (*Its* Price list 78)   Z1223.A191 no. 78

Supreme Court

Established in 1789.

Reports on decisions and other publications of the Supreme Court have been listed in Superintendent of Documents' *Catalog of the Public Documents,* 1893–1940 (Z1223.A13), in its *Checklist of United States Public Documents,* 1789–1909 (Z1223.A113), as well as in its *Monthly Catalog,* 1895+ (Z1223.A18), and its Price list 54 (*Political Science, Government, Crime,* 1911+ Z1223.A191 no. 54). Following bibliographies deal with such matters as the history, powers, and decisions of the Supreme Court:

Haines, Charles G.   Histories of the Supreme Court of the United States written from the federalist point of view ... Reprinted from the Southwestern political and social science quarterly, vol. 4, no. 1, June, 1923. Austin, Tex. [1923?] 35 p.
Z1249.S9H2

Senior, Mildred R., *comp.*   The Supreme Court: its power of judicial review with respect to congressional legislation; selected references. Washington, D.C. [Division of Library Science, the George Washington University] 1937. 75 [1] p. (Publications of Division of Library Science, the George Washington University. no. 1)
Z1249.S9S4

Tompkins, Dorothy L. C. C.   The Supreme Court of the United States: a bibliography. Berkeley, Bureau of Public Administration, University of California, 1959. 217 p.
DLC LL

U.S. *Library of Congress. Division of Bibliography.* List of references on the Supreme
Court of the United States with particular reference to the doctrine of judicial
review, comp. by Florence S. Hellman. [Washington] 1935. 17 p.   Z1249.S9U58

——— List of works relating to the Supreme Court of the United States; comp. under
the direction of Hermann H. B. Meyer. Washington, Govt. Print. Off., 1909. 124 p.
                                                                          Z1249.S9U6

——— Supplementary list of references on judicial legislation by decisions of the U.S.
Supreme Court declaring laws unconstitutional, including power of Congress to
review these decisions. [Washington] 1924. 15 p.   Z1249.S9U62   1924

——— The Supreme Court issue: a selected list of references, comp. by Florence S.
Hellman. [Washington] 1938. 42 p.   Z1249.S9U64   1938

Tariff Commission
Established in 1916.

U.S. *Tariff Commission.* List of publications. 1920+ Washington.   Z1223.T22
    List for 1920 issued as its Tariff Information Series (HF1756.A425). Title
    varies: 1920, *Subject Index of United States Tariff Commission Publications;*
    1921–27, *List of Principal Subjects Investigated and Reported Upon;* 1939+
    Publications. Published irregularly. Latest covers the period 1951–71.

Tennessee Valley Authority
Established in 1933.

Tennessee Valley Authority. *Library.* A bibliography for the TVA program. [1952–53?]
Knoxville.   Z7164.P97T29

——— An indexed bibliography of the Tennessee Valley Authority, compiled by Harry
C. Bauer, technical librarian. Knoxville, Tenn., 1936. 60 p.   Z7164.P97T3   1936
    "This bibliography of periodical articles covers the period January 1933 to
    June 1936, inclusive. It supersedes *A Bibliography of the Tennessee Valley Au-
    thority,"* published in 1935.
    ——— ——— Supplement. July/Dec. 1936+ Knoxville, Tenn., 1937+
                                                                    Z7164.P97T3 Suppl.

——— Congressional hearings, reports, and documents relating to TVA. 1933+ Knoxville.   Z7164.P97T32
    Each volume contains data from 1933.

Veterans Administration
Established in 1930.

U.S. *Veterans Administration.* Index to publications. [1945+] Washington. Z1223.V4

Weather Bureau
Established in 1890 within the Department of Agriculture. Transferred
to Department of Commerce in 1940. From 1965 within the Environmental Science Services Administration (ESSA) in the Department of Com-

merce. In 1970 ESSA was abolished and its functions transferred to National Oceanic and Atmospheric Administration. The name in 1970 was changed to National Weather Service.

Swartz, John R.   Selective guide to published climatic data sources, prepared by U.S. Weather Bureau. Washington, U.S. Dept. of Commerce, Weather Bureau; U.S. Govt. Print. Off., 1963. 84 p. (U.S. Weather Bureau. Key to meteorological records documentation no. 4.11)   Z6685.U64 no. 4.11

U.S. *Superintendent of Documents.*   Weather, astronomy and meteorology. [1909+] Washington. (*Its* Price list 48)   Z1223.A191 no. 48

Weather Bureau publications are listed also in the *United States Department of Commerce Publications* (1952. Z1223.C75) and Supplements 1951/52+ (Z1223.C75 Suppl.).

Welfare Administration

Established in 1963 in the Department of Health, Education, and Welfare. Components consisted of Bureau of Family Services, Children's Bureau, Office of Juvenile Delinquency and Youth Development, and the Cuban Refugee Staff. Functions of the Welfare Administration reassigned to the Social and Rehabilitation Service in 1967.

U.S. *Welfare Administration.*   Welfare Administration publications list. [April 1964– 67] Washington.   Z7164.C4U51
    Continued by *Publication List of the Social and Rehabilitation Service.*

Women's Bureau

Established originally as Woman-in-Industry Service in 1918 within the Department of Labor, it became the Women's Bureau in 1920.

U.S. *Women's Bureau.*   Publications of the Women's Bureau currently available. [Washington, 1943+] (Leaflet 10)   HD6093.A354 no. 10
    Before 1943, the bureau issued *Women's Bureau of Department of Labor. What It Is, What It Does, What It Publishes* (from about 1923, title varies 1923–26).

Work Projects Administration

Established as Works Progress Administration in 1935, absorbing the Federal Emergency Relief Administration, created in 1933. Name changed to Work Projects Administration in 1939, when it became a unit in the Federal Works Agency. Abolished in 1943.

U.S. *Federal Emergency Relief Administration.*   Index to policies, reports, and other publications (May 31, 1933–December 31, 1934) Issued by Publications Division. [Washington, 1934] 55 p.   HV85.A55 1934

—— Subject index of research bulletins and monographs issued by Federal Emergency Relief Administration and Works Progress Administration, Division of Social Research. September 1937. [Washington, 1937] 110 (i.e. 121) numb. l.
Z7164.U56U52

U.S. *Work Projects Administration.* Catalog of publications, 1933–1937. [Washington] 1937. 16 numb. l. Z1223.W9
At head of title: Works Progress Administration. Division of Research, Statistics, and Records.

—— Catalogue of research and statistical publications. Sept. 1, 1936–[Nov. 1941?] [Washington] Z7164.U56U562

—— W. P. A. technical series: research and records bibliography. no. 1–8. Washington, 1940–43. 8 v. in 5. Z1223.W85
Contents: no. 1–3, 5–6, 8, *Bibliography of Research Projects Reports;* no. 4, 7, *Bibliography of Research Projects Reports: Checklist of Historical Records Survey Publications.*

Wilcox, Jerome K. Unemployment relief documents; guide to the official publications and releases of F. E. R. A. and the 48 state relief agencies. New York, H. W. Wilson Co., 1936. 95 p. Z1223.Z7W64
Contents: Checklist of final state CWA reports.—Checklist of the publications and releases of the Federal Emergency Relief Administration and the Federal Surplus Relief Corporation.—Checklist of the publications and releases of the National Youth Administration and the Works Progress Administration.—List of the publications and releases of the 48 state relief agencies (and of the territories).—Partial list of transient camp newspapers.

SPECIALIZED BIBLIOGRAPHIES

Under the headings "Bibliography," "Catalogs," and "Indexes," the *Monthly Catalog of United States Government Publications* lists, in alphabetical order of subjects, most bibliographic tools issued by federal agencies. Following are a few bibliographies covering science, technology, and statistical categories of U.S. government publications:

SCIENCE AND TECHNOLOGY

Bradshaw, Nina H. PB–AD reports index;BSIR, BTR, USGRR, USGRDR, 1946–1967. Washington, Technical Information Service [c1968] xxxiii, 265 p. Z7916.B475

Government reports announcements. v. 1+ Jan. 11, 1946+ Springfield, Va., National Technical Information Service. semimonthly. Z7916.B47
Title varies: 1946–June 1949, *Bibliography of Scientific and Industrial Reports;* July 1949–Sept. 1954, *Bibliography of Technical Reports* (varies slightly); Oct. 1954–Dec. 1964, *U.S. Government Research Reports;* Jan. 1965–March 1971, *U.S. Government Research & Development Reports;* April 1971+ *Government Reports Announcements.*

Government reports index. [1965+] Springfield, Va., National Technical Information
    Service   Z7405.R4U513
        Title from Feb. 1965 through 1967, *Government-Wide Index to Federal Re-
    search & Development Reports* (numbered as vol. 1 and 2, for 1965 and 1966;
    vol. 67+ from Jan. 1967) ; *U.S. Government Research & Development Reports
    Index,* from Jan. 1968 to Mar. 10, 1971.

Keywords index to U.S. government technical reports. v. 1–2, June 15, 1962–Sept. 1,
    1963. Washington, U.S. Dept. of Commerce, Office of Technical Services. Z7916.K45
    Discontinued with vol. 2, no. 6.

Special Libraries Council of Philadelphia and Vincinity. Correlation index: document
    series and PB reports, compiled by the Science–Technology Group . . . with the
    cooperation of Office of Technical Services, U.S. Dept. of Commerce. New York,
    Special Libraries Association, 1953. 271 p.   Z7916.S65

Technical Information Service, *Washington, D.C.* Alpha-numerical index with cor-
    relations: United States government research reports. v. 1+ Washington, 1965+
                                                                     Z7916.B4715
        "This cumulation is intended as a reference guide primarily for research
    librarians and literature searchers who need to know at a glance, (a) the sub-
    ject division under which a given AD report is classified, (b) its PB number
    . . ., (c) the bibliographic reference to the abstract."

—— Index to PB reports listed in U.S. government research reports. Washington.
                                                                     Z7916.B473

Technical translations. v. 1–18, Jan. 2, 1959–Dec. 1967. Washington, U.S. Dept. of Com-
    merce, Office of Technical Services.   Z7401.T712
        Superseded *Translation Monthly.* Absorbed by *U.S. Government Research &
    Development Reports* from Jan. 1968. (See *Government Reports Announce-
    ments* above.)

U.S. *Dept. of Commerce. Office of Technical Services.* Correlation index of technical
    reports (AD–PB reports) Washington, 1958. 184 p. "PB151567S"   Z7913.U46

—— OSRD reports: bibliography and index of declassified reports having OSRD num-
    bers. Ed. by W. Kenneth Lowry. [Washington] Bibliographic and Reference Divi-
    sion, 1947. 105 p. "PB78000"   Z7916.U5
    Reports of the Office of Scientific Research and Development (1941–47) .

STATISTICS

Guide to U.S. government statistics. 3d ed. [Arlington, Va.] Documents Index, 1961.
    402 p.   Z7554.U5G8
    4th edition published in 1973.

U.S. *Bureau of the Budget. Office of Statistical Standards.* Statistical services of the
    United States government. [Washington]   HA37.U16
    Revised editions are issued irregularly.

U.S. *Bureau of the Census.* Directory of federal statistics for states; a guide to sources,
    1967. Prepared by Diane B. Gertler, with the assistance of Beatrice Guttenberg.
    Washington, U.S. Govt. Print. Off., 1967 372 p.   HA37.U52

STATES, TERRITORIES, AND LOCAL GOVERNMENT

Efforts to bring better control to the distribution, depository practice, and bibliographic listing of state documents have been discussed for many decades. In a circular letter calling for an annual conference of state librarians, Talbot H. Wallis, California State Librarian, proposed in 1887 the development of uniform laws and policies to ensure efficient distribution and preservation of documents through the state libraries and standardization of public reports as to printing, title page information, binding, and indexing.[3] Since 1889, when the first meeting of the state librarians was held and the Association of State Librarians organized, there has been increased appreciation of the historical importance of state documents, their distribution, preservation, and exchange. In 1902, a model state law for the distribution of state publications was adopted at the meeting of the National Association of State Librarians, to be submitted to legislatures of states which did not have a similar statute yet.

Up to the middle of the first decade of the 20th century, bibliographic control of state documents did not receive much attention at the meetings of the association, in spite of the efforts of Richard R. Bowker to encourage such work. Through his endeavors, the first lists of publications of several states were included in the appendixes of *The American Catalogue* (New York) for 1884–90 and 1890–95 (Z1215.A5). His *State Publications; a Provisional List of the Official Publications of the Several States of the United States from Their Organization* (New York, 1899–1908. Z1223.5.A1B7), covering state publications up to 1900, is still the best bibliographic source for the early official documents of the states, together with Adelaide R. Hasse's *Index of Economic Material in Documents of the States of the United States* (Washington, 1907–22. Z1223.-5.A1H2), extending coverage of 13 states' publications up to 1904.

Probably the first discussion of bibliographic control of state documents in the reports of the National Association of State Librarians came at its seventh convention, in 1904, when Adelaide R. Hasse commented on a plan for bibliographic work dealing with state official literature. A statement by the Committee on Exchanges also concerned

---

[3] *Library Journal*, v. 12 (1887) : 284–285 (Z671.L7).

the need for a current checklist of the publications of various states and a bibliography of state publications for reference and research purposes.[4]

Occasional attempts to compile current lists of state documents were made in several states, but it was not until 1910 that the first issue of the *Monthly Checklist of State Publications* (called until 1921 *Monthly List of State Publications*) was published by the Library of Congress. It was the first current bibliography of the publications of all the states, including publications of territories and insular possessions of the United States. The *Monthly Checklist* remains the only comprehensive bibliography of the documents of the individual states.

Progress during the first half of this century in the distribution, exchange, and bibliographic control of state documents cannot be characterized as very encouraging. In spite of the increasing percentage of documents being recorded bibliographically, a considerable number still remain unknown and thus unavailable to researchers. A strong bid for a more active effort in this area was made in the thirties at the annual conferences of the American Library Association (ALA). In 1933, A. F. Kuhlman, associate director of the University of Chicago Library, presented a paper at the conference on "The Need for a Check-list Bibliography of State Publications," which was later published in an enlarged version in the *Library Quarterly* (v. 5, 1935: 31–58. Z671.L713). At this conference and at each ALA conference through 1937, there were discussions concerning various aspects of the problems of state publications. Two important projects—the State Document Center Plan and the Public Document Clearing House—were discussed extensively.[5]

These discussions and the resolutions that were adopted, as well as the Second World War and the realization of the increased importance of government documents in wartime, intensified considerably the interest in official publications, state documents included. Before the Second World War, only eight states published periodical checklists of their official publications; during the war, their number increased to 22, which doubled in the post-war period. At the present time, only a few states have no current checklists.

For a more detailed discussion of state document checklists and other aspects of the problems concerning state documents, see the special issue of *Library Trends* devoted entirely to "Federal, State and Local Government Publications" (v. 15, July 1966. Z671.L6173), which was produced under the editorial guidance of Thomas Shuler Shaw. James B. Childs gives considerable attention in his article "Bibliographic Control of Federal, State and Local Documents" to the problems of state documents and includes a state-by-state examination of their checklists and other

---

[4] *Proceedings and Addresses*, 7th Convention, 1904. p. 17–33 (Z673.N27).

[5] American Library Association. Committee on Public Documents, *Public Documents*, 1933–38 (Chicago. Z7164.G7A4).

bibliographies (p. 11–23). Margaret T. Lane, in her article "State Documents Checklists" (p. 117–134), presents a study of the bibliographic control of state documents.

For a comprehensive look at the retrospective developments in the field of state documents and their bibliographic control, the following works should be consulted:

American Library Association. *Committee on Public Documents.* Public documents . . . with Archives and Libraries. Papers presented at the 1933–[38] conference, of the American Library Association. Chicago. American Library Association, 1934– 38.   Z7164.G7A4

The Book of the States. v. 1+ 1935+ Chicago, Council of State Governments. biennial.
                                                                     JK2403.B6 ⌐
     Each volume contains selected bibliographies concerning the problems of state governments.

Council of State Governments. Index to Council of State Governments publications, 1950–1960. Chicago, 1960. 19 l.   Z7165.U5C68
     Continues from 1960 as an annual index, with cumulations (latest, 1960–69) .

Kuhlman, A. F. The need for a comprehensive check-list bibliography of American state publications. Library Quarterly, v. 5, Jan. 1935: 31–58.   Z671.L713
     Appendix A: "Bibliographies, Catalogs, Check-lists, etc. of American State Publications"; Appendix B: "Rules for Preparing Check-list Bibliographies of American State Publications."

Lloyd, Gwendolyn. The status of state document bibliography. Library Quarterly, v. 18, July, 1948: 192–199.   Z671.L713
     Includes a "Bibliography of Bibliographies of State Publications, 1940–47."

Reece, Ernest J. State documents for libraries. Urbana, University of Illinois, 1915. 162 p. (*On cover*: University of Illinois bulletin. v. 18, no. 36)   Z1223.5.A1R3
     "Bibliographical matter": p. 103–156.

Tompkins, Dorothy L. C. C. State government and administration; a bibliography. [Berkeley] Bureau of Public Administration, University of California [1955, c1954] 269 p.   Z7165.U5T63
     "This volume presents a guide to primary sources of information which are basic to a study of state government and administration."

Wilcox, Jerome K., *ed.* Bibliography of new guides and aides to public documents use, 1953–56. New York, Special Libraries Association, 1957. 16 p. (SLA bibliography no. 2)   Z7164.G7W5
     Includes state documents lists and other materials concerning state publications.

——— Manual on the use of state publications. Chicago, American Library Association, 1940. 342 p.   Z1223.5.A1W66
     Includes a bibliography of bibliographies of state publications (p. 75–91) , legislative digests and indexes (p. 125–131) , law compilations (p. 139–149) .

In recent years there have been several attempts to compile lists of current checklists of state documents. In 1962 the Tennessee State Library and Archives in Nashville published "Current Checklists of

State Publications, as of May 1962" in *Library Resources and Technical Services* (v. 6, Fall 1962: 357–59). In the same journal, Margaret T. Lane published "List of Current State Documents Checklists" (v. 10, Fall 1966: 504–06. Z671.L7154). The New York State Library in Albany issued in 1957 a mimeographed pamphlet entitled *Current Checklists of State Publications*, prepared by the Legislative Reference Library (Albany, N.Y., 1967. 5 l. Z1223.5.N57N554). It includes checklists of publications of the provinces of Canada.

The *Library Journal* (Z671.L7), in its vol. 97 (1972): 1393–1398 and vol. 99 (1974): 2810–2819, published reviews of state checklists and other sources which list state publications. The *Monthly Checklist of State Publications,* issued by the Library of Congress, includes state checklists in its semiannual listing of state periodicals (June and December issues).

GENERAL LISTS OF STATE PUBLICATIONS

Following are current and retrospective lists of state publications which cover several or all of the states:

Current:

U.S. *Library of Congress. Exchange and Gift Division.* Monthly checklist of state publications. v. 1+ Jan. 1910+ Washington, U.S. Govt. Print. Off.   Z1223.5.A1U5
Title varies: 1910–21, *Monthly List of State Publications.* Issued Jan. 1910–June 1943 by Division of Documents; July 1943–Nov. 1947 by Acquisition Dept.; Dec. 1947–Dec.1954 by Processing Dept. Annual indexes issued at the end of calendar year. List of state periodicals published in the June and December issues. A reprint of vols. 1–29, covering the years 1910–38, published by Kraus Reprint Co., New York, in 1970.

U.S. *Superintendent of Documents.* States and territories of the United States and their resources, including beautification, public buildings and lands, recreational resources. Washington. 1967+ (*Its* Price list 87)   Z1223.A191 no. 87
Although not a list of state publications alone, it covers many subjects of interest to researchers in material on the states.

Another source of current information on state publications is the weekly *Bulletin* issued by the Public Affairs Information Service, New York, cumulated five times a year, the fifth cumulation being the annual volume for permanent reference (Z7163.P9).

Retrospective:

The American catalogue . . . July 1, 1876–Dec. 31, 1910. New York, 1941. 8 v. in 13.
                                                                                                Z1215.A52
"Copyright 1880 by R. R. Bowker & Co. Reprinted, 1941, by special arrange-

ment with R. R. Bowker & Co." Published by Peter Smith. Vols. for 1884–90 and 1890–95 include lists of state publications in their appendixes.

Bowker, Richard R. State publications; a provisional list of the official publications of the several states of the United States from their organization. New York, Publishers' Weekly, 1908. 1 v. in 4. Z1223.5.A1B7
Issued in four parts, each with special title page, 1899–1908. Contents: pt. 1. New England States. 1899.—pt. 2. North Central States. 1902.—pt. 3. Western States and Territories. 1905.—pt. 4. Southern States. 1908.

Childs, James B. Government document bibliography in the United States and elsewhere. 3d ed., Washington, U.S. Govt. Print. Off., 1942. xviii, 78 p. Z7164.G7C5
Reprinted in 1964 and 1966 by Johnson Reprint Corp., New York. State publication bibliographies, p. 13–33.

Hasse, Adelaide R. Index of economic material in documents of the states of the United States ... Washington, Carnegie Institution of Washington. [1907–22]
Z1223.5.A1H2
In 13 volumes, it lists state documents for the following 13 states: California, Delaware, Illinois, Kentucky, Maine, Massachusetts, New Hampshire, New Jersey, New York, Ohio, Pennsylvania, Rhode Island, and Vermont. Material for a South Carolina volume also prepared, but never published.[6]

National Association of State Libraries. Collected public documents of the states; a check list, comp. by William S. Jenkins. Boston, 1947. 87 p. Z1223.5.A1N24
The checklist gives locations for very rare items.

U.S. Library of Congress. A guide to the microfilm collection of early state records, prepared by the Library of Congress in association with the University of North Carolina. Collected and compiled under the direction of William S. Jenkins; edited by Lillian A. Hamrick. [Washington] Library of Congress, Photoduplication Service, 1950. 1 v. (various pagings) Z1223.5.A1U47
——— ——— Supplement. [Washington] Library of Congress, Photoduplication Service, 1951. xxiii, 130, xviii p. Z1223.5.A1U47 Suppl.

Following are bibliographies of documents of state constitutional conventions, legislative publications, and some specialized bibliographies of state documents:

Chicago. University. Library. Official publications relating to American state constitutional conventions. New York, H. W. Wilson Co., 1936. 91 p. Z6457.A1C5

Cole, Theodore L. Bibliography of the statute law of the Southern states. Washington, D.C., Statute Law Book Co., 1897. 3 v. Z6457.A1C6
From Publications of the Southern History Association, Jan.–July, 1897. Covers Alabama, Arkansas, and Florida only.

Council of State Governments. Legislative research checklist no. 1–37; Dec. 22, 1947–Nov. 1958. Chicago. 37 no. Z7161.C75
Reports arranged by subject. Includes news notes on legislative activities, notes on research assignments, and occasionally changes in state offices. There is no index. Superseded in March 1959 by a publication with the same title but different approach.

——— Legislative research checklist. v. 1, no. 1+ Mar. 1959+ Chicago. DLC LL

[6] James B. Childs. "Bibliographic Control of Federal, State and Local Documents," Library Trends, v. 15, July 1966: 20.

Giefer, Gerald J., *and* David K. Todd.   Water publications of state agencies; a bibliography of publications on water resources and their management published by the states of the United States. Port Washington, N.Y., Water Information Center [1972] xxvii, 319 p.   Z7935.G55

Massachusetts. State Library, *Boston.*   Hand list of legislative sessions and session laws, statutory revisions, compilations, code, etc., and constitutional conventions of the United States and its possessions and of the several states to May 1912. Published by the trustees. Prepared by Charles J. Babbitt under direction of Charles F. D. Belden, State Librarian. [Boston, Wright & Potter Printing Co., State Printers, 1912] 634 p.   Z6457.A1M2

Morse, Lewis W.   A checklist of judicial council reports from their beginning through 1935. [New York, 1936] 7 p.   Z6455.J9M8
    Arranged alphabetically by states. "Reprinted with additions to Illinois, New Jersey, New York and Oregon. from *Law Library Journal,* v. 29, Jan. 1936."

————Historical outline and bibliography of attorneys general reports and opinions from their beginning through 1936. Law library journal, v. 30, 1937: 39–247.
                                                                      DLC LL

———— State Tax Commissions, their history and reports. Taxes, the tax magazine, Chicago [1940–43]   HJ2360.T4
    Published as follows: v. 18, 1940: 227–232, 302–308, 376–381, 400, 444–448, 499–507, 572–576, 582, 636–638, 648, 755–760, 763; v. 19, 1941: 38–41, 166–174, 234–238, 287–293, 320, 361–363, 415–421, 480–482, 550–557, 565, 613–617, 734–738, 745; v. 20, 1942: 34–37, 286–294, 309, 550–553; v. 21, 1943: 13–15, 89–90, 103, 144, 186–187.

National Association of State Libraries. *Public Document Clearing House Committee.* Check-list of legislative journals of states of the United States of America, compiled by Grace E. Macdonald. Providence, Oxford Press, 1938. 274 p.
                                                    Z1223.5.A1N27   1938

———— ———— Supplement . . . compiled by William S. Jenkins for the National Association of State Libraries. Boston, 1943. 107 p.   Z1223.5.A1N27   1938 Suppl.
    Continued by William R. Pullen in *A Check List of Legislative Journals* (see below).

———— Check-list of session laws, compiled by Grace E. Macdonald. New York, H. W. Wilson Co., 1936. 266 p.   Z6457.A1N34
    Provisional edition issued in 1934 and 1935 as two separate volumes with titles: *Preliminary Check-List of Session Laws. 1850–1933; Preliminary Check-List of Session Laws Prior to 1850.* A "Twenty year supplement to Macdonald's Check-List of Session Laws" for 1934–54, published in *Law Library Journal,* v. 49, Feb. 1956: Suppl. i-xxx. (DLC LL)

———— Check-list of statutes of states of the United States of America, including revisions, compilations, digests, codes and indexes, compiled by Grace E. Macdonald. Providence, Oxford Press, 1937. 147 p.   Z6457.A1N36   1937

Pullen, William R.   A check list of legislative journals issued since 1937 by the states of the United States of America. Chicago, American Library Association, 1955. 59 p.
                                                   Z1223.5.A1P8
    Continues the *Check-List* by Grace E. Macdonald and its supplement by William S. Jenkins, compiled for the Public Document Clearing House of the National Association of State Libraries (see above).

Shearer, Augustus H.   A list of official publications of American state constitutional conventions, 1776–1916. Compiled for use in the Newberry Library. Chicago, 1917.

39 p. (*Half-title:* Bulletin of the Newberry Library, no. 6)   Z6457.A1N6   1917
   A revision of the library's Bulletin no. 4 issued in 1915 under title *A List of Documentary Material Relating to State Constitutional Conventions, 1776–1912.*

State law index. v. 1–12; 1925–26—1947–48. Washington, U.S. Govt. Print. Off. 12 v. biennial.   DLC LL
   Compiled by the Legislative Reference Service of the Library of Congress. Vols. 1–5 (1925–26 to 1933–34) include digests of important state legislation: statutory changes and changes in state laws relating to administrative organization and personnel. Beginning in 1938, digests on selected subjects were published separately as numbers of the series: State Law Digest Report.

Tompkins, Dorothy L. C. C. Civil defense in the states; a bibliography. [Berkeley] Bureau of Public Administration, University of California, 1953. 56 l. (Defense bibliographies, no. 3)   Z6724.C6T6

U.S. *Bureau of Labor.* Index of all reports issued by bureaus of labor statistics in the United States prior to March 1, 1902. Prepared under the direction of Carroll D. Wright for the use of the United States Department of Labor. With a new introduction by Herbert G. Gutman. New York, Johnson Reprint Corp., 1970. 287 p. (History of American Economy)   Z7164.L1U6   1970
   Reprint of the 1902 edition, with Gutman's introduction added.

U.S. *Bureau of the Census.* Directory of non-federal statistics for states and local areas; a guide to sources, 1969 [prepared by Francine E. Shacter] [Washington, U.S. Govt. Print. Off., 1970] 678 p.   HA37.U52   1970

U.S. *Library of Congress. Census Library Project.* State censuses 1790–1948. An annotated bibliography of censuses of population taken after the year 1790 by states and territories of the United States. Prepared by Henry J. Dubester. Washington, U.S. Govt. Print. Off., 1948. 73 p.   Z7554.U5U63   1948
   Reprinted in 1969 by Burt Franklin, New York.

U.S. *Library of Congress. Division of Documents.* Tentative check list of state publications relating to the European war, 1917–1919. Washington, Govt. Print. Off., 1920. (*In its* Monthly list of state publications. Washington, 1920, v. 10, no. 12, December 1919, p. [579]–648)   Z1223.5.A1U5 v. 10, no. 12
   "Includes state war publications issued during 1917–1919 which were received by the Library of Congress."

U.S. *Office of Aging.* A handbook of aging in the states; organization and action. v. 1+ Sept. 1964+ Washington.   HQ1064.U5A275
   Includes lists of state publications on aging.

Wilcox, Jerome K. Official defense publications; guide to state and federal publications. Berkeley, Bureau of Public Administration, University of California, 1941–45. 9 v.   Z1361.D4W56
   Title varies: v. 3–9, *Official War Publications; Guide to State, Federal and Canadian Publications.*

———— Unemployment relief documents; guide to the official publications and releases of F. E. R. A. and the 48 state relief agencies. New York, H. W. Wilson Co., 1936. 95 p.   Z1223.Z7W64
   Contents:—Checklist of final state CWA (Civil Works Administration) reports;—Checklist of the publications and releases of the Federal Emergency Relief Administration and the Federal Surplus Relief Corporation;—Checklist of the publications and releases of the National Youth Administration and the Works Progress Administration;—List of the publications and releases of the 48 state relief agencies (and of the territories) ;—Partial list of transient camp newspapers.

INDIVIDUAL STATES

ALABAMA

Part was in the Mississippi Territory, 1789; part was ceded by Spain, 1813; territory, 1817; state, 1819.

No current checklist published at the present time.

Retrospective:

Alabama. *History Commission.* Report of the Alabama History Commission to the Governor of Alabama. December 1, 1900. Ed. by Thomas McAdory Owen. Vol. 1. Montgomery, Ala., Brown Printing Co., 1901. 447 p. (Publications of the Alabama Historical Society. Miscellaneous collections, vol. 1)   F321.A24
　　　No more published. Contents. pt. 1. An account of manuscripts, papers and documents pertaining to Alabama in official repositories beyond the state.—pt. 2. An account of manuscripts, papers and documents in official repositories within the state of Alabama.—pt. 3. An account of manuscripts, papers and documents in private hands.—pt. 4. War records of Alabama.—pt. 5. Aboriginal and Indian remains in Alabama.

Cole, Theodore L.　Bibliography of the statute law of the Southern states. Washington, D.C., Statute Law Book Co., 1897. 3 v.   Z6457.A1C6
　　　Part 1: Alabama.

Ellison, Rhoda C.　A check list of Alabama imprints, 1807–1870. University, Ala. University of Alabama Press, 1946. 151 p.   Z1253.E55

Historical Records Survey. *Alabama.* Check list of Alabama imprints, 1807–1840. Birmingham, Ala., Alabama Historical Records Survey Project, 1939. 159 p. (American imprints inventory, no. 8)   Z1215.H67 no. 8

Markley, Anne E.　Author headings for the official publications of the state of Alabama. Chicago, American Library Association, 1948. xviii, 123 p.   Z695.1.G7M3

Olcott, Margaret T.　Alabama: an index to the state official sources of agricultural statistics. Washington, 1926. 96 [2] p. (U.S. Dept. of Agriculture. Bureau of Agricultural Economics. [Library] Agricultural economics bibliography no. 15)
          Z5074.E3U35 no. 15

Owen, Thomas McAdory.　A bibliography of Alabama. (*In* American Historical Association. Annual report for . . . the year 1897. Washington, 1898: 777–1248.)
          E172.A60 1897
          Z1253.O97
　　　Includes Alabama state documents.

ALASKA

Purchased from Russia in 1867; district, 1867; territory, 1912; state, 1959.

Current:

Alaska. Division of State Libraries.　State publications received. [1965+] Juneau. [annual]   Z1223.5.A4A3
　　　From 1971, also a monthly list.

Retrospective:

Judson, Katharine B. Subject index to the history of the Pacific northwest and of Alaska as found in the United States government documents, congressional series, in the American state papers, and in other documents, 1789–1881; prepared . . . for the Seattle Public Library. Pub. by the Washington State Library, Olympia, 1913. Olympia, Wash., F. M. Lamborn, Public Printer, 1913. 341 p.   Z1251.N7J92

U.S. *Dept. of the Interior.* Government publications on Alaska. [Washington, D.C., 1909] Sheet fold, to 10 p. On verso of U.S. Geological Survey, Map of Alaska, 1909.
Z1255.U59

U.S. *Library of Congress. Division of Bibliography.* Alaska: a selected list of recent references. Comp. by Grace Hadley Fuller, under the direction of Florence S. Hellman. Washington, 1943. 181 p.   Z1255.U62
"While it is mainly a supplement to the Wickersham bibliography, we have not attempted to make it so all-inclusive, but have limited it to the more important writings, chiefly in the English language." Arranged by subject, it includes Alaskan and U.S. official documents.

U.S. *National Archives.* List of National Archives microfilm publications. 1947+ Washington. (*Its* Publication)   CD3027.M514
Includes: "Records of the Russian-American Company, 1802–1867." M–11 (p. 81). The Russian-American Company, created in 1799, had both economic and political control of Alaska before its purchase by the United States in 1867. These records, which were maintained by the company in Alaska and are in Russian longhand, were transferred to the U.S. government in accordance with provisions of the treaty of cession.

U.S. *Superintendent of Documents.* Territories and insular possessions. 1914–[1960] Washington. (*Its* Price list 60)   Z1223.A191 no. 60
Title varies: 1914, *Alaska Territory;* 1916–28, *Alaska;* 1929–45, *Alaska and Hawaii;* 1946–55?, *Territories and Insular Possessions;* 1956?–60, *Alaska, Guam, Hawaii.* Publications on Alaska before 1914 were included in Price list no. 32: *Insular Possessions;* after 1967, in Price list no. 87, *States and Territories.*

Wickersham, James. A bibliography of Alaskan literature, 1724–1924; containing the titles of all histories, travels, voyages, newspapers, periodicals, public documents, etc., printed in English, Russian, German, French, Spanish, etc., relating to, descriptive of, or published in Russian America or Alaska, from 1724 to and including 1924. Cordova, Alaska, Cordova Daily Times Print [1928] xxvii, 635 p. (Alaska Agricultural College and School of Mines [Fairbanks] Miscellaneous publications, v. 1)   Z1255.W63
The compiler was assisted in his work by Hugh A. Morrison, George A. Jeffery, Richard H. Geoghegan, Henry W. Elliott, and Harry E. Morton. "Alaska Territory, Public documents of," p. 46–56.

An unfinished manuscript by Melvin B. Ricks, *Basic Bibliography of Alaskan Literature; Annotated,* is reported at the Alaska Historical Library in Juneau, containing entries up to 1961.

ARIZONA
Ceded by Mexico, 1848; territory, 1863; state, 1912.

Current:
Arizona. *Dept. of Library and Archives.* Annual checklist of publications of the state

of Arizona received by the Dept. of Library and Archives during the fiscal year.
[1956/57+] Phoenix.   Z1223.5.A75A25
   Issues for 1956/57 to 1962/63, typewritten copies only.

Retrospective:

Arizona. State Library, *Phoenix.* Check list of annual reports. Arizona law and other
   current publications issued by or under authority of the state of Arizona. [1]—16th;
   1915/16–1930/31. [Phoenix, 1916–31] 16 v.   Z1223.5.A75
      Prepared by C. P. Cronin. Continued in the *State Library Newsletter* (later
      Arizona Newsletter).

Arizona newsletter. no. 1– ?, July 1933–? Phoenix.   Z732.A8A7
      No. 1–8 issued under the title *State Library Newsletter.* Includes printed
      checklists for 1931/33 (issue no. 1); 1933/35 (issue no. 2); 1935/36 (issue no. 4);
      1938/39 (issue no. 12). For years 1941/42–1951/52 (nos. 19–30), only typed
      copies exist.

Historical Records Survey, *Arizona.* A check list of Arizona imprints, 1860–1890.
   Chicago, Historical Records Survey, 1938. 81 p. (American imprints inventory, no.
   3)   Z1215.H67 no. 3

Los Angeles. Southwest Museum. *Munk Library of Arizoniana.* Bibliography of Arizona; being the record of literature collected by Joseph Amasa Munk, M.D. and
   donated by him to the Southwest Museum of Los Angeles, California; by Hector
   Alliot, Curator, Southwest Museum. Los Angeles, Southwest Museum, 1914. 431,
   [1] p.   Z1257.Z9S6
      Territorial and state documents are listed under Arizona in the subject sec-
      tion.

Arkansas

Louisiana Purchase, 1803; territory, 1819; state, 1836.

Current:

Arkansas. University. *Library.* Checklist of Arkansas state publications received by
   the University of Arkansas Library. no. 1+ 1943+ Fayetteville, 1944+ semiannual.
                                                                      Z1223.5.A6

Retrospective:

Allen, Albert H., *ed.* Arkansas imprints, 1821–1876. New York, Pub. for the Bibliographical Society of America by R. R. Bowker Co., 1947. xx, 236 p.   Z1259.A4
      Based upon the original sources from which *A Check List of Arkansas Im-
      prints, 1821–1876,* published in 1942 by the Arkansas Historical Records Survey,
      was compiled. Lists a considerable number of official documents. Entries under
      Arkansas are collected in the index, p. 207–209.

Arkansas. *History Commission.* Arkansas history catalog. By Dallas T. Herndon. [Ft.
   Smith, Calvert–McBride Printing Co., 1923] 164 p.   Z1259.A72
      Official documents are found under broad subjects in the first part of the
      catalog (Public documents, history, etc. p. 11–79).

Arkansas. *Library Commission.* Arkansas books and materials; a compilation of Arkansas shelf lists of the public libraries of Arkansas. [Comp. by LaNell Compton
   and Lorene Bryant] Little Rock, 1967. 224 p.   Z1259.A74
      Public state documents are listed under Arkansas in the alphabetical arrange-
      ment. Other official publications under names of counties, cities, etc.

Arkansas. University. *Industrial Research and Extension Center.* Publications on the state of Arkansas. Marsha A. Walters [and] Sherry H. Hogan, editors. Linda R. Seamon, compiler. Little Rock, 1967. 2 v. (*Its* Publication L4–I and L4–II)
                                                     HC107.A8A66 no. L4, v. 1–2
    A considerable number of state and local documents included, mostly studies published since 1945. "Listings were selected for their pertinence to present-day problems of growth and development of the state." (Preface).

Cole, Theodore L. Bibliography of the statute law of the Southern states. [Pt. 2, Arkansas] Washington, D.C., Statute Law Book Co., 1897. 3 v.   Z6457.A1C6

Historical Records Survey, *Arkansas.* A check list of Arkansas imprints, 1821–1876. Prepared by the Arkansas Historical Records Survey, Division of Community Service Programs. Work Projects Administration. Little Rock, Ark., 1942. 139 numb. 1., 2 1. (American imprints inventory, no. 39)   Z1215.H67 no. 39
                                                     Z1259.H57
    Reproduced from typewritten copy.

Mathews, Jim P. A bibliographical study of Arkansas state publications. Urbana, Ill. 335 1.   Z1223.5.A6M38
    An unpublished (typewritten) M.A. thesis, prepared for the Graduate School of Library Science, University of Illinois, 1933.

CALIFORNIA

Ceded by Mexico, 1848; state, 1850.

Current:

California state publications. v. 1+ ; July/Sept. 1947+ Sacramento, Printing Division, Documents Section.   Z1223.5.C2C4
    Published quarterly 1947–56, with cumulation for Sept. 15, 1945–Sept. 3, 1947, in v. 1, no. 2, and annual cumulations in no. 5 of each volume. From Jan. 1957 published monthly, with no. 12 the annual cumulation.
    For listings of state publications prior to 1947, see *News Notes of California Libraries.* (Z732.C2A).

Retrospective:

California. *Bureau of Printing.* California state publications and documents. [Sacramento, California State Printing Office] [1936–40?]   Z1223.5.C2C2
    Distributed by Supervisor of Documents.
    A sales list of California publications.

———— Official catalog of documents—reports. maps. Published by agencies of the state of California. Sacramento [1940] 1 v.   Z1223.5.C2C21
    Looseleaf; photoprinted. Covers the period July 1, 1939, to Apr. 1, 1940.

California. State Library, *Sacramento.* News notes of California libraries. v. 1+ May, 1906+ Sacramento.   Z732.C2A
    In each number, beginning with v. 1, no. 4, to v. 42, no. 4 (Oct. 1947), are lists of California state publications received in the State Library, and beginning with v. 9 through v. 52, no. 2 (April 1957), lists of California city publications are included. County publications are listed beginning with v. 3 (1936).

California. State Library, *Sacramento. Government Publications Section.* GPS Publication. 1+ 1966+ Sacramento.   Z1223.Z7C35
    "The California State Library is initiating this series of monographs as part
of its program to provide information on the acquisition, processing and use
of government documents, particularly California and U.S."
    GPS publication no. 3 deals with California legislative publications. Publica-
tion no. 1 outlines approaches to California published and unpublished sources
of information.

California Library Association. *Documents Committee.* California state publications;
manual for acquisition, processing, use. 2d ed. rev. by California State Library.
[Sacramento] 1961. unpaged.   Z695.1.G7C22   1961

Conlan, Eileen M. A checklist of California imprints for the year 1870, with a historical introduction. Washington, 1967. 150 l.   Z1261.C63
    M. S. thesis, Catholic University of America, typescript (carbon copy).
    Public documents are listed under California and the names of cities.

Cowan, Robert E. A bibliography of the Spanish press of California, 1833–1845. San
Francisco, 1919. 31 p.   Z209.C25C69
    Includes a number of official documents.

Fahey, Herbert. Early printing in California, from its beginning in the Mexican
territory to statehood, September 9, 1850. San Francisco, Book Club of California,
1956. 141 p.   Z209.C25F3

Greenwood, Robert, *ed.* California imprints, 1833–1862; a bibliography. Compiled
by Seiko June Suzuki & Marjorie Pulliam and the Historical Records Survey. Los
Gatos, Calif., Talisman Press, 1961. 524 p.   Z1261.G7
    Includes state and municipal publications. Bibliography, p. xxii–xxiv. Im-
prints are arranged in chronological order by year and alphabetically within
each year by author or title.

Groves, Esther P. A checklist of California imprints for the years 1863 and 1864 with
a historical introduction. Washington, 1960. 147 l.   Z1261.G74
    M. S. thesis, Catholic University of America, typescript (carbon copy).

Hasse, Adelaide R. Index of economic material in documents of the states of the
United States: California, 1849–1904. [Washington] Carnegie Institution of Washington. 1908. [Carnegie Institution of Washington. Publication no. 85 (California)]
                                                              Z1223.5.Z1H2 v. 1
                                                                    Z1261.H25
                                                              AS32.A5 no. 85

Parma, Rosamond, *and* Elizabeth Armstrong. A bibliography for the codes and statutes, not included in Hasse. Law library journal (Richmond, Va.) v. 22, 1929:
41–56.   DLC LL

Sacconaghi, Charles D. A checklist of California imprints for the years 1865 and 1868,
with a historical introduction. Washington, 1963. 219 l.   Z1261.S35
    M. S. thesis, Catholic University of America, typescript (carbon copy).

Wagner, Henry R. California imprints, August 1846–June 1851. Berkeley, Calif., 1922.
97 p.   Z209.C25W21
    "Documents of the first and second sessions of the legislature," p. 67–77.

COLORADO

Louisiana Purchase, 1803; territory, 1861; state, 1876.

Current:

Colorado. *Division of State Archives and Public Records.* Checklist [of] Colorado
   publications received. v. 1+ Oct./Dec. 1964+ Denver. quarterly.   Z1223.5.C6A3
      From Jan. 1971, called *Colorado Checklist,* published monthly.

Retrospective:

Checklist of Colorado official state publications. Apr./June 1940–[Sept. 1941] Denver,
   Colorado State Library. *(Its* Extension bulletin no. 7, pt. 1–6)   Z881.C709C6

Colorado. *State Board of Library Commissioners.* Checklist of Colorado public documents. Denver, Smith-Brooks Printing Co., state printers, 1910. 203 p.   Z1223.5.C76
      "Prepared in Document department, Public library, Denver."
      "Purports to present an entry for every document from earliest territorial
      days to September 1, 1910 and also to give sufficient information to readily
      identify each, viz: title-page, date, pagination and size."

Colorado. State Museum, *Denver.* Checklist of Colorado public documents. Denver,
   Colorado State Historical Society, 1950. 32 p.   Z1223.5.C6C6
      First part of a supplement to the 1910 *Checklist of Colorado Public Documents*
      (see above). Covers only the following agencies: Office of the Governor, Divi-
      sion of Accounts and Control, Division of Purchasing, Division of Public Build-
      ings, and the Colorado National Guard.

A list of Colorado state publications. [1958–61 and May 1961–May 1963] Denver, Colorado State Library.   Z1223.5.C6L5
      The 1958–61 list was published under the title *Colorado State Publications; a
      Selected Check List.* The May 1961–May 1963 list was compiled by Sarah L. Judd.

McMurtrie, Douglas C., *and* Albert H. Allen. Colorado imprints not listed in the
   bibliography on "Early Printing in Colorado." Evanston, Priv. print., 1943. 4
   numb. 1.   Z1263.M15
      Reproduced from typewritten copy.

——— Early printing in Colorado, with a bibliography of the issues of the press, 1859
   to 1876, inclusive, and a record and bibliography of Colorado territorial newspapers. Denver, A. B. Hirschfeld Press, 1935. 305 p.   Z1263.M17   1935
      Includes official documents of the territory of Colorado.

CONNECTICUT

Fifth of the original 13 states.

Current:

Connecticut. State Library, *Hartford.* Checklist of publications of Connecticut state
   agencies received by the Connecticut State Library. April 1964+ Hartford. monthly.
                                                                                  DLC
      Published quarterly from 1964 through 1969; monthly from Jan. 1970. Ar-
      ranged by state agencies, it also includes publications of temporary commissions
      and committees and those of the University of Connecticut. A list of state serials
      is included once a year.

Before 1964, a list of "Connecticut State Publications Received at the State Library" was published in *Quarterly Acquisitions* (Connecticut. State Library, Hartford. DLC). These lists cover state documents from Jan. 1961 through Mar. 1964, and municipal publications from July 1962.

Retrospective:

Adams, Regina M. A check-list of Connecticut imprints from 1801 through 1805, with a historical introd. Washington, 1954. 214 l.   Z1265.A4
    Typescript (carbon copy).
    Thesis (M.S.), Catholic University of America. Bibliography: leaves 185–190.

Bates, Albert C. Connecticut statute laws: a bibliographical list of editions of Connecticut laws from the earliest issues to 1836. [Hartford, Case, Lockwood & Brainard Co.] 1900. 120 p. (Acorn Club, Connecticut. [Publication no. 31])   Z6457.C7B3

——— A list of official publications of Connecticut, 1774–1788, as shown by the bills for printing. [Hartford, Press of the Hartford Printing Co.] 1917. 54 p. (Acorn Club of Connecticut. [Publication no. 14])   Z1223.5.C8A3

Connecticut. State Library, *Hartford.* Connecticut state publications, their binding and distribution. By George S. Godard, State Librarian. Hartford, the Library, 1925. 27 p. (*Its* Bulletin no. 11)   Z1223.5.C8C7
    Reprinted from the *Report of the State Librarian* for the two years ending June 30, 1922.

——— Public documents of the state of Connecticut; four volumes bound in six parts, 1929. Hartford, 1929. 13 p. (*Its* Bulletin, no. 14)   Z1223.5.C8C8

——— Report of the state librarian. Hartford, 1855+   C733.C755
    Each report includes information on and often lists of state and municipal documents. The biennial report 1907–8 contains "Connecticut State Publications," (p. 17–19), which includes a list of printed departmental reports, with the date when first printed (p. 18–19), and "Connecticut Town and Municipal Reports in the State Library" (p. 20–28).

——— Select list of manuscripts in the Connecticut state library [September 30, 1916], by George S. Godard, State Librarian. Hartford, 1920. 32 [3] p. (*Its* Bulletin, no. 9)   Z6621.C745

Winkler, Paul W. Author headings for the official publications of the state of Connecticut, 1818–1947. Urbana, Ill., 1949.   Microfilm Z–26
    Microfilm copy of typewritten manuscript. Collation of the original, as determined from the film: xiii, 247 leaves.
    Thesis (M.S.), University of Illinois.

Delaware

First of the original 13 states.

Current:

Delaware. *Public Archives Commission.* List of accessions. v. 1+ Oct. 1951+ Dover.   CD3154.A3
    A mimeographed list, issued quarterly, which includes Delaware state publications. From October 1970 issued by the Dept. of State, Division of Historical and Cultural Affairs, under the title *Accessions List.*

Retrospective:

Checklist of official Delaware publications. v. 1, no. 1–6; Jan. 1968–Apr. 1969? Dover State Library Commission. quarterly.   Z1223.5.D3C47

Delaware. *State Planning Office.* Bibliography of Delaware State agency publications. [Dover] 1971. 47 p.   Z1223.5.D3A5

Hasse, Adelaide R. Index of economic material in documents of the states of the United States: Delaware, 1789–1904. [Washington] Carnegie Institution of Washington, 1910. 137 p. [Carnegie Institution of Washington. Publication no. 85 (Delaware)]   Z1223.5.A1H2 v. 2
    Z1267.H25
    AS32.A5 no. 85

Reed, Henry C., *and* Marion B. Reed. A bibliography of Delaware through 1960. Newark, Published for the Institute of Delaware History and Culture by the University of Delaware Press, 1966. 196 p.   Z1267.R4
    A classified bibliography. Official documents are listed mainly under subjects: Government and Politics, Towns and Cities, Public Finance, etc.

Rink, Evald. Printing in Delaware, 1761–1800; a checklist. Wilmington, Del., Eleutherian Mills Historical Library, 1969. 214 p.   Z1267.R5

Ryden, George H. Bibliography of Delaware history. [n. p., University of Delaware, 1927] 25 numb. l.   Z1267.R98
    Includes a substantial listing of Delaware official documents.

The following three M.S. theses (typescript, carbon copies) submitted to the Catholic University of America include a considerable number of official documents:

Carpenter, Malinda F. A check list of imprints of Delaware, 1836–1862, with a historical introduction. Washington, 1957. 89 l.   Z1267.C3

Gibbons, Rosaria. A check list of Delaware imprints from 1801 through 1815, with an historical introd. of the period. Washington, 1956. 102 l.   Z1267.G5

Loughran, Clayton D. A checklist of Delaware imprints from 1816 through 1835, with a historical introduction. Washington, 1956. 110 l.   Z1267.L6

DISTRICT OF COLUMBIA

City incorporated, 1802; present form of government since 1878.

Current:

Official publications of the District of Columbia are currently listed in the *Monthly Catalog* of the Superintendent of Documents, and non-GPO imprints are given in the *Monthly Checklist of State Publications* (Library of Congress).

Retrospective:

Early documents of the District of Columbia, up to 1909, are listed
in the Superintendent of Documents' *Checklist of United States Public
Documents* (3d ed., 1911, p. 387–406. Z1223.A113), and those up to and
including 1940, in its biennial *Catalog of the Public Documents* (1893/
95–1939/40. Z1223.A13).

The following bibliographies and checklists also include official
documents:

Bryan, Wilhelmus B.   Bibliography of the District of Columbia, being a list of books,
    maps, and newspapers, including articles in magazines and other publications to
    1898. Prepared for the Columbia Historical Society. Washington, U.S. Govt. Print.
    Off., 1900. 211 p. ([U.S.] 56th Cong., 1st sess. Senate. Doc. 61)   DLC LL
                                                                            Z1269.B92

Historical Records Survey, *District of Columbia.*   Inventory of the municipal archives
    of the District of Columbia. Prepared by District of Columbia Historical Records
    Survey, Division of Professional and Service Projects, Work Projects Administra-
    tion. Sponsored by the Board of Commissioners of the District of Columbia. [Pre-
    liminary edition no. 1] Washington, 1940. 31 p.   CD3160.H55
        Only part of the projected first volume, it deals with the records of the Board
    of Accountancy, Board of Examiners and Registrars of Architects, Board of
    Barber Examiners, and Board of Cosmetology.

Madigan, Angela M.   A check-list of Georgetown, D.C. imprints with an historical
    introd. from 1789–1871. Washington, 1950. 97 l.   Z1270.C4M3
        Typescript (carbon copy). Thesis (M.S.), Catholic University of America.

Slaughter, Peggy.   A check list of Washington, D.C. imprints from 1838–39, with a
    historical introduction. Washington, D.C., 1964. 111 l.   Z1269.S4
        Typescript (carbon copy). Thesis (M.S.), Catholic University of America.

Townsend, Dorothea B.   A checklist of official and nonofficial imprints for Wash-
    ington City, District of Columbia, 1800–1801, with a historical introduction. Wash-
    ington, 1960. 80 l.   Z1270.W3T6
        Thesis (M.S.), Catholic University of America.

FLORIDA

Ceded by Spain, 1819; territory, 1822; state, 1845.

Current:

Florida public documents. Feb. 1968+ Tallahassee, Florida State Library.
    Issued monthly, with annual cumulations.   Z1223.5.F5F57

Retrospective:

Cole, Theodore L.   Bibliography of the statute law of the Southern states. [Pt. 3:
    Florida] Washington, D.C., Statute Law Book Co., 1897. 3 v.   DLC LL

Florida. Atlantic University, *Boca Raton. Library.* A keyword-in-context index to
Florida public documents in the Florida Atlantic University. Ed. by Nancy P.
Sanders. Tallahassee, Dept. of State, Florida State Library [1969?] 163 p.
                                                                          Z1223.5.F5F45
Contains titles of all documents distributed by the State Library.

Florida. *Laws, statutes, etc. (Indexes).* Index to special and local laws, 1845–1951.
Tallahassee [Attorney General's Office, Statutory Revision Dept., 1952] 1 v. (unpaged)   DLC LL

Florida. *Legislative Council. Committee on Governmental Organization.* Bibliography
of Florida government. Tallahassee, Legislative Reference Bureau, 1960. 95 p.
                                                                          Z7165.U6F63

Florida. University, *Gainesville. Libraries. Documents Dept.* Short-title checklist of
official Florida publications received by the University of Florida libraries. no.
1–62, July/Aug. 1942–May/June 1968. [Gainesville]   Z1223.5.F5F5

Florida Library Association. Preliminary check list of Floridiana, 1500–1865, in the
libraries of Florida. Florida library bulletin (Jacksonville, Fla.) , vol. 2, no. 2.
(1930) , 16 p.   Z673.F63 vol. 2, no. 2
Some official documents included, mainly under the "Florida" heading.

Floridiana, a bibliography on Florida for use by public school teachers and others
[by] Carita D. Corse, A. R. Mead, J. M. Leps and others. Gainesville, Fla., 1945.
11, 13, 15–207, 209–225 numb. 1. (Bulletin 32, Bureau of Educational Research,
University of Florida)   LB5.F6 no. 32
Official publications are entered under individual authors, as well as Florida
agencies. Reproduced from typewritten copy. Prepared from a master bibliography, compiled and published earlier (1936?) under direction of State Work
Projects Administration. Two supplements to *Bulletin* 32 provide an "Index,
a subject matter index for use with the bibliography on Florida and supplementary references" (Gainesville, Fla., 1945, 19 numb. 1.) , and "additional
materials from 1941–1945" (Gainesville, Fla., 1945. 35 numb. 1.) .

Lloyd, Dorothy G. Official publications of Florida, 1821–1941. Urbana, Ill., 1943.
                                                                          Microfilm Z–24
Microfilm copy of typewritten manuscript, made by the University of Illi-
nois Library. Collation of the original, as determined from the film: 537 1.
Thesis (M.A.) , University of Illinois.

McMurtrie, Douglas C. The first printing in Florida. Atlanta, Ga., Priv. print., 1931.
5–18 p.   Z209.F6M2
"Reprinted, with additions from the *Southern Printer* for March 1931...."
Contains a list of the imprints of the acts of the Legislative Council, Aug. 1822–
Jan. 6, 1845.

——— A preliminary short-title check list of books, pamphlets and broadsides printed
in Florida, 1784–1860. Jacksonville [Historical Records Survey] 1937. 15 numb. 1.
(American imprints inventory. Imprints memoranda, no. 1)   Z1215.H66 no. 1
Includes a considerable number of official documents.

Taylor, Grace E. W., *and* A. Elizabeth Alexander. A bibliography and subject index
of publications issued by official Florida agencies, January 1942–December, 1951.
Gainesville, Fla., 1953, 376 p. (Florida. University, Gainesville. Libraries. Bibliographic series, no. 5)   Z1223.5.F5T3

GEORGIA

Fourth of the original 13 states.

Current:

Georgia. State Library, *Atlanta*. Checklist of official publications of the state of
　　Georgia. Feb./Aug. 1954+ Atlanta. quarterly.   DLC
　　　　Continues the "Checklist of Georgia Documents Entered at the State Library,"
　　　　published in issues no. 1–9 of *Georgia Commentary* (Atlanta, State Library)
　　　　and covering the period Jan. 1948/Aug. 1949 to March 1953/Jan. 1954.

Retrospective:

Georgia. State Library, *Atlanta*. Trial checklist of Georgia state documents. Comp.
　　by Ella May Thornton, State Librarian. Atlanta, 1940. 70 1.   Z1223.5.G4G4
　　　　The checklist covers documents from the early 1800's to 1940.

Larwood, James. Georgia, 1800–1900. A series of selections from the Georgiana library
　　of James Larwood: historical, biographical, bibliographical & critical. Atlanta, At-
　　lanta Public Library, 1956. xv, 295 p.   Z1273.L3
　　　　Under the heading "Georgia Banks and Banking," a description of colonial
　　and confederate currency is included.

McMurtrie, Douglas C. Located Georgia imprints of the eighteenth century not in
　　the DeRenne catalogue. Savannah, Ga., Priv. print., 1934. 44 p.   Z1273.M17
　　　　"Two hundred copies reprinted, with additional illustrations, from the
　　Georgia historical quarterly for March, 1934."

Wymberley Jones DeRenne Georgia Library, *Wormsloe*. Catalogue of the Wymber-
　　ley Jones DeRenne Georgia Library at Wormsloe, Isle of Hope near Savannah,
　　Georgia. Wormsloe, Privately printed, 1931. 3 v.   Z1273.D46 1931
　　　　Includes listings and facsimiles of a number of official state publications.

HAWAII

Kingdom until 1893; republic, 1894; annexed by United States, 1898;
territory, 1900; state, 1959.

Current:

Hawaii documents. no. 1/2+ Jan./Feb. 1967+ [Honolulu] Hawaii State Library. bi-
　　monthly, annual cumulation.   DLC

Current Hawaiiana. v. 1+ June 1944+ [Honolulu] quarterly.   Z4703.C8
　　　　Issued by the Hawaii Library Association. 1944–64; from June 1964, by the
　　Hawaiian and Pacific Collection, Gregg M. Sinclair Library, University of Ha-
　　waii. In two parts: Books, Pamphlets, Leaflets, etc., and Serials. Includes state
　　documents.

Retrospective:

Carter, George R. Preliminary catalogue of Hawaiiana in the library of George R.
　　Carter . . . collected largely by Professor H. M. Ballou. [Boston, Heintzemann Press,
　　priv. print] 1915. 1 v.   Z4709.C28

Official documents are listed under corporate entries and broad subjects (Government Reports, Laws, Territorial Reports, etc.)

Hawaii. *Dept. of Planning and Economic Development.* Hawaii state research inventory, 1961–1966. Honolulu, 1967. 199 l.   Z4705.A5
"...lists all research reports completed and/or published by or for the State of Hawaii, between July 1, 1961 and December 31, 1966, or in progress as of January 1, 1967."

Hawaii. University, *Honolulu, Library, Hawaiian Collection.* Dictionary catalog. Boston, G. K. Hall, 1963. 4 v.   Z4709.H22

Hawaii Library Association. *Hawaiiana Section.* Official publications of the Territory of Hawaii, 1900–1959. Honolulu, Public Archives, Dept. of Accounting and General Services, 1962. 250 p.   Z4705.H35
Compiled by Janet Bell, Agnes Conrad, Margaret Holden, and Clare Murdoch. Documents are listed under names of agencies. Numerous cross-references by keywords. Gives date of establishment and a brief history of agencies.

Phillips, James T.   A preliminary check list of the printed reports and correspondence of the Minister of Foreign Relations of the government of the Hawaiian Islands, 1845 to 1862, inclusive, together with a list of the printed government documents referred to, or quoted therein. Honolulu, Printed for private circulation by the Hawaiian Historical Society, 1928. 16 p.   Z4705.P5

U.S. *Library of Congress.* List of books relating to Hawaii (including references to collected works and periodicals), by A. P. C. Griffin. Washington, Govt. Print. Off., 1898. 26 p.   Z4706.U5
A number of official documents are listed. covering the period 1886–98.

U.S. *Superintendent of Documents.* Insular possessions. [1910–45] Washington. (*Its* Price list 32)   Z1223.A191 no. 32
After 1929, Hawaii was included in Price list 60, *Alaska and Hawaii* (title varies), and after 1960, in Price list 87, *States and Territories.*

IDAHO

Ceded by Great Britain, 1846; part of Oregon Territory, 1848; territory, 1863; state, 1890.

Current:

The Idaho librarian. v. 1+ April 1945+ [Moscow, Idaho] Idaho Library Association, University of Idaho Library. quarterly.   Z671.A3
Brief lists of state documents were published in the issues of October 1955, January and October 1956. A list for the period 1960–63 appeared in January 1964 issue. From 1965 on, a "Checklist of Idaho Publications" for the previous year is included in the April issue.

Retrospective:

Historical Records Survey.   A check list of Idaho imprints, 1839–1890. Chicago, WPA Historical Records Survey Project, 1940. 66, 66a–66b, 67–74 numb. l. (American imprints inventory, no. 13)   Z1215.H67 no. 13
    Z1275.H57

"The present list was preceded in 1938, by *A Short-Title Check List of Books, Pamphlets and Broadsides Printed in Idaho, 1839–1890,* which was issued as no. 2 of the American imprints inventory, Imprints memoranda" (compiled by Douglas C. McMurtrie, Chicago, Historical Records Survey, 1938. Z1215.H66 no. 2 and Z1275.M16).

ILLLINOIS

Part of Northwest Territory, 1787; part of Indiana Territory, 1800; Illinois Territory, 1809; state, 1818.

Current:

Illinois. *Secretary of State.* Publications of the state of Illinois. [Springfield] Z1277.A3
"...a list of Illinois documents deposited with the Illinois State Library." Issued first as a separate publication in 1957. From January 1959 to December 1960, issued as *Illinois State Publications,* in a mimeographed form, semiannually. From Jan./June 1961 issued in printed form.

Illinois documents list. Mar. 15, 1971+ Springfield, Illinois State Library, Documents Unit. semimonthly.   Z1223.5.I3I44
From Jan. 1968 to Feb. 28, 1971, issued under the title *Illinois State Publications (Documents) Shipping List* (Z1223.5.I3I439).

Retrospective:

Buck, Solon J. Travel and description, 1765–1865, together with a list of county histories, atlases, and biographical collections, and a list of territorial and state laws. Springfield, Ill., Trustees of the Illinois State Historical Library, 1914. 514 p. (Collections of the State Historical Library, v. 9. Bibliographical series, v. 2)
F536.I25 v. 9
Z1277.B89
"Territorial and state laws, 1788–1913," p. 383–426.

Byrd, Cecil K. A bibliography of Illinois imprints, 1814–58. Chicago, University of Chicago Press [1966] xxv, 601 p.   Z1277.B9
"It was decided arbitrarily to exclude all state documents except legislative journals, session laws, a few laws that were separately printed, Supreme Court reports, and a few publications relating to the constitutional conventions of 1818 and 1847."

Hasse, Adelaide R. Index of economic material in documents of the states of the United States: Illinois, 1809–1904. [Washington] Carnegie Institution of Washington, 1909. 393 p. [Carnegie Institution of Washington. Publication no. 85 (Illinois)]   AS32.A5 no. 85
Z1277.H25
Z1223.5.A1H2 v. 3
"The present volume follows the preceding volumes in form, except that perhaps a little more space has been given to checklist entries." Hasse deals mainly "with the printed reports of administrative officers, legislative committees, and special commissions of the states, and with governors' messages for the period since 1809. It does not refer to constitutions, laws, legislative proceedings or court decisions."

Illinois. *Secretary of State.* List of documents published by state of Illinois, for distribution by Secretary of State. Springfield, Ill. [1911–18?]   Z1223.5.I3
A simple enumeration of publication titles, arranged by agencies.

Illinois libraries. v. 1+ Jan. 1919+ Springfield, 1919+ quarterly, 1919–37; monthly, 1938+   Z732.I2I3
   "Illinois Documents, a Checklist 1812–1850," by Margaret Cross Norton, v. 32, no. 8–10, and v. 33, no. 1–6 (Oct. 1950–June 1951); "Illinois State Documents," by Dorothy G. Bailey, published irregularly from October 1939 (v. 21, no. 10) to October 1954 (v. 36, no. 8). "Publications of the State of Illinois Pertaining to the Illinois Constitution," v. 51, no. 9 (1969). Lists can be located through cumulative indexes for 1919–47, 1948–52, etc.

INDIANA
Part of Northwest Territory, 1787; territory, 1800; state, 1816.

Current:
Indiana documents received at the State Library. Library occurrent. Indiana State Library, Indianapolis.   Z732.I43
   A list of publications received during the past quarter has been published regularly in each quarterly issue since 1924.

Retrospective:
Byrd, Cecil K., *and* Howard H. Peckham. A bibliography of Indiana imprints, 1804–1853. Indianapolis, Indiana Historical Bureau, 1955. xxi, 479 p. (Indiana historical collections, v. 35)   Z1281.B8
   Of government documents, it includes "session laws, revised statutes, separate printings of single laws, Supreme Court reports, official documents on the constitutional conventions, and the House and Senate Journals." Omits "the documents comprising the so-called Documentary Journals . . . even though they also exist, in some instances, in separate and variant state."

Howe, Daniel W. A descriptive catalogue of the official publications of the territory and state of Indiana from 1800 to 1890, including references to the laws establishing the various state offices and institutions, and an index to the official reports. Indianapolis, Bowen-Merrill Co., 1890, p. [135]–230 (Indiana Historical Society. Publications. vol. 2, no. 5)   F521.I4
   Originally issued as no. 5 of the Indiana Historical Society pamphlets. *A Bibliography of the Laws of Indiana, 1788–1927,* by Rauch and Armstrong and Titus' *Indiana State Documents* (see below) supersede and extend this catalog through 1927 and 1909 respectively.

Indiana. *Executive Dept. Division of Accounting and Statistics.* Yearbook of the state of Indiana. 1917–[1950] Indianapolis.   JK5630.A26
   Includes annual reports of the state officers, departments, bureaus, boards, and commissions. From 1935 to 1950, a list of "Regular Publications of the State of Indiana" was included.

Indiana. State Library, *Indianapolis.* Biennial report. Indianapolis.   Z733.I39
   "Index to Documentary Journal of Indiana to 1899," 23d report, 1899/1900, Appendix B (p. 291–326); "State Documents and Publications Distributed by the State Library," 29th–31st reports, 1910/12–1914/16.

——— Bulletin. Indianapolis. bimonthly.   Z881.I39B
   "State Documents Received," v. 4, no. 6 (Nov. 1909) to v. 10 (1915).

Library occurrent. v. 1+ Apr. 1906+ Indianapolis, Indiana State Library, quarterly.
                                                                             Z732.I43

In addition to the quarterly listing (since 1924) of "Indiana Documents Received at the State Library," the following will be of interest: "Indiana State Documents; Some Checklists," by Nellie M. Coats, v. 18, 1954: 49–50; and "Public Documents of Indiana," by J. A. Lapp. v. 2, 1910; 108–111 and 130–133.

Rauch, John G., *and* Nellie C. Armstrong. A bibliography of the laws of Indiana, 1788–1927, beginning with the Northwest Territory. Indianapolis, Historical Bureau of the Indiana Library and Historical Department, 1928. xxxix, 77 p. (Indiana historical collections, vol. 16) F521.I38 v. 16
Z6457.I39R2
Arranged chronologically. "List of Authorized and Private Revisions of the Laws," p. 75–77. Completely replaces the very few pages of laws in Howe (see above) and extends the record to 1927. Based on Rauch's private collection.

Titus, Edna M. B. Indiana state documents. Urbana, Ill. [1930?] 87 l.   Z1223.5.I5T56
Thesis (M.A.), University of Illinois. Photocopy of typescript.
"Bibliography of Documents Issued by the State of Indiana During the Years 1890–1909": leaves 62–84. Bibliography: leaves 85–87. It fills the gap between Howe and the *Monthly Checklist of State Publications* issued by the Library of Congress.

IOWA

Louisiana Purchase, 1803; part of the territories of Missouri, Michigan, and Wisconsin, 1812–38; Territory of Iowa, 1838; state, 1846.

Current:

Iowa documents; list. no. 1+ Jan./Mar. 1956+ [Iowa City] State University of Iowa Libraries. quarterly.   Z1223.5.I6I58
Annual cumulations published since 1969. "Beginning with List no. 61, Jan.–Mar. 1971. the *Iowa Documents* list is being experimentally produced by computer. The list will now cumulate quarterly to the end of the calendar year, and each issue will include a key-word-out-of-context index."

Retrospective:

Budington, Margaret. Bibliography of Iowa state publications for [1898/99 to 1904/5] Iowa journal of history, v. 1, July 1903: 362–403; v. 2, July 1904: 399–429; v. 3, Jan. 1905: 101–145; v. 5, July, 1907: 337–408.   F616.I5

Carpenter, Zoe I. A check list of Des Moines, Iowa, imprints from 1861 through 1865, with a historical introduction. Washington, 1961. 64 l.   Z1284.D4C3
Thesis (M.A.), Catholic University of America. Includes official documents of the state of Iowa.

Cole, Theodore L. Historical bibliography of the statute law of Iowa. Law bulletin of the State University of Iowa (Iowa City) no. 2, 1891: 38–48.   DLC LL

Fitzpatrick, Thomas J. Bibliography of the Iowa territorial documents. Iowa journal of history, v. 5, April 1907: 234–269.   F616.I5

Iowa. *State Document Editor.* Iowa publications. Report of the State Document Department. [1st–3d, July 1, 1915/Dec. 31, 1916 to June 30, 1920] by Ora Williams, State Document Editor. Des Moines [1917–21]   Z1223.5.I7S

Each report includes list of publications. The Office of State Document Editor, created July 1, 1915, was abolished in 1921 and duties transferred to the State Superintendent of Printing.

Iowa. State Library, *Des Moines.* Report [1860?+] Des Moines.　　　Z733.I64
　　Issued biennially, it includes an accessions list of Iowa state documents received at the State Library, up to 1916. "Laws, journals, documents, etc. published by Iowa, 1838–1890," in the *Report* for 1889–91, p. 164–203 (Appendix).

Iowa. *State Library Commission.* Check list of the publications of the state of Iowa. With an index to the Iowa documents. Prepared under the supervision of the Iowa Library Commission . . . Lavinia Steele, compiler. Des Moines, B. Murphy. State Printer, 1904. 65 p.　　　Z1223.5.I6I6
　　Publications are listed by agencies, arranged in alphabetical order. Includes date of establishment of indiviudal agencies. "An effort has been made to provide a list as complete as possible of the official publications of the territory and state of Iowa."

Stewart, Helen. Iowa state publications. Urbana, Ill. 360 1.
　　An unpublished M.A. thesis prepared for the Graduate School of Library Science, University of Illinois, in 1937.

KANSAS

Part acquired in the Louisiana Purchase, 1803; the rest ceded by Mexico, 1848; territory, 1854; state, 1861.

Current:

Kansas. State Library, *Topeka. State Documents Division.* Checklist of official publications of the state of Kansas. v. 1, no. 1+ May/Oct. 1953+ Topeka, Kans.
　　　Z1223.5.K2A3
　　Continues list published in *Kansas Library Bulletin* from 1936 (see below) .

Retrospective:

A comprehensive bibliography of Kansas state publications up to 1958, including territorial publications, is:

Wilder, Bessie E. Bibliography of the official publications of Kansas, 1854–1958. [Lawrence] Governmental Research Center, University of Kansas, 1965. Z1285.W5
　　"This publication is the product of an attempt to complete a comprehensive bibliography of all printed material by the territory and state, 1854 through 1958." Only one volume, *Territorial and State Publications,* was published. Volume two, planned to cover state institutions and societies, was prepared but remained unedited and unpublished due to Miss Wilder's death. The first volume (318 p.) is arranged by agencies in alphabetical order. Symbols indicate location of the material. It does not include legislative bills, which for 1858–70 are itemized in the *Check List of Kansas Imprints, 1854–1876* (Historical Records Survey, see below) .

The following bibliographic tools will also be of assistance to researchers in Kansas state documents:

Historical Records Survey. Check list of Kansas imprints, 1854–1876. Topeka, WPA Historical Records Survey Project, 1939. xxxvii, 773 1. (*Its* American imprints inventory, no. 10)　　　Z1215.H67 no. 10

———— Kansas imprints, 1854–1876; a supplement. Compiled by Lorene A. Hawley and Alan W. Farley. Topeka, Kansas State Historical Society, 1958. 89 p.
Z1215.H67 no. 10 Suppl.
The main checklist includes in its chronological arrangement all the official documents that were located, and lists separately legislative bills for 1858–70.

Holt, Beatrice H. Kansas state publications since 1898. Urbana, Ill. 1932. 138 p.
An unpublished M.A. thesis prepared for the University of Illinois.

Kansas. *Laws, statutes, etc.* General statutes of Kansas (annotated) 1949; containing all general laws and laws of a general nature in force...Compiled, edited nd indexed by Franklin Corrick. Topeka, Printed and bound by F. Voiland, Jr., State Printer, 1950 [i.e. 1951] lxxxvi, 3388 p.   DLC LL
Supplements, published biennially, include "Bibliography of Kansas Statute Law."

Kansas. *Traveling Libraries Commission.* Kansas library bulletin. Topeka. 1932+ quarterly.   Z732.K2K37
A selected list of documents received in the State Library was published once or twice a year from 1936 to 1952 under the title "Kansas State Publications." Continued currently in the *Checklist of Official Publications of the State of Kansas,* issued from 1953 by the State Library.

Kansas State Historical Society. *Library.* Catalog of the Kansas territorial and state documents in the library of the State Historical Society, 1854–1898. Topeka, W. Y. Morgan, State Printer, 1900. 93 p.   Z1285.K21
Prepared by Zu Adams. Issued originally in *Transactions of the Kansas State Historical Society,* 1897–1900, v. 6: 383–475; revised and reissued in 1905 in Bowker's *State Publications.*

Ruppenthal, J. C. A bibliography of the statute law of Kansas. Law library journal, v. 23, July 1930: 79–103.   DLC LL
Lists laws in chronological order, official and unofficial compilations, partial compilations, indexes, and official supplements.

Shafer, J. D. Index to the laws of Kansas, comprising all general, special and private acts contained in the original authorized editions of the laws from the organization of the territory of Kansas in 1855 to the close of the 17th annual session of the state legislature in 1877. Leavenworth, Kans., Ketcheson & Durfee, Steam Printers and Engravers, 1877. 315 p.

Wilder, Bessie E. Author headings for the official publications of the state of Kansas. Chicago, American Library Association, 1956. 136 p. (State author headings)
Z695.1.G7W5

———— Governmental agencies of the state of Kansas, 1861–1956. [Lawrence] Governmental Research Center, University of Kansas, 1957. 141 p. (Governmental research series, no. 4, rev.)   JK6831 1957 .W5

KENTUCKY

Part of Virginia until 1787; part of Territory of the United States South of the River Ohio, 1790; state, 1792.

Current:

Kentucky. *State Archives and Records Service.* Checklist of Kentucky state publications. 1962+ Frankfort. annual.   Z1223.5.K4A33

"All items listed in the checklist are microfilmed at the University of Kentucky and are available for sale by the University of Kentucky Libraries." A directory of state officials is included in the checklist.

Kentucky; monthly checklist of Kentucky state publications. Lexington University of Kentucky Libraries. Z1223.5.K4K45
Vol. 1, no. 1 issued in April 1973.

Retrospective:

Clift, Garrett G. Bibliography of the House and Senate Journals, Commonwealth of Kentucky, 1792–1966. Frankfort, Kentucky Historical Society, 1967. 58 p. (Kentucky Historical Society. Research contribution no. 3) Z1223.5.K4C56

Hasse, Adelaide R. Index of economic material in documents of the states of the United States: Kentucky, 1792–1904. [Washington] Carnegie Institution of Washington, 1910. 452 p. [Carnegie Institution of Washington. Publication no. 85 (Kentucky)] Z1223.5.A1H2 v. 4
Z1287.H25
AS32.A5 no. 85

Kentucky. *Laws, statutes, etc.* The statute law of Kentucky; with notes, praelections, and observations on the public acts. Comprehending also, the laws of Virginia and acts of Parliament in force in this commonwealth; the charter of Virginia, the federal and state constitutions, and so much of the King of England's proclamation in 1763, as relates to the titles to land in Kentucky. Together with a table of reference to the cases adjudicated in the Court of Appeals. By William Littell. Frankfort, Ky. Printed by and for William Hunter. 1809–19. 5 v. DLC LL

—— A complete index to the names of persons, places and subjects mentioned in Littell's laws of Kentucky; a genealogical and historical guide, prepared by W. T. Smith, Lexington, Ky., Bradford Club Press, 1931. 213 p. DLC LL

Kentucky. *Secretary of State.* Catalogue: records, documents, papers, etc., Kentucky governors, 1792–1926. Comp. by Emma G. Cromwell, Secretary of State. Frankfort, State Journal Co., Printer to the Commonwealth, 1926. 185 p. CD3254.A5 1926
Documents are listed in chronological order successively under the names of 43 governors of Kentucky.

Kentucky. *University. Libraries.* Kentucky session laws, legislative journals, collected documents: checklists revised to November 1954. Lexington, 1954. 24 p. (*Its Occasional contributions, no. 67*) Z1009.K4 no. 67

McMurtrie, Douglas C. A bibliography of Kentucky statute law. Louisville, Filson Club, 1935. p. [95]–120 incl. Z6457.K3M2
Running title: *Kentucky Statute Law, 1792–1830.* "Extract from the Filson Club History Quarterly for April 1935." Updated and completed by *A Bibliography of Kentucky Statute Law, 1792–1830, by Douglas C. McMurtrie; Addition of Titles in the Kentucky Historical Society, the University of Kentucky, and the Filson Club Only, 1831–1952,* by Garrett G. Clift, issued as Occasional contribution no. 49, University of Kentucky Libraries (1953, 41 p. Z1009.K4 no. 49)

McMurtrie, Douglas C., *and* Albert H. Allen. Check list of Kentucky imprints, 1787–1810. Louisville, Historical Records Survey, 1939. xxvii, 205 p. (American imprints inventory, no. 5) Z1215.H67 no. 5

—— Check list of Kentucky imprints, 1811–1820, with notes in supplement to the Check list of 1787–1810 imprints. Louisville, Historical Records Survey, 1939. 235 p. (American imprints inventory, no. 6) Z1215.H67 no. 6

LOUISIANA

Part acquired in the Louisiana Purchase, 1803; the rest ceded by Spain, 1810; territory, 1804; state, 1812.

Current:

Louisiana. *Dept. of State.* Official publications. v. 1+ 1935/48+ [Baton Rouge]
Z1223.5.L7A29
    Continues the *Bibliography of the Official Publications of Louisiana, 1803–1934*, prepared by Foote (see below). Volumes 2+ are cumulations of the semi-annual *Public Documents [of the] State of Louisiana.*

———— Public documents [of the] state of Louisiana. no. 1+ Feb. 1949+ [Baton Rouge]
semiannual.   Z1223.5.L7A32
    Title varies: no. 1, *Publications of State Agencies;* no. 2–10, *Semiannual List of the Public Documents of Louisiana* (varies slightly). Nos. 11, 25, and 37 not issued separately. Documents for those periods are included in the depart-ment's *Official Publications,* vols. 2–4. A mimeographed monthly list called *Public Documents of Louisiana Distributed to Depository Libraries* has also been issued since March 1949, to supplement the semiannual list.

Retrospective:

Foote, Lucy B.   Author headings for the official publications of the state of Louisiana.
[1803–1947] Chicago, American Library Assn., 1948. 125 p.   Z695.1.G7F6
———— ———— Supplement, 1948–1953 [by Margaret T. Lane. Baton Rouge] Wade
O. Martin, Jr., Secretary of State [1955] 32 p.   Z695.1.G7F6 Suppl.
    Supplements for 1954–64 were published in the semiannual *Public Documents,* issued by the Department of State, nos. 13, 17, 21, 27, 29, and 33. A cumulative supplement for 1948–73 was included in no. 50 (Jan.–Dec. 1973).

———— Bibliography of the official publications of Louisiana, 1803–1934. Baton Rouge,
La., Hill Memorial Library, Louisiana State University, 1942. 579 p. ([Histori-cal Records Survey] American imprints inventory, no. 19)   Z1215.H67 no. 19
Z1223.5.L7F7
    Territorial documents for 1803–12 precede the state documents for 1812–1934. Arrangement of the latter and of the main section is alphabetical by agency. "A brief statement outlining the establishment and functions of each govern-mental unit, including the latest form of name as found in the law up to the final date of this bibliography, accompanies the list of its publications." Con-tinued in Dept. of State's *Official Publications.*

Louisiana. State Library, *Baton Rouge.* The Louisiana union catalog. Baton Rouge,
1959. 912 p.   Z1289.L6
    Official documents are listed separately (p. 458–549). Kept up to date by sup-plements, 1959+. A *Pre–1968 Index* was issued in 1968 (497 p.) .

The following bibliographic tools relate to Louisiana laws, statutes, etc.:

Dart, Benjamin W.   Combined general indexes and parallel reference tables, Louisiana
constitution, codes and statutes, 1942. Indianapolis, Bobbs-Merrill Co. [1942]
1291 p.   DLC LL

Louisiana. *Dept. of State.* Index to legislative resolutions, 1941–1966. Compiled by
Wade O. Martin, Jr., Secretary of State. [Baton Rouge, 1967] 79 p.   KFL10 1967

Louisiana. Law Library, *New Orleans.* Catalogue of the Louisiana State Library, Law Department. Compiled by Albertine F. Phillips. [New Orleans] 1905. 199 p.
Z6459.L87

Louisiana. *Laws, statutes, etc.* The Louisiana digest, embracing the laws of the legislature of a general nature, enacted from the year 1804 to 1841, inclusive, and in force at this last period. Also, an abstract of the decisions of the Supreme Court of Louisiana on the statutory law, arranged under the appropriate articles in the digest. By Meinrad Greiner. vol. 1. New Orleans, B. Levy, 1841. xvii, 579 p.
DLC LL
Only the first volume was published.

Wallach, Kate. Research in Louisiana law. Baton Rouge, Louisiana State University Press [1958] 238 p. (Louisiana University studies. Social science series, no. 6)
DLC LL
"Bibliographical history of Louisiana civil law sources, Roman, French, and Spanish," p. 150–218.

MAINE
Part of Massachusetts until 1820; state, 1820.

Current:

Maine. State Library, *Augusta.* Checklist of state of Maine publications received by the Maine State Library. 1941–44+ [Augusta] quarterly. Z1223.5.M25M3
Cumulations of the quarterly checklist issued only for 1941–44 and 1945 to June 1947.

Retrospective:

Friedman, Rebecca. Index of Maine state publications, 1904–1934. [Augusta? 1934]
Microfilm 3208 Z
Microfilm copy of typescript, made by the Library of Congress Photoduplication Service. Collation of the original, as determined from the film, 50 leaves. "Supplements Hasse's Index, published by Carnegie Institution" (below).

Hasse, Adelaide R. Index of economic material in documents of the states of the United States: Maine, 1820–1904. [Washington] Carnegie Institution of Washington, 1907. 95 p. [Carnegie Institution of Washington. Publication no. 85 (Maine)]
Z1223.5.A1H2 v. 5
Z1291.H25
AS32.A5 no. 85

McMurtrie, Douglas C. Maine imprints, 1792–1820; an open letter to R. Webb Noyes, Esq., by Douglas C. McMurtrie. Chicago, Priv. print., 1935. 12 numb. l. Z1291.M17

Maine, State Library, *Augusta.* Maine library bulletin. v. 1–[18?] Apr. 1911–[Jan./Apr. 1933?] Augusta. quarterly. Z881.M219
"State Publications" (title varies slightly) included more or less regularly.

—— Report of the librarian of the Maine State Library. Augusta. Z733.M22
"Bibliography of Maine laws," report for 1891–92 (p. 34–41), reprinted from the *Collections and Proceedings* of the Maine Historical Society, 2d series, v. 2 (p. 391–402).
"Executive, legislative and judicial departments of Maine (and their publications)," report for 1895–96 (p. 23–32).
"Index to Maine public documents, 1834–1867," report for 1905–6 (p. 26–90).

Noyes, Reginald W. A bibliography of Maine imprints to 1820. Stonington, Me.,
	Printed by Mrs. and Mr. R. W. Noyes, 1930. 22 p. 1 l. [132], xvii p. Z1291.N95
		Chronologically arranged with complete author and partial title and subject
		index.
	—— Supplement to a bibliography of Maine imprints to 1820. Stonington, Me.,
	1934. 11 l.																Z1291.N95 Suppl.
		Douglas C. McMurtrie's *Maine Imprints* (see above) constitutes another sup-
		plement to Noyes' bibliography.

Williamson, Joseph. A bibliography of the state of Maine from the earliest period
	to 1891. Portland, Thurston Print, 1896. 2 v.							Z1291.W73
		"Compiled under the auspices of the Maine Historical Society."

Willis, William. A descriptive catalogue of books and pamphlets relating to the his-
	tory and statistics of Maine, or portions of it. Norton's literary letter (New York),
	v. 4, 1859: 11–30.														Z1219.N88v.4
																		Microfilm 22182 Z

In the Library of Congress there are five unpublished M.S. theses on
Maine imprints. Collected under the general title *A Checklist of Maine
Imprints,* the papers were presented originally at the Catholic University
of America and are typewritten carbon copies.

1821–25: Donnelly, Joan A. (1951, 189 l., Z1291.D6)
1826–30: Woolery, Rosemary J. M. (1951. 167 l., Z1291.W76)
1831–35: Kuhn, John C. (1950. 132 l. Z1291.K8)
1836–38: Lo, Chi-hua. (1959. 1061 l. Z1291.L6)
1844–46: Wilkins, Otto (1960. 114 l. Z1291.W7)

MARYLAND
Seventh of the original 13 states.

Current:
Maryland manual. Annapolis, Md., Hall of Records Commission. biennial.   JK3831
		Since 1950 it includes a list of Maryland state publications issued during the
		preceding two years.

The Hall of Records Commission also issues a monthly typewritten
list under the title *Maryland State Documents Received at the Hall of
Records.* Since 1946, *Maryland Libraries,* issued by Maryland Library
Association and the Association of School Librarians of Maryland (Bal-
timore, Z673.M393), has included "Maryland State Documents; a Selected
List."

Retrospective:
"For the Maryland collected documents, 1829–1920, the Hall of Records, Annapolis, has a typewritten index, and for documents since 1920,
a card index, thus serving the purpose of a comprehensive record, con-

tinuously kept up to date." [7] The following bibliographies also relate to Maryland state documents and may be of assistance to researchers:

Alexander, John H. Index to the Calendar of Maryland state papers. Baltimore, J. S. Waters, 1861. 66 p.　　　　　　　　　　　　　　　　　　　　　CD3284.A6
　　Index to the first volume of a manuscript calendar of Maryland documentary material covering in general the period 1637–1702.

Bristol, Roger P. Maryland imprints, 1801–1810. Charlottesville, Published by the University of Virginia Press for the Bibliographical Society of the University of Virginia, 1953. xxviii, 310 p.　　　　　　　　　　　　　　　　Z1293.B75

Lee, John W. M. A hand list of laws, journals and documents of Maryland to the year 1800. Baltimore [London printed] 1878. 16 p.　　　　　　Z1293.L45
　　"Preliminary list"; no more published. "Privately printed at the Chiswick press . . . for Jno W. M. Lee."

Maryland. *Court of Appeals.* Catalogue of manuscripts and printed matter in the possession of the Court of Appeals of Maryland, November, 1926. [Baltimore, Daily Record Co., 1926] 29 p.　　　　　　　　　　　　　　　Z1293.M39
　　Compiled by William Baxter. Includes lists of "Original Acts of Assembly in Manuscripts" for 1640–92 and 1732–99; "Record of Laws Enacted by the General Assembly," 1711–1908; "Court Documents," etc.

Maryland. *Hall of Records Commission.* Publication. no. 1+ Annapolis [c1942+]
　　　　　　　　　　　　　　　　　　　　　　　　　　　　　　CD3280.A16
　　Title varies slightly. Reprinted by the Genealogical Pub. Co. in Baltimore, 1967+ (CD3280.A17). Following are titles of individual volumes:

　　no. 1: *Calendar of Maryland State Papers,* no. 1, *The Black Books,* 1943.
　　no. 2: *Catalogue of Archival Material,* 1942.
　　no. 4: *Land Office and Prerogative Court Records of Colonial Maryland,* 1946.
　　no. 5: *Calendar of Maryland State Papers,* no. 2, *The Bank Stock Papers,* 1947.
　　no. 6: ——— no. 3, *The Brown Books,* 1948.
　　no. 7: ——— no. 4, pt. 1, *The Red Books,* 1950.
　　no. 8: ——— no. 4, pt. 2, *The Red Books,* 1953.
　　no. 10: ——— no. 4, pt. 3, *The Red Books,* 1955.
　　no. 11: ——— no. 5. *Executive Miscellaneous,* 1958.
　　no. 13: *The County Courthouses and Records of Maryland,* pt. 2, *The Records,* 1963.

Minick, Amanda R. A history of printing in Maryland, 1791–1800, with a bibliography of works printed in the state during the period. Baltimore, Enoch Pratt Free Library, 1949. 603 p.　　　　　　　　　　　　　　　　　　Z209.M39M5
　　Thesis (M.S.), Columbia University.

Wheeler, Joseph T. The Maryland press, 1777–1790; with an introduction by Lawrence C. Wroth. Baltimore, Maryland Historical Society, 1938. 226 p.　Z209.M39W91
　　A continuation of Lawrence C. Wroth's *History of Printing in Colonial Maryland* (see below). "A bibliography of Maryland imprints," p. [77]–206.

Wroth, Lawrence C. A history of printing in colonial Maryland, 1686–1776. Baltimore, Typothetae of Baltimore, 1922. 275 p.　　　　　　　　　　Z209.M39W9
　　"Maryland imprints; an annotated bibliography of books, broadsides and newspapers printed in Maryland from 1689 to 1776," p. 157–256.

---

[7] James B. Childs, "Bibliographic Control of Federal, State and Local Documents," *Library Trends,* v. 15, July 1966: 17.

In the Library of Congress there are the following unpublished M.S. theses on Maryland imprints. Collected under the general title *A Check List of Maryland Imprints*, the papers were presented originally at the Catholic University of America and are typewritten carbon copies.

1811–14: Webb, Erna M. (1954. 136 l. Z1293.W4)
1815–18: Alagia, Damian P. (1951. 159 l. Z1293.A6)
1819–22: Franklin, Aurelia W. (1951. 297 l. Z1293.F7)
1823–26: Dunegan, Florence M. (1952. 151 l. Z1293.D8)
1831–34: Murphy, Robert B. (1952. 199 l. Z1293.M8)
1839: Titus, Thomas R. (1963. 86 l. Z1293.T55)
1840: Nelson, Cecil P. (1958. 154 l. Z1293.N4)
1841–42: Luney, Alice W. (1959. 144 l. Z1293.L8)
1843–46: Donnelly, Frederic D. (1953. 241 l. Z1293.D6)
1847–49: King, Sarah B. (1954. 201 l. Z1293.K5)
1850–52: Spencer, Helen I. (1953. 215 l. Z1293.S7)
1853–54: Rodriguez, Adelaide V. (1953. 175 l. Z1293.R6)
1855–57: Davis, Vashti A. (1953. 209 l. Z1293.D3)
1859: Gildea, Matthew E. (1965. 116 l. Z1293.G53)
1860: O'Neill, Maureen (1963. 135 l. Z1293.O5)
1861: Neavill, Helen A. (1962. 106 l. Z1293.N27)
1863: Rosenthal, Elaine P. (1962. 88 l. Z1293.R67)
1864–66: Chin, Elisabeth M. (1963. 253 l. Z1293.C45)
1867–69: Thompson, John H. (1953. 265 l. Z1293.T5)
1870–71: Bennett, Emily F. (1953. 230 l. Z1293.B4)
1872–73: Raymond, Anne F. (1954. 111 l. Z1293.R3)
1874–76: Quigg, Dorothy (1954. 260 l. Z1293.Q5)

MASSACHUSETTS
Sixth of the original 13 states.

Current:

Massachusetts. State Library, *Boston.* Commonwealth of Massachusetts publications received. [Feb. 1962+] Boston. monthly.   DLC

―――― Massachusetts Executive Department publications, 1962–1966. [Boston, 1968] 77 l.   Z1223.5.M35M3
   Cover title: "Cumulative listing of publications of Massachusetts Executive Agencies (with some selected publications of the General Court) received at Massachusetts State Library during 1962–66, with Index." According to the introduction: "The listing is not an exact total of all the entries that would be found in the monthly bulletins.... Eliminated are all Legislative Documents (which are separately indexed in our *Index of Special Reports Authorized by the General Court.*) Also omitted are the various listings of Acts, Resolves, etc. of the Commonwealth, and separates of the laws of specific agencies." Since 1967, the list has been issued annually.

Retrospective:

American Imprints Inventory Project, *Massachusetts.* A check list of Massachusetts imprints, 1801. Prepared by the American Imprints Inventory Project in Massachusetts from material furnished by the Historical Records Survey in all the states. Boston, Mass., 1942, xxxiii, 157 numb. l. (American imprints inventory, no. 40)   Z1215.H67 no. 40

—— A check list of Massachusetts imprints, 1802. Boston, Mass., 1942. xxxiii, 158 numb l. (American imprints inventory, no. 45)   Z1215.H67 no. 45

Blouin, Francis X.   Index and guide to Massachusetts state legislative documents, 1802–1882. Boston, Massachusetts State Library, 1972. 186 l.   Z1223.5.M35B55

Ford, Worthington Ch., *and* Albert Matthews.   A bibliography of the laws of the Massachusetts Bay, 1641–1776. Cambridge, Priv. print. [University Press, J. Wilson and Son] 1907. 186 p.   Z6457.M4F7
    "Reprinted from the *Publications of the Colonial Society of Massachusetts,* vol. 4."

—— A bibliography of the Massachusetts House Journals, 1715–1776. Cambridge, Priv. print., 1905. 87 p.   Z1295.F75
    "Reprinted from the *Publications of the Colonial Society of Massachusetts,* v. 4."

—— Broadsides, ballads, etc. printed in Massachusetts 1639–1800. [Boston] Massachusetts Historical Society, 1922. xvi, 483 p. (Massachusetts Historical Society. Collections v. 75)   F61.M41 v. 75
    Z1295.F76
    Includes a considerable number of official documents.

Hasse, Adelaide R.   Index of economic material in documents of the states of the United States: Massachusetts, 1789–1904. [Washington] Carnegie Institution of Washington, 1958. 310 p. [Carnegie Institution of Washington. Publication no. 85 (Massachusetts)]   Z1223.5.A1H2 v. 6
    Z1295.H25
    AS32.A5 no. 85

Massachusetts. *Executive Office for Administration and Finance. Office of Planning and Program Coordination.*   Massachusetts inventory of state agency periodicals [by John Bauer. Boston] 1970. 95 p.   DLC

Massachusetts. State Library, *Boston.*   Catalogue of the State Library of Massachusetts. Boston, Rand, Avery & Co., 1880. 1048 p.   Z881.M41C
    State documents listed mostly under Massachusetts. Supplements to the catalogue listed in the annual report of the State Librarian until 1910 (see below).

—— Index of special reports authorized by the General Court. 1900–57+ [Boston]   Z1295.M36
    Prepared by the Library and the Legislative Research Bureau.
    Revised and updated editions issued in 1966 and 1970.

—— Index to reports and selected bills and resolves of the General Court, 1806–1899. Boston, 1964. 145 p.
    A manuscript in the Massachusetts State Library.

—— Report [of the Librarian] Boston. annual.   Z733.M41
    From 1849 to 1878, those state documents received at the State Library are listed under the headings "Volumes Received from Officers of the Government" and "Received from Other Sources." From 1879/80 to 1910 they are listed in the section "Annual Supplement to the General Catalogue [of 1880]."

—— Report on annual reports of the departments and agencies of the Commonwealth. Boston, 1960. 1 v.
    A typewritten copy, in the Massachusetts State Library.

MICHIGAN
Part of the Northwest Territory, 1787; territory, 1805; state, 1837.

Current:

Michigan documents. no. 1+ July/Sept. 1952+ Lansing. irreg.   Z1223.5.M5M5
    Continues selected list published in *Michigan Library News* (Z732.M6M78)
    under title "Michigan Material" up to Nov. 1949, and "Michigan Documents,"
    1950–52. Issued by the Michigan Department of Education, Bureau of Library
    Services.

Retrospective:

Citizens Research Council of Michigan. A quarter-century of citizen concern with
    government; a preface and a bibliography of the Detroit Bureau of Governmental
    Research, 1916–1941. [Detroit] 1941. 62 p.   Z1298.D4C5
    Includes comments on various problems of state administration and a class-
    ified bibliography of reports made by the bureau.

Greenly, Albert H. A selective bibliography of important books, pamphlets, and
    broadsides relating to Michigan history. Lunenburg, Vt., Stinehour Press, 1958.
    xvii, 165 p.   Z1297.G7
    Includes a section on the laws of early Michigan.

Historical Records Survey, *Michigan*. Preliminary check list of Michigan imprints,
    1796–1850. Detroit, Mich., Michigan Historical Records Survey Project, 1942.
    (American imprints inventory, no. 52)   Z1215.H67 no. 52
                                                     Z1297.H5
    Reproduced from typewritten copy. "Publications of the Michigan Historical
    Records Survey": 4 leaves at end.

McMurtrie, Douglas C. Early printing in Michigan, with a bibliography of the
    issues of the Michigan press, 1796–1850. Chicago, John Calhoun Club, 1931. 351 p.
                                                     Z209.M59M2
    Official documents can be identified through the index.

Michigan. *Dept. of State*. Michigan official directory and legislative manual. Lansing.
                                                     JK5831
    From 1887 to 1925, includes lists of public documents.

Michigan. *Historical Commission*. Michigan bibliography. A partial catalogue of
    books, maps, manuscripts and miscellaneous materials relating to the resources,
    development and history of Michigan from earliest times to July 1, 1917; together
    with citation of libraries in which the materials may be consulted, and a complete
    analytique index by subject and author. Prepared by Floyd B. Streeter. Lansing,
    Michigan Historical Commission, 1921. 2 v.   Z1297.M62
    "Michigan state and territorial publications": v. 1, p. 295–575.

Michigan. State Library, *Lansing*. Catalogue of the Michigan State Library. United
    States documents, state documents, foreign exchanges. Lansing, Robert Smith
    Print. Co., 1898. 276 p.   Z7164.G7M62

——— Report [of the State Librarian] Lansing [1850–1936]   Z733.M62
    Published annually from 1850 to 1860, biennially 1861/62 to 1935/36. "Docu-
    ments received from the state of Michigan" listed from 1860 to 1916. Reports
    for 1892–94 include "List of Publications of the Territory and State of Michigan,
    1806–1891."

MINNESOTA
Northwest Territory, 1787; territory, 1849; state, 1858.

Current:

Minnesota. State Library, *St. Paul.* Checklist. no. 1+ Aug. 1946+ St. Paul. annual. DLC

Minnesota state documents. [v. 1, no. 1+ Jan./Mar. 1970+] St. Paul, Minnesota Historical Society Library. quarterly. Z1223.5.M58M5

Minnesota state publications. v. 1, no. 1+ July/Sept. 1957+ St. Paul, Department of Administration. Documents Section. irregular. DLC
A price list of Minnesota documents placed on sale.

Retrospective:

Jerabek, Esther. A bibliography of Minnesota territorial documents. St. Paul, Minnesota Historical Society, 1936. xvi, 157 p. (Publications of the Minnesota Historical Society. Special bulletins 3) Z1223.5.M58J5

———— Check list of Minnesota state documents, 1858–1923. St. Paul, Minnesota Historical Society, 1972. 216 p. (Publications of the Minnesota Historical Society) Z1223.5.M58J52
"The present list is arranged as follows: State agencies, with their publications, in alphabetical order; the contents of the *Executive Documents,* arranged chronologically; supplement to *Check List of Minnesota Public Documents,* August 1923–December 1940; and additions to *A Bibliography of Minnesota Territorial Documents.*"

Minnesota Historical Society. Check list of Minnesota public documents. no. 1–86; July 1923–Oct./Dec. 1940. St. Paul. Z1223.5.M6
———— ———— [Cumulation] July 1, 1923–June 30, 1925. St. Paul. 39 p. (Publications of the Minnesota Historical Society) Z1223.5.M61
Issued monthly from July 1, 1923 to June 30, 1925; quarterly from July/Sept. 1925 to Oct./Dec. 1940. Superseded by a publication of the same title (see below) .

———— Checklist of Minnesota public documents. 1941–50. St. Paul. 303 p. Z1223.5.M62
Superseded the monthly, later quarterly, publication of the same title. Compiled by Esther Jerabek. Includes a supplement covering titles omitted from the monthly (or quarterly) lists, 1923–40. Although planned to continue as an annual publication, only the first issue was published.

MISSISSIPPI
Territory, 1798; state, 1817.

Current:

Mississippi. Public documents. no. 1+ July/Dec. 1966+ Jackson. semiannual. DLC
Issued by the Secretary of State.

Retrospective:

Chambers, Moreau B. C. A check list of Mississippi imprints, 1865–1870, with a historical introduction. 1968. 121 l. Z1301.C45
Thesis (M.A.) , Catholic University of America. Typescript (carbon copy) .

Cole, Theodore L. Statute laws of Mississippi. *In* Mississippi. Secretary of State. Biennial report, 1896–97, Jackson, Miss., 1897: [107]–109.   J87.M74a

Colliflower, Charles E. A check-list of Mississippi imprints from 1831 through 1840, with a historical introduction of the period. Washington, 1950. 126 l.   Z1301.C6
Thesis (M.S.) , Catholic University of America. Typescript (carbon copy) .

McMurtrie, Douglas C. A bibliography of Mississippi imprints, 1798–1830. Beauvoir Community, Miss., The Book Farm, 1945. 168 p. (Heartman's historical series no. 69)   Z1301.M15
At least half of the 230 items are territorial and state documents.

Mississippi. *Laws, statutes, etc. (Indexes)* Index of Mississippi session acts, 1817+ By Rena Humphreys and Mamie Owen. Jackson, Miss., Tucker Printing House, 1937+   DLC LL

Owen, Thomas McAdory. A bibliography of Mississippi. Washington, U.S. Govt. Print. Off., 1900. p. [633]–828.   Z1301.097
A reprint from the *Annual Report* of the American Historical Association for 1899 (v. 1) . Official documents are listed under broad subject headings (Codes, Conventions and Constitutions, Laws, State Offices, etc.) .

Missouri
Louisiana Purchase, 1803; territory, 1812; state, 1821.

Current:
Missouri. State Library, *Jefferson City. Reference and Circulation Dept.* Checklist of official publications of state of Missouri. 1951+ Jefferson City.   Z1223.5.M7M5
Published irregularly.

Missouri state government documents. [Jan. 1962+] Jefferson City, Missouri State Library. monthly.   Z1223.5.M7M53
Title 1972+: *Missouri State Government Publications,* issued bimonthly. Not published in 1971.

Retrospective:
Historical Records Survey. A preliminary check list of Missouri imprints, 1808–1850. Washington, D.C., Historical Records Survey, 1937. 225 p. (American imprints inventory, no. 1)   Z1215.H67 no. 1
                                                                                      Z1303.H67

Missouri. *Division of Commerce and Industrial Development.* A bibliography of economic reports in the state of Missouri. Jefferson City, 1965. 101 p.   Z7165.U5M55
Reports are listed under broad subject headings and cover approximately the period 1955–65.

Missouri. *State Dept.* Official manual. 1878+ [Jefferson City]   JK5431
From 1903 to 1915, it included a "List of Printed Public Documents of Missouri."

Sampson, Francis A. Bibliography of Missouri state official publications. [1905–9]
Missouri historical review, v. 1: 85–100; v. 2: 303–318; v. 4: 182–201.   F461.M59

Saylor, Cerilla E. Official publications of the state of Missouri. [Urbana, Ill., 1941] 375 l.   Microfilm Z–24
This unpublished M.S. thesis presented at the University of Illinois includes territorial as well as state publications.

MONTANA
Part of Louisiana Purchase, 1803; territory, 1864; state, 1889.

Current:
Montana state publications. 1969+ Helena, Montana State Library. annual.   DLC
The first annual list, covering publications received by Montana State Library in 1968, was published in *Montana Libraries*, v. 22, Jan. 1969: 18–23 (Z732.M9M6) .

Retrospective:
McMurtrie, Douglas C. Montana imprints, 1864–1880; bibliography of books, pamphlets and broadsides printed within the area now constituting the state of Montana. Chicago, Black Cat Press, 1937. 82 p.   Z1305.M17

Montana. *State Bureau of Mines and Geology*. Publications of Montana Bureau of Mines and Geology, 1919–1968. Butte, Montana College of Mineral Science and Technology [1968] 21 p.   Z6034.U5M92

Speer, Lucile. Montana state documents: a preliminary bibliography. Missoula, Mont., Bureau of Government Research, Montana State University, 1958. 56 p. (Bureau of Government Research. Montana State University. Publication no. 1)   Z1305.S7

NEBRASKA
Louisiana Purchase, 1803; territory, 1854; state, 1867.

Current:
Nebraska state publications checklist [Abstracts; Index] vol. 1, 1973+ [Lincoln] Nebraska Publications Clearinghouse.   Z1223.5.N4N4
To be used in conjunction with the *Guide to Nebraska State Agencies. January 1973* (Lincoln, Nebraska Publications Clearinghouse).

Retrospective:
Gilmore, Sylvia C. The official publications of Nebraska. Urbana, Ill., 1935. 206 l.
Microfilm Z–69
Unpublished M.S. thesis prepared for the Graduate School of Library Science, University of Illinois. Covers period 1855–1934.

Historical Records Survey, *Nebraska*. A check list of Nebraska imprints, 1847–1876. Lincoln, Neb., 1942. (American imprints inventory, no. 26 and 27)
Z1215.H67 no. 26
Pt. 1, Non-documentary; pt. 2, Documentary. Part 2 (no. 27) was prepared as a typewritten draft but never published.

Nebraska. *Legislative Council.* Report ... [Lincoln, 1938+]   JK6674.A3
    Report no. 13, entitled *State Publications in Nebraska* (1940, 33 p.), contains
    four lists of agency reports; laws, regulations, and legislative proceedings; and
    books, bulletins and miscellaneous publications, arranged by agencies. The re-
    port covers 1938 and 1939.

Nebraska. *Legislative Reference Bureau.* Subject index of legislative bills with other
    legislative information, March 5, 1937. Lincoln, Neb. [1937] 59 p.   J87.N2

Omaha. Public Library. Nebraska, material in the Omaha Public Library. [Omaha,
    1931] 21 1.   Z1307.O54
    Compiled by Bertha Baumer. The bibliography includes a considerable num-
    ber of state documents.

NEVADA
Ceded by Mexico, 1848; part of Utah territory, 1850; territory, 1861;
state, 1864.

Current:
Nevada. State Library, *Carson City.* Nevada official publications. List no. 1+ Feb.
    1953+ Carson City. monthly.   Z1309.N43
    Title before 1968 (no. 90) : *Official Nevada Publications.* There is a semi-
    annual and an annual index.

Nevada official publications periodical index. List no. 1+ Jan./June 1969+ Carson
    City, Nevada State Library. semiannual.   Z1223.5.N49N45

Retrospective:
Armstrong, Robert D. A preliminary union catalog of Nevada manuscripts. Foreword
    by David W. Heron. Reno, University of Nevada Library, 1967. 218 p.   Z1309.A75
    Official documents listed under Nevada. Covers mainly early territorial and
    state documents.

Historical Records Survey. A check list of Nevada imprints, 1859–1890. Chicago, His-
    torical Records Survey, 1939. 127 1. (American imprints inventory, no. 7)
                                                                       Z1215.H67 no. 7
    "Among the 520 imprints recorded in this list, 416 (80%) are official docu-
    ments of the territory or state of Nevada."

Nevada. *Superintendent of State Printing.* Biennial report. Carson City. Nev.
                                                                         Z1223.5.N49
    Reports for 1899/1900 to 1921/22 include a detailed statement of printing for
    the various state agencies, listing publications, forms, etc., printed during the
    period.

Poulton, Helen J. Nevada state agencies: from territory through statehood. [Reno]
    University of Nevada Press [1964] 97 p. (University of Nevada Press. Bibliographi-
    cal series, no. 5)   Z695.1.G7P6
    "Author headings for the official publications of the State of Nevada."

New Hampshire
Ninth of the original 13 states.

Current:

New Hampshire. State Library, *Concord.* Checklist of New Hampshire state departments publications. 1942/44+ [Concord] biennial.   Z1223.5.N5
> Superseded its *Checklist of New Hampshire State Documents Received at the State Library* (1938–May 1943).

Retrospective:

Hasse, Adelaide R. Index of economic material in documents of the states of the United States: New Hampshire, 1789–1904. [Washington] Carnegie Institution of Washington, 1907. 66 p. [Carnegie Institution of Washington. Publication no. 85 (New Hampshire)]   Z1222.5.A1H2 v. 7
                                                                         Z1311.H25
                                                                         AS32.A5 no. 85

New Hampshire. State Library, *Concord.* Biennial report. 1846/47+ Concord.
                                                                         Z733.N49
> Published annually from 1846/47 to 1891/92. Before 1890, New Hampshire state documents were included in the lists of accessions. Between 1889 and 1894 special lists were included in the report as follows:

Report for 1889/90:
> "A list of official publications..." March 1889–Oct. 1890, p. [91]–94.
> "List of reports of departments of the state of New Hampshire and other documental matter, as found in appendices of legislative journals, and subsequently in the 'Annual reports'," p. [95]–137. (Also reprinted by J. B. Clarke, Public Printer, Manchester, 1890. 44 p. Z1311.N55) The list covers the period 1822–89.
> "Check list of New Hampshire laws, 1789–1889," by Theodore L. Cole, p. [145]–152. (Also reprint, 1890?, 8 p. Z6457.N3C7).
> "Table of sessions of the legislature, 1776–1889," p. [153]–160.

Report for 1890/91:
> "A list of official publications... 1890/91," p. [75]–82.
> "Index list of reports of departments... and other documental matter published in the appendices to legislative journals, 1822–69, and in the 'Annual reports' 1870–90," p. [85]–119.

Report for 1891/92:
> "Condensed list of reports of departments and some other state publications of New Hampshire," p. [77]–104 (Departmental reports, Special reports, Judicial reports, New Hampshire legislative journals).
> "Check list of New Hampshire laws, 1789–1891; public acts, 1789–1834; public and private acts, 1835–1891," p. [105]–117. Includes also "Early laws," 1699–1780.
> "A list of official publications, state of New Hampshire, issued during the year ending Oct. 1, 1892," p. [119]–125.

Report for 1892/94:
> "List of New Hampshire state publications issued during the report period," p. [101]–112.

> In the reports for 1938/40 to 1942/44, the monthly *Checklist of New Hampshire State Documents Received at the State Library* (see below) is cumulated as follows: 1938/40: p. 23–32; 1940/42: p. 10–20; 1942/44: p. 19–30.

—— A checklist of New Hampshire state documents received at the State Library.
Jan. 1938–May 1943. [Concord] 6 v. monthly.   Z1223.5.N52
   Issues for July 1938–May 1943 are cumulated in the library's *Biennial Report*
   for 1938/40–1942/44. Superseded by a biennial publication with the same title.

NEW JERSEY
Third of the original 13 states.

Current:

Checklist of official New Jersey publications. v. 1+ July 1965+ Trenton, New Jersey
   State Library. bimonthly.   Z1223.5.N55C45

Retrospective:

Fannan, Mary E. New Jersey state publications on history, geology, geography, cli-
   mate, resources, industries and other topics. Newark, N.J., Pub. for the Free
   Public Library, 1907. 15 p.   Z1223.5.N55F2
      "Mary E. Fannan . . . has selected and entered in the following list alphabet-
   ically by subject those [publications] that seem to be most serviceable in a New
   Jersey library" (explanatory note) .

Hasse, Adelaide R. Index of economic material in documents of the states of the
   United States: New Jersey, 1789–1904. [Washington] Carnegie Institution of Wash-
   ington, 1914. 705 p. [Carnegie Institution of Washington. Publication no. 85 (New
   Jersey)]   Z1223.5.A1H2 v. 8
                                                                               Z1313.H22
                                                                               AS32.A5 no. 85

Humphrey, Constance H. Check-list of New Jersey imprints to the end of the Revolution. The papers of the Bibliographical Society of America. Chicago. Ill. 1931,
   v. 24, pt. 1–2, 1931, p. 43–149 incl. tab.   Z1008.B51P vol. 24
      "Chronological List, 1723–1783": p. 68–133; "Appendix: a Partial List of New
   Jersey Official Publications Not Printed in New Jersey": p. 134–149.

Lucas, Dorothy F. Bibliography of New Jersey official reports, 1905–1945, following
   A. R. Hasse, Index of economic material in documents of New Jersey, 1789–1904.
   [Trenton] N.J. State Dept. of Education, Division of State Library, Archives and
   History, 1947. 256 p.   Z1223.5.N55L8

      —— —— Supplement, 1945–1960. [By the cataloging staff of the New Jersey
   Bureau of General Reference under Rebecca Schlam] Trenton, N.J. State Dept.
   of Education, Division of State Library, Archives and History, 1961. 197 p.
                                                                               Z1223.5.N55L8 Suppl.

Morsch, Lucile M. Check list of New Jersey imprints, 1784–1800. Baltimore, WPA
   Historical Records Survey Projects, 1939, xvii, 189 p. (American imprints inventory,
   no. 9)   Z1214.H67 no. 9
                                                                               Z1313.M89

Nelson, William. Bibliography of the printed proceedings of the Provincial Assembly
   [of New Jersey] 1707–1776 [and of the printed acts of the Legislature of New
   Jersey, 1703–1800, and ordinances of the governors] *In* New Jersey. Public Record
   Commission. Report . . . 1899. Somerville. N.J., 1899. v. 1, p. 31–93.
                                                                               CD3380.A2
                                                                               Z6629.N54

New Jersey. State Library, *Trenton.* Check list of annual reports and other current publications issued by or under the authority of the state of New Jersey. July 1, 1915. Comp. by John P. Dullard, State Librarian. [Trenton, N.J., 1915] 12 p.
Z1223.5.N55N4

State documents. New Jersey library bulletin, v. 2, June 1913: 6–9.   Z732.N6N65 v. 2

Stevens, Henry, *and* William A. Whitehead.   An analytical index to the colonial documents of New Jersey in the State Paper Offices of England. New York, Pub. for the Society, D. Appleton and Co., 1858. xxix, 504 p. (New Jersey Historical Society, Collections, v. 5)   F131.N62 v. 5
    Appendix: A. List of the minutes of Council of the province of New Jersey ...[1681–1775]. List of the minutes of Council in Assembly, of the province of New Jersey...[1738–1775]. List of journals of the House of Representatives ...[1703–1775]. B. Catalogue of books, pamphlets and other publications referring in whole, or in part, to New Jersey during the colonial period...C. Titles of the several editions of the laws of New Jersey [1723–1852] D. List of newspapers in New Jersey prior to 1800. E. Notices of some of the public records.

NEW MEXICO

Ceded by Mexico, 1848; territory, 1850; state, 1912.

Current:

New Mexico. *State Records Center and Archives. Publications Division.* Publications of New Mexico state agencies. Santa Fe. 1968+   DLC
    The first issue covers publications for the period 1960 to spring 1968. Supplements issued in 1970 and in 1972. A monthly list, called *Publications Filed,* is also issued.

Retrospective:

Historical Records Survey. *Illinois.* Check list of New Mexico imprints and publications, 1784–1876. Imprints, 1834–1876; publications, 1784–1876. Prepared by the Illinois Historical Records Survey. [Detroit] Michigan Historical Records Survey, 1942. 115 p. (American imprints inventory, no. 25)   Z1215.H67 no. 25
Z1315.H5

New Mexico. University. *Library.* New Mexico official publications. no. 1–15. Jan./ Mar. 1956–Aug. 1960. Albuquerque.   DLC
    Not a complete list but partly fills the gap between Wilma L. Shelton's *Checklist of New Mexico Publications, 1850–1953* (see below) and the current checklist issued by the State Records Center and Archives.

Shelton, Wilma L. Checklist of New Mexico publications, 1850–1953. [Albuquerque] University of New Mexico Press, 1954. 240 p.   Z1315.S47
    "The publications in this list include all official literature which has been printed and published from 1850 through 1953 by or for the state." State Government Publications, p. 1–197; Associations, Institutions, p. 197–236.

NEW YORK
Eleventh of the original 13 states.

Current:

New York. State Library. *Albany.* A checklist of official publications of the state of
New York. v. 1+ Oct. 1947+ Albany.   Z1223.5.N57N55
    Published monthly with annual cumulation. A 15-year cumulation (v. 1–15,
Oct. 1947–June 1962. Z1223.5.N57N552) and a five-year cumulation (v. 16–21,
July 1962–Dec. 1967) issued in 1969. An author-index to the *Checklist*, covering
v. 1–23, Oct. 1947–Dec. 1969, issued in 1970, and an index to state serials,
covering the same period, issued in 1971. A *Subject Index* is in preparation.

Retrospective:

Breuer, Ernest H. Constitutional developments in New York 1777–1958; a bibliography
of conventions and constitutions with selected references for constitutional research. Albany, University of the State of New York, State Education Dept., 1958.
103 p. (New York. State Library, Albany. Bibliography bulletin 82)
                                                          Z1009.N56 no. 82

—— Constitutional developments in New York 1958–1967; a temporary supplement.
Albany, University of the State of New York, State Education Dept., New York
State Library, 1967. 142, A–17, B–8, 41 p. [various pagings]   Z1009.N56 no. 82

Hasse, Adelaide R. Index to economic material in documents of the states of the
United States: New York, 1789–1904. [Washington] Carnegie Institution of Wash-
ington, 1907. 553 p. [Carnegie Institution of Washington. Publication no. 85
(New York)]   Z1223.5.A1H2 no. 9
                                                           Z1317.H2
                                                           AS32.A5 no. 85

—— Some materials for a bibliography of the official publications of the General
Assembly of the colony of New York, 1693–1775. [New York, Public Library, 1903]
73 p.   Z1317.H18
    Just 25 copies reprinted from the New York Public Library *Bulletin*, Feb.–
April 1903, v. 7: 51–79, 95–116, 129–151 (Z881.N6B) .

Jewett, Alice L. Official publications of the state of New York relating to its history
as colony and state. Albany, University of the State of New York, 1917. 62 p.
(New York. State Library, Albany. Bibliography bulletin 59)   Z1009.N56 no. 59

New York (*State*) *Legislature.* General index to the documents of the state of New
York. 1777–1857—1777–1888. Albany. 6 v.   J87.N75d
    Title varies: 1842–54, *Index to the Documents of the Legislature of New York.*

New York (*State*) *Legislature. Senate. Secretary.* Cumulative index to joint legislative
committees and selected temporary state commissions, and alphabetical list of
chairmen and vice-chairmen thereof, 1900–1950. Rev. ed. Albany, Reprinted and
distributed by the New York State Library, 1966. 224 p.   JK3466.A54
—— —— Supplement [1951–65] Albany.   JK3466.A542

New York. State Library, *Albany. Gift and Exchange Section.* Materials and services
available to law libraries from the Gift and Exchange Section, New York State
Library, by Peter J. Paulson. [Albany, 1960] 17, 7 p.   Z690.N4
    "Reprinted from the *Proceedings of the Third Annual Law Library Institute,
Law Library Association of Greater New York, April 29–30, 1960.*"

Recent New York state publications of interest to libraries. [1907–17] New York
libraries (New York State University, Albany), v. 1–5, 1907–17. Z732.N7N8
    Lists of important New York state publications included irregularly. Lists
    can be located through index to vols. 1–10, in vol. 10, p. xxvi: "New York
    State Publications."

Works relating to the state of New York in the New York Public Library. *In* New
York. Public Library. Bulletin. v. 4, 1900: 163–178, 199–220. Z881.N6B
    Includes lists of constitutions and other legislative and documentary ma-
    terials.

NORTH CAROLINA
Twelfth of the original 13 states.

Current:

North Carolina. University. *Library. Documents Dept.* North Carolina publications.
no. 1+ Aug./Sept. 1952+ Chapel Hill. Z1319.N873
    Superseded the department's *Monthly Checklist of Official North Carolina
    Publications,* issued 1940 to 1946. Title from Aug. 1952 to Dec. 1956, *Checklist
    of Official North Carolina Publications Received by the University of North
    Carolina Library.* Issued in cooperation with North Carolina State Library in
    Raleigh.

Retrospective:

Lambert, Fred L. North Carolina bibliography; a critical history. Chapel Hill, 1970.
70 l. Z1319.L28
    Thesis (M.S.L.S.), University of North Carolina. Bibliographies of North
    Carolina official publications: p. 32–44.

McMurtrie, Douglas C. A bibliography of eighteenth century North Carolina imprints, 1761–1800. Raleigh, N.C., Priv. print., 1936. p. 47–86, 143–166, 219–254.
  Z1319.M16
    "Extract from the North Carolina historical review for January, April and
    July, 1936."
    "Continuation of a bibliography of the issues of the press of the colony dur-
    ing its first twelve years of existence (1749–1760) which appeared in the North
    Carolina historical review for July, 1933" (p. 47). Reprint of the July 1933
    article in 1933, 23 p. Z209.N75M16.

—— Eighteenth century North Carolina imprints, 1749–1800. Chapel Hill, University
of North Carolina Press, 1938. 198 p. Z1319.M16 1938
    Much of the material was published in the *North Carolina Historical Review*
    (F251.N892) and also separately in 1936 in *A Bibliography of Eighteenth Century
    North Carolina Imprints, 1761–1800* (see above).

North Carolina. The state records of North Carolina, collected and edited by Walter
Clark. Raleigh, P. M. Hale, 1886–1907. 26 v. F251.N6
    Vols. 1–10 have title: *The Colonial Records of North Carolina,* collected and
    edited by William L. Saunders.

—— Index to the colonial and state records of North Carolina, compiled and edited
by Stephen B. Weeks. Goldsboro, Nash, 1909–14. 4 v. F251.N61
    Published as vols. 27–30 of the main work, *State Records.*

North Carolina. University. *Library. Documents Dept.* Monthly checklist of official
North Carolina publications. v. 1–7; Jan./Mar. 1940–July/Dec. 1946. [Chapel Hill]
7 v.   Z1319.N875
    Superseded in 1952 by the department's *Checklist of Official North Carolina
Publications,* now *North Carolina Publications.*

Thornton, Mary L.   Official publications of the colony and state of North Carolina,
1749–1939; a bibliography. Chapel Hill, University of North Carolina Press, 1954.
347 p.   Z1319.T5
    Arranged in alphabetical order of agencies, the bibliography is a quasi-union
catalog of the holdings of a group of the principal North Carolina libraries.

NORTH DAKOTA
Part of the Louisiana Purchase, 1803; the rest ceded by Great Britain,
1818; territory, 1861; state, 1889.

Current:

North Dakota. *State Library Commission.* North Dakota state publications. 1965+
Bismarck. semiannual.   Z1321.A3

Retrospective:

Allen, Albert H., *ed.* Dakota imprints, 1858–1889. New York, Pub. for the Bibliographical Society of America by R. R. Bowker Co., 1947. xxi, 221 p.   Z1321.A4
    Includes documents of the Dakota territory and of the first year of the states
of North and South Dakota.

McMurtrie, Douglas C.   Preliminary check list of North Dakota imprints, 1874–1890,
issued as manuscript for checking and revision. Evanston, Ill., 1943. 32 numb. l.
                                                                                  Z1321.M25

OHIO
Part of the Northwest Territory, 1787; state, 1803.

Current:

Ohio documents: a list of publications of state departments. v. 1, no. 1+ Jan./March,
1971+ Columbus, State Library of Ohio.   Z1223.5.O4A43
    Superseded *Selected Publications of the State of Ohio,* 1968–70 (called *Ohio
State Publications,* 1945–67).

Retrospective:

Hasse, Adelaide R.   Index of economic material in documents of the states of the
United States: Ohio, 1787–1904. [Washington] Carnegie Institution of Washington, 1907. 553 p. [Carnegie Institution of Washington. Publication no. 85 (Ohio)]
                                                                           Z1223.5.A1H2 v. 10
                                                                                  Z1323.H25
                                                                                  AS32.A5 no. 85

Hayes, Rutherford P., *comp.* Publications of the state of Ohio, 1803–1896. Together
with an index to the executive documents. Norwalk, Ohio. Laning Printing Co.,
1897. 71 p.   Z1323.H42P

Historical Records Survey, *Ohio.* A check list of Ohio imprints, 1796–1820. Columbus, Ohio Historical Records Survey, 1941. 202 1. (American imprints inventory, no 17)
Z1215.H67 no. 17
Z1323.H6

Houk, Judith A. Classification system for Ohio state documents. Columbus, Printed and distributed by the Ohio State Library, 1962. 27 1. Z697.G7H6
"This notation system is intended to facilitate recording and retrieving state documents. The scheme is similar to the Government Printing Office classification."

Missar, Charles D. A checklist of Ohio imprints from 1821 to 1825; with a historical introduction. Washington, 1960. 161 1. Z1323.M56
Thesis (M.S.). Catholic University of America.

Ohio. *Dept. of Printing and Binding.* Annual report. Columbus [1864–1914?]
Z1223.5.O4
Each report contains a list of public documents in alphabetical order of agencies, printed by the Dept. of Printing and Binding.

Ohio. *Laws, statutes, etc.* (*Indexes*) An index to all the laws and resolutions of the state of Ohio: including the laws adopted and enacted by the governor and judges, and the territorial legislature; from the commencement of the territorial government, to the year 1844–5, inclusive. Prepared by Zechariah Mills. Columbus, Scott and Co.'s Steam Power Press, 1846. 181 p. DLC LL

—— Index to Ohio laws, general and local, and to the resolutions of the General Assembly, from 1845–6 to 1857, inclusive. With an appendix, containing an index to the documents in the journals of the House and Senate from 1802 to 1836. By William T. Coggeshall. Columbus, R. Nevins, State Printer, 1858. 302 p. DLC LL

Ohio. *Secretary of State.* Checklist of Ohio public documents. v. 1–4, Sept. 1933–Dec. 1937. Columbus. 4 v. in 1. Z1223.5.O4A4

Ohio. State Library, *Columbus.* Checklist, publications of the state of Ohio, 1803– 1952. Columbus, Ohio Library Foundation, 1964. 131 p. Z1223.5.O4A18
"This compilation is a union list of publications on file in the Ohio State Library, Ohio State University Library, Ohio Historical Society, Legislative Reference Library and Supreme Court Library." Entries are arranged by the keyword of state agencies. An author index is included. A new updated edition of the checklist is prepared, to cover the period 1803–1970, by the Ohio Historical Society.

—— Ohio state publications. no. 1–100, Dec. 1945–Dec. 1970. Columbus. quarterly (irregular) . DLC
Title varies: 1945–67, *Ohio State Publications;* 1968–70, *Selected Publications of the State of Ohio.*
Superseded from Jan./Mar. 1971 by *Ohio Documents; a List of Publications of State Departments.*

OKLAHOMA
Louisiana Purchase, 1803; territory, 1890; state, 1907.
No current checklist published at the present time.

Retrospective:
Checklist of state publications. *In* Oklahoma. State Library, *Oklahoma City.* Bulletin. v. 1–7; Jan./Mar. 1948–July/Dec. 1954. Z881.O49

Cramer, Rose F. Author headings for the official publications of the state of Oklahoma. Rev. and extended by Carolyn Curtis Mohr. Chicago, American Library Association, 1954. 114 p.   Z695.1.G7C7 1954
"Originally prepared as a master's thesis at the University of Illinois Library School by Rose F. Cramer in 1944."

Foreman, Carolyn T. Oklahoma imprints, 1835–1907; a history of printing in Oklahoma before statehood. Norman, University of Oklahoma Press, 1936. xxiv, 499 p.   Z1325.F71
Session laws, legislative journals, statutes and Supreme Court decisions of Oklahoma, p. 249–253. Publications of the Indian nations, in chapter 4 ("Mission and other presses"), p. 33–54.

Hargrett, Lester. Oklahoma imprints, 1835–1890. New York, Published for the Bibliographical Society of America [by] Bowker, 1951. xvii, 267 p.   Z1325.H3
Includes official publications of the Indian nations and of the first year of Oklahoma territory.

Historical Records Survey, *Oklahoma*. A list of records of the state of Oklahoma. Oklahoma City, Okl., Historical Records Survey, 1938. 277 l.   CD3454.H5
"Cover-title: State archives, a list of records of the State of Oklahoma."

OREGON

Ceded by Great Britain, 1846; territory, 1848; state, 1859.

Current:

Oregon. State Library, *Salem*. Checklist of official publications of the state of Oregon. no. 1+ Jan./Mar. 1951+ Salem. quarterly.   DLC

Retrospective:

Belknap, George N. Oregon imprints, 1845–1870. Eugene, University of Oregon Books [1968] 305 p.   Z1327.B4
Annotates 1,521 books, pamphlets, and broadsides printed in Oregon through 1870. It includes imprints recorded in McMurtrie's *Oregon Imprints, 1847–1870* (see below) and in four supplements published in the *Oregon Historical Quarterly*.

McMurtrie, Douglas C. Oregon imprints, 1847–1870. Eugene, University of Oregon Press, 1950. xxi, 206 p. (University of Oregon Library. Studies in bibliography, no. 2)   Z881.O67S7 no. 2
Four supplements to this work by George N. Belknap were published in *Oregon Historical Quarterly*, Dec. 1950, June 1954, Sept. 1958, and June 1963 (F871.O47). Belknap also wrote "Early Oregon Documents," which appeared in the June 1955 issue of the quarterly.

Rockwood, Eleanor R. Oregon state documents; a check list, 1843 to 1925. Portland, Oregon Historical Society [1947] 283 p.   Z1223.5.O7R6
". . . covers all that could be found in the libraries of Oregon, for the period from the beginning of the provisional government in 1843 down to and including 1925." Reprinted from the *Oregon Historical Quarterly*, 1944–46. Arranged in the following main groups: Legislative branch, with analysis of committees; Officials, boards and commissions (p. 92), in alphabetical order; State institutions for defectives, dependents and delinquents (p. 271), in alphabetical order. No index.

PENNSYLVANIA

Second of the original 13 states.

Current:

Pennsylvania. *Bureau of Publications.* Publications of the Commonwealth of Pennsylvania. no. 1+ Feb. 1937+ Harrisburg. irregular. Z1329.A32
Current title: *Directory of State Publications.*

Pennsylvania. State Library, *Harrisburg.* A checklist of the official publications of the state of Pennsylvania. v. 1, no. 1+ Sept. 1963+ [Harrisburg] DLC
Current title: *Checklist of Official Pennsylvania Publications.*

Retrospective:

Ellis, Elizabeth G., *and* Robert C. Stewart. List of basic Pennsylvania state publications for depository libraries. Prelim. ed. Harrisburg, Government Publications Section, Pennsylvania State Library, 1967. 23 l. Z1223.5.P4E4
"Titles have been chosen on the basis of their value as reference and information sources relating to Pennsylvania." Entries are arranged alphabetically by issuing agency, as found in the Library of Congress' *National Union Catalog.* Many entries are annotated.

General index to the colonial records, in 16 volumes, and to the Pennsylvania archives [1st series] in 12 volumes, prepared and arranged by Samuel Hazard, under an act of the General Assembly of Pennsylvania. Philadelphia, Printed by J. Severns & Co., 1860. 653 p. F146.P409 Index
F146.P435

Hasse, Adelaide R. Index of economic material in documents of the states of the United States: Pennsylvania, 1790–1904. [Washington] Carnegie Institution of Washington, 1919–22. 3 v. (1711 p.) [Carnegie Institution of Washington. Publication no. 85 (Pennsylvania)] Z1223.5.A1H2 v. 11
Z1329.H28
AS32.A5 no. 85

Pennsylvania. *Dept. of Internal Affairs. Bureau of Statistics.* Index of statistical sources for Pennsylvania. 1955+ [Harrisburg] Z7554.U6P4
Issue 1955–57 has title: *Index of State Sources of Statistical Data.*

Pennsylvania. *Historical and Museum Commission.* Guide to the published archives of Pennsylvania covering the 138 volumes of colonial records and Pennsylvania archives, series 1–9, by Henry Howard Eddy, with an alphabetized finding list and two special indexes compiled by Martha L. Simonetti. Harrisburg, 1949. 101 p. F146.P432

Pennsylvania. State College. *Library.* Pennsylvania author headings, compiled by Olive S. Holt. State College, Pa., Library, the Pennsylvania State College, 1941. 54 p. (*Its* Library studies, no. 3) Z695.1.G7P4
An issue of the Pennsylvania State College *Bulletin,* v. 35, no. 39.

Pennsylvania. State Library, *Harrisburg.* Annual report. Harrisburg, 1855+ Z733.P41
Pennsylvania state documents are covered to some extent in the list of accessions included in the report, mainly for years 1906–22. In addition, more comprehensive lists of laws, statutes, etc., were included in the following reports:
1903: "Checklist of the Laws, Minutes, Journals, and Documents of the State of Pennsylvania, 1682–1901," p. 115–213. Similar lists, covering shorter periods were included in reports for 1888/89, p. 103–190; 1899, p. 175–268; 1900, p. 314–407; 1901, p. 325–421; 1902, p. 185–283.

1904: "Checklist of Laws and Statutes of Pennsylvania from 1714 to 1801 in the Pennsylvania State Library," p. 103–120.

Pennsylvania. *Superintendent of Public Printing and Binding.* Annual report. Harrisburg, 1881–1918.   Z1223.5.P42
Includes lists of public documents of Pennsylvania.

Pennsylvania. University. *Fels Institute of Local and State Government.* Bibliography on Pennsylvania government, a compilation published in connection with the work of the Research committee of the Pennsylvania political science and public administration association. [Philadelphia] 1941. 188 l.   Z7165.U6P46
A supplement to the *Bibliography on Pennsylvania Government* was published in 1959 under the title *Annotated Bibliography on Pennsylvania State Government,* by Rosalind L. Branning (prepared for the Dept. of Political Science, University of Pittsburgh, Pittsburgh, 1959. 42 p. Z7165.U6P38).

Stewart, Robert C.   Union list of selected Pennsylvania serial documents in Pennsylvania libraries. Pittsburgh, Pennsylvania Library Association, 1971. 68 p.
                                                                          Z1223.5.P4S73
"The cooperative efforts of eighty libraries have made possible this list of their holdings of 175 Pennsylvania documents. This selection of titles from the totality of Pennsylvania serial documents has been made on the basis of extensive working experience with major collections of those documents." Serials are arranged in alphabetical order of issuing agencies. Some monographs have been included which complement certain series, or form sets of related publications (e.g., constitutional convention debates, early laws, court reports).

RHODE ISLAND
Thirteenth of the original 13 states.

Current:

Rhode Island. State Library, *Providence.*   Check-list of departmental publications of the state of Rhode Island, 1935–1955. [Compiled by Alice E. Caldwell, cataloger. Providence, 1955? 33 p.]   Z1331.R56
———— ———— Supplement. 1956+ Providence. irregular.   Z1331.R5612

Retrospective:

Alden, John E.   Rhode Island imprints, 1727–1800. New York, Published for the Bibliographical Society of America [by] Bowker, 1949 [i.e. 1950] xxiv, 665 p.
                                                                             Z1331.A6
Included are some 370 items not listed in an earlier bibliography published in 1915 (*Rhode Island Imprints . . . 1727–1800,* Providence, 88 p. Z1331.R55), edited by George P. Winship. Entries are arranged by years. Most official documents are found under "Rhode Island".

Bongartz, J. Harry.   Check list of Rhode Island laws. Containing a complete list of the public laws and acts and resolves of the state of Rhode Island to date. Providence, J. A. & R. A. Reid, Printers, 1893. 8 p.   Z6457.R6B7

Hasse, Adelaide R.   Index of economic material in documents of the states of the United States: Rhode Island, 1789–1904. [Washington] Carnegie Institution of Washington, 1908. 95 p. [Carnegie Institution of Washington. Publication no. 85 (Rhode Island)]   Z1223.5.A1H2 v. 12
                                                                            Z1331.H25
                                                                        AS32.A5 no. 85

Rhode Island. *Laws, statutes, etc.* Index to the printed acts and resolves of, and of the petitions and reports to the General Assembly of the state of Rhode Island and Providence Plantations, from the year 1850 to 1862. By John Russell Bartlett, Secretary of State. Providence, A. Anthony, Printer to the State, 1863. xxxiv, 104 p.
                DLC LL
    Similar indexes exist for the period 1758–1850, 1863–73, and 1873–99.

Rhode Island. State Library, *Providence.* Check-list of legislative documents in the Rhode Island state archives, by Grace E. Macdonald. Providence, Oxford Press, 1928. 24 p. (Office of the Secretary of State, State Bureau of Information. Annual bulletin no. 1)   Z1223.5.R47

—— Check list of state documents of Rhode Island, annual departmental publications. [Providence] Rhode Island State Library, 1931. 36 l.   Z1223.5.R475

In the Library of Congress there are two groups of unpublished masters theses on Rhode Island imprints, one of which concentrates on those from Providence. The papers were presented originally at the Catholic University of America and are typewritten carbon copies.

A Checklist of Providence, Rhode Island Imprints

1801–5: St. Denis, Gaston P. (1952. 81 l. Z1332.P7S3)
1835–38: Tsao, Wei-i. (1958. 107 l. Z1332.P7T75)
1842–43: Hancock, Eva W. (1960. 75 l. Z1332.P7H3)
1848–50: Cutting, Helen F. (1961. 93 l. Z1332.P7C8)

A Checklist of Rhode Island Imprints

1821–30: Mendeloff, Nathan N. (1954. 189 l. Z1331.M4)
1831–34: Cairns, Margaret T. (1959. 100 l. Z1331.C3)
1839–41: Moeson, Florence T. T. (1959. 57 l. Z1331.M6)
1845–47: Vambery, Joseph T. (1959. 150 l. Z1331.V3)
1854–56: Bachmann, George T. (1961. 113 l. Z1331.B22)
1860–61: Farkas, Cathrine A. (1965. 79 l. Z1331.F36)

SOUTH CAROLINA
Eighth of the original 13 states.

Current:

South Carolina. State Library, *Columbia.* Checklist of South Carolina state publications. 1969/70+ Columbia. annual.   Z1223.5.S6A232
    Report year ends June 30. Superseded a publication with the same title issued by the Archives Department.

Retrospective:

Leverette, Sarah E., *and* Charles E. Lee. A checklist of S.C. session laws. Columbia, S.C., 1963. 35 l.   Z6457.S6L4
    Divided into three parts: Colonial Period, 1670–1775; Revolutionary Period, 1776–90; National Period, 1791–1962.

McMurtrie, Douglas C. A bibliography of South Carolina imprints, 1731–1740. Charleston, Priv. print., 1933. 23 p.   Z1333.M15
    "Two hundred copies reprinted from the *South Carolina Historical and Genealogical Magazine* of July 1933, vol. xxxiv, p. 117–137." (F266.S55)

—— Four South Carolina imprints of MDCCXXXI, together with complete facsimiles of these imprints from the presses of George Webb and Thomas Whitmarsh. Chicago, Ill., John Calhoun Club, 1933. 6 p.   Z1333.M16

—— Some nineteenth century South Carolina imprints, 1801–1820. South Carolina historical magazine, v. 44, 1945: 87–106, 155–172, 228–246.   F266.S55

Meacham, Miriam D.   A checklist of South Carolina imprints for the years 1811–1818. Washington, 1962. 83 l.   Z1333.M4
      Thesis (M.S.) , Catholic University of America. Typescript (carbon copy) .

Moore, John H.   Research materials in South Carolina; a guide, compiled and edited for the South Carolina State Library Board. [1st ed.] Columbia, University of South Carolina Press, 1967. 346 p.   Z732.S72M6

South Carolina. *Archives Dept.*   A checklist of South Carolina state publications. 1950/51–[1966/67?] Columbia. annual.   Z1333.A3
      Superseded in 1969/70 by State Library's *Checklist of South Carolina State Publications.*

South Carolina. University. *Library.*   Author list of Caroliniana in the University of South Carolina library, compiled by Elisabeth D. English. Columbia, S.C., 1923. 337 p.   Z1333.S72
      Official documents are listed under "South Carolina."

South Carolina Historical Society.   A list and abstract of documents relating to South Carolina, now existing in the State Paper Office, London. Prepared for the South Carolina Historical Society by an authorized agent in London. (*Its* Collections. Charleston, 1857–59. v. 1:[85]–307; v. 2: [118]–326; v. 3:[272]–343.   F266.S71

Turnbull, Robert J.   Bibliography of South Carolina, 1563–1950. Charlottesville, University of Virginia Press [1956–60] 6 v.   Z1333.T8
      Official documents can be identified under names of agencies in the index.

Whitney, Edson L.   Bibliography of the colonial history of South Carolina. *In* American Historical Association. Annual report . . . for the year 1894. Washington, 1895, p. 563–586.   Z1333.W61
                                                                              E172.A60 1894

—— Government of the colony of South Carolina. Baltimore, Johns Hopkins Press, 1895. 121 p. (Johns Hopkins University. Studies in historical and political science)
                                                                              JK99.S5W6
      Reprinted by Haskell House, New York, in 1970.

SOUTH DAKOTA

Part of Louisiana Purchase, 1803; territory, 1861; state, 1889.

No current checklist published at the present time.

Retrospective:

Allen, Albert H. *ed.* Dakota imprints, 1858–1889. New York, Pub. for the Bibliographical Society of America [by] R. R. Bowker Co., 1947. xxi, 221 p.   Z1321.A4
      Includes documents of the Dakota territory and the first year of the states of North and South Dakota.

Helgeson, Estella H.   South Dakota state documents; a report presented to the School of Library Science, University of Southern California. South Dakota library bulletin, v. 55, 1969: [51]–108.   Z732.S9S6

"The writer had proposed the compilation of a bibliography to bring up to date the one compiled by Miss Krueger in 1935. . . . [see below] All publications included in Miss Krueger's bibliography have been omitted from the list except those serials which continued publication after 1936. Other publications omitted include compilations of laws other than codes and session laws, the publications of the state educational institutions and the experiment stations." The bibliography gives a brief history of state agencies.

Krueger, Ruth C. South Dakota state publications. Urbana, Ill., 1936. 182 l.
Microfilm Z-69
    Thesis (M.A.) , University of Illinois. Microfilm copy of a typescript.

South Dakota. *State Legislative Research Council.* Bibliography of South Dakota State Legislative Research Council publications, July 1, 1951, through July 31, 1965; staff memorandum. Pierre, 1965. 18 p.   Z1223.5.S6A5

South Dakota. *State Planning Board.* Bibliography of South Dakota State Planning Board publications. Brookings, S. Dak., 1939. 12 p.   Z1335.S73

Tipton, Merlin J., Cleo M. Christensen, *and* Allen F. Agnew. Bibliography of reports containing maps on South Dakota geology published before January 1, 1959. Vermillion, Science Center, University of South Dakota, 1966. 71 p. (South Dakota State Geological Survey. Circular no. 33)   Z6034.U5S75

TENNESSEE

Part of North Carolina until 1789; in the Territory of the United States South of the River Ohio, 1790; state, 1796.

Current:

Tennessee. State Library and Archives, Nashville. *State Library Division.* A list of Tennessee state publications. no. 1+ April 1954+ Nashville. annual.   Z1337.A516

Retrospective:

Cheney, Frances N. Historical and bibliographical study of the administrative departments of the state of Tennessee. [New York?] 1940. 245 l.   Microfilm JK–8
    Unpublished M.S. thesis presented at Columbia University. Microfilm copy of a typescript.

Gass, Frances S., Eleanor Goehring, *and* Mary L. Ogden. Guide to reports of state departments and institutions found in the appendix volumes of Tennessee House and Senate journals. [Knoxville? Tenn., 1936?] [58] l.   Z1223.5.T4G3
    Compiled for the University of Tennessee Library.

Harbison, Mary C., *and* Betty C. Tilley, *comp.* Index to information available from state agencies. [Nashville?] Tennessee State Planning Commission [1955] 1 v. (unpaged) (Tennessee. State Planning Commission. Publication no. 261)
Z1223.5.T4H3

Historical Records Survey, *Illinois.* A check list of Tennessee imprints, 1793–1840. Chicago, Ill., Illinois Historical Records Survey, 1942. xv, 285 p. (American imprints inventory, no. 32)   Z1215.H67 no. 32
Z1337.H52

Historical Records Survey, *Tennessee.* Check list of acts and codes of the state of Tennessee, 1792–1939. Prepared by the Tennessee Historical Records Survey Project, Division of Professional and Service Projects, Work Projects Administration,

Tennessee State Library, sponsor. Nashville, Tenn., 1940. 21 numb. 1. (Special publications series, no. 5)   F431.H57 no. 5

——— Check list of Tennessee imprints, 1841–1850. Prepared by the Tennessee Historical Records Survey, Division of Community Service Programs, Work Projects Administration. Sponsored by the Tennessee State Planning Commission. Nashville, Tenn., 1941. 138 numb. 1. (American imprints inventory, no. 20)
Z1215.H67 no. 20
Z1337.H56

——— List of Tennessee imprints, 1793–1840, in Tennessee libraries. Prepared by the Tennessee Historical Records Survey, Division of Community Service Programs ... Nashville, Tenn., Tennessee Historical Records Survey, 1941. 97 1. (American imprints inventory, no. 16)   Z1215.H67 no. 16
Z1337.H55

Hyde, Grace V. A bibliographical checklist of Nashville imprints, 1867–1876, with an introductory essay on Nashville literature and publishers of the Reconstruction Era. Nashville, University of Tennessee, 1953. 325 1.
An unpublished M.A. thesis, typewritten.

Mitchell, Eleanor D. A preliminary checklist of Tennessee imprints, 1861–1866. Charlottesville, Bibliographical Society of the University of Virginia, 1953. 98 1.
Z1337.M58

Springer, Patricia. Bibliography of historical material of Tennessee in Nashville libraries. [Nashville] 1930. 245 1.   Z1337.S6
Thesis (M.A.) , George Peabody College for Teachers. Official publications are included mainly in the first part: Economic, Military, Political, Social History.

Tennessee. State Library, *Nashville.* Catalogue-Tennesseana. *In its* Biennial report 1911/12: 31–133.   Z733.T3B 1911/12

Tennessee. State Library and Archives, *Nashville. State Library Division.* Preliminary checklist of Tennessee legislative documents. Nashville, 1954. unpaged.   Z1337.T4
Year by year statement (1794–1953) of the session laws, legislative journals, and the collected documents.

TEXAS
Part of Mexico until 1835; republic, 1836; state, 1845.

Current:
Texas state documents. Jan. 1968+ Austin, Texas State Library, Archives Division. Texas Documents.   DLC
Superseded *Checklist for Official State Publications* (1921–67) , and *List of State Publications Issued* (1963–67) .

Retrospective:
Raines, Cadwell W. A bibliography of Texas, being a descriptive list of books, pamphlets, and documents relating to Texas in print and manuscript since 1536, including a complete collation of the laws; with an introductory essay on the materials of early Texan history. Austin, Tex., Published for the author by Gammel Book Co., 1896 [1934] xvi, 268 p.   Z1339.R15 1934
"Reprint copyright by Gammel's Inc., Austin, Texas, 1934." "Conventions

and constitutions relating to Texas, and the collation of the laws of the Republic and State, all in chronological order," p. 227–236 (Appendix, no. 1).

Streeter, Thomas W. Bibliography of Texas, 1795–1845. Cambridge, Harvard University Press, 1955–60. 3 pts. in 5 v.   Z1339.S8
    Contents. pt. 1. Texas imprints. 1817–1845. 2 v.—pt. 2. Mexican imprints relating to Texas, 1803–1845.—pt. 3. United States and European imprints relating to Texas, 1795–[1845] 2 v.

Texas. Laws, statutes, etc. (Indexes) Vernon's annotated civil and criminal statutes of the state of Texas, revision of 1925. General index and tables, including tables of session laws 1923–1925, tables of corresponding articles in Revised statutes 1911 and Vernon's former compilations. Kansas City, Mo., Vernon Law Book Co., 1927. lxxxvii, 628 p.   DLC LL

—— Vernon's annotated statutes of the state of Texas, comprising all laws of a general and permanent nature with annotations from state and federal courts. Index. Kansas City, Mo., Vernon Law Book Co. [c1941] 2 v.   DLC LL
    "Kept to date by cumulative annual pocket parts."

—— Vernon's annotated statutes of the state of Texas. General index. Kansas City, Mo., Vernon Law Book Co., 1958. 4 v.   DLC LL

Texas. Library and Historical Commission. Biennial report. Austin, Tex., 1911+
                                                   Z732.T25
    From 1920/22 to 1960/62, a cumulated list of "Documents Distributed" was included in the report.

Texas. State Library, Austin. Texas state departmental publications in the State Library, 1900–1944. [Austin] 1953. 1 v. (unpaged)   Z1223.5.T47T47
    Issued as a special edition of Texas Libraries (Sept. 1943. Z671.T46).

Texas. State Library, Austin. Archives Division. Checklist for official state publications. no. 1–220; Oct. 1921–Dec. 1967. Austin.   Z1223.5.T47T47a
    Title, 1921–46, Document Checklist. After 1946 title varies slightly. Superseded in January 1968 by Texas State Documents, issued by the State Library.

—— List of state publications issued. Sept. 1963–Dec. 1967. Austin.   DLC
    Superseded from January 1968 by Texas State Documents, issued by the State Library.

Winkler, Ernest W. Check list of Texas imprints. With a foreword by Thomas W. Streeter. Austin, Texas State Historical Association, 1949–63. 2 v.   Z1339.W5
    An expansion of a checklist begun by the Historical Records Survey for the American Imprints Inventory and continued under the State-Wide Library Project in Texas. Vol. 2 edited by Ernest W. Winkler and Llerena Friend. Vol. 1 covers period 1846–60; vol. 2, 1861–76.

UTAH
Ceded by Mexico, 1848; territory, 1850; state, 1896.

Current:
Official publications of the state of Utah. v. 1, no. 1+ July 1, 1970+ Salt Lake City, Utah State Library Commission.   DLC
    The first issue covers state publications for the period Jan.–June 1970.

Utah. Dept. of Finance. *State Archives and Records Service.* Checklist of Utah state
publications. [July 1, 1967/June 30, 1969+ Salt Lake City]   DLC

Retrospective:

Checklist of Utah state publications. [1960–61] Salt Lake City, Utah State Library.
                                                                        Z1341.C48

Utah. *State Planning Board. Library.* A selective list of references. Utah State Planning Board Library. [Salt Lake City, 1937] 29 p.   Z7164.O7U8
    "This work was prepared with the assistance of the Works Progress Ad-
ministration."

Utah Foundation. State and local government in Utah; a description of the structure,
operations, functions and finances of all branches of state and local government
in Utah—their departments, commissions and agencies. [Rev. ed.] Salt Lake City
[1962] 233 p.   JK8425 1962 .U8
    Originally published in 1954. Both editions include a bibliography of state
and other publications relating to Utah.

VERMONT

Part of territory of New Hampshire and New York until it declared its
independence in 1777; state, 1791.

Current:

Vermont. *Dept. of Libraries.* Checklist of available Vermont state publications. 1970+
    Montpelier. annual.   Z1223.5.V48C44

Retrospective:

From September 1928 on, Vermont state publications were listed
occasionally in the Vermont Free Public Library Commission's *Bulletin*
(Z732.V5V63) under titles "Recent Vermont Documents," "Recent State
Publications," etc. Other bibliographies listing or including state documents are the following:

Cooley, Elizabeth F. Vermont imprints before 1800; an introductory essay on the
history of printing in Vermont, with a list of imprints, 1779–1799. Montpelier,
Vt., Vermont Historical Society, c1937. xxxii, 133 p.   Z1343.C77

Gilman, Marcus D. The bibliography of Vermont, or a list of books and pamphlets
relating in any way to the state. Burlington, Printed by the Free Press Association,
1897. 349 p.   Z1343.G48B
    Official documents: p. 291–316.

Hasse, Adelaide R. Index of economic material in documents of the states of the
United States: Vermont, 1789–1904. [Washington] Carnegie Institution of Wash-
ington, 1907. 71 p. [Carnegie Institution of Washington. Publication no. 85
(Vermont)]   Z1223.5.A1H2 v. 13
                                                              Z1343.H22
                                                            AS32.A5 no. 85

McCorison, Marcus A. Vermont imprints, 1778–1820; a check list of books, pamphlets,
and broadsides. Worcester, Mass., American Antiquarian Society, 1963. xxiv, 597 p.
                                                                    Z1343.M3
    For official Vermont documents, see index, p. 593.

In the Library of Congress there are seven unpublished M.A. theses on Vermont imprints, grouped under the titles *A Check List of Vermont Imprints* or *Vermont State-wide Imprints*. The papers were presented at the Catholic University of America and are typewritten carbon copies.

1821–35: Ready, James K. (1955. 235 l. Z1343.R4)
1836–50: Snoddy, Alice L. (1959. 226 l. Z1343.S6)
1851–56: Maki, Suiko. (1964. 124 l. Z1343.M34)
1860–62: Zeke, Zoltan. (1960. 76 l. Z1343.Z4)
1863–65: Levant, Muriel R. (1964. 96 l. Z1343.L47)
1869–72: Verner, Mathilde M. (1959. 122 l. Z1343.V4)
1873–76: Wright, Lottie M. (1960. 33, 79 l. Z1343.W7)

VIRGINIA

Tenth of the original 13 states.

Current:

Virginia. State Library, *Richmond*. Checklist of Virginia state publications. 1926+
  Richmond, 1927+ (*Its* Bulletin [Publication]) Z881.V81B
  Z1223.5.V81
    Checklists no. 1–21 (1926–54) were published as *Bulletin* v. 16/4, 17/2 and 4, 18/1, 3–4, 19/1–4, 20/1–4, 21/1–4, 22/1–4, 23/1, 3, 4, 24/1–4. Checklists no. 22+ (1955+) were published as State Library's *Publication* no. 2, 6, 7, 8, 15, 17, 19, 20, 24, 26, 27, 29, 30, 31, 34, 35, etc. The checklists are published annually.

——— Virginia state publications in print. 1965+ [Richmond] annual. DLC

Retrospective:

Cappon, Lester J. Bibliography of Virginia history since 1965. [Charlottesville] University, Va., Institute for Research in the Social Sciences, 1930. xviii, 900 p. (University of Virginia. Institute for Research in the Social Sciences. Institute monograph no. 5) Z1345.C25
    Government documents are listed under each part and section.

Hall, Wilmer L. Bibliography of Virginia state documents; scope and methods. [Richmond, 1930] 14 p. Z1223.5.V81H2
    Reprinted from *Virginia Libraries,* v. 3, no. 2/3, July–Oct. 1930.

——— The missing journals of the General Assembly of the state of Virginia. Richmond, 1950. 161 p. Z1223.5.V81H23
    Reprinted from the *Bulletin of the Virginia State Library,* v. 23, no. 2.

Kraus, Joe W. Notes on Virginia state publications. 2d ed. Richmond, Virginia State Library, 1960. 23 p. Z1223.5.V81K7 1960

Swem, Earl G. A bibliography of Virginia. Richmond, D. Bottom, Superintendent of Public Printing. 1916–55. 5 v. (Virginia. State Library, Richmond. Bulletin. v. 8, no. 2–4; v. 10, no. 1–4; v. 12, no. 1–2; v. 18, no. 2; v. 25, no. 1–4) Z881.V81B
    Official documents arel listed as follows: pt. 2. Titles of the Printed Official Documents of the Commonwealth, 1776–1916;—pt. 3. The Acts and the Journals of the General Assembly of the Colony, 1619–1776;—pt. 4. Three Series of the Sessional Documents of the House of Delegates: extra session, January 7–April 4, 1861; called session, September 15–October 6, 1862; and adjourned session, January 7–March 31, 1863;—pt. 5. Titles of the Printed Documents of

the Commonwealth, 1916–1925.

With part 5 of this *Bibliography*, the bibliographical coverage of the official documents of Virginia was completed through 1925, when the annual *Checklist of Virginia State Publications* began publication.

—— The Jamestown 350th anniversary historical booklets. Williamsburg, Virginia 350th Anniversary Celebration Corp.; Garrett & Massie, Sales Agent, Richmond [1957] 23 v.   F229.S93

    Vol. 1: *A Selected Bibliography of Virginia, 1607–1699*, by E. G. Swem and J. M. Jennings. Includes early official documents.

Virginia. *Division of State Planning and Community Affairs.* State informational directory. Richmond, 1969. 75 p.   Z1223.5.V5A3

    "This publication serves as a basic source of information in regard to the variety of facts and figures available. ..."

    The directory lists "various governmental units followed by a list of their publications and persons to contact."

Virginia. *Laws, statutes, etc.* Index to enrolled bills of the General Assembly of Virginia, 1776 to 1910. Comp. by John W. Williams. Richmond, D. Bottom, Superintendent of Public Printing, 1911. 1155 p.   J87.V907

Virginia. *Laws, statutes, etc. (Indexes)* Index of Acts of the General Assembly of the Commonwealth of Virginia, 1912–1959. Richmond, Dept. of Purchases and Supply, 1959 [i.e. 1960] 477 p.   DLC LL

    Compiled by Alice C. Peirce. Supplements the *Index to Enrolled Bills ...* (see above).

Virginia. State Library, *Richmond.* A trial bibliography of colonial Virginia. Richmond, D. Bottom, Superintendent of Public Printing, 1908–10. 2 v. (*In* Virginia. State Library, Richmond. 5th–6th annual report, Richmond, 1908–10)   Z733.V64

    Covers the periods 1607–1754 and 1754–76.

WASHINGTON

Ceded by Great Britain, 1846; part of Oregon Territory, 1848; territory, 1853; state, 1889.

Current:

Washington state publications. v. 1+ Apr./June 1952+ Olympia, Washington State Library. monthly, with annual cumulations.   DLC

    Before 1964, issued quarterly or semiannually. Superseded list called "Washington State Publications Received at the Washington State Library," published in the library's *Library News Bulletin* from July 1947 to Mar. 1952 (Z732.W28W27).

Retrospective:

Historical Records Survey. *Washington (State).* A check list of Washington imprints, 1853–1876 ... Edited by Geraldine Beard. Seattle, Wash., Washington Historical Records Survey, 1942. 89 p. (American imprints inventory, no. 44) Z1215.H67 no. 44
                                                                         Z1347.H57

McMurtrie, Douglas C. A record of Washington imprints, 1853–1876. Seattle, University of Washington Press [1943] 27–38 p.   Z1347.H57M2

    "Reprinted from the Pacific Northwest Quarterly, volume 34, no. 1, January

1943." Represents a supplement to and commentary on the *Check List of Washington Imprints, 1853–1876* (Historical Records Survey, 1942) .

Tucker, Lena L. Author headings for the official publications of the state of Washington. Seattle, University of Washington Press, 1950. 75 p.   Z695.1.G7T8
Kept updated with a card file at Washington State Library.

Washington (*State*) *Laws, statutes, etc.* (*Indexes*) Index, laws of Washington, including all the general, local and private laws, memorials and resolutions. Also miscellaneous laws affecting land titles. 1854–1897. By Frank Pierce. Seattle, Wash., Tribune Printing Co., 1898. 67 p.   DLC LL

Washington (*State*) *State Legislative Council.* Distribution of state publications [by] Washington State Legislative Council, Subcommittee on State and Local Government and Legislative Procedure. Prepared by Kenneth A. Hammond, research associate. [Olympia?] 1961–62. 2 pts.   Z1223.5.W3A48

Washington (*State*) State Library, *Olympia.* A reference list of public documents 1854–1918, found in the files of the State Library. Published by the State Librarian. Olympia, Wash., F. M. Lamborn, Public Printer, 1920. 51 p.   Z1223.5.W31

Washington (*State*) University. *Bureau of Governmental Research and Services.* Publications of the state of Washington. Seattle, Bureau of Governmental Research, University of Washington [1941] 31 l. (*Its* Report no. 52)   JA37.W3 no. 52
"A revision of a previous report of the Bureau of Governmental Research (Report no. 41) issued under the same title March 1, 1940."

WEST VIRGINIA

Part of Virginia until 1861, when a state government was formed; admitted to the Union, 1863.

Current:

West Virginia. *Dept. of Archives and History.* Short-title checklist of West Virginia state publications. 1947/48+ Charleston.   Z1223.5.W4A32
Issued annually 1947/48 to 1965/66, semiannually from Sept. 1966, quarterly(?) from 1971.

Retrospective:

Historical Records Survey. A check list of West Virginia imprints, 1791–1830. Chicago, WPA Historical Records Survey Project, 1940. 62 l. (American imprints inventory, no. 14)   Z1215.H67 no. 14
                                                                                    Z1349.H57

Kreyenbuhl, Jeannine. A check list of West Virginia imprints from 1864–1876, with a historical introduction. Washington, 1957. 162 l.   Z1349.K7
Thesis (M.S.) , Catholic University of America. Typescript (carbon copy) .

Norona, Delf., *ed.* West Virginia imprints, 1790–1863; a checklist of books, newspapers, periodicals and broadsides. Moundsville, West Virginia Library Association, 1958. 316 p. (West Virginia Library Association. Publication no. 1) Z1349.N6
Official documents, p. 153–177; index, p. 281–316.

West Virginia. *Dept. of Archives and History.* A bibliography of West Virginia, parts I and II, compiled by Innis C. Davis, State Archivist, with the assistance of Emily Johnston, librarian, and other members of the staff of the Department of Ar-

chives and History. [Charleston, 1939] 143, 392 p. (*In its* Biennial report, 1936/38)
F236.W31   1936/38
Part 2 includes the printed official documents of the state and documents
(printed and manuscript) preceding and relating to the formation of the state.
A bibliography of the legislative journals and public documents of West
Virginia had been published in 1908, in the second *Biennial Report* of the
department (p. 13–63).

———— Checklist of West Virginia state documents. [Feb. 1942–June 1943] Charleston.
DLC
Only four issues published, covering periods: Feb. 1–June 1, 1942; June 1–
Oct. 1, 1942; Oct. 1942–Feb. 1943; Feb.–June 1943. Compiled by Nancy Wilson.

WISCONSIN

Part of Northwest Territory, 1787; successively part of Indiana, Illinois,
and Michigan territories, beginning 1815; territory, 1836; state, 1848.

Current:

Wisconsin. State Historical Society. Wisconsin public documents, a checklist. v.
[1]+ Feb. 1917+ Madison.   Z1223.5.W6W65
Frequency varies. Currently issued monthly with annual cumulation. It includes a list of Wisconsin documents, dated Dec. 1916, prepared by the society's
library.

Retrospective:

Historical Records Survey. *Wisconsin.*   A check list of Wisconsin imprints, 1833–1849
[–1864–1869] Madison, Wis., Wisconsin Historical Records Survey, 1942–53. 5 v.
Z1215.H67 no. 23–24, 41–42
Z1351.H6
Vols. 1–4 issued as no. 23–24 and 41–42, American imprints inventory of the
Historical Records Survey. Vol. 5 published by the State Historical Society.

Jackson, Ruth L. W.   Author headings for the official publications of the state of
Wisconsin. Chicago, American Library Association, 1954. 211 p.   Z695.1.G7J3   1954
"An earlier version . . . was prepared as a master's thesis at the University of
Illinois Library School in 1941."

Knudson, William.   Wisconsin legal research guide. Madison, University of Wisconsin,
Extension Law Dept., 1962. 1 v. (various pagings)   DLC LL
Includes bibliographies.

Wisconsin. *Free Library Commission.*   Check list of the journals and public documents
of Wisconsin. Madison, Democrat Printing Co., State Printer, 1903. 179 p.
Z1223.5.W5
Covers territorial and state documents. Prepared in the documents department of the commission under the direction of Charles McCarthy, and revised
by Adelaide R. Hasse.

———— Wisconsin state publications. July 1, 1902–Sept. 30, 1903. [Madison] 5 p.
Z1223.5.W55

Wisconsin. Legislative Reference Library, *Madison.*   Summary of the measures before
the regular session of the Wisconsin Legislature which became law, including joint
resolutions which were adopted. 1961+ sess. Madison. (*Its* Research bulletin)
JK6074.A34

Wisconsin. State Historical Society. Checklist of Wisconsin public documents. 1917–
19. [Madison] (*Its* Bulletin of information, no. 91, 95, 96) F576.W78
Z1223.W6W62

Wisconsin library bulletin. v. 1+ Jan. 1905+ Madison, Wis., Div. of Library Services.
Z732.W8W6
"Wisconsin Documents," v. 1 (Nov. 1905) : 85–87.
"Public Documents," v. 6 (Mar.–Apr. 1910) : 40–41.
"Wisconsin Documents," v. 10 (Apr. 1914) : 71–73.
Wisconsin documents are also listed occasionally in vols. 34–38 (1938–42) .

An unpublished manuscript, entitled "Checklist of Wisconsin Public
Documents Down to 1912," is reported to be on file at the Wisconsin
State Historical Society. Located in the Division of Archives and Manuscripts, it constitutes the so-called Isaac Bradley Papers, together with
annotations, additions, etc.

WYOMING

Part acquired in the Louisiana Purchase, 1803; another part ceded by
Great Britain, 1846; a third part ceded by Mexico, 1848; territory, 1868;
state, 1890.

No current checklist published at the present time.

Retrospective:

"The most complete collection [of state documents] is in the Wyoming
State Library, Cheyenne, and in the University of Wyoming Library at
Laramie. The latter can supply Xerox copies of the relevant catalog
cards. . . ." [8] For earlier documents, the following works will be of
assistance:

Fischer, Hail. Author headings for the official publications of the state of Wyoming.
Chicago, American Library Association, 1951. 60 p. (State author headings)
Z695.1.G7F5

Historical Records Survey. *Illinois.* A check list of Wyoming imprints, 1866–1890.
Chicago, Ill., Illinois Historical Records Survey, 1941. 70 l. (American imprints
inventory, no. 18) Z1215.H67 no. 18
Z1353.H57
Of the 178 items listed, 73 are state documents.

McMurtrie. Douglas C. Early printing in Wyoming and the Black Hills. Hattiesburg,
Miss., Printed for the Book Farm, 1943. 78 p. (Heartman's historical series, no. 67)
Z209.W95M17
"Reprinted with revisions and additional illustrations from the Papers of the
Bibliographical Society of America, vol. 36, 1942, pages 267–304, and vol. 3
[i.e. 37] 1943, pages 37–60." Some early territorial documents. p. 40–50.

—— Pioneer printing in Wyoming. Cheyenne, Priv. print., 1933. 16 p. Z209.W95M2
"Two hundred copies reprinted from the Annals of Wyoming, January 1933."
"Wyoming Bibliography," p. 16.

[8] James B. Childs, "Bibliographic Control of Federal, State and Local Documents,"
Library Trends, 15 (July 1966) : 22.

TERRITORIES

There are no special bibliographies covering the outlying territories of the United States. The basic bibliographic tools on U.S. government publications (*Document Catalog, Monthly Catalog*) list a considerable number of official documents concerning territorial possessions. Mention should be made, however, of the following price lists of the Superintendent of Documents:

U.S. *Superintendent of Documents.* Insular possessions [1910–45] Washington. (*Its* Price list 32)   Z1223.A191 no. 32
    Merged with no. 60 (below).

—— Territories and insular possessions [1914–60] Washington. (*Its* Price list 60)
Z1223.A191 no. 60

—— States and territories of the United States and their resources, including beautification, public buildings and lands, recreational resources. 1967+ Washington. (*Its* Price list 87)   Z1223.A191 no. 87

The library of the Department of the Interior has in its collections a considerable number of documents of outlying territories. An offset reproduction of its catalog of some 724,000 cards, representing the collections of the department library, has been published in 1968 under the title *Dictionary Catalog of the Department Library* (New York, G. K. Hall, 38 vols.). The catalog is kept up to date by supplements.

COMMONWEALTH OF PUERTO RICO

Alemany, Ana R. de   Las publicaciones oficiales del gobierno del Estado Libre Asociado de Puerto Rico: bibliografía. Cayey, P.R., Univ. de Puerto Rico, Biblioteca del Colegio Regional de Cayey, 1968. 76 1.   DLC
    Preliminary list of official publications of Puerto Rico, arranged by agencies. Coverage and completeness of bibliographical data vary widely from agency to agency.

Anuario bibliográfico puertorriqueño; indice alfabético de libros, folletos, revistas y periódicos publicados en Puerto Rico. 1948+ Río Piedras, Biblioteca de la Universidad.   Z1551.A6
    Official publications are listed mostly under the heading Puerto Rico.

Bird, Augusto.   Bibliografía puertorriqueña de fuentes para investigaciones sociales, 1930–1945. Ed. provisional. [Río Piedras] Centro de Investigaciones Sociales, Universidad de Puerto Rico, 1946–47. 2 v.   Z1551.B5
    Continuation of the *Bibliografía puertorriqueña, 1493–1930*, by Pedreira (see below).

Current Caribbean bibliography. v. 1+ June 1951+ [Hato Rey, P.R., Biblioteca Regional del Caribe] annual.   Z1595.C8
    Until 1965 published by the Caribbean Commission (Organization) in Port of Spain, Trinidad. Includes official publications of Puerto Rico in a classified arrangement. Monthly supplements also issued.

Handbook of Latin American studies. no. [1]+ 1935+ Gainesville, University of Florida Press. annual. Z1605.H23
Includes selected official publications.

Pedreira, Antonio S. Bibliografía puertorriqueña (1493–1930). Madrid, Imprenta de la Librería y casa editorial Harnando (s.a.) 1932. xxxii, 707 p. (Monografías de la Universidad de Puerto Rico. Serie A. Estudios Hispánicos, núm. 1) Z1551.P37
Official documents are listed mainly in section "Historia Politica y Administrativa." Classified, with author and subject indexes.

Puerto Rico. *Bureau of the Budget.* Report on surveys, research projects, investigations and other organized fact-gathering activities of the Government of Puerto Rico. 1949/50+ San Juan. annual. Z1555.A3

U.S. *Library of Congress. Division of Bibliography.* Puerto Rico; a selected list of recent references. Comp. by Ann D. Brown. Washington, 1943. 44 p. Z1551.U5

U.S. *National Archives.* Records of the Bureau of Insular Affairs relating to Puerto Rico, 1898–1934; a list of selected files. Comp. by Kenneth Munden and Milton Greenbaum. Washington, 1943. 47 p. (*Its* Special list no. 4) CD3028.P9U6 1943

GUAM

Reid, Charles F. Bibliography of the Island of Guam. New York, H. W. Wilson Co., 1939. 102 p. Z4741.R35
"Prepared with the assistance of the Federal Works Agency, Work Projects Administration...." Preliminary edition issued as series A in U.S. Work Projects Administration, New York (City), *Compilation of Sources of Information on the Territories and Outlying Possessions of the United States* (1937. Z1251.T32U56 1937a).

VIRGIN ISLANDS

[Bibliography of West Indian materials in the National Library of Denmark. n. p., n. d.] 1 v. Z1561.V8B5
Photocopy of a manuscript.

Reid, Charles F. Bibliography of the Virgin Islands of the United States. New York, H. W. Wilson Co., 1941. xvi, 225 p. Z1561.V8R4
"Prepared with the assistance of the Federal Works Agency, Work Projects Administration for the City of New York...."

U.S. *Library of Congress. Division of Bibliography.* A list of books (with references to periodicals) on the Danish West Indies. By A. P. C. Griffin. Washington, Govt. Print. Off., 1901. 18 p. Z881.U5
Z1561.V8U5

——— The Virgin Islands of the United States; a list of references, 1922–1936, compiled by Helen F. Conover. [Washington] 1937. 12 p. Z1561.V8U54

U.S. *National Archives and Records Service.* Preliminary inventory of the records of the Government of the Virgin Islands of the United States (Record group 55). Comp. by H. Don Hooker. Washington, 1960. 31 p. (*Its* Publication 61–1. Prelim. inventories, no. 126) CD3026.A32 no. 126

Virgin Islands of the United States. A bibliography of the Virgin Islands of the
United States. Formerly the Danish West Indies. St. Thomas, Government Printing
Office, 1922. 11 p.   Z1561.V8V8

COLONIAL PERIOD

The following bibliographies relate principally to or include a substantial number of official documents of the colonial period:

Andrews, Charles McLean. List of the journals and acts of the councils and assem-
blies of the thirteen official colonies and the Floridas, in America, preserved in the
Public Record Office, London. (*In* American Historical Association. Annual report . . . for the year 1908. Washington, 1909. v. 1: 399–509)   E172.A60   1908

Evans, Charles. American bibliography; a chronological dictionary of all books, pamphlets, and periodical publications printed in the United States of America from
the genesis of printing in 1639 down to and including the year 1820. With bibliographical and biographical notes. Chicago, Priv. print. for the author by the
Blakely Press, 1903–59. 14 v.   Z1215.E92
   Includes official documents, which can be identified through the index (vol.
14). Vol. 5 printed by Hollister Press; vols. 6–12 by Columbia Press; vols. 13–14
have imprint: Worcester, Mass., American Antiquarian Society.
   Reprinted, 1941–59, by Peter Smith, New York (Z1215.E923); photocopy in
reduced size, by Mini-Print Corp., Metuchen, N.J., 1967 (Z1215.E9232   1967).

Following publications supplement Charles Evans' *American Bibliography*:

Bristol, Roger P. Supplement to Charles Evans' American bibliography. Charlottesville, Published for the Bibliographical Society of America and the Bibliographical
Society of the University of Virginia [by] University Press of Virginia [1970] xix,
636 p.   Z1215.E92334
   A chronological list, 1646–1800, of "not-in-Evans" items. Bibliography: p.
xiii-xvi. Index to *Supplement* published in 1971.

Henry E. Huntington Library and Art Gallery, *San Marino, Calif.* American imprints,
1648–1797, in the Huntington Library, supplementing Evans' American bibliography, compiled by Willard O. Waters. Cambridge, Mass., Printed at the Harvard
University Press, [1933] 95 p.   Z1215.E92 Suppl.
   "Reprinted from the Huntington library bulletin, number 3, February, 1933."

New York. Public Library. *Rare Book Division.* Checklist of additions to Evans'
American bibliography in the Rare Book Division of the New York Public Library.
Compiled by Lewis M. Stark and Maud D. Cole. New York, New York Public
Library, 1960. 110 p.   Z1215.E95

Shipton, Clifford K. National index of American imprints through 1800; the short-title
Evans. [Worcester, Mass.] American Antiquarian Society, 1969. 2 v. (xxv, 1028 p.)
                                                                        Z1215.S495
   A combined alphabetical index to Evans' *American Bibliography*, with cor-
rections, and R. Bristol's "not-in-Evans" items.

Other bibliographies relating to the colonial period:

Hasse, Adelaide R. Materials for a bibliography of the public archives of the thirteen
original states, covering the colonial period and the state period to 1789. (*In*
American Historical Association. Annual report ... for the year 1906. Washington, 1908. v. 2: 239–561)   E172.A60 1906 v. 2

Henry E. Huntington Library and Art Gallery, *San Marino, Calif.* Check list of American laws, charters and constitutions of the 17th and 18th centuries in the Huntington Library, compiled by Willard O. Waters. San Marino, Calif., 1936. 140 p.
(Huntington Library lists. no. 1)   Z6457.A1H5

Pennsylvania. Historical Society. *Library.* The Charlemagne Tower collection of American colonial laws. [Philadelphia] Priv. print. for the Historical Society of Pennsylvania, 1890. 7–298 p.   Z1237.P4
    Compiled by C. S. R. Hildeburn.

CONFEDERATE STATES OF AMERICA

Alabama. University. *Library.* Confederate imprints in the University of Alabama
Library. Compiled by Sara Elizabeth Mason with the collaboration of Lucile
Crutcher and Sarah A. Verner. Foreword by Wm. Stanley Hoole. University, Ala.,
1961. 156 l.   Z1242.5.A4
    Official publications of the Confederate States of America, and of individual
states, p. 1–113.

Beers, Henry P. Guide to the archives of the Government of the Confederate States
of America. Washington, National Archives. General Services Administration;
[U.S. Govt. Print. Off.] 1968. 536 p. (National Archives publication no. 68–15)
                                                            CD3047.B4
    Companion volume to *Guide to Federal Archives Relating to the Civil War.*

Boston Athenaeum. Confederate literature; a list of books and newspapers, maps,
music, and miscellaneous matter printed in the South during the Confederacy,
now in the Boston Athenaeum. Prepared by Charles N. Baxter and James M.
Dearborn, with an introduction by James Ford Rhodes. [Boston] Boston Athenaeum, 1917. 213 [1] p. (Robert Charles Billings Fund. Publications, 5) Z1242.5.B65
    Confederate States of America publications, p. 1–31; state publications, p.
32–79.

Cobb, Jessie E. Publications in Alabama during the Confederacy, located in the State
Department of Archives and History. The Alabama Historical Quarterly, v. 23,
1961: 73–137.   F321.A17 v. 23
    Official publications, p. 73–87.

Crandall, Marjorie L. Confederate imprints; a check list based principally on the
collection of the Boston Athenaeum. With an introduction by Walter Muir White-
hill. [Boston] Boston Athenaeum, 1955. 2 v. (xxxv, 910 p.) (Robert Charles Billings Fund publications, no. 11)   Z1242.5.C7
    Contents: v. 1. Official publications.—v. 2. Unofficial publications.

Harwell, Richard B. The Confederate hundred; a bibliophilic selection of Confederate books. [Urbana. Ill.] Beta Phi Mu, 1964. xxiii, 58 p. (Beta Phi Mu. Chapbook
no. 7)   Z1242.5.H314
    Includes some official publications.

—— Confederate imprints in the University of Georgia Libraries. Athens, University of Georgia Press, 1964. 49 p. (University of Georgia Libraries. Miscellanea publications, no. 5)   Z1242.5.H315

—— More Confederate imprints. Richmond, Virginia State Library, 1957. 2 v. (xxxvi, 345 p.) (Virginia. State Library, Richmond. Publications, no. 4–5)
                                                                        Z1242.5.H33
    Supplement to Marjorie L. Crandall's *Confederate Imprints; a Check List Based Principally on the Collection of the Boston Athenaeum.* Vol. 1, *Official Publications.*

Leiter, Levi Z.   The Leiter Library; a catalogue of the books, manuscripts and maps relating principally to America, collected by the late Levi Ziegler Leiter. With collations and bibliographical notes by Hugh Alexander Morrison. Washington, Priv. print., 1907. 533 p.   Z977.L533
    Confederate States of America. p. 241–341.

Morrison, Hugh A.   A bibliography of the official publications of the Confederate States of America. (*In* Bibliographical Society of America. Proceedings and papers. New York, 1908, v. 3, p. 92–132)   Z1008.B51P v. 3

U.S. *National Archives.*   List of National Archives microfilm publications. 1947+ Washington. (*Its* Publication)   CD3027.M514
    The 1968 ed. includes: War Department collection of Confederate records (RG 190) , p. 81; Treasury Department collection of Confederate records (RG 365) , p. 82; Official records of the War of the Rebellion: Official records of the Union and Confederate Armies, 1861–65 (M–262) , and Official Records of the Union and Confederate Navies, 1861–65 (M–275) , p. 88.

Virginia. State Library, *Richmond.*   A list of the official publications of the Confederate States government in the Virginia State Library and the Library of the Confederate Memorial Literary Society. (*In its* Bulletin. Richmond, 1911, v. 4, no. 1, p. [1]–72)   Z881.V81B v. 4
                                                                        Z1242.5.V6

Walker, Evans and Cogswell Company, *Charleston, S.C.*   War-time publications (1861– 1865) from the press of Walker, Evans & Cogswell Co., Charleston, S.C., an addendum to "One hundred years of Wecco," by Yates Snowden. Charleston, S.C., 1922. 30 p.   Z1242.5.W18

Waters, Willard O.   Confederate imprints in the Henry E. Huntington Library, unrecorded in previously published bibliographies of such material. Papers of the Bibliographical Society of America, Chicago, Ill. [1930] v. 23, pt. 1, 1929, p. 18–109.
                                                                 Z1008.B51P v. 23, pt. 1
                                                                        Z1242.5.H52

LOCAL GOVERNMENT

The bibliographic control of local government publications has progressed very slowly during the past few decades. The following two quotations characterize the situation well, though dated three decades apart. James G. Hodgson, in a report presented at the 1936 conference of the American Library Association, said: "County government, once called the dark continent of American politics, has been studied with increased interest in recent years, but is still an almost virgin field as far as library collecting is concerned." [9] In 1966, James B. Childs, in his article "Bibliographic Control of Federal, State and Local Documents," published in *Library Trends* (v. 15, July 1966: 22), said: "To turn to . . . bibliographical control over local government publications, the picture is very meager. Indeed it is almost as though there were an iron curtain over the vast output of local government publications, despite the never-ceasing urban sprawl."

The difficulties seem to derive both from the vast output and from the very nature of local government publications. In the majority of local jurisdictions, especially rural, the most common form of reporting government decisions is in local newspapers, for which legal provisions exist in practically all the states. In larger jurisdictions, decisions and reports are also published in separate pamphlet form. In addition, many local government reports are included in state documents. This array of sources makes it difficult to compile a thorough checklist of local publications.

The picture changes considerably in large local jurisdictions, where there are regular publication channels. New York, Chicago (and Cook County), Honolulu (city and county), and other large jurisdictions have had for some time a fairly good bibliographic control of their publications. For other local jurisdictions, however, printed material is rare, and the only remaining source of documentation is the local archives.

During the 1930's the Historical Records Survey in the Work Projects Administration began compiling inventories of county and municipal archives; only a few inventories had been published when the program was discontinued, although a large amount of additional material was prepared.

In recent years, there have been a few attempts to improve this situation, and one project is particularly notable. In 1972 Greenwood Press, Inc., of Westport, Conn., commenced publishing the *Index to Current Urban Documents* (v. 1, no. 1/2, July-Oct. 1972), a quarterly bibliography with annual cumulations. Complete and detailed bibliographic data for some 2,400 documents are provided in the first number, including a subject index. The goal is to catalog and index documents issued by 154 cities of 100,000 or more inhabitants and 24 counties of a million or more inhabitants, as determined by the 1970 census. Greenwood Press is depending on the cooperation and assistance of municipal officials, local public libraries, municipal reference libraries, and major research libraries to achieve this goal. In conjunction with the indexing program, the Microform Division of Greenwood Press is planning to produce and offer subscriptions to the Urban Documents Microfiche

---

[9] "Publishing activities of American counties," in American Library Association's *Public Documents: Papers Presented at the 1936 Conference.* (Chicago, 1936), p. 215. (Z7164.C7A4)

Collection. This will provide libraries with a means of acquiring comprehensive sets of government publications from the larger cities and counties.

Several attempts at the state level to improve on the acquisitions and indexing of local documents should be noted. In 1966–67 California organized a series of workshops dealing with government documents at all levels.[10] At the New York Public Library, David K. Beasley initiated in 1966 a "Bibliography Program for County and City Publications" to encourage local libraries, preferably public libraries, to acquire local government publications.

In New Jersey, Catharine M. Fogarty, librarian of Fairleigh Dickinson University in Rutherford, N.J., began publishing a checklist entitled *Documents of New Jersey Local Governments* (Rutherford, 1967, 40 p. Z7165.U6N37), with supplements for 1968 and 1969. Several states also began including local government documents in their checklists of state publications (e.g., *Nevada Official Publications*, since April 1968).

Following are bibliographies and other publications dealing with local government in the United States, which may be of assistance to researchers:

American Library Association. *Committee on Public Documents.* Public documents ... with archives and libraries. Papers presented at the 1933–[38] conference[s] of the American Library Association. Chicago, American Library Association, 1934– [38]   Z7164.G7A4
      1936: "Publishing Activities of American Counties," by James G. Hodgson, p. 215–237; "American City Charters," by Ione E. Dority, p. 238–246.
      1937: "Municipal Document Indexes, Guides and Problems of Pacific Coast States," by Josephine B. Hollingsworth, p. 140–145; "Municipal Reporting in Michigan Since 1930," by Ione E. Dority, p. 146–167.

Boston University. *Bureau of Public Administration.* Bibliography on state and local government in New England. Boston, 1952. 233 p. (*Its* Bulletin no. 1)   Z7164.L8B6

Chicago. Municipal Reference Library. Index to municipal legislation; a cumulative, alphabetical, subject index of municipal ordinances, proposed or adopted by city councils, boards of aldermen, city commissions and similar bodies, as recorded in their printed official proceedings and journals. Compiled, arranged and edited by Frederick Rex. [Chicago] 1937. 15 p. l., 250 (i.e. 251) numb. l.   Z7164.L8C521
      "Cumulation of forty-two numbers of the publication 'What Our City Councils Are Doing,' issued irregularly during the period from June 15, 1922 to January 1, 1936, by the Municipal Reference Library of the city of Chicago."— Introd. (Z7164.L8C52)
      Included in the index are proceedings of some 38 U.S. and four foreign cities.

Duncombe, Herbert S. County government in America. Washington, National Association of Counties Research Foundation [1966] 288 p.   JS411.D8
      Includes bibliographical references, p. 265–279.

---

[10] See California, State Library, Sacramento, Government Publications Section, *GPS Publication*, no. 1 (Sacramento, 1966). (Z1223.Z7C35).

Government Affairs Foundation. Metropolitan communities: a bibliography with special emphasis upon government and politics. Chicago, Public Administration Service [1957, c1956] xviii, 392 p. Z7164.L8G66
—— —— Supplement. 1955–57+ Chicago, Public Administration Service.
Z7164.L8G662
Issued in cooperation with the Bureau of Public Administration, University of California.

Guide to county organization and management. Washington, National Association of Counties [1968] 453 p. JS411.G84
Includes bibliographical references; also a chapter on public information and the problem of communication between county administration and its citizens (p. 140–149).

Hodgson, James G., *comp.* The official publications of American counties, a union list, with an introduction on the collecting of county publications. Fort Collins, Colo., 1937. xxii, 594 p. Z7164.L8H72
On cover: "Official County Publications."

The Municipal year book; [the authoritative résumé of urban data and developments] 1934+ [Washington, D.C., International City Management Association]
JS344.C5A24
Title varies: *The Municipal Year Book; an Authoritative Résumé of Activities and Statistical Data of American Cities.* Published originally in Chicago by International City Managers' Association. Under the heading "References (Sources of Information)" the yearbook lists publications on local government.

Munro, William B. A bibliography of municipal government in the United States. 2d ed. Cambridge, Harvard University Press, 1915. 472 p. (Harvard University. Publications of the Bureau for Research in Municipal Government, 2) Z7164.L8M9
Includes a considerable number of official documents.

New York. Public Library. Checklist of municipal documents in the New York Public Library, May 1899. [New York, 1899] 15 p. Z7164.G7N57
Covers municipal publications of New York and a number of other U.S. municipalities for the greater part of 19th century.

—— County government, including county publications; references to material in the New York Public Library. [New York] New York Public Library, 1915. 40 p.
Z7164.L8N55
Compiled by Rollin A. Sawyer, Jr. Reprinted from the *Bulletin* of the New York Public Library (May 1915).

New York. Public Library. *Municipal Reference Library.* County government; an annotated list of references, June 1, 1915 to December 31, 1931, comp. by M. Margaret Kehl. New York, Municipal Reference Library, Branch of the New York Public Library, 1932. 28 p. Z7164.L8N56
Classified. Supplements *County Government, Including County Publications* (see above). Reprinted from *Municipal Reference Library Notes,* Jan. 27, Feb. 3 and 10, 1932 (Z7164.L8N6).

—— List of works relating to city charters, ordinances and collected documents. New York, 1913. 383 p. Z7164.L8N53
Lists municipal documents of a number of U.S. cities. A number of foreign cities are included.

Special Libraries Association. *Special Committee on Municipal Documents.* Basic list of current municipal documents; a checklist of official publications issued periodically since 1927 by the larger cities of the United States and Canada. New York, Special Libraries Association, 1932. 71 p. Z7164.L8A15

U.S. *Advisory Commission on Intergovernmental Relations.* ACIR publications list.
Washington.   DLC
An annotated list, occasionally updated.

—— Report. [1st+ 1960+] [1961+] annual.   JK325.A2
Includes a list of publications issued during the year, as well as those from
previous years currently available.

U.S. *Bureau of the Census.* Semi-monthly list of selected acquisitions of the Municipal Reference Service (exclusive of periodic governmental documents) v. 1–4;
Feb. 15, 1948–Dec. 31, 1951. Washington. 4 v.   Z7164.L8U43

—— State and local government special studies. no. 1+ Washington.   JK2403.A35
Some 60 special studies on various aspects of the state and local government.
No. 27 is "Checklist of Basic Municipal Documents" (1948, 92 p.).

U.S. *Work Projects Administration.* W. P. A. technical series: research and records
bibliography. no. 1–8. Washington, 1940–43. 8 v. in 5.   Z1223.W85
"Inventories of County Archives," v. 7, p. 17–31; "Inventories of Municipal
and Town Archives," v. 7, p. 32–39.

Among bibliographies and checklists issued for or by individual local
governments, mention should be made of the following, in alphabetical
order of states concerned:

CALIFORNIA

California. *Historical Survey Commission.* Guide to the county archives of California.
By Owen C. Coy. Sacramento, California State Printing Office, 1919. 622 p.
CD3111.A5 1919

California. State Library, *Sacramento.* News notes of California libraries. v. 1+ May
1906+ Sacramento.   Z732.C2A
Beginning with v. 9 (1914), lists of California city publications received at
the State Library were included. Vol. 9, no. 1 also includes: "California City
Publications Received up to December 31, 1913". From v. 31 (1936), lists of
county publications are included. Lists discontinued in 1957.

California Library Association. California local history; a centennial bibliography.
Edited by Ethel Blumann and Mabel W. Thomas. Stanford, Calif., Stanford
University Press, 1950. xvi, 576 p.   Z1261.C12
A considerable number of official documents listed under corporate entries
(counties, cities, etc.).

—— A union list of local documents in libraries of Southern California. Los Angeles
Sixth District, California Library Association, 1935. 166 l. (*Its* Publication, no. 1)
Z1261.C15
In three parts: County Publications, City Publications, and District Publica-
tions (School Districts). Includes a name and subject index.

CONNECTICUT

Connecticut. State Library, *Hartford.* Connecticut town and municipal publications,
December 1908. Hartford, Conn., 1909. 11 p. (Bulletin of the Connecticut State
Library, no. 3)   Z1265.C89

HAWAII

Hawaii (County) Dept. of Research and Development. Bibliography of Hawaii county studies, 1960–68. [Hilo?] (Its Research memorandum no. 2, March 1969)
A comprehensive listing of materials about Hawaii county, including documents.

Honolulu. Mayor. Municipal Reference Library. Honolulu Hale quarterly bibliography; publications by and about the city and county of Honolulu received in the Municipal Reference Library. July–Dec. 1964+ Honolulu.
An acquisition list of the Municipal Reference Library which includes city and county documents.

ILLINOIS

Chicago. Municipal Reference Library. Annual report. Chicago.   Z733.C5238
Report for 1937 includes "A Bibliography of the Reports and Publications of the Library During the Past 25 years." The bibliography contains, under 137 subject headings, reports and studies on many aspects of the activities of the city government during the period 1912–37.

—— Checklist of publications issued by local governing bodies in Chicago and Cook county. v. 1, no. 1+ June 1936+   Z1278.C5A28

—— Checklist of publications issued by the city of Chicago. v. 1, no. 1+ Jan./Mar. 1958+ Chicago. quarterly.   Z1278.C5A27

Chicago and Cook county; a union list of their official publications, including the semi-official institutions. University of Chicago Libraries, Documents Section. Chicago, 1934. 230 l.   Z1278.C5C
"This list attempts to record the publications of the local governments which have jurisdiction within the limits of Chicago and Cook county, and to show in which libraries they are available." Includes name-subject index and also a brief history of agencies.

Historical Records Survey. Check list of Chicago ante-fire imprints, 1851–1871. Chicago, Historical Records Survey, 1938. xvii, 727 p. ([Historical Records Survey] American imprints inventory, no. 4)   Z1215.H78 no. 4
                     Z1278.C5H6
Arranged in chronological order. Includes official documents.

MARYLAND

Maryland. Hall of Records Commission. Publication, no. 1+ Annapolis. CD3280.A16
Publication no. 12–13: Morris L. Radoff, The County Courthouses and Records of Maryland (1960–63, v. 2, The Records).

MASSACHUSETTS

Boston. City Council. A list of the documents, not serially numbered, published by the town or city of Boston prior to A.D. 1891. Boston, 1894. 40 l.   Z1296.B7B74

MICHIGAN

Dority, Ione E. Municipal reporting in Michigan since 1930. *In* American Library Association. Committee on Public Documents. Public documents, 1937: 146–167.
Z7164.G7A4
Includes a list of publications of cities over 30,000 population.

NEVADA

Nevada. State Library, *Carson City.* Nevada official publications. List no. 1+ Feb. 1953+ Carson City. monthly.   Z1309.N43
Lists Nevada state, county, and city publications received at the State Library. County and city publications are listed from April 1968.

NEW JERSEY

Messler Library. Documents of New Jersey local governments, compiled and edited by Catharine M. Fogarty. Rutherford, N.J., Fairleigh Dickinson University, 1967. 40 p.   Z7165.U6N37
———— ———— Supplement. no. 1+ 1968+ Rutherford, N.J. annual. Z7165.U6N372

NEW YORK

New York. Public Library. *Municipal Reference Library.* Municipal Reference Library notes. v. 1+ Oct. 28, 1914+ New York.   Z7164.L8N6
Issued weekly to Feb. 1933, then monthly.
New York City publications listed from vol. 1, no. 16 (Feb. 10, 1915). From Sept. 1960, also: "List of Other City Publications" and "List of Metropolitan Area Publications."
Publication suspended with May 1971 issue (v. 45, no. 5). "Efforts are being made to secure sufficient funding to resume publishing as soon as possible" (notice, May 1971 issue).

Parker, Ted F., *and* Virginia E. Parker. Local government in New York state during the Dutch period; bibliography. Albany, Govt. Affairs Foundation [1968] 41 p.
Z7165.U6N64
"This bibliography lists and briefly describes major sources of information of value to a person interested in the development of local government during the Dutch period of New York State history." A subject index is included.

OREGON

Oregon. University. *Bureau of Municipal Research and Service.* Community planning in Oregon; a list of publications [1946–1967. Eugene] 1967. 100 p.   Z7165.U6O73
Includes some reports of local governments.

PENNSYLVANIA

Pennsylvania. University. *Fels Institute of Local and State Government.* Bibliography on Pennsylvania government. [Philadelphia] 1941. 188 numb. l.   Z7165.U6P46
On cover: "Bibliography on Pennsylvania Local and State Government."

In 1959, Rosalind L. Branning prepared for the Department of Political Science, University of Pittsburgh, a supplement to the *Bibliography on Pennsylvania Government* (see above) entitled *Annotated Bibliography on Pennsylvania State Government* (Pittsburgh, 1959, 42 p. Z7165.U6P38). The supplement is limited to Pennsylvania government at the state level and includes publications on local government "only insofar as they fall in the category of intergovernmental relations."

TENNESSEE

Millirons, Martha W. A bibliographical checklist of Tennessee imprints in small towns, 1867–1876. With an introductory essay: An inquiry into Reconstruction publications of village Tennessee, 1867–1876. [Knoxville, Tenn.] 1965. xxxiv, 64 l.

Z1337.M56

Thesis (M.A.) —University of Tennessee.

VIRGINIA

Virginia imprint series, no. 1+ Richmond, Virginia State Library, 1946+ [i.e. 1947+]

Z1345.V9

"Sponsored jointly by the Library of Congress, the University of Virginia, the Virginia State Library, the College of William and Mary [and] the Virginia Historical Society."

Based on the W. P. A. Imprints Inventory List, with additions and corrections. Issued only: no. 1, Abingdon, 1807–1876 (1946); no. 4, Fredericksburg, 1778–1876 (1947); no. 9, Petersburg, 1786–1876 (1949).

International Governmental Organizations

With the considerably increased number of international governmental organizations after the Second World War, and with the constantly growing amount of printed and processed material emanating from these organizations, the bibliographic control of such documents becomes a matter of great concern. There is no comprehensive bibliographical work which lists all or even a selection of the most important official documents of international governmental organizations. Very few organizations have compiled and published comprehensive individual bibliographies or checklists of their own publications. With the exception of the League of Nations and the United Nations, only a handful of other large organizations are covered by satisfactory bibliographic tools for their great output of documentary and informational material. One example is the International Labor Organization which has issued several bibliographies and catalogs covering its publications since 1919, the year of its establishment. In recent years, UNESCO, Food and Agriculture Organization, World Health Organization, European Communities, and a few others have made good progress toward more comprehensive bibliographic tools covering their publications. It is to be hoped that other organizations will follow, not only for the sake of improving the control of international documentation in general, but also to make the results of their own work more accessible to the world's research community.

As stated, the problem of a more general comprehensive bibliography of international governmental organizations' documents remains largely unsolved. The reasons are varied because of the extremely complex nature of these organizations and their documents. It is possible, however, that the stagnation in this vast field of documentation is caused mainly by the lack of reliable checklists and indexes of publications of individual organizations on which a more general bibliography or index could be based. Such considerations probably dominated the General Assembly of the Association of International Libraries, held in 1965 in Helsinki, when a working party was set up to examine the possibility of some centralized listing or indexing of documentation published by international governmental organizations, excluding the United Nations. The first step in this direction was the compilation of an "Inventory of Lists, Indexes and Catalogues of Publications and Documents of Intergovernmental Organizations other than the United Nations," produced

153

since the *United Nations Documents Index* had ceased to index the documentation of the specialized agencies in 1963. The "Inventory" was published in the *UNESCO Bulletin for Libraries* (v. 21, Sept./Oct. 1967: 263–270).

The fate of this project seems to be uncertain after 1967. The Association of International Libraries, in its *Newsletter* no. 9 (July 1967), published the following note:

"It was also learned, from an article in the *UNESCO Bulletin for Libraries* (Vol. XXI, No. 3, May–June 1967, p. 137) that the newly created International Advisory Committee on Documentation, Libraries and Archives (of UNESCO), will include 'among the subjects which (it) will examine . . . the bibliographical processing of the publications and documents of international organizations.'

"Under these circumstances, the Executive Committee decided at its meeting on 22 June 1967, to terminate the AIL's interest in this question and to transmit officially to the UNESCO Department of Documentation, Libraries and Archives, an account of its activities in this connection as a contribution to whatever action the Committee may think fit to take in future."

Listing and indexing of U.N. specialized agency publications after 1962 was the subject of several meetings of an Inter-Agency Working Party on Indexing (and Documentation) created by the U.N. Administrative Committee on Co-ordination. The participants at the meetings, held in Geneva (February 1966), Rome (June 1967), and Paris (November 1968), discussed mainly preparatory steps for coordinating indexing activities among the specialized agencies

The International Symposium on Documentation of the United Nations and Other Intergovernmental Organizations, organized by the United Nations Institute for Training and Research (UNITAR) and held in Geneva in August 1972, represents an important step forward in the coordination of bibliographic control of international documentation. A considerable number of "Working documents" presented at the symposium form a valuable contribution toward the clarification of some problems in this field; see, for example, Théodore D. Dimitrov, *Documentation of the United Nations and Other Intergovernmental Organizations* (UNITAR/EUR/SEM.1/WP.III/15).

Turning now to the existing general bibliographic tools which can guide the researcher through the vast field of international documentation, particular mention should be made here of the following three publications: *International Scientific Organizations; a Guide To Their Library, Documentation, and Information Services*, published by the Library of Congress (Washington, 1962); *Yearbook of International Organizations*, published by the Union of International Associations (Brussels); and *International Governmental Organizations; Constitutional Documents*, by Amos J. Peaslee (The Hague, 1961).

The *United Nations Documents Index* is, of course, the most comprehensive bibliographic tool to documents of the organizations belonging to the United Nations family up to and including 1962, when it ceased indexing documents of the specialized agencies. These and other bibliographic sources of a general character describing publications of intergovernmental organizations, or international documents of specialized character, will be listed in the following pages. It should be noted, however, that the list of general bibliographies, as well as the following lists of publications of individual organizations, is based mainly on materials available in the Library of Congress. Also, a considerable number of the lists, many of which are sales catalogs in pamphlet form, are not preserved permanently in the Library.

The listing of bibliographic tools will be limited to the largest organizations only, which in one form or another keep control of their publications. Generally the current and the most helpful tools are cited first. Additional and secondary sources, as well as retrospective tools, are listed next. A number of annotations or parts of annotations are quoted from the forewords and the introductions to the works cited.

GENERAL AND
SPECIALIZED BIBLIOGRAPHIES

For more or less current listing of publications of a number of international organizations, the following catalogs of official publications and some yearbooks will be of assistance:

Annuaire européen. European yearbook. v. 1+ La Haye, Nijhoff, 1955+ JN3.A5
Published under the sponsorship of the Council of Europe, the yearbook lists individual European intergovernmental organization publications of the past year.

Canada. *Dept. of Public Printing and Stationery.* Canadian government publications. Publications du gouvernement canadien. Catalogue. Ottawa. Z1373.C22
In part three, the catalog lists publications of some 15 international governmental organizations in its monthly and annual editions.
Published from 1970 by Information Canada.

The Europa year book. 1st+ ed.; 1959+ London, Europa publications. JN1.E85
Lists selected publications of intergovernmental organizations.

International organisations and overseas agencies publications. 1955+ [London] H. M. Stationery Off. annual. Z6464.I6I62
Includes publications of international governmental organizations listed in the monthly issues of *Government Publications* (London, H. M. Stationery Off. Z2009.G822). It is issued as a supplement to the annual cumulation of *Government Publications.*

Das Schweizer Buch; bibliographisches Bulletin der Schweizerischen Landesbibliothek, Bern. Le livre suisse. Il libro svizzero. 1.+ Jahrg.; Jan./Feb. 1901+ [Bern] Verlag des Schweizerischen Buchhändler– und Verleger–Vereins, 1901+ Z2775.S35
Publications of international organizations are noted.

Yearbook of international congress proceedings. 1st+ ed.; 1960/67+ Brussels, Union of International Associations. (Union of International Associations. Publication) Z5051.Y4
"Bibliography of reports arising out of meetings held by international organizations."
Second ed., published in 1970, covers years 1962–69.

Yearbook of international organizations. Annuaire des organisations internationales. 1st+ year; 1948+ Brussels, Union of International Associations. JX1904.A42
In its alphabetical listing of organizations, it includes titles of their principal, mainly periodical, publications.

The following retrospective bibliographies and other tools should be

156

of assistance in identifying documents and solving special research problems:

[Aufricht, Hans] World organization, an annotated bibliography. 7th rev. ed. New York, Woodrow Wilson Memorial Library, 1946. 28 p.   Z6464.I6A8   1946a
    Includes works on international organizations and international conference documents (e.g. Bretton Woods, Dumbarton Oaks, San Francisco Conference, Foreign ministers conferences in London and Moscow, etc.).

Boehm, Eric. H., *ed.* Bibliographies on international relations and world affairs; an annotated directory. Santa Barbara, Calif., Clio Press, 1965. 33 p. (Bibliography and reference series, no. 2)   Z1002.B65
    "This is primarily a bibliography of bibliographic sources published in English-speaking countries. An attempt was made to include the major bibliographies published in Western languages."

Carnegie Endowment for International Peace. *Library.* International organization, with emphasis on the United Nations. A guide to published sources of documentation, bibliographies, and general information, compiled by Helen Lawrence Scanlon. Washington, 1947. 8 p. (*Its* Memoranda series, no 4. August 25, 1947)
                                                                JX1906.A35 no. 4

Childs, James B. Current bibliographical control of international intergovernmental documents. Library resources & technical services, v. 10, no. 3, summer 1966: 319–331.   Z671.L7154
    "Revision of a paper presented at the program meeting on documents, July 5, 1965, ALA Conference in Detroit."

Dimitrov, Théodore D. Documentation of the United Nations and other intergovernmental organizations: information and functional purposes, processing and utilization, a bibliography. Geneva, 1972. 111 p.   Z6481.D55
    Working document (UNITAR/SEM.1/WP.III/15) presented at the International Symposium on Documentation of the United Nations and Other Intergovernmental Organizations, Geneva, Aug. 1972, published by the United Nations Institute for Training and Research (UNITAR). "Bibliographic Control," p. 30–81.

Dimitrov, Théodore D. Documents of international organisations: a bibliography handbook covering the United Nations and other intergovernmental organisations. London, International University Publications; Chicago, American Library Association, 1973. xv, 301 p.   Z6481.D56

Documents of international organizations; a selected bibliography. v. 1–3; Nov. 1947–Sept. 1950. Boston, World Peace Foundation. 3 v. quarterly.   Z6464.I6D6
    Includes publications of the United Nations, its specialized agencies, and a number of other intergovernmental organizations; also several "War and Transitional Organizations." Discontinued in 1950 because of the publication of the *United Nations Documents Index.*

Peaslee, Amos J., *and* Dorothy P. Xydis, eds. International governmental organizations: constitutional documents. Rev. 2d ed. [The Hague, M. Nijhoff, c1961] 2 v. (lviii, 1962 p.)   JX1995.P4   1961
    Contents. v. 1. African Postal Union to Intergovernmental Maritime Consultative Organization. –v. 2. International Atomic Energy Agency to World Meteorological Organization.

Roussier, Michel, *and* Maryvonne Stephan. Les publications officielles des institutions européennes. Paris, Dotation Carnegie pour la paix internationale, Centre européen, 1954 73 p.   Z2000.R6

Speeckaert, Georges P. Bibliographie sélective sur l'organisation internationale. 1885–1964. Select bibliography on international organization. Bruxelles, Union des associations internationales, 1965. 150 p. (Publication FID no. 361) Z6464.I6S68 1965 Publication UAI no. 191.
First published in 1956 in English under title: *International Institutions and International Organization, a Select Bibliography;* and in French under title: *Les organismes internationaux et l'organisation internationale, bibliographie sélective.*

Union of International Associations. Bibliographie courante des documents, comptes rendus et actes des réunions internationales. Bibliographical current list of papers, reports and proceedings of international meetings. [v. 1–7; Jan. 1961–Dec. 1967] Brussels. monthly. Z6463.U512
Continued in 1968 as part of *Associations internationales; International Associations* (AS4. U583) , and called vol. 8. From January 1969, the material is included in the *Yearbook of International Congress Proceedings* (Z5051.Y4) .

——— Bibliography of proceedings of international meetings. Bibliographie des comptes rendus des réunions internationales. 1957–[1959] Brussels. (*Its* Publication [no. 183, 187, 196]) Z5051.U48

——— Directory of periodicals published by international organizations. 3d ed. Brussels [1969] 240 p. (*Its* Publication no. 212) AS8.U38 1969
FID publication no. 449.
Published jointly with the International Federation for Documentation, it includes some 260 periodicals of intergovernmental organizations.

United Nations. *Dag Hammarskjold Library.* United Nations documents index. v. 1+ Jan. 1950+ [New York] monthly. (United Nations. [Document] ST/LIB/ser. E) JX1977.A2 ST/LIB/ser. E Z6482.U45
Includes publications of specialized agencies from 1950 to 1962 only (v. 1–13) .

United Nations. *Dept. of Public Information.* Selected bibliography of the specialized agencies related to the United Nations. Lake Success, Library Services, Dept. of Public Information, 1949. 28 p. (United Nations. Library. Bibliographical series, no. 1) Z6481.A4
Lists publications for the period 1946–48.

U.S. *Library of Congress. International Organizations Section.* International scientific organizations; a guide to their library, documentation, and information services, prepared under the direction of Kathrine O. Murra. Washington U.S. Govt. Print. Off. 1962 [i.e. 1963] 794 p. Q10.U5 Z663.295.I5
Some 60 international governmental organizations are included, with a selection of their publications. "Bibliography of General Sources of Information," p. 731–741.

Winton, Harry N. M. Publications of the United Nations system; a reference guide. New York, R. R. Bowker Co., 1972. 202 p. Z6481.W55
Covers publications of the United Nations and its specialized agencies (part one) ; specialized bibliographies (part two) ; periodicals of the United Nations system (part three) .
Includes a subject index.

Specialized bibliographies dealing with particular aspects of international affairs are numerous. Most of them include official documents of intergovernmental organizations. The United Nations has published a number of such bibliographies. The Organization for Economic Cooperation and Development (OECD), and its predecessor, the Organization for European Economic Cooperation (OEEC), have published a series of such bibliographies, and other intergovernmental organizations have made valuable contributions in their own fields.

It would be impossible within the framework of this guide to enumerate even the most important of these works. They can, however, be identified in larger libraries under appropriate subject headings. The following specialized bibliographies or bibliographical series are cited only as examples:

International Atomic Energy Agency. List of bibliographies on nuclear energy (with annotations) v. 1+ June 1960+ Vienna. irregular.   Z7144.N8I525 "STI/DOC/11."

—— List of periodicals in the field of nuclear energy. no. 1+ 1961+ Vienna. irregular.
                                                                          Z5160.I4
"STI/DOC/30."

Organization for Economic Cooperation and Development. *Library.* Bibliographie spéciale analytique. Special annotated bibliography. 1+ [Paris] 1964+ Z7164.E2O68 Supersedes its *Bibliographie spéciale. Special Bibliography.*

Organization for European Cooperation. Bibliographies de l'OECE. OEEC bibliographies. no. 1–[37] Paris [1956–?]   Z7165.E8O7 Continued in OECD library's *Bibliographie spéciale analytique. Special Annotated Bibliography,* of which no. 1–7 are called also no. 38–44, continuing OEEC bibliographies' numbering.

Treaties and alliances of the world: a survey of international treaties in force and communities of states. Bristol, Keesing's Publications; New York, Scribner's, 1968. 158 p.   JX4005.T7 A survey of important contemporary treaties as of March 31, 1968. Includes a review of international agreements of the 19th century and of the World War II period.

United Nations. Treaty series; treaties and international agreements registered or filed and recorded with the Secretariat of the United Nations. Recueil des traités; traités et accords internationaux enregistrés ou classés et inscrits au répertoire au Secrétariat de l'organisation des Nations unies. v. 1+ 1946/47+ New York.
                                                                       JX170.U35 Supersedes Treaty Series issued by the League of Nations (JX170.L4). Indexes published about once a year, in separate English and French editions, each number covering 15 or more volumes. Cumulative indexes cover generally 100 volumes.

United Nations. *Office of Legal Affairs.* List of treaty collections. Liste de recueils de traités. Lista de colecciones de tratados. [Compiled by the Codification Division] New York, United Nations, 1956. xv, 174 p. (United Nations. [Document. Documento] ST/LEG/5)   JX1977.A2 ST/LEG/5 Introduction in English, French, and Spanish. Includes entries for approximately 700 treaty collections.

United Nations. *Office of Public Information.* The United Nations and disarmament, 1945–1965. New York, United Nations [1967] 338 p.   JX1974.U453

United Nations. *Secretariat.* Disarmament: a select bibliography, 1962–1964. [New York] United Nations, 1955. 95 p. (United Nations [Document] ST/LIB/15)
JX1977.A2 ST/LIB/15

United Nations juridical yearbook. 1962+ New York, United Nations. (United Nations. [Document] ST/LEG/SER. C)   JX1977.A2 ST/LEG/SER. C
JX1977.A1U54
  Part 4: "Legal documents index of the United Nations and related intergovernmental organizations."

U.S. *Library of Congress. Law Library.* Air laws and treaties of the world. Washington, U.S. Govt. Print. Off., 1965. 3 v. (4483 p.)   DLC LL
  At head of title: 89th Congress, 1st session. Committee print.
  "Prepared at the request of Senator Warren G. Magnuson, Chairman of the Committee on Commerce, United States Senate."
  Vol. 1 is a revision of a publication compiled by William S. Strauss issued in 1961.

U.S. *Library of Congress. Science and Technology Division.* Aeronautical and space serial publications; a world list. Washington, 1962. 255 p.   Z5063.A2U64
  Serials and conference documents of intergovernmental organizations listed p. 1–7. Alphabetical title index included.

Winton, Harry N. M. Man and the environment: a bibliography of selected publications of the United Nations system, 1946–1971. New York, Unipub, 1972. xxi, 305 p.
Z5322.E2W56

UNITED NATIONS

United Nations. *Dag Hammarskjold Library.* United Nations documents index. v. 1+
Jan. 1950+ [New York.] (United Nations [Document] ST/LIB/ser.E)

JX1977.A2 ST/LIB/Ser. E
Z6482.U45

Vols. 1–13 (1950–62) included an annual cumulative subject index which superseded indexes of monthly issues. Beginning with v. 14 (1963), an annual cumulative edition supersedes both the checklist and the index in monthly issues. It consists of a *Cumulative Checklist* and a *Cumulative Index.* The latter is issued in two parts: subject index; and lists of documents and publications issued, documents republished, sales publications, new document series symbols, and a list of libraries and U.N. information centers receiving United Nations material. Since 1963 (v. 14), the *United Nations Documents Index* does not list documents and publications of specialized agencies, but continues listing of documents and publications of the International Court of Justice and U.N. subsidiaries.

An experimental, computer-assisted index to United Nations documents and publications has been issued since January 1970:

United Nations. UNDEX; United Nations documents index. Series A: subject index. v.
1+ Jan. 1970+ New York. (United Nations [Document] ST/LIB/SER.I/A)

JX1977.A2 ST/LIB/SER./I/A
Z6481.U4

—— UNDEX; United Nations documents index. Series B: country index. v. 1+ Jan.
1970+ New York. (United Nations [Document] ST/LIB/SER.I/B)

JX1977.A2 ST/LIB/SER.I/B
Z6481.U42

"At present UNDEX is issued for official distribution only. Its coverage is limited to selected documents and publications issued currently by the United Nations, mostly in the economic, social and human rights fields. It is expected that . . . UNDEX will cover documents and publications issued currently by the United Nations in all fields."

UNDEX consists of eight series (A–H). In addition to series A and B, cited above, series C is "List of Documents Issued"; D—"List of Documents Analysed"; E—"Index to Reports"; F—"Index to Resolutions and Decisions"; G—"Compendium of Resolutions"; H—"Index to Speeches." Series D–H are produced at present for internal use of the U.N. library.

United Nations documents issued before 1950 are listed in:

United Nations. *Dag Hammarskjold Library.* Check list of United Nations documents.
New York. (United Nations. [Document] ST/LIB/ser. F)

JX1977.A2 ST/LIB/ser. F
Z6481.A3

Issued in 9 parts, each one devoted to the documents of a particular organ.
Included in every part is a subject index and introductory notes on the or-

161

ganization of the United Nations bodies concerned. Parts 1 (General Assembly and Subsidiary Organs) ; 6G (Economic and Social Council. Commission on Narcotic Drugs) ; 7A (Economic and Social Council. Economic Commission for Europe) ; and 9 (Secretariat Publications) have not yet been issued. The *Check List* covers publications 1946–49.

Printed publications of the United Nations that are for sale are listed in catalogs published at irregular intervals. Generally, the catalogs are cumulative from 1945; supplementary catalogs are issued in the intervals between cumulative catalogs:

United Nations. *Dept. of Public Information.*   United Nations publications. 1945/48+
New York. annual.   Z6485.U5
    Issued first in 1947 as *Catalogue* no. 1. The 1949 edition was issued as United Nations [Document] ST/DPI/1; from 1950 to 1957 (?), as [Document] ST/DPI/ser. F. The 1954 edition was issued under the title *Ten Years of United Nations Publications, 1945–1955, a Complete Catalogue.*

From 1963 on, several cumulative catalogs have been issued by the various services of the United Nations:

United Nations.   United Nations publications; a reference catalogue. 1945–63. [New York, 1964] 71 p. (United Nations [Document] ST/CS/ser. J/3)
                                                    JX1977.A2 ST/CS/ser. J/3
                                                       Z6485.U46
    Prepared by the Sales Section, Publishing Service, Office of Conference Services. Supplement issued for 1964.

United Nations. *Office of Conference Services.*   United Nations official records, 1948–1962; a reference catalogue. New York, United Nations, 1963. 107 p. (United Nations [Document] ST/CS/ser. J/2)   JX1977.A2 ST/CS–ser. J/2
                                                       Z6485.U53
    Includes official records of various organs of the United Nations, documents of the United Nations Conference on International Organization (1945), and documents of the Preparatory Commission of the United Nations (1945).

—— United Nations publications, 1945–1966. [New York] United Nations, 1967. 175 p. (United Nations [Document] ST/CS/ ser. J/8)   JX1977.A2 ST/CS/ser. J/8
    "... lists all sales publications of the United Nations, including publications of the International Court of Justice, issued from 1945 to 1966. Mimeographed documents as prepared by the Economic Commission for Europe are not listed."

An *Index to Microfilm of United Nations Documents in English, 1946–1961,* was published by the United Nations Archives as Special guide no. 14, in 1963, and a supplement to the *Index* for 1962–67 appeared in 1970 (Special guide no. 14, Suppl. 1). It supersedes the *Index to Microfilm of United Nations Documents in English, 1946–1950,* issued by Dag Hammarskjold Library in 1955 as U.N. Document ST/LIB/ser. B/4 (Bibliographical series, no. 4).

The following indexes offer a bibliographical guide to the documentation of the General Assembly and the three councils. They generally include an introduction, agenda, subject index, index to speeches, and a numerical list of documents, arranged by document symbols:

United Nations. *Dag Hammarskjold Library.* Index to proceedings of the General
Assembly. 5th+ sess.; 1950/51+ New York. (United Nations [Document]
ST/LIB/ser. B/A)   JX1977.A2 ST/LIB/ser. B/A
                                                                     JX1977.A44
"Continues . . . the mimeographed series entitled *Disposition of Agenda Items*"
(see below) .

―――― Index to proceedings of the Economic and Social Council. [14th+ sess; 1952+]
New York. (United Nations [Document] ST/LIB/ser. B/E)
                                                        JX1977.A2 ST/LIB/ser. B/E
                                                                     HC59.A173
"Continues . . . the mimeographed series entitled *Disposition of Agenda Items*"
(see below) .

―――― Index to proceedings of the Security Council. 19th+ year; 1964+ New York.
(United Nations [Document] ST/LIB/ser. B/S)   JX1977.A2 ST/LIB/ser. B/S
A related secondary source, covering the period 1946–64, is John Deardorff's
*United Nations Security Council Index; Document Number Index to Material
Located in the Official Records of the Security Council, 1946–1964* (Columbus,
United Nations Collection, O.S.U. Libraries, 1969. 100 l. JX1977.D364) .

―――― Index to proceedings of the Trusteeship Council. 11th+ sess.; 1952+ New York.
(United Nations [Document] ST/LIB/ser. B/T)   JX1977.A2 ST/LIB/ser. B/T
                                                                    JX4021.U32
"Continues . . . the mimeographed series entitled *Disposition of Agenda Items*"
(see below) .

―――― Index to resolutions of the General Assembly, 1946–1970. New York, 1972. (*Its
Indexes to resolutions, no. 1*)   JX1977.A2 ST/LIB/SER.H/1
In two parts: pt. 1. Numerical index.—pt. 2. Subject index. Issued as Docu-
ment ST/LIB/SER.H/1.

United Nations. *General Assembly.* Disposition of agenda items. [1st–4th sess., 1946–
49] New York. (United Nations [Document] A, A/INF)   JX1977.A2 A, A/INF
                                                                   JX1977.A4265
Similar series were published for the Economic and Social Council (Document A, E/INF) and for the Trusteeship Council (Document A, T/INF) .

The following bibliographies and other works may clarify certain
specific aspects of the United Nations publications:

Brimmer, Brenda, *and others.* A guide to the use of United Nations documents (including reference to the specialized agencies and special U.N. bodies) . Dobbs
Ferry, N.Y., Oceana Publications, 1962. xv, 272 p.   Z674.B7 1962a

McConaughy, John B., *and* Hazel J. Blanks. A student's guide to United Nations
documents and their use. With a pref. by Joseph Groesbeck. New York, Council on
International Relations and United Nations Affairs [1969] 17 p.   Z6481.M3
"This short guide pretends to nothing except a simplification of the steps
required in locating and, thereby, using United Nations documents. . . . If any-
thing, its purpose is to introduce the student to the best guides available at
the present time, by referring him to specific pages in these publications."

Thompson, Elizabeth M. Resources for teaching about the United Nations, with
annotated bibliography. Prepared for the Committee on International Relations.
Washington, National Education Association of the United States, 1962. 90 p.
                                                                       Z6481.T5
"Replaces *A Selected and Annotated Bibliography of Resource Materials for*

Teaching About the United Nations, published by the Committee on International Relations in 1958" (Z6481.N3) .

United Nations. *Dag Hammarskjold Library.* A bibliography of the Charter of the United Nations. [New York] United Nations. 1955. 128 p. *(Its* Bibliographical series, no. 3)   JX1977.A2 ST/LIB/ser.B/3
                                                                         Z6483.C45U5
    [United Nations. Document ST/LIB/ser.B/3]

—— List of United Nations document series symbols. Sept. 1952+ New York, United Nations. (United Nations [Document] ST/LIB/ser.D)   JX1977.A2 ST/LIB/ser.D
                                                                         Z6482.U44

United Nations. *Dept. of Conference and General Services.* Guide to the records of the United Nations Conference on International Organization, San Francisco, 1945, prepared in Archives Section, Communications & Records Division. [Lake Success] 1949. 11 p. *(Its* United Nations archives reference guide no. 10)
                                                                 JX1977.A2 ST/CGS/ser.A/10
                                                                         Z6482.U5 no. 10
    [United Nations. Document ST/CGS/ser. A/10]

—— Index to the documents of the Executive Committee of the United Nations Preparatory Commission, 1945. [Lake Success] 1948. 85 l. *(Its* United Nations archives reference guide no. 2)   JX1977.A2 ST/CGS/ser.A/2
                                                                         Z6482.U5 no. 2
    [United Nations. Document ST/CGS/ser. A/2]

—— Index to the documents of the United Nations Preparatory Commission, 1945–46. [Lake Success] 1947. *(Its* United Nations archives reference guide, no. 1)
                                                                 JX1977.A2 ST/CGS/ser. A/1
                                                                         Z6482.U5 no. 1
    [United Nations. Document ST/CGS/ser. A/1]

United Nations. *Dept. of Economic Affairs.* Guide to documents by the regional economic commissions on economic development and related subjects. New York, Overseas and Special Feature Services, Press and Publications Bureau, DPI, United Nations, 1953. 35 p.   Z7164.E2U42

Various organs of the United Nations issue periodically or occasionally bibliographies, lists, or indexes to their own documents to supplement the *United Nations Documents Index.* Most of these bibliographic tools are issued in the mimeographed document series. Following are some that may be of assistance to researchers:

Economic Commission for Africa (eca)

United Nations. *Economic Commission for Africa.* List of documents by subjects. New York, 1965. 128 p. (United Nations [Document] E/CN 14/DOC/9)
                                                                 JX1977.A2 E/CN 14/DOC/9
    Kept up to date by supplements (Addition 1+) .

—— List of ECA documents distributed up to 1 April 1964. [New York] 1964. (United Nations [Document] E/CN 14/DOC/1)   JX1977.A2 E/CN14/DOC/1

—— List of ECA documents reproduced from 1 April to 1 July 1964 and 1 October to 31 December 1965. [New York] 1966. (United Nations [Document] E/CN14/

DOC/3–8, 10)   JX1977.A2 E/CN14/DOC/3–8, 10
Bilingual, English and French. Kept up to date by quarterly lists ("List of
ECA Documents Issued").

ECONOMIC COMMISSION FOR ASIA AND THE FAR EAST (ECAFE)

United Nations. *Economic Commission for Asia and the Far East.* Check list of Economic Commission for Asia and the Far East documents. [Bangkok, Thailand,
1959] 2 v.   Z7164.E2U44
The two volumes issued cover periods June 1947–Feb. 1954 and March 1954–
Feb. 1959. Include documents not listed in the *United Nations Documents Index.*

—— Report. 1st/2d. sess., 1947. [Lake Success] (United Nations [Document] E/606,
E/CN11/53)   JX1977.A2 E/606 and E/CN11/53
                                                                   HC411.U4A338

—— Report. 1948/49+ New York. annual. (United Nations [Document] E,E/CN11)
                                                            JX1977.A2 E,E/CN11
                                                                    HC411.U4A34
Each annual report includes a list of ECAFE publications and documents issued
during the year. 1950/51+ issued as supplements to the *Official Records* of the
Economic and Social Council.

ECONOMIC COMMISSION FOR EUROPE (ECE)

United Nations. *Economic Commission for Europe.* Bibliography of reports issued
1 January 1953–31 August 1957. [n.p., 1958?] 259 p.   Z7161.U35
"Compiled from the *Monthly Bulletins* issued by the Economic Commission
for Europe (ECE).... Each issue contains an Annex which lists the ECE documents that were distributed during the period covered."

—— Compendium of resolutions and decisions, 1947–1964. Prepared by the ECE
Secretariat pursuant to Commission resolution 4 (xix). [New York] United Na-
tions, 1965. 179 p. (United Nations [Document] E/ECE/574)   HC240.A1U5317
Includes alphabetical subject index.

—— ECE, the first ten years, 1947–1957. Geneva, 1957. 1 v. (various pagings) (United
Nations [Document] E/ECE/291)   JX1977.A2 E/ECE/291
                                                                   HC240.A1U532
Includes a "Selected and Classified List of ECE Publications" (Appendix H:
p. 1–8).

—— Report. 1947/48+ New York. annual. (United Nations [Document] E, E/ECE)
                                                            JX1977.A2 E, E/ECE
                                                                    HC240.A1U484
Issued 1949/50+ as Supplements to the Official Records of the Economic and
Social Council.
Report for 1960/61 includes "List of ECE Publications for Sale" for the period
1956–60. Thereafter each report lists publications issued during the year.

ECONOMIC COMMISSION FOR LATIN AMERICA (ECLA)

United Nations. *Economic Commission for Latin America.* List of ECLA documents
distributed. Jan./Apr. 1968+ New York. (United Nations [Document]
E/CN12/DOC/1+)   JX1977.A2 E/CN12/DOC/1+
Published every four months.

—— Catálogo de la Comisión Económica para América Latina. Catalogue of the Economic Commission for Latin America. New York, 1965. 12 p. (United Nations [Document] ST/CS/ser. J/4) JX1977.A2 ST/CS/ser. J/4

—— Indice de trabajos preparados por la Comisión Económica para América Latina desde 1948 a junio de 1963. New York, 1963. 208 p. (United Nations [Document] E/CN12/LIB/1) JX1977.A2 E/CN12/LIB/1
Additions 1+ bring the index up to date.

The following retrospective indexes relate to U.N. organizations no longer in existence, or special indexes no longer published:

United Nations. *Atomic Energy Commission.* Index to documents, 1 January 1946 to 30 April 1951. New York, 1951. 72 p. (United Nations [Document] AEC/C.1/81/rev. 1) JX1977.A2 AEC/C.1/81/rev. 1
HD9698.A24O35

United Nations. *Children's Fund.* Index of UNICEF documents. [Lake Success] 1950. 70 p. Z7164.C5U45
No document series indicated. In two parts: "Subject Index" and "Numerical Index."

United Nations. *Dept. of Conference and General Services.* Index to document series of the United Nations Relief and Rehabilitation Administration (UNRRA), 1943–1949, prepared in Archives Section, Communications and Records Division. [New York] 1951. 17 p. (*Its* United Nations archives reference guide no. 18) [United Nations. Document ST/CGS/ser.A/18] JX1977.A2 ST/CGS/ser.A/18
Z6482.U5 no. 18

United Nations. *Technical Assistance Administration.* Index of final reports issued as United Nations Documents or prepared as papers for governments. Aug. 5, 1953–[June 30, 1960?] New York. (United Nations [Document] ST/TAA/Inf.) JX1977.A2 ST/TAA/Inf.
Z7164.E2U45

LEAGUE OF NATIONS

The Covenant of the League adopted by the Paris Peace Conference April 28, 1919, came into effect on January 10, 1920. Dissolved by the League Assembly resolution of April 18, 1946. Final report on liquidation, July 31, 1947.

Aufricht, Hans. Guide to League of Nations publications; a bibliographical survey of the work of the League, 1920–1947. New York, Columbia University Press, 1951. xix, 682 p. Z6473.A85

The guide is a selective rather than a complete list of League documents. Arranged by subjects, it deals also with publications of the principal autonomous organs of the League: Permanent Court of International Justice, International Labor Organization, International Institute of Intellectual Cooperation, International Educational Cinematographic Institute, and International Institute for the Unification of Private Law.

Breycha-Vauthier, Arthur C. von   Sources of information; a handbook on the publications of the League of Nations. Preface by James T. Shotwell. London, G. Allen and Unwin; New York, Columbia University Press [1939] 118 p. Z6473.B84

Analyzes League publications up to December 1, 1938. Previously published also in German (1934), Czech (1936), French (1937) and an abridged edition in Russian (1937).

League of Nations. Publications. Jan. 1st, 1940–Mar. 31st, 1945. New York, Columbia University Press, International Documents Service, 1945. 21 p. Z6472.L429

—— Publications issued by the League of Nations. [Geneva, Publications Dept., League of Nations] 1935. 312 p. Z6472.L43 1935

"The present edition gives the titles of all the publications offered for sale up to the end of May 1935."

—— —— Supplement to general catalogue, 1935. 1st–4th. Geneva, League of Nations, Publications Dept., 1936–38. 4 v. Z6472.L43 1935 Suppl.

Also issued in French as *Catalogue des publications éditées de 1920 à 1934* (Genève, 1935. 312 p.), with supplements covering the period 1935–38. (Z6472.L43F7 1935)

—— Subject list of documents distributed to the Council and members of the League . . . [1921–28] Geneva, 1922–31. Z6472.L45

Published also in French under the title *Répertoire analytique des documents distribués aux états membres*. Continued after 1928 only as a periodical mimeographed list.

League of Nations. *Library*. Guide sommaire des publications de la Société des nations. Brief guide to League of Nations publications. [Genève, Impt. Vitte, 1929] 32 p. Z6472.A1L4

—— Index to Council documents prepared by the Library. Provisional English edition. Geneva, Offices of the Secretariat, 1920. 81 p.   Z6472.L4

—— Short bibliography of the publications of the League of Nations. Geneva, 1931. 14 p.   Z6472.A1L5
   A list of principal publications of the League, arranged in 14 chapters by subject. Reprinted from *Ten Years of World Cooperation* (Geneva, League of Nations, 1930. 467 p. JX1975.A49)

Reno, Edward A. League of Nations documents, 1919–1946; a descriptive guide and key to the microfilm collection. New Haven, Conn., Research Publications, 1973–   Z6473.R45
   "The present guide is the first volume of a projected three volume set. Together these volumes will serve as a guide to all of the League of Nations documents published by Research Publications as part of its microfilm project: League of Nations documents and publications, 1919–1946."

U.S. *Library of Congress. Division of Bibliography.* The League of Nations and disarmament; a bibliographical list. [Washington] 1929. 18 p.   Z6475.D5U53

U.S. *Library of Congress. General Reference and Bibliography Division.* The League of Nations, intellectual cooperation program; a list of references. Washington, 1945. 20 p.   Z6475.I5U5
   Reproduced from typewritten copy.

World Peace Foundation, *Boston.* Key to League of Nations documents placed on public sale, 1920–1929, by Marie J. Carroll. Boston, Mass., World Peace Foundation, 1930. 340 p.   Z6471.A1W8
   Arranged chronologically, with classification according to the various activities of the League. Numerical index of official numbers and series of League of Nations publications numbers, p. 316–340.
   —— —— Supplement. 1–[3]; 1930–[1931, 1932–33] by Marie J. Carroll. Boston, Mass., World Peace Foundation, 1931–[34] 3 v.   Z6471.A1W8 Suppl.
   —— —— Supplement. 4. 1934–36. New York, Columbia University Press, 1938. xxiii, 188 p.   Z6471.A1W8 Suppl.
   —— —— Supplement [5?] 1937–47. New York, Columbia University, [Law Library] 1 v. (unpaged)   Z6471.A1W8 Suppl.
   Undated, typewritten copy (62 leaves). "Prepared in the Law Library of Columbia University, listing the documents in its collection."

OTHER ORGANIZATIONS

BANK FOR INTERNATIONAL SETTLEMENTS (BIS) 1930–

Bank for International Settlements. Annual report. 1st+ 1930/31+ Basle, 1931+
HG1997.I6A3
Index to annual reports 1930–50.

New York. Public Library. The Bank for International Settlements; a list of references compiled by Rollin A. Sawyer. New York, 1932. 16 p.   Z7164.F5N45
"Reprinted from the Bulletin of the New York Public Library of April, 1932."
Contents: Publications of the Bank.—Books, monographs and pamphlets.—
Periodical articles.

BENELUX ECONOMIC UNION 1944–

Benelux; bulletin trimestriel de statistique. Statistisch kwartaalbericht. [1954–65]
Bruxelles, Secrétariat général de l'Union douanière Néerlando-belgo-luxembourgeoise.   HC310.5.B4
Lists Benelux publications on the back cover of each issue. Includes also "Benelux bibliografie-Bibliographie Benelux."

Benelux; economisch en statistisch kwartaalbericht. Bulletin trimestriel économique et statistique. Bruxelles, 1966+   DLC
Issues no. 4 for 1966, 1967, and 1968, and issue no. 3/4 for 1969 continue the "Benelux bibliografie-Bibliographie Benelux."

The following bibliographies also list Benelux publications:

Belgium. *Ministère des affaires économiques. Bibliothèque.* Bibliographie; livres, documents, brochures, périodiques, articles de revues et textes officiels traitant de l'Union douanière néerlando-belgo-luxembourgeoise (Benelux) catalogués à Bibliothèque centrale du Ministère des affaires économiques et des classes moyennes (Fonds Quetelet) à la date du 15 août 1952. [Bruxelles, 1952] 66 l.   Z7165.N4B43

———— ———— (15 septembre 1953) 2. éd. [Bruxelles, 1953] 81 p.   Z7165.N4B43 1953
Includes works on the development of the economic union between Belgium, Netherlands, and Luxemburg since 1922, as well as a list of official documents.

Netherlands. *(Kingdom, 1815–) Economische Voorlichtingsdienst. Bibliotheek.* Literatuur over economische Benelux-vraagstukken. 's-Gravenhage [1950] 16 p.
Z7165.N4N43
A general bibliography on Benelux, including official documents.

169

CARIBBEAN COMMISSION; CARIBBEAN ORGANIZATION 1942–

Caribbean Organization. *Central Secretariat.* A catalogue of Caribbean Commission and Caribbean Organization publications. Catalogue des publications de la Commission des Caraibes et de l'Organisation des Caraibes. Hato Rey, Puerto Rico, 1962. 11 p.   Z7165.C3C36
    Lists publications of the Caribbean Commission, including reports of the Anglo-American Caribbean Commission (1942–45), and publications of the Caribbean Organization, by general subject groups. Also periodicals and occasional publications.

Current Caribbean bibliography. v. 1+ June 1951+ Port of Spain, Trinidad [Hato Rey, Puerto Rico]   Z1595.C8
    Includes official publications of the Caribbean Commission and the Caribbean Organization up to 1965. Published from 1965 by the Caribbean Regional Library.

CENTRAL TREATY ORGANIZATION (BAGHDAD PACT) (CENTO) 1955–

Lawrence, Mary M. Decade of development: compendium of United States sponsored CENTO economic publications, 1959–1969. [Ankara, Turkey, Office of United States Economic Coordinator for CENTO Affairs 1970. 201 p.   Z7164.U5L33
    Arranged by broad subject headings, it contains brief summaries of each publication.

Most monographic publications of the Central Treaty Organization include lists called "CENTO Publications."

COLOMBO PLAN (Council for Technical Co-operation in South and South-east Asia). 1950–

Colombo Plan Bureau. The Colombo plan; facts and figures. 3d ed. [Colombo? Ceylon] 1962. 20 p.   HC412.C57 1962
    "Some Colombo Plan Publications," p. 20. Similar lists were included in the first (1958) and second (1960) editions.

——— The Colombo Plan; questions and answers. 4th ed. Colombo, 1962. 18 p.
                                                                      HC412.C575 1962
    "Some Publications on the Colombo Plan," p. 18.

Council for Technical Co-operation in South and South-east Asia. Technical co-operation under the Colombo plan; report. 1950/51+ [Colombo] Ceylon, Printed at the Govt. Press. annual.   HC411.C64
    Under the heading "Colombo Plan Information Activities—Publications," the annual report lists publications issued or "under production" during the year covered.

COUNCIL FOR MUTUAL ECONOMIC ASSISTANCE (COMECON) 1949–
(Sovet ékonomicheskoĭ vzaimopomoshchi)

There are very few original publications or documents of this organization available to the public; most of them seem to be reserved for official use only. Summary reports on meetings are released to the press and published in the daily press or other periodicals. Monographic works and periodical articles on COMECON and its activities are numerous and several comprehensive bibliographies cover such material. They occasionally include citations for a few official documents.

The Library of Congress' *International Scientific Organizations; a Guide to Their Library, Documentation and Information Services* describes in general terms what publications of or about COMECON are available to researchers. The following two bibliographies cover considerable material in this field:

Akademiĭa nauk SSSR. *Fundamental'naĭa biblioteka obshchestvennykh nauk.* Razvitie mirovoĭ sotsialisticheskoĭ sistemy khoziaĭstva i ekonomicheskoe sotrudnichestvo evropeĭskikh sotsialisticheskikh stran-uchastnits SEV; bibliografiĭa. Knigi i stati 1957–1962 gg. Moskva, 1964. 167 p.   Z7165.E82A56
    Lists monographic works and articles in periodicals concerning economic cooperation between COMECON countries. An alphabetical index of authors and titles of anonymous works is included.

Teich, Gerhard. Der Rat für Gegenseitige Wirtschaftshilfe 1949–1963. 15 Jahre wirtschaftliche Integration im Ostblock. Bibliographie. Kiel (Institut für Weltwirtschaft, Bibliothek), 1966. 445 p. (Kieler Schrifttumskunden zu Wirtschaft und Gesellschaft, 14)   HB41.K55 Bd. 14
    In seven sections, the bibliography lists works and periodical articles concerning COMECON and the economic cooperation between the countries of East Europe. Includes an index of excerpted periodicals and an index of personal names.

The East German Deutsche Akademie für Staats- un Rechtswissenschaft "Walter Ulbricht," Prorektorat Aussenpolitik, published in 1963: *Dokumente und Materialien zur Tätigkeit des Rates für Gegenseitige Wirtschaftshilfe (RGW).* Teil B.: *Sammlung von Dokumenten und Materialien.* (Stand vom 1.4.1963). Ausgewählt, zusammengestellt und herausgegeben von [Werner] Hänisch, [Wolfgang] Spröte [und] Süss. (Berlin, 1963, 144 p.) [1] The work includes documents for the period 1949–63.

One of the freely available COMECON publications is the agricultural periodical *Mezhdunarodnyĭ sel'skokhoziaĭstvennyĭ zhurnal* (International Journal of Agriculture), published in Moscow, as well as in the COMECON member countries in their national languages.

COUNCIL OF EUROPE 1949–

Annuaire européen. European yearbook. v. 1+ La Haye, Nijhoff, 1955+   JN3.A5
    A complete catalog of its publications printed in v. 11 (1963).

---

[1] Gerhard Teich, *Der Rat für Gegenseitige Wirtschaftshilfe 1949–1963* (Kiel, 1966), p. 140.

Council of Europe. Publications; catalogue. [Strasbourg] annual.   Z2000.C6
    Lists publications of the Consultative Assembly, European treaty series, Records of proceedings of the Consultative Assembly and other organs, as well as other publications of the Council.

Council of Europe. *Consultative Assembly.* Index of the official records. 1st+ sess.;
    1949+ Strasbourg.   JN22.A353
    Indexes the documents, working papers, the official report of debates, and texts adopted.

CUSTOMS CO-OPERATION COUNCIL (CCC) 1950–

Études comparées des méthodes douanières. Bruxelles, 1957+   HJ6041.E78
    Each issue includes a complete list of "Publications du Conseil de Coopération Douanière." Issued also in English.

EUROPEAN COMMUNITIES

The establishment of the European Coal and Steel Community in 1951 constituted the first step toward the economic integration of Western Europe. This was followed in 1957 by the European Atomic Energy Community and the European Economic Community. Belgium, France, the German Federal Republic, Italy, Luxembourg, and the Netherlands were the original members. In 1972 two EFTA countries (Denmark and Great Britain) and the Republic of Ireland joined the European Economic Community, effective January 1, 1973. Norway, which originally applied for membership, withdrew following the referendum of September 1972. The functions assigned to the three communities are discharged by a number of institutions which are common to all three communities, such as the European Parliament, the Court of Justice, and, since 1965, a single Council and a single Commission which superseded separate organs for each community.

    Documents of the European Communities have been listed in various catalogs and periodical publications. Currently, a single catalog is being issued and kept up to date by supplements:

Publications of the European Communities. Catalogue. Luxembourg [Publications Dept.
    of the European Communities]   Z7165.E8P8
    The March 1964–July 1967 edition of the catalog printed the following notice: "We are now able to offer for 1967 a single full catalogue of publications by all the Institutions and Joint Services of the three European Communities." The catalog lists publications for the following community organs and institutions: European Parliament, Court of Justice of the European Communities, Councils of Ministers of the European Communities, European Coal and Steel Community, European Economic Community, European Investment Bank, European Atomic Energy Community, Legal Service of the European Executives, Press and Information Service of the European Communities, Statistical Office of the European Communities, Economic and Social Committee of the EEC and Euratom, and European Schools.

The catalog "supersedes the separate editions hitherto issued by individual institutions, and more especially by the EEC Commission, and ties up with the Bibliographical Supplement brought out in 1964 by the High Authority of ECSC. The present Catalogue accordingly contains particulars of all European Community publications, whether issued free of charge and/or for limited distribution, or for sale."

The following retrospective catalog of the European Communities' official publications was issued in 1972 as a supplement (Supplément hors série) to the Bulletin des Communautés européennes (HC241.2.A152) :

Commission of the European Communities. Catalogue des publications, 1952-1971. Bruxelles, 1972+   Z7165.E8C59
     To be published in two volumes. Vol. 1 includes publications of the communities, and publications of their institutions and organs (European Parliament, Council, Commission, Court of Justice, Economic and Social Committee, and European Investment Bank).
     Vol. 2 will list mainly technical publications of Euratom.

———— List of the publications of the European Communities in English; supplement to the French edition of the Catalogue of publications of the European Communities 1952-1971. [Bruxelles] 1972. 127 p.   Z7165.E8C6
     "Provisional edition for the internal use in the departments of the Commission of the European Communities."

Other general bibliographic publications of the European Communities:

Court of Justice of the European Communities. Publications juridiques concernant les trois Communautés européennes. [Luxembourg] Service de documentation, Cour de justice des Communautés européennes, 1961. 267 1.   DLC LL

European Parliament. Annuaire. 1958/59+ Luxembourg.   HC240.A1E888
     Vol. 1963/64 lists legislative acts concerning all three European Communities for 1958-63. The 1964/65 vol. lists legislation concerning the European Coal and Steel Community for 1952-64.

———— Vierteljährliche methodische Bibliographie. Bd. 1–[11?] Jan./März 1956–[Okt./Dez. 1966?] [Luxembourg?]   Z7163.E8
     Quarterly bibliography. Superseded Monatliches bibliographisches Verzeichnis, issued 1953-55 by the Common Assembly of the European Coal and Steel Community. From 1958, it covers publications and periodical articles concerning all three communities.

Information Service of the European Communities. A guide to the study of the European Community. [Rev. ed. Brussels] European Community Information Service [1956] 19 p.   Z7165.E8I47 1965

———— Relevé bibliographique mensuel. Monatliches Veröffentlichungsverzeichnis. Bruxelles, 1965–[70?]   Z2000.I53
     Monthly catalog, listing periodical and nonperiodical publications of the three European Communities.

Following are bibliographies issued by individual communities or institutions of European Communities which concern their own publications or publications in specialized fields:

Court of Justice of the European Communities 1957–

Bibliographie zur europäischen Rechtsprechung betreffend die Entscheidung zu den Verträgen über die Gründung der Europäischen Gemeinschaften. Bibliographie de jurisprudence européenne concernant les décisions judiciaires relatives aux traités instituant les Communautés européennes. [Den Haag, 1965] 261 p. DLC LL
—— —— Supplément. [La Haye, 1967+]   DLC LL
Bibliography of European case law concerning Court rulings on the treaties establishing the European Communities.

—— Publications juridiques concernant l'intégration européenne, 1952–1966. [n.p.] Service de documentation de la Cour de justice des communautés européennes, 1966. lxviii, 994 p.   DLC LL
—— —— Supplément 1+ [n.p.] Service de documentation de la Cour de justice des communautés européennes, 1967+   DLC LL
Table of contents and indexes in French, German, Italian and Dutch.

—— Sammlung der Rechtsprechung des Gerichtshofes der Europäischen Gemeinschaften. Recueil de la jurisprudence de la Cour de justice des communautés européennes ... Indices. v. 1–5+ 1954–59+ Luxembourg.   DLC LL
Indexes to the decisions of the Court of Justice of the European Communities. (Compendia of Community case law.)
Documents of the Court of Justice are also listed in *Publications of the European Communities, Catalogue.*

European Atomic Energy Community (EURATOM) 1957–

Euro abstracts. v. 8+ Jan. 1970+ [Brussels]   Z5160.E78
Continues *Euratom Information* (v. 1–7, May 1963–Dec. 1969) .
Published by the Commission of the European Communities, Directorate-General Dissemination of Information. In three parts, part one being a list of publications issued by EURATOM.

European Coal and Steel Community (ECSC) 1951–

Belgium. *Ministère des affaires économiques. Bibliothèque.* Bibliographie; publications officielles, livres, documents, brochures diverses et articles de revues traitant de la Communauté européenne du charbon et de l'acier, catalogués à la Bibliothèque centrale du Ministère des affaires économiques et des classes moyennes (Fonds Quetelet) à la date du 15 janvier 1953. [2. ed. Bruxelles, 1953] 25 l.
          Z6738.C6B42 1953
Bibliography of official publications, books, documents, pamphlets, and periodical articles concerning the European Coal and Steel Community, cataloged at the Central Library of the Ministry of Economic Affairs.

Deutsche Gesellschaft für Auswärtige Politik. *Forschungsinstitut.* Bibliographie zum Schumanplan, 1950–1952. Bibliographischer Index der amtlichen Unterlagen, Bücher, Broschüren und Beiträge in Periodica über die Schaffung der Europäischen Gemeinschaft für Kohle und Stahl. Bearb. unter Mitwirkung der Hohen Behörde der Europäischen Gemeinschaft für Kohle und Stahl, Luxemburg, 2. Aufl. Frankfurt am Main, 1954. 151 l.   Z6334.E8D4 1954
Bibliography to the Schuman plan. An index of official documents, books,

pamphlets, and periodical articles concerning the establishment of the European Coal and Steel Community, prepared with the assistance of the High Authority of the ECSC.

European Coal and Steel Community. *Common Assembly.* Bibliographie analytique du plan Schuman et de la C.E.C.A. Luxembourg, Communauté européenne de charbon et de l'acier, Assemblée commune, Service d'études et de documentation, 1955–? Z6334.E8E8

Subject bibliography of the Schuman plan and of the publications of the European Coal and Steel Community.

—— Monatliches bibliographisches Verzeichnis. Bd. 1–3, Jan. 1953–Dez. 1955 [Luxembourg] Z7161.E79

Superseded from Jan. 1956 by *Vierteljährliche methodische Bibliographie,* issued 1956–57 by the ECSC and from Jan. 1958 by the Secretariat of the European Parliament. Lists works and articles on coal and steel, as well as works on European integration in general, accessioned at the library of European Parliament (formerly Common Assembly).

European Coal and Steel Community. *Common Assembly. Library.* Catalogue analytique du fonds Plan Schuman-CECA, conservé à la Bibliothèque de l'Assemblée commune. Luxembourg, 1955+ Z6334.E8E83

Subject catalog of the documents concerning the Schuman plan at the library of the Common Assembly.

European Economic Community (EEC) 1957–

European Economic Community. Bulletin. [Feb. 1959–Dec. 1967] [Brussels] Executive Secretariat of the Commission of the European Economic Community. monthly. (irregular) HC241.2.A2

Superseded from Jan. 1968 by the *Bulletin of the European Communities.* "Publications of the European Economic Community" listed regularly in the Oct./Nov. issue. "Publications de la Communauté économique européenne," published in the French edition since January 1961 (HC241.2.A22).

—— Publications. [1958?+] Brussels. DLC

Published irregularly. After 1967, superseded by *Publications of the European Communities, Catalogue,* except for the Spanish edition, which continues to be issued.

European Economic Community. *Commission.* Cahier bibliographique. 1+ Brussels. 1967+ DLC

Each issue covers a special subject.

Weil, Gordon L., *ed.* A handbook on the European Economic Community. New York, Published in cooperation with the European Community Information Service, Washington, by F. A. Praeger [1965] 479 p. (Praeger special studies in international economics) HC241.2.W43

"This bibliography includes a complete listing of official documents of the EEC which are available to the public ... listed here by institution and ... by groups of documents or by major subjects."

Wild, John E. The European Common Market and the European Free Trade Association. 3d rev. ed. London, Library Association, 1962. 64 p. (Library Association. Special subject list no. 35) Z7165.E8W5 1962

The bibliography includes a considerable number of official documents.

EUROPEAN FREE TRADE ASSOCIATION (EFTA) 1960–

European Free Trade Association. Publications issued by the European Free Trade Association (1960–69), [Washington] EFTA Washington Information Office, 1969. 3 l.   Z7164.C8E825

———— Selected publications on the European Free Trade Association and European integration. Rev. Washington, European Free Trade Association, Washington Information Office, 1963. 52 p.   Z7165.E8E82 1963
———— ———— Supplement. Washington, European Free Trade Association, Washington Information Office, 1964. 18 p.   Z7165.E8E82 1963a

Selected EFTA publications are also listed in EFTA Bulletin (Geneva. HF1531.E2) and EFTA Reporter (Washington. HF10.E2).

EUROPEAN NUCLEAR ENERGY AGENCY (ENEA) 1957–

Organization for Economic Cooperation and Development. Catalogue of publications. 1964+ Paris. biennial.   DLC
   Includes publications of the ENEA under classified heading "Energy."

EUROPEAN ORGANIZATION FOR NUCLEAR RESEARCH (CERN) 1954–

European Organization for Nuclear Research. Répertoire des communications scientifiques. Index of scientific publications. [1955/57–?] Genève.   Z5160.E84
   Volume for 1955/57 includes a chronological list and subject-author indexes for its CERN reports. Volume for 1955/59 indexes the CERN reports, CERN reprints and bibliographies.
   Publications issued during the year are listed in its annual report (QC770.E83).

EUROPEAN PAYMENTS UNION (EPU) 1950–58

Belgium. Ministère des Affaires Economiques. Bibliothèque. Bibliographie; textes officiels, livres, documents, brochures diverses et articles de revues traitant de l'Union européenne de paiments catalogués à la Bibliothèque centrale du Ministère . . . à la date du ler Novembre 1953. Bruxelles. 65 p.   Z7164.F5B38
   A bibliography of official documents and other works concerning the European Payments Union cataloged at the Central Library of the Belgian Ministry of Economic Affairs on Nov. 1, 1953.

Organization for European Economic Cooperation. Bibliographies de l'OECE. OEEC bibliographies. no. 1+ Paris, 1956+   Z7165.E8O7 no. 1
   Bibliography no. 1: European Payments Union-Convertibility of Currencies. Lists basic documents, articles and other works concerning the Union.

———— Documents relating to the European Payments Union. London, H. M. Stationery Office, 1950. 27 p.   HG3881.O7

———— General catalogue of books published from 1948 to 1958. Paris [1958] 110 p. DLC
   Publications of the European Payments Union are included under the heading "Intra-European Payments" (p. 17).
   In 1958, the European Payments Union was replaced by the European Monetary Agreement.

EUROPEAN SPACE RESEARCH ORGANIZATION (ESRO) 1962–

Annuaire européen. European yearbook. v. 1+ La Haye, Nijhoff, 1955+   JN3.A5

European Space Research Organization. General report. 1st+ 1964/65+ Paris.
                                                                    TL858.E95

EUROPEAN SPACE VEHICLE LAUNCHER DEVELOPMENT ORGANIZATION (ELDO) 1962–

Annuaire européen. European yearbook. v. 1+ La Haye, Nijhoff, 1955+   JN3.A5
    The *ESRO/ELDO Bulletin,* issued jointly by the European Space Research
    Organization and the European Space Vehicle Launcher Development Organ-
    ization, lists currently publications of both organizations.

FOOD AND AGRICULTURE ORGANIZATION (FAO) 1945–

Food and Agriculture Organization of the United Nations. Catalogue of publications.
    [1945+ Rome]   Z5076.Z9
    Published every two years, each volume is cumulative from 1945. Catalog for
    1945–54 includes available publications of the former International Institute of
    Agriculture, 1910–46.
    A supplement, published quarterly, lists new and forthcoming publications.

FAO documentation: Current index. [Jan. 1967+] Rome, Food and Agriculture Organi-
    zation of the United Nations. Documentation Centre.   Z5073.F2
    Published monthly with semiannual (1967–68) or annual (1969+) cumula-
    tion. From January 1972 called *FAO Documentation: Current Bibliography,*
    with 11 monthly issues and one cumulative annual issue.

FAO documentation: Quarterly list of documents and ETAP final reports. [no. 1+ Feb.
    1962+] Rome, Food and Agriculture Organization of the United Nations.   DLC
    From February 1962 to October 1963, a checklist of working papers; from
    October 1963, it includes "publications and main documents." From January
    1965, a supplement entitled "Abstracts of UN Special Fund and EPTA Reports"
    was published, containing indexes by subject matter and country.
    Note: ETAP or EPTA: Expanded Program of Technical Assistance.

The FAO Documentation Centre is also publishing a series of special
indexes in the technical, economic, and other fields, numbered SP 1+,
for the years 1945–66+. Lists of these special indexes appear in the
FAO Documentation: Current Index (Bibliography).

GENERAL AGREEMENT ON TARIFFS AND TRADE (GATT) 1947–

Contracting Parties to the General Agreement on Tariffs and Trade. GATT bibliog-
    raphy, 1947–1953; the text of the GATT, selected GATT publications, a chronological
    list of references to the GATT. 1st ed. Geneva, GATT Secretariat, 1954. 40 p.
                                                                    Z7164.T2C6
————— ————— Supplement. 1st+ Jan. 1954/June 1955+ Geneva, GATT Secretariat.
                                                                    Z7164.T2C612
    Ceased publication with the 16th supplement (1970).

Official publications of GATT and the International Trade Centre (established in 1964), are listed currently in an annual sales catalog, called *GATT Publications* (title varies). Other lists (published generally in the document series) are: *Documents Index; List of Documents Issued; List of Official Material Published by the Secretariat of the General Agreement on Tariffs and Trade.*

INTERGOVERNMENTAL COMMITTEE FOR EUROPEAN MIGRATION (ICEM) 1951–

Intergovernmental Committee for European Migration. *Council.* [Document] PIC/1–PIC/106, Dec. 6, 1951–Dec. 15, 1952; MC/1+ Jan. 29, 1953+ [Geneva?] JV6008.I384
  After each annual session, a *List of Documents Issued* is published as one of MC documents. A *Subject Index to the Documents of the Brussels Migration Conference, the Provisional Intergovernmental Committee for the Movement of Migrants from Europe (PICMME), and the First to Eighth Sessions of the Intergovernmental Committee for European Migration (ICEM)*, was published as Document MC/62/Rev. 1, dated March 15, 1955.

INTERGOVERNMENTAL MARITIME CONSULTATIVE ORGANIZATION (IMCO) 1958–

Intergovernmental Maritime Consultative Organization. IMCO publications. London.
                                                                              DLC
  A sales catalog, issued currently. Earlier (before 1968?), printed in the *IMCO Bulletin*. From 1958 to 1962, publications of IMCO were listed in the *United Nations Documents Index.*

INTERNATIONAL ATOMIC ENERGY AGENCY (IAEA) 1956–

International Atomic Energy Agency. Publications in the nuclear sciences. [1958/61+]
  Vienna.   Z5160.I47
  "A complete catalogue of the publications of the International Atomic Energy Agency." Title for 1958/61, *IAEA Publications Catalogue;* 1970, *IAEA Nuclear Science Publications-Catalogue;* 1972, *International Atomic Energy Agency Publications-Catalogue.*
  From 1957 to 1962, publications of IAEA were listed also in the *United Nations Documents Index.*
  A *Cumulative Index to Resolutions and Decisions, 1957–1965,* was published in 1966 as Document GC/Res/Index/3 (HD9698.5.A2).

INTERNATIONAL BANK FOR RECONSTRUCTION AND DEVELOPMENT (IBRD) 1945–

Publications of the IBRD (World Bank) and the associated institutions—International Centre for Settlement of Investment Disputes (ICSID), International Development Association (IDA), International Finance Corporation (IFC)—were listed for 1950–62 in the *United Nations Documents Index.* The Bank also occasionally issues lists of its publications, called

Free Publications and *Sale Publications.* A *Catalog of Studies* has been issued from time to time by its Central Economic Staff until 1973 when it was replaced by the annual *World Bank Catalog; Studies, Reports, Statistics, References.*

INTERNATIONAL BUREAU OF EDUCATION (IBE) 1925–

International Bureau of Education, *Geneva.* Bulletin. [Éd. française] Genève. quarterly. L10.I69512

—— Bulletin. [English ed.] Geneva. quarterly. L10.I695
   Each issue of the *Bulletin* included until about 1968 lists of IBE publications. The Bureau occasionally issues a sales catalog, called *List of Publications.*

INTERNATIONAL CIVIL AVIATION ORGANIZATION (ICAO) 1945–

International Civil Aviation Organization. Catalogue des publications en vente. [Montreal] annual. Z5066.I5

—— Catalogue of salable publications. [Montreal] annual. DLC
   Each volume cumulative from 1946. The 1971 ed. is called *Catalogue of ICAO Publications.* Kept up to date by the *Weekly List of Publications, ICAO Technical Publications* (issued as documents), and *New ICAO Publications.*

—— Index of ICAO documents. Cumulated ed. Montreal. annual. Z5063.A1I47
   Current title: *Index of ICAO Publications.*
   A combined author and subject index. Issued since 1955 in its document series (TL500.5.A2).

—— Library index of PICAO documents. Montreal, 1947. 2, 37 l. Z5063.A1I5
   Index to documents of the Provisional International Civil Aviation Organization (1945–47).

Publications of the International Civil Aviation Organization are also listed in the *United Nations Documents Index* for the period 1950–62, in the Canadian catalog *Government Publications* (Z1373.C22) and the British *International Organisations and Overseas Agencies Publications* (Z6464.I6162), a supplement to Stationery Office's *Government Publications* (Z2009.G822).

INTERNATIONAL COUNCIL FOR THE EXPLORATION OF THE SEA (ICES) 1902–

International Council for the Exploration of the Sea. Index to publications by the International Council for the Exploration of the Sea, 1899–1938. Copenhague, En Commission chez A. F. Høst & Fils, 1939. 1 v. GC1.I67
   Covers "protocols" of the Stockholm and Christiania conferences (1899 and 1901).

INTERNATIONAL COURT OF JUSTICE (ICJ) 1945–

Hague. International Court of Justice. Bibliography of the International Court of Justice. no. 1+ The Hague, 1947+ Z6464.Z9H27

"A continuation of the bibliographical lists which have appeared in chapter IX of the Annual reports (Series E, nos. 2–16) of the Permanent Court of International Justice."
Reprinted from the *Yearbook* of the ICJ up to 1963/64, then published separately.

—— Publications of the International Court of Justice; catalogue. The Hague.
                                                                      Z6464.Z9H275
Issued in English and French.
"It is brought up to date as of 1 January each year, by means either of an addendum or of a new edition." (*Yearbook 1969–1970*, p. 122).

—— Yearbook. 1946/47+ [Hague]   JX1971.6.A25
Included, up to 1963/64: "Bibliography of the International Court of Justice." Also, from 1946/47, a chapter on "Publications of the Court," with a more or less extensive list of ICJ publications and publications of the Permanent Court of International Justice.

The *United Nations Documents Index* lists publications of the International Court of Justice from 1950. A list of "all the publications issued in respect of each case submitted to the Court" is included in the *United Nations Publications 1945–1966* (New York, United Nations, 1967. JX 1977.A2 ST/CS/ ser. J/8; Z6485.U535), p. 101–115.

The following bibliographies cover publications and documents of both the International Court of Justice and its predecessor, the Permanent Court of International Justice:

Hague. Permanent Court of International Justice. Bibliographical list of official and unofficial publications concerning the Permanent Court of International Justice. Prepared for the second annual report of the Court by J. Douma, Assistant Librarian of the Peace Palace. The Hague, 1926. 159 p.   Z6464.Z9H4
—— —— Supplement. 1927–[40/45] The Hague, 1927–[46]
Includes official publications of the Court since 1922, as well as other official or unofficial publications concerning the Court.
Reprinted from the Court's annual reports.

—— The case law of the International Court; a repertoire of the judgements, advisory opinions and orders of the Permanent Court of International Justice and of the International Court of Justice [by] Edvard Hambro, with a bibliography prepared by J. Douma and an index prepared by Audrey Welsby. Leyden, A. W. Sijthoff, 1952+   JX1971.5.A615
Five volumes published from 1952 to 1968 (v. 1–5B), covering Court documents up to 1966. Vol. 4C contains *Bibliography on the International Court, Including the Permanent Court, 1918–1964*, prepared by J. Douma. Divided in two parts, the first dealing with the Permanent Court (1918–45), the second with the International Court of Justice (1946–64).

—— Publications. Leyden, A. W. Sijthoff.   Z6464.Z9H45
Lists of Court publications, generally issued annually, covering the period 1922–38. Issued in English and French.

INTERNATIONAL HYDROGRAPHIC BUREAU (IHB) 1921–

International Hydrographic Bureau. List of publications of the International Hy-

drographic Bureau. Monaco, 1938+   Z6004.P5I62
Issued in English and French.

INTERNATIONAL INSTITUTE OF AGRICULTURE (IIA) 1905–48

International Institute of Agriculture. Bibliographie concernant l'histoire et l'activité
de l'Institut international d'agriculture (1905–1945). Bibliography of the history
and activity of the International Institute of Agriculture (1905–1945). Rome,
1945. 38 p.   Z5073.I605

—— Index décennal des publications éditées par l'Institut international d'agriculture (1930–1939). Rome [Imprimerie C. Colombo] 1941. 55, [1] p.   Z5076.Z9I57
In three parts; part one contains an index of monographs, yearbooks and
periodicals by broad subject groups; part two is an index to the French ed. of
the *International Review of Agriculture (Revue internationale de l'agriculture)* ;
part three is an alphabetical subject index.

—— Liste des publications. Rome, 1936–[47]   Z5076.Z9I6
Last issue published by FAO in October 1947.

INTERNATIONAL INSTITUTE OF INTELLECTUAL COOPERATION (IIIC) 1925–46

International Institute of Intellectual Cooperation. List of publications [1933–36?]
Boston, Mass., World Peace Foundation. irregular.   Z5051.I6

—— Publications of the International Institute of Intellectual Cooperation. Paris.
irregular.   Z5051.I614
Title varies: *List of publications.*

International Institute of Intellectual Cooperation. *Distribution Section.* Liste
périodique des documents. [1926–28] [Paris] irregular, mimeographed. Z5051.I617

United Nations Educational, Scientific and Cultural Organization. Publications; general catalogue. [1952] Paris.   Z6483.U5A47
"Listed for the first time in UNESCO's general catalogue are the publications
of the former International Institute of Intellectual Cooperation (IIIC)" (introduction to June 1952 edition).

INTERNATIONAL LABOR ORGANIZATION (ILO) 1919–

Publications of the International Labor Organization are covered both
currently and retrospectively in catalogs, indexes, and several retrospective bibliographies. A *Catalogue of Publications* has been issued since
1919, supplemented by lists of new publications. Current publications
of ILO and publications on labor legislation and labor problems in general, are covered in the following catalogs and indexes:

International Labor Office. Publications of the International Labour Office. Geneva,
1919?+   Z7164.L1I63
Published at irregular intervals, occasionally in cumulative editions. Title
varies: *Catalogue of Publications of the International Labour Office* (1919?–22;
1948–?). The 1969 ed. called *Catalogue of ILO Publications.* Occasional supplements issued.

New publications are covered in the *Official Bulletin* since 1963, and in *ILO Publications* since 1969.

────── Legislative series. 1919+ Geneva.   DLC LL
Chronological Index and *General Subject Index*, both cumulative from 1919, issued occasionally.

International Labor Office. *Library*. International labour documentation. Documentation internationale du travail. Geneva.   Z7164.L1I646
Published irregularly since 1919 to 1956, weekly from 1957 to 1964, with annual indexes. A *Subject Index to International Labour Documentation, 1957–1964* published in 1968 by G. K. Hall, Boston. From 1965, published as New Series, v. 1, no. 1+

The following retrospective bibliographies and catalogs cover publications of the International Labor Office from 1919:

International Labor Office. *Central Library and Documentation Branch*. ,Subject guide to publications of the International Labour Office, 1919–1964. Geneva, 1967. 478 p. (*Its* Bibliographical contributions, no. 25)   Z7164.L1I56
────── ────── Geographical index. Geneva, 1968. 14 p. (*Its* Bibliographical contributions, no. 25, suppl.)   Z7164.L1I56 Index

International Labor Office. *Library*. Bibliography on the International Labour Organisation. 1919/26–[1959?] Geneva.   Z7164.L1I59
Vols. for 1929/53–? issued as its Bibliographical contributions.

────── Catalogue des publications en langue française du Bureau international du travail, 1919–1950. Geneva, 1951. 411 p. (*Its* Contributions bibliographiques, no. 6)
Z7164.L1I64 1951

────── ────── Supplément, 1951–1955. Genève, 1957. 88 p. (*Its* Contributions bibliographiques, no. 6, suppl.)   Z7164.L1I64 1951 Suppl.

────── Catalogue of publications in English, 1919–1950. Geneva, 1951. 379 p. (*Its* Bibliographical contributions, no. 5)   Z7164.L1I642
"This volume represents the first attempt at a complete listing of publications of the International Labour Office in English."

INTERNATIONAL MONETARY FUND (IMF) 1945–

International Monetary Fund. Catalogue of publications, 1946–1971. Washington, 1972, 104 p.   Z7164.F5I56
Lists all publications and documents issued for public use, with brief annotations for most entries. Appendix one lists, by subject, articles published in IMF's *Staff Papers;* appendix three cites selected articles on the Fund, published in its *Finance and Development*.

────── Report of the executive directors. 1946/47+ Washington. annual.   HG3881.I634
The chapter on IMF activities includes a report on publications issued during the year.

────── Staff papers. v. 1+ Feb. 1950+ [Washington] 3 no. a year.   HG3810.I5
"The International Monetary Fund...; a selected bibliography," compiled by Martin L. Loftus, appeared in the *Staff Papers* for the following periods: 1946–50: v. 1 (April 1951), 471–491; 1951–52: v. 3 (April 1953), 171–180; 1953–

54: v. 4 (Aug. 1955), 467–481; 1955–58: v. 6 (Nov. 1958), 476–496; 1959–61: v. 9 (Nov. 1962), 449–489; 1962–65: v. 12 (Nov. 1965), 470–524; 1965–67: v. 15 (March 1968), 143–195; 1968–71: v. 19 (March 1972), 174–258; 1972–73: v. 21 (July 1974), 484–534.

The International Monetary Fund, 1945–1965; twenty years of international monetary cooperation, [edited] by J. Keith Horsefield. Washington, International Monetary Fund, 1969. 3 v.   HG3881.I637
    A list of IMF publications covering the period 1945–68 is included in vol. 3, p. 545–549.

U.S. *Board of Governors of the Federal Reserve System. Library.* Bretton Woods agreements: a bibliography. April 1943–December 1945. Washington, D.C. [1946] 48 p.   Z7164.F5U455
    "A consolidation, with additions and revisions, of the bibliography and three supplements originally issued under the title 'Bibliography of comment in English language publications on the post-war international monetary and investment proposals' compiled by Caroline M. Burgess of the library staff."

INTERNATIONAL REFUGEE ORGANIZATION (IRO) 1946–52

United Nations. *Dag Hammarskjold Library.* United Nations documents index. v. 1+ Jan. 1950+ [New York] monthly. (United Nations. [Document] ST/LIB/ser. E)
                                   JX1977.A2 ST/LIB/ser. E
                                             Z6482.U45
    IRO publications listed for the period 1950–52.

United Nations. *Dept. of Public Information.* Selected bibliography of the specialized agencies related to the United Nations. Lake Success, Library Services, Dept. of Public Information, 1949. 28 p. (United Nations. Library. Bibliographical series, no. 1)   Z6481.A4

INTERNATIONAL SOCIAL SECURITY ASSOCIATION (ISSA) 1927–

Although not a true intergovernmental organization, it has strong ties to the International Labor Organization and to national governments, since in most countries social security is administered by government agencies.

Bibliographie universelle de sécurité sociale. World bibliography of social security. v. 1+ 1963+ [Genève] quarterly.   Z7164.L1B52
    Prepared by the Documentation Service of the International Social Security Association and published by the association's General Secretariat. It superseded the *World Bibliography of Social Security,* issued as a special section of the association's *Bulletin.* It contains a bibliography of nonperiodical literature on social security, a selection of articles and studies, published in social security periodicals, and notes on current social security legislation. Entries are listed by country. Each quarterly issue has a subject index.

International Labor Office. Publications of the International Labour Office. Geneva, 1919?+   Z7164.L1I63
    The catalog, as well as other bibliographies of ILO, include publications on social security.

International Social Security Association. In the service of social security, the International Social Security Association, 1927–1957: origins, development, activities, publications, members. [2d ed. Geneva, 1957?] 142 p.   HD7090.I6664 1957
>   A list of ISSA publications, p. 125–128.

INTERNATIONAL TELECOMMUNICATION UNION (ITU) 1932–

The General Secretariat occasionally issues lists of publications, called *Publications of the General Secretariat of the International Telecommunication Union,* or simply *List of Publications.* It includes publications of the International Telegraph and Telephone Consultative Committee (CCITT), and of the International Radio Consultative Committee (CCIR). An annual list is published in:

International Telecommunication Union. Report on the activities of the International Telecommunication Union. Geneva. annual.   HE7700.I474
>   Includes in the annex "List of publications issued by the Union" during the past year.

For retrospective listing of ITU publications, see also the *United Nations Documents Index* for the period 1950–62 (Z6482.U45); *Selected Bibliography of the Specialized Agencies Related to the United Nations* (Lake Success, Library Services, Dept. of Public Information, 1949. Z6481.A4); and *International Scientific Organizations; a Guide to Their Library, Documentation, and Information Services* (Washington, Library of Congress, 1962 [i. e. 1963] Q10.U5).

LATIN AMERICAN INSTITUTE FOR ECONOMIC AND SOCIAL PLANNING 1962–

Latin American Institute for Economic and Social Planning. Catálogo de publicaciones. Santiago de Chile.   DLC
>   A sales catalog, issued occasionally.
>   Documents of the Institute are also listed in the *United Nations Documents Index* (Z6482.U45).

LEAGUE OF ARAB STATES 1945–

American University at Cairo. *Library.* Guide to U. A. R. Government publications at the A. U. C. Library. [Cairo] Periodicals and Documents Dept., American University in Cairo Library, 1965. 20, 41 p.   Z3655.A5
>   Includes titles in Arabic and Western languages.
>   "Arab League publications," p. 19–20.

NORDIC COUNCIL 1952–

Annuaire européen. European yearbook. La Haye, 1955+   JN3.A5
>   Documents and other publications of the Nordic Council are listed at the end of the chapter on Nordic Council.

Bibliografi over Danmarks offentlige publikationer. 1+ årg. 1948+ København. annual.
Z2569.A25
Includes publications of the Nordic Council (Nordisk Råd) under the heading Folketinget.

NORTH ATLANTIC TREATY ORGANIZATION (NATO) 1949–

North Atlantic Treaty Organization. Bibliography. Paris, NATO–OTAN, 1967. 136 p.
JX1393.N63 1967
English edition of the *NATO bibliographie,* published in French (Paris, 1962, 165 p.) Coverage extended to 1963 only. Lists NATO official publications (p. 65–68), official publications of member countries, as well as other publications on NATO.

North Atlantic Treaty Organization. *Advisory Group for Aeronautical Research and Development.* Index to AGARD publications, 1952–1963. Comp. by A. G. Vannucci and J. C. Dunne. [Paris, 1963?] 446 p. TL500.N63A25 1963
Kept up to date by supplements.
The Advisory Group is now the Advisory Group for Aerospace Research and Development.

ORGANIZATION FOR ECONOMIC COOPERATION AND DEVELOPMENT (OECD) 1961–

Successor body to Organization for European Economic Cooperation, established in 1948.

Organization for Economic Cooperation and Development. Catalogue of publications. 1964+ Paris. biennial. DLC
Title varies: 1964, *General Catalogue of OECD Publications.*
The catalog is arranged by broad subject groups based on the main general activities of the organization. Includes an alphabetical index of titles, authors, and series. Kept up to date by supplements entitled *Recent Publications,* issued twice a year (Feb. and Aug.). Supersedes the *General Catalogue of Books,* published previously by OEEC.

Organization for European Economic Cooperation. General catalogue of books published from 1948 to 1958. Paris [1958] 112 p. DLC
"Covers all works published by OEEC since its inception."
Supplements to 1948–58 catalog published until 1962.

ORGANIZATION OF AFRICAN UNITY (OAU) 1963–

Organization of African Unity. *Scientific, Technical and Research Commission.* Liste des publications en vente. Price list of publications. March 1968. Niamey, Niger.
DLC
Issued by its Bureau des publications, Maison d'Afrique, Niamey. Includes publications of its predecessor, the Commission for Technical Cooperation in Africa, South of Sahara, from 1957.

ORGANIZATION OF AMERICAN STATES (OAS) 1890–

Pan American Union. Publications in English, Spanish, Portuguese, and French. 1950+ Washington.   Z1610.I6214
    Title varies: 1951–54, *Catalogue of Pan American Union Publications;* 1960+ *Catalog of Publications.*
    Divided into two parts: Technical and Informational Publications, and Official Records. The catalog includes publications of the following specialized organizations of OAS: Inter-American Commission of Women, Inter-American Commission on Human Rights, Inter-American Commission on Nuclear Energy, Inter-American Institute of Agricultural Sciences, Inter-American Peace Committee, Inter-American Statistical Institute, Pan-American Institute of Geography and History, and Special Consultative Committee on Security.

Pan American Union. *Columbus Memorial Library.* Documentos oficiales de la Organización de los Estados Americanos. Indice y lista general. v. 1+ 1960+ Washington, Unión Panamericana. (OEA/ser.Z/I.1, OEA/ser.Z/II.1)   F1402.A169
    Vols. 1–3 consist of two sections, each with its own title and series notation: Lista general, OEA/ser.Z/I.1; and Indice analítico, OEA/ser. Z/II.1. Vol. 4, 1963+ issued in separate parts: no. 1–2, Lista general; no. 3, Indice analítico.

Pan American Union. *Office of Council and Conference Secretariat Services. Official Records Section.* Official records series of the Organization of American States: guide, outline, and expanded tables. Washington, Pan American Union, 1961. 68 p.
                                                                                F1402.P37
    The series includes official records published by the General Secretariat and the various organs and specialized organizations of OAS. "Multilateral agreements, conventions, and treaties; bilateral and regional agreements deposited at the Pan American Union; agreements and arrangements to which the OAS is a party; final acts of conferences and meetings of the OAS; and collections of OAS official records are also included in the OAS Official Records Series, as are indexes to the Series and guides to its use. . . . It should be noted that the OAS Official Records Series does not include the informational or technical publications of the General Secretariat; these publications are to be classified within a new series, PAU Informational and Technical Publications."

Current publications of the Organization of American States and its specialized agencies are also listed in:

Inter-American review of bibliography. Revista interamericana de bibliografía. v. 1+ Jan./Mar. 1951+ Washington. quarterly (irregular) .   Z1007.R4317
    Issued by the Pan American Union. Before 1955, publications of the OAS listed in the section "Notas y noticias"; after 1955, listed separately under the title "Publications of the OAS and Its Specialized Organizations."

Pan American Union. *Columbus Memorial Library.* List of books accessioned and periodicals indexed. Washington. monthly.   Z881.W3254
    Official documents listed under the heading "Documents of the OAS and Publications of the Pan American Union."

For retrospective publications of the predecessor organizations of the OAS—International Union of American Republics, 1890–1910, and the International (sometimes called Commercial) Bureau of the American Republics, in Washington; and the Union of American Republics, 1910–48, and the Pan American Union, in Washington—the following catalogs and lists should be consulted:

International Bureau of the American Republics, *Washington, D.C.* International Union of American Republics. Washington, D.C. [Press of W. F. Roberts] 1901. 37 p. Z1610.I61
"Publications of the Bureau of the American Republics, 1891–1901," p. 33–37.

—— International Bureau of the American Republics. Washington, Govt. Print. Off., 1906. 35 p. F1403.B972
"Publications of the Bureau . . . 1891–1906," p. 31–35.

Pan American Union. List of publications published or distributed by the Pan American Union, Washington, D.C. [Washington, 1907–?] Z1610.I62
List issued before 1910 by the Bureau of the American Republics.

U.S. *Superintendent of Documents.* Monthly catalog of United States government publications. Washington, U.S. Govt. Print. Off., 1895+ Z1223.A18
Publications before 1910 are listed under the heading "American Republics Bureau"; after 1910, under "Pan American Union." Publications ceased to be listed in the *Monthly Catalog* after 1950.

—— Catalog of the Public documents . . . no. [1]–25; Mar. 4, 1893/June 30, 1895–Jan. 1, 1939/Dec. 31, 1940. Washington, U.S. Govt. Print. Off. 25 no. Z1223.A13
Until 1910 publications were listed under "American Republics Bureau"; after 1910, under "Pan American Union."

ORGANIZATION OF CENTRAL AMERICAN STATES (OCAS, ODECA) 1951–

Summaries of the meetings and conferences of the organization are printed in its *Boletin Informativo.* The issue of August 1961 (no. 26) contains texts of agreements and treaties covering the period 1956–60, and the issue of May-August 1964 (no. 30) includes a list of treaties, with dates of ratification, covering the period 1956–63.

The relationship between the Organization of Central American States and the Central American Common Market, as well as the basic documents of the latter, are analyzed in Andrew B. Wardlaw's *Achievements and Problems of the Central American Common Market* (Washington, Office of External Research, Dept. of State, U.S. Govt. Print. Off., 1969. 46 p. HC141.W35).

PAN AMERICAN HEALTH ORGANIZATION (PAHO) 1902–

Created in 1902 as the International Sanitary Bureau, its name was changed in 1923 to Pan American Sanitary Bureau. In 1947 the structure was modified and its name changed to Pan American Sanitary Organization. The Pan American Sanitary Bureau became its executive organ. In 1958 the present name, Pan American Health Organization, was adopted. The Pan American Sanitary Bureau in Washington serves as the regional office for the Americas of the World Health Organization (WHO). Retrospectively, its publications are covered in the *Catalog of the Public Documents* (U.S. Superintendent of Documents, Washington,

U.S. Govt. Print. Off. Z1223.A13) and the *Monthly Catalog of United States Government Publications* (U.S. Superintendent of Documents. Washington, U.S. Govt. Print. Off. Z1223.A18). Currently the publications are listed in:

Pan American Health Organization. Catálogo de publicaciones. [Washington] irregular.   Z6673.P3
    The catalog lists its numbered publications under three series: Documentos oficiales, Publicaciones cientificas, and Publicaciones varias. Supplementary lists to the catalog for 1964+ are issued annually under the title *Publicaciones Especiales*.

PERMANENT COURT OF ARBITRATION 1899–

Carnegie Endowment for International Peace. *Library*. The Permanent Court of Arbitration; select list of references on arbitrations before the Hague tribunals and the international commissions of inquiry, 1902–1928. [Washington, D.C., 1931] 29 p. (*Its* Reading list no. 30)   Z6464.Z9C3 no. 30
    A list of cases before the Permanent Court is published annually in its *Rapport du Conseil administratif* (JX1925.A53).

SOUTHEAST ASIA TREATY ORGANIZATION (SEATO) 1954–

Southeast Asia Treaty Organization. SEATO publications. Bangkok, Thailand, 1965. 13 p.   Z3221.S67
    "This list of SEATO publications, the most detailed so far produced, is primarily intended for reference use. . . . Publications currently available are listed in each issue of SEATO *Record*."

SEATO record. v. 1+ May 1960+ [Bangkok, Thailand, Public Information Office, SEATO] bimonthly.   DS501.S7916
    Title varies: May-June/July 1960, SEATO *News-Bulletin*. Each issue includes "SEATO Publications."

SOUTH PACIFIC COMMISSION (SPC) 1947–

South Pacific bulletin. v. 1+ Jan. 1951+ [Nouméa, New Caledonia, South Pacific Commission] quarterly.   DU1.S582
    Title varies: Jan. 1951-Oct. 1959, *Quarterly Bulletin*. Includes regularly a subject list of its "technical papers."

South Pacific Commission. Catalogue of the SPC library on co-operation. Nouméa, 1963. 306 p. (*Its* Technical Paper no. 138)   DU1.S586 no. 138
    SPC publications can be identified through the author list (pt. 5).

——— Checklist of principal documents; health (1949–January, 1969) Nouméa, 1969. 125 1.   DLC

——— Checklist of principal documents, 1949–1970; economic development. Nouméa, 1971. 194 1.   DLC

——— Report. 1948+ Wellington, N.Z. annual.   DU1.S584
    Title varies: 1958–63, *Progress in the South Pacific; Report of the South*

Pacific Commission for the Year.
Included in each report is "Selected List of spc Publications."

South Pacific Commission. *Library.* Catalogue of technical papers published by the Commission. Nouméa, New Caledonia, South Pacific Commission, 1966, 9 l.
Z5055.N65S6

South Pacific Commission. *Literature Bureau.* Publications index; a guide to the publications produced by the South Pacific Commission Literature Bureau in cooperation with the territories in the region. Nouméa, New Caledonia, 1963. 28 p.
DLC

UNION POSTALE UNIVERSELLE, UNIVERSAL POSTAL UNION (UPU)   1874–

Codding, George A. The Universal Postal Union, coordinator of the international mails. [New York] New York University Press, 1964. 296 p.   HE6261.C6
Bibliography, p. [267]–285, includes "upu publications."

Union Postale Universelle. *Bureau international.* Liste des publications du Bureau international. Berne.   DLC
Published occasionally, it covers upu publications since 1874. New upu publications listed in the monthly review *Union postale,* issued by the Bureau international (HE6251.A1U5).

UNITED INTERNATIONAL BUREAUX FOR THE PROTECTION
OF INTELLECTUAL PROPERTY (BIRPI)   1893–

A joint office for the International Union for the Protection of Industrial Property and International Union for the Protection of Literary and Artistic Works. The convention which established the World Intellectual Property Organization (wipo or Organisation mondiale de la propriété intellectuelle, ompi) was signed in Stockholm in 1967 and went into force in April 1970. wipo and its International Bureau of Intellectual Property will gradually take over the functions of birpi, as its members become members of wipo.

United International Bureaux for the Protection of Intellectual Property. BIRPI bibliography of the official publications of the International Industrial Property offices. Geneva.   DLC

────── Publications. Geneva, 1965. 21 p.   DLC

A catalog, called *Publications de l'Organisation mondiale de la propriété intellectuelle, Publications of the World Intellectual Property Organization,* has been published in Geneva since 1972.

UNITED NATIONS EDUCATIONAL, SCIENTIFIC AND CULTURAL
ORGANIZATION (UNESCO)   1945–

United Nations Educational, Scientific and Cultural Organization. Catalogue général

des publications de l'Unesco et des publications parues sous les auspices de l'Unesco. General catalogue of Unesco publications and Unesco sponsored publications. 1946–59+ [Paris]   Z6483.U5A4
—— —— Supplement. 1960–63+ [Paris]   Z6483.U5A42
Published first in 1962 for the period 1946–59, "the catalogue lists all works produced throughout the world with the Organization's assistance, whether published by Unesco itself, by some other body under contract, or under Unesco auspices." Publications are arranged by subject, and a general index of authors, titles, and series titles is included. Supplements include also a cumulative list of Unesco periodicals. Publications of the International Institute for Educational Planning, created in 1962, are included in the 1964–67 *Supplement*.

—— List of UNESCO documents and publications. Jan. 1951+ Paris. (*Its* [Document] CPG/List/1–124; ARC/List/1–)   AS4.U8A15
Frequency varies. Supersedes the Organization's *Subject List of UNESCO Documents* (1949–50. Z6483.U5A48). Title varies: 1951–56, *Subject List of Publications and Documents of UNESCO;* 1957–58, *Bibliographical List of UNESCO Documents and Publications.* The list includes documents for general distribution, sales publications and free publications issued from headquarters, documents and publications issued from regional centres or offices, and works published by other publishers. A cumulative annual index is issued separately.

In 1973, a new index entitled *UNESCO List of Documents and Publications* has begun publication, issued by UNESCO's Computerized Documentation Service. It will appear six times a year. The list covers all General Conference, Executive Board, main series and working series documents, and field project reports. A three volume listing of 1972 UNESCO materials preceded the 1973 issues and a similar cumulative author-title-series listing will be issued for 1973. The new list supersedes in part the *List of UNESCO Documents and Publications* (see above).

In addition to the preceding basic catalogs, the *United Nations Documents Index* (for the period 1950–62) and the following sales catalogs should be of assistance as supplementary sources of bibliographic information on UNESCO publications:

United Nations Educational, Scientific and Cultural Organization. Publications. [Paris] (UNESCO publication)   Z6483.U5A47
Published annually from 1949 to 1954, with occasional supplements. "Every effort has been made to supply as complete information as possible on the whole range of publications which have so far appeared under Unesco's imprint or sponsorship."
The 1952 ed. lists for the first time publications of the former International Institute of Intellectual Co-operation, which are still available.

—— UNESCO publications check list. [1st] + ed.; [1956]+ Paris   Z6483.U5A52
Issued irregularly (5th ed. rev., 1962). Only publications issued under the UNESCO imprint are listed.

From 1963 to 1969, sales catalogs were issued under the title *Current List of UNESCO Publications*, with occasional supplements: 1966–67, *Quarterly List;* cumulative supplement for 1968–69 was called *New Publications.* Subject lists are occasionally issued under the titles: *Art and*

Literature; Documentation, Libraries, Archives (earlier, *Libraries and Librarians*); *Education; Mass Media* (earlier, *Press, Film, Radio, Television*); *Periodicals; Science; Social and Human Sciences* (earlier, *Social Sciences*).

From 1970, the *Catalogue of UNESCO Publications* includes only books and periodicals published directly by UNESCO. Publications are listed first alphabetically, then by subject.

UNITED NATIONS INDUSTRIAL DEVELOPMENT ORGANIZATION (UNIDO) 1967–

United Nations. *Industrial Development Organization.* Documents list. [1967/70+]
    New York. (United Nations [Document] ID/SER.G)   JX1977.A2 ID/SER.G
                                                           Z6483.I5
        Cumulative list from 1967, issued annually. Monthly lists up to no. 18 called
    Index to UNIDO Publications, no. 19+ (March 1971) *Checklist of UNIDO Documents.*

UNITED NATIONS INSTITUTE FOR TRAINING AND RESEARCH (UNITAR) 1963–

United Nations Institute for Training and Research. UNITAR news. [v. 1, no. 1+; 1969+]
    New York.   JX1977.A1U535
    "Publications available or in preparation" included in nearly all issues.

WESTERN EUROPEAN UNION (WEU) 1955–

Established originally in 1948 as the Brussels Treaty Organization. After an unsuccessful attempt in 1952 to create a European Defense Community, the Brussels Treaty Organization was expanded in 1955 to include the Federal Republic of Germany and Italy, and renamed Western European Union. Publications concerning some phases of the early period, as well as current developments, are listed in:

Annuaire européen. European yearbook. v. 1+ La Haye, 1955+   JN3.A5

Council of Europe. *Research Directorate.* Documentation sur la Communauté euro-
    péenne de défense. [Documentation] on the European Defense Community. Stras-
    bourg, Centre de documentation, 1953. 38 p.   Z6725.E8C6
    Contains official documents, selected articles, and monographs on the pro-
    posed European Defense Community.

WORLD HEALTH ORGANIZATION (WHO) 1946–

World Health Organization. Catalogue of World Health Organization publications.
    Geneva.   Z6660.W56
    Published first in 1951 (?), cumulative from 1947. Entries are arranged by
    subject. Includes an author and a subject-title index.

—— Publications; a bibliography. 1947–57+ Geneva.   Z6660.W57
Quinquennial, 1958–62+
The bibliography covers, besides regular publications of the World Health
Organization, all articles published in the *Bulletin of the World Health Organ-
ization* and other WHO periodical publications. It includes author and country
indexes, and a list of WHO publications by series.

—— World Health Organization publications catalogue 1947–1971. Geneva, 1971.
171 p.   Z6660.W58
Includes publications of the International Agency for Research on Cancer,
an author index, and a subject index.

WORLD METEOROLOGICAL ORGANIZATION (WMO)   1947–

World Meteorological Organization. Catalogue of publications. Meteorology and re-
lated fields, such as hydrology, marine sciences and human environment. Geneva,
Secretariat of the World Meteorological Organization, 1970. 108 p.   Z6681.W67
"This catalogue contains all the publications of WMO from the date of its
formation in 1951 until 1970. It was prepared on a project worked out by Mr.
G. A. Bull, formerly librarian of the United Kingdom Meteorological Office.
Supplements will be issued from time to time."

—— Report. 1951+ Geneva. annual. (*Its* WMO [publications])   QC851.W6445
Each annual report includes a list of WMO publications issued during the year.

—— WMO bulletin. v. 1+ Apr. 1952+ [Geneva] quarterly.   QC851.W63
Lists called "Recent WMO Publications" or "Selected WMO Publications" are
printed in nearly every issue. In 1968–71, a separate pamphlet called "Selected
List of WMO Publications" or "List of Available Publications" was inserted in
individual issues.
Cumulative lists of WMO publications have been printed in the following
issues: v. 4, no. 1 and 4 (1955) ; v. 5, no. 2 and 3 (1956) ; v. 6, no. 1 and 2 (1957) ;
v. 7, no. 1 (1958) ; v. 8, no. 1 and 2 (1959) ; v. 10, no. 1 (1961) ; v. 11, no. 1
(1962) ; v. 14, no. 1 (1965) .
Vol. 1, no. 1 (1952) includes a list of post-World War II publications of the
International Meteorological Organization, the predecessor of the WMO.

A sales list called *Publications in Print* is issued occasionally by the
WMO Publications Center (Division of Unipub, Inc., New York).

Foreign Countries

GENERAL BIBLIOGRAPHIES

Bibliographic tools for official publications of individual countries presented in this part are arranged by countries, grouped in the following geographical areas: Western Hemisphere, Europe, Africa, Near East, and Asia and the Pacific area. Such an arrangement provides for convenient access to the materials listed, facilitates comparison between countries and areas, and conforms to the probable pattern of use of the materials. Also, existing bibliographies of a general character but limited to a certain area can be cited under the appropriate geographic heading.

The arrangement generally follows that of Jean Meyriat's *Étude des bibliographies courantes des publications officielles nationales; A Study of Current Bibliographies of National Official Publications* (Paris, UNESCO, 1958). Exceptions are based on existing conditions and divisions in the world community of nations and on other practical considerations. Since the United States has been treated extensively in the first part, the remaining countries of the Western Hemisphere are divided into three groups: Canada, Caribbean area, and Central and South America. In Europe, countries of the Communist bloc are treated in separate sections (East Central Europe, U.S.S.R.), due to special characteristics of their official publications. All other European countries, including Scandinavian and Mediterranean areas, are in the section on Western Europe. Similarly, North African countries are considered separately from the countries situated south of Sahara.

As in previous parts, current bibliographies, catalogs, lists, etc. of official publications or, in their absence, current national bibliographies or other bibliographic tools listing official publications, will be cited first, followed by retrospective bibliographies. As a rule, only bibliographies of national coverage are cited. Bibliographies or other bibliographic tools covering provincial or state publications, bibliographies of significant central government agencies, or specialized bibliographies are mentioned in exceptional cases.

General bibliographies, guides, library catalogs, and similar bibliographic tools described in the first chapter of this guide ("Government Publications in General") furnish basic information on bibliographic control of official documents of foreign countries both for current and for retrospective coverage and should be consulted.

A valuable source of information on foreign official documents, mainly those in the so-called difficult languages, are the translations prepared by the United States Joint Publications Research Service, issued since 1957. These translations have been listed since 1958 in the *Monthly Catalog of United States Government Publications* (Washington, U.S. Superintendent of Documents), as well as in various indexes prepared and published by private sources (see U.S. federal agencies).

Listed below are additional sources of information on official publications of foreign countries, including bibliographies covering more or less comprehensive areas and specialized fields, mainly official gazettes and statistics.

Ball, Joyce, *and* Roberta Gardella. Foreign statistical documents; a bibliography of general, international trade, and agricultural statistics, including holdings of the Stanford University libraries. Stanford, Calif., Hoover Institution on War, Revolution and Peace, Stanford University, 1967. 173 p. (Hoover Institution bibliographical series 28)   Z7551.B3

Childs, James B. The official gazettes of foreign countries. *In* American Library Association. Committee on Public Documents. Public documents ... Paper presented at the 1938 conference of the American Library Association (Chicago, 1938), p. 129–174.   Z7164.G7A4 1938

Cormier, Reine. Les Sources des statistiques actuelles, guide de documentation. Paris, Gauthier-Villars, 1969. 287 p. (Documentation et information)   Z7551.C65

Koren, John, *ed.* The history of statistics, their development and progress in many countries, in memoirs to commemorate the seventy fifth anniversary of The American Statistical Association. New York, B. Franklin [1970] 773 p. (Burt Franklin research & source works series, 453. Selected essays in history, economics, and social science, 124)   HA19.K7 1970
        Reprint of the 1918 ed.

Lancaster, Henry O. Bibliography of statistical bibliographies. Edinburgh, London, published for the International Statistical Institute by Oliver & Boyd, 1968. 103 p.
                                                          Z7551.L3

List of the serial publications of foreign governments, 1815–1931, edited by Winifred Gregory for the American Council of Learned Societies, American Library Association, National Research Council. New York, The H. W. Wilson Co., 1932. 720 p.
                                                          Z7164.G7L7

New York. Public Library. Checklist of newspapers and official gazettes in the New York Public Library; compiled by Daniel C. Haskell. [New York] The New York Public Library, 1915. 579 p.   Z6945.N6
        Reprinted from the *Bulletin of the New York Public Library*, July-December 1914 and July 1915.

——— National and local gazettes microfilming program. New York [1962] 37 1.
                                                          Z7164.G7N6
        "236 national and local gazettes from all parts of the world available on microfilm as of the end of 1961."

A supplement, *African Official Gazettes Being Filmed in N. Y. P. L. Official Gazettes Program,* was issued in January 1967.

New York (State). *Foreign Area Materials Center.* Guide to reference sources on Africa, Asia, Latin America and the Caribbean, Middle East and North Africa, and Russia and East Europe: selected and annotated. Williamsport, Pa., Bro-Dart Pub. Co., 1972. 73 p. (*Its* Occasional publication no. 17)   Z1009.N54 no. 17

Staatsbibliothek der Stiftung Preussischer Kulturbesitz. Abteilung Internationaler Amtlicher Schriftentausch. Bestands-Verzeichnis laufend erscheinender ausländischer Amtsdruckschriften. 1967. 2 v.   Z7164.G7S84
———— ———— Nachtrag. Berlin, 1969+   Z7164.G7S84 Suppl.
    Offset reproduction of cards of serial publications of foreign governments in the collections of the Staatsbibliothek, issued by its Section for International Exchange of Official Publications.

Technical co-operation; a monthly bibliography. v. 1+ Jan. 1964+ [London] monthly.
                                                                     Z2021.C7A35
———— Supplement. 1964+ [London]   Z2021.C7A35 Suppl.
    In 1964 issued by the Dept. of Technical Co-operation Library; 1964–70, by the Ministry of Overseas Development Library; from 1971 by the Overseas Development Administration Library.
    The bibliography covers official publications of all countries of the British Commonwealth. The supplement extends the coverage to bills and subsidiary legislation.

Texas. University. *Population Research Center.* International population census bibliography. Austin, Bureau of Business Research, University of Texas, 1965–67. 6 v. (*Its* Census bibliography no. 1–6)   Z7164.D3T45
———— ———— Supplement 1968. Austin, Bureau of Business Research, University of Texas, 1968. 154 p. (*Its* Census bibliography no. 7)   Z7164.D3T45 Suppl.

United Nations. *Dag Hammarskjold Library.* Constitutions of the world; a selected bibliography of titles in the official languages of the United Nations and in the languages of the various countries. 2d draft. New York, 1951. 70 1.   Z6455.C8U53
    Preliminary draft published under title: *Bibliography of Constitutions* (New York, 1951).

———— Government gazettes; an annotated list of gazettes held in the Dag Hammarskjold Library. New York, United Nations, 1964. 50 p. (United Nations [Document] ST/LIB/ser. B/10)   JX1977.A2 ST/LIB/ser. B/10

United Nations. *Library, Geneva.* Répertoire des données publiées regulièrement dans les journaux officiels. Analysis of material published regularly in official gazettes. Genève, 1958. 39 p. (*Its* Listes bibliographiques, nouv. sér. Miscellaneous bibliographies, new ser., no. 1)   Z7164.G7U5
    "This list is an analysis of important material published regularly in the 199 official gazettes currently received by the United Nations Library in Geneva."

U.S. *Bureau of the Census.* Foreign social science bibliographies. Ser. P–92, no. 1–22, 1961–65. Washington.   Z7161.U43
    The Bureau of the Census published 22 bibliographies under the title *Bibliography of Social Science Periodicals and Monograph Series,* for countries of the "Communist bloc and other countries using so-called 'difficult' languages." The bibliographies, arranged by broad subjects, cover generally the post-war period (1945–61/63) and contain a substantial number of government publications. The following countries are included in the series:
    no. 1. *Rumania, 1947–1960.*
    „ 2. *Bulgaria, 1944–1960.*

  „   3. *Mainland China, 1949–1961.*
  „   4. *Republic of China, 1949–1961.*
  „   5. *Greece, 1950–1961.*
  „   6. *Albania, 1944–1961.*
  „   7. *Hong Kong, 1950–1961.*
  „   8. *North Korea, 1945–1961.*
  „   9. *Republic of Korea, 1945–1961.*
  „ 10. *Iceland, 1950–1962.*
  „ 11. *Denmark, 1945–1961.*
  „ 12. *Finland, 1950–1962.*
  „ 13. *Hungary, 1947–1962.*
  „ 14. *Turkey, 1950–1962.*
  „ 15. *Norway, 1945–1962.*
  „ 16. *Poland, 1945–1962.*
  „ 17. *U.S.S.R., 1950–1963.*
  „ 18. *Yugoslavia, 1945–1963.*
  „ 19. *Czechoslovakia, 1948–1963.*
  „ 20. *Japan, 1950–1963.*
  „ 21. *Soviet Zone of Germany, 1948–1963.*
  „ 22. *Sweden, 1950–1963.*

Zahn, Friedrich. Die amtliche Statistik in den einzelnen Staaten. Handwörterbuch der Staatswissenschaften, herausgegeben von D. Dr. Ludwig Elster, Dr. Adolf Weber, Dr. Friedrich Wieser. 4. Aufl. (Jena, F. Fischer, 1923–28), v. 7: 886–942.

                                       H45.H23 v. 7

WESTERN HEMISPHERE

CANADA

Before 1928 bibliographic control of official documents in Canada was practically nonexistent. The *Price List of Government Publications*, first issued in 1895 by the Department of Public Printing and Stationery (King's Printer), included only publications for sale by its distribution branch. The *Catalogue of Official Publications of the Parliament and Government of Canada*, a so-called complete catalogue, was issued in April 1928 and included for the first time titles of official publications of all kinds, whether copies were procurable from the King's Printer or from the issuing agency. The year 1953 marked the beginning of a comprehensive scheme for the control and recording of Dominion government publications with the issuance of a daily checklist and the monthly and annual catalogs entitled *Canadian Government Publications*. In 1954 *Canadiana*, issued by the National Library of Canada, began listing provincial official publications received at the library.

Current:

Canada. *Dept. of Public Printing and Stationery.* Canadian government publications.
   Publications du gouvernement canadien. Catalogue. Ottawa.   Z1373.C22
      Began publication in 1895 under the title *Price List of Government Publications,* in English and French editions. From April 1928 through 1939, published under the title *Catalogue of Official Publications of the Parliament and Government of Canada,* with occasional supplements. From 1943 to 1948, published as *Government Publications; Annual Catalogue,* with supplements through 1952. In 1953 a "Consolidated Catalogue" was issued under the present title, with a daily checklist and a monthly edition. It includes in its monthly and annual cumulations a list of international organizations for which the Queen's Printer acts as a sales agent. Since 1957, the following sectional catalogs have been issued to provide "a subject aproach to the many thousands of publications which form the sales stock of the Queen's Printer": no. 10, *Labour;* no. 11, *Northern Affairs and National Resources*; no. 12, *Mines Branch*; no. 13, *Forestry*; no. 14, *Dominion Bureau of Statistics*; no. 15, *Canada Treaty Series*; no. 16, *National Museums of Canada.*

Canadiana. Jan. 15, 1951+ [Ottawa]   Z1365.C23
      Issued monthly, with annual cumulations. Issues for 1951–52 published by the Canadian Bibliographic Centre; 1953+ by the National Library of Canada. From 1951 to 1953 published in two parts, part two being Dominion official publications. From 1954, part three listed provincial official publications. From 1968, published in six parts, part five listing federal publications, part six, provincial publications. There are quarterly, semiannual, and annual indexes.

Retrospective:

Bhatia, Mohan. Canadian federal government publications: a bibliography of bibliographies. Saskatoon, University of Saskatchewan, 1971. 33 1.   Z1373.B45
    In its three parts, it lists general bibliographies, bibliographies of parliamen-
tary publications, and bibliographies of departmental publications.

Bishop, Olga B. Publications of the Government of the Province of Canada, 1841–
1867. Ottawa, National Library of Canada, 1963 [i.e. 1964] 351 p.   Z1373.B5
    "The purpose of this study has been to investigate the type of documents
published and to prepare a bibliography of the publications issued by the
government of the Province of Canada from 1841 to June 1867." The bibliography covers the period between the unification of the provinces of Lower and
Upper Canada (1841) and the beginning of the federal system.

Childs, James B. Author entries for Canadian government publications. Chicago,
1934. 6 p.   Z695.1.G7C5
    Reprinted from the Library Quarterly, April 1934, for private distribution.

—— Canadian government publications: developments in control, use, and bibliography. [Washington, 1969] 256–262 p.   Z1313.C37
    Reprinted from the Australian Library Journal, v. 18, no. 7.

Higgins, Marion V. Canadian government publications; a manual for librarians. With
an introduction by Gerhard R. Lomer. Chicago, American Library Association,
1935. 582 p.   Z1373.C2H6
    Dominion government only. "Brief outline histories of the various govern-
mental bodies, with a list of their publications."

Ontario library review. v. 1, no. 1+ June 1916+ Toronto, Ontario Dept. of Education.
                                                                          Z671.O57
    From November 1933 to February 1951, it included with each issue a list of
Dominion official publications, as well as some provincial publications, the
latter listing continuing through May 1953.

Following are catalogs, indexes, and lists, issued by individual agencies, and specialized bibliographies covering particular fields:

Bligh, Harris H. The Dominion law index, embracing all the legislation of the
Dominion Parliament; and such unrepealed provincial enactments, and imperial
statutes, treaties and orders as bear a special relation to Canada. (1867–1914)
3d ed. Toronto, The Carswell Co., 1915. 549 p.   DLC LL

Boult, Reynald. A bibliography of Canadian law. Montreal, Wilson and Lafleur,
1966. 393 p.   DLC LL
    Text partly in English, partly in French.

Canada. Bureau of Statistics. Current publications. [Ottawa]   Z7554.C2C2
    Issued first in 1922 as Reports, Bulletins, Press Releases, etc.; 1925–38? as
List of Publications, Including Reports, Bulletins, Press Releases; 1942–48 as
Publications, Including Reports, Bulletins, Press Releases.... From 1950 published as Current Publications of the Dominion Bureau of Statistics and from
1959, as part of Canadian Government Publications, Catalogue (1964+, as Sectional catalogue no. 14)

Canada. Bureau of Statistics. Library. Historical catalogue of Dominion Bureau of
Statistics publications, 1918–1960. Catalogue rétrospectif des publications du
Bureau fédéral de la statistique. Ottawa, DBS Library [and] Canada Year Book
Division, 1966 [i.e. 1967] 298 p.   Z7554.C2A5

Canada. *Dept. of Agriculture. Economics Division.* List of published material, 1930–1956, by members of the Economics Division. Ottawa, 1957, 64 p. Z5075.C2C33

Canada. *Dept. of Agriculture. Information Division.* Publications of the Canada Department of Agriculture, 1867–1959, compiled by Ella S. G. Minter. [Ottawa] Available from the Queen's Printer, 1963. 387 p. Z5075.C2C34
"The purpose of this list is to have available a permanent record of all known publications issued officially by the Department from its inception until its reorganization in 1959."

Canada. *Dept. of Agriculture. Library.* Index to publications of the Federal Department of Agriculture of Canada as follows: Bulletins 1–100, n. s.; Pamphlets 1–100, n.s.; Circulars 1–70, n. s.; Acts, orders and regulations 1–29. Ottawa, 1930. 62 p. (Canada. Dept. of Agriculture. Pamphlet, new. ser., no. 122) S133.A3467 no. 122

Canada. *Dept. of Agriculture. Publicity and Extension Division.* List of publications. 1912+ Ottawa, 1912+ Z5075.C2C2
Lists up to 1935 issued as the *Pamphlet,* new series (S133.A3467), later, as *Publication* and the *Farmers' Bulletin* (1936–40). From 1949 issued by its Information Service (Division).

Canada. *Dept. of External Affairs.* Report. 1909/10+ Ottawa, 1910+ JX352.A3
Publications of the department, issued during the year, are listed in Appendix I. Also issued in French (JX352.A32). The Information Division of the department occasionally issues lists called *Publications Available in Canada* and *Publications Available Outside Canada,* in English and French.

Canada. *Dept. of Forestry and Rural Development.* List of available publications. Liste des publications disponibles. Ottawa. DLC

Canada, *Geological Survey.* Catalogue of publications of the Geological Survey, Canada. (Revised to January 1, 1909) Ottawa, Printed by C. H. Parmelee, 1909. 181 p. Z6034.C19C2

―――― Index of publications of the Geological Survey of Canada, 1845–1958, by A. G. Johnston. [Ottawa] Dept. of Mines and Technical Surveys, Canada [1961] 378 p. Z6034.C19A5
―――― ―――― Supplement. Ottawa Dept. of Mines and Technical Surveys, Canada. Z6034.C19A512
Supplements issued biennially, with occasional cumulations. A 10-year (1959–69) cumulation issued in 1970.

―――― Index to reports of Geological Survey of Canada, from 1927–50. Compiled by W. E. Cockfield, E. Hall, and J. F. Wright. [Ottawa, Dept. of Mines and Technical Surveys] 1962. 723 p. Z6034.C19A515

Index to 1927–50 annual reports, economic geology series, geological bulletins, maps without reports, museum bulletins; geological papers, 1935–50, and summary reports, 1927–33. This index is the sixth in a series issued by the Geological Survey of Canada. The previous five covered the following periods: *General Index to the Reports of Progress, 1863–1884* (1900, 475 p. QE185.A12); *General Index to Reports, 1885–1906* (1908, 1014 p. QE185.A13); *Index to Separate Reports 1906–1910 and Summary Reports 1905–1916* (1923, 305 p. QE185.A13); *Index to Paleontology (Geological Publications ...)* pt. 1, 1847–1916, pt. 2, 1917–26 (1925, 1930, QE748.A43 no. 1, 2) ; *Index to Memoirs, 1910–1926, Bulletins, 1913–1926, Summary Reports, 1917–1926, Sessional Papers (Administrative) 1921–1926.* (1932, 666 p. QE185.A2; QE748.A43 no. 3).

—— Index to reports of Geological Survey of Canada from 1951–59. Compiled by
J. F. Wright. Ottawa Dept. of Mines and Technical Surveys, 1965. 379 p.
                                                                    Z6034.C19A517
Seventh in the series of indexes issued by the Geological Survey of Canada.

—— Misc. G series. Ottawa.   Z6034.C19A34
Under the title *Geological Reports and Maps of . . .*, the following lists were
published, revised occasionally:
Misc. G–50, [*List of General Geological Reports and Maps of Canada. Rev. 1970.*]
Misc. G–51, *Reports and Maps Yukon Territory, 1917–1959* (1959, 16 p.)
Misc. G–52, . . . *British Columbia, 1917–1960* (1960, 35 p.)
Misc. G–53, . . . *Alberta, 1917–1960* (1960, 27 p.)
Misc. G–54, . . . *Saskatchewan, 1914–1970* (rev. 1970, 9 p.)
Misc. G–55, . . . *Manitoba, 1917–1960* (1960, 23 p.)
Misc. G–56, . . . *Northwest Territories, 1916–1968* (rev. 1968, 17 p.)
Misc. G–57, . . . *Ontario, 1917–1959* (rev. 1959, 30 p.)
Misc. G–58, . . . *Quebec, 1917–1959* (rev. 1959, 34 p.)
Misc. G–59, . . . *the Atlantic Provinces, 1917–1959* (rev. 1959, 31 p.)

—— Publications of the Geological Survey and National Museum of Canada.
Ottawa.   Z6034.C19C22
Issues cumulative from 1909.
An *Annotated Catalogue of and Guide to the Publications of the Geological
Survey Canada, 1845–1917,* compiled by Walter F. and Dorothy J. Ferrier
(Ottawa, J. de Labroquerie Taché, 1920. Z6034.C19F3), and *Publications of the
Geological Survey of Canada, 1917–1952,* compiled by Lorne B. Leafloor (Ottawa,
E. Cloutier, Queen's Printer, 1952. Z6034.C19L4), cover Canadian Geological
Survey publications for more than 100 years.

Canada. *Parliament. House of Commons.* General index to the Journals of the House
of Commons of the Dominion of Canada and of the sessional papers of Parliament
from 1867 to [1930] inclusive. Ottawa, 1880–1932, 5 v.   J103.K3 Index

Canada. *Parliament. Legislative Assembly.* General index to the Journals of the
Legislative Assembly of Canada in the 1st, 2d, and 3d Parliaments. 1841–1851.
By Alfred Todd. Montreal, Printed by John Lovell, 1855. 575 p.   J102.K3 Index

—— General index ... in the 4th, 5th, 6th, 7th and 8th Parliaments. 1852–1866.
By Alfred Todd. Ottawa, Printed by Hunter, Rose & Co., 1867. 943 p.
                                                                    J102.K3 Index
The *General Indexes* for both the House of Commons and the Legislative
Assembly were reprinted in 1971 by the United States Historical Documents
Institute, Inc., Washington, D.C., in *Canadian Parliamentary Proceedings and
Sessional Papers 1841–1970,* a dual-media edition (proceedings, etc. on microfilm,
indexes in print) .

Canada. *Wartime Information Board.* List of Dominion government publications.
Jan. 1944–Sept. 1945. Ottawa, 1944–45.   DLC
Published quarterly, it includes "all publications issued by the various depart-
ments of the Dominion Government ..."

Carter, Neal M. Index and list of titles, Fisheries Research Board of Canada and
associated publications, 1900–1964. Ottawa, Queen's Printer 1968. xviii, 649 p.
(Canada. Fisheries Research Board. Bulletin no. 164)   SH223.A344 no. 164
A subject-author index and a list of titles. A considerable expansion of *Bulletin* no. 110, published in 1957, covering 1901–54.

Henderson, George F. Federal royal commissions of Canada, 1867–1966; a checklist.
[Toronto] University of Toronto Press [1967] xvi, 212 p.   Z1373.H4

Lists all located reports of Royal Commissions, with full name of the commission, date of appointment, names of members, etc.

Maxwell, William H., *comp.* A complete list of British and colonial law reports and legal periodicals, arranged in alphabetical and in chronological order with bibliographical notes. 3d ed., with a check list of Canadian statutes. Toronto, The Carswell Co., Ltd., 1937. 141, 59 p. DLC LL
"Issued for private circulation only." The "Check List of Canadian and Newfoundland Statutes" has separate paging (2 l., 59 p.) at end.

National Research Council, *Canada.* Publications. [1st]+ ed.; 1918–38+ Ottawa, 1939+ Z5055.C2N3
Kept up to date by supplements. Lists and indexes reprints of papers and other miscellaneous reports which form part of the N.R.C. numbered series, and provides bibliographical information on publications which are not included in numbered series.

Wilcox, Jerome K. Official defense publications; guide to state and federal publications. Berkeley, Bureau of Public Administration, University of California, 1941–45. 9 v. Z1361.D4W56
Vol. 3, entitled *Official War Publications; Guide to State, Federal, and Canadian Publications; Second Supplement to Official Defense Publications,* and v. 4–9 include Canadian publications issued from the time of Canada's declaration of war to January 1, 1945.

CANADIAN PROVINCES

The publications of Canadian provinces were not systematically listed until 1954 when *Canadiana,* the monthly national bibliography issued by the National Library, undertook "to list publications forwarded by the provincial governments." Provincial publications were listed in part three of the bibliography, with a personal author and distinctive title index to part two, "Publications of the Government of Canada," and part three, "Publications of the Provincial Governments of Canada." Beginning in 1968 provincial publications have been listed in part six.

The following works deal with Canadian provincial government publications in general:

Bhatia, Mohan. Bibliographies, catalogues, checklists and indexes of Canadian provincial government publications. Saskatoon, University of Saskatchewan, 1970 16 l. Z1373.5.A1B45
After a list of general works, provinces are grouped in three regions: Atlantic provinces, Ontario and Quebec, and Western provinces.
A new, enlarged edition was issued in 1971 under the title *Canadian Provincial Government Publications; Bibliography of Bibliographies.* (Saskatoon, University of Saskatchewan, 1971. 19 l. Z1373.5.A1B48 1971)

Pross, A. Paul, *and* Catherine A. Pross. Government publishing in the Canadian provinces; a prescriptive study. [Toronto] University of Toronto Press [c1972] 178 p. Z484.P76
"Finding aids," p. [62]–82.

Other bibliographies and lists mainly covering the Atlantic provinces both retrospectively and currently are the following:

Atlantic provinces checklist; a guide to current information in books, pamphlets, government publications. v. 1–[9?] 1957–[65?] [Halifax, N.S.] Atlantic Provinces Economic Council. annual.   Z1392.M37A8

Bishop, Olga B. Publications of the governments of Nova Scotia, Prince Edward Island, New Brunswick, 1758–1952. Ottawa, National Library of Canada, 1957. 237 p.   Z1373.5.A1B5

Tremaine, Marie. A bibliography of Canadian imprints 1751–1800. Toronto, University of Toronto Press, 1952. xxvii, 705 p.   Z1365.T7
    Includes early official publications of the provinces of Ontario, Quebec (Upper and Lower Canada), New Brunswick, Nova Scotia, Prince Edward Island, in chronological order.

Following are current and retrospective bibliographies and lists published by governments of individual Canadian provinces:

ALBERTA

Catalogue of Alberta government publications. v. 1, no. 1+ 1954+ Edmonton, Queen's Printer.   DLC
        Cover title, Catalogue, Acts, Regulations and Publications of the Government of the Province of Alberta.

BRITISH COLUMBIA

British Columbia government publications. Monthly checklist. v. 1, no. 1+ Jan. 1970+ Victoria, Provincial Library.   DLC
        "The Monthly Checklist includes all British Columbia government publications received by the Provincial Library. Its aim is to provide a current bibliographical guide to Provincial Government publications rather than to be an order catalogue."
        In the 1940's a Price List of Government Publications and British Columbia Gazette Advertising Rates was occasionally issued by the Government Printing Bureau (Z1373.5.B8).

Holmes, Marjorie C. Publications of the government of British Columbia, 1871–1947. Being a complete revision and enlargement of Publications of the Government of British Columbia 1871–1937, by Sydney Weston. [Victoria ? 1950]   Z1373.5.B8H6
        Includes a supplement to Marjorie C. Holmes' Royal Commissions and Commissions of Inquiry (see next entry).

——— Royal commissions and commissions of inquiry under the "Public Inquiries Act" in British Columbia, 1872–1942; a checklist. [Victoria, Printed by C. F. Banfield, 1945] 68 p.   Z1373.5.H6
        "Includes all documents that are known to exist up to date, either in print or in manuscript." Printed for the Provincial Library. A supplement was included in Marjorie C. Holmes' Publications of the Government of British Columbia, 1871–1947 (see preceding entry).

Weston, Sydney M. Publications of the government of British Columbia, 1871–1937; a checklist. Victoria, Printed by C. F. Banfield, Printer to the King, 1939. 167 p.
Z1373.5.B8W5

MANITOBA

Manitoba. *Legislative Assembly. Library.* A checklist of publications of the Government of Manitoba received in the Legislative Library. 1st+ 1970+ Winnipeg. 3 no. a year. Z1373.5.M3A27

Morley, Marjorie. A bibliography of Manitoba, selected from holdings in the Legislative Library of Manitoba. [Winnipeg] 1948. 16 l. Z1392.M35M67
Official publications listed relate mainly to the period 1938–48.

NEW BRUNSWICK

New Brunswick. Legislative Library. *Fredericton.* New Brunswick government documents; a checklist of government documents received at the Legislative Library. no. 1+ 1955+ Fredericton, 1956+ annual. Z1373.5.N4N4

For New Brunswick statutes, the following indexes should be mentioned:

New Brunswick. *Laws, statutes, etc. (Indexes)* General index to statutes of New Brunswick from 1854 to 1st July 1867; with supplementary index to statutes for 1868. Ottawa, Printed by Hunter, Rose & Company, 1869. 55 p. DLC LL

—— A general index to the statutes of New Brunswick, now in force, other than those contained in the Consolidated Statutes, being chiefly local and private acts, with a table of acts which, since 1854, have expired or become obsolete or have been repealed otherwise than by chapter 120 of the Consolidated Statutes. By George W. Burbidge. Fredericton, 1878. 112 p. DLC LL

—— An index to the statutes of New Brunswick passed during the years 1917–1921, consisting of two parts. Part I. A tabulation of the changes effected in the Consolidated Statutes, 1903, and the acts relating thereto. Part II. A general index to the statutes, both public and private; being a continuation of the index to the statutes of New Brunswick prepared in 1916 by George Bidlake, Esq., under the authority of the attorney general. Fredericton, Printed by R. W. L. Tibbits, Printer to the King, 1922. 15, 35 p. DLC LL

—— New Brunswick alphabetical index of all the acts passed by the General Assembly from the time of the Consolidated Statutes [1877] down to and including the year 1890. By C. A. Steeves. Toronto, Carswell & Co., 1891. 127 p. DLC LL

NEWFOUNDLAND

No checklist of official publications issued.

Nova Scotia

Nova Scotia. Legislative Library, *Halifax*. A finding list of Royal Commissions appointed by the Province of Nova Scotia, 1877–1965. Halifax, 1965. 9 1.   DLC
    A revised and enlarged edition of a 1956 list, covering the period 1908–54 (Halifax, 1956 5 1.)

—— Publications of the Province of Nova Scotia; a checklist. 1967+ Halifax. annual.
                                                                        DLC
    Publications are listed by agency. An author index is included.

Ontario

Currently Ontario government documents are listed in the following two publications:

Ontario. Government publications check list. v. 1, no. 1+ May 1971+ Toronto, Queen's Printer and Publisher. monthly.   DLC
    Annual cumulation published from 1972+ (Z1373.5.O7O55) .

Ontario, *Dept. of Tourism and Information*. Directory and guide to services of Ontario Government. Toronto, 1948?+   JL270.A3
    "Presents the publications prepared and distributed by the various departments, which are available upon request."

The earliest period of the present Province of Ontario is covered by Marie Tremaine's *A Bibliography of Canadian Imprints, 1751–1800* (Toronto, University of Toronto Press, 1952) and the period 1841–67 by Olga B. Bishop's *Publications of the Government of the Province of Canada* (Ottawa, National Library of Canada, 1963). Legislative documents for earlier periods and documentation published after 1900 are covered by the following bibliographies and indexes:

Bligh, Harris H. The Ontario law index, embracing all the legislation of the province of Ontario, down to and including the year 1895. Toronto, The Carswell Co., 1895. 268 p.   DLC LL
—— Supplement to the Ontario law index (1867–1895) embracing all the legislation of the province of Ontario from 1896 to 1900. Toronto, The Carswell Co., 1900. 104 p.   DLC LL

MacTaggart, Hazel I. Publications of the government of Ontario, 1901–1955; a checklist compiled for the Ontario Library Association. Toronto, Printed and distributed by the University of Toronto Press for the Queen's Printer, 1964. 303 p.
                                                       Z1373.5.O7M3

Ontario. *Legislative Assembly*. General index to the journals and sessional papers, together with an index to debates and speeches, and list to appendices to the journals. Toronto, 1888–1927. 6 v.   J108.M2
    Vol. 1–5 compiled by Arthur H. Sydere; v. 6, by Alex C. Lewis.

Ontario. *Parliament. House of Assembly*. Journal of the House of Assembly of Upper Canada. [1825–1840] Toronto.   J101.K3
    The index volume title: *General Index to the Journals of the House of Assem-*

bly of the Late Province of Upper Canada; Commencing with the First Session of the Ninth Provincial Parliament (1825) and Ending with the Fifth Session of the Thirteenth Parliament (1839–40), (Being the Last Session before the Union of the Canadas). By Alfred Todd, Clerk of Committees. Printed by order of Legislative Assembly. Montreal, Lovell & Gibson, 1848. 585 p.   J101.K3 Index

PRINCE EDWARD ISLAND

Prince Edward Island. *Laws, statutes, etc. (Indexes)* General index to the statutes of Prince Edward Island, public and private, passed during the years 1869–1918 (both included). Prepared under the authority of the attorney-general by A. D. Fraser. Charlottetown, Printed by F. L. Dillon, 1918. 116 p.   DLC LL

—— Index to the statutes of Prince Edward Island, in force in the year 1845. Together with a table of acts repealed, executed, &c., which remain in print. Compiled by William Cundall. Printed by order of the legislature of P. E. Island. Charlottetown, Printed by J. D. Haszard, Printer to the Queen, 1845. 96 p.
DLC LL

QUEBEC

Bibliographie du Québec. avril 1969+ [Montréal] Bibliothèque nationale du Québec. quarterly.   Z1392.Q3B5
   In two parts, part two being a list of official publications. Includes an alphabetical index which is cumulated annually and every three years. A special issue, covering 1968, as well as a cumulative index 1968–69, were published in 1970.

Current publications of the government of Quebec are also listed in sales catalogs published occasionally by the Office d'information et de la publicité and the Bureau de l'éditeur officiel du Quebec *(Publications en vente au Bureau de l'éditeur officiel.* Z1373.5.Q4Q44)

Retrospective bibliographies and indexes of Quebec official publications are the following:

Beaulieu, André, Jean-Charles Bonenfant, *and* Jean Hamelin.   Répertoire des publications gouvernementales du Québec de 1867 a 1964. Québec, Imprimeur de la reine, 1968. 554 p.   Z1373.5.Q4B4
—— —— Supplément, 1965–1968 [par] André Beaulieu, Jean-Charles Bonenfant [et] Gaston Bernier. Québec Editeur officiel du Québec 1970. 388 p.
Z1373.5.Q4B4 Suppl.
   Annotated list of publications of the legislative branch and of the 19 executive departments existing in 1965, giving a short history of each department (ministère).

Quebec *(Province). Legislature. Legislative Assembly.* Journals of the Legislative Assembly. v. 1–76, Dec. 27th, 1867-May 17, 1941. Quebec, 1868–1941. 77 v.
J107.K3
   "General index to the journals of the Legislative Assembly of the province of Quebec in the 1st to 6th legislatures, 1867–1887, by Paul Ernest Smith." 1 v. (J107.K3 Index)
   From the 77th volume, the journals are bilingual. Indexes are included in each volume.

—— Journaux de l'Assemblée législative, v. [1]–76, 27.déc. 1867–17.mai 1941. Québec.
1868–1941. 77 v.   J107.K33
   "Index général des Journaux de l'Assemblée législative de la province de
Québec . . . depuis la session 1867–68 à la 2 ème session de 1890 . . . par Louis
Fortier." (J107.K3 Index)

SASKATCHEWAN

MacDonald, Christine. Publications of the governments of the North-west Territories, 1876–1905, and of the Province of Saskatchewan, 1905–1952. Regina, Legislative Library, 1952. 109 p.   Z1373.5.N6M32
   Omits "maps, posters, items relating to office routine, office consolidations of
acts, and acts printed separately unless accompanied by regulations and similar
data, and items put out by crown corporations of purely commercial nature."
   A mimeographed preliminary checklist for 1877–1947 was issued in 1948.
(Z1373.5.N6M3)

CARIBBEAN AREA

The concept of the Caribbean area, as used here, will be limited mainly
to the six independent island countries and the Federation of the West
Indies, as it existed between 1958 and 1962.[1] A survey of the former area
of the West Indies Federation reveals that after the secession of Jamaica
and Trinidad and Tobago in 1962, six of the remaining member states
(Antigua, Dominica, Grenada, St. Kitts-Nevis-Anguilla, St. Lucia, and
St. Vincent) received in 1967 the status of "Associated State of the United
Kingdom," under which each island state has complete self-government,
with Great Britain retaining the responsibility for foreign affairs and
defense. The status of the other member, the island state of Montserrat,
was not settled at that time.

   Other dependent island territories of the area are treated along with
countries of which they form a part: Puerto Rico and the Virgin Islands,
as outlying territories of the United States; Guadeloupe and Martinique,
as départements of France; Netherlands Antilles (Curaçao, Aruba, Bo-
naire, St. Eustatius, Saba, and St. Marteen), as autonomous parts of the
Netherlands.

GENERAL BIBLIOGRAPHIES

Current Caribbean bibliography. v. 1+ June 1951+ [Hato Rey, Puerto Rico, Caribbean Regional Library] irregular.   Z1595.C8

   [1] The Association of Caribbean University and Research Institute Libraries (ACURIL),
the professional library group for the area, founded in 1969, includes not only the
island countries and dependent territories but also continental members from countries bordering the Caribbean Sea (United States, Mexico, Central America, etc.) .

Published originally by the Central Secretariat of the Caribbean Commission, later Caribbean Organization. From 1965, published by the Caribbean Economic Development Corporation, Caribbean Regional Library. It includes official publications of countries of the Caribbean area. V. 4: French Caribbean Departments; v. 5; British West Indies; v. 6: Netherlands Antilles and Surinam. A monthly supplement is published beginning with January 1969.

Handbook of Latin American studies. no. [1]+ 1935+ Gainesville, University of Florida Press. annual.											Z1605.H23
Includes selected official publications of several Caribbean countries. These can be identified through the author indexes in individual volumes and the *Author Index* to volumes 1–28 (1936–66).

Technical co-operation; a monthly bibliography. v. 1+ Jan. 1964+ [London] monthly.
											Z2021.C7A35
———— Supplement. 1964+ [London]						Z2021.C7A35 Suppl.
Issued in 1964 by the Dept. of Technical Co-operation Library; 1964–70, by the Ministry of Overseas Development Library; from 1971 by the Overseas Development Administration Library. It covers official publications of former and present British possessions in the Caribbean area.

For retrospective documentation, the following bibliographies will be of assistance to students of the Caribbean area:

Baker, Edward C.   A guide to records in the Leeward Islands. Oxford, Published for the University of the West Indies by B. Blackwell, 1965. 102 p.   CD3985.L4B3
"This guide . . . outlines the history and scope of the records of the Leeward Islands (administrative, legal, ecclesiastical, commercial and private material); also includes hitherto unpublished lists of records concerned with the Leeward Islands in the United Kingdom and the United States of America."

———— A guide to records in the Windward Islands. Oxford, published for the University of the West Indies by B. Blackwell, 1968. 95 p.   CD3985.W5B3
A record of manuscripts, official documents, newspapers, etc., for the islands of Grenada, St. Lucia, St. Vincent, and Dominica. Includes an index.

Bishop, Crawford M., *and* Anyda Marchant.   A guide to the law and legal literature of Cuba, the Dominican Republic and Haiti. Washington, Library of Congress, 1944. 276 p. ([U.S.] Library of Congress. Latin American series, no. 3)   DLC LL

Childs, James B.   The memorias of the republics of Central America and of the Antilles. Washington, U.S. Govt. Print. Off., 1932. 170 p.   Z881.U5
Issued by the Library of Congress. It includes, besides documents of the former Central American federations and six Central American republics, the memorias of Cuba, Dominican Republic, and Haiti.

Ragatz, Lowell J. *comp.*   A check-list of House of Commons sessional papers relating to the British West Indies and to the West Indian slave trade and slavery, 1763–1834. London, The Bryan Edwards Press [1928] 32 p.   Z1502.B5R2   1928

———— A check-list of House of Lords sessional papers relating to the British West Indies and to the West Indian slave trade and slavery, 1763–1834. London, The Bryan Edwards Press [1932] 13 p.   Z1502.B5R21   1932

———— A guide for the study of British Caribbean history, 1763–1834, including the abolition and emancipation movements. New York, Da Capo Press, 1970. 725 p.
											Z1502.B5R22 1970
A reprint of the first edition, published in 1932 by the U.S. Government

Printing Office. Parts I–V list bibliographies, catalogs, indexes, manuscripts, official documents, and legislative materials.

U.S. *Dept. of State. Library Division.* Point four, Latin America and European dependencies in the Western Hemisphere; a selected bibliography of studies on economically underdeveloped countries. Washington, 1950. 110 p. (*Its* Bibliography no. 55) Z7165.S75U52 1950

U.S. *Library of Congress.* A guide to the official publications of the other American republics. Washington [1945–49] 19 v. (*Its* Latin American series)   Z1605.U64
Vol. 7, Cuba; v. 8, Dominican Republic; v. 12, Haiti.

U.S. *Library of Congress. Division of Bibliography.* British possessions in the Caribbean area: a selected list of references. Compiled by Ann Duncan Brown. Washington, 1943. 192 p.   Z1502.B5U6

The individual countries are listed below.

BARBADOS

Formerly under British rule; independence: 1966.

Barbados. *Dept. of Archives.* List of printed accessions, 1964–1967. [Bridgetown] 1968. 74 p.   CD3985.B3A45
Includes a list of official publications.

Chandler, Michael J. A guide to records in Barbados. Oxford, Published for the University of the West Indies by Basil Blackwell, 1965. 204 p.   CD3985.B3C5
Lists official, semi-official, and private records (published or in manuscript). Some of the material is available on microfilm. A short history of agencies and institutions is outlined.

Gt. Brit. *Colonial Office.* Annual report on Barbados. [1947–62/63?] London, H. M. Stationery Office. (*Its* Colonial annual reports)   F2041.A33
Previously issued in the numbered series, *Colonial Reports-Annual,* which was suspended in 1940 (JV33.G7A4). Includes lists of official publications in its "reading list."
For the years 1919/20–1946/47, the *Barbados Blue Book* (J137.R2) also included a list of official publications.

Pan American Institute of Geography and History. *Commission on History.* Barbados; guía de los documentos microfotografiados por la Unidad Móvil de Microfilm de la UNESCO. México, 1965. 141 p. (*Its* [Publicación] 113. Fuentes documentales para la historia de América, Guías 2) Instituto Panamericano de Geografía e Historia. Publicación no. 270   F1401.P153 no. 270
Detailed record of filmed Blue Books, minutes of the Council, official gazettes, etc.

Sevillano Colom, Francisco. List of microfilmed materials at the Barbados Public Library. Barbados, 1960. 23 l.   Z1502.B35S4

Shilstone, E. M. A descriptive list of maps of Barbados. Journal of the Barbados Museum and Historical Society, Bridgetown, v. 5, Feb. 1938: 57–84   F2401.B217
A chronological list of maps, 1657–1936.

CUBA

Formerly under Spanish rule; independence: 1898.

Anuario bibliográfico cubano; bibliografía cubana. v. [1] –30, 1937–1966. Gainesville, Fla.   Z1511.A65
   Volumes for 1937–59 published in Havana; the last (30th), in Coral Gables, Fla., by its editor from 1937, Fermín Peraza Sarausa. Volumes for 1937–52 have no numbering but constitute v. 1–6, and volumes for 1937–48 were issued without subtitle.

———— Complementos. 1937/61. Gainesville, University of Florida Libraries. 1966.   Z1511.A652
   First volume is a cumulation of addenda originally issued in v. 2–23 of the main work, plus additional entries for the years 1960–61, covered in v. 24–25. Arranged by author (pt. A) and subject (pt. B) up to v. 25, then by author only in alphabetical order. Includes official publications. Superseded in 1967 by *Revolutionary Cuba; a Bibliographical Guide.* (See below)

Bibliografía cubana. 1959/62+ La Habana, Consejo Nacional de Cultura.   Z1511.B5
   Volumes for 1959/62–1963/64 issued by the Departamento Colección Cubana of the Biblioteca Nacional "José Marti"; 1965+ by the Library. Includes official publications.

Mesa, Rosa Q. Cuba. Ann Arbor, University Microfilms, 1969. xvi, 207 p. (Latin American serial documents, v. 3)   Z6954.C9M45
   Compiled at the University of Florida Libraries, in cooperation with several other university libraries, the New York Public Library, and the Library of Congress. It includes official serial titles of Cuba, published since the date of national independence, held in major libraries in the United States and Canada.

Revolutionary Cuba; a bibliographical guide. 1966+ Coral Gables, Fla., University of Miami Press. annual. (Research Institute for Cuba and the Caribbean, University of Miami. Research study series.)   Z1511.A653
   Supersedes *Anuario bibliográfico cubano.*

Trelles y Govín, Carlos M. Bibliografía cubana de los siglos xvii y xviii. 2.ed. Habana, Impr. del Ejército, 1927. xix, 463 p.   Z1511.T85   1927

———— Bibliografía cubana del siglo xix. Matanzas, Imp. de Quirós y Estrada, 1911–15. 8 v.   Z1511.T86

———— Bibliografía cubana del siglo xx. Matanzas, Impr. de la vda. de Quirós y Estrada, 1916–17. 2 v.   Z1511.T87

U.S. *National Archives.* Records of the Bureau of Insular Affairs, relating to the United States military government of Cuba, 1898–1902, and the United States provisional government of Cuba, 1906–1909; a list of selected files. Comp. by Kenneth Munden. Washington, 1943. 43 p. (*Its* Special list no. 3)   CD3028.C9U65

U.S. *Treaties, etc., 1933–1945 (Franklin D. Roosevelt)* Exchange of official publications. Agreement between the United States of America and Cuba. [May 1938] Washington, U.S. Govt. Print. Off., 1938. 14 p. ([U.S. Dept. of State. Publication 1206] Executive agreement series 123)   JX236 1929 no. 123
                                                                         Z690.U6155
   Includes a list of official publications of Cuba.

DOMINICAN REPUBLIC

Formerly under Spanish and French rule; independence: 1821 (1844);
occupied by Haiti, 1822–44; occupied by United States, 1916–24.

There is no current bibliography of official publications. Between
1945 and 1950 an attempt was made to list at least some official documents in *Anuario bibliográfico dominicano* (Ciudad Trujillo, 1946+
Z1533.A58), which superseded the *Boletín bibliográfico dominicano*
(Ciudad Trujillo, 1945. Z1533.B6).

In addition to general bibliographies listed earlier, the following
sources may be of assistance to researchers:

Florén Lozano, Luis. Bibliografía de la bibliografía dominicana. Ciudad Trujillo,
    Roques Román, 1948. 66 p.   Z1531.F57

Hitt, Deborah S., *and* Larman C. Wilson. A selected bibliography of the Dominican
    Republic: a century after the restoration of independence. Washington, American
    University, Center for Research in Social Systems, 1968. 142 p.   Z1536.H56
    An annotated bibliography of books, articles, and official documents.

U.S. *Treaties, etc., 1933–1945* (*Franklin D. Roosevelt*) Exchange of official publications.
    Agreement between the United States of America and the Dominican Republic.
    [Dec. 1942] Washington, U.S. Govt. Print. Off., 1943. 10 p. ([U.S. Dept. of State.
    Publication 1906] Executive agreement series 297)   JX236 1929 no. 297
                                                                      Z690.U7D6
    Includes a list of official publications of the Dominican Republic.

HAITI

Under French rule from 1677; independence: 1804; occupied by United
States, 1915–34.

No current bibliography or list of official publications issued. A considerable number of official documents are listed in:

Bissainthe, Max. Dictionnaire de bibliographie haïtienne. Washington, Scarecrow
    Press, 1951. 1052 p.   Z1531.B5
    Official publications mainly under corporate entry "Haiti."

Duvivier, Ulrick. Bibliographie générale et méthodique d'Haiti. Port au Prince,
    Imprimerie de l'État, 1941. 2 v.   Z1531.D88
    Arranged by broad subject headings, it includes official, mainly legislative
    documents.

U.S. *Treaties, etc., 1933–1945* (*Franklin D. Roosevelt*) Exchange of official publications.
    Agreement between the United States of America and Haiti. [June 1941] Washing-
    ton, U.S. Govt. Print. Off., 1941. 7 p. ([U.S. Dept. of State. Publication 1666]
    Executive agreement series 210)   JX236 1929 no. 210
                                                                      Z690.U7H25
    Includes a list of official publications of Haiti.

JAMAICA

Under Spanish rule until 1655, then British rule; independence: 1962.

Government publications on sale at the Government printing office. Kingston. Revised
to 30th September 1964. Kingston, the Government Printer, 1964. 16 p.   DLC

Gt. Brit. *Colonial Office.* Report on Jamaica. 1946–[61] London, H. M. Stationery
Office. annual.   F1861.G7
    Previously issued in the numbered series, *Colonial Reports-Annual,* which
was suspended in 1940 (No. 1–1936, 1891–1940. JV33.G7A4). Title varies: 1946–
48, *Annual Report on Jamaica.* Includes a list of selected official publications
in its bibliography.

Handbook of Jamaica. 1881+ Kingston.   F1861.H23
    The Handbook lists since 1948, "Government publications, on sale at the
Government Printing Office" in the chapter "Literature, Art, etc." It includes
current as well as retrospective publications.

Institute of Jamaica, *Kingston. West India Reference Library.* Jamaican accessions.
1964+ Kingston. annual.   Z1549.I5
    Official publications entered mostly under corporate entries.

Jamaica. Blue book. Kingston, Government Printing Office. annual.   J138.R2
    From 1920, it has included a more or less complete list of official publications.

Jamaica. *Laws, statutes, etc. (Indexes)* An index to the laws of Jamaica in force on
the 30th day of June 1953. The rev. ed. (1953) and supplement thereto, by D. O.
Swane with the assistance of H. H. Dunn, K. C. Henry, and H. C. Stedman.
[London?] Printed by Eyre and Spottiswoode, H. M. Printers, 1957. 469 p.
                                                              DLC LL

Jamaica Library Service. Jamaica: a select bibliography, 1900–1963. [Kingston?]
Jamaica Independence Festival Committee, 1963. 115 p.   Z1541.J35
    Under broad subject headings, it includes a substantial number of official
documents.

TRINIDAD AND TOBAGO

Under British rule from 1802; independence: 1962.

The "List of publications obtainable from the Government Printer,
Trinidad and Tobago" is published occasionally in the *Trinidad and
Tobago Gazette.* It includes both current and retrospective publications.
There are no retrospective bibliographies which cover only official publications. The *Current Caribbean Bibliography* presents a fairly representative selection from 1951. Other sources which include official
publications are the following:

Dow, Henry. *comp.* Bibliography of Trinidad and Tobago. Trinidad and Tobago
Yearbook, 1956: 533–549.   F2121.T833 1956

Franklin, C. B. Bibliography of Trinidad and Tobago. Trinidad and Tobago Yearbook, 1923: Appendix.   F2121.T833 1923

Gt. Brit. *Colonial Office.* Annual report on Trinidad and Tobago. 1946–[57?] London, H. M. Stationery Off. (*Its* Colonial annual reports)   F2121.G8
  Includes a list of official publications in its "reading list." Previously issued in the numbered series of *Colonial Reports-Annual* which was suspended in 1940 (JV33.G7A4).

Trinidad and Tobago. Blue book. Port Spain.   F2121.T7
  From 1920, it included a section listing government publications.

WEST INDIES FEDERATION (1958–62)

Established in January 1958, the Federation was dissolved in February 1962, after Jamaica and Trinidad and Tobago withdrew and opted for independence. The original members of the Federation were Antigua, Barbados, Dominica, Grenada, Jamaica, Montserrat, St. Kitts (St. Christopher)-Nevis-Anguilla, St. Lucia, St. Vincent, and Trinidad and Tobago.

The *Current Caribbean Bibliography* (v. 5, Z1595.C8) lists official publications of the Federation. A substantial number of official publications issued by the various organs of the Federation and documents issued by the British government and governments of member states concerning the Federation are listed in bibliographies included in the following two works:

Hoyos, F. A. The rise of West Indian democracy; the life & times of Sir Grantley Adams. [n.p.] Printed by Advocate Press, 1963. 228 p.   F2041.A65H6
  Bibliography: p. i–iv.

Mordecai, *Sir* John. Federation of the West Indies. Evanston, Northwestern University Press, 1968. 484 p.   F2134.M6 1968
  Official documents are listed in section A, "official sources," of its bibliography, p. [470]–476.

CENTRAL AND SOUTH AMERICA

Attempts at comprehensive bibliographic control of official documents of Latin American countries date from the 1930's. Previously, only in rare instances were official publications of several countries compiled in a single bibliography. In the late 1940's the first systematic record of official publications of all Latin American republics was compiled and published by the Library of Congress in the series *A Guide to the Official Publications of the Other American Republics* (Washington, 1945–49. Z1605.U64). The Seminar on the Acquisition of Latin American Library Materials (SALALM), founded in June 1956 and continuing to date, has sponsored numerous bibliographical studies of Latin American government publications and documents of inter-American organizations. The "Report on Bibliographic Activities," published annually as a working paper in the *Final Report and Working Papers* of SALALM meetings, includes titles on government documents recently published and on works in progress. A short documented survey of developments in Latin American government document bibliography was made in an article by J. B. Childs, "Forty Years of Latin American Document Bibliography," published in the *Herald of Library Science* v. 7, April 1968: 71–78.

In 1961 the University of Florida Libraries, Gainesville, Fla., with the support of SALALM, initiated a project of compiling the holdings of Latin American official publications in major repositories in the United States and Canada. The first volume of a projected 19-volume series of this union list, entitled *Latin American Serial Documents; a Holdings List,* was published in 1968. Edited by Rosa Quintero Mesa, the following volumes have been published to date: 1. Colombia (1968), 2. Brazil (1968), 3. Cuba (1969), 4. Mexico (1970), 5. Argentina (1971), 6. Bolivia (1972), 7. Chile (1973), 8. Ecuador (1973), 9. (Paraguay (1973), 10. (Peru). (1973).

Following are bibliographies listing official documents for all or for several countries and general bibliographies listing a considerable number of official documents of Latin American countries:

Bibliografías corrientes de la América Latina. [1962+] Medellín, Colombia, Ediciones Anuario Bibliográfico Cubano. (Biblioteca del bibliotecario)   Z1601.A2B5
    Latest edition, 1969, published in Coral Gables, Fla., was compiled by Dr. Fermín Peraza Sarausa.

Childs, James B. Latin American treaty collections. Inter-American bibliographical review, v. 3, 1943: 197–205   Z1008.I583
    Lists treaty collections and existing catalogs or lists of treaties for individual countries. It also indicates where treaties were first published.

——— The memorias of the republics of Central America and of the Antilles. Washington, U.S. Govt. Print. Off., 1932. 170 p.   Z881.U5
    Issued by the Library of Congress. It includes the Central American Federations (1821–38), Costa Rica, El Salvador, Guatemala, Honduras, Nicaragua, Panama, Cuba, Dominican Republic, Haiti.

Dillon, Dorothy R. Latin America, 1935–1949; a selected bibliography. New York, United Nations, 1952. 1 v. (United Nations. Library. Bibliographical series, no. 2)
                                           Z1601.D5
    "The publications listed are all of the past ten or fifteen years, except for some older works included for comparative purposes or for want of more recent available works. Books, pamphlets, periodicals and official publications of the governments of the Latin American countries are included."

Gropp, Arthur E. A bibliography of Latin American bibliographies. Metuchen, N.J., Scarecrow Press, 1968. 515 p.   Z1601.A2G76
    Arranged by broad subjects. It includes a section on government publication bibliographies (p. 224–228). Other references to bibliographies of official docu-

ments are listed under various subjects. Brings up to date the 1942 edition compiled by Cecil K. Jones and published by the Library of Congress. A supplement published in 1971. (277 p.)

Handbook of Latin American studies. no. [1]+ 1935+, Gainesville, University of Florida Press. annual.   Z1605.H23
    Includes selected official publications. These can be identified through author indexes to individual volumes and through the *Author Index* to volumes 1–28 (1936–66).

Harrison, John P.   Guide to materials on Latin America in the National Archives. Washington, General Services Administration, National Archives and Records Service, 1961+ (National Archives publication, no. 62–3)   CD3028.S7H3
    The first volume covers records of the Departments of State, Treasury, War, and Navy and the general records of the government. Volume two will cover records of the remaining departments and independent agencies, as well as legislative and judicial branches of the government.

Hill, Roscoe R.   The national archives of Latin America. Cambridge, Mass., Harvard University Press, 1945. xx, 169 p. (*Half-title*: Joint Committee on Latin American Studies of the National Research Council, American Council of Learned Societies, and Social Science Research Council. Miscellaneous publication no. 3)
                                                               CD3683 1945 .H5
    Lists publications of the national archives.
    Issued also in Spanish as *Los archivos nacionales de la América Latina* (Habana, 1945 [cover 1948] 166 p. Publicaciones del Archivo Nacional de Cuba, 19. CD3683.H557)

Inter-American Statistical Institute.   Bibliography of selected statistical sources of the American nations. Washington, 1947. xvi, 689 p.   Z7554.S75I4
    Annotations are given in English and the language of the particular publication (Spanish, Portuguese, or French). Quarterly supplements published in *Estadística*, the journal of the institute (HA1.E8) .

Pan American Institute of Geography and History. *Commission on History.*   Guía de los documentos microfotografiados por la Unidad Móvil de Microfilm de la UNESCO. México, 1963. xxv, 317 p. (*Its* [Publicación] 112. Guías, 2) Instituto Panamericano de Geografía e Historia. Publicación 225   F1401.P153 no. 225 1963
    The guide lists published and unpublished documents microfilmed by UNESCO in the archives and libraries of the following countries: Barbados, Dominican Republic, El Salvador, Honduras, Panama, Paraguay, and Peru.

Peraza Sarausa, Fermín.   Bibliografías sobre publicaciones oficiales de la América Latina. Gainesville, Fla., 1964. 25 l. (Biblioteca del bibliotecario, 70)
                                                             Z1609.G7P4 1964
    In three sections the bibliography lists: 1. bibliografías especiales, 2. bibliografías generales, 3. bibliografías nacionales de publicaciones oficiales.

Sable, Martin H.   A guide to Latin American studies. Los Angeles, Latin American Center, University of California, 1967. 2 v. (lxxv, 783 p.) (Reference series, no. 4)
                                                              Z1601.S25
    Contains approximately 5,000 annotations in English of text and reference books, government documents, and conference proceedings.

Schuster, Edward.   Guide to law and legal literature of Central American republics. New York, 1937. 153 p. (American Foreign Law Association. Bibliographies of Foreign Law Series, no. 11)   Z6458.A1A5
    Includes Costa Rica, El Salvador, Guatemala, Honduras, Nicaragua, Panama, as well as the Central American federations.

Seminar on the Acquisition of Latin American Library Materials. Final report and working papers. 1st+ 1956+ annual. Z688.L4S38
Volumes for 1962+ issued as *Reuniones bibliotecológicas* of the Columbus Memorial Library, Pan American Union (Z673.A1P3). Generally referred to as SALALM seminars.
An annual working paper provides information on developments concerning bibliographical activities, including official publications.

Statistical activities of the American nations, 1940; a compendium of the statistical services and activities in 22 nations of the western hemisphere, together with information concerning statistical personnel in these nations. Edited under the direction of the temporary organizing committee of the Inter-American Statistical Institute, by Elizabeth Phelps. Washington, Inter-American Statistical Institute, 1941. xxxi, 842 p. HA175.S75

U.S. *Dept. of State. Library Division.* Point four, Latin America and European dependencies in the Western Hemisphere; a selected bibliography of studies on economically underdeveloped countries. Washington, 1950. 110 p. (*Its* Bibliography no. 55) Z7165.U52 1950

U.S. *Library of Congress.* A guide to the official publications of the other American republics. Washington [1945–49] 19 v. (*Its* Latin American series, no. 9–11, 15, 17, 19, 22–25, 27, 29–31, 33–37) Z1605.U64
Contents: 1. Argentina, by James B. Childs (1944) — 2. Bolivia, by James B. Childs (1945) — 3. Brazil, by John de Noia (1948) — 4. Chile, by Otto Neuburger (1947) — 5. Colombia, by James B. Childs (1948) — 6. Costa Rica, by Henry V. Besso (1947) — 7. Cuba, by James B. Childs (1945) — 8. Dominican Republic, by John de Noia (1947) — 9. Ecuador, by John de Noia (1947) — 10. El Salvador, by John de Noia (1947) — 11. Guatemala, by Henry V. Besso (1947) — 12. Haiti, by Otto Neuburger (1947) — 13. Honduras, by Otto Neuburger (1947) — 14. Nicaragua, by John de Noia (1947) — 15. Panama, by John de Noia (1947) — 16. Paraguay, by James B. Childs (1947) — 17. Peru, by John de Noia (1948) — 18. Uruguay, by John de Noia and Glenda Crevenna (1948) — 19. Venezuela, by Otto Neuburger (1948).
No volume for Mexico was issued as part of this series since the Library of Congress published in 1940 *Mexican Government Publications*, by Annita M. Ker.

U.S. *Library of Congress. Census Library Project.* General censuses and vital statistics in the Americas. An annotated bibliography of the historical censuses and current vital statistics of the 21 American republics, the American sections of the British Commonwealth of Nations, the American colonies of Denmark, France and the Netherlands, and the American territories and possessions of the United States. Washington, U.S. Govt. Print. Off., 1943. 151 p. Z7553.C3U45

U.S. *Library of Congress. Hispanic Law Division.* Index to Latin American legislation, 1950–1960. Boston, G. K. Hall [1961] 2 v. (1474 p.) DLC LL
——— ——— First supplement, 1961–1965. Boston, G. K. Hall, 1970. 2 v. DLC LL
Covers laws, decrees, regulations, and administrative rulings of the Latin American republics.

Villalón Galdames, Alberto. Bibliografía jurídica de América Latina, 1810–1965. [Santiago de Chile] Editorial Jurídica de Chile, 1969+ DLC LL
——— ——— Indices provisorios del tomo 1+ [Santiago de Chile] Editorial Jurídica de Chile, 1969+ DLC LL
"This legal bibliography of Latin America lists 17,000 publications issued from 1810 up to 1965, including important legal texts, collections of jurisprudence, treaties, periodical publications, monographs, acts and agreements of national and international conferences, etc. The first four volumes comprise the

bibliography and the fifth volume contains the indexes, list of abbreviations, and list of publishers and printers." [2]

Zimmerman, Irene. Current national bibliographies of Latin America; a state of the art study. [Gainesville, Fla.] Center for Latin American Studies, University of Florida, 1971. 139 p. (A Center for Latin American Studies Publication)
Z1602.5.Z55
Describes Latin American bibliographies in general and bibliographic tools for government publications wherever available. (See Index: "Official government publications")

—— A guide to current Latin American periodicals; humanities and social sciences. [1st ed.] Gainesville, Fla., Kallman Pub. Co., 1961. 357 p.   Z6954.S8Z5
Includes official periodicals. Arranged by countries and by subjects.

INDIVIDUAL COUNTRIES

As previously noted, very few Latin American countries currently issue special bibliographies or checklists of their official publications. In several countries, national bibliographies include selected government documents. Partial bibliographies or lists covering publications of individual agencies or special fields (statistics, etc.) will be cited more as an example, than as a rule. For retrospective coverage, the *Guide to the Official Publications of the Other American Republics* (U.S. Library of Congress) still remains the basic tool. The *Guide* and the other general bibliographies listed in the preceding chapter will not be cited under individual countries to which their coverage may extend. As before, bibliographic tools covering current publications will be listed first.

ARGENTINE REPUBLIC
Independence: 1816.

There is no current coverage of official publications. The *Boletín bibliográfico nacional,* published irregularly since 1937 (issue no. 33, covering years 1955–56, published in 1963), included some official publications (Z1615.B69). A new bibliographic journal *Los libros,* published since July 1969, occasionally mentions official or semiofficial publications.

Other bibliographies which shed some light on special fields of official documentation are:

Argentine Republic. *Comisión Nacional de Energía Atómica.* Lista de informes publicados por la Comisión Nacional de Energía Atómica. Buenos Aires, 1967. [10] p.
Z5160.A7

Argentine Republic. *Consejo Federal de Inversiones.* Catálogo de publicaciones, 1959–1966. Buenos Aires, 1966. 245 p.   Z7165.A7A45

———
[2] *Unesco Bulletin for Libraries,* 25 (March/April 1971): 102–103.

Argentine Republic. *Dirección General de Navegación e Hidrografía.* Catálogo de cartas, libros y otras publicaciones de ayuda a la navegación. Buenos Aires.

Z6027.A6A48

Before 1941 the catalog was published by the Servicio Hidrográfico of the Ministerio de Marina under the title *Catálogo de cartas y libros para navegación* (Z6026.H9A7).

Argentine Republic. *Dirección Nacional de Geología y Minería.* Catálogo de publicaciones de la Dirección Nacional de Geología y Minería, incluyendo los informes inéditos. Ordenado y clasificado por Antonio Amato. Buenos Aires, 1960. 113 p.

Z6034.A7A5

Clagett, Helen L. A guide to the law and legal literature of Argentina, 1917–1946. Washington, 1948. 180 p. ([U.S.] Library of Congress. Latin American series, no. 32)

DLC LL
Z6458.A8C5

Instituto Torcuato di Tella. *Centro de Investigaciones económicas.* Catálogo de estadísticas publicadas en la República Argentina [por] Lelia I. Boeri. 2. ed. [Buenos Aires] Editorial del Instituto [1966] 2 v. (824 p.) *(Its* Serie ocre: Economía)

Mesa, Rosa Q. Argentina. New York, R. R. Bowker, 1971. xxxii, 693 p. (Latin American serial documents, v. 5)   Z1619.M47

Compiled at the University of Florida Libraries in cooperation with several other university libraries, the New York Public Library, and the Library of Congress. It includes official serial titles of Argentine Republic held in major U.S. and Canadian libraries.

Turco Greco, Carlos A. Catálogo cartográfico de la República Argentina. Consejo Nacional de Investigaciones Científicas y Técnicas. [Buenos Aires] Editorial Universitaria de Buenos Aires [1967] 262 l. (Biblioteca de América. Documentos)

Z6027.A6T9

U.S. *Treaties, etc., 1933–1945 (Franklin D. Roosevelt)* Exchange of official publications. Agreement between the United States of America and Argentina. [Oct. 1939] Washington, U.S. Govt. Print. Off., 1940. 19 p. ([U.S. Dept. of State. Publication 1427] Executive agreement series 162)   JX236 1929 no. 162
X690.U7A7

Includes a list of official publications of Argentina.

The following bibliographies include provincial official publications:

Figuerero, Manuel V. Bibliografía de la Imprenta del estado en Corrientes desde sus orígenes en 1826 hasta su desaparición en 1865. Buenos Aires, Impr. y casa editora "Coni," 1919. xxxiv, 323 p.   Z213.C82F4

Solá, Miguel. La imprenta en Salta, cien años de prensa (1824–1924) y bibliografía antigua de la imprenta salteña. Buenos Aires, Tall. gráf. Porter hnos., 1924. 131 p.

Z213.S17S6

The bibliography, which extends only to 1885/86, includes official publications of the province of Salta.

BOLIVIA

Independence: 1825.

No current bibliography of official documents published. A number of official publications are listed in the annual *Bibliografía boliviana,* issued since 1962 (Cochabamba, Amigos del Libro. Z1641.B5). Compiled by Werner Guttentag Tichauer, it includes official publications under personal or corporate authors.

For retrospective listing, the following works will be of assistance:

Bolivia, *Congreso. Biblioteca.* Catálogo. [La Paz] Bolivia, Impr. y lit. Boliviana, H. H. Heitman & Cia, 1915. 72 p.   Z907.L35

Bolivia. *Ministerio de Colonización y Agricultura. Sección de Estadística y Biblioteca.* Catálogo general de las publicaciones ingresadas durante el año de 1906–[8?] La Paz.   Z907.L2

Clagett, Helen L.   A guide to the law and legal literature of Bolivia. Washington, The Library of Congress, 1947. 110 p. ([U.S.] Library of Congress. Latin American series, no. 12)   DLC LL
                                                                    Z6458.B75C6

Mesa, Rosa Q.   Bolivia. New York, R. R. Bowker, 1972. xxxiii, 156 p. (Latin American serial documents, v. 6)   Z1649.M44
      Compiled at the University of Florida Libraries, in cooperation with several other university libraries, the New York Public Library, and the Library of Congress. It includes official serial titles of Bolivia held in major U.S. and Canadian libraries.

U.S. *Treaties, etc., 1933–1945 (Franklin D. Roosevelt)*   Exchange of official publications. Agreement between the United States of America and Bolivia. [Jan. 1942] Washington, U.S. Govt. Print. Off., 1942. 9 p. ([U.S. Dept. of State. Publication 1786] Executive agreement series, 242)   JX236 1929 no. 242
                                                                    Z690.U7B6
      Includes a list of official publications of Bolivia.

BRAZIL

Independent Empire, 1822; republic, 1889–.

Although there is no current bibliography of official documents, a considerable number are listed in several bibliographical publications. The Departamento de Imprensa Nacional has issued since 1942 an annual alphabetical-title list of all books, pamphlets, and periodical publications printed there. The *Bibliografia brasileira* and the *Boletim bibliográfico* of the Biblioteca Nacional also include official publications. Following are bibliographies and lists which cover more or less current official publications:

Bibliografia brasileira. 1938/39+, Rio de Janeiro, 1941+   Z1671.B5
      Published irregularly by the Instituto Nacional do Livro (Ministério da Educação e Cultura), it includes official publications under corporate entries. From 1956, published as a supplement to *Revista do livro* (PQ9500.R4), under the title "Bibliografia brasileira corrente." From 1963 to 1966 published as separate annual volumes.

Bibliografia brasileira mensal. [ano 1, no. 1–ano 5, no. 12, Nov. 1967–Dec. 1972. Rio de Janeiro]   Z1675.B5

A classified bibliography, published by the Instituto Nacional do Livro (MEC), continuing the *Bibliografia brasileira*. Includes official publications. Continued from Jan. 1973 by *Boletim bibliográfico da Biblioteca Nacional* (see below).

Brazil. *Departamento de Imprensa Nacional*. Mostra de livros. 1.+ 1941–42+ Rio de Janeiro. [annual]   Z1679.R582
  Lists publications printed by the Imprensa Nacional.

Rio de Janeiro. Biblioteca Nacional. Boletim bibliográfico da Biblioteca Nacional. Rio de Janeiro, 1918+ [quarterly]   Z907.R585B
  Arranged by subjects, it includes official publications which can be identified through the author index, under corporate entries. Not published 1922–30, 1932–37, 1939–44, 1946–50 and 1968–72. Resumed publication in 1973 (v. 18, no. 1).

Another bibliographical bulletin, published bimonthly by the Sindicato Nacional das Emprêsas Editoras de Livros e Publicações Culturais, entitled *BBB, Boletim bibliográfico brasileiro* (v. 1+ Nov. 1952/Feb. 1953+, Rio de Janeiro. Z1671.B6), includes selected official documents.

Bibliographies for particular agencies or certain fields are issued occasionally by various government institutions, covering both retrospective and current publications:

Brazil. *Congreso. Câmara dos Deputados. Biblioteca*. Boletim. Brasilia. [1952+] semiannual.   Z770.B7
  Publications of the Câmara dos Deputados are listed in the *Boletim* as follows: "Anais de Câmara dos Deputados," v. 12, Jan./Jun. 1963: 217–279; "Atas, Sinopse, Resenha legislativa," v. 12, Jul./Dez. 1963: p. 575–577; "Diários do Congresso e das Assembléias Constituintes," v. 13, Jan./Jun. 1964: p. 137–139; "Indices: Relação de oradores, Relação de assuntos, Súmula de discursos," v. 14, Jan./Abr. 1965; "Documentos parlamentares," v. 14, Set./Dez. 1965: p. 585–596 and v. 16, Set./Dez. 1967: p. 785; "Publicações avulsas," v. 15, Jan./Abr. 1966: p. 98–106, v. 15, Mai./Agô. 1966: p. 239–255, v. 16, Jan./Abr. 1967: p. 136–146, v. 16, Set./Dez. 1967: p. 784.
  The "Publicações avulsas" and other lists of documents are published periodically in the *Boletim*.

Brazil. *Conselho Nacional de Proteção aos Indios*. Catálogo geral das publicações de Comissão Rondon e do Conselho Nacional de Proteção aos Indios. Rio de Janeiro, 1950. 32 p. (*Its* Publicação, no. 96)   F2501.B792 no. 96

Brazil. *Departamento Administrativo do Serviço Público*. Catálogo de publicações do D. A. S. P. seguido de uma lista de títulos de obras editadas pelo D. A. S. P. de 1938 a 1946. Rio de Janeiro, 1947. 82 p.   Z1679.B83
  The catalog has been updated in later years. Publications of the D. A. S. P. also listed regularly in its *Revista do serviço público* (JL2445.A3).

Brazil. *Departamento de Imprensa Nacional*. 150 [i.e. Cento e cinqüenta] anos de tipografía oficial; seleção de cento e cinqüenta livros e periódicos impresos de 1808 a 1958, nas oficinas do Departamento de Imprensa Nacional. Rio de Janeiro, 1958. 1 v. (unpaged)   Z1679.B84

—— Relatorio. Rio de Janeiro.   Z232.B83B715
  Includes at the end of each volume for the years 1939–43 (?) a list of the Brazilian official publications printed by the Imprensa Nacional.

Brazil. *Directoria de Hidrografia e Navegação.* Catálogo de cartas náuticas e publicações: Brasil. Correto até 31 de dezembro de 1966. [Rio de Janeiro] 1966. 44 p.
                                                                                          Z6027.B82A5

Brazil. *Diretoria do Serviço Geografico do Exercito.* Catálogo das cartas e obras diversas. 2. ed. [Rio de Janeiro] Oficinas Gráficas da DSG, Ministério da Guerra, 1959.
45 p.   Z6027.B82A52 1959

Brazil. *Ministério da Educação e Cultura. Serviço de Documentação.* Catálogo das publicações do Serviço de Documentação, 1947–1965. Organizado pelos bibliotecários Xavier Placer, Edson Nery da Fonseca e José Alcides Pinto. [Rio de Janeiro] 1965. 156 p.   Z1679.B86

Brazil. *Ministério das Relações Exteriores. Serviço de Publicações.* Lista de publicações, 1826–1950. [Rio de Janeiro, 1950?] 67 p.   Z6465.B7A5

Brazil. *Ministério do Planejamento e Coordenação Geral.* Catálogo das publicações do MINIPLAN. Rio de Janeiro, 1968+   Z7164.E15B67

Mesa, Rosa Q. Brazil. Ann Arbor, Mich., University Microfilm, 1968. 2, 343, 12 p.
(Latin American serial documents, v. 2)   Z1679.M4
    Compiled at the University of Florida Libraries in cooperation with several other university libraries, the New York Public Library, and the Library of Congress. It includes official serial titles of Brazil, published from the date of national independence to Dec. 1966, held by major U.S. and Canadian libraries.

Revista do serviço público. ano 1+ Nov. 1937+ Rio de Janeiro.   JL2445.A3
    Lists official publications (national and state) received by the Departamento Administrativo do Serviço Público.

Richardson, Ivan L. Bibliografia brasileira de administração pública e assuntos correlatos. Rio de Janeiro, Fundação Getulio Vargas, Serviço de Publicações, 1964.
xxii, 840 p.   Z7165.B7R5
    Includes a considerable number of official documents on public administration, covering mainly the period 1940–61.

Rio de Janeiro. Biblioteca Nacional. Catálogo de exposição de historia do Brasil realizada pela Biblioteca nacional do Rio de Janeiro a 2 de dezembro de 1881. Rio de Janeiro, Typ. de G. Leuzinger & filhos, 1881. 2 v. (1612 p.)   Z1686.R6
——— ——— Suplemento. Rio de Janeiro, Typ. de G. Leuzinger & filhos, 1883.
p. 1613–1758; 98, 5 p.   Z1686.R6 Suppl.
    The sections "Historia administrativa" and "Historia constitucional" include principally the official publications of both the national and provincial governments.

Russo, Laura G. M. Entradas de entidades governamentais do Brasil. List of headings for Brazilian Government agencies. Submitted for the eighth Seminar on the Acquisition of Latin American Library Materials, University of Wisconsin, Madison, Wisconsin, July 11–13, 1963. Madison, Wis., 1963 39 p. (Working paper no. 9)
                                                                           Z688.L4S448 no. 9

U.S. *Treaties, etc., 1933–1945. (Franklin D. Roosevelt)* Exchange of official publications. Agreement between the United States of America and Brazil. [June 1940] Washington, U.S. Govt. Print. Off., 1940. 17 p. ([U.S. Dept. of State. Publication 1527] Executive agreement series 176)   JX236 1929 no. 176
                                                                                 Z690.U7B7
    Includes a list of Brazilian official publications. Amended in 1950 by exchange of notes (U.S. Dept. of State publication 4564. Series: U.S. *Dept. of State.* Treaties and other international acts series 2402. JX235.9.A32 no. 2402)

Valle Cabral, Alfredo. Annaes da Imprensa nacional do Rio de Janeiro de 1808 a 1822. Rio de Janeiro, Typographia nacional, 1881. lxv, 339 p.   Z232.R6V2
    1154 items arranged alphabetically by title under each year from the establishment of the Imprensa Nacional in 1808 to the year 1822, with an appendix containing items 1155–1251, which are works published from other printing offices in Rio de Janeiro during 1821 and 1822.
—— —— Suplemento, 1823–1831. Rio de Janeiro. 1954. 87 p.   Z232.R6V2
    Published originally in vol. 73 of the *Anais da Biblioteca Nacional* (Z1675.R58)

Official documents concerning the Northeast Region (Nordeste) are listed in *Bibliografia cartográfica do Nordeste* (Recife, 1965, 209 p.), *Bibliografia sôbre a SUDENE e o Nordeste* (Recife, 1969, 385 p.), and *Catálogo das publicações editadas pela SUDENE*. (Recife, 1969, 133 p. Z7165.B7A5), all issued by Brazil, Superintendencia do Desenvolvimento do Nordeste, Divisão de Documentação.

The following two publications list documents of two Brazilian states:

Pernambuco, *Brazil (State)*. *Arquivo Público*. Catálogo das publicações da Imprensa Oficial do Estado, 1926–1966. Recife, 1967. 36 p.   Z1679.P4

São Paulo, *Brazil (State)*. *Departamento Estadual de Estatistica*. Índice alfabético das publicações de 1938 a 1943. São Paulo, [1944] 133 p.   Z7554.B8S3

CHILE

Independence: 1810.

No separate bibliography or list, current or retrospective, of official publications has been or is being issued in Chile. The following general bibliographies include official documents:

Feliú Cruz, Guillermo. Bibliografía histórica de la imprenta en Santiago de Chile [1818–1964]. Santiago de Chile, Talleres de la Editorial Nascimento, 1964. 162 p.   Z1724.S3F4
Medina, José T. Bibliografía de la imprenta en Santiago de Chile desde sus orígenes hasta febrero de 1817. Seguida de las adiciones y ampliaciones del mismo autor. Edición facsimilar. Introd. de Guillermo Feliú Cruz. Santiago de Chile, Fondo Histórico y Bibliográfico José Toribio Medina, 1961. 2 v. in 1. (Homenaje al sesquicentenario de la independencia nacional, 3)   Z1724.S3M4 1961

Santiago de Chile. Biblioteca Nacional. Anuario de la prensa chilena. [1877+] Santiago de Chile.   Z1701.S23
    Includes official publications.

—— Anuario de publicaciones periódicas chilenas. [Santiago de Chile]   Z6954.C5S23
    Lists official and non-official periodicals by title, geographic location and subject. Title varies: 1921–25, *Lista de las publicaciones periódicas chilenas*; 1926–29, *Revistas, diarios y periódicas chilenas*; 1930–37/38, *Publicaciones periódicas chilenas*.

Servicio bibliográfico chileno (Chilean bibliographic news service). núm. 1+, Sept. 1940+ Santiago de Chile, Librería y Editorial Zamorano y Caperan [1940+]
    Z1705.S4

U.S. *Treaties, etc., 1933–1945 (Franklin D. Roosevelt)* Exchange of official publications. Agreement between the United States of America and Chile [Oct. 1937] Washington, U.S. Govt. Print. Off., 1938. 25 p. ([U.S. Dept. of State. Publication 1123] Executive agreement series 112)   JX236   1929 no. 112
                                                                                                            Z690.U7C53
    Includes a list of official publications of Chile.

Other bibliographies and catalogs covering agency publications or certain subjects are the following:

Chile. *Departamento de Navegación e Hidrografía.* Catálogo de cartas náuticas. Valparaiso.   Z6027.C53A3
    Title varies: 1941–45, *Indice de las cartas en uso en la Armada Nacional.*

Chile. *Dirección de Estadística y Censos.* Guía de publicaciones estadísticas. Santiago de Chile, 1966. 27 p.   DLC
———— ———— Supplemento. Santiago de Chile, 1967. 5 p.   DLC

Chile. *Instituto Geográfico Militar.* Catálogo de mapas y cartas para la venta. [Santiago de Chile. 1963?+]   Z6027.C53A35

Chile. *Superintendencia de Seguridad Social.* Bibliografía de la seguridad social chilena. Santiago de Chile, 1967. 228 p.   Z7165.C45C45

Clagett, Helen L. A guide to the law and legal literature of Chile, 1917–1946. Washington, The Library of Congress, 1947. 103 p. ([U.S.] Library of Congress. Latin American series, no. 28)   DLC LL
                                                                                                            Z663.5.G8C5

Correa Saavedra, Mario. Bibliografía del derecho constitucional. [Santiago de Chile, C. E. Gibbs A.] 1967. 352 p.   DLC LL

Molina Arias, Evaristo. Ensayo bibliográfico chileno sobre hacienda publica. Chilean bibliographical sketch of the public finances. Santiago de Chile, Impr. Nacional, 1901. 64 p.   Microfilm Z–49

Santiago de Chile. Biblioteca Nacional. Las publicaciones de la Biblioteca Nacional, 1854–1963; informe elevado al Ministerio de Educación [par] Guillermo Feliú Cruz, director de la Biblioteca Nacional. [Santiago de Chile] Dirección de Bibliotecas, Archivos y Museos, 1964. lxxxi p. [3]

COLOMBIA

Independence: 1819; 1819–30 was Gran Colombia with Ecuador [1822–30] and Venezuela [1821–30]. Panama was part of Colombia, 1821–1903.

    There is a current bibliography of official publications, issued by the Escuela Interamericana de Bibliotecología:

Bibliografía oficial colombiana. no. 1+ 1964+ Medellín, Escuela Interamericana de Bibliotecología.   Z1740.B5
    Announced as a quarterly publication, issues have appeared irregularly.

---

[3] Cited in Arthur E. Gropp, *A Bibliography of Latin American Bibliographies* (Metuchen, N.J.: Scarecrow Press, 1968), p. 226. (Z1601.A2G76 1968)

The bibliography lists official publications in three parts: Gobierno central, Gobiernos departamentales, and Organismos autónomos.

The following bibliographies should also be helpful in identifying official documents:

Anuario bibliográfico colombiano. [1951/56+] Bogotá, Instituto Caro y Cuervo.
Z1731.A58
Official documents are included in the various sections and are cited under agency in the index.

Bibliografía colombiana. t. 1–[13?] enero/jun. 1961–[68?] Gainesville, Florida. semi-annual.   Z1731.B5
Published by Dr. Fermín Peraza Sarausa. Title from 1961 to Jan./June 1964, *Fichas para el Anuario bibliográfico colombiano.* Includes official publications.

Childs, James B. Colombian government publications. Washington [Library of Congress], 1941. 41 p.   Z1739.C5
Originally printed in the proceedings of the Third Convention of the Inter-American Bibliographical and Library Association (New York, H. W. Wilson Co., 1941), then reprinted in separate form by the U.S. Government Printing Office (1941).

Colombia. *Congreso. Biblioteca.* Indice general de la Biblioteca del Congreso. Bogotá, Imp. Nac., 1936. 203 p.   Z1739.C71
Includes mainly Colombian official publications, arranged by title.

Colombia. *Departamento Administrativo Nacional de Estadística, División de Información, Publicaciones y Biblioteca.* Publicaciones periódicas en Colombia, 1964. Bogotá, 1965. 52 p.   Z6954.C7A3
An alphabetical list of periodicals, including official periodicals. New, updated edition published in 1967.

Colombia. *Imprenta Nacional.* Informe. [1895+] Bogotá. annual.   Z232.C71
Includes lists of official publications printed at the Imprenta Nacional during the report period.

Florén Lozano, Luis. Obras de referencia y generales de la bibliografía colombiana. Medellín, Editorial Universidad de Antioquia, 1968. 204, 22 l. (Publicaciones de la E. I. B. Serie: Bibliografía no. 28)   Z1731.F54
Chapter E: "Publicaciones oficiales."

Mesa, Rosa Q. Colombia. Ann Arbor, Mich., University Microfilms, 1968. 140 p. (Latin American serial documents, v. 1)   Z1739.M4
Compiled at the University of Florida Libraries, in cooperation with several other university libraries, the New York Public Library, and the Library of Congress. It includes official serial titles of Colombia, published since the date of national independence to Dec. 1966, held in major libraries in the United States and Canada.

Peraza Sarausa, Fermín, *and* José Ignacio Bohórquez C. Publicaciones oficiales colombianas. Gainesville, Fla., 1964. 31 l. (Biblioteca del bibliotecario, 69)   Z1739.P4
Covers official publications 1958–62. Published originally as Doc. 35 of the Conferencia sobre Administración Pública en los Países en Desarrollo, held at the Escuela Superior de Administración Pública, Bogotá, in April 1963.

226 FOREIGN COUNTRIES

The following two bibliographies cover the Colombian legal and statistical publications:

Backus, Richard C., *and* Phanor J. Eder. A guide to the law and legal literature of Colombia. Washington, Library of Congress, 1943. 222 p. ([U.S.] Library of Congress. Latin American series, no. 4)   Z6458.C7B3

Colombia. *Departamento Administrativo Nacional de Estadística.* Trayectoria bibliográfica del Departamento Administrativo Nacional de Estadística, 1952–1966. By Armando Moreno Mattos. Bogotá, 1967. 10 1.   Z7165.A64A5

COSTA RICA

Independence: 1821; member of Federation of Central America, 1824–39.

No separate bibliography of official publications has been or is being published in Costa Rica. Official documents are, however, listed currently in:

Anuario bibliográfico costarricense. [1956+] San José, Imprenta Nacional [1958+]   Z1453.A65
    Prepared by the Comité Nacional de Bibliografía "Adolfo Blen" of the Asociación Costarricense de Bibliotecarios. Official publications are included since 1959/60 in the alphabetical topic arrangement and are listed mainly under Costa Rica in the "Indice de autores." From 1956 to 1958, the publications were listed in two groups: "por autores" and "por materias." The *Anuario* is a continuation of the annual *Boletín bibliográfico,* published by Biblioteca Nacional (see below).

San José. Costa Rica. Biblioteca Nacional. Boletín bibliográfico. [1946–55] San José, Imprenta Nacional.   Z1451.S27
    Includes official publications mostly under corporate entries.

——— Publicaciones nacionales. San José, Costa Rica [1935/38–45?]   Z1451.S3
    The Library of Congress has photostat copies of this typewritten publication, which includes a considerable number of official documents. Its title varies: 1935/38–39, *Lista de algunas de las obras publicadas.*

Other bibliographies covering certain categories of Costa Rican official publications are:

Costa Rica. *Dirección General de Estadística y Censos.* Bibliografía estadística de Costa Rica, por Manuel García Valverde. San José, 1950. 9 1.   Z7554.C6C6 1950
    Lists statistical publications of Costa Rica issued since 1883.

Dobles Segreda, Luis. Indice bibliográfico de Costa Rica. [v. 1–9] San José, Imprenta Lehmann, 1927–36.   Z1451.D63
    Occasionally includes listing of official documents, e.g., v. 2, "Lista de mapas parciales o totales de Costa Rica" (p. 545–608); v. 5, "Nómina de las memorias anuales presentadas al Congreso Constitucional por los secretarios de estado de Costa Rica" (p. 473–540); v. 5, "Bibliografía de las publicaciones hechas por el Departamento Nacional de Estadística" and "Otras publicaciones" (p. [541]–623); v. 6 "Perez Zeledón, Pedro: Costa Rica-Panama Arbitration," 1910 (p. 172–327).

Lines, Jorge A. Libros y folletos publicados en Costa Rica durante los años 1830–1849. San José, C. R., 1944. xxxv, 151 p. Z1451.L5
Published by the Universidad de Costa Rica, Facultad de Letras y Filosofía.
Official publications are listed in chronological order.

ECUADOR

Independence: 1821; 1822–30, part of Gran Colombia.

No bibliography of official publications has been published to date. Some official publications are listed in:

Ecuador. *Junta Nacional de Planificación y Coordinación Económica. División de Estadística y Censos.* Boletín bibliográfico. año 1, no. 1+ 1964+ Quito. DLC

The following bibliographies and indexes to laws and legislation will be of assistance:

Clagett, Helen L. A guide to the law and legal literature of Ecuador. Washington, 1947. 100 p. ([U.S.] Library of Congress. Latin American series, no. 18) DLC LL

Ecuador. *Laws, statutes, etc. (Indexes)* Clave de la legislación ecuatoriana, 1899–1921. Quito, Imprenta Nacional, 1922. 1 v. DLC LL

——— ——— 1922–1935. Quito, Imprenta Nacional, 1936. 1 v. DLC LL

——— Indice de la legislación ecuatoriana desde 1898 hasta 1918. Quito, 1918–21 112 p. DLC LL
Issued in installments with *Revista forense*; órgano del Colegio de abogados de Quito, no. 59–60, 63–66, 68, by the Academia de abogados de Quito.

——— Indice general y clave de la legislación publicada en el Registro oficial. v. 1+ 1925–29+ Quito. DLC LL

EL SALVADOR

Independence: 1821; member of Federation of Central America, 1824–39.

There is no current bibliography of official publications. A considerable number of these are listed in:

Anuario bibliográfico salvadoreño. 1952+ San Salvador. Z1493.A63
Issued by the Biblioteca Nacional of Salvador.
Previously, from May 1951, published in *Anaqueles* (see below).
Official publications are listed mostly under corporate entries in both the subject section and in the author section.

For retrospective listing of official publications, there are the following general sources:

Anaqueles. año 1 (no. 1)+ 30 jul. 1929+ San Salvador, [Biblioteca Nacional] irregular.
Z887.S23
    Title varies: 1929—*Revista bibliográfica científico-literaria*; 1932—Boletín; 1948—*Revista de la Biblioteca Nacional;* 1951—*Anaqueles.* Until 1948, some official publications of El Salvador were included in the list of publications received. From January/April 1948 (Epoca IV, no. 1) a special section, entitled "Bibliografía salvadoreña," was included in the periodical, listing publications printed in El Salvador from 1945. The title of the section was changed to "Anuario bibliográfico salvadoreño" beginning with issue for May 1951/Apr. 1952 (Epoca V, no. 2). In 1954 the "Anuario" published as a separate anexo to issue May 1953/April 1954 (Epoca V, no. 4), covering the year 1952.

[El] Salvador. *Imprenta Nacional.* Nómina de las obras editadas en la Imprenta Nacional y existentes en el Archivo de la misma. [San Salvador, 1943] 54 l. Type-written.   Z1495.S3
    A list of publications issued by Imprenta Nacional, arranged by title.

—— Nómina de las obras editadas en la Imprenta Nacional y en el Departamento Editorial del Ministerio de Cultura, existentes en el archivo de los mismos. San Salvador, Imprenta Nacional, 1960.[4]

San Salvador. Biblioteca Nacional. Bibliografía salvadoreña; lista preliminar por autores. [San Salvador, 1953?] 430 l.   Z1491.S27
    Official publications listed mainly under corporate entries.

GUATEMALA

Independence: 1821; member of Federation of Central America, 1824–39.

Official publications printed at the Tipografía Nacional are listed in its annual report, *Memoria de las principales labores realizadas por la Dirección de la Tipografía Nacional.* The report was published in the past under varied titles: *Labores de la Tipografía Nacional, Informe de los trabajos realizados por la Tipografía Nacional* (Z232.G91). From 1934 to 1941/42(?), the list was included in the annual *Memoria* of the Secretaría de Gobierno y Justicia (J179.R2). A retrospective list of publications printed at the Tipografía Nacional from 1892 to 1943 was published in 1944 and kept up to date by supplements:

Guatemala. *Tipografía Nacional.* Catálogo general de libros, folletos y revistas editados en la Tipografía Nacional de Guatemala. 1892/1943+ Guatemala, 1944+
Z1465.A3
    The catalog lists publications by years. An *Appendice* for 1892–1944 was issued in 1945. Supplements covering individual years have been published for the following periods: 1944–53 (1954); 1954–62 (1963); 1963–65 (1966). The pagination of supplements is continuous with the main work.

Other bibliographic sources listing official publications are the following:

---

[4] Cited in UNESCO, *Handbook on the International Exchange of Publications.* 3d ed. [Paris, 1964].

Dardón Córdova, Gonzalo. Series guatemaltecas en el campo de las humanidades, 1886–1962. [l. ed.] Guatemala, Instituto Guatemalteco Americano, 1962. 137 l. (Cooperación interbibliotecaria, 3)   Z1033.S5D3

Guatemala *(City)* Biblioteca Nacional. Anuario bibliográfico guatemalteco. [1960+] Guatemala.   Z1461.G8
    In two sections (monographs and periodicals), the *Anuario* lists official publications mainly under "Guatemala" and other corporate entries. The 1960 *Anuario* was reprinted in the *Revista de la Biblioteca Nacional,* año 1, núm. 1, 1962: 137–170.

———— Boletín. año 1+ mayo 1932+ Ciudad de Guatemala, 1932+   Z887.G91B
    Title varies: 1941–45, *Boletín de museos y bibliotecas.*
    From 1936 (no. 2), it includes a list of publications subject to legal deposit.

Indice bibliográfico guatemalteco. [1951?+] Guatemala, Servicio Extensivo, Biblioteca Nacional.   Z146.I5
    A combined dictionary and subject bibliography. Issues for 1958 and 1959/60 published by Instituto Guatemalteco-Americano.

Medina, José T. La imprenta en Guatemala (1660–1821). Santiago de Chile, Impreso en casa del autor, 1910. lxxxv, 696 p.   Z1461.M4   1910
    Includes official documents. Reprinted by Tipografía Nacional, Guatemala in 1960 (Colección Tri-Centenario, v. 2) and in Amsterdam by N. Israel in 1964 (Reprint series of José Toribio Medina's bibliographic works, 2).

U.S. *Treaties, etc., 1933–1945 (Franklin D. Roosevelt)* Exchange of official publications. Agreement between the United States of America and Guatemala. [March 1944] Washington, U.S. Govt. Print. Off., 1944. 13 p. ([U.S. Dept. of State, Publication 2209] Executive agreement series 412)   JX236   1929 no. 412
                                                                              Z690.U7G9
    Includes a list of Guatemalan official publications.

Valenzuela, Gilberto. Bibliografía guatemalteca; catálogo de obras, folletos, etc., publicados en Guatemala desde la independencia hasta el año de 1850. Guatemala, 1933. 459 p.   Z1461.V16

———— Bibliografía guatemalteca, y catálogo general de libros, folletos, periódicos, revistas, etc., 1821–1930. Guatemala, 1961. 319 p. (Colección bibliográfica del tercer centenario de la fundación de la primera imprenta en Centro América, t. 3)
                                                                              Z1461.V162

Further volumes of Valenzuela's *Bibliografía guatemalteca* were published as follows:

1831–40 (1961. 206 p. Colección—t. 4)   Z1461.V17
1841–60 (1961. 185 p. Colección—t. 5)   Z1461.V173

Volumes for 1861–1960 were compiled by Gilberto Valenzuela's son, Gilberto Valenzuela Reyna, and published between 1962 and 1964, as follows:

Valenzuela Reyna, Gilberto. Bibliografía guatemalteca, y catálogo general de libros, folletos, periódicos, revistas, etc., 1861–1900. Guatemala, 1962. 485 p. (Colección—t. 6)   Z1461.V18

———— ———— 1901–1930. Guatemala, 1962 [i.e. 1963] 537 p. (Colección–t. 7)
Z1461.V182

———— ———— 1931–1940. Guatemala, 1963. 288 p. (Colección–t. 8)   Z1461.V183

———— ———— 1941–1950. Guatemala, 1963 [i.e. 1964] 383 p. (Colección–t. 9)
Z1461.V1835

———— ———— 1951–1960. Guatemala, 1964. 573 p. (Colección–t. 10)   Z1461.V184

GUYANA

Dutch rule until 1796; British Guiana until 1966; independence: 1966.

Since 1951 the *Current Caribbean Bibliography* has listed publications
of British Guiana. These were also listed in British general bibliogra-
phies (see Gt. Britain: General bibliographies). Currently, the *Technical
Cooperation; a Monthly Bibliography* (Gt. Brit. Overseas Development
Administration Library) lists official publications of Guyana.
Other retrospective bibliographic sources on British Guiana:

British Guiana. *Bibliography Committee.* Bibliography of British Guiana . . . by
   Vincent Roth. [Georgetown?] 1948.   Microfilm Z–38
   Microfilm copy of a typescript. Lists a considerable number of official publica-
   tions up to 1946.

Gt. Brit. *Colonial Office.* Annual report on British Guiana. 1946–[61?] London, H. M.
   Stationery Off. (*Its* Colonial annual reports)   F2368.G75
   In its "reading list," it includes selected official publications of British
   Guiana. Previously issued in the numbered series of *Colonial Reports-Annual,*
   which was suspended in 1940 (JV33.G7A4). Also, from 1920 the British Guiana
   Blue Book included a short list of official publications (J146.R2).

HONDURAS

Independence: 1821; member of Federation of Central America, 1824–39.

There is no bibliography of official publications, current or retrospective. These may be identified in the following general bibliographies:

Durón, Jorge F. Indice de la bibliografía hondureña. Tegucigalpa, D.C., Impr. Cal-
   derón, 1946. 211 p.   Z1471.D77
   An annotated general bibliography, which includes government publications.
   It covers the period 1821–Aug. 1946. The *Indice* is a much enlarged edition of the
   author's *Repertorio bibliográfico hondureño.* (Tegucigalpa, 1943. 68 p. Z1471.D8)

Honduras. Biblioteca Nacional, *Tegucigalpa.* Anuario bibliográfico, 1961+ Tegucigalpa, 1963+   Z1471.H6
   A classified bibliography. Official publications can be identified through author
   index. A list of periodicals is included.

Pan American Institute of Geography and History. *Commission on History.* Honduras;
   guía de los documentos microfotografiados por la Unidad Móvil de Microfilm de
   la UNESCO. México, 1967. 245 p. (*Its* [Publicación] 120. Guías 3) Instituto Panamericano de Geografía e Historia. Publicación no. 307.   F1401.P153 no. 307

A record of 2,721 manuscripts, official gazettes, and other government publications. A person and place name index is included.

U.S. *Treaties, etc., 1933–1945 (Franklin D. Roosevelt)* Exchange of official publications. Agreement between the United States of America and Honduras. [Dec. 1940] Washington, U.S. Govt. Print. Off., 1941. 6 p. ([U.S. Dept. of State. Publication 1654] Executive agreement series 194) JX236 1929 no. 194
Z690.U7H6
Includes a list of Honduran official publications.

MEXICO

Independence: 1821.

No special current bibliography of government publications is issued. The *Bibliografía mexicana,* issued bimonthly since January/February 1967 by the Biblioteca Nacional and the Instituto Bibliográfico Mexicano of the Universidad Nacional Autónoma, includes some official publications in its section "Ciencias sociales."

Retrospective coverage of the Mexican official publications is found in the following three works:

Fernández Esquivel, Rosa M. Las publicaciones oficiales de México; guía de publicaciones periódicas y seriadas, 1937–1967. México, 1967. 269 p. (Universidad Nacional Autónoma de México. Seminario de Investigaciones Bibliotecológicas. [Publicaciones] Ser. B, no. 4) Z1419.F42
A thesis for "licenciatura en bibliotecología," it deals first with official publications in general, then lists some 1,200 serials issued since 1937.

Ker, Annita M. Mexican government publications: A guide to the more important publications of the national government of Mexico, 1821–1936. Washington, U.S. Govt. Print. Off., 1940. xxi, 333 p. Z1419.K4
Published by the Library of Congress. "The following have been considered of primary importance: the official gazette, the regular (annual or semiannual) messages of the president to Congress, the annual reports (*memorias*) of the cabinet members to Congress. Next in importance are the long or otherwise significant publications of individual departments, and all their current serial publications."

Mesa, Rosa Q. Mexico. Ann Arbor, Mich., University Microfilms, 1970. 351, 4 p. (Latin American serial documents, v. 4) Z1419.M46
Compiled at the University of Florida Libraries, in cooperation with several other university libraries, the New York Public Library, and the Library of Congress. It includes official serial titles of Mexico, published since the date of national independence to 1969, held in major United States and Canadian libraries.

The following works may be helpful in supplementing the three basic bibliographies mentioned above as far as the Mexican colonial period (before 1821) is concerned and for some particular aspects and fields of Mexican official documentation:

Carpenter, Edwin H. Government publication in late eighteenth-century Mexico. [New York] Bibliographical Society of America, ᶜ1952. 69 p. Z1419.C37

Reprinted from the *Papers of the Bibliographical Society of America*, v. 46, second and third quarters, 1952. Covers official publications of 1789–94, partly supplementing José Toribio Medina's work for the period (see below).

Castillo, Ignacio B. del.   Bibliografía de la imprenta de la Cámara de Diputados para servir a los historiadores de la época de Madero, Huerta y la convención, 1912– 1915. México, 1918. 48 p. (*In* Iguiniz, Juan B. Concurso de bibliografía y biblioteconomía convocado por la Biblioteca Nacional. 1918. II.)   Z1426.5.I53
277 titles arranged in chronological order.

Clagett, Helen L.   A guide to the law and legal literature of the Mexican states. Washington, The Library of Congress, 1947. 180 p. ([U.S.] Library of Congress. Latin American series, no. 13)   DLC LL

Medina, José Toribio.   La imprenta en México (1539–1821). Santiago de Chile, Impreso en casa del autor, 1907–12. 8 v.   Z1411.M49
Reprinted in 1965 by N. Israel, Amsterdam (Z1411.M492). Includes a number of early official documents.

Mexico. Biblioteca Nacional, *Mexico*.   Anuario bibliográfico. 1958+ México, 1967+
Z1411.M5
Arranged by decimal classification, it includes official publications under the subject headings. An author index is included.

Mexico. *Comisión de Estudios Militares. Biblioteca del Ejército*.   Apuntes para una bibliografía militar de México, 1536–1936. Recopilación de fichas bibliográficas hecha por los delegados de la Secretaría de Guerra y Marina, en ocasión del primer Congreso Bibliográfico, convocado por el Ateneo Nacional de Ciencias y Artes de México. Sessión de estudios militares del Ateneo: Mayor M. C. Néstor Herrera Gómez, Mayor Silvino M. González. México, D. F. [Tall. Gráf. de la Nación] 1937. 469, [1] p.   Z6725.M6M6
Mainly official publications included.

Mexico. *Departamento de Informaciones Sociales y Estadística. Biblioteca*.   Feria del libro y exposición nacional del periodismo, 1943. México, 1943. 32 p.   Z1764.L1M6
Cover title: *Bibliografía de la Secretaría del Trabajo y Previsión Social*.

Mexico. *Dirección General de Educación Higiénica*.   Bibliografía, que el Departamento de Salubridad Pública presenta en la Feria del libro y exposición nacional del periodismo. México, 1943. 63 p.   Z1419.M56   1943

Mexico. *Ministerio de Comunicaciones y Obras Públicas*.   Bibliografía. Secretaría de Comunicaciones y Obras Públicas, 1891–1943. México [1943] 189 p. (Biblioteca de la Feria del libro y exposición nacional del periodismo)   Z1419.M57

Mexico. *Ministerio de Hacienda y Crédito Público*.   Bibliografía de la Secretaría de Hacienda y Crédito público. [1821–1942] México, D. F., 1943. 226 p. (Biblioteca de la Feria del libro y exposición nacional del periodismo)   Z1419.M58   1943

―――― Memoria. 1821/22+ México.   HJ15.A25
The *Memoria* presented to the Congress of the Union by the Secretario de Hacienda in 1870 contains an analysis of the previous memorias, 1822–69, a statement giving all the secretaries of state for the various departments, 1821–60, and a list of the works used in preparation of this memoria including all of the earlier memorias of the various government departments, etc.

Mexico. *Secretaría de Industria y Comercio*.   Publicaciones oficiales, Secretaría de la Economía Nacional (1933–1942). México [1943] 62 p. (Biblioteca de la Feria del libro y exposición nacional del periodismo)   Z1419.M6

Mexico. *Secretaría de la Defensa Nacional.* Algunas fichas para una bibliografía general de la Secretaría de la Defensa Nacional, recopiladas por . . . Silvino M. González. México, 1943. 206 p. (Biblioteca de la Feria del libro y exposición nacional del periodismo)   Z1419.M59

Mexico. *Secretaría de Relaciones Exteriores.* Catálogo de las publicaciones. México, Imprenta de la Secretaría de Relaciones Exteriores, 1926. 14 p.   Z1419.M62

Mexico. (City) Universidad Nacional. *Instituto de Derecho Comparado.* Ensayo bibliográfico de derecho constitucional mexicano y de garantías y amparo. México, Imprenta Universitaria, 1947. xvii, 173 p.   Z6458.M4M4

New York. Public Library. List of works in the New York Public Library relating to Mexico. New York, 1909. 186 p.   Z1431.N56
    Reprinted from the *Bulletin of the New York Public Library,* Oct.–Dec., 1909.
Includes a section, "Public Documents."

Saldívar, Gabriel. Bibliografía de la Secretaría de Relaciones Exteriores. México, 1943. 96 p. ([Mexico] Departamento de información para el extranjero. Series bibliográficas mexicanas, no. 2)   Z1419.S3
    "Biblioteca de la Feria del libro y exposición nacional del periodismo, 1943."

Spain. *Archivo General de Indias, Seville.* Indice de documentos de Nueva España existentes en el Archivo de Indias de Sevilla. México [Imprenta de la Secretaría de Relaciones Exteriores] 1928–[31] 4 v. (Monografías bibliográficas mexicanas, núm. 12, [14, 22, 23])   CD1859.S3A5 no. 12, etc.
    Z1417.M75

Vance, John T., *and* Helen L. Clagett. A guide to the law and legal literature of Mexico. Washington, The Library of Congress, 1945. 269 p. ([U.S.] Library of Congress. Latin American series no. 6)   Z6458.M4V3
    An updated edition published in 1973.

NICARAGUA

Independence: 1812; member of Federation of Central America, 1824–39.

No current bibliography of official publications is issued in Nicaragua. The *Handbook of Latin American Studies* lists a few selected publications. For retrospective listing, the *Guide to the Official Publications of the Other American Republics* (v. 14, *Nicaragua*) and the two sources listed below, cover official publications to the late 1940's.

Managua. Biblioteca Americana de Nicaragua. Bibliografía de trabajos publicados en Nicaragua. Bibliography of works published in Nicaragua. [Managua, Editorial Nuevos Horizontes, 1944–48] 4 v. (Serie bibliográfica, 1, 4, 6–7/9).   Z1481.M3
    Government publications are listed in a separate section. Volume 4, part 1, published in January 1945, covers publications "with 1942 or earlier as date of publication."

U.S. *Treaties, etc., 1933–1945 (Franklin D. Roosevelt)* Exchange of official publications. Agreement between the United States of America and Nicaragua. [Feb. 1940] Washington, U.S. Govt. Print. Off., 1940. 7 p. ([U.S. Dept of State. Publication 1490] Executive agreement series 171)   JX236 1929 no. 171
    Z690.U7N6
    Includes a list of Nicaraguan publications.

PANAMA

Independence: 1903; 1821–1903, part of Colombia.

No current bibliography of official publications issued. In addition to general bibliographies listed previously, for retrospective listings the following tools will be of assistance. They include some official publications under corporate entries or personal authors:

Panama (City) Biblioteca Nacional. Guía de organismos oficiales y sus publicaciones. Panamá, 1960. 29 p.   DLC

Panama (City) Universidad. *Biblioteca*. Bibliografía panameña existente en la Biblioteca de la Universidad. [Año del cincuentenario, 1903–1953. Panamá, 1953] 109 l.
Z1500.P16

Panama (City) Universidad. *Grupo Bibliográfico*. Bibliografía retrospectiva de libros y folletos, 1957–1955. Panamá, 1958. 63 p.   Z1500.P165

Susto Lara, Juan A. Introducción a la Bibliografía panameña (1619–1945). Panamá [Impr. La Nación] 1946. 35 p. (Publicaciones de la Biblioteca Nacional, no. 4)
Z744.P3 no. 4

U.S. Treaties, etc., 1933–1945 (Franklin D. Roosevelt) Exchange of official publications. Agreement between the United States of America and Panama. (Nov. 1941) Washington, U.S. Govt. Print. Off., 1942. 7 p. ([U.S. Dept. of State. Publication 1760] Executive agreement series 243)   JX236 1929 no. 243
Z690. U7P3
    Includes a list of official publications of Panama.

PARAGUAY

Independence: 1811.

No current bibliography of official publications issued. In addition to general bibliographies, listed previously, there are a few bibliographies or lists which may be of assistance:

Asunción. Biblioteca Nacional. Bibliografía paraguaya: catálogo de la biblioteca paraguaya "Solano López." Asunción, Talleres nacionales de H. Kraus, 1906. 984 p.
Z907.A86

—— Catálogo de la sección paraguaya de la Biblioteca Nacional. Asunción, 1925. 24 l.
Z1849.A8

Clagett, Helen L. A guide to the law and legal literature of Paraguay. Washington, Library of Congress, 1947. 59 p. ([U.S.] Library of Congress. Latin American series, no. 14)   DLC LL
Z6458.P7C6

Decoud, José S. A list of books, magazine articles, and maps relating to Paraguay. Books, 1638–1903. Maps, 1599–1903. A supplement to the Handbook of Paraguay, published in September 1902, by the International Bureau of the American Republics. Washington, Govt. Print. Off., 1904. 53 p.   Z1821.D27

U.S. *Treaties, etc., 1933–1945* (*Franklin D. Roosevelt*) Exchange of official publications. Agreement between the United States of America and Paraguay. [Nov. 1942] Washington, U.S. Govt. Print. Off., 1943. 9 p. ([U.S. Dept. of State. Publication 1926] Executive agreement series 301) JX236 1929 no. 301
Z690.U7P35
Includes a list of official publications of Paraguay.

PERU

Independence: 1821.

There is no current bibliography of official publications and no comprehensive retrospective bibliography has been published in Peru. Some official documents are listed, although with considerable delay, in the following three publications:

Anuario bibliográfico peruano. 1943+ Lima [Talleres gráficos de la editorial Lumen S. A.] 1945+ (Ediciones de la Biblioteca Nacional) Z1851.A5
A classified general bibliography. Official publications are listed under individual subject headings, most in the section "Legislación y estudios jurídicos."

Lima. Universidad de San Marcos. *Biblioteca.* Boletín bibliográfico. v. 1+ jul. 1923+ Lima. Z782.L77B
Official publications are listed under corporate entries, personal authors, or titles. Several more substantial contributions have been published in the *Boletín* as follow:

1928, v. 3, no. 6, p. 317–342; "Contribución a la bibliografía del derecho administrativo peruano," by Enrique Dammert Elguera.

1937, v. 7, no. 3, p. 188–205: "El Peruano," by Constanza Raggio, Beatriz Normand, and Teresa Umlauff.

1937, v. 7, no. 4, p. 329–361: "Los 'Diarios de los debates'," by Constanza Raggio, Beatriz Normand, and Teresa Umlauff.

1942, v. 12, nos. 3–4, p. 141–152: "Al servicio de una bibliografía de historia internacional y diplomática del Perú," by Pedro Ugarteche and José Pareja Paz-Soldán. Ministerio de Relaciones Exteriores.

1950, v. 20, nos. 1–2, p. 65–175; "Bibliografía de derecho y ciencias políticas (1936–1950)," by Alberto Benavides Balbín and Dagoberto García Ramos.

1950, v. 20, nos. 3–4, p. 235–262: "Para una bibliografía diplomática del Perú; publicaciones oficiales de la cancillería peruana," by José Pareja Paz-Soldán and José Carlos Mariategui.

1953, v. 23, nos. 1–4, p. 3–86: "Bibliografía de educación (1936–1952)."

1963, v. 35, nos. 3–4, p. [215]–340: "Cuarenta años del 'Boletín Bibliográfico' (1923–1962)," by Alejandro Tumba Ortega.

Peru. Biblioteca Nacional, *Lima.* Boletín. año 1, no. 1+ enero 1919+ Lima. Z907.L72
Occasionally lists some official publications in its acquisitions list. From 1952 to 1955 it published three lists of memorias, as follows:

1952, v. 9, p. 29–64: "Catálogo de las memorias de Ministros de estado del Peru."

1953, v. 10, p. 341–368: "Catálogo de las memorias de prefectos, alcaldes y presidentes de juntas departamentales del Perú," by A. Ballon and Caridad Esparzam.

1954–55, v. 11–12, p. [103]–137: "Catálogo de memorias de los presidentes de las Cortes de Justicia del Perú."

Other bibliographies covering official Peruvian publications, mainly for retrospective periods, which may occasionally be of help, are the following:

Clagett, Helen L. A guide to the law and legal literature of Peru. Washington, 1947. 188 p. ([U.S.] Library of Congress. Latin American series, no. 20)   DLC LL
                                                                                      Z6458.P5C5
An updated edition is in preparation.

Peru. *Congreso. Cámara de Senadores. Biblioteca.* Catálogo de la biblioteca, formado por el oficial primero Don Rafael Belaunde. Lima, Emp. tip. "Unión," 1913. 75 p.
                                                                                      Z907.L7 1913

——— Catálogo de las obras de la Biblioteca de la h. Cámara de Senadores. Lima, Impr. la Industria, 1906. 67 p.   Z907.L7 1906

Peru. *Oficina de Reparto, Depósito y Canje Internacional de Publicaciones.* Catálogo de las publicaciones que la Oficina de Reparto, . . . tiene disponibles para distribuir. [Lima, 1905] 10 p.   Z1859.P44

Texas. University. *Library.* Recent Peruvian acquisitions of the Latin American collection of the University of Texas Library. no. 1+ 1962/64+ Austin.   Z881.T382

U.S. *Treaties, etc., 1933–1945 (Franklin D. Roosevelt)* Exchange of official publications. Agreement between the United States of America and Peru. [Oct. 1936] Washington, U.S. Govt. Print. Off., 1936. 11 p. ([U.S. Dept. of State. Publication 1049] Executive agreement series 103)   JX236.1929 no. 103
                                                                                      Z690.U7P47
Includes a list of Peruvian official publications.

URUGUAY
Independence: 1825.

As in most Latin American countries, no current bibliographies or lists of official publications are being issued. A number of official documents are listed in *Bibliografía uruguaya*, issued irregularly since 1962 by the Biblioteca del Poder Legislativo (Z1881.M76). According to a note in UNESCO's *Bibliography, Documentation, Terminology* (v. 8, no. 4, July 1968), "In 1966 a bibliography of official publications issued in Uruguay during the last ten years was compiled by the students of the bibliography course no. 2 (Methods) of the University Library School, under the direction of one of their teachers, Miss Elvira Lerena Martínez. This bibliography (unpublished) includes monographs and periodicals."

For retrospective publications, these other tools, which include official publications, may be of assistance:

Anuario bibliográfico uruguayo. 1946–[49] Montevideo, Biblioteca Nacional. Z1881.A5
Resumed publication in 1969.

Clagett, Helen L.   A guide to the law and legal literature of Uruguay. Washington, Library of Congress, 1947. 123 p. ([U.S.] Library of Congress. Latin American series, no. 26)   DLC LL
                                                                        Z6458.U8C5

Estrada, Dardo.   Historia y bibliografía de la imprenta en Montevideo 1810–1865. Montevideo, Librería Cervantes, 1912. 318, [2] p.   Z213.M7E8

Musso Ambrosi, Luis A.   Autores corporativos uruguayos: guía para su catalogación: organizaciones de gobierno, organizaciones particulares, reuniones. Montevideo, 1965. 71 l.   Z695.8.M8   1965
     First published under title: *Guía de encabezamientos de autores corporativos uruguayos* in 1961. Lists corporate entries with short history of agencies.

——— Bibliografía de bibliografías uruguayas, con aportes a la historia del periodismo en el Uruguay. Pref. de James B. Childs. Montevideo, 1964. 102 p.   Z1881.A1M8

——— Bibliografía del poder legislativo desde sus comienzos hasta el año 1965. Montevideo, Centro de Estudios del Pasado Uruguayo, 1967. 236 p.   DLC LL
     Lists publications of Uruguayan legislative bodies. Includes: "Indice de autores y personas citadas," "Indice geográfico y de institutos citados," and "Indice de materias."

Otero Mendoza, Gabriel.   Prontuario; índice general de las leyes vigentes 1825–1924. Montevideo, Peña hnos., Impresores, 1924. 23 p.   DLC LL

Uruguay. *Oficina de Depósito, Reparto y Canje Internacional de Publicaciones*.   Lista de las publicaciones existentes en la Oficina de Depósito . . . (Año 1890) Montevideo, 1891 75 p.   Z1881.U88
     "Publicaciones oficiales," p. 48–75.

Uruguay. *Servicio de Hidrografía*.   Catálogo de cartas y publicaciones; índice alfabético de nombres geográficas. 2. ed. Corregido hasta el 31 de diciembre de 1956. [Montevideo] Taller Tip. de la Marina, 1956. 121 p.   Z6027.U8A5   1956

——— Catálogo del archivo cartográfico histórico. 1. ed. [Montevideo] 1956. 393 p.
                                                                        Z6028.U7

VENEZUELA

Independence: 1811; 1821–30, part of Gran Colombia.

No lists or bibliographies of government publications are issued currently. A number of official documents are listed in:

Bibliografía venezolana. año 1+ enero/marzo 1970+ Caracas, Centro Bibliográfico Venezolano. quarterly.   Z1911.B5

Venezuela. *Archivo General de la Nación*.   Boletín. t. 1, no. 1+ marzo 1923+ Caracas.
                                                                        CD4260.A3
     The *Boletín*, published semiannually from 1965 (quarterly until 1960, with cumulated editions of issues 1–4, for 1961–64), includes official publications of Venezuela in its section "Publicaciones recibidas."

Other, mainly restrospective bibliographies, which include official publications and cover certain periods or fields, are:

Anuario bibliográfico venezolano. 1942+ Caracas, Tip. Americana, 1944+   Z1911.A7
Separate *Alcance: Escritores venezolanos fallecidos entre 1942 y 1947*, published in 1948 (Z1911.A72).

Childs, James B.   Venezuelan government publications. Inter-American bibliographical review, v. 3, 1943: 120–125.   Z1008.I583 v. 3

Clagett, Helen L.   A guide to the law and legal literature of Venezuela. Washington, 1947. 128 p. ([U.S.] Library of Congress. Latin American series, no. 16)   DLC LL
Z6458.V4C5

Venezuela. Biblioteca Nacional, *Caracas*. Indice bibliográfico. año 1, no. 1+ jun. 1956+ Caracas.   Z907.V4
Includes an author and title index. Official publications are listed mostly under corporate entries.

Venezuela, *Laws, statutes, etc.* (*Indexes*)   Indice de leyes vigentes hasta el 31 de marzo de 1963 [por] Carlos Romero Zuloaga [y] Luis Guillermo Arcay. Caracas, Mene Grande Oil Co., Departamento Legal [1963] 441 p.   DLC LL

Venezuela. *Ministerio de Fomento.*   Memoria y cuente. *Caracas*, [1863]+   HC236.A4
Lists current publications of the Dirección General de Estadística y Censos Nacionales. In its issue for 1912 (p. 830–835), it printed a list of annual reports of various ministries, under the title: "Estado de la existencia de memorias de los ministerios, etc. de Venezuela en las colecciones de la Bibliografía Nacional para 31 de marzo de 1912."

Venezuela. *Ministerio de Hacienda.*   Bosquejo histórico de la vida fiscal de Venezuela; ofrenda del Ministerio de Hacienda en el primer centenario de la batalla de Ayacucho. Caracas, Tip. Vargas, 1924. xxii, 167 p.   HJ990.A5 1924
An exhaustive bibliography of the publications of the Ministry of Finance, for the period 1830–1924 is included (p. [67]–163). Also issued in English under the title: *Historical Sketch of the Fiscal Life of Venezuela; Offering of the Department of Finance in the First Centennial of the Battle of Ayacucho* (HJ990.A5 1925).

Venezuela. *Presidencia.* Catálogo de publicaciones, 1959–1963. Caracas [1963] 111 p.
Z1934.C3A5

EUROPE

GENERAL BIBLIOGRAPHIES

Bibliographic control of official publications of European governments varies considerably from country to country. Although most West European countries issue separate bibliographies and lists of their official documents, the countries of East and East Central Europe limit the bibliographic control of their official documents to listings in their general bibliographies.

The British Stationery Office began issuing retrospective lists of official publications in the 1880's, but the more systematic listing of official documents dates generally from the 1920's and 1930's. In 1924 Italy issued the first volume of *Pubblicazioni edite dello stato o col suo concorso, 1861–1923* (Italy, Provveditorato Generale dello Stato), and Germany in 1928 started issuing *Monatliches Verzeichnis der reichsdeutschen amtlichen Druckschriften* (Germany, Reichsministerium des Innern, 1928–44). Other West European countries initiated systematic control of their official publications after the Second World War. In East European countries, the only known attempt to compile a list of selected official or semi-official publications was made in Poland, when in 1967 the Biblioteka Narodowa published a *Katalog polskich wydawnictw urzędowych i polurzędowych, dostępnych do wymiany międzynarodowej. Catalogue of Polish Official and Semi-Official Publications Available for Exchange, compiled by Waclaw Słabczyński.* In the USSR, Oleg Pavlovich Korshunov, in his *Izdaniiă i bibliografiiă dokumentov Kommunisticheskoĭ partii Sovetskogo Soiuza i Sovetskogo Gosudarstva* (Moskva, 1955), attempted to describe official documents of the Communist Party and of the Soviet government and to emphasize the importance of providing good bibliographic control of them.

There are few general bibliographies, besides those cited earlier in the sections Government Publications in General, Guides, General Bibliographies and Foreign Countries, General Bibliographies, which cover official publications of European countries. The following are cited here as examples:

American Library in Paris, Inc. *Reference Service on International Affairs.* Official publications of European governments. Paris [1926] 284 p.   Z7164.G7A5
   Compiled by Miss José Meyer. Reproduced from typewritten copy. Includes

Austria and provinces, Belgium, Bulgaria, Czechoslovakia, Denmark, Estonia, Finland, France and colonies, Germany and the German States, Greece, Hungary, Irish Free State, Italy, Latvia, Lithuania, Luxemburg, Netherlands, Norway, Poland, Portugal, Rumania, Serbia and the Serb-Croat-Slovene State, Spain, Sweden, Switzerland, Union of Soviet Socialist Republics and the United Kingdom.

—— Official publications of European governments; an outline bibliography of serials and important monographs, including diplomatic documents issued by European government offices and ministries. Compiled by José Meyer. Paris, 1929. [255 p.]   Z7164.G7A5 1929
   "Revision and expansion of the mimeographed list of *Official publications of European governments* issued in December 1926."
   Only Part I published, covering Albania, Austria, Belgium, Bulgaria, Czechoslovakia, Denmark, Estonia, Finland and France.
   Reprinted in 1971 by B. Franklin, New York (Z7164.G7M4).

Blake, Judith, *and* Jerry J. Donovan. Western European censuses, 1960; an English language guide. Berkeley, Institute of International Studies, University of California [1971] 421 p. (Population monograph series, no. 8)   HA37.E93B5
   Includes bibliographical references.

Cabeen, Violet A. Publications of the European governments in exile and of groups of their nationals in North America and Great Britain. *In* American Library Association. *Committee on Public Documents.* Public documents and World War II. Chicago, 1942. p. 91–110.   Z7164.G7A43
   Includes official publications of the governments of Belgium, Czechoslovakia, Free France, Greece, Luxemburg, Netherlands, Norway, Poland, and Yugoslavia.

Carnegie Endowment for International Peace. *Library.* European governments in exile. Compiled by Helen Lawrence Scanlon. [Washington, 1943] 24 p. *(Its* Memoranda series, no. 3a. Revised Jan. 25, 1943)   JX1906.A35
   "This memorandum attempts to set forth the organization, personnel, diplomatic activities and publications of the European governments which are now functioning outside their own territories."

Childs, James B. Exiled governments, their official records. American Political Science Review, v. 35, Dec. 1941: 1158–60.   JA1.A6

Harvey, Joan M. Statistics Europe: sources for market research, 2d ed., rev. and enl. Beckenham, Kent. C. B. D. Research Ltd., 1972. 255 p. (A CBD research publication)   Z7554.E8H35 1972

London. University. *Institute of Advanced Legal Studies.* Union list of West European legal literature; publications held by libraries in Oxford, Cambridge and London. London, 1966. 426 p. *(Its* Union catalogue, no. 5)   DLC LL

U.S. *Dept. of the Army. Army Library.* Bibliography on foreign law of Europe, Africa, Iceland and USSR. Washington, Law Branch, Army Library, 1953. 25 l.   DLC LL

U.S. *Library of Congress. Census Library Project.* National censuses and vital statistics in Europe, 1918–1939; and annotated bibliography. Prepared by Henry J. Dubester. Washington, U.S. Govt. Print. Off., 1948. 215 p.   Z7553.C3U46

—— —— 1940–48 supplement. Washington, 1948. 48 p.   Z7553.C3U46 Suppl.
   Reprinted in 1967 by Gale Research Co., Detroit, and in 1969 by B. Franklin, New York.

WESTERN EUROPE

AUSTRIA

Until 1918, Austria-Hungary; 1938–45, under German occupation; 1945–55, under Allied occupation.

No bibliography or catalog of official publications issued. Official publications are listed, but without special indication, in the classified arrangment of:

Oesterreichische Bibliographie; Verzeichnis der österreichischen Neuerscheinungen. 1954+ Wien, Verein der Österr. Buch-, Kunst-, Musikalien-, Zeitungs- und Zeitschriftenhändler.   Z2105.O33
    Compiled by the Austrian National Library.

From 1938 to 1944, Austrian official documents were listed in *Monatliches Verzeichnis der reichsdeutschen amtlichen Druckschriften* (Germany, Reichsministerium des Innern, Z2229.A15). Before 1938, the Austrian Government Printing Office and still earlier, before 1918, the Imperial Printing Office, occasionally published catalogs listing official publications for sale:

Austria. *Staatsdruckerei*. Katalog des Verlages der österreichischen Staatsdruckerei. Wien.   Z2109.V7
    Before 1918, published by the K. K. Hof- und Staatsdruckerei. Title varies.

In 1906 the library of the Imperial Printing Office issued the following catalog of its holdings:

Austria. *Staatsdruckerei. Bibliothek*. Katalog der Bibliothek der K. K. Hof- und Staatsdruckerei. Wien, K. K. Hof- und Staatsdruckerei, 1906. 381 p.   Z925.V74
    Entries are arranged by subjects in alphabetical order, with author and subject index.

The following bibliographic tools relate to statistics and law:

Austria. *Laws, statutes, etc. (Indexes)* Wegweiser durch Österreichs Bundesgesetzgebung seit 1945. [1.] + Aufl.; 1948+ Klangenfurt. annual.   DLC LL

Austria. *Statistisches Zentralamt*. Publikationen. 1960/70+ [Wien]   Z7554.A9A3

—— Verzeichnis der Veröffentlichungen des österreichischen statistischen Zentralamtes, 1945–1959. Wien, 1960. 18 l.   Z7554.A8A5

Österreichische Rechtsdokumentation. 1. Jahrg. Heft 1+ Mai 1969+ Wien, Hollinek Verlag. 10 issues a year.   DLC LL
    Lists Austrian laws and statutes, as well as regulations of provincial and local

governments. Includes a list of excerpted gazettes and other sources, and geographical, subject, and author indexes.

Silvestri, Gerhard. Die deutschsprachigen Gesetzblätter Österreichs. Eine Bibliographie. Berg a. Starenberger See, Haller [1967] 39 p.   DLC LL

BELGIUM

Until 1830, under various forms of foreign rule; 1914–18 and 1940–44, under German occupation.

There is no current list of Belgian official publications, but they are listed in:

Bibliographie de Belgique. Belgische bibliographie. 1+ année; jan. 1875+ Bruxelles.
                                                                                     Z2405.B58
    Currently issued monthly by the Bibliothèque royale Albert I. Since 1912 it has listed official publications under broad subject headings. Most of them are indexed under corporate entries.

Retrospectively, Belgian official publications for the period 1794–1914, which includes the periods of French rule (1794–1815) and Dutch rule (1815–30), are listed in the following work:

De Weerdt, Denise. Bibliographie rétrospective des publications officielles de la Belgique 1794–1914. In Centre interuniversitaire d'histoire contemporaine. Cahiers. Bijdragen, no. 30, 1963. 427 p.   DH403.C42 no. 30
    Divided into "Période française," "Période hollandaise," and "Période 1830–1914." Publications are listed in alphabetical order by title or personal author. The bibliography includes an index of personal authors and an index of geographical names and subject matter, as well as a bibliography of lists, catalogs, and other bibliographic sources of official publications (p. 424–426).

Other bibliographic tools describing official publications:

Belgium. Commission nationale belge de coopération intellectuelle. Périodiques belges, répertoire par titres et par sujets. Bruxelles, A. Dewit [1928] 471 p.   Z6956.B4B4
    The official periodicals are grouped in the alphabetical arrangement under the headings: Chambres législatives, Ministère, Moniteur, Conseil provincial, Villes et communes.

Belgium. Commission royale belge des échanges internationaux. Section littéraire. Liste des documents officiels de la Belgique. Parlement, ministères, provinces, communes, institutions et établissements officiels. Bruxelles, 1912. 45 p.
                                                                                     Z2409.B47   1912
    The publication lists official documents issued between 1900 and 1912, as well as official periodicals currently published in 1912. Similar lists were published in 1890 and 1905.

Belgium. Parlement. Documents parlementaires (Chambre et Sénat). Répertoire méthodique et alphabétique. 1901/02–1910/11+ Bruxelles.   Z2409.B46

Supersedes *Table décennale et alphabétique des pièces imprimées par ordre de la Chambre des représentants* (1831+ J393.K6) and *Table vicennale alphabétique des matières contenues dans le Recueil des pièces imprimées par ordre du Sénat* (1831+, Z2409.B455). The title from 1901/02–10/11, *Table alphabétique décennale des pièces imprimées par ordre de la Chambre des représentants et du Sénat.*

Bibliographie nationale. Dictionnaire des écrivains belges et catalogue de leurs publications 1830–1880. Bruxelles, P. Weissenbruch, 1886–1910. 4 v.   Z2401.B586
   Includes official publications for the period 1830–80, listed by title in its alphabetical arrangement, e.g., loi, mémoire, rapport, etc.

Hove, Julien van. Répertoire des périodiques paraissant en Belgique. Bruxelles, Librairie encyclopédique, 1951. 358 p.   Z6956.B4H6
—— —— Supplément. 1+ Bruxelles, Librairie encyclopédique, 1955+
      Z6956.B4H62
   Includes official periodicals. The list is arranged in alphabetical order. Also contains subject index, publishers' index, and geographical index.

Keppenne, Marie G. Les publications périodiques éditées par les services centraux des ministères, 1954. Bruxelles, Commission belge de bibliographie, 1957. 63 p. (Bibliographia Belgica, 22)   Z2405.B57 no. 22
   List of periodicals issued by agencies of the central government, arranged by agencies, with an alphabetical index of titles.

Picard, Edmond, *and* Ferdinand Larcier. Bibliographie générale et raisonnée du droit belge. Relevé de toutes les publications juridiques parues depuis la séparation de la Belgique et de la France (1814) jusqu'au 1er Octobre 1889. Bruxelles, F. Larcier, 1882–90. 4 v. in 1.   Z6458.B4P5
   Continued in *Bibliographie générale et raisonnée du droit belge. Tome II (1889–1903)*, issued in Brussels by the Institut international de bibliographie, 1906–13 (Z6458.B4P6).

Publications scientifiques de l'État. Choix de publications récentes éditées par: les Archives générales du Royaume, la Bibliothèque royale de Belgique, l'Institut d'aéronomie spatiale de Belgique, l'Institut royal météorologique de Belgique, l'Institut royal du patrimoine artistique, l'Institut royal des sciences naturelles de Belgique, le Jardin botanique de l'État, le Musée royal de l'Afrique centrale, les Musées royaux d'art et d'histoire, les Musées royaux des beaux-arts de Belgique, l'Observatoire royal de Belgique. (Exposition organisée à la Bibliothèque Albert Ier, Bruxelles, du 11 au 15 janvier 1966). (Bruxelles) [Bibliothèque royale de Belgique] 1966. 54 p.   Z2409.P8
   A list of scientific publications, in a classified arrangement, of 11 official institutions. It also gives a short history of institutions (p. 6–13) and includes an alphabetical index of authors and titles of anonymous works. Published also in Flemish under the title *Wetenschapelijke publikaties uitgegeven van het Rijk.* (Brussel [Koninklijke Bibliotheek van België] 1966. Z2409.W4).

Répertoire bibliographique du droit belge. [Liège] Presses universitaires de Liège, 1947–62. 3 v.   DLC LL
   Covers Belgian law for the period 1919–60.

Senelle, Robert, *and* Maurice Mees. Guide de références légales et réglementaires. Bruges, La Charte, [1967+]   DLC LL
   Looseleaf indexes to Belgian laws and statutes.

For official publications of or relating to the former Belgian administration of Belgian Congo and Ruanda-Urundi, the bibliographic works of Théodore Heyse, as well as the lists of publications of the Belgian Ministry of African Affairs (formerly Ministère des colonies, Ministère du Congo belge et du Ruanda-Urundi), should be of great assistance to the researcher:

Belgium. *Ministère des affaires africaines.* Liste des publications. Lijst der uitgaven. [Bruxelles] annual.   Z3631.B4
    Issued earlier by Ministère des Colonies and Ministère du Congo belge et du Ruanda-Urundi. It lists publications of the Ministry, the Institut national pour l'étude agronomique du Congo belge, and other institutions concerned with colonial affairs.

Heyse, Théodore. Bibliographie du Congo belge et du Ruanda-Urundi (1939–1951) L'Afrique centrale dans le conflit mondial. Bruxelles, G. Van Campenhout, 1953. 2 v. (Cahiers belges et congolais, no. 21–22)   Z3631.H427

——— Bibliographie du Congo belge et du Ruanda-Urundi (1939–1949) Documentation générale, histoire et expansion belge, biographies, Stanley, articles et ouvrages généraux. Bruxelles, G. Van Campenhout, 1950. 73 p. (Cahiers belges et congolais, no. 12)   Z3631.H4

——— Bibliographie juridique du Congo belge et du Ruanda-Urundi, période 1939– [1951. n. p., n. d.] 26 pts in 1 v.   DLC LL
    Detached pages from several numbers of the two periodicals in which this bibliography has appeared: *Anglo Belgian Trade Journal* (London) July/Aug. 1944–Jan./Apr. 1947 and *Belgique coloniale et commerce international* (Brussels) Feb. 1949–June 1953.

——— Bibliographie juridique du Congo belge et du Ruanda-Urundi, 1939–1951: Droit et administration. Tableau d'assemblage. Bruxelles, G. Van Campenhout, 1953. 12 p.   DLC LL

——— Le travail bibliographique colonial belge de 1876 jusqu'en 1933. [Bruxelles?] Éditions universitaires, 1948. 20 p.   Z2451.C7H48
    "Extrait de Zaïre, juin 1948."

Under the title *Documentation générale sur le Congo et le Ruanda-Urundi,* Théodore Heyse published a number of bibliographies, containing a considerable number of official publications. The bibliographies, covering the period 1950–60, were published in the *Bibliographia Belgica* (Z2405.B57), under the following numbers: no. 4 (1950–53); no. 18 (1953–55); no. 39 (1955–58); no. 56 (1958–60). No. 26, by the same author, entitled *Bibliographie des Territoires d'Outre-Mer, (soumis à l'autorité de la Belgique),* and no. 43, by Jean Berlage, entitled *Répertoire de la presse du Congo belge (1884–1958) et du Ruanda-Urundi (1920–1958),* also include publications issued by the Belgian government, or the colonial administration.

CYPRUS

Up to 1878, Turkish possession; 1878–1960, British; independence: 1960.

There is no bibliography or list of government publications issued currently. The Government Printer issues a *Price List of Publications for Sale at the Government Printing Office, Nicosia, Cyprus.* Some official publications are listed in the *Kypriakē Bibliographia (Bibliography of Cyprus)*, compiled annually since 1960/61 by Costas D. Stefanou. For retrospective listing of official documents, the following works will be of interest:

Cyprus. *Laws, statutes, etc. (Indexes)* Index to the statute laws of Cyprus compiled by M. Shemi. Nicosia, Printed by Government Printer, 1939. 134 p.   DLC LL
"...a complete index to the laws and subsidiary legislation, and to orders of the King in Council, acts of the imperial Parliament, treaties and conventions applicable to Cyprus, in force on the 31st December 1938."

Gt. Brit. *Colonial Office.*
Annual report on Cyprus. 1946–[59] London, H. M. Stationery Off. (*Its* Colonial annual reports)   DS54.A2A33
Previously issued in the numbered series *Colonial Reports—Annual,* suspended in 1940. Includes a list of official publications in its "reading list."

DENMARK

Union with Norway, 1380–1814; with Sweden, 1388–1523; German occupation, 1940–44.

Since 1948 the Danish Institute for International Exchange of Publications has annually issued:

Bibliografi over Danmarks offentlige publikationer. 1+ arg.; 1948+ København, Dansk bibliografisk kontor. annual.   Z2569.A25
At head of title: *Impressa publica Regni Danici.*
Title, 1948–59: *Bibliografisk fortegnelse over statens tryksager og statsunderstøttede publikationer.* Includes municipal publications of Copenhagen and Århus (from 1951). Preface and main entries of the subject index also in English.

Bibliographies listing Danish official publications retrospectively or currently for certain fields:

Denmark. *Grønlands styrelse.* Registre til Kundgørelser, Tjenestemeddelelser og Beretninger vedrørende Grønlands styrelse og Landsraads forhandlinger. København.   Z2569.A3
Index to official publications concerning the administration of Greenland and to the debates of the provincial parliament of Greenland (1913–47).

Denmark. *Rigsarkivet.* Skrifter udgivet af Rigsarkivet 1852–1968. København, 1968.
8 p.   Z2569.A5
A mimeographed list of the publications of National Archives.

Denmark. *Statistiske departement.* Statistisk aarbog. Annuaire statistique. København,
1896+   HA1477
A list of publications of the Statistical Department has been included since
1896.

[Hansen, Karl A.] *comp.* Oversigt over beretninger, betaenkninger m. v. udgivet ved
statens foranstaltning i tiden 1848–1929. København, trykt hos J. H. Schultz a.-s.,
1929. 86 p.   Z2569.H24
Provisional print, arranged by subject in 16 groups, of a proposed retrospective checklist of Danish official publications.

Lund, Torben. Den danske retslitteratur, 1950–1955. København, Nyt nordisk forlag,
1956. 94 p.   DLC LL
A bibliography of Danish legal literature.

—— Juridiske litteraturhenvisninger. København, Nyt nordisk forlag, 1950. 229 p.
                                                                                    DLC LL
Reference works of Danish legal literature.

Søndergaard, Jens K. Jura. Fortegnelse over juridisk litteratur. København, Gads
Boghandel, 1966. 159 p.   DLC LL
An index to legal literature.

U.S. *Bureau of the Census.* Bibliography of social science periodicals and monograph
series: Denmark, 1945–1961. [Washington, 1963] 111 p. (*Its* Foreign social science
bibliographies. Series P–92, no. 11)   Z7161.U43 no. 11
Contains a substantial number of official publications in its classified arrangement. Includes subject, title, personal author, and issuing agency indexes.

FINLAND

Until 1809, part of Sweden; 1809–1917, part of Russia; independence:
1917.

The Finnish Parliamentary Library (Eduskunnan Kirjasto) has issued
since 1961 an annual catalog of Finnish official publications. Official
publications for sale are covered in catalogs and their supplements, issued
by the Government Publishing Office (Valtion julkaisutoimisto; since
1967, Valtion painatuskeskus):

Finland. *Eduskunta. Kirjasto.* Valtion virallisjulkaisut. Statens officiella publikationer.
Government publications in Finland. 1961+ Helsinki. annual.   Z2520.A3F25
Arranged in alphabetical order by the Finnish name of agencies, references
being made from the Swedish names. Contains printed publications issued during
the year, with the exclusion of maps and publications of state-controlled or
subsidized organizations. Includes name index and subject index in Finnish,
Swedish, and English.

Finland. *Valtion painatuskeskus.* Luettelo. [1967+] Helsinki.   Z2520.A3F34
—— Lisäluettelo. Helsinki.   Z2520.A3F342

Classified, general catalog of Finnish official publications, issued irregularly by the Government Publishing Office and kept up to date by annual supplements (*Lisäluettelo*). The catalog has been issued since 1926 under the earlier names of the Publishing office: 1926–49, *Valtioneuvoston julkaisuvaraston luettelo* (issued by Valtioneuvoston kirjapaino ja julkaisuvarasto); 1956, 1961, *Valtion julkaisutoimiston luettelo* (issued by Valtion julkaisutoimisto, Z2520.A3F33). Supplements (*Lisäluettelo*) also published occasionally (Z2520.A3F332). In earlier years the catalog was occasionally also published in Swedish (1927, 1935), and special sales catalogs of official statistics, committee reports, maps, and older publications, supplementary to the general catalog, have also been issued by the publishing office.

The following bibliographies and lists may also be of assistance:

Finland. *Eduskunta. Kirjasto.* Valtion komiteanmietinnöt. Statens kommittebetänkanden. 1930–1960. Toimittaneet/Redigerad av Aune Autti & Kaarina Einola. Helsinki, Valtion painatuskeskus, 1966 [i.e. 1967] 326 p. (*Its* Julkaisuja, 4)
JN6713.A513
    This list of state committee reports includes printed and mimeographed reports, both in Finnish and Swedish, in chronological order.

Finland. *Geologinen tutkimuslaitos.* Guide to the publications of the Geological Survey of Finland, 1879–1960. Compiled by Marjatta Okko and Marjetta Hannikainen. Helsinki, 1960. 104 p.   Z6034.F5A53
    Includes area, subject, and author indexes.

Finland. *Maanmittaushallitus.* Karttaluettelo.
1. tammikuu 1946+ [Helsinki, Valtioneuvoston kirjapaino]   Z6027.F5A23
    List of maps issued by the Surveyor General's Office. Catalogs of Finnish charts have been published by the Hydrographic Office (Merikarttaosasto).

Finland. *Merikarttaosasto.* Luettelo Merenkulkuhallituksen merikarttalaitoksen merikorteista ja muista julkaisuista. Catalogue of Finnish charts and other publications. Helsinki, 1947. 7 p.   Z6027.F5A25

────── Merikarttaluettelo. Catalogue of Finnish charts. Helsinki, 1956. 16 p.
Z6027.F5A27
Reissued occasionally.

Finland. *Tilastollinen päätoimisto.* Suomen tilastollinen vuosikirja. Statistical yearbook of Finland. 1+ 1879+ Helsinki.   HA1448.F53
    Includes a list of the Statistical Office publications in Finnish, Swedish, and English. Also issued separately.

U.S. *Bureau of the Census.* Bibliography of social science periodicals and monograph series: Finland, 1950–1962. [Washington, 1963] 85 p. (*Its* Foreign social science bibliographies. Series P–92, no. 12)   Z7161.U43 no. 12
    Contains a substantial number of official publications in its classified arrangement. Includes subject, title, personal author, and issuing agency indexes.

U.S. *Treaties, etc. 1933–1945 (Franklin D. Roosevelt)* Exchange of official publications. Agreement between the United States of America and Finland. [Dec. 1938] Washington, U.S. Govt. Print. Off., 1939. 4 p. ([U.S. Dept. of State. Publication 1294] Executive agreement series no. 139)   JX236 1929 no. 139
Z690.U73
    Includes a list of Finnish official publications.

FRANCE

Monarchy up to 1789 (1792); First Republic, 1792–1804; First Empire, 1804–14; Monarchy, 1814–48; Second Republic, 1848–52; Second Empire, 1852–70; Third Republic, 1871–1946 (German occupation and Vichy government, 1940–44); Fourth Republic, 1946–58; Fifth Republic, 1958– .

Two bibliographies cover currently the official publications of France:

Bibliographie de la France; ou, Journal général de l'imprimerie et de la librairie. 1.+ année; nov. 1811+ Paris, Au Cercle de la librairie. weekly.   Z2165.B58
   Supplément F: Publications officielles, issued since 1950 at irregular intervals, 4–7 times a year, presents the most complete listing of official publications received at the Service of legal deposit of the Bibliothèque Nationale. Official publications are listed in the following categories: Budgets, lois et traités; Assemblées constitutionelles; Cours et jurisdictions; Administration centrale; Administration locale; Administration Outre-Mer; Établissements publics et entreprises nationalisées; États étrangers; Organisations intergouvernementales. The supplement lists in full only publications of purely administrative character and makes references to items, such as official scientific and technical publications, periodicals, maps, etc. to listings in the main section of the bibliography and in the other supplements. There is an annual index of corporate authors.
   Before 1950, official publications were listed only in the main section, marked since 1937 by an asterisk.

Bibliographie sélective des publications officielles françaises. 1.+ année; 15 jan. 1952+ Paris, Documentation française. semimonthly.   Z2169.B5
   The bibliography, prepared by an editorial committee composed of representatives of the Bibliothèque Nationale and several government agencies, is issued in two parts: "Documents administratifs," arranged by categories, similar to the arrangement of the *Supplément F* of the *Bibliographie de la France;* and "Bulletin des sommaires," analyzing contents of selected official periodicals. The bibliography is highly selective and contains citations to parliamentary and other documents, in particular to the contents of the *Journal officiel,* which otherwise would be likely to escape notice. A subject, agency, and name index is issued annually.

The following works will clarify many aspects of French official documentation, both retrospectively and currently:

Childs, James B.   French government document bibliography. [n.p., 1953] 13 p.
                                                                          Z2169.C47
   Reprinted from *Library Science in India; Silver Jubilee Volume Presented to the Madras Library Association* (Madras, 1953. Z674.C38) . Presents a brief history of French government printing, with citations of retrospective bibliographies of French official documents.

Dampierre, Jacques *marquis* de.   Les publications officielles des pouvoirs publics; étude critique et administrative. Paris, A. Picard et fils, 1942. 628 p.   Z7164.G7D3
   Describes official publications in general and French official publications in particular, including special chapters on: "Principales publications officielles françaises" (p. 594–612) , "Documents diplomatiques français de la période 1920–

1940" (p. 613–614), and "Journaux officiels de la France et de son empire" (p. 615–618), within its "Index bibliographique."

Doré, Robert.   Bibliographie des "Livres jaunes" à la date du 1er janvier 1922. Paris, H. Champion, 1922. 28 p.   Z6465.F7D6
    Reprinted from *Revue des bibliothèques* (Paris, 32e année, 1922, p. [109]– 136). It lists French diplomatic documents from approximately 1860 to 1920. The listing is extended to 1940 in Dampierre's *Les publications officielles des pouvoirs publics*.

France. *Ministère de l'éducation nationale*.   Inventaire général des publications officielles. Première série: Institutions centrales de l'état, tome premier: Publications administratives et techniques, 1937–1938. Paris, Librairie Berger-Levrault, 1940. 100 p.   Z2169.A1F85
    A Commission des Publications Administratives was set up by order of the minister of finance in August 1937, to prepare a continuing catalog of French official publications. Due to war conditions, only the first hundred pages of this publication, containing the preface and the listing of parliamentary publications, were printed. Jacques Dampierre, who was in charge of this project, later published his *Publications officielles des pouvoirs publics* (see above).

[La Peyrie,] Bibliographie administrative, ou Nomenclature méthodique et raisonnée des recueils de lois et d'arrêts, des instructions et réglements ministériels, des traités de jurisprudence et de doctrine administratives, suivie d'une liste des documents officiels et des principaux ouvrages publiés en France sur les diverses matières de l'administration, par un employé du Ministère de l'intérieur. Paris, Joubert, 1848. 208 p.   Z2169.L31
    Includes legislative and other statutory documents, documents of various administrative agencies and works on administrative matters.

Paris. Bibliothèque nationale. *Département des imprimés*.   Catalogue de l'histoire de France. Paris, Firmin Didot frères, 1855–79. 11 v.   Z2176.P23
    The classes of constitutional and administrative history in v. 6–7 include many official publications. The class "Législation" is not included. In addition to the 11 volumes, there have been issued: "Table des auteurs" (1895), "Table générale alphabétique des ouvrages anonymes" (1905–32), and "Table des divisions" (1966). Six autographed supplements, including one on constitutional history and one on military and maritime history, have been published from 1880 to 1895. A reprint of the *Catalogue* was published by the Bibliothèque nationale, Paris, in 1968–69 (Z2176.P234).

—— Catalogue général des livres imprimés de la Bibliothèque nationale. Actes royaux. Paris, Impr, nationale, 1910–60. 7 v.   Z2176.P26
    Lists royal decrees and other acts from the earliest times to 1789. Volume seven is a subject index (Table analytique).

Paris. *Imprimerie nationale*.   Catalogue des publications mises en vente par l'Imprimerie nationale. Paris [1923?+]   Z2169.P23
    A sales catalog, usually revised annually.

Répertoire de la presse et des publications périodiques françaises. [1.]+ ed.; 1957+ Paris, La Documentation française.   Z6956.F8R39
    Includes government periodicals in its classified arrangement. Its section N4 lists official periodicals issued by central government agencies, départements (préfectures), and municipalities. There is also a "Table des collectivités" and "Table générale alphabétique des titres périodiques."

Répertoire des publications périodiques et de série de l'administration française.
[Paris, La Documentation française, 1973] 368 p.   Z2169.C64 1973
   List of French government serials. Arranged by agencies, with alphabetical
index.

The following two lists relate to official publications issued by the
French Committee of National Liberation and by French and German
authorities in occupied France during World War II:

Comité français de la libération nationale. *Commissariat à l'information.* Catalogue
des publications de la France combattante, juin 1940–juin 1943. Alger, 1943. 18 l.
Typescript (carbon copy).   Z2187.F7C6
   Includes publications issued in London and other centers of Free French
authorities.

Paris. Chambre de commerce et d'industrie. *Bibliothèque.* Liste de références aux
principales dispositions législatives et administratives parues au Journal officiel
de l'État français ... et au Journal officiel des ordonnances allemandes pour les
territoires français occupés. [Paris] monthly. 23 no. in 1 v.   DLC LL
   Lists main legislative and administrative decisions published in the official
gazette of the French State (Vichy) and in the official gazette of German authorities for occupied French Territory.

The French parliamentary records are printed in two editions. The
debates are first printed in the *Journal officiel* (not mentioning the
Compte rendu analytique, which is the original record of debates, distributed to members of the respective chambers). Later revised by the
Service des archives, they are issued in numbered volumes, with indexes
(Table des débats) usually included in the last volume of the session.
Both the *Journal officiel* and the parliamentary edition print documents as annexes to the debates. The documents are also printed separately (often as single sheets) and numbered individually. These *Impressions* include legislative bills (projet de loi, proposition de loi), budgets,
committee reports, messages of the president, etc.
   The following indexes are issued to current parliamentary records:

France. Journal officiel. Tables. [Paris]   J7.F2H
   Issued annually and separately for each part of the *Journal* (Lois et décrets,
Débats, Documents, etc.) Indexes for parliamentary debates (both for Assemblée
nationale and Sénat) are issued in three sections "Table nominative," "Table
des matières" and "Table des questions écrites." There is a separate index for
the documents.
   The *Journal officiel* since 1868 and its predecessor *Moniteur universel* from
1789 to 1868 printed records of the French legislative bodies.

France. *Parlement (1946–) Assemblée nationale.* Tables générales des documents et
débats parlementaires rédigées par les Services des procès-verbaux et des archives.
1.+ législ.; 28 nov. 1946–4 juil. 1951+ Paris, Impr. de l'Assemblée nationale.
                                                                    J341.H27625

An index to documents and debates of the Assemblée nationale, covering a legislative period. Issued in two parts, the first being a subject index, which includes an annex listing the *Impressions* by number, and cross-reference to the subject index; the second part, an index of names of the Assembly members, lists in chronological order their legislative activities. This index, compiled exclusively for the Assemblée nationale, is not to be confused with the annual (sessional) indexes included in the last sessional volume of the debates of the Assemblée nationale and the Sénat.

Retrospectively, from 1861, annual or sessional indexes to debates and documents have been included in the parliamentary records at the end of each session. For the period 1787–1860, the records and indexes are printed in:

Archives parlementaires de 1787 à 1860; recueil complet des débats législatifs & politiques des chambres françaises imprimé par ordre du Sénat et de la Chambre des députés. Paris, Librairie administrative de P. Dupont, 1862+   J341.H2
     The publication, first issued in 1862, prints records of the French legislative bodies in two series, the first covering the period 1787–99, the second, 1800–60. In the first series, the period covered up to date is 1787–94, in 89 volumes; in the second series, 1800–39, in 127 volumes.
     Indexes covering longer periods or certain sectors of parliamentary documentation were issued as follows:
     First series: v. 1–6 (États généraux), 1787–89, in v. 7; v. 8–32 (1789–91), in v. 33; v. 34–50 (1791–92), in v. 51; v. 52–70 (1792–93), in v. 71.
     Second series: v. 1–13 (1800–15), in v. 14; v. 15–61 (1815–30), in v. 62.

France. *Assemblée consultative provisoire. 1943–1945.* Débats de l'Assemblée consultative provisoire. Paris, Imp. des journaux officiels, 1945. 3 v.   J341.H27
     Includes a subject and name index at end of v. 2 and 3. Index also issued separately as *Table analytique des débats.* Sessions d'Alger (3 nov. 1943–25 Juil. 1944) et de Paris (7 nov. 1944–3 août 1945).

——— Documents. Annexes aux procès-verbaux des séances. Demandes d'avis, propositions de résolution, rapports. [Paris, 1946] 2 v.   J341.H2732
     Volume 2 bound with *Documents parlementaires. Assemblée consultative provisoire et Assemblée nationale constituante élue le 21 octobre 1945. Table chronologique, 1944–45.*

——— [Impressions] No. 1–631; séance du 3 nov. 1943–3 août 1945. [Paris]   J341.H273
     Includes: *Table alphabétique (nominative et méthodique) des impressions.*

France. *Assemblée nationale, 1871–1942.* Table alphabétique (nominative et méthodique) des Impressions du Sénat et de la Chambre des députés. 12 fév. 1871/31 déc. 1875–1 Juin 1936/31 mai 1942. Paris, 17 v.   J341.H55

France. *Assemblée nationale, 1871–1942. Chambres des députés.* Tables analytiques des Annales. 3.–16. législature; 1881/85–1936/40. Paris. 14 v. in 28.   J341.K212
     Each volume in 2 pts.: "Table des matières," "Table nominative." Includes references to other publications of the Chamber, as *Impressions, Fascicules, Feuilletons,* and some references to the *Journal officiel.*

France. *Assemblée nationale constituante, 1945–1946.* Tables générales des documents et débats parlementaires, rédigées par les Services des procès-verbaux et des

archives. t. 1–3; 6 nov. 1945–10 juin 1946. Paris, Impr. de l'Assemblée nationale
constituante. 3 v. in 1.   J341.H27623
    In 3 parts: "Table des matières," "Table nominative," and "Questions di-
verses."

France. *Assemblée nationale constituante, June–Oct. 1946.* Tables générales des documents et débats parlementaires, rédigées par les Services des procès-verbaux et des
archives. t. 1–3; 11 juin–27 nov. 1946 Paris, Impr. de l'Assemblée nationale constituante. 3 v. in 1.   J341.H27624
    In 3 parts: "Table des matières," "Table nominative," and "Questions di-
verses."

A number of official or semi-official agencies issue lists of their own
publications, or if they use private publishing facilities, their publications are likely to be included in the catalogs of their publishers. In the
following, some of the more substantial bibliographies or lists concerning
agencies, periods, or fields, will be listed:

Charbonnages de France. *Centre d'études et recherches.* Publications des stations
centrales de recherches minières françaises, 1907–1952 [par M. Ferrari] Paris
[1953] 54 p.   Z6738.C6C45
    Lists publications of the French research stations on coal mining.

Cormier, Reine. Les sources des statistiques actuelles; guide de documentation. Paris,
Gauthier-Villars, 1969. 287 p. (Documentation et information).   Z7551.C65
    Lists sources of statistical information under broad subjects (general statistics,
demographic and health statistics, economic statistics, cultural statistics, etc.).
Includes international sources with detailed listing of French statistical publications.

David, René. Bibliographie du droit français, 1945–1960, établie pour le Comité
international pour la documentation des sciences sociales. Paris, Mouton, 1964.
252 p. (Maison des sciences de l'homme. Publications. Série A: Bibliographies, 1).
                                                                            DLC LL

France. Journal officiel. Tables. Paris.   J7.F2H
    Issued annually and separately for each part of the *Journal* (Lois et décrets,
Débats parlementaires, Documents parlementaires, etc.).

France. *Armée. Service géographique.* Catalogue des cartes, plans et ouvrages divers.
Paris.   Z6028.F81
    Lists maps and other related publications up to 1939. Continued under In-
stitut géographique national.

France. *Commissariat à l'énergie atomique.* Liste récapitulative des Notes de C.E.A.
publiées par le Commissariat à l'énergie atomique, 1953–1962. Gif-sur-Yvette
(Seine-et-Oise), Service central de documentation du C. E. A., Centre d'études
nucléaires de Saclay [1963] 53 p. (*Its* Série "Bibliothèque" 1001)   Z5160.F688

———— Liste récapitulative des Rapports C. E. A. [Gif-sur-Yvette (S. et O.)] Z5160.F69
    Began publication with issue covering July 1948–Oct. 1956. Some volumes
cumulative from July 1948. The 1948–62 issues included both original reports
and reprints (Première série). From 1963, limited to original reports (Deuxième
série).

—— Liste récapitulative des textes C.E.A. publiés dans la presse scientifique, 1962–1964. [Gif-sur-Yvette (S. et O.)] 1965. 573 p. (*Its* Série "Bibliothèque," BIB 1005).
Z5160.F72

France. *Direction de la documentation.* Catalogue méthodique. 1945/55+ Paris. annual.   AI1.F7
An index to publications of the Documentation française, mainly to *Notes et études documentaires* and *Textes du jour.* Cumulated editions have been issued for 1945–55 and 1956–60.

—— Documentation française. Index général. Paris, 1948+   DLC
Publications of the Documentation française indexed in two parts: 1. by country; 2. by subject if publication or article deals with general subjects or international problems.

France. *Institut géographique national.* Catalogue des cartes en service publiées par l'Institut géographique national. Paris [1953+]   Z6027.F8A52

—— Catalogue des cartes publiées par l'Institut géographique national. Paris, 1943.
Z6027.F83A2
Contents. 1. fasc. Cartes de France et publications diverses. 2. fasc. Cartes de l'Afrique du Nord, des départements et territoires d'outre-mer . . . publications diverses.

France. *Institut national de la statistique et des études économiques.* Répertoire des sources statistiques françaises. Paris, Imprimerie nationale, 1962+   Z7554.F7A5
A looseleaf guide to French statistical sources, with a subject index.

France. *Service hydrographique.* Catalogue des cartes, plans et ouvrages qui composent l'hydrographie française. Paris, Imprimerie nationale [1873?+] Z6026.H9F82

Legeard, Claude. Guide de recherches documentaires en démographie. Paris, Gauthier-Villars, 1966. 322 p. (Documentation et information)   Z7164.D3L4
Includes general documentation on demographic statistics, with detailed account of French statistical sources (p. [91]–189).

Stumberg, George W. Guide to the law and legal literature of France. Washington, U.S. Govt. Print. Off., 1931. 242 p.   Z6458.F8S78

U.S. *Library of Congress. Census Library Project.* National censuses and vital statistics in France between two world wars, 1921–1942; a preliminary bibliography. Washington, 1945. 22 p.   Z7554.F7U5
Reproduced from typewritten copy.

Overseas departments and territories of France

For official publications of French outlying departments and territories (Départements d'outre-mer, Territoires d'outre-mer), the sources listed below may be of some assistance. A number of comprehensive retrospective bibliographies, mainly in English, listing both official and unofficial publications of or on former French colonies will also be cited here. Others will be found in the chapter on Africa—General bibliographies and under the names of respective countries.

Current Caribbean bibliography. v. 1+, June 1951+ [Hato Rey, Puerto Rico, Caribbean Regional Library] irregular.   Z1595.C8
Lists selected official publications of the French possessions in the Caribbean area. Volume 4, *The French Caribbean Departments; Sources of Information, 1946–1955* by Berthe E. Canton, lists a substantial number of official publications.

France. *Institut national de la statistique et des études économiques. Service de coopération.* Bibliographie démographique 1945–1967. Travaux publiés par l' I. N. S. E. E. (Service de la coopération), les services de statistique des États africains d'expression française ou de Madagascar, et le Ministère de la Coopération. Paris, 1967. 67 p.   Z7165.F8A48
Lists statistical works on demography published by the French Statistical Institute, statistical services of African countries (formerly French), Madagascar, and the Ministry of Cooperation.

—— Bulletin bibliographique. no. 1+ août 1948+ [Paris] monthly (irregular).
Z7165.F8A3
Published originally by Ministère de la France d'outre-mer, Service des statistiques. The *Bulletin* lists a considerable number of official publications of French overseas possessions.

French Union. *Assemblée. Service de la bibliothèque et de la documentation.* Index des articles relevés dans les revues et périodiques metropolitains et d'outre-mer. [Paris?] monthly.   AI7.F72
Includes articles published in official periodicals.

U.S. *Library of Congress. African Section.* Africa south of the Sahara; index to periodical literature, 1900–1970. Boston, G. K. Hall, 1971. 4 v.   Z3503.U47
"The arrangement of the *Index* is by area (region or country) and by subject within areas..."
Contents: v. 1, Africa-General-Central Africa.-v. 2, Central African Republic-Ivory Coast.-v. 3, Kenya-Somalia.-v. 4, South Africa-Zambia. Literary index.
Includes official periodicals of France and former French possessions. A list of excerpted periodicals is included in v. 1.

—— Madagascar and adjacent islands; a guide to official publications. Compiled by Julian W. Witherell, African Section. Washington, General Reference and Bibliography Division, Reference Department, Library of Congress; [U.S. Govt. Print. Off.] 1965. 58 p.   Z3702.U5
Includes official publications of or relating to the Comoro Islands and Réunion.

—— Official publications of French Equatorial Africa, French Cameroons, and Togo, 1946–1958; [a guide] compiled by Julian W. Witherell, African Section. Washington, General Reference and Bibliography Division, Reference Department, Library of Congress. [U.S. Govt. Print. Off.] 1964. 78 p.   Z3691.U5

—— Sub-Saharan Africa; a guide to serials. Washington, Library of Congress [U.S. Govt. Print. Off.] 1970. xx, 409 p.   Z3503.U49
Includes a considerable number of official serials.

U.S. *Library of Congress. Library of Congress Office, Nairobi.* Accessions list, Eastern Africa. v. 1+ Jan. 1968+ Nairobi. quarterly.   Z3516.U52
Includes the French Territory of the Afars and the Issas (formerly French Somaliland) and the Réunion.

Witherell, Julian W. French-speaking central Africa; a guide to official publications in American libraries. Washington, Library of Congress [U.S. Govt. Print. Off.] 1973. 314 p.   Z3692.W5

——— French-speaking West Africa; a guide to official publications. Washington, General Reference and Bibliography Division, Library of Congress [U.S. Govt. Print. Off.] 1967. 201 p.   Z3672.W5
    Lists official publications of the government of French West Africa from 1895 to 1959 (p. 1–37). French colonial administration (p. 146–175), French Union (p. 176), and French Community (p. 177); also Organisation Commune Africaine et Malgache (p. 178). Publications of former colonies are listed under the names of present countries: Dahomey, Guinea, Ivory Coast, Mali, Mauritania, Niger, Senegal, Togo, Upper Volta.

GERMANY

Up to 1870, various forms of government over constantly changing territory; Deutscher Bund, 1815–66; Deutscher Zollverein, Norddeutscher Bund, 1867–70; empire, 1871–1918; republic, 1919–33; Third Reich, 1933–45.

Presented in this section are official publications of Germany up to 1945, followed by publications of the Federal Republic of Germany. The German Democratic Republic publications are included with "People's Democracies" of East Central Europe in the next section of this guide.

The first systematic listing of German official publications did not appear until 1928, when the German Ministry of the Interior, through the Deutsche Bücherei, began publishing its *Monatliches Verzeichnis der reichsdeutschen amtlichen Druckschriften*. Almost simultaneously the Preussische Staatsbibliothek began issuing an accessions list of official publications, *Deutsche amtliche Druckschriften, Erwerbungen der Staatsbibliothek zu Berlin*, which, however, had only an ephemeral lifespan (1928–30).

For the earlier periods of German official documentation, the bibliographic control is almost nonexistent, although some categories of official publications have been listed in special catalogs (e.g., the White Books). Several central or provincial agencies have issued lists of their own publications. Further sources of bibliographic control, even if not satisfactory, are the library catalogs or accessions lists, such as *Berliner Titeldrucke* (Berlin, Preussische Staatsbibliothek, 1892–1936. Z926.B5N), which is a list of the accessions of the Prussian State Library. The *Handbuch für das Deutsche Reich* (Berlin, C. Heymann. JN3204), published from 1874 to 1936, listed some official documents in its editions after the First World War. Another source is the *Handwörterbuch der preussischen Verwaltung*, originally compiled by Rudolf von Bitter (3d ed., Berlin, W. de Gruyter & Co., 1928. JN4529.H2 1928). Winifred Gregory's *List of the Serial Publications of Foreign Governments, 1815–1931* (New York, H. W. Wilson, 1932. Z7164.G7L7), is probably one of the most useful bibliographic tools for early German official documents, listing serial publications of the central government, as well as those of the

German states. It also includes some official serials of former German colonies (East and Southwest Africa and German New Guinea).

Bibliographies on German history constitute another source for tracing official documents. One of the most useful tools in this respect is *Quellenkunde der deutschen Geschichte,* by Friedrich C. Dahlmann and Georg Waitz, 10. Aufl. (Stuttgart, A. Hiersemann, 1965+ Z2236.D14). In chapters devoted to political, legal, constitutional, and administrative history, many primary and secondary sources to official documentation are indicated. Similar source is *Quellenkunde der Geschichte des preussischen Staats,* by Karl Kletke (Berlin, Verlag von E. H. Schroeder, 1958–61. Z2244.P9K4).

The following bibliographies deal with official publications in general, mainly for the post-First World War period:

Berlin. Preussische Staatsbibliothek. Deutsche amtliche Druckschriften, Erwerbungen der Staatsbibliothek zu Berlin. Berlin, Staatsbibliothek, 1928–[30]   Z2229.B51
    An accessions list of German official publications. Divided into two parts: Publications of central agencies, state agencies and public corporations; publications of local governments and church communities. Covers only 1927 and 1929. The list for 1928, although announced as "in preparation," was apparently never published.

Germany. *Reichsministerium des Innern.* Monatliches Verzeichnis der reichsdeutschen amtlichen Druckschriften. Herausgegeben und bearbeitet von der Deutschen Bücherei. 1–17. Jahrg. 1928–März/Juni 1944. Berlin, Reichs– und Staatsverlag, 1928–44.
    Includes official and semi-official publications of the central government, the state governments, including Austria from March 1938, and the larger municipalities. Monthly and annual indexes.

—— Die Veröffentlichungsorgane des Deutschen Reichs und der deutschen Länder nebst den laufenden amtlichen Veröffentlichungen der obersten Reichs—und der Reichsmittelbehörden. (Stand 15. September 1925) [Berlin, 1926?] 39 p. mimeographed.   Z2229.A14
    The list includes mainly the official bulletins and other publications of the federal ministries and those of the state ministries.

Neuburger, Otto. Official publications of present-day Germany; government, corporate organizations and National Socialist Party, with an outline of the governmental structure of Germany. Washington, U.S. Govt. Print. Off., 1942. 130 p.   Z2229.N4
    The publication emphasizes serial publications and generally indicates the starting year. Besides federal and provincial publications, it also includes the gazettes of the territories occupied by Germany from the beginning of World War II.

Schwidetzky, Georg. Deutsche Amtsdrucksachenkunde; ein methodisches Handbuch für Parlamentarier, Verwaltungsbeamte, Bibliothekare, Archivare und Lehrer der Staatsbürgerkunde. Leipzig, Otto Harrasowitz, 1927. 109 p. (Beiheft zum Zentralblatt für Bibliothekswesen, 59)   Z2229.S41
    The publication is the first attempt in Germany to define government publications and to point out their importance for research.

Parliamentary documents for both the Bundesrat and the Reichstag
have been regularly indexed in the cumulative and sessional indexes:

Germany. *Bundesrat.* Protokolle [und Drucksachen] zu den Verhandlungen des
Bundesrats des Deutschen Reichs. Berlin.   Z351.J58

—— Generalregister . . . einschliesslich des Bundesraths des Zoll– und Handelsvereins
und des Bundesraths für Elsass-Lothringen für die Jahre 1867 bis 1881. Berlin,
1882. 330 p.   J351.J58 Index

—— Sachregister zu den Protokollen und Drucksachen des Bundesraths einschliesslich des Bundesraths des Zoll– und Handelsvereins für die Jahre 1867 bis 1890.
Bearbeitet im Reichsamt des Innern. Berlin, Reichsdruckerei, 1891. 230 p.
                                                                J351.J58 Index

—— Sachregister zu den Protokollen und Drucksachen des Bundesraths für die
Jahre 1891 bis 1900. Bearbeitet im Reichsamt des Innern. Berlin, Reichsdruckerei, 1902. 109 p.   J351.J58 Index

Germany. *Reichstag.* Verhandlungen. Stenographische Berichte. [1871–1938] Berlin,
Reichsdruckerei. 440 v.   J351.K22 Index
    The index for the period 1871–94/95 also includes the proceedings of the
North German Confederation (Konstituierender Reichstag, Zollverein, Zoll-
parlament) . From 1897, sessional indexes issued.

Staatsbibliothek der Stiftung Preussischer Kulturbesitz. *Abteilung Amtsdruckschriften.*
Deutsche Parlamentaria; ein Bestandsverzeichnis der bis 1945 erschienenen Druckschriften. Berlin, 1970. 140 p.   DLC
    A chronological catalog of German parliamentary papers from 1816 to 1945.
In two parts: 1. Deutsche Bundesversammlung, 1816–66; Deutsche National-
versammlung, 1848–49; Deutscher Zoll- und Handelsverein, 1868–70; Norddeutscher Bund, 1867–70; Deutscher Reichstag, 1871–1933; Deutsche Nationalver-
sammlung, 1919–20; Bundesrat (des Deutschen Reichs) 1871–1918; Reichsrat,
1919–33. 2. Provincial parliaments (Länderparlamente) .

Parliamentary publications, as well as law collections and other documents, for both the federal government and some state governments,
are included in the following works:

Facius, Friedrich. Die Verwaltungs-Drucksachen der Thüringischen Staaten vom 18.
Jahrhundert bis 1922. Bibliographische Übersicht der periodisch erschienen amtlichen Veröffentlichungen. *In* Verein für Thüringische Geschichte und Alter-
tumkunde. Zeitschrift. Jena, N. F. 33, 1938/39: 190–232; 467–475.   DD801.T4V3
    Includes a considerable number of Thüringian official publications from 1920
and those of its component states before 1920.

Germany. *Reichstag. Bibliothek.* Katalog der Bibliothek des Reichstages. Berlin,
1890–99. 5 v.   Z7166.G37
    Official publications are listed mainly in the first three volumes, with additions
in the supplements.

Germany. *Statistisches Reichsamt.* Die Veröffentlichungen des Kaiserlichen statisti-
chen Amts 1873 bis Ende 1899. Berlin, Puttkammer & Mühlbrecht, 1900. 32 p.
                                                                Z7554.G3G3
    Later, updated editions issued occasionally.

Prussia. *Landtag. Haus der Abgeordneten. Bibliothek.* Bücher-Verzeichnis des Hauses der Abgeordneten. Berlin, 1900–1917 (?)   Z7166.P965

U.S. *Library of Congress. Law Library.* Guide to the law and legal literature of Germany, by Edwin M. Borchard. Washington, Govt. Print. Off., 1912. 226 p.
                                                                        DLC LL

Wolfstieg, August. Bibliographie der Schriften über beide Häuser des Landtags in Preussen. Berlin, W. Greve, 1915. 757 p.   Z7165.P9W8

The following group of bibliographies, catalogs, and indexes relates mainly to the documents concerning the German foreign policy:

American Historical Association. *Committee for the Study of War Documents.* A catalogue of files and microfilms of the German Foreign Ministry archives, 1867–1920. [Washington] 1959. 1290 columns.   CD1261.A52
    "The present catalogue ... is both a record of files of the Political Depart- ment of the German Foreign Ministry ... and a guide to all the microfilming programs. The catalogue shows the filming which has been done and identifies the holders of negative copy."

—— Guides to German records microfilmed at Alexandria, Va. Washington, Na- tional Archives and Records Service, 1958–[1969] [1 v.]   D735.A58
    "The microfilm ... has been deposited in the National Archives."

California. University. *Library.* An index of German Foreign Ministry archives, 1867– 1920, microfilmed at Whaddon Hall for the General Library, University of Cali- fornia, Berkeley. Berkeley, 1957. 1 v. (various pagings) .   CD1261.C3

Michigan. University. *Library.* A catalogue of German Foreign Ministry Archives, 1867–1920, microfilmed at Whaddon Hall for the University of Michigan under the direction of Howard M. Ehrmann. [Ann Arbor] 1957. 73 1.   CD1261.M5
    "The University of Michigan collection does not duplicate other collections. In some instances it supplements or completes other filming programs."

Moeller, Johannes. Zeitgeschichtliche Dokumentation; vom Farbbuch zum Aktenwerk —von Lüge zur Wahrheit. Geist der Zeit, v. 18, 1940: 243–250; 298–304; 365–381; 560–575.   AP30.G33 v. 18
    Includes bibliographies of German "white books" and other documents con- cerning the First World War, the growth of the Third Reich, and the Second World War. Some Austro-Hungarian, Serbian, Russian, French, Belgian, British, Italian, and United States official documents concerning the two World Wars are also listed.

Sass, Johann. Die deutschen Weissbücher zur auswärtigen Politik, 1870–1914; Ges- chichte und Bibliographie. Berlin und Leipzig, W. de Gruyter & Co., 1928. 224 p.
                                                                        DD221.5.S3
    Lists German "white books" published between 1870 and 1914.

Schwandt, Ernst. Index of microfilmed records of the German Foreign Ministry and the Reich's Chancellery covering the Weimar Period, deposited at the National Archives. Washington, National Archives, 1958. 95 p.   Z2240.S3

U.S. *Dept. of State. Historical Office.* A catalog of files and microfilms of the German Foreign Ministry archives, 1920–1945. Stanford, Calif., Hoover Institution, Stan- ford University, 1962–66— (Hoover Institution publications)   CD1261.A65
    Compiled by George O. Kent, of the Historical Office of the Dept. of State, the catalog continues and completes for the period 1920–45, the *Catalogue of*

Files and Microfilms of the German Foreign Ministry Archives, 1867–1920, published by the American Historical Association in 1959. (See above).

Weinberg, Gerhard L. Guide to captured German documents. Prepared... under the direction of Fritz T. Epstein. [Maxwell Air Force Base, Alabama, Air University, Human Resources Research Institute, 1952] 90 p. (Columbia University. Bureau of Applied Social Research. War documentation project study no. 1) Human Resources Research Institute. Research memorandum no. 2., v. 1. Z2240.W4
—— —— Supplement. [Washington, National Archives and Records Service, 1959] 69 p. Z2240.W4 Suppl.

For the German African colonies (1880–1918), a comprehensive select bibliography, which includes government publications, is Jon Bridgman's *German Africa: A Select Annotated Bibliography,* published by the Hoover Institution, Stanford University (Stanford, Calif., 1965. 120 p. Z3751.B7). It includes the official publications on German East and Southwest Africa, Togo, and Cameroon in the Hoover collections. A "Note on German official and semiofficial publications" is printed on p. v-viii.

GERMANY

Federal Republic, 1949– , including the period 1945–55, under allied occupation.

Current official publications are covered in the following special biennial edition of the *Deutsche Bibliographie,* published by the Deutsche Bibliothek in Frankfurt am Main. Official documents are also listed in the weekly edition of the *Deutsche Bibliographie,* but without any special distinction, in alphabetical order of titles within various subject groups:

Deutsche Bibliographie; Verzeichnis amtlicher Druckschriften. 1957–58+ Frankfurt a. M., Buchhändler-Vereinigung [1962+] biennial. Z2229.D48
   Compiled by the Deutsche Bibliothek, it includes in alphabetical order of the names of agencies, federal (Bund), provincial (Länder), municipal (Kommunen), and church (Kirchen) publications in that order. The indexes are by agency, place, title and keyword, and by personal names.

Deutsche Bibliographie. Wöchentliches Verzeichnis. März 1947+ Frankfurt a.M., Buchhändler-Vereinigung. weekly. Z2221.F75
   Issued in two main parts (A, in the book trade; B, outside the book trade). Both parts list official publications received at the Deutsche Bibliothek. A third part lists maps. Periodical indexes (monthly, quarterly) should be of assistance in identifying official publications through corporate authors. The quinquennial cumulative indexes also list publications in German, issued in Austria, Switzerland, and other countries.

An explanation of the complex problems of bibliographic control of official publications in Western Germany during the post-World War II period, as well as the listing of official documents, is contained in the following works:

Childs, James B.   Corporate author entry as regards the German Federal Republic.
[n. p.] 1964. 12 p.   Z695.8.C5
Reprinted from *Library Science Today (Ranganathan Festschrift*, v. I)
chapt. E3, p. 151–162.

———— German Federal Republic official publications, 1949–1957, with inclusion of
preceding zonal official publications; a survey. Washington, Library of Congress,
Reference Dept., Serial Division, 1958. 887 p.   Z663.44.G4
"This study attempts to identify all official publications of the Federal Republic and of the earlier zonal organizations, insofar as it has been possible to
identify these publications from sources available in the Library of Congress.
The official publications of the Länder, however, are not included."

Germany *(Federal Republic, 1949–) Press und Informationsamt.* Das amtliche Schrift-
tum der Bundesrepublik. [1] Aufl., 1952. Bonn, Deutscher Bundesverlag. 47 p.
                                                                                              Z2229.A12
Includes only federal publications. A second, enlarged (114 p.) edition was
published in 1957.

Marburg. Westdeutsche Bibliothek. *Abteilung Internationaler Amtlicher Schriftenaus-
tausch für die Bundesrepublik Deutschland.* Verzeichnis amtlicher Veröffentlichungen der Bundesrepublik Deutschland. Marburg/Lahn, 1959. 93 p.
Only federal government publications listed. Includes an index of agencies.

Price, Arnold H.   The Federal Republic of Germany; a selected bibliography of
English-language publications, with emphasis on the social sciences. Washington,
Library of Congress [U.S. Govt. Print. Off.] 1972. 63 p.   Z2240.3.P75
Official publications are listed under broad subject headings. An index of au-
thors and titles includes names of government agencies.

A considerable number of German federal and provincial agencies
occasionally or periodically issue lists of their own publications which
may supplement the *Deutsche Bibliographie.* Following are listed only
a few of the works which may help the researcher to identify the agencies
or which cover certain categories of official publications (parliament,
laws, statistics, etc.):

Ämter und Organisationen der Bundesrepublik Deutschland. [1+] Frankfurt am Main.
[1966+]   JN3971.A125A62
Each issue contains a description of the history and organization of an individual agency.

Die Bundesrepublik Deutschland. Köln, C. Heymann.   JN3971.A485
A looseleaf handbook describing the German governmental organization on
the federal and provincial (Länder) level.

Germany *(Federal Republic, 1949–) Bundesrat.* Verhandlungen; Stenographische Ber-
ichte. 1+ Sitzung; 7, Sept. 1949+ Bonn.   J351.J23
Subject and speakers index issued periodically, covering a number of sessions.
Cumulative subject index covering sessions no. 1–227 (1949–60) .

Germany *(Federal Republic, 1949–) Bundestag.* Verhandlungen. Stenographische
Berichte. 1+ Wahlperiode; Sept. 7, 1949+ Bonn.   J351.K25

———— ———— Anlagen zu den stenographischen Berichten. Drucksachen. 1+ Wahlperiode; Nr. 1+ Bonn, 1950+   J351.K25 Anlagen
Subject and speakers indexes issued for each legislative period (Wahlperiode) .

Germany. *(Federal Republic, 1949–)* *Bundestag. Wissenschaftliche Abteilung.* Bibliographien. [no. 1+ 1962+] Bonn.   Z7161.G4
   Specialized bibliographies on various subjects concerning German political, economic, and social problems. Includes newspaper and periodical articles.

Germany *(Federal Republic. 1949–)* *Laws, statutes, etc. (Indexes)* Fundstellen der Bundesgesetzgebung und Fortschreibung der Sammlung des Bundesrechts, Bundesgesetzblatt, Teil 3, nach dem Stande vom 31. Dez. 1951+ Bonn, Bundesanzeiger Verlagsges. annual.   DLC LL
   Published as a supplement to the *Bundesgesetzblatt,* Jan. 1, 1959+. A cumulative index to the legislation and statutory orders in effect, as published in the *Bundesgesetzblatt* and in the *Bundesanzeiger.*

Germany *(Federal Republic, 1949–)* *Statistisches Bundesamt.* Verzeichnis der Veröffentlichungen des Statistischen Bundesamtes. Stuttgart, Kohlhammer. Z7554.G3A25
   A list of publications of the Federal Office of Statistics, published annually.

Kapferer, Clodwig. Quellen für statistische Marktdaten; Führer durch die amtliche Statistik der Bundesrepublik Deutschland. Hamburg, Verlag Weltarchiv, 1964. 139 p.   HA37.G3K33
   A description of the scope of official statistics on both the federal and provincial level.

GREAT BRITAIN

The complex nature and the great variety of British official publications and the numerous changes in the governmental structure create intricate problems in the use of these publications. For this reason, experts in government publishing, and the Stationery Office itself, felt the need to provide more or less detailed guides to facilitate the use of this vast documentation. Following are guides describing retrospective or current publications, as well as the British governmental organization:

Cowell, Frank R. Brief guide to government publications. London, H. M. Stationery Off., [1938] 43, [1] p.   Z2009.A1C8
   Describes pre-World War II publications by broad subjects.

Gt. Brit. *Stationery Office.* Published by HMSO; a brief guide to official publications. London, 1960. 58 p.   Z232.G867
   "This booklet is intended to serve as a guide under broad subject headings to the very wide range of publications issued and sold by H. M. Stationery Office."

Gt. Brit. *Treasury.* Official publications. London, H. M. Stationery Off., 1958. 19, [1] p.   Z2009.A1G73
   "... intended to give civil servants a general description of the various types of papers produced by the Government or Parliament ... It includes some reference to the publications of the nationalized industries."

Mallaber, K. A. The sale catalogues of British Government publications, 1836–1965. Journal of librarianship [London] v. 5, April 1973: 116–131.   Z671.J66

Morgan, Annie M. British Government publications: an index to chairmen and authors, 1941–1966. London, Library Association, 1969. [3] 193 p.   Z2009.M64
   "The purpose of this index is to assist librarians and research workers to identify reports where they are known only by the name of the chairman or author."

Ollé, James G. An introduction to British government publications. London, Association of Assistant Librarians, 1965. 128 p.   Z2009.04
    Includes bibliographies. A revised edition issued in 1972.

Pemberton, John E. British official publications. [1st ed.] Oxford, New York, Pergamon Press, [1971] 315 p. (The Commonwealth and international library. Library and technical information division)   Z2009.P45 1971
    "This book sets out to describe, within the context of the parliamentary and governmental processes from which they derive, all the different categories of British official publications." More than half of the work is devoted to parliamentary documents, with a detailed listing of indexes, a concordance of command papers (1833–1968), alphabetical lists of royal commissions (1900–69), and of departmental committees, working parties, and tribunals of inquiry (1900–69). Nonparliamentary publications are described in the second part, with special chapters devoted to "Science, technology and medicine" and "Statistics." An index of subjects, titles, authors, and committee chairmen is included. Second revised edition published in 1973.

Royal Institute of Public Administration. The organization of British central government 1914–1964: a survey by a group of the Royal Institute of Public Administration; edited by D. N. Chester; written by F. M. G. Willson. 2d ed. London, Allen & Unwin, 1968. 521 p.   JN425.R67 1968
    Bibliographical references included in "Notes," p. [414]–435. Includes a "table of changes" in the British governmental organization to October 1964, p. [436]–480. For recent changes, consult the British Museum's *Check List of British Official Serial Publications.*

General catalogs and lists

Most of the British official publications are printed and distributed by Her Majesty's Stationery Office (HMSO) in London. The lists and catalogs of this office date back to about the 1880's. Currently, HMSO issues a mimeographed daily list, a monthly catalog with an insert (*HMSO Monthly Selection*), and an annual cumulative catalog:

Gt. Brit. *Stationery Office.* Government publications. Jan. 1936+ [London] monthly, with annual cumulations.   Z2009.G822
    Title of the annual volume varies: 1936–50, *Consolidated List of Government Publications;* 1951–55, *Government Publications, Consolidated List* (or *Catalogue)* ; 1956+, *Catalogue of Government Publications.* Indexes are included in monthly and annual editions and cumulated quinquennially. Supersedes *Monthly List of Government Publications* and *Monthly Circular.*
    The catalog includes only publications placed on sale. Does not include *Statutory Instruments* (published separately), free publications, admiralty charts, maps, or publications distributed by issuing agencies. Publications of overseas agencies and international organizations, available from the Stationery Office, included in the monthly list, are cumulated in a special supplement to the annual catalog (*International Organisations and Overseas Agencies Publications.* Z6464.I6I62). A number of publications entitled *Sectional List,* each one devoted to the publications of an agency or a subject, have been published occasionally since 1947, continuing the pre-World War II lists. Numbered from 1 to 70 (not all of them republished), the sectional lists are revised from time to time. The *Daily List of Government Publications from Her Majesty's Stationery Office* (Z2009.G774) is published daily except Saturday and Sunday. Unlike the monthly and the annual editions, it lists *Statutory Instruments.*

The current catalog is the continuation of the following lists:

Gt. Brit. *Stationery Office.* Monthly circular of recent selected publications. Nov. 1922–[1935] [London, H. M. Stationery Office]   Z2009.G782

—— Monthly list of government publications. Jan. 1922–[1935] [London, H. M. Stationery Off.]   Z2009.G82

     Formed in 1922 by a combination of the *Monthly* and *Quarterly Lists of Parliamentary Publications* and the *Monthly* and *Quarterly Lists of Official Publications,* issued 1897–1921 (see below). Annual volumes 1922–35 issued as no. 12 of the *Monthly List* under the title *Consolidated List of Government Publications.* (1922 has title: *Consolidated List of Parliamentary and Stationery Office Publications.*) From 1923 to 1935, a semiannual cumulation was also published (as no. 6). In January 1936 it combined with the *Monthly Circular,* as *Consolidated List of Government Publications.*

—— Quarterly list (with prices and postage affixed) of official and parliamentary publications. London, [1894–96]   Z2009.G794

     Published from March 1894, with annual cumulations. A continuation of the periodical *List of Parliamentary Papers for Sale,* which was issued annually beginning with 1836 and quarterly beginning with 1873, by Hansard and Son, printer to the House of Commons until 1886, when *List* was taken over by the Stationery Office. (Z2009.G793)

—— Quarterly list of official publications (with prices ... and postage affixed) issued by H. M. Stationery Office. 1897–1921. London.   Z2009.G796

     No. IV of each year cumulative for the year. A monthly list was also issued during the same period (Z2009.G786). Continued in the *Monthly List* ... Jan. 1922–[1935]

—— Quarterly list of parliamentary publications (with prices ... and postage affixed), issued by H. M. Stationery Office. 1897–1921. London.   Z2009.G8

     No. IV of each year cumulative for the year. A *Monthly List of Parliamentary Publications* (issued since 1881?) was also published during the same period (Z2009.G79). Continued in the *Monthly List* ... Jan. 1922–[1935]

Other bibliographic tools which may supplement retrospective lists cited previously:

Gt. Brit. *Stationery Office.* Catalogue of works (other than parliamentary papers and acts of Parliament) published by H. M. Stationery Office ... Revised to 31st December 1920. London, H. M. Stationery Office, 1921. 352 p.   Z2009.G77 1921

     Last cumulative consolidated sales catalog of nonparliamentary publications, its place having been taken by departmental and subject lists. After World War II, continued in *Sectional Lists.*

—— List of official & parliamentary publications, available for exchange with foreign and colonial governments. [London] H. M. Stationery Off. [1882–1906?] Z2009.G78

—— List of works published on account of Her Majesty's Stationery Office. London, Printed by George E. Eyre and William Spottiswoode. [1867–87?]   Z2009.G781

A practical instrument for the control of the most important British official serial publications is:

British Museum. *State Paper Room.* Check list of British official serial publications.
1967+ London. annual.   Z2009.B87
   "The main object of producing the check list is to give those who are re-
sponsible for serials maintenance an opportunity of verifying quickly the currency of their files."
   Includes, from 1969, a list of new, changed, and defunct official bodies, with
dates of changes.

Parliamentary publications

Besides John E. Pemberton's *British Official Publications* (Oxford, New
York, 1971), the following works will be of assistance to researchers in
the field of the British parliamentary publications:

Ford, Percy, *and* G. Ford.   A guide to parliamentary papers; what they are, how to
find them, how to use them. [New ed.] Oxford, Blackwell, 1956. 79 p.
                                                            Z2009.A1F6   1956

Gt. Brit. *Parliament. House of Commons. Library.* A bibliography of parliamentary
debates of Great Britain. London, H. M. Stationery Off., 1956. 62 p. (*Its* Document, no. 2)   Z2009.G7

Lees-Smith, Hastings B.   A guide to parliamentary and official papers. London, New
York, Oxford University Press, 1924. 23 p. (London. School of Economics and
Political Science. Series of Bibliographies, no. 5)   Z2009.A1L4

Menhennet, David.   The journal of the House of Commons; a bibliographical and
historical guide. London, H. M. Stationery Off., 1971. 95 p. (Gt. Brit. House of
Commons. Library. Document no. 7)   DLC
   Appendix one: *Availability of the Printed Commons Journals Volumes and
of the General Indexes.* A partial union list of the holdings of journals by
British libraries other than the Parliamentary libraries.

The Parliamentary history of England from the earliest period to the year 1803, from
which last-mentioned epoch it is continued downwards in the work entitled
"Hansard's parliamentary debates." v. 1–36; 1066/1625–1801/03. London, Printed
by T. C. Hansard, 1806–20. 36 v.   J301.H2
   Title varies: 1066/1625–1741/43, *Cobbett's Parliamentary History of England,
from the Norman Conquest in 1066 to the Year 1803, From Which Last Mentioned Epoch It Is Continued Downwards in the Work Entitled "Cobbett's
Parliamentary Debates."* Detailed tables of contents and indexes of names of
speakers are included in individual volumes.

The Parliamentary or constitutional history of England; being a faithful account of
all the most remarkable transactions in Parliament, from the earliest times. Collected from the journals of both houses, the records, original manuscripts, scarce
speeches, and tracts; all compared with the several contemporary writers, and
connected, throughout, with the history of the times. By several hands. London,
Printed and sold by T. Osborne and W. Sandby, 1751–61. 24 v.   J301.H178
   Covers parliamentary history to the restoration of King Charles II (1660).
Volume 24: *A General Index to the Twenty-Three Volumes of the Parliamen-
tary or Constitutional History of England.*
   A second edition (title varies slightly) was published in London, printed for
J. and R. Tonson, 1761–63. (J301.H18)

Rodgers, Frank, *and* Rose B. Phelps. A guide to British Parliamentary papers. [Urbana] 1967. 35 p. (Illinois. University. Graduate School of Library Science. Occasional papers, no. 82)   Z674.I52 no. 82

Indexes to parliamentary journals, debates, and sessional papers are numerous and rather difficult to use. The guides listed earlier should be of great assistance in this respect. Following are the main official indexes:

Gt. Brit. *Parliament. House of Commons.* Journals. [London]   J301.K3
    There are indexes for each session and cumulative indexes exist for various periods (the first one being 1547–1714) until 1880, when decennial indexes began.

—— Parliamentary debates (Hansard). Official report. v. 1+, Feb./Mar. 1909+ London, H. M. Stationery Off.   J301.K22
    The last volume for each session is (or includes) a general index for the volumes in that session.
    There were four series (1909+ being the fifth of the series) of debates published before 1909, beginning with 1803. The volumes up to 1803, entitled *The Parliamentary History of England from the Earliest Period to the Year 1803* ... v. 1–36; 1066/1625–1801/03 (London, Hansard, 1806–1820. J301.H2), are not actual reports of debates but a collection of records of parliamentary proceedings compiled from original sources. Also: *The Parliamentary or Constitutional History of England ... from the Earliest Times.* (London, T. Osborne and W. Sandby, 1751–61. 24 v. J301.H178) Volume 24 is a general index.

—— Sessional papers. [London]   J301.K6
    The last volume of each session is index for that session. Since 1870, these are consolidated into decennial indexes. There is a *General Index* for the period 1801–52, issued in three volumes: *General Index to the Bills* ..., *General Index to the Reports of Select Committees* ..., and *General Index to the Accounts and Papers, Reports of Commissioners, Estimates, etc.* ...; a *General Alphabetical Index to the Bills, Reports, Estimates, Accounts, and Papers, Printed by Order of the House of Commons, and to the Papers Presented by Command, 1852–1899.* In 1960 a *General Index to the Bills, Reports and Papers Printed by Order of the House of Commons and to the Papers Presented by Command, 1900 to 1948/49* was published.

The following two official catalogs to sessional papers relate to the pre-1800 period:

Gt. Brit. *Parliament. House of Commons.* Catalogue of papers printed by order of the House of Commons from the year 1731 to 1800. In the custody of the clerk of the journals. [London, H. M. Stationery Off., 1953] 101 p.   J301.A2   1800a
    A reprint of the 1807 edition.

—— Hansard's catalogue and breviate of parliamentary papers, 1696–1834. Reprinted in facsimile, with an introduction by P. Ford and G. Ford. Oxford, Blackwell, 1953. 220 p.   J301.K62 1953
    A reprint of the 1836 edition.

For the House of Lords publications, indexes have been compiled, as follows:

Gt. Brit. *Parliament. House of Lords.* Journals [London]   J301.J3
Each sessional volume has its own index. Cumulative indexes have been compiled for various periods until 1852/53. Beginning with 1854–63, decennial indexes have been published.

—— The parliamentary debates (Hansard). Official report. v. 1+, Feb./May 1909+
London, H. M. Stationery Off.   J301.J22
Up to 1965 there was a weekly index and a sessional index. From 1965/66, a progressively cumulative index is also being published, covering all previous debates. The final edition is the general index for the session.

—— Sessional papers. [London]   J301.J6
From 1921, only sessional lists are published. A numerical list of the Lords' sessional papers is also published in the annual *Catalogue of Government Publications* (HMSO). Between 1886 and 1920 an index, entitled: *Tables of the Papers Ordered by the House of Lords and of the Papers Presented by His Majesty's Command . . . Followed by an Alphabetical Index to the Titles of All the Papers of the Session*, was issued. Papers from 1801 to 1884/85 are covered by three cumulative indexes, entitled *A General Index to the Sessional Papers Printed by Order of the House of Lords or Presented by Special Command* (1801–59; 1859–70; 1871–84/85). A facsimile reprint of 1801–59 index was made by H. M. Stationery Office in 1938.

Following are nonofficial works and indexes relative to parliamentary papers, including the reports of Royal Commissions, blue books, etc.:

Clokie, Hugh McDowall, *and* J. William Robinson. Royal commissions of inquiry; the significance of investigation in British politics. London, H. Milford, Oxford University Press, c1937 242 p.   JN407.C6
Reprinted in 1969 by Octagon Books, New York.

Cole, Arthur H. A finding list of British royal commission reports: 1860 to 1935. Cambridge, Mass., Harvard University Press, 1935. 66 p.   Z2009.C68

Di Roma, Edward, *and* Joseph A. Rosenthal. A numerical finding list of British command papers published 1833–1961/62. New York, New York Public Library, 1967. 148 p.   Z2009.D5

Ford, Percy, *and* G. Ford. A breviate of parliamentary papers, 1900–1916. Oxford, Blackwell, 1957. xlix, 470 p.   JN549.F59
Reprinted in 1969 by Irish University Press, Shannon.

—— A breviate of parliamentary papers, 1917–1939. Oxford, Blackwell, 1951. xlviii, 571 p.   JN549.F6
Reprinted in 1969 by Irish University Press, Shannon.

—— A breviate of parliamentary papers, 1940–1954: war and reconstruction. Oxford, Blackwell, 1961. 1, 515 p.   JN549.F62

—— Select list of British parliamentary papers, 1833–1899. Oxford, Blackwell, 1953. xxii, 165 p.   J301.M3
Reprinted in 1969 by Irish University Press, Shannon.

Gt. Brit. *Parliament. House of Commons.* List of House of Commons sessional papers, 1701–1750; edited by Sheila Lambert. London, Swift (P. & D.), 1968. 155 l. (List & Index Society. Special series, v. 1)   CD1042.A2L56 vol. 1

King. (P. S.) & Son, Ltd., *London.* Catalogue of parliamentary papers, 1801–1900, a few of earlier date. London [1904] 317 p. Z2009.K55

"Does not pretend to be a complete and exhaustive list of all the papers ordered to be printed by Parliament, but it is claimed that the most important papers, diplomatic correspondence, reports of commissions and select committees are given here in a form more easily referred to than in the official general indexes." Compiled by Hilda V. Jones.

—— Catalogue of parliamentary papers, 1901–1910, being a supplement to Catalogue of parliamentary papers, 1801–1900. London [1912] 81 p. Z2009.K55 Suppl.

—— Catalogue of parliamentary papers, 1911–1920, being the second decennial supplement to the Catalogue of parliamentary papers, 1801–1900. London [1922] 58 p. Z2009.K55 Suppl. 2

The three volumes of the *Catalogue* were reprinted in 1972 by Burt Franklin, New York.

Rodgers, Frank. Serial publications in the British Parliamentary papers, 1900–1968; a bibliography. Chicago, American Library Association, 1971. xix, 146 p. Z2009.R63

Serials which have appeared in the House of Commons *Sessional Papers* are listed by issuing agencies. The bibliography also provides a key to the subject headings used in the principal indexes of parliamentary papers. A brief summary of the history of agencies is also included.

Temperley, Harold W. V., *and* Lillian M. Penson. A century of diplomatic blue books, 1814–1914. Lists edited, with historical introduction. Cambridge [Eng.] The University Press, 1938. xvi p. 600 p. Z2009.T28

Reprinted in 1966 by Cass, London, and Barnes & Noble, New York.

Vogel, Robert. A breviate of British diplomatic blue books, 1919–1939. Montreal, McGill University Press, 1963. xxxv, 474 p. Z2009.V6

"The general purpose of this work . . . is to continue the task undertaken by Temperley and Penson in their *A Century of Diplomatic Blue Books, 1814–1914.*"

In 1968, the Irish University Press, Shannon, began reprinting the 19th century British parliamentary papers in a projected 700 volume subject set. The general indexes were published in 8 vols. (Z2009.I73).

Nonparliamentary publications

Publications of British governmental agencies are covered satisfactorily in the HMSO catalogs and its sectional lists. Additional lists are published either periodically or occasionally by individual agencies. Guides to British government publications, listed earlier, also furnish much information on this category of official publications. Following are only a few examples of more important bibliographies or lists, covering certain subjects:

Edlin, Herbert L. Check list of Forestry Commission publications, 1919–65. London, H. M. Stationery Off. [1966] 36 p. ([Gt. Brit.] Forestry Commission. Forest record, no. 58) SD1.G66 no. 58

Gt. Brit. *Central Statistical Office.* List of principal statistical series available. London, H. M. Stationery Off., 1965. 36 p. *(Its* Studies in official statistics no. 11)
    HA37.G583 no. 11

Gt. Brit. *Hydrographic Office.* Catalogue of Admiralty charts and other hydrographic publications. [1849?+] London. annual.   Z6026.H9G7

Gt. Brit. *Ordnance Survey.* Catalogue of the maps and plans and other publications. London [1881–1924?]   Z6027.G7G7
—— —— Supplement to catalogue. London [1921–38?]   Z6027.G7G73

—— Publication report. Chessington, Eng. [1953?+]   DLC

—— Report. London, H. M. Stationery Off. annual.   GA66.G7A32
Called *Report of the Progress* from 1871 to 1938/39. (GA66.G7A3)
Includes lists of maps published during the year.

Gt. Brit. *Permanent Consultative Committee on Official Statistics.* Guide to current official statistics of the United Kingdom. [no. 1–vol. 17, 1922–38] London, H. M. Stationery Off., 1924–[1939] annual.   Z7554.G7G7

Gt. Brit. *Public Record Office.* Maps and plans in the Public Record Office. London, H.M.S.O., 1967+   Z6028.G767
Contents: 1. British Isles, c. 1410–1860. [648 p.]

Harvey, Joan M. Sources of statistics. [Hamden, Conn.] Archon Books [1969] 100 p.
    Z7554.G7H3
List of unpublished documents of economic and social interest. [London?] Interdepartmental Committee on Social and Economic Research [1948–58] 8 no. in 1 v.
    Z7165.G8L5

Newby, Frank. How to find out about patents. [1st ed.] Oxford, New York, Pergamon Press, [1967] 177 p.   T210.N4 1967
Includes bibliographies.

United Kingdom National Committee of Comparative Law. A bibliographical guide to the law of the United Kingdom, the Channel Islands, and the Isle of Man. London, Institute of Advanced Legal Studies, 1956. 219 p.   DLC LL
An updated edition published in 1973.

Northern Ireland

Gt. Brit. *Stationery Office, Belfast.* Consolidated list of the publications of the Government of Northern Ireland. 1921–1937. Belfast, H. M. Stationery Off., 1938. 141 p.
    Z2035.G79
Supplementary lists published 1938+

—— Government of Northern Ireland annual list of publications. [1961+] Belfast.
    DLC

—— Monthly list of publications [July 1938?+] Belfast.   Z2035.G82

Northern Ireland. *Laws, statutes, etc. (Indexes)* Chronological table and index of the statutes affecting Northern Ireland. 1st+ ed. Belfast, H. M. Stationery Off., 1930+
    DLC LL
Formerly included in *Chronological Table and Index to the Statutes of Great*

Britain. Issued in two volumes: 1. *Chronological Table;* 2. *Index to the Statutes in Force.*

—— Index to the statutory rules and orders of Northern Ireland in force on 31st December 1961, shewing the statutory powers under which they are made. 9th ed. Belfast, H. M. Stationery Off., 1962. 449 p.   DLC LL

The Commonwealth

This section includes only a few general works which list official publications, retrospective and current, concerning the British Commonwealth in general, its member states, associated states, and dependent territories. Some of the retrospective works will, of course, include publications related to former colonies, now independent countries. In many instances, bibliographic tools to retrospective publications of these former colonies, listed in this guide, will be found under the countries concerned.

A number of these tools have been and are published by the British central authorities concerned with commonwealth (or formerly colonial) affairs. Before July 1925, the affairs of all the British outlying territories (except India) were conducted by the Colonial Office. At that date, the Dominions Office was created to handle the relations with the independent members of the Commonwealth. In July 1947 the Dominions Office became the Commonwealth Relations Office, and on August 1, 1966, the Colonial Office was merged with the Commonwealth Relations Office under the new name, the Commonwealth Office. Finally, in October 1968, the Commonwealth Office was merged with the Foreign Office to form the Foreign and Commonwealth Office. Naturally, these changes are reflected in the official publications concerning the Commonwealth affairs.

The following works deal with the Commonwealth (and colonial) publications:

Adam, Margaret I. Guide to the principal parliamentary papers relating to the dominions, 1812–1911. Edinburgh, Oliver and Boyd, 1913. 190 p.   Z2021.C7A3

Cole, Arthur H. A finding-list of royal commission reports in the British dominions. Cambridge, Mass., Harvard University Press, 1939. 134 p.   Z2021.C7C6

Gt. Brit. *Colonial Office.* Colonial reports-annual. no. 1–1936. London, H. M. Stationery Off., 1891–1940. 1936 v.   JV33.G7A4
These annual reports have included a more or less full section listing official publications for certain colonies.
After the second World War, beginning with 1946, this publication was superseded by the *Colonial Annual Reports* (later only *Colonial Reports*). Individual reports ceased publication when the territory attained independence but are still being published currently by the Foreign and Commonwealth Office for the "dependent territories." Official publications are listed in the "Reading list."

Gt. Brit. *Colonial Office. Library Reference and Research Section.* Monthly list of official colonial publications. June 1948–[1963?] London.   Z2021.C7A32
    Regularly includes a record of official gazettes with notes as to special supplements as well as the map additions list of the Directorate of Colonial Surveys.

Gt. Brit. *Ministry of Overseas Development. Library.* Public administration: a select bibliography. Revised ed. London. 1967. 101 p.   Z7164.A2G695 1967
    Each field is covered both by general studies and national studies of the British Commonwealth countries. Part VIII contains a list of periodicals concerned with the study of public administration.

Gt. Brit. *Public Record Office.* List of Colonial Office confidential print to 1916. London, H. M. Stationery Off., 1965. 179 p. (*Its* Handbooks no. 8)   CD1052.A55

––––– List of Colonial Office records, preserved in the Public Record Office. New York, Kraus Reprint Corp., 1963. 337 p. (*Its* Lists and indexes, no. 36)
CD1040.A25 no. 36

King (P.S.) & Son Ltd., *London.* Catalogue of parliamentary reports, papers, &c., relating to Africa, 1800 to 1899. London. [1899] 16 p. (*Its* Special lists of parliamentary papers no. 18)   Z3509.K5

London. University. *Institute of Advanced Legal Studies.* Union list of Commonwealth and South African law: a location guide to Commonwealth and South African legislation, law reports and digests held by libraries in the United Kingdom at May 1963. 1963 ed. London [1963] 129 p.   DLC LL

Overseas official publications. Quarterly bulletin of official publications received by the Royal Empire Society . . . and issued in the Overseas British Empire, or relating thereto. v. 1–5. April, 1927–Jan. 1932. London, [1927–32] 5 v.   Z2021.C7O9

Ragatz, Lowell J. A check-list of House of Commons sessional papers relating to the British West Indies and to the West Indian slave trade and slavery, 1763–1834. London, The Bryan Edwards Press, [1928] 32 p.   Z1502.B5R2

––––– A check-list of House of Lords sessional papers relating to the British West Indies and to the West Indian slave trade and slavery, 1763–1934. London, The Bryan Edwards Press, [1932] 13 p.   Z1502.B5R21

Royal Commonwealth Society. *Library.* Subject catalogue of the library of the Royal Empire Society, formerly Royal Colonial Institute. By Evans Lewin. v. 1–4. [London] 1930–37. 4 v.   Z7164.C7R82
    "There have been included . . . most of the official literature published since the year 1910, as well as a selection of earlier official publications."
    Reprinted in 1967 with a new introduction by Donald H. Simpson (London, Dawsons for the Royal Commonwealth Society, 1967).
    Vol. 1: British Empire generally and Africa; vol. 2: Australia, New Zealand, South Pacific, voyages and travels, Arctic and Antarctic; vol. 3: Canada, Newfoundland, West Indies, Colonial America; vol. 4: Mediterranean colonies. India and the East.

Technical co-operation; a monthly bibliography. v. 1+ Jan. 1964+ [London] monthly.
Z2021.C7A35
––––– Supplement. 1964+ [London]   Z2021.C7A35 Suppl.
    Issued in 1964 by the Dept. of Technical Co-operation Library; 1964–70, by the Ministry of Overseas Development Library; from 1971 by the Overseas Development Administration Library. It covers official publications of all countries of the British Commonwealth. The supplement extends the coverage to bills and subsidiary legislation.

U.S. *Library of Congress. Census Library Project.* Population censuses and other official demographic statistics of British Africa; an annotated bibliography, prepared by Henry J. Dubester. Washington, U.S. Govt. Print. Off., 1950. 78 p.   Z7554.A35U5

A Year book of the Commonwealth. 1969+ London, H. M. Stationery Off.   JN248.C5912
Published currently by the Foreign and Commonwealth Office, the yearbook includes a list of British parliamentary and nonparliamentary publications relating to Commonwealth relations. The yearbook is the continuation of the following lists and yearbooks issued since 1803, listed here in chronological order: *The India Office and Burma Office List,* 1803–1947 (JQ202.A3) ; *The Dominions Office and Colonial Office List,* 1862–1940 (JV1005; published from 1862 to 1925 under the title, *Colonial Office List*) ; *The Colonial Office List,* 1946–66 (JV33.G7A2) ; *The Commonwealth Relations Office Yearbook,* 1951–66 (JN248.C58; title 1951–65, *The Commonwealth Relations Office List*) ; *The Commonwealth Office Yearbook,* 1967–68 (JN248.C59) .
The 1940 edition of the *Dominions Office and Colonial Office List* includes a "List of Parliamentary papers and nonparliamentary publications on the affairs of the dominions and colonies," covering the period 1877–1940. The 1963 edition of the *Commonwealth Relations Office List* (preamble to Chapter 11, p. 123) explains where lists of earlier official publications relating to the affairs of Commonwealth countries could be found.

The official *Blue Books* for certain former colonies have also, since about 1920, included a list of government publications and newspapers.
At the end of 1970, British dependent territories (including protectorates and protected states), administered through the Foreign and Commonwealth Office, were the following: Bahamas, Bermuda, British Honduras, British Indian Ocean territory, British Solomon Islands (protectorate), British Virgin Islands, Brunei (protected state), Cayman Islands, Falkland Islands, Gibraltar, Gilbert and Ellice Islands, Hong Kong, Montserrat, New Hebrides (Anglo-French condominium), Pitcairn, St. Helena, Seychelles, Tonga (protected state), Turks and Caicos Islands.
The group of the so-called associated states in the Caribbean area (Antigua, Dominica, Grenada, St. Christopher-Nevis-Anguilla, St. Lucia, and St. Vincent) were dealt with previously. (See Caribbean area.)
Official publications of the dependent territories, as well as those of the associated states, are currently listed in the Overseas Development Administration Library's *Technical Co-operation: a Monthly Bibliography* (London, 1964+, Z2021.C7A35).
The following individual bibliographies or lists concerning some of the dependent territories may be of assistance:

Bahamas, Bermuda, Caribbean area

British Honduras Library Service, *Belize.* A bibliography of the national collection in the Central Library, Bliss Institute, Belize. [Belize?] 1960. 52 l.   Z1449.B7
A considerable number of official publications are included. Entries are arranged by subject, with a title index.

U.S. *Library of Congress. Division of Bibliography.* British possessions in the Caribbean area: a selected list of references. Washington, 1943. 192 p.   Z1502.B5U6
Reproduced from typewritten copy. Includes government publications.

Gibraltar

Abbott, Wilbur C. An introduction to the documents relating to the international status of Gibraltar, 1704–1934. New York, Macmillan Company, 1934. 112 p.
Z2704.G44A2
"General bibliography of books, pamphlets, articles, etc. relating to Gibraltar," p. 18–94. Includes official publications, mainly parliamentary papers.

Hong Kong

Braga, José M. A Hong Kong bibliography, 1965. Hong Kong, Government Press. [1965] 17 p.   Z3107.H7B7
"This bibliography is intended only as a brief guide to some of the recent publications about Hong Kong, including those issued by the Government."

Hamilton, Geoffrey C. Government departments in Hong Kong, 1841–1969. Hong Kong, S. Young, Govt. Printer, 1969. 87 p.   JQ674.H32

Hong Kong. List of government publications. Hong Kong. quarterly.   DLC
Published currently by the Government Printer.

U.S. *Bureau of the Census.* Bibliography of social science periodicals and monograph series: Hong Kong, 1950–1961. [Washington, 1962] 13 p. (*Its* Foreign social science bibliographies. Series P–92, no. 7)   Z7161.U43 no. 7
Annotated. Some official publications are included.

Seychelles

U.S. *Library of Congress. African Section.* Madagascar and adjacent islands; a guide to official publications. Compiled by Julian W. Witherell. Washington, 1965. 58 p.
Z3702.U5
Includes official publications of the Seychelles.

Greece

Independence, 1830; republic, 1925–35; monarchy, 1935–74; (German, Italian, Bulgarian occupation, 1941–44); republic, 1974–.

No bibliography of official publications is issued. In 1956–57 two issues of *Bulletin for the Exchange of Greek Official Publications,* covering the year 1956, were published by the Office for Exchange of Official Publications, Directorate of Letters, Ministry of Religion, and National Education.

Some official publications are included in the following works:

Brooks, E. Willis. A list of materials for the study of the history of Greece, with a note of holdings in the libraries of Stanford University. [n.p.] 1963. 31 l. Z2296.B7
Official publications, p. [1]–7.

Bulletin analytique de bibliographie hellénique. Athènes [1940?+] (Collection de l'Institut Français d'Athènes)   Z2285.A75
Originally published quarterly, it became an annual after World War II. It includes some official publications in a classified arrangement.

Greek bibliography. v. I. no. 1+, 1960+ Athens. semiannual.   DLC
A classified bibliography, published by the Research and Cultural Relations Division of the Prime Minister's Office, in English and Greek. Includes official publications. Indexes covering several issues are occasionally included.

Hannay, Annie M. M. *comp.* Greece: a guide to official statistics of agriculture, population and food supply. Washington, 1932. 142 p. (U.S. Dept. of Agriculture. Bureau of Agricultural Economics [Library] Agricultural economics bibliography, no. 39)   Z5074.E3U35 no. 39
An annotated list of Greek official publications in the Library of the U.S. Dept. of Agriculture and in the Library of Congress.

U.S. *Bureau of the Census.* Bibliography of social science periodicals and monograph series: Greece, 1950–1961. [Washington, 1962] 19 p. (*Its* Foreign social science bibliographies. Series P–92, no. 5)   Z7161.U43 no. 5
An annotated bibliography. Official publications are included.

U.S. *Library of Congress. Division of Bibliography.* Greece: a selected list of references. Washington, 1943. 101 p.   Z2296.U5
A classified bibliography. Some official publications are included.

ICELAND
Under Danish rule, 1380–1918; sovereign state, king common with Denmark, 1918–41; republic, 1944– .

There is no separate list of government publications of Iceland. These are, however, included in the following works:

Reykjavík. *Landsbókasafnið.* Árbók. [1+] 1944+ Reykjavík.   Z824.R4
The yearbook includes a list of publications printed in Iceland during the year, the official publications being entered in alphabetical order under title or personal author.

——— Ritaukaskrá. Reykjavík, Ísafoldarprentsmiðja. annual.   Z941.R46
This catalog of acquisitions of the National Library covers the Icelandic government publications for the period 1886–1943.

U.S. *Bureau of the Census.* Bibliography of social science periodicals and monograph series: Iceland, 1950–1962. [Washington, 1962] 10 p. (*Its* Foreign social science bibliography. Series P–92, no. 10)   Z7161.U43 no. 10
An annotated bibliography. Includes official publications.

U.S. *Treaties, etc., 1933–1945 (Franklin D. Roosevelt)* Exchange of official publications. Agreement between the United States of America and Iceland. [Aug. 1942] Washington, U.S. Govt. Print. Off., 1942, 5 p. ([U.S. Dept. of State. Publication 1837] Executive agreement series 269)   JX236 1929 no. 269
Z690.U7I3
Includes a list of official publications of Iceland.

The *Catalogue of the Books Printed in Iceland from A.D. 1578 to 1880* (British Museum, Dept. of Printed Books, London, 1885. Z2556.B86) and the *Catalogue of the Icelandic Collection* (Cornell Univ., Libraries, Ithaca, N.Y., 1960. Z2556.C6) include Icelandic government documents.

IRELAND

Dominion status (Irish Free State) 1922–37; Dominion status (Eire-Ireland) 1937–48; republic, 1948– .

Official publications of Ireland are currently listed weekly in *Iris Oifigiúil,* the official gazette. Separately, they are listed in the following catalogs:

Ireland *(Eire) Stationery Office.* Catalogue [of] Government publications. [1948+]
    Dublin. annual.   Z2035.A12
        From 1953, also a quarterly edition published.

—— Consolidated list of official publications. 1922/25+ Dublin [1927+]   Z2035.A23

For pre-1948 official publications, the following lists will be of assistance:

Dublin. National Library of Ireland. List of publications deposited under the terms
    of the Industrial and Commercial Property (Protection) Act, 1927. no. 1–[5] Aug.
    1927/Dec. 1929–[1935/36] Dublin, Stationery Off. [1930–1937]   Z921.D82
        Each number includes a special section of official publications issued by the
        Stationery Office.

Irish Free State. *Stationery Office.* A list of government publications issued by the
    Stationery Office. [1924–?] annual.   Z2035.A15
        A monthly edition was also issued from 1925. (Z2035.A14)

—— A list of parliamentary publications. Dublin [1923]   Z2035.A19

—— A list of Stationery Office publications. Dublin. [1923]   Z2035.A22

Official publications of Ireland for the pre-1922 period are listed in the British Stationery Office catalogs.

The following are indexes to the statutes of Ireland:

Irish Free State. *Laws, statutes, etc. (Indexes)* Index to the statutes, 1922 to 1953,
    with chronological tables showing their effect on pre-Union Irish statutes, British
    statutes, Saorstat Eireann statutes, Acts of the Oireachtas, and the Local govern-
    ment (application of enactments) order, 1898. [Prepared in the Statute Law Re-
    form and Consolidation Office] Dublin, Stationery Office [1954?] 388 p.   DLC LL

—— Index to the statutes, 1922 to 1963, with chronological tables and 1964–1965
    supplement. [Prepared in the Statute Law Reform and Consolidation Office]
    Dublin, Stationery Off., [1966] 583 p.   DLC LL

ITALY

Kingdom until 1946; republic, 1946– .

The *Bibliografia nazionale italiana* (Firenze, 1958+ Z2341.B5) and its annual cumulation (Z2341.B52), includes official publications in its classified arrangement but without any indication as to their official character. From 1958 the Libreria dello Stato has issued the following catalog:

Italy. *Libreria dello stato.* Catalogo delle pubblicazioni ufficiali, legislative e varie. [1958+] Roma, Istituto poligrafico dello stato. Z2349.I82

For retrospective coverage, the main bibliographic sources are:

Italy. *Provveditorato generale dello stato.* Pubblicazioni edite dallo stato o col suo concorso (1861–1923). Catalogo generale. Roma, Libreria dello stato, 1924. 668 columns. Z2349.I88
This general document checklist is divided into the following groups: 1. Parliament from the first legislature in 1848; 2. Foreign affairs; 3. Colonies; 4. Internal administration; 5. Justice and religious affairs; 6. Finance and the Treasury; 7. War; 8. Navy; 9. Public instruction; 10. Public works; 11. National economy; 12. Posts, telegraphs and telephones; 13. Railways. Includes the royal universities and technical colleges, academies, societies and royal institutes. Indexed by authors and by topics.

———— ———— Supplemento, 1924–30+ e aggiunte al periodo anteriore. Roma, Libreria dello stato, 1931+ Z2349.I88 Suppl.
Supplements issued up to 1944.

———— Pubblicazioni edite dallo stato o col suo concorso. Spoglio dei periodici e delle opere collettive, 1901–1925+ Roma, Libreria dello stato, 1926+ AI11.I82
Indexes to periodicals and collective works. Latest, 1935–40.

The following catalogs and lists will also be of assistance:

Italy. *Istituto centrale di statistica.* Catalogo delle pubblicazioni. [1946?+] Roma. Z7554.I8I85

Italy. *Libreria dello stato.* Catalogo delle pubblicazioni dello stato. [Roma] 1940. xxvii, 327 p. Z2349.I83 1940
Supplements issued to June 1941?

———— Catalogo delle pubblicazioni e prontuario di legislazione. Roma, Istituto poligrafico dello stato, 1935. 489 p. (Italy. Libreria dello stato. Pubbl. spec. 1247) Z2349.I83 1935

———— Catalogo delle pubblicazioni legislative (alphabetico-oggettivo) 1949+ Roma. DLC LL
Continued from 1958 as *Catalogo delle pubblicazioni ufficiali, legislative e varie* (see above) .

———— Elenco delle legi e dei decreti emanati dal 1851 al 31 dicembre 1941–xx, con indicazione delle corrispondenti pubblicazioni ufficiali messe in vendita dalla Libreria dello stato. Roma, [Istituto poligrafico dello stato, 1942] 224 p. Z2349.I8415

—— Elenco numerico delle pubblicazioni della Libreria dello stato al 31 dicembre 1942. Roma, 1943. 251 p.   Z2349.I842

Italy. *Ministero dell'Africa italiana. Ufficio studi e propaganda. Biblioteca.* Catalogo delle pubblicazioni edite dall'amministrazione coloniale, presentate all'Esposizione coloniale di Anversa. Roma, 1930. 48 p.   Z2361.C7I82

Italy. *Parlamento.* Atti parlamentari, 1.–30. legislatura; 8 magg. 1848–5 ag. 1943. Roma.
                                                                          J388.H2
    Includes *Indice generale degli atti parlamentari 1848–1897* (2 v.) for the publications of the Parlamento and index 1848–1904 (1 v.) for the publications of the Camera dei Deputati.

Italy. *Parlamento. Camera dei deputati.* Atti parlamentari. Discussioni. [1]+ legislatura; 8 magg. 1948+ Roma.   J388.K23
    Includes annual indexes and a general index for the legislative session.

Italy. *Parlamento. Senato.* Atti parlamentari. Resoconti delle discussioni. [1]+ legislatura; 8 magg. 1948+ Roma.   J388.J22
    Includes annual indexes and a general index for the legislative session.

U.S. *Library of Congress. Census Library Project.* National censuses and official statistics in Italy since the First World War, 1921–1944. Washington, 1945. 58 p.
                                                                          Z7554.I8U5

LUXEMBURG
Grand duchy; under various rules until 1815; part of German Confederation, 1815–66; German occupation, 1914–18 and 1940–44.

The government printing office (Office des imprimés de l'état) occasionally issues a leaflet entitled *Publications de l'état luxembourgeois.* Official publications are also listed in:

Bibliographie luxembourgeoise. [1]+ année; 1944/45+ Luxembourg, P. Linden.
                                                                          Z2461.B5
    Includes government publications. Since 1962 official publications are designated with +. Volume for 1947 includes a list of maps and plans of the country and the city of Luxemburg.

Hury, Carlo. Luxemburgensia; eine Bibliographie der Bibliographien. Luxembourg, Impr. Saint-Paul, 1964. xxvi, 186 p. (Publications nationales du Ministère des arts et des sciences)   Z2461.A1H8
    Includes a number of bibliographies and lists which contain official publications.

MALTA
Formerly under British control; independence, 1964.

The Royal Malta Library periodically published in the Malta *Government Gazette* a list of its accessions, classified by subject, including official publications. For other listings, see bibliographies under British Commonwealth.

The following list includes a number of British and Maltese official publications:

Simpson, Donald H. Malta. London, Library Association, 1957. 6 p. (Library Association. A special subject list, no. 15)   Z2375.S5

MONACO

Principality; from 1861 under French protection.

Handley-Taylor, Geoffrey. Bibliography of Monaco. 2d ed. Chicago, St. James Press, 1968. 62 p.   Z2191.H3 1968
   First published in 1961. Includes official documents of and related to Monaco.

NETHERLANDS

Under Spanish rule until 1581; under French rule, 1795–1813; independent kingdom, 1815– ; under German occupation, 1940–44.

The Netherlands government publishing office (Staatsuitgeverij) issues a monthly sales catalog entitled *Maandlijst rijksoverheidsuitgaven,* which includes publications of Benelux and other European intergovernmental organizations.

Since 1929 the Royal Library has issued the following bibliography of official and semiofficial publications:

Hague. Koninklijke Bibliotheek. Bibliografie van in Nederland verschenen officiële en semi-officiële uitgaven. 1+ 1929+ 's–Gravenhage, Staatsdrukkerij. annual.
                                                                                            Z2439.H18
   From 1929 to 1952 the title was: *Nederlandse [Nederlandsche] overheidsuitgaven.* The arrangement is alphabetical by agency. Provincial publications are included. There is a personal name and a subject index.

The following works may be found helpful in identifying various categories of Dutch official publications:

Franken, T. J. H. Nederlandse periodieke overheidspublicaties. 's–Gravenhage, Uitgeversfonds der Bibliotheekverenigingen, 1959. 15, [75] p. (Bibliotheekstudies; monografieën over praktische en theoretische problemen van het bibliotheekvak, no. 2)   Z2439.F7
   Describes Dutch parliamentary publications, *Staatsblad, Tractatenblad* and *Nederlandsche Staatscourant.* Second edition published in 1964. Based on F. K. van Iterson's work of same title.

Iterson, F. K. van. Nederlandse periodieke overheidspublicaties. 's–Gravenhage, 1930. 23 p.   Z2439.I8
   Describes parliamentary, as well as other Dutch official publications, including provincial and municipal publications. Second edition published in 1948.

Netherlands (*Kingdom, 1815–*) *Staatsdrukkerij-en uitgeverijbedrijf.* Catalogus van rijksuitgaven (bijgewerkt t/m 31 maart 1939) verkrijgbaar gesteld bij de Rijksuit-

geverij. 's–Gravenhage, Rijksuitgeverij, 1939. 234 p.   Z2439.N37   1939
Fifth edition of the general sales catalog of the state publication office.

Netherlands (*Kingdom, 1815—*) *Staten-Generaal.* Verslag der handelingen. 1814/15+
's–Gravenhage.   J391.H2
Indexes (Register) issued for 1847–53, 1853–63, 1863/64–1872/73, 1873/–
1879/80. From 1880/81 indexes issued every 10 years, up to 1939/40. Currently
indexes are issued annually in two parts: by persons and by topics.

U.S. *Library of Congress. Netherlands Studies Unit.* A guide to Dutch bibliographies,
prepared by Bertus H. Wabeke. Washington, 1951. 193 p.   Z2416.U6
A considerable number of bibliographies, catalogs and lists of official publications are included in its classified arrangement, both for Netherlands and its
overseas territories. These are found mainly in chapters II, L "Law and government" (p. 65–72) and III, B "Government publications" (p. 110–113).

Dutch overseas territories in the Caribbean are currently covered in
the *Current Caribbean Bibliography* (Hato Rey, Puerto Rico. Z1595.C8).
Volume 6 of the bibliography contains a special feature entitled "Netherlands Antilles and Surinam; developments 1946–1956, as reflected in
publications on these countries." The bibliography includes a considerable number of government documents.

NORWAY

1380–1814, united with Denmark; 1814–1905, with Sweden; 1905– ,
constitutional monarchy; 1940–44, German occupation.

Current official publications are listed in:

Oslo. Universitet. *Bibliotek.* Bibliografi over Norges offentlige publikasjoner. 1956+
Oslo, Universitetsforlaget. annual.   Z2599.08
Publications are listed in alphabetical order of agencies in the first section.
The second section lists parliamentary papers. There are separate indexes by
persons and by subjects.

Official publications are also listed in the Norwegian national bibliography, the *Norsk bokfortegnelse* (1814–47+ Z2591.N865) and in the *Norsk
bokhandlertidende* (1880+ Z2593.N7) a weekly publication of the Norske
bokhandlerforening. In both, the official publications are treated as
other publications, without special distinction.

For retrospective publications there are the following bibliographies,
lists, and indexes:

Haffner, Vilhelm. Instillinger og betenkninger fra kongelige og parlamentariske
komisjoner, departementale komiteer m.m. 1814–1924. Oslo, Fabritius & Sønners
Boktrykkeri, 1925, xlvi, 823 p.   Z2599.H13
————— ————— 1925–34, med tilleg for tidsrummet 1814–1924. Oslo, O. Fred. Arne-
sens bok- og akcidenstrykkeri, 1936. xviii, 203 p.   H2599.H13 Suppl.
A retrospective bibliography of governmental and parliamentary publications,
covering the period 1814 through 1934.

Norway. *Statistisk Sentralbyrå.* Fortegnelse over Norges offisielle statistikk, 1828–1950.
Oslo. I Komisjon hos Aschehoug, 1951. 97 p. *(Its* Norges offisielle statistikk, 11.
[Raekke, nr.] 63)   HA1501 no. XI/63
Official statistics are listed in chronological order and by subject.

Norway. *Stortinget.* Stortings-forhandlinger. Oslo [1814+]   J405.H4
Cumulative indexes *(Hovedregister)* for Norwegian parliamentary papers
were published for the periods 1814–70; 1871–91; 1892–99/1900; 1901–10;
1911–24; 1925–34.

U.S. *Bureau of the Census.* Bibliography of social science periodicals and monograph
series: Norway, 1945–1962. [Washington, 1964] 59 p. *(Its* Foreign social science
bibliographies. Series P–92, no. 15)   Z7161.U43 no. 15
An annotated classified bibliography. Includes a considerable number of official
publications.

PORTUGAL

Kingdom to 1910; republic, 1910– .

There is no current bibliography or list of official publications. In
1969, at the occasion of the opening of the new building of Biblioteca
Nacional, the following two bibliographies of selected official publications were issued: *Actividade editorial do estado, Catálogo da exposição*
(Lisbon, Biblioteca Nacional, 1969), and *Bibliografia das publicações
oficiais portuguesas,* 1967–68 (Lisbon, Biblioteca Nacional, 1969). The
two bibliographies cover official publications from 1926 to 1968. The
following tools include official publications currently or retrospectively:

Lisbon. Biblioteca Nacional. Boletim de bibliografia portuguesa. v. 1+ ano de 1935+
Lisboa, 1937+   Z2715.L6
Includes official publications in its classified arrangement.

Portugal. *Direcção de Hidrografia e Navegação.* Catálogo de cartas hidrográficas e
outras publicações de Portugal Continental, ilhas adjacentes, e províncias ultra-
marinas. 3. ed. Lisboa, 1960. 9 (i.e. 18) p.   Z6027.P8A52 1960
Fifth edition, issued by Instituto Hidrográfico in 1967, has title *Catálogo de
cartas hidrográficas e outras publicações do Instituto Hidrográfico.*

Portugal. *Imprensa Nacional de Lisboa.* Catálogo de livros à venda em 1927–? Lisboa,
Imprensa Nacional, 1927–?   Z2719.P84
Previously, similar sales catalogs were issued occasionally (e. g., 1879, 1891,
1913, 1924) .

—— Catálogo dos livros editados pela extinta Imprensa da Universidade de Coimbra
à venda na Imprensa Nacional de Lisboa, 1937. 21 p.   Z5055.P8C69

Portugal. *Secretariado Nacional da Informação.* Catálogo geral das Edições SNI,
Lisboa, 1933–1948. [Lisboa] Secretariado Nacional da Informação, Cultura Popular
e Turismo, 1948. 93 p.   Z2719.P875
List of publications of the Secretariat of Information, issued in Portuguese, as
well as in other languages (English p. 78–84).

Portugal. Serviços Geológicos. Catálogo, por ordem cronológica, das publicações dos
Serviços Geológicos de Portugal e organismos que os antecederam, 1865–1948.
Lisboa, 1949. 36 p.   Z6034.P8P64

Later ed. published in 1969 under title: *Catálogo das publicações dos Serviços Geológicos de Portugal, 1865–1968.*

Repertório das publicações periódicas portuguesas. 1961+ Lisboa, Biblioteca Nacional.
                                                                                    Z6956.P8R4
—— Suplemento. 1963+ Lisboa, Biblioteca Nacional. annual. Z6956.P8R4 Suppl.
Includes official publications in its classified arrangement.

The following works list publications of or related to Portuguese overseas possessions:

Gibson, Mary J. Portuguese Africa, a guide to official publications. Compiled [in the] African Section. Washington, General Reference and Bibliography Division, Reference Dept., Library of Congress [U.S. Govt. Print. Off.] 1967. 217 p.   Z3871.G5

Lisbon. Biblioteca Nacional. *Secção Ultramarina.* A Secção Ultramarina da Biblioteca Nacional. Inventários. 1. Códices do Extincto Conselho Ultramarino. 2. Códices vindos de Moçambique. 3. Códices do Arquivo da Marinha. Lisboa, Oficinas Gráficas da Biblioteca Nacional, 1928. 333 p. (Publicações da Biblioteca Nacional)
                                                                                    Z2731.C7L57

Portugal. *Agencia Geral do Ultramar.* Catálogo bibliográfico da Agencia Geral das Colónias. Lisboa, 1943. 302 p.   Z2731.C7P6

—— Catálogo das publicações, didascálico. Lisboa, 1965. 224 l.   Z2731.C7P62

Portugal. *Ministério do Ultramar.* Catálogo das cartas publicadas pela extinta Comissão de Cartografia e pela Junta das Missões Geográficas e Investigações Coloniais, 1883–1937. Lisboa, Papelaria Fernandes, 1937. 27 p.   Z6027.P8P85

SPAIN

Monarchy until 1931; republic, 1931–39; (Civil War, 1936–39) Estado Español, 1939–.

There is no separate bibliography or list of current official publications. These are listed in the *Bibliografía española* (published annually since 1958), under the various classes and indexed by agency so far as they are entered under the agency (Z2685.B583). From 1969 a monthly edition is being issued which replaced the *Boletín del depósito legal de obras impresas* (Spain. Dirección General de Archivos y Bibliotecas. Z2685.S76), published since April 1958.

Retrospectively, Spanish official publications have been listed in the following works:

Bibliografía española. año 1–22; 1 mayo 1901–dic. 1922. Madrid, Asociación de la librería, 1901–22. 22 v.   Z2685.B58

Bibliografía general española e hispanoamericana. enero/abril 1923–marzo/abril 1942. [Madrid] 1925–[1942] 16 v.   Z2685.B59
    Published monthly 1923–36, bimonthly 1941–42. Publication suspended July 1936–Jan. 1941.

Bibliografía hispánica. año 1–[16]; mayo/junio 1942–[dic. 1957] Madrid, Sección de Ordenación Bibliográfica del Instituto Nacional del Libro Español. 1942–[1958]
Z2685.B6
Index for v. 1–16, 1942–57.

Childs, James B. Spanish government publications after July 17, 1936; a survey. Washington, Library of Congress, Reference Dept., Serial Division, 1965–69 6 v. (2304 p.) Z2689.C5
Z663.44.S6
". . . an operational document for limited distribution issued in an edition of 50 copies." The bibliography lists the Government agencies of Spain and their publications, including a brief history of each agency.

Spain. *Ministerio de Información y Turismo. Secretaría General Técnica. Servicio de Documentación.* Censo de las publicaciones oficiales españolas, 1939–1964. Coordinador: Ricardo de la Cierva, Madrid, 1966–? [6 v.] Z2689.A52
Contents: t. 1. Ministerios de Trabajo, Información y Turismo, Vivienda. —t. 2. Ministerios de Ejército, Marina, Aire. —t. 3., pt. 1. Ministerios de Agricultura, Comercio, Hacienda; pt. 2. Ministerios de Industria, Obras Públicas. —t. 4. Ministerio de Educación Nacional. (2 v.) —t. 5. Ministerio de Asuntos Exteriores, Jefatura del Estado, Presidencia del Gobierno. [—t. 6. Ministerios de Gobernación, Justicia, Secretaría General del Movimiento, in preparation.]

A number of Government agencies issue more or less extensive catalogs or lists of their own publications.

Following are a few bibliographies covering special fields:

Banco Urquijo, Madrid. *Servicio de Estudios en Barcelona.* Guía de fuentes estadísticas de España. Edición 1970. [Madrid] Editorial Moneda y Crédito [1970+] 3 v. (loose-leaf) HA37.S77B3

Barcelona (*Province*) *Diputación Provincial.* Catálogo de publicaciones de la Diputación Provincial de Barcelona y de sus instituciones y servicios. Barcelona, 1966. 182 p. Z2704.B24A5
Covers a period of about 140 years through 1965.

Bibliografía general sobre la Guerra de España (1936–1939) y sus antecedentes históricos: fuentes para la historia contemporánea de España. Madrid, Secretaría General Técnica del Ministerio de Información y Turismo, 1968. xxxix, 729 p. (Horas de España) Z2700.B52

Cierva y de Hoces, Ricardo de la. Cien libros básicos sobre la guerra de España. Madrid, Publicaciones Españolas, 1966. 348 p. (Claves de España, 4) Z2700.C52

Madrid. Universidad. *Cátedra de Historia Contemporánea de España.* Cuadernos bibliográficos de la Guerra de España, 1936–1939. Madrid, 1966+ Z2700.M34
Contents. ser. 1. Folletos e impresos menores del tiempo de la guerra. v. 1+; ser. 2. Periódicos publicados en tiempo de la guerra. v. 1+; ser. 3. Memorias y reportajes de testigos. v. 1+ Four more series are planned, the fifth relating to documents.

Spain. *Instituto Nacional de Estadística.* Publicaciones estadísticas de España. Madrid. 1956. 202 p. (Publicaciones del primer centenario de la estadística española) Z7554.S7A5
In two sections, it lists Spanish statistical publications first in chronological order, then by subject. Covers 1856–1956, with some earlier works cited.

SWEDEN
Union with Denmark, 1388–1523, and with Norway until 1905.

Currently, Swedish official publications are listed in:

Sweden. *Riksdagen. Bibliotek.* Årsbibliografi över Sveriges offentliga publikationer
utgiven av Riksdagsbiblioteket. 1931+ Uppsala, Almqvist & Wiksells boktryckeri.
1934+   Z2629.S94
    The first volume covers 1931–33. Published annually. The arrangement is
alphabetical by agencies. It includes a detailed listing of two general series:
Statens offentliga utredningar and *Sveriges officiella statistik,* and from 1966, also
Riksdagens protokoll. Personal name and subject indexes are also included.

Official publications are also listed currently in the Swedish national
bibliography *Svensk bokförteckning,* prepared at the Kungl. Biblioteket
(Z2625.S952) and in the weekly *Svensk bokhandel* (Z407.S84).
    For retrospective, parliamentary, and other specialized bibliographies
and indexes, the following works will be of assistance:

Holmstedt, Sven, *and* Bengt Olsson. Statistiknyckel. [Stockholm] Rabén & Sjögren
[1965] 325 p.   Z7555.S9H6
    A guide to Swedish statistics.

Hutchinson, Edward P. Guide to the official population data and vital statistics of
Sweden. Washington, 1942. 72 p.   Z7554.S8H8
    At head of title: The Library of Congress. Consultant service. Reproduced
from typewritten copy.

Lundstedt, Bernhard W. Aperçu de la principale littérature bibliographique de la
Suède. Stockholm, Samson & Wallin, 1900. 34 p.   Z2621.L96 1900
    Includes bibliographies and indexes to early Swedish official publications
(p. 15–16).

Sweden. *Laws, statutes, etc.* Svensk författningssamling. 1.+ årg.; 1825+ Stockholm,
Kungl. boktryckeriet, P. A. Norstedt & Söner, 1825+   DLC LL
    Indexes (Allmänt sakregister) have been issued for periods 1825–74; 1875–94;
1895–1904; 1905–19.

Sweden. *Riksdagen.* Register till Riksdagens protokoll med Bihang. 1809–66+ Stockholm, Tryckt i Centraltryckeriet.   J406.M3
    Irregular, 1809–1910; decennial, 1911+ Title 1809–66: *Sakregister till rikets
ständers protokoll med Bihang.* Latest decennial index 1921–30. From 1931 continued with sessional indexes.

Sweden. *Riksdagen. Bibliotek.* Förteckning över statliga utredningar 1904–1945.
Norrköping, Östergötlands dagblads tryckeri, 1953. 1405 p.   Z2629.S943
    A list of government commission reports, arranged first by departments, then
chronologically. A continuation of Thyselius' list (see below). A mimeographed
continuation for 1946–65 prepared by Lars Frykholm, librarian, in 1971.

―――― Svenska riksdagarnes från och med 1786 till och med år 1866 tryckta protokoller
med bihang. Förtecknade af D. M. Sandahl. Stockholm, I. Marcus, 1871. 56 p.
                                                                         Z2629.S945
    A description of parliamentary papers.

Sweden. *Riksgäldskontoret.* Förteckning över i Riksgäldskontoret förvarade kommitte- och sakkunnigbetänkanden, efter uppdrag av fullmäktige i Riksgäldskontoret utgiven av Henrik Ekedahl [Stockholm, P. A. Nymans Efterträdare, 1920] 126 p.
Z2629.S95
Government committee reports on file in the Swedish National Debt Office, arranged by topic.

Sweden. *Sjöfartsstyrelsen.* Katalog över sjökort och seglingsbeskrivningar m.m. Catalogue of charts, sailing directions and other publications. [Stockholm, Statens Reproduktionsanstalt]
Z6027.S96A3

Sweden. *Statistiska Centralbyrån.* Statistisk årsbok för Sverige. 1+, 1914+ Stockholm.
HA1253.A46
Includes a cumulative list, by broad subjects, of official statistical reports.

Sweden. *Statskontoret.* Statlig publicering. Stockholm, Nordiska bokhandeln, 1967. 153 p. (Statens offentliga utredningar, 1967:5)
J406.R15 1967:5
Report on the printing and distribution of official publications, with a list of publications by agencies (p. 111–124).

Thyselius, Erik. Förteckning öfver komitébetänkanden afgifne under åren 1809–1903. Stockholm, Iduns Boktryckeri A.-B., 1896–1904. 2 v.
Z2629.T54
Chronological annotated list of government commission reports. Continued by *Förteckning över statliga utredningar 1904–1945,* published by Riksdagen, Bibliotek (see above).

U.S. *Bureau of the Census.* Bibliography of social science periodicals and monograph series: Sweden, 1950–1963. [Washington, 1964] 83 p. (*Its* Foreign social science bibliographies. Series P–92, no. 22)
Z7161.U43 no. 22
An annotated classified bibliography. Includes a considerable number of official publications.

There are several indexes to early Swedish legal and other official documents. The Library of Congress has in its holdings an incomplete collection of *Kongl. placater, resolutioner, förordningar och påbud, samt andre allmänne handlingar* for the years 1646 to 1824, with annual indexes (DLC LL).

Two indexes, listed in the Swedish Riksdagsbibliotek catalog [5] cover this period:

Höppener, Johan Pehr. Förtekning uppå alla k. placater, förordningar påbud, resolutioner, privilegier, manifester, fredsfördrager, relationer, domar och andre allmenne handlingar, som ifrån år 1522 til och med år 1750 af trycket serskilt utgångne äro. Stockholm, 1754.
DL603.H64

Förteckningar på k. placater, resolutioner, förordningar och påbud, samt andre publique handlingar som äro genom trycket utgångne år 1751–1833. [Stockholm]

SWITZERLAND

Independence: 1648.

Since 1946, official publications have been listed in a separate bib-

---

[5] Sweden, Riksdagen. Bibliotek, *Katalog,* 1927 (Stockholm, 1928–30), p. 156. (Z7166.- S93)

bliography of official publications, as well as in the Swiss national bibliography:

Bern. Schweizerische Landesbibliothek. Bibliographie der schweizerischen Amtsdruckschriften. Bibliographie des publications officielles suisses. Bd. 1+, 1946+ Bern.
Z2779.B4
   Entries are arranged by agencies. Included are publications of cantons and cities. From 1968 the bibliography is published in two parts: the main part includes only monographs and is published annually or biennially; part two, published as special issue (Sonderheft, Numéro spécial) with the subtitle *Periodische Amtsdruckschriften von Bund, Kantonen und Gemeinden; Publications officielles périodiques de la Confédération, des cantons et des communes,* lists government periodicals and will be published approximately every five years.

Das Schweizer Buch; bibliographisches Bulletin der Schweizerischen Landesbibliothek, Bern. Le livre suisse. Il libro swizzero. 1.+ jahrg.; Jan./Feb. 1901+ [Bern] Verlag des Schweizerischen Buchhändler-und Verleger-Vereins, Zürich.   Z2775.S35
   Since 1943, issued in two series: Serie A (semi-monthly) lists publications in the book trade; Serie B (bimonthly) lists publications outside the book trade. Official Swiss publications and publications of international organizations with headquarters in Switzerland are each distinguished by special marks.

For retrospective and specialized bibliographies, the following works may be of assistance:

Bern. Schweizerische Landesbibliothek. Verzeichnis der laufenden schweizerischen Zeitschriften mit Einschluss der Zeitungen, Jahrbücher, Kalender, Serien, usw. 2d ed. Bern-Bümpliz, 1925. 217 p.   Z6956.S92B3   1925
   "Amtliche Periodica des Bundes und der Kantone," p. 153–161. With supplements.

Switzerland. *Bundeskanzlei. Drucksachenverwaltung.* Liste des imprimés en vente au Bureau des Imprimés de la Chancellerie Fédérale. [Bern, 1936] 10 l. mimeographed
Z2779.S93
   A selected list of publications "most in demand."

Switzerland. *Landestopographie.* Katalog der Eidg. Landestopographie. Catalogue du Service topographique fédéral. [1892–1947?]   Z6027.S97S9

Switzerland. *Statistisches Amt.* Veröffentlichungen, 1860–1959. Publications [1860–1959] Bern, Eidgenössisches Statistisches Amt [1959] 23 p.   Z7554.S9S86

—— Veröffentlichungen, 1880–1964. Publications [1880–1964. Bern] Eidgenössisches Statistisches Amt [1964] 26 p.   Z7554.S9S87

—— Veröffentlichungen. Publications; 1860–1970. Bern, 1971. 31 p.   Z7554.S9A55
   Parallel text in German and French.

Schweizer Zeitschriftenverzeichnis. Répertoire des périodiques suisses. 1951/55+ Zürich, Schweizerischer Buchhändler– und Verlegerverein. (Schweizerische Nationalbibliographie [Teil] 2)   Z6956.S92S33
   Published under the direction of the Schweizerische Landesbibliothek. Includes important government periodicals.

Schweizerische Bibliographie für Statistik und Volkswirtschaft. Bibliographie suisse de statistique et d'économie politique. 1+ jahrg.; 1937+ [Bern, 1938+]   Z7552.S42

Published 1937–50, as a supplement to *Schweizerische Zeitschrift für Volkswirtschaft und Statistik;* from vol. 14 (1950–52) , by the Swiss Society for Statistics and Economics with the cooperation of the Swiss Office of Statistics. A classified bibliography includes all Swiss statistical publications, as well as important foreign publications dealing with Swiss statistics or economics.

EAST CENTRAL EUROPE

"That all publications are official publications in a 'people's democracy' is a common misconception. The number of 'people's democracies' has increased since 1917 sufficiently to present a need for more precise understanding. With the exception of one work, now much outdated,[6] there had been no overall bibliographical control of official publications in or for any 'people's democracy.' "[7]

Earlier Jean Meyriat in *Étude des bibliographies courantes des publications officielles nationales. A Study of Current Bibliographies of National Official Publications* (International Committee for Social Sciences Documentation, UNESCO, 1958), explained on page 253 (footnote 2), that in countries where all publications are considered government publications because their production is under government control, he would regard as official only those publications issued by the legislative, executive (head of government, ministries, and administrative services), and judicial branches of the government.

Since there are no separate bibliographies or lists of official publications for the countries of East Central Europe and the Soviet Union, we will cite a few general bibliographies and other bibliographic tools which at least partially cover official publications of these countries. Preference will be given to bibliographic tools in English. For individual countries, the same selection will be followed, citing national bibliographies or other works which may be of help in identifying official publications. Some of these works, of course, cover retrospectively the pre-World War II or earlier publications of these countries.

National bibliographies of these countries are generally classified in the following 31 subject groups: 1. Marxism-Leninism; 2. Communist and workers' parties; 3. Communist and progressive youth organizations; 4. Social sciences; 5. Philosophy; 6. History; 7. Economics; 8. Internal and economic conditions (in socialist states, in other states); 9. International relations; 10. Planning administration; 11. Finance; 12. Labor; 13. State and law; 14. Armed forces; 15. Natural sciences, mathematics; 16. Technology, industry; 17. Agriculture; 18. Transportation; 19. Tele-

---

[6] *List of the Serial Publications of Foreign Governments, 1815–1931,* comp. by Winifred Gregory. (New York: Wilson, 1932. Z7164.G7L7) .

[7] *Government and Official Publications in a People's Democracy,* Library science today, Ranganathan Festschrift, 1 (1965) : 163–170 (Z665.R33) and updated reprint, 1968 (Z695.1.G7C56) .

communication; 20. Commerce; 21. Communal economy, services; 22. Public health, medicine; 23. Physical education, sports; 24. Culture, education, science; 25. Philology, linguistics; 26. Literature; 27. Children's literature; 28. Arts; 29. Atheism, science and religion, religion; 30. Printing, library science, libraries, bibliography; 31. Handbooks, encyclopedias, calendars (yearbooks), collected works.

Official publications are included in most of the subject classes. Generally, class 13 (State and law) will contain the most important entries. Since the Communist Party is the dominant factor in these countries, its decisions are the determining factor in the activities of the legislative and executive bodies. Therefore documents of the Communist Party are considered official in the Soviet Union and other countries of Eastern Europe.[8]

GENERAL BIBLIOGRAPHIES

Apanasewicz, Nellie M.   Eastern Europe education: a bibliography of English-language materials. [Washington] U.S. Dept. of Health, Education and Welfare, Office of Education. [U.S. Govt. Print. Off., 1966] 35 p. ([U.S. Office of Education] Bulletin 1966, no. 15) [9]   L111.A6 1966 no. 15

East European accessions index. v. 1–[10] Sept./Oct. 1951–[Dec. 1961] Washington [U.S. Govt. Print. Off.]   Z881.A1U35
    Published by the Library of Congress bimonthly in 1951, monthly 1952–61, it is a classified index of monographic and serial accessions received by the Library of Congress and a group of cooperating libraries.

Gsovski, Vladimir, and Kazimierz Grzybowski.   Government, law and courts in the Soviet Union and Eastern Europe. New York, F. A. Praeger, [c1959] 2 v. (xxxii, 2067 p.)   DLC LL

Horecky, Paul L.   East Central Europe; a guide to basic publications. Chicago, University of Chicago Press [1969] xxv, 956 p.   Z2483.H56
    Part 1. Overview of the East Central European area; pt. 2. Czechoslovakia; pt. 3. East Germany; pt. 4. Hungary; pt. 5. Poland.

——— Southeastern Europe; a guide to basic publications. Chicago, University of Chicago Press [1969] xxii, 755 p.   Z2831.H67
    Similar arrangement as in the preceding entry. Covers Albania, Bulgaria, Romania, and Yugoslavia.

Johann Gottfried Herder-Institut, Marburg. Bibliothek.   Bibliothek des Johann Gottfried Herder Instituts . . .; alphabetischer Katalog. Boston, G. K. Hall, 1964. 5 v.   Z2483.J6
    West Germany's largest research center for East Central European studies. Holdings of the library cover the political, legal, economic, and cultural history of the area, including the Baltic states. The catalog includes some 75,000 entries.

[8] See Korshunov, Oleg Pavlovich, Izdaniia i bibliografiia dokumentov Kommunistich-eskoi partii sovetskogo Soiuza i Sovetskogo Gosudarstva (Moskva, 1955), p. 4 (Z366.K68)
[9] Nellie M. Apanasewicz also published individual studies on education in Bulgaria, Czechoslovakia, Poland, USSR, and Yugoslavia.

U.S. *Library of Congress. Slavic and Central European Division.* The U.S.S.R. and Eastern Europe; periodicals in Western languages. Compiled by Paul L. Horecky and Robert G. Carlton. 3d ed. rev. and enl. Washington, 1967. 89 p. Z2483.U5 1967

ALBANIA

Up to 1812 under Turkish rule; 1912, kingdom; 1914–20, occupation by various countries; 1925–28, republic; 1928–39, kingdom; 1939–44, occupation by Italy, Germany, etc.; 1944, people's republic.

Bibliografia e Republikës Popullore të Shqipërisë. Vepra origjinale dhe përkhtime. Tiranë. [v. 1–5, 1960–64]   DLC
    A classified bibliography, published quarterly by Biblioteka Kombëtare. Annual volumes only published under the same title, 1958–59 (?) Includes mostly official publications.

Bibliografia kombëtare e Republikës Popullore të Shqipërisë. Libri shqip. [v. 6+, 1965+] Tiranë, Biblioteka Kombëtare, quarterly.   DLC
    Seemingly a continuation of the preceding bibliography. Covers monographic publications, including those ot the government.

Periodical publications and articles in periodical publications are covered since 1965 in:

Bibliografia kombëtare e Republikës Popullore të Shqipërisë. Artikujt e periodikut shqip. [v. 5+ 1965+] Tiranë, Biblioteka Kombëtare. monthly.   DLC
    Seemingly a continuation of the *Bibliografia e periodikut të Republikës Popullore të Shqipërisë* (v. 1–4, 1961–64). Also includes, in a classified arrangement, articles in official periodicals and a list of periodicals published in Albania.

Brooks, E. Willis. A list of materials for the study of the history of Albania, with a note of holdings in the libraries of Stanford University. [n.p.] 1962. 20 1. Z2854.A5B7
    Includes parliamentary debates, documents, laws, statutes, memoirs, etc. Also publications of Albanian exile parties and groups.

Kastrati, Jup. Bibliografi Shqipe (29. XI. 1944– 31. XII. 1958). Tiranë, N. Sh. Batimeve "Naim Frasheri," 1959, 498 p.   Z2854.A5K3
    A considerable number of official publications are included under personal authors, and in chapters two, six, seven, and eight, under titles (pt. 2).

U.S. *Bureau of the Census.* Bibliography of social science periodicals and monograph series: Albania, 1944–1961. [Washington, 1962] 12 p. (*Its* Foreign social science bibliographies. Series P–92, no. 6)   Z7161.U43 no. 6
    An annotated bibliography. Includes mostly official publications of ministries and other government agencies.

BULGARIA

Under Turkish rule, 1393–1908; principality under Turkish rule, 1878–1908; independent kingdom, 1908–46; people's republic, 1946–.

Bibliografiĭa na bŭlgarskata bibliografiĭa, knigoznanie i bibliotechno delo. 1963+
Sofiĭa.   Z1002.B5687
    A bibliography of Bulgarian bibliographies issued annually by Narodna
biblioteka "Kiril i Metodiĭ." Includes bibliographies and lists of publications of
a number of government agencies, mainly in chapters XI—Law and state, and
XII—Military matters, Armed forces.

Bulgaria. *Dŭrzhavna pechatnitsa.* Spisŭk na zakonitĭe pravilnitsitĭe i drugi drzhavni
izdaniĭa. [Sofiĭa, 1908–33?]   Z2895.B93
    A price list of laws, ordinances, and other government publications available
from the government printing office. Issued irregularly.

Bulgaria. *Laws, statutes, etc. (Indexes)* Pŭlen ukazatel' na zakonitĭe v Bŭlgariĭa ot
osvobozhdenieto ù do 30 iŭnī 1939 g. Sofiĭa, Dŭrzh. kn–vo 1939. 1025 p.   DLC LL
    A complete index of laws in Bulgaria from the liberation to June 30, 1939.

——— Ukazatel' na zakonitĭe, naredbi-zakonitĭe, pravilnitsitĭe, dogovoritĭe, konventsiitĭe
i dr. obnarodvani v "Dŭrzhaven vestnik" ot 1 iŭliĭ 1939 do 31 dekemvri 1949
godina. Sofiĭa, Nauka i izkustvo, 1950. 339 p.   DLC LL
    Index to laws, decrees with force of law, resolutions, treaties, conventions,
etc. published in the official gazette.

Bŭlgarski knigopis. god. 1+ 1897+ Sofiĭa.   Z2893.B85
    Published 1897 to 1952 by the National Library and from 1953 by the Bul-
garian Institute of Bibliography. Includes official publications, listed in alphabetical arrangement without special indication, but with an annual index to
corporate authors and series.

Dimitrov, Liŭben. Spravochnik po zakonodatelstvoto na Narodna republika Bŭlgariĭa.
Zakoni, ukazi, postanovlenniĭa i razporezhdanniĭa na Minist. sŭvet, pravilnitsi,
naredbi, okruzhni, zapovedi i dr. [Predmeten bibliogr. ukazatel] Sofiĭa, Nauka i
izkustvo, 1969. 219 p.   DLC LL
    Guide to the legislation of the People's Republic of Bulgaria. A subject index
included.

Dzherova, Liŭba. Bibliografiĭa na bulgarskata statisticheska literatura, 1878–1960.
Sofiĭa, 1961. 105 p.   Z7555.B8D9
    Issued by the State Statistical Office, it covers all official statistics.

Letopis na periodichniĭa pechat. g. 1+ 1952+ Sofiĭa.   AI15.L37
    Issued monthly by the Bŭlgarski bibliografski institut, it covers periodical
articles, including those published in official periodicals.

Mid-European Law Project. Legal sources and bibliography of Bulgaria, by Ivan
Sipkov. Vladimir Gsovski, general editor. New York, Published for Free Europe
Committee by F. A. Praeger [c1956] 199 p. (Praeger publications in Russian his-
tory and world communism, no. 18)   DLC LL

Novaĭa literatura po Bolgarii. 1960+ Moskva.   Z2893.N6
    Issued monthly by Fundamental'naĭa biblioteka obshchestvennykh nauk of
of the Akademiĭa nauk SSSR, it is an accessions list of Bulgarian monographic
and serial literature received in several Soviet libraries.

Pundeff, Marin V. Bulgaria; a bibliographic guide. Washington, Slavic and Central
European Division, Library of Congress, 1965. New York, Arno Press, 1968. 98 p.
                                                                   Z2896.P8 1968
    Includes a number of official publications in its "Bibliographic listing of
publications discussed," mainly under Bulgaria.

Sofia. Narodna biblioteka. Pŭtevoditel po literaturata v Narodna biblioteka "Kiril i Metodiĭ." [Sŭstavil Khristo Trenkov] Sofiĭa, 1966+   Z1035.6.S58
     A guide to the holdings of the National Library. Ten volumes published between 1966 and 1970. Vol. 3 (1967) deals with state and legal sciences.

Topalov, T. ed. Petnadeset godini narodna vlast. Preporuchitelna bibliografiĭa. Sofiĭa, Nauka i izkustvo, 1959. 169 p.   Z2891.T57
     A selective bibliography published on the 15th anniversary of the September 9, 1944 uprising. Includes party and government documents.

U.S. Bureau of the Census. Bibliography of social science periodicals and monograph series: Bulgaria, 1944–1960. [Washington, 1961] 36 p. (Its Foreign social science bibliographies. Series P–92, no. 2)   Z7161.U43 no. 2
     Includes a considerable number of government agencies' publications.

CZECHOSLOVAKIA

Independence: 1918; German occupation, 1939–45; people's democracy, 1945 (1948)–60; socialist republic, 1960– ; federal republic, 1969–.

Official publications are included in the *Bibliografický katalog ČSSR*, the Czechoslovak national bibliography, issued by the National Library in Prague (and Matica slovenská in Martin), but without any special indication and without use of corporate entries.

Bibliografický katalog ČSSR is published in several separate parts and supplements, listing monographs, articles in periodical publications, musical scores, graphic works and maps, etc., separately for Czech provinces (by National Library in Prague) and for Slovakia (by Matica slovenská in Martin). The principal parts are the following:

České knihy. 1951+ V Praze. weekly.   Z2131.C437
     From 1951 to 1954 called *Česká kniha*. It has annual subject, title, and author indexes. Lists monographic publications of the Czech provinces, including publications of the Federal government and its agencies, as well as a few publications of local authorities. The last annual issue lists Czechoslovak standards issued during the year.

Články v českých časopisech. [1955+] V Praze, Národní knihovna. monthly   AI15.C55
     A bibliography of articles in Czech periodicals. It superseded an earlier title, *České časopisy* (1953–54, AI15.C4)

Články v slovenských časopisoch. roč. 1+ 1955+ V Martine, Matica slovenská. monthly.   AI15.C57
     A bibliography of articles in Slovak periodicals. Superseded an earlier title, *Slovenské časopisy* (1954 only, AI15.S55), and still an earlier publication, called *Slovenská bibliografia* (v. 1–7, 1947–53, Z2124.S56S5).

Slovenské knihy. roč. 2+ 1951+ V Martine, Matica slovenská. monthly.   Z2124.S56S53
     From 1951 to 1954 called *Slovenská kniha*. Volume 1 issued as vol. 18 of the preceding *Bibliografický katalog*. It lists Slovak monographic publications. Author, title and subject indexes are included annually.

From January 1970, the Slovak parts of the *Bibliografický katalog ČSSR (Články v slovenských časopisoch* and *Slovenské knihy)*, appear as parts of *Slovenská národná bibliografia, rad A-Knihy*, and *Slovenská národná bibliografia, rad C-Články*, both issued monthly.

For retrospective general bibliographies, which include some official publications, the following works may be of assistance:

Bibliografický katalog. [1933–50] V Praze, [Národní knihovna] weekly.   Z2133.B5813
    Issues for 1946–50 published in 3 parts: *Knihy české, Knihy slovenské, Hudebniny.*

Bibliografický katalog. [1922–28] V Praze, Melantrich [Národní knihovna] weekly.
    Z2133.B58

Bibliografický katalog Československé republiky. [1929–46] Praha, Nákl. Nár. a universitní knihovny. annual.   Z2133.B582

Československá bibliografie. [1920–21] Praha, 1921–22.   Z2133.C43
    Compiled and published privately by Jan Gotthard.

Czechoslovak Republic. *Národní shromáždění. Knihovna.* Liste des publications offertes en échange par le Service tchécoslovaque des échanges internationaux en 1926. Prague, 1926. 50 p.   Z2135.C97

Novaîã literatura po Chekhoslovakii. 1960+ Moskva.   Z2133.N6
    A monthly classified accessions list of monographic and serial publications of Czechoslovakia, received at several Soviet libraries, issued by Fundamental'naîã biblioteka obshchestvennykh nauk of the Akademiîã nauk SSSR

Seznam oficiálních a poloofíciálních periodických publikací Československé socialistické republiky. List of Czechoslovak official and semi-official periodicals and serials, 1973. Praha, Státní knihovna. 68 p.   DLC

Sturm, Rudolf. Czechoslovakia; a bibliographic guide. Washington, Slavic and Central European Division, Library of Congress, [U.S. Govt. Print. Off.] 1967 [i.e. 1968]   Z2136.S7
    Official publications listed mainly under Czechoslovak Republic (p. 103–109).

U.S. *Bureau of the Census.* Bibliography of social science periodicals and monograph series: Czechoslovakia, 1948–63. [Washington, 1965] 129 p. (*Its* Foreign social science bibliographies. Series P–92, no. 19)   Z7161.U43 no. 19
    A substantial number of official publications are included and can also be identified through the "Index of issuing agencies."

Verzeichnis tschechoslowakischer Amtsdruckschriften, [Prague, 1965] 17 l.   Z2135.V4
    Prepared by the Státní knihovna in Prague, it includes some 330 titles of official and semi-official publications.

Following are works covering special categories of publications:

Agricultural literature of Czechoslovakia. Sept. 1960+ Prague.   Z5073.A48
    Published by the Institute of Scientific and Technical Information of the Ministry of Agriculture, Forestry and Water Management.

Bibliografie československé statistiky. 1966+ Praha, Výzkumný ústav statistiky a účetnictví, 1967+   Z7554.C9B52
    Lists Czechoslovak statistical publications.

Česká grafika a mapy. 1958+ V Praze, Státní knihovna ČSSR.   Z5949.C9C4

Special supplement to *Bibliografický katalog, České knihy,* listing maps printed during the year.

Czechoslovak Republic. *Laws, statutes, etc.* (*Indexes*) Index ke sbírce zákonů a nařízení republiky československé, 1918–1947. V Praze, Státní tiskárna, 1948. 299 p.   DLC LL
   Index to the collection of laws and decrees, 1918–47.

———— Rejstřík československého práva. Praha, Nákl. "Československého kompasu," 1936. 654 p.   DLC LL
   Index to Czechoslovak law.

Czechoslovak Republic. *Ministerstvo spravedlnosti.* Přehled platných právních předpisů, vyhlášených ve Sbírce zákonů ČSSR, Sbírce zákonů SNR, v Úředním listu a Úředním věstníku od doby osvobození ČSSR do konce roku 1964. Praha, Nákl. Statistického a evidenčního vydavatelství tiskopisů, 1965. 155 p.   DLC LL
   A new updated edition of this survey of legal regulations in force, was published in 1968 covering the period 1945–67. Supplements published annually, as a subject index to Sbírka zákonů ČSSR.

Jeřábek, Josef. Rejstřík právních předpisů vyhlášených ve Sbírce zákonů v letech 1945 až 1957. Praha, Nákl. stát. a evid. vyd. tiskopisů, 1958. 202 p.   DLC LL
   Index to legal regulations published in the collection of laws, 1945–57.

———— Rejstřík vyhlášek uveřejněných v Úředním listě Čs. soc. republiky v letech 1952 až 1959. Praha, Nákl. stát. a evid. vydavatelství tiskopisů, 1960. 259 p.
                                                                                                                DLC LL
   Index to notices published in the *Úřední list* (*Official Gazette*).

Mid-European Law Project. Legal sources and bibliography of Czechoslovakia, by Alois Bohmer [and others] Vladimir Gsovski, general editor. New York, published for Free Europe Committee, by F. A. Praeger [1959] 180 p. (Praeger publication in Russian history and world communism, no. 19)   DLC LL

Podzimek, Jaroslav. Bibliografie československé statistiky a demografie, 1945–1968. 1. vyd. Praha, Výzkum. ústav statistiky a účetnictví, 1969+   Z7551.A2P6
   A bibliography of Czechoslovak statistical and demographic publications. Published in two parts: pt. 1. Statistics (2 v.); pt. 2. Demography (v. 1+).

Prague. *Vojenský zeměpisný ústav.* Katalog map a publikací. IV. doplněné vyd. Praha, 1937. 38 p.   Z6027.C9P8
   Catalog of maps and publications issued by the Military Geographic Institute.

U.S. *Joint Publications Research Service.* JPRS. 1+ July 3, 1957+ Washington.
                                                                                                                AS36.U57
   A *Subject Index of Regulations Published in Sbírka zákonů ČSSR During
...Year,* has been published as JPRS no. 35282, 42427, 45378 and 48120, for years 1965–68, "as a supplement to the *Survey of Legal Regulations in Force ...
from the Time of Liberation to the End of...*" (See above: Czechoslovak Republic. Ministerstvo spravedlnosti. *Přehled platných právních předpisů, vyhlášených ...*

GERMANY
Democratic republic, 1949–.

Childs, James B. German Democratic Republic official publications, with those of the preceding zonal period, 1945–1958; a survey. Washington, Library of Congress,

Reference Dept., Serial Division, 1960–(61). 4 v. (1448 p.)   Z2229.C44
                                                                     Z663.44.G39
    An operational document for limited distribution issued in an edition of 50
copies. Based on the holdings of and information available at the Library of
Congress, the "study attempts to identify all official publications of the Democratic Republic and of the earlier zonal organizations. . . . The following have
been included: the legislative branch; the executive branch, including the
ministries and state secretariats with subordinate and attached agencies, and
other central organs, agencies and institutions of the national administration;
the national courts; and the previous German zonal authorities of the Soviet
Zone." A brief history of each agency is given. Includes an index of agency
headings (also in inverted form).

Deutsche Nationalbibliographie. Jan. 1931+ Leipzig, Verlag für Buch- und Bibliothekswesen.   Z2221.H67
    Issued in two series: Reihe A, New publications in book trade (weekly) and
Reihe B, new publications outside book trade (semimonthly). Official publications are listed under personal authors or under titles. The annual "Register
der korporativen Verfasser" (index of corporate authors) helps in locating
official publications.

Germany (Democratic Republic, 1949–) Laws, statutes, etc. (Indexes) Das geltende
Recht; Verzeichnis der geltenden gesetzlichen Bestimmungen der Deutschen Demo-
kratischen Republik [vom 7.10.1949 bis 31.12.1966.] [Berlin] Staatsverlag der
Deutschen Dem. Rep., [1967] 670 p.   DLC LL
    Index to laws, 1949–66.

Novaià literatura pro Germanskoĭ Demokraticheskoĭ Respublike 1962+ Moskva.
                                                                     Z2243.N6
    A monthly classified accessions list of monographic and serial publications of
the German Democratic Republic, received at several Soviet libraries, issued by
Fundamental'naià biblioteka obshchestvennykh nauk of the Akademiià nauk
SSSR.

Price, Arnold H. East Germany, a selected bibliography. Washington, Library of
Congress, 1967. 133 p.   Z2244.E38P7
    Official publications are listed under broad subject headings. An index of
authors and titles includes names of government agencies.

U.S. Bureau of the Census. Bibliography of social science periodicals and monograph
series: Soviet zone of Germany, 1948–1963. [Washington, 1965] 190 p. (Its Foreign
social science bibliographies. Series P–92, no. 21)   Z7161.U43 no. 21
    An annotated classified bibliography. Official publications are included and
can also be identified through an "index of issuing agencies."

U.S. Library of Congress. Slavic and Central European Division. East Germany: a
selected bibliography, compiled by Fritz T. Epstein. Washington, 1959. 55 p.
                                                                     Z2244.E38U5
    Contains a considerable number of official publications, under broad subject
headings.

HUNGARY

Part of Austria-Hungary until 1918; republic, 1918–20; monarchy(with
regent) 1920–44; republic 1945–; people's republic, 1949–.

Magyar nemzeti bibliográfia; Bibliographia Hungarica. Jan./Márc. 1946+ Budapest.
[fortnightly, since 1962]   Z2143.M32

Published by the Országos Széchényi Könyvtár, it includes official monographic publications in its classified (U.D.C.) arrangement, together with yearbooks and similar serials, without special designation. Annual indexes, published until 1961, included listing of official publications by government agencies. From 1961/62, annual indexes are published, together with annual cumulations of the national bibliography, as *Magyar könyvészet* (Budapest, Országos Széchényi Könyvtár. Z2141.M255).

Official periodicals are included in a separate supplement to the national bibliography, *Magyar folyóiratok repertóriuma. Repertorium bibliographicum periodicorum Hungaricorum*, with an annual index (AI19.H8M27).

A special annual supplement to both, the national bibliography and the repertory of periodicals, contains a guide to the utilization of the bibliography (in Hungarian and in French), a numerical index to classification (U.D.C.), an alphabetical index of subjects and a list of periodicals excerpted, with abbreviations.

For other current and retrospective, both general and specialized bibliographies, the following works will be of assistance:

Budapest. *Országos könyvforgalmi és bibliográfiai központ*. A nemzetközi csere céljaira az országos könyvforgalmi és bibliográfiai központ rendelkezésére álló magyar hivatalos és tudományos kiadványok címjegyzéke. Liste des publications officielles et scientifiques, mises à la disposition du Bureau central bibliographique des bibliothèques publiques de Hongrie pour l'échange international. Budapest, 1928. 13 p. Z2145.B92

A list of official and scientfic publications for exchange.

Hungary. *Központi Statisztikai Hivatal. Könyvtár. Bibliográfiai Osztály*. Statisztikai adatforrások. bibliográfia, 1867–1967. Sources of statistical data; bibliography. Budapest, 1967. 344 p. Z7554.H8A5

Hungary. *Laws, statutes, etc. (Indexes)* Hatályos jogszabályok mutatója, 1945–1957. Budapest, Közgazdasági és Jogi Könyvkiadó, 1958. 208 p. DLC LL
Index of legal regulations in force, 1945–1957.

———— Magyar törvények és egyéb jogszabályok mutatója. Budapest, 1928. 812 p.
Index of laws and other legal regulations. DLC LL

———— ———— Pótkötet. 1.+ 1928/32+ Szombathely, Martineum Könyvnyomda, 1933+ DLC LL
Supplemental indexes 1928/32+

———— Törvényeink betüsoros mutatója, 1836–1927. Összeállította Somogyi István. Budapest, [Bíró M. Nyomda] 1928. 128 p. DLC LL
Alphabetical index of laws, 1836–1927.

Hungary. *Országgyülés. Könyvtár*. A Magyar Tanácsköztársaság kiadványai és az elsö komunista kiadványok. [Budapest] 1958. 496 p. Z2141.A45
Official publications of the Hungarian Soviet Republic (1919, March-August).

———— Az Országgyülési Könyvtár magyar országgyülések irásai gyüjteménye. [Budapest] 1962. 30 p. Z794.H812
A brief description of Hungarian parliamentary papers in the Hungarian parliamentary library, from the earliest times.

Magyar könyvészet, 1945–1960; a Magyarországon nyomtatott könyvek szakosított jegyzéke. [Föszerkesztö Sebestyén Géza] Közreadja az Országos Széchényi Könyvtár. Budapest, 1964–[68] 5 v. Z925.M29

A cumulated classified bibliography of the Hungarian book production during the period 1945–60. Volume 5 is the alphabetical index to volumes 1–4.

Magyar Tudományos Akadémia, *Budapest. Állam és Jogtudományi Intézet.* Állam és jogtudományi bibliográfia. Bibliographia juridica hungarica 1945–51+, Közgazdasági és Jogi Könyvkiadó. (*Its* Állam- és Jogtudományi Intézet Tudományos könyvtára) DLC LL
A bibliography of political and juridical science publications: Title 1952–53: *Jogi és államigazgatási bibliográfia.*

Mid-European Law Project. Legal sources and bibliography of Hungary, by Alexander Kálnoki-Bedö and George Torzsai-Biber. New York, Published for Free Europe Committee by F. A. Praeger [1956] 156 p. (Praeger publications in Russian history and world communism, no. 20) DLC LL

Nagy, Lajos. Bibliography of Hungarian legal literature, 1945–1965. Budapest, Akadémiai Kiadó, 1966. 315 p. DLC LL

Novaîa literatura po Vengrii. 1960+ Moskva. Z2143.N6
A monthly classified accessions list of monographic and serial literature published in Hungary and received in several Soviet libraries, issued by Fundamental'naîa biblioteka obshchestvennykh nauk of the Akademiîa nauk SSSR.

Paxton, Roger V. A list of materials for the study of the history of Hungary, with a note of holdings in the Libraries of Stanford University. [Stanford? Calif.] 1962. 18 l. Z2146.P3
Contents: 1. Parliamentary debates and government documents; 3. Laws, statutes, decrees and official legal publications; 9. Statistical publications.

Szeged, Hungary. Tudományegyetem. *(Founded 1940) Könyvtár.* A Magyar Tanácsköztársaság dokumentumai Szegeden; bibliográfia. Szeged, 1959. 159 p. Z2145.S9
Official documents of the Hungarian Soviet Republic (1919, March-August).

U.S. *Bureau of the Census.* Bibliography of social science periodicals and monograph series: Hungary, 1947–1962. [Washington, 1964] 137 p. (*Its* Foreign social science bibliographies. Series P–92, no. 13) Z7161.U42 no. 13
An annotated bibliography. Official publications are included in its classified arrangement. There is also an index of issuing agencies.

POLAND

Kingdom until 1772; divided between Austria, Prussia and Russia until 1918; republic 1918–39; under German and Russian occupation 1939–44; people's republic, 1944–.

Przewodnik bibliograficzny; urzędowy wykaz druków wydanych w Rzeczypospolitej Polskiej. rocz. 1+ [1944+] Warszawa, Biblioteka Narodowa. weekly (irregular). Z2523.P93
The weekly classified national bibliography, published by the National Library, includes official publications without special designation. There is a monthly index of authors, with annual cumulation and an annual subject index. This bibliography continues (with interruption during the Second World War) the *Urzędowy wykaz druków wydanych w Rzeczypospolitej Polskiej* (1928–39. Z2523.U83) and the *Przewodnik bibliograficzny,* published from 1878–1933 (Z2523.P92).

In 1967 the Bureau for the International Exchange of Publications of the Polish National Library (Biuro Miedzynarodowej Wymiany Wydawnictw) published the following list of official and semiofficial publications, available for exchange:

Słabczyński, Wacław, *comp.* Katalog polskich wydawnictw urzędowych i połurzędowych, dostępnych do wymiany międzynarodowej. Catalogue of Polish official and semi-official publications available for exchange. Warszawa, 1967. 28 p.
Z2525.S55

Other bibliographic tools which may be of assistance in identifying Polish official publications are the following:

Cytowska, Maria. Bibliographia druków urzędowych xvi wieku [Wyd. 1] Wrocław, Zakład Narodowy im. Ossolińskich, 1961. 217 p. (Książka w dawnej kulturze polskiej, 11)
Z2525.C9
A bibliography of official publications of the 16th century, listing constitutional documents, royal ordinances, and ordinances of lower authorities.

Dąbrowski, Stefan, Wiesław Majewski, and Edward Pigoń. Bibliografia polskich bibliografii wojskowych. Warszawa, Wydawn. Ministerstwa Obrony Narodowej. 1967+
Z6721.D27
A bibliography of bibliographies of military publications.

Gawryszewski, A. comp. Polskie mapy narodowościowe, wyznaniowe i językowe; bibliografia (lata 1827–1967). Warszawa, 1969. 154 p. (Instytut Geografii Polskiej Akademii Nauk. Dokumentacja geograficzna, zesz. 4)   G23.D63 1969, zesz. 4
A bibliography of maps relating to ethnic, religious, and language groups of population.

Keck, Zdzisław. Skorowidz przepisów prawnych ogłoszonych w Dzienniku ustaw i Monitorze polskim w latach 1918–1939 i 1944–1967. Stan prawny na dzień 31 grudnia 1967 r. Warszawa, Wydawn. Prawnicze, 1968. 720 p.   DLC LL
Index of legal regulations, 1918–39 and 1944–67.

Mid-European Law Project. Legal sources and bibliography of Poland, by Peter Siekanowicz. Vladimir Gsovski, general editor. New York, Published for Free Europe Committee by F. A. Praeger [1964] 311 p. (Praeger publications in Russian history and world communism, no. 22)   DLC LL

Novaîa literatura po Pol'she. 1960. Moskva.   Z2523.N58
A monthly classified accessions list of Polish monographic and serial publications, including official publications, received at several Soviet libraries. Issued by Fundamental'naîa biblioteka obshchestvennykh nauk of the Akademiîa nauk SSSR.

Poland. *Główny Urząd Statystyczny.* Bibliografia wydawnictw Głównego Urzędu Statystycznego, 1918–1968. Warszawa, 1968. 466 p.   Z7554.P6A5
A bibliography of publications of the Polish statistical office, 1918–68.

Poland. *Ośrodek Informacji o Energii Jądrowej.* List of reports of Polish nuclear institutes, 1964. Warsaw, Nuclear Energy Information Center, 1965. 27 p   QC770.P6

——— Polskie publikacje z zakresu energii jądrowej w 1964 roku; bibliografia. Polish papers on nuclear energy published in 1964 a bibliography. Warsaw, Nuclear Energy Information Center, 1966. 244 p. (*Its* Review report, no. 22)   Z7144.N8P6

Polska Akademia Nauk. *Instytut Nauk Prawnych.* Bibliographie juridique polonaise, 1944–1956. Rédaction collective sous la direction de Witold Czachórski. Warszawa, Państwowe Wydawn. Naukowe, 1958. 136 p.   DLC LL

Rżewski, Kazimierz. Bibliografia wydawnictw geodezyjnych Państwowego Przedsiębiorstwa Wydawnictw Kartograficznych (1945–1965). Warszawa, Państwowe Przedsiębiorstwo Wydawnictw Kartograficznych, 1969, 81 p.   Z6000.R96
    A bibliography of geodesical publications issued by the state enterprises of cartography.

Szporluk, Roman. A list of materials for the study of the history of Poland. With a note of holdings in the Libraries of Stanford University, [Stanford, Calif.] 1962, 32 1.   Z2526.S9
    Chapter 7: Journals of laws. Parliamentary proceedings; 8. Collections of laws; 9. Parliament, Constitution, studies and monographs; 10. Statistical yearbooks.

U.S. *Bureau of the Census.* Bibliography of social science periodicals and monograph series: Poland, 1945–1962. [Washington, 1964] 312 p. (*Its* Foreign social science bibliographies. Series P–92, no. 16)   Z7161.U43 no. 16
    An annotated classified bibliography. Official publications can also be located through an "Index of issuing agencies."

U.S. *Library of Congress.* Poland in the collections of the Library of Congress; an overview, by Kazimierz Grzybowski. Washington [U.S. Govt. Print. Off.] 1968 [i.e. 1969] 26 p.   Z2526.U5

Warsaw. Centralna Biblioteka Wojskowa. *Pracownia Bibliograficzna.* Ludowe Wojsko Polskie w odbudowie i rozbudowie kraju, 1944–1969; materiały do bibliografii. [Oprac. zespół Pracowni Bibliograficznej Eugenia Drążek et al.] Warszawa, 1969. 89 p.   Z6725.P6W37
    A bibliography of materials concerning the role of the army in the reconstruction and development of the country.

Warsaw. *Państwowy Instytut Hydrologiczno-Meteorologiczny.* Katalog publikacji PIHM, 1946–1968. [Wyd. 1.] Warszawa, Wydawnictwa Komunikacji i Łaczności, 1969. 46 p.   Z6004.H9W3
    Catalog of publications of the State Institute of Hydrology and Meteorology.

Wepsiec, Jan. Polish national and local government serial publications on legislation and administration published in 1955. Highlights on current legislation and activities in Mid-Europe, (Washington, Library of Congress) v. 4, 1956: 333–343.
                                                                                        Z663.55.H5 v. 4

—— Polish serial publications 1953–1962, an annotated bibliography. Chicago, 1964. 506 p.   Z2523.W4
    Includes government serials.

ROMANIA

Under Turkish rule until 1877; kingdom, 1881–1947; people's republic, 1947–65; socialist republic, 1965–.

Bucharest. Biblioteca Centrală de Stat. Bibliografia Republicii Populare Romîne; cărţi, albume, hărţi, note muzicale. [Bucureşti] semimonthly.   Z2923.B82
    Published since 1952, it includes official publications in its classified arrangement, but without any special designation.

—— Bibliografia Republicii Populare Romîne; articole din publicații periodice și
seriale. [București] semimonthly.   Z2923.R8B8
Lists articles in periodical and serial publications, including official publications, and lists laws, decrees, resolutions, etc., when published in the periodical
press.

Fischer-Galați, Stephen A. Rumania; a bibliographic guide. Washington, Slavic and
Central European Division, Library of Congress, 1963. New York, Arno Press, 1968.
75 p.   Z2921.F53 1968

Mid-European Law Project. Legal sources and bibliography of Romania, by Virgiliu
Stoicoiu. New York, Published for Free Europe Committee by F. A. Praeger
[1964] 237 p. (Praeger publications in Russian history and world communism,
no. 24)   DLC LL

Newspapers and periodicals from Romania. București, Cartimex. [1959?+]   DLC
Includes official periodicals.

Novaiă literatura po Rumynii. 1960+ Moskva.   Z2923.N6
A monthly classified accessions list of Romanian monographic and serial publications, including official publications received at several Soviet libraries. Issued
by Fundamental'naiă biblioteka obshchestvennykh nauk of the Akademiiă nauk
SSSR.

Rock, Kenneth. A list of materials for the study of the history of Romania, showing
holdings in the Libraries of Stanford University. [Stanford, Calif.] 1962. 45 l
                                                                          Z2926.R6
Contents: 1. Parliamentary debates and government journals; 2. Documents,
laws, statutes, decrees . . . ; 10. Statistics.

Romania. *Institutul Meteorologic. Biroul de Schimburi Internaționale.* Lista publica-
tiunilor oficiale oferite în schimb de Biroul de Schimburi Internaționale din
România, în 1930–? [București] Tip. Copuzeanu, 1930–? (*Its* [Publicațiune] no.
1+?)   Z2925.B9
A list of official publications available for exchange. Publications are listed
by agencies.

Romania. *Laws, statutes, etc.* (*Indexes*) Repertoriu general alfabetic al tuturor
codurilor, legilor, decretelor-legi, convențiuni decrete. regulamente, etc., 1 ianuarie
1860– 1 ianuarie 1940, publicate in Monitorul oficial, Colecția C. Hamangiu,
Consiliul legislativ și în alte collecțiuni similare. Întocmit de: prof. George Alexia-
nu. București, Monitorul oficial și imprimeriile statului, Imprimeria Centrală,
1940. 2 v.   DLC LL
A general alphabetic index of laws and other statutes, 1860–1940.

—— Repertoriul analitic al legilor în vigoare. București, Monitorul oficial și Imprimeriile Statului, Imprimeria Centrală. [1942?+]   DLC LL
A subject index of laws in force.

—— Repertoriul general al legislației în vigoare, pe materii, cronologic, alfabetic.
București, Editura Științifică. [1966. 1103 p.]   DLC LL
A cumulative general index of legislation in force.

U.S. *Bureau of the Census.* Bibliography of social science periodicals and monograph
series: Rumania, 1947–1960. [Washington, 1961] 27 p. (*Its* Foreign social science
bibliographies. Series P–92, no. 1)   Z7161.U43 no. 1
An annotated classified bibliography. Includes official publications. There is
an index of issuing agencies.

YUGOSLAVIA
Under Turkish rule until 1878; kingdom, 1878–1945 (Occupied by
foreign powers during the First and Second World War); Federal
People's Republic, 1945–63; Federal Socialist Republic, 1963–.

Bibliografija Jugoslavije; knjige, brošure i muzikalije. The bibliography of Yugoslavia;
books, pamphlets and music. god. 1+ 1950+ Beograd.   Z2951.B37
   Published semimonthly since 1954 (previously monthly) by Jugoslovenski
   bibliografski institut, it includes official publications marked with an asterisk.
   Periodical articles and other similar materials are listed in a separate part
   of the national bibliography, with the subtitle: Članci i književni prilozi u
   časopisima (Articles and Literary Contributions in Periodicals), published
   quarterly since 1950 (AI15.B47)

Jugoslovenski bibliografski institut. Jugoslovenska retrospektivna bibliografska građa:
knjige, brošure i muzikalije, 1945–1967. [Glavni i odgovorni urednik: Jovan
Janičijević] Beograd, Jugoslovenski bibliografski institut, 1969–71. 21 v.
                                                                        Z2951.J79
   A retrospective bibliography, covering the period 1945–67. In a classified
   arrangement (UDC), it includes official publications, some marked with an
   asterisk (mainly in vol. 2, Statistics, and vol. 5, Law), but a substantial number
   in other classes, unmarked.

A number of Yugoslav official institutions issue specialized bibliographies or bibliographies of their own publications. The Jugoslovenska
retrospektivna bibliografska građa . . ., issued by the Jugoslovenski bibliografski institut (see above), lists a number of them in its first volume
(p. 13–37, 41–63). The following selected bibliographies, catalogs, and
indexes may also be of assistance to researchers:

Belgrad. Vojnoistorijski institut. Bibliografija izdanja u Narodnooslobodilačkom ratu,
1941–1945. Red. Vinko Branica et al. Beograd, 1964. 815 p.   Z6207.W8B4
   A bibliography of publications relating to the national liberation war, 1941–45.
   Preface also in English, French, and Russian.

Blagojević, Borislav T. Bibliographie du droit yougoslave 1945–1967. Établie pour
le Comité international pour la documentation des sciences sociales sous le pa-
tronage de l'Association internationale des sciences juridiques. [Maison des sciences
de l'homme, Service de l'échange d'informations scientifiques] 2me éd. Paris, La
Haye, Mouton [1971] 157 p. (Maison des sciences de l'homme. Service d'échange
d'informations scientifiques. Publications. Série A: Bibliographies, 2)   DLC LL
   A bibliography of Yugoslav law, 1945–1967.

——— Bibliographie juridique yougoslave. Beograd, 1959. lii, 262 p.   DLC LL
   Translation of Pravna bibliografija, an annotated bibliography of yugoslav
   jurisprudence.

Đorđević, Nenad, ed. Zakoni, uredbe i ostali propisi izdani od 1. dec. 1918 do 31.
dec. 1933 . . . Beograd, Izdavačko i knjižarsko preduzeče G. Kon, 1934. xxxii, 227 p.
                                                                        DLC LL
   Laws, regulations, etc., 1918–33. A second edition, covering the period 1918–
   36, issued in 1937.

Informatorov registar važećih saveznih propisa objavljenih u Službenom listú SFRJ of 1945. do 1.I.1970. Pripremili: Milan Dajčić [ì dr.] Zagreb, Informator, 1970. xxvii, 355 p. (Informatorov registar propisa)   DLC LL
Index of federal legal provisions, published in the official gazette 1945–Jan. 1, 1970.

Krivokapić, Radovan V. Bibliografija vojnih izdanja, 1945–1968. Beograd, Vojnoizdavački zavod, 1969. 368 p. (Vojna biblioteka. Naši pisci)   Z6725.Y8K73
An annotated bibliography of military publications.

Mid-European Law Project. Legal sources and bibliography of Yugoslavia, by Fran Gjupanovich and Alexander Adamovitch. Vladimir Gsovski, general editor. New York, published for Free Europe Committee by F. A. Praeger [1964] 353 p. (Praeger publications in Russian history and world communism, no. 21) DLC LL

Mihailović, Mihailo, comp. Registar pravnih propisa objavljenih u "Službenom listu SFNR." Beograd, Savremena administracija, 1945–53+   DLC LL
Title 1945–55: Registar saveznih propisa. Each issue cumulative from 1945.

Mihelčić, Stanko. Splošni register veljavnih predpisov (Zveznih in republiških) 1945–1968. Ljubljana, "Uradni list SR Slovenije," 1969. 442 p.   DLC LL
Index of legal provisions (Federal and related to the Republic of Slovenia). Continued with supplements.

Novaîa literatura po ĨUgoslavii. 1960+   Z2953.N56
A monthly classified accessions list of Yugoslav publications (including official publications), received in several Soviet libraries, issued by Fundamental'naîa biblioteka obshchestvennykh nauk of the Akademiîa nauk SSSR.

Split, Yugoslavia. Hidrografski institut. Katalog pomorskih karata i navigacijskih publikacija. [1950?+] Split.   Z6026.H9S75
A catalog of hydrographic charts and related publications. Published irregularly (1950, 1952, 1962), and kept up to date by monthly additions, issued as a section of Oglas za pomorce (Split. VK798.O35)

Sukijasović, Miodrag. Pravni propisi Jugoslavije 1941–1944. Beograd, "Naučno delo," 1966. 88 p. (Srpska akademija nauka i umetnosti. Spomenik, knj. 115)
                                                                    DR303.S65 vol. 115
Chronological list of legal acts of Yugoslavia, 1941–44. Summary in English.

U.S. Bureau of the Census. Bibliography of social science periodicals and monograph series: Yugoslavia, 1945–1963. [Washington, 1965] 152 p. (Its Foreign social science bibliographies. Series P–92, no. 18)   Z7161.U43 no. 18
An annotated classified bibliography. Includes a considerable number of official publications. There is an "Index of issuing agencies."

Yugoslavia. Direkcija za informacije. Gradja za bibliografiju o Narodnooslobodilačkoj borbi; knjige, brošure, listovi, časopisi i bilteni. Beograd, 1948. 200 p.   Z6207.W8Y8
A bibliography of publications related to the national liberation war (1941–45).

Yugoslavia. Laws, statutes, etc. (Indexes) Registar saveznih propisa 1961–1966. Beograd, "Službeni list SFRJ," 1967. 360 p.   DLC LL
An index of federal regulations.

——— Splošni register predpisov za Uradni list FLRJ, Uradni list LRS, Uradni vestnik Prezidija Ljudske skupščine FLRJ, Vestnik organov za cene in Finančni zbornik. 1945/47+ Ljubljana. annual.   DLC LL
Index of regulations published in various official gazettes.

Following bibliographies and indexes relate to individual federated republics:

Bosnia and Herzegovina *(Federated Republic, 1945–)* Laws, statutes, etc. *(Indexes)* Registar važećih republičkih propisa objavljenih u "Službenom listu SRBiH" od 1945, do 31. marta 1968. Sarajevo, "Službeni list SRBiH," 1968. 136 p.   DLC LL
 Index of legal provisions in force in the Federated Republic of Bosnia and Herzegovina.

Ivanković, Zvonko, *comp.* Registar važećih propisa SR Hrvatske 1945–1968 (sa 31. xii. 1968). Zagreb, "Narodne novine," 1969. 249 p. (Zbirka pravnih propisa, 53)
                                                                      DLC LL
 Index of legal provisions in force in the Federated Republic of Croatia.

Kitarović, Igor. Registar propisa objavljenih u "Službenom glasniku SRS," 1945–1965. godine. Beograd, "Savremena administracija," 1966. xxii, 78, 322 p.   DLC LL
 Index of legal provisions in the Federated Republic of Serbia.

Macedonia *(Federated Republic, 1945–)* Laws, statutes, etc. *(Indexes)* Registar na republički propisi 1945–1968. Sostavil: Ljupka Šukarova. Skopje, Služben vesnik na SRM, 1969. 254 p.   DLC LL

Macedonia *(Federated Republic, 1945–)* Zavod na statistika. Bibliografija na statis-tičkata dokumentacija. Dopolnenie. Skopje [1954–62]   Z7554.Y8M3
 Bibliography of statistical documentation. Besides federal statistics and sta-tistics concerning other republics, it includes detailed lists of Macedonian statistics.

Register republiških predpisov, 1945–1962. Ljubljana, 1963. 585 p.   DLC LL
 Index to legal provisions of the Federated Republic of Slovenia, 1945–62.

UNION OF SOVIET SOCIALIST REPUBLICS

Russia, empire until 1917; Russian Socialist Federal Soviet Republic, 1917–22; Union of Soviet Socialist Republics, 1922–.

In the "Explanatory notes" to the section on Russia in *List of the Serial Publications of Foreign Governments, 1815–1931*, edited by Wini-fred Gregory (New York, H. W. Wilson Co., 1932, p. 578), Vladimir Gsovski, the compiler of the section on Russia, gave the following inter-pretation of "official publications" in the USSR.:

Since almost the entire publishing activity in Soviet Russia is in the hands of gov-ernment institutions, all publications are in a sense official. For this list it was decided to select only those Soviet serials which are issued in a way similar to that of the official publications of other countries.... Accepted as official were the publications of institutions with a jurisdiction which, in other countries, is exercised by the central government offices, i.e. those of Soviet central authorities such as the People's com-missariats, the Congress of Soviets, etc. By central authorities are meant not only the federal authorities of the whole Soviet Union, but also those of the individual re-publics in it.

Added to these legislative and executive agencies were institutions closely connected with government offices, which in other countries have an official status, such as central geological, meteorological, geodetic, and similar institutions. Other institutions considered official were central directive bodies of national economy, such as Supreme economic councils, planning commissions, etc. Publications of the Communist party and Communist International were also included in the section on Soviet Union "inasmuch as the publications... often contain official or semi-official material."

The *List*, as indicated in the title, covers official serials from 1815 to 1931. The Russian section is divided into three parts: 1. Imperial Russia (1815–1917) with two appendices: Kingdom of Poland and Grand Duchy of Finland; 2. Russia under the Provisional government (Feb./Mar.–Oct./Nov. 1917); 3. Soviet Russia (Federal Government, Communist Party, Individual republics).

Publications covered in the *List* are those issued by the central authorities of the Federal government and of the individual republics. Publications of local authorities, i.e., provinces, regions, cities, and so-called autonomous republics, are not included in the *List*.

Current Soviet official publications are covered in the following bibliographies and catalogs:

Knizhnaiă letopis'; organ gosudarstvennoĭ bibliografii SSR. g. 1+ 1907+ Moskva. weekly. Z2491.K5
    Classified national bibliography, issued by Vsesoiuznaiă knizhnaiă palata. It includes official publications without any special distinction. Corporate entries are used seldom. Indexes have been issued in various forms and frequencies. Currently, annual author, subject and geographical indexes are issued. An annual list of serial publications has been issued in recent years, as a supplement to *Knizhnaiă letopis'* (*Ukazatel' seriĭnykh izdaniĭ*, Z2491.K522), and also a monthly supplement, listing selected official documents, scientific and other publications (Z2491.K52).

Entries listed in *Knizhnaiă letopis'*, with omissions of minor publications, are cumulated annually in:

Ezhegodnik knigi SSSR. Sistematicheskiĭ ukazatel'. 1925+ Moskva, Vsesoĭuznaiă knizhnaiă palata, 1927+ Z2491.E9
    Published irregularly (some years omitted), it includes index to authors, titles, and subjects.

The following general bibliographies of Russian literature, published in Russia and abroad, may be of assistance in identifying official publications:

Berthold, Arthur B. Russkie kollektivnye zagolovki. Russian corporate headings. A list of over one thousand Russian headings for official and semi-official bodies, based chiefly on the holdings of the Union Library Catalogue, with an attempt at their identification for cataloguing purposes. [Philadelphia] Union Library Catalogue of the Philadelphia metropolitan area, 1939. 52 l. Z695.8.B4

Horecky, Paul L. Basic Russian publications; an annotated bibliography on Russia and the Soviet Union. [Contributors: Robert V. Allen and others. Chicago] Uni-

versity of Chicago Press [1962] xxvi, 313 p.   Z2491.H6
Bibliographies (p. 1–24), government, law, etc. p. 84–123.

Korshunov, Oleg P. Izdaniĩa i bibliografiĩa dokumentov Kommunisticheskoĭ partiĭ Sovetskogo Soĩuza i Sovetskogo Gosudarstva. Moskva, Gos. izd-vo kul'turno-prosvetitel'noĭ lit-ry, 1955. 46 p.   Z366.K68
A description of official documents of the Communist party of the USSR, of official (mainly legislative) documents of the Soviet government, and of their indexes. The publication lists main collections of laws, decrees, and decisions of the USSR government, of the government of RSFSR (Russian republic), and indexes to them.

Kulazhnikov, Mikhail N. Teoriĩa gosudarstva i prava. Bibliografiĩa. 1917–1968. Moskva, "IŪrid. lit.", 1969. 272 p.   DLC LL
Theory of state and law.

Leningrad. Publichnaĩa biblioteka. Opisanie izdaniĭ napechatannykh pri Petre Pervom. Moskva, Izd-vo Akademii Nauk SSSR, 1955–58. 2 v.   Z2492.L43
A union catalog of the Library Saltykov-Shchedrin and the Library of the Academy of Sciences of the USSR. Official publications 1708–25 (Jan.), in pt. 1.

Maichel, Karol. Guide to Russian reference books. Edited by J. S. G. Simmons. [Stanford, Calif.] Hoover Institution, Stanford University, 1962+ (Hoover Institution. Bibliographical series 10, 18, 32+)   Z2491.M25
When completed, the guide will consist of six volumes, the sixth being an index.

Russia (1917– R.S.F.S.R.) Gosudarstvennoe izdatel'stvo. Biŭlleten. [g. 1–8]; 30 iĩuliĩa 1921–28. Moskva.   Z2495.R83
Bulletin of the State Publishing House, superseded from 1929 by Na knizhnom fronte, later Sovetskiĭ knizhnik. (See below)

Shamurin, Evgeniĭ I. Katalogizatsiĩa ofitsial'nykh i vedomstvennykh izdaniĭ. Moskva, Gos. izd-vo kul'turno-prosv. lit-ry, 1947. 117 p.   Z695.1.G7S5
Deals with cataloging of government publications, and includes, in the second part, a chapter on corporate entries.

Smits, Rudolf. Half a century of Soviet serials, 1917–1968; a bibliography and union list of serials published in the USSR. Washington, Library of Congress, 1968. 2 v. (1661 p.)   Z6956.R9S58
     Z663.23.H3
Government serials are included mostly under corporate entries for Russia, union republics, autonomous republics, autonomous regions, provinces, cities, etc., but also under titles.

Sovetskiĭ knizhnik. g. 8–[19]; 1929–40. Moskva.   Z2495.S68
Superseded Biŭlleten published 1921–28 by Gosudarstvennoe izdatel'stvo. Title: 1929–31, No knizhnom fronte; 1932–35 Knizhnyĭ front.

U.S. Bureau of the Census. Bibliography of social science periodicals and monograph series U.S.S.R., 1950–1963. [Washington, 1965] 443 p. (Its Foreign social science bibliographies. Series P–92, no. 17)   Z7161.U43
An annotated classified bibliography. Includes a substantial number of official publications. There are indexes of subjects, titles, authors, and issuing agencies.

U.S. Library of Congress. Eighteenth century Russian publications in the Library of Congress; a catalog. Prepared by Tatiana Fessenko. Washington, Slavic and Central European Division, Reference Department, Library of Congress, 1961. 157 p.   Z2502.U5
Official publications included under Russia and other corporate and title entries.

U.S. *Library of Congress. General Reference and Bibliography Division.* Guide to Soviet bibliographies; a selected list of references. Compiled by John T. Dorosh. New York, Greenwood Press [1968] 158 p.   Z1002.U584 1968
A reprint of the 1950 edition.

U.S. *Library of Congress. Processing Dept.* Monthly index of Russian accessions. v. 1–22, Apr. 1948–May 1969. Washington, U.S. Gov't. Print. Off.   Z2495.U6
                                                            Z663.7.A45
Classified list of monographic and serial accessions received by the Library of Congress and a group of cooperating libraries.

The following works cover official publications in certain important fields:

Akademiiā nauk sssr. *Institut gosudarstva i prava.* Literatura po sovetskomu pravu; bibliograficheskiĭ ukazatel'. Moskva, Izd-vo Akademii nauk sssr, 1960. 279 p.
                                                            DLC LL
A bibliographic index of the literature on Soviet law. In Russian and English.

—— Sovetskoe grazhdanskoe pravo. Sovetskoe semeĭnoe pravo. Bibliografiiā 1917–1960. Moskva, Gos. izd-vo iūrid. lit-ri, 1962. 663 p.   DLC LL
A bibliography of Soviet civil and family law.

Akademiiā nauk sssr. *Institut prava.* Sovetskoe gosudarstvennoe pravo; bibliografiiā 1917–1957. Moskva, Gos. izd-vo iūrid. lit-ri, 1958. 774 p.   DLC LL
A bibliography of Soviet law.

Degras, Jane T. Calendar of Soviet documents on foreign policy, 1917–1941. London and New York, Royal Institute of International Affairs [1948] 248 p.   Z6465.R9D4

Grigor'ev, Vasiliĭ N. Predmetnyĭ ukazatel' materialov v zemsko-statisticheskikh trudakh s 1860-kh godov po 1917 g. Vypuski 1–ĭ i 2–ĭ. (Iz rabot kabineta C.–Kh. Statistiki imeni A. F. Fortunatova pri Nauchno-Issledovatel'skom Institute c.–kh. ekonomiki. Vypuski 16–ĭ i 25–ĭ). Izdanie TŜSU Soiūza S.S.R. Moskva, 1926–27. 2 v.
                                                            Z7554.R9G8
Subject index ot the materials printed in the zemstvo statistical transactions from 1860 to 1917.

Harvard University. *Law School. Library.* Soviet legal bibliography; a classified and annotated listing of books and serials published in the Soviet Union since 1917, as represented in the collection of the Harvard Law School Library as of January 1, 1965. Edited by Václav Mostecký and William E. Butler. Cambridge, 1965. 288 p.
                                                            DLC LL

Hungary. *Központi Statisztikai Hivatal. Könyvtár.* A Szovietúnió hivatalos statisztikai kiadványainak bibliografiája, 1917–1967. Budapest, Statisztikai Kiadó Vállalat, 1967. [1169]–1188 p.   Z7554.R9H9
A bibliography of Soviet statistical publications. Reprint from *Statisztikai szemle* (vol. 45, Nov. 1967. HA1.H83).

Izdatel'stvo "Statistika." Statistika i uchet. Annot. katalog knig izd-va "Statistika." 1966–1970 gg. Moskva, "Statistika," 1971. 423 p.   Z7551.I96
An annotated catalog of publications of the "Statistika" publishing house.

Levental', IĀ. Spravochnîe posobiiā po zakonodatel'stvu. Bibliotekar (Moskva), 1950, no. 12: 13–17.   Z671.B5804 1950
A description of Soviet reference books on Soviet legislation.

Mezhov, Vladimir I.   Trudy central'nago i gubernskikh statisticheskikh komitetov . . .
   s samago nachala ikh uchrezhdeniiă vplot do 1873 g. S.–Peterburg, Tip. V. Bezobrazova i komp., 1873 [1883] 128 p.   (Bibliograficheskiiă monografii, T. I, vyp. I)
                                                                                Z2491.M45 pt. 1
   Transactions of the central and government district statistical administrations
   from the beginning of their establishment to 1873.

———— Vklad pravitel'stva, uchennykh i drugikh obshchestv na pol'zu russkago pro-
   svieshcheniiă. S.–Peterburg [Tip. V. Bezobrazova i komp.] 1886. 348 p.   Z2491.M47
   Classed catalog of government and society publications on education.

Russia (1923– U.S.S.R.) Laws, statutes, etc. (Indexes) Khronologicheskiĭ perechen'
   zakonov SSSR, po sostoiănniŭ na 1. iiŭliă 1937 g. Moskva, ĬUridicheskoe izdatel'-
   stvo NKĬU SSSR, 1938. 200 p.   DLC LL
   Chronological list of Soviet laws to July 1, 1937.

Russia (1923– U.S.S.R.) Statisticheskoe izdatel'stvo. Katalog izdaniĭ. Moskva, 1929. 46 p.
                                                                            Z7554.R9R85   1929
   Catalog of publications of the statistical publishing house.

Russia (1923– U.S.S.R.) Tsentral'noe statisticheskoe upravlenie. Bibliograficheskiĭ obzor
   izdaniĭ Tsentral'nogo statisticheskogo upravleniiă Soiŭza S.S.R. za 10 let (1918–
   1928). Moskva, 1928. 70 p.   Z7554.R9R86
   Bibliographical review of the publications of the central statistical administration.

Slusser, Robert M., and Jan F. Triska.   A calendar of Soviet treaties, 1917–1957. Stan-
   ford, Calif., Stanford University Press, 1959. 530 p. (Hoover Institution on War,
   Revolution, and Peace. Documentary series, no. 4)   JK756   1917
   Bibliography: p. [450]–460.

Constituent republics of the USSR

The official publications of the Soviet Republics are included, similarly
to those of the USSR, in their national bibliographies (called generally
Knizhnaiă letopis', Letopis' pechati, etc.) Titles are listed mostly in
the particular language of the republic, often giving the Russian translation.   Works dealing mainly with official publications are rare and are
limited mostly to indexes to laws.   The index covering the official collection of laws of the Russian Federated Republic (Russian SFSR), also
includes decrees of the Supreme Soviet and basic decisions of the government.   Another bibliographic tool which separates official documents
from other publications is *Ukraïns'ka Radiăns'ka Sotŝialistychna Respublika 1917–1967*, compiled by Mykyta P. Rud' (Kiïv, Naukova dumka,
1969).

   There are few bibliographies which cover publications of more than
one federated republic.   A considerable number of official publications of
Soviet Republics are included in U.S. Bureau of the Census' *Bibliography of Social Science Periodicals and Monograph Series: U.S.S.R.,
1950–1963,* (Washington, 1965), under individual subject classes.   Baltic
states' legal literature has been covered in *Legal Sources and Bibliog-*

raphy of the Baltic States (Estonia, Latvia, Lithuania), compiled by Johannes Klesment, Mid-European Law Project, Library of Congress (New York, F. A. Praeger [c1963]).

The following bibliographies and indexes refer to law collections or include official documents of individual Soviet Republics:

BELORUSSIAN SSR

Akademiiā navuk BSSR, *Minsk. Fundamental'naiā bibliātēka*. Bibliografiiā belorusskoĭ sovetskoĭ bibliografii, 1922–1961; ukazatel' bibliograficheskikh materialov, izdannykh v Belorusskoĭ SSR. Minsk. Izd-vo Akademii navuk BSSR, 1963. 268 p. Z1002.A45

Under the headings, "state and law" and "state bibliographic registration" a number of official publications are listed. Indexes to collections of laws, decrees of the Supreme Soviet and decisions of the government of the Belorussian SSR are also listed (p. 45).

Minsk. Dziārzhaŭnaiā bibliātēka BSSR. *Addzel belaruskaĭ litaratury i bibliiāgrafii*. Russkaiā dorevoliūtsionnaiā kniga o Belorussii, 1802–1916 gg.; bibliografiiā. [Sostavil A. A. Sakol'chik] Minsk, 1964. 311 p. Z2514.W5M5

Includes a substantial number of official publications, mainly under "laws, administration" (p. 114–149), "statistics" (p. 156–158), etc.

Vakar, Nicholas P. A bibliographical guide to Belorussia. Cambridge, Harvard University Press, 1956. 63 p. (Russian Research Center studies, 22) Z2514.W5V3

A classified bibliography, with official publications included in several subject groups.

ESTONIA
Independent, 1918–40.

Estonia. *Laws, statutes, etc. (Indexes)* Sundnormide (seaduste ja määruste) süsteemiline nimestik. Riigi teataja üldine sisujuht. [Tallinn] Kohtuministeeriumi Kodifikatsiooniosakonna wäljaanne, 1925. 692 p. DLC LL

Index to *Riigi Teataja* (government gazette). Covers years 1918–25. Later, annual indexes covered laws and regulations published in *Riigi Teataja*.

U.S. *Library of Congress. Slavic and Central European Division*. Estonia: a selected bibliography, compiled by Salme Kuri. Washington, 1958. 74 p. Z2533.U5

U.S. *Treaties, etc. 1933–1945 (Franklin D. Roosevelt)* Exchange of official publications. Agreement between the United States of America and Estonia. (Dec. 1938) Washington, U.S. Govt. Print. Off., 1939. 14 p. ([Dept. of State. Publication 1301] Executive agreement series, no. 138) JX236 1929 no. 138
  Z690.U7E78

Includes a list of Estonian official publications.

KAZAKH SSR
1920–36, part of the Russian SFSR.

Alma-Ata. Kazakhstan. Gosudarstvennaiā respublikanskaiā biblioteka Kazakhskoĭ SSR. Kazakhskaiā SSR k 40-letiiū Velikoĭ Oktiābr'skoĭ sotsialisticheskoĭ revoliūtsii; kratkie spravochnyie svedeniiā i ukazatel' literatury. Alma-Ata, 1957. 233 p.
  Z3413.K3A6

A bibliography of Kazakh literature, published on the 40th anniversary of the October revolution. Includes constitutional and other documents, as well as a listing of laws and decisions of the government from 1920 to 1956.

LATVIA

Independent, 1918–40.

Latvia, *Laws, statutes, etc.* (*Indexes*) Alfabētiskais rādītājs "Pagaidu valdības vēstnesī", "Latvijas sargā" un "Valdības vēstnesī" izsludinātiem likumiem, noteikumiem, instrukcijām, rīkojumiem un pavēlēm no. 1918. g. 14. decembra līdz 1937. g. 31. decembrim. Sastādījis Rob. Lapsinš. Rīgā, Grāmatu draugs, 1938. 533 p.   DLC LL
An alphabetical index to official gazettes, regulations, notices, etc., 1918–37.

―――― Rokas grāmata likumkrājuma lietotājiem (1919.–1927.g) Saeimas kodifikacijas nodajas 1927. gada izdevums. Rīgā [1927] 312 p.   DLC LL
A guide to the collection of laws, 1919–27.

Latvia. *Starptautiskais drukas darbu apmainas birojs.* Latvijas oficialo izdevumu saraksts. Liste des documents officiels de Lettonie. Rīgā, 1925–?   Z2535.A3
A list of official publications, prepared by the International Exchange Service of the State Library.

Ozols, Selma A.   Latvia, a selected bibliography. [1st ed.] Washington, K. Karusa, 1963. 144 p.   Z2535.O9 1963
A classified bibliography. Official publications are included under broad subject headings, mainly under "Constitution and Law" and "Government and Politics," p. 46–49. Issued also as thesis, Catholic University of America, 1958.

Riga. Valsts biblioteka. *Bibliogrāfijas un metodiskā darba nodala.* Latvijas PSR, 1940–1960.; literatūras rādītājs. Latviĭskaĭa SSR, 1940–1960; ukazatel' literatury. [Sastādītāji: O. Pūce un J. Veinbergs] Rīgā, 1961+   Z2535.R577
Volume I is divided into periods 1940–41, 1941–44, and 1944–59 and includes a substantial number of official publications for each period under broad subject headings.

LITHUANIA

Independent, 1918–40.

Adomonienė, O., V. Milius, *and* A. Tautavičius.   Lietuvos TSR istorijos bibliografija 1940–1965. Vilnius, 1969. 708 p.   Z2537.A6
Includes some official publications. Also covers the Russian rule before 1918.

Lithuania. *Laws, statutes, etc.* (*Indexes*) Vyriausybės žinių 1927–1929 metų rodyklė. Kaunas, "Spindulio" b-vės spaustuvė, 1930. 46 p.   DLC LL
An index to laws, 1927–29.

Stanka, Elena.   Lithuania: a selected bibliography, with a brief historical survey. Washington, 1958. 124 1.   Z2537.S77
Thesis (M.S.) –Catholic University of America. Typescript (carbon copy).
Includes some official publications.

MOLDAVIAN SSR

Surilov. A. V. Istorii︠a︡ gosudarstva i prava Moldavskoĭ SSR, 1917–1959 gg. Kishinev, Kartī︠a︡ moldovenī︠a︡ske, 1963. 334 p.   DLC LL
A history of the Moldavian government and law. Some official documents cited in bibliographical footnotes.

RUSSIAN SFSR

Russia (*1917– R.S.F.S.R.*) *Laws, statutes, etc.* Khronologicheskoe sobranie zakonov, ukazov Prezidiuma Verkhnogo Soveta i postanevleniĭ Pravitel'stva R.S.F.S.R. Moskva, Gos. izd-vo ︠i︡urid. lit-ry.   DLC LL
Vol. 1, covers period 1917–28; v. 2, 1929–39; v. 3, 1940–47; v. 4, 1948–53; v. 5, 1954–56; v. 6+ annual. Indexes: Vols. 1–6, 1917–57 (1 v.) A chronological collection of laws, decrees of the Supreme Soviet and of decisions of the government of the Russian S.F.S.R., from 1917.

UKRAINIAN SSR

Rud', Mykyta P. Ukraïns'ka Radi︠a︡ns'ka Sofsialistychna Respublika 1917–1967; bibliografichnyĭ pokazhchyk literatury. Kiïv, Naukova dumka, 1969. 474 p.   Z2514.U5R78
A bibliography of Ukrainian literature covering the period 1917–67. Divided into parts, it covers successively 1917 (March–Dec.), 1918–20, 1921–25, 1926–32, 1933–41, 1941–45, 1946–50, 1951–58, 1959–67. Official publications of the Communist Party and the government are listed at the head of each period. There are separate indexes of the documents of the Communist Party and of the government, an index of collected works, index of statistical publications, and index of authors. Also included is a list of Ukrainian bibliographies (p. 415–418).

Ukraine. *Tsentral'ne statystychne upravlinni︠a︡.* Publications de la Direction centrale de la statistique de l'Ukraine. Kharkoff [Typo-litographie du Conseil de rédaction de la circonscription militaire de l'Ukraine du nom de Frounsé] 1923. 10 p.
Z7554.R9U3
A list of statistical publications covering the period 1920–23.

AFRICA

During the last decade, when most of the former European possessions achieved independent status, an urgent need for bibliographic control of the official publications of these new countries has arisen. In individual African countries, with a few exceptions, bibliographic tools to official publications are rare. Researchers have to rely on occasional lists inserted in official gazettes or published separately by government printing offices. For former British possessions, the *Colonial Annual Reports* (1946+) and the *Blue Books* include lists of official publications. The *Colonial Reports—Annual* (1889–1940), include lists mainly from 1930 to 1940. Comprehensive bibliographies of official publications for individual countries or for certain areas or groups of countries have mostly been published abroad. The Library of Congress, during the post-World War II years, has made a serious effort to provide the researcher with such bibliographies. Similar efforts have been made by other libraries and centers on African studies in the United States and abroad.

Following are bibliographies covering all or some African countries, as well as a few other works which may furnish information on governmental changes, etc.:

Afrique contemporaine: documents d'Afrique noire et de Madagascar. v. 1+ 1962+
[Paris, Centre d'études et de documentation sur l'Afrique et l'Outre-Mer]
DT348.A36
Published bimonthly in the Documentation française, it includes reports on governmental changes, international conferences relating to African affairs, lists important legislative acts by countries, and reviews books on Africa.

Alderfer, Harold F. A bibliography of African government, 1950–1966. [2d rev. ed.] Lincoln University, Pa., Lincoln University Press; [distributed by Livingston Pub. Co,. Narberth, Pa., 1967] 163 p. Z3501.A6 1967
Includes studies on the constitutional and governmental developments of African countries with numerous citations of official documents.

Boston University. *Libraries.* Catalog of African government documents and African area index. Compiled by Mary D. Herrick. 2d ed., rev. and enl. Boston, G. K. Hall, 1964. 471 p. Z3508.G6B6 1964

East African Common Services Organization. Catalogue of publications. Nairobi. Information Division, Office of Secretary General. [1965?] DLC

France. *Institut national de la statistique et des études économiques. Service de coopération.* Bibliographie démographique 1945–1967. Paris, 1967. 67 p.   Z7165.F8A48
Covers publications of all French-speaking countries in Africa.

Gibson, Mary J. Portuguese Africa, a guide to official publications. Washington, Library of Congress, Reference Dept., General Reference and Bibliography Division, 1967. 217 p.   Z3871.G5
Z663.285.P6
Lists official publications of Angola, the Cape Verde Islands, Mozambique, Portuguese Guinea, São Tomé and Principe Islands, and Portuguese government documents pertaining to Portuguese Africa.

Gt. Brit. *Colonial Office.* Colonial reports—annual. no 1–1936. London, H. M. Stationery Off. 1891–1940. 1936 v.   JV33.G7A4
Lists of official publications appear in these reports mainly after 1930.

Harvey, Joan M. Statistics Africa: sources for market research. Beckenham (Kent), C. B. D. Research Ltd., 1970. 175 p.   Z7554.A34H37

Jwaideh, Zuhair E. African law collections in the Library of Congress. *In* U.S. *Library of Congress.* Quarterly journal, v. 27, July 1970: [213]–221.   Z881.U49A3 v. 27

King (P. S.) & Son, Ltd., *London.* Catalogue of parliamentary reports, papers, &c, relating to Africa. 1800 to 1899. London [1899] 16 p. (*Its* Special lists of parliamentary papers from 1800 to 1899, no. 18)   Z3509.K5

Library bulletin and accessions list. [no. 1+ Jan./Feb. 1956+] [Kampala] Makerere University College [Library] quarterly.   Z965.L5
Published bimonthly to Sept. 1966. Official publications of the East African Community, Kenya, Tanzania, and Uganda are listed separately, as well as selected official documents of other African countries.

Moses, Larry. Kenya, Uganda, Tanganyika, 1960–1964, a bibliography. Washington, External Research Staff, Dept. of State, 1964. 13 p. (U.S. Dept. of State. External Research Staff. External research paper 152)   JX231.A3 no. 152

Rishworth, Susan K. Spanish speaking Africa; a guide to official publications. Washington, Library of Congress, 1973. 66 p.   Z2689.R57

Staatsbibliothek der Stiftung Preussischer Kulturbesitz. Catalogue of African official publications available in European libraries as of 1 May 1971. Berlin, International Federation of Library Associations, Committee for Official Publications, 1971. 251 p.   Z3508.G6S7
Arranged by countries, in alphabetical order. Within each country publications are listed in alphabetical order by title. Included are indexes of corporate authors, personal authors, and titles.

Technical co-operation; a monthly bibliography. v. 1+ Jan. 1964+ [London]   Z2021.C7A35
——— Supplement. 1964+ [London]   Z2021.C7A35 Suppl.
Issued in 1964 by the Dept. of Technical Cooperation Library; 1964–70 by the Ministry of Overseas Development Library; from 1971 by the Overseas Development Administration Library.
Lists official publications of African countries, members of the British Commonwealth.

Texas. University. *Population Research Center.* International population census bibliography. Austin, Bureau of Business Research, University of Texas, 1965–67. 6 v. (*Its* Census bibliography, no. 1–6)   Z7164.D3T45

No. 2 of the series lists works on population censuses in African countries.
——— ——— Supplement 1968. 154 p. (*Its* Census bibliography no. 7)
Z7164.D3T45 Suppl.

United Nations. *Economic Commission for Africa.* Bibliography of African statistical publications. [New York] 1962. 206 p. (United Nations [Document] E/CN.14/112)
JX1977.A2 E/CN.14/112
Z7554.A34U46
Also covers the United Arab Republic.

United Nations. *Economic Commission for Africa. Library.* Bibliography: Economic and social development plans of African countries. Bibliographie: plans de développement économique et social des pays africains. [New York] 1968. 40 p. (United Nations [Document] E/CN.14/LIB/Ser.C/4)
JX1977.A2 E/CN.14/LIB/C4

——— Bibliography of African statistical publications, 1950–1965. [New York] 1966. 256 p. (United Nations [Document] E/CN.14/LIB/Ser.C/2)
JX1977.A2 E/CN.14/LIB/C2
Covers also the United Arab Republic.

——— New acquisitions in the UNECA library. v. 1+ Oct. 1962+ Addis Ababa. monthly. (United Nations [Document] E/CN.14/LIB/Ser.B/1+)
JX1977.A2 E/CN.14/LIB/Ser.B/1+

——— Periodicals received in the UNECA library. Addis Ababa, 1961+ 113 p. (United Nations [Document] E/CN.14/LIB/Sed.A/1+)
JX1977.A2 E/CN.14/LIB/Ser.A/1+
"Kept up to date by periodic supplements."

U.S. *Dept. of State. Library Division.* Point four, Near East and Africa; a selected bibliography of studies on economically underdeveloped countries. New York, Greenwood Press [1969] 136 p.   Z3013.U5   1969
Reprint of the 1951 edition.

U.S. *Library of Congress. African Section.* Africa south of the Sahara; index to periodical literature, 1900–1970. Boston, G. K. Hall, 1971. 4 v.   Z3503.U47
Includes official periodicals of France and former French possessions. A list of excerpted periodicals is included in v. 1. First supplement issued in 1973.

U.S. *Library of Congress. African Section.* Official publications of British East Africa, compiled by Helen F. Conover. Washington, 1960–63. 4 v.   Z3582.U5
Contents: pt. 1. *The East Africa High Commission and Other Regional Documents.* —pt. 2. *Tanganyika.* —pt. 3. *Kenya and Zanzibar.* —pt. 4. *Uganda.* A new edition (*East Africa: a Guide to Official Publications of Kenya, Tanzania and Uganda*) is in preparation.

——— Official publications of French Equatorial Africa, French Cameroons and Togo, 1946–1958; [a guide] compiled by J. W. Witherell. Washington, 1964. 78 p. Z3691.U5
A new guide (*French-Speaking Central Africa; a Guide to Official Publications in American Libraries*) issued in 1973 (see below).

——— Sub-Saharan Africa; a guide to serials. Washington, 1970. 409 p.   Z3503.U45
Official serials are included, mostly under corporate entries, in alphabetical order.

U.S. *Library of Congress. Census Library Project.* Population censuses and other official demographic statistics of Africa, not including British Africa; an annotated bibliography, prepared by Henry J. Dubester. Washington, U.S. Govt. Print. Off., 1950 [i.e. 1951] 53 p.   Z7554.A34U5

——— Population censuses and other official demographic statistics of British Africa; an annotated bibliography, prepared by Henry J. Dubester. Washington, U.S. Govt. Print Off., 1950. 78 p.   Z7554.A35U5

U.S. *Library of Congress. General Reference and Bibliography Division.* Official publications of French West Africa, 1946–1958; a guide compiled by Helen F. Conover. Washington, 1960. 88 p.   Z3672.U5

U.S. *Library of Congress. Library of Congress Office, Nairobi.* Accessions list, Eastern Africa. v. 1+ Jan. 1968+ Nairobi. quarterly.   Z3516.U52
"The area covered by this office includes the Comoros, Ethiopia, the French Territory of the Afars and the Issas, Kenya, the Malagasy Republic, Malawi, Mauritius, Réunion. the Seychelles, the Somali Republic, the Sudan, Tanzania, Uganda and Zambia." (Introduction, v. 4, no. 1, Jan. 1971)

Vanderlinden, Jacques. African law bibliography. Bibliographie de droit Africain, 1947–1966. Bruxelles, Presses universitaires de Bruxelles, [1972] 471 p.   DLC LL
Includes references to printed books and articles, including official publications. Prepared at the Centre for African Legal Development of the Faculty of Law, Haile Selassie I University, Addis Ababa.

Witherell, Julian W. French-speaking central Africa; a guide to official publications in American libraries. Washington, Library of Congress [U.S. Govt. Print. Off.] 1973. 314 p.   Z3692.W5
"Includes documents of former Belgian and French possessions from the beginning of colonial rule to the time of independence, as well as publications of national governments and regional and provincial administrations from independence to 1970." Also included are some documents of international and regional organizations pertaining to this area.

——— French speaking West Africa; a guide to official publications. Washington, General Reference and Bibliography Division, Library of Congress [U.S. Govt. Print. Off.] 1967. 201 p.   Z3672.W5
Covers publications of the former French administration of West Africa, Dahomey, Guinea, Ivory Coast, Mali (Federation) , Mali (Republic) , Mauritania, Niger, Senegal, Togo (including League of Nations mandate and United Nations trusteeship documents) , Upper Volta; also French official publications and publications of the French Union and French Community, concerning these countries. Some documents of the Organisation Commune Africaine et Malgache are also included.

NORTH AFRICA

The following two publications list or reproduce many official documents of the North African countries:

Annuaire de l'Afrique du Nord. 1+ 1962+ [Paris] Centre national de la recherche scientifique.   DT181.A74
Issued currently by the Centre de recherches et d'études sur les sociétés mediterranéennes, Aix-en-Provence. Includes: "Chronologie," listing important laws, decrees, etc., "Documents," and "Bibliographie systématique."

Maghreb; études et documents Algérie, Libye, Maroc, Tunisie. no. 1+ Jan./Fév. 1964+ [Paris, Centre d'étude des relations internationales, Section Afrique du Nord]   DLC
Published bi-monthly. Includes in its ' Rubrique législative" listing of im-

312 FOREIGN COUNTRIES

portant treaties and agreements, laws, decrees, and other statutes. From 1964
to 1969 (July), Libya not included.

ALGERIA
From 1518–1830, Turkish rule; 1830–1962, French rule; independent
republic, 1962–.

Currently, the Bibliothèque nationale issues an annual bibliography
of Algeria which includes official publications:

Algiers (City) al-Maktabah al-Waṭanīyah. al-Bībliyūghrāfyā al-Jazā'irīya Bibliographie
de l'Algérie. no. 1+ Oct. 1963+ Algiers.   Z3681.B5 Orien Arab
   Publications are listed by broad subjects. A substantial number of entries are
   government publications. Volumes one and three list periodicals only.

For retrospective coverage, the following works include official
documents:

Algeria. Direction des Territoires du sud. Les Territoires du sud de l'Algérie. [2. éd.]
   Alger, Imprimerie algérienne, 1929–30. 5 v.   DT298.S6A5
   Volume 3, Essai d'une bibliographie, includes many official documents.

Archives départementales de Constantine. Centre de documentation. Répertoire de
   documentation nord-africaine dressé par E-Th. Lemaire, Constantine, Attali imprimeurs [1954] 134 p.   Z3681.A73
   ——— ——— Supplément. Constantine, Attali imprimeurs, 1956+ Z3681.A73 Suppl.
   Includes a considerable number of official documents published mainly in the
   official collection Documents algériens. Synthèse de l'activité algérienne. 1945/46–
   [1960?] (Alger, Imprimerie officielle. DT271.D6)

Cairo. Dār al-Kutub al-Miṣrīyah. Qā'imah bi-al-kutub wā-al-marāji' 'an al-Jazā'ir. A
   bibliography of Algeria. Cairo, 1963. 47, 87 p.   Z3681.C33 1963 Orien Arab
   Includes publications in Arabic and Western languages.

Études sociales nord-africaines. Essai de bibliographie algérienne, ler Janvier 1954–30
   juin 1962; lectures d'une guerre. [Paris, 1962] 115 p. (Cahiers nord-africains, 92)
                                                              Z3681.E8
   Some official documents concerning the war of resistance are included.

LIBYA
Until 1911 under Turkish rule; 1911–42, Italian colony; 1942–51, British
(Tripolitania and Cyrenaica) and French (Fezzan) military administra-
tion; independent kingdom, 1951–69; republic, 1969–.

There is no bibliography of official publications and no national
bibliography. Some official documents are included in the following
works:

Cairo. Dār al-Kutub al-Miṣrīyah. Qā'imah bi-al-kutub wā-al-marāji' 'an Lībiyā. A
   bibliographical list of Libya. Cairo, 1961. 21, 30 p.   Z3971.C33 Orien Arab
   Includes publications in Arabic and Western languages.

Hill, Roy Wells. A bibliography of Libya. [Durham, Eng.] 1959. 100 p. (Durham Colleges in the University of Durham. Dept. of Geography. Research papers series, no. 1)   Z3971.H5
Includes an extensive list of maps (p. 11–14). Official documents of Italy Gt. Britain, France, United Nations, concerning Libya are cited.

Murabet, Mohammed. A bibliography of Libya, with particular reference to sources available in libraries and public archives in Tripoli. Valetta, Malta, Progress Press, 1959. 86 p.   Z3971.M8

MOROCCO

Kingdom under various dynasties; 1912–56, under French protectorate, with some sections under Spanish protectorate; independent kingdom, 1956–.

There is no bibliography of official publications; currently these are registered in:

Rabat, Morocco. al-Khizānah al-ʻĀmmah lil-Kutub wa-al-Mustanadāt. Bibliographie nationale marocaine. Nouvelle série. no. 1+ Janv. 1963+   DLC

—— Anbāʼal-bībliyūghrāfīyah al-Maghribīyah. Informations bibliographiques marocaines. [1931–62?] Rabat.   Z3836.R34

—— Liste des publications déposées au titre du dépôt légal. [Rabat, 1948–?] Z965.R33
Up to and including 1959, divided into two parts: A. Publications officielles; B. Autres publications. From 1960, works in Arabic and works in French and foreign languages.

TUNISIA

Monarchy under Turkish rule until 1881; under French protectorate, 1881–1956; independent monarchy, 1956; republic, 1957–.

Official publications are to be listed in part two of the semiannual Bibliographie nationale de Tunisie. (Part one issued first in 1969.)

From 1950 to 1955, the Bulletin économique et social de la Tunisie, issued monthly by the Résidence générale (HC547.T8B8), included about 10 times a year "Informations bibliographiques," listing some official publications.

Lists of official publications of Tunisia were published in the above Bulletin as follows:

"Publications officielles parues en Tunisie durant l'année 1954" (no. 99, avril 1955).

"Publications officielles parues en Tunisie en 1952 et 1953" (no. 88, mai 1954).

"Récapitulation des publications administratives de langue française publiées en Tunisie du 1er janv. 1950 au 1er janv. 1952" (no. 71, dec. 1952).

"Récapitulation des publications officielles parues en Tunisie de 1881 à 1951" (no. 79 and 82, août, nov., 1953; no. 85, 87, 90, 91, 93, fév., avril, juillet, août, oct., 1954; no. 96, janv. 1955).

The following two bibliographies will also be of interest:

Cairo. Dār al-Kutub al-Miṣrīyah. Qā'imah bi-al-kutub wa-al-marāji' 'an Tunis. A bibliographical list of Tunisia. [Cairo 1961]   Z3681.C34 Orien Arab

Tunis. Dār al-Kutub al-Qawmīyah. Récapitulation des périodiques officiels parus en Tunisie de 1881 à 1955 [par] Hélène Pilipenko [et] Jean Rousset de Pina. Tunis, 1956. 108 p.; 10 p.   Z6960.T8T8

SUB-SAHARAN AFRICA

BOTSWANA

Formerly Bechuanaland, a British protectorate; independence: 1966–.

Current official publications are listed in:

The national bibliography of Botswana. v. 1+ 1969+ [Gaberones] Botswana National Library Service.   Z3559.N38
      A classified bibliography. Most entries are official publications.

For retrospective listing, the following bibliographies list official publications:

Balima, Mildred G. Botswana, Lesotho, and Swaziland; a guide to official publications, 1868–1968. Washington, General Reference and Bibliography Division, Library of Congress [U.S. Govt. Print. Off.] 1971. xvi, 84 p.   Z3559.B3

Gt. Brit. *Office of Commonwealth Relations.* Annual report on the Bechuanaland Protectorate. 1946–[1965?] London, H.M. Stationery Off. ([Gt. Brit. Colonial Office] Colonial annual reports)   DT791.A55
      Includes official publications in its "reading list."

Middleton, Coral. Bechuanaland, a bibliography. [Cape Town] University of Cape Town, School of Librarianship, 1965. 37 p. ([Cape Town] University of Cape Town. School of Librarianship. Bibliographical series)   Z3559.M5
      Includes official publications.

Stevens, Pamela. Bechuanaland: Bibliography. [Cape Town] University of Cape Town. School of Librarianship, 1947 [i.e. 1964] 27 p. ([Cape Town] University of Cape Town. School of Librarianship. Bibliographical series)   Z3559.S75 1964
      First published in 1947 under title, *Bibliography of Bechuanaland.* Includes official publications.

BURUNDI

Part of German East Africa, 1890–1918; League of Nations Mandate and United Nations Trust Territory, administered by Belgium, 1919–62; independence: 1962.

No national bibliography or list of official publications issued. For retrospective bibliographies, see Belgium and also:

Clément, Joseph R. **Essai de bibliographie du Ruanda-Urundi.** [Usumbura, Service des A. I. M. O., 1959] 201, xxii l.   Z3971.C5
   Includes some official publications.

Webster, John B. **The political development of Rwanda and Burundi.** [Syracuse, N.Y., Maxwell Graduate School of Citizenship and Public Affairs, Syracuse University] 1966. 121 l. ([Syracuse University] Program of Eastern African Studies. Occasional paper no. [16])   DT1.S915 no. 16
   "Bibliographies" (leaves 101–121) include official publications.

CAMEROON

German colony, 1884–1916; French and British occupation, 1916–19; French and British administration, 1919–22; League of Nations Mandate and United Nations Trusteeship, 1922–60, administered by France and Great Britain; independence: 1960– ; in October 1961 united with Southern Cameroons, formerly administered by Gt. Britain, to form the Federal Republic of Cameroon; United Republic of Cameroon, 1972–.

No national bibliography or list of official publications issued. Some official publications are occasionally listed in the *Bibliographie de la France* (Supplément F). For other listings, see Africa, general bibliographies.

CENTRAL AFRICAN REPUBLIC

Formerly Ubangi-Shari, part of French Equatorial Africa; independence: 1960.

There is no national bibliography or list of official publications. Occasionally some official publications are listed in the *Bibliographie de la France* (Supplément F). For other listings, see Africa, general bibliographies.

CHAD

Formerly part of French Equatorial Africa; independence: 1960.

There is no national bibliography or list of official publications. For listings of official publications, see Africa, general bibliographies.

CONGO, PEOPLE'S REPUBLIC

Formerly part of French Equatorial Africa; independence: 1960.

No national bibliography or list of official publications issued. For retrospective listing of official publications, see Africa, general bibliographies.

DAHOMEY
Formerly part of French West Africa; independence: 1960.

No national bibliography or list of official publications issued. For retrospective listing of official publications, see Africa, general bibliographies and also:

Silva, Guillaume da. Contribution à la bibliographie du Dahomey. Études daho-
    méennes, no. 12, t. 2 and 3 (1968–69)   DT541.E8
        An alphabetical bibliography by authors or titles. Includes official publica-
    tions. There is an index by broad subjects.

EQUATORIAL GUINEA
Formerly Spanish colony; independence: 1968.

For retrospective listing of official publications of the former Spanish Guinea (Rio Muni and Fernando Poo), see:

Childs, James B. Spanish government publications after July 17, 1936; a survey.
    Washington, Library of Congress, Reference Dept., Serial Div. 1965–69. 6 v.
    (2304 p.)   Z2689.C5
                                                                                     Z663.44.S6
        Under the heading Dirección General de Plazas y Provincias Africanas, the
    bibliography lists official publications concerning Spanish Guinea (p. 77–88).

An unpublished dissertation for M.S. degree in library science at the Catholic University of America, by Sanford Berman, entitled *Spanish Guinea, an Annotated Bibliography* (Washington, 1961. 597 l. DLC), also lists official publications.

ETHIOPIA
Kingdom; Italian occupation, 1936–41; Eritrea returned to Ethiopia, 1952.

Addis Ababa. Haile Selassie I University. *Institute of Ethiopian Studies.* Ethiopian
    publications; books, pamphlets, annuals and periodical articles. 1936/64+ Addis
    Ababa, 1965+ annual.   DLC
        A classified bibliography in two parts: pt. 1, Works in Ethiopian languages;
    pt. 2, Works in foreign languages. Includes official publications. There is a
    subject and an author index.

—— List of current periodical publications in Ethiopia. Addis Ababa, 1964+ irreg-
    ular.   DLC
        Classified by broad subjects. Includes official periodicals. There is a subject and
    a title index, also an index in Ethiopian languages.

Baylor, Jim. Ethiopia, a list of works in English. [2d ed. Berkeley? Calif.] 1967. 60, 10 l.   Z3521.B35 1967
   Includes government publications.

Bibliography of publications on Ethiopian education. [no. 1+] Addis Ababa, Educational Research and Curriculum Library [1968?+]   Z5815.E8B52
   Arranged by broad subjects, it includes mainly publications of the Ethiopian Ministry of Education and Fine Arts.

GABON
Formerly part of French Equatorial Africa; independence: 1960.

No national bibliography or list of official publications issued. See Africa, general bibliographies, for retrospective coverage.

GAMBIA
Former British crown colony; independence: 1965.

The Government Printer occasionally issues a list, called *Government Publications.* The following bibliographies list Gambian official publications:

Gamble, David P. Bibliography of the Gambia. [Bathurst, Gambia Gvt. Printer, 1967] 153 p.   Z3735.G3 1967
   A revised and considerably enlarged edition of the 1958 publication of the same title, issued in London (?) In two parts, part one being a classified bibliography, part two, entitled "Gambia government publications," lists sessional papers, departmental reports, other recurrent reports, administrative publications, and miscellaneous publications.

Gt. Brit. *Colonial Office.* Annual report on the Gambia. 1946– [1962/63?] London, H.M. Stationery Off.   DT509.A33
   Biennial from 1950/51. Includes official publications in its "reading list."

U.S. *Library of Congress. African Section.* Official publications of Sierra Leone and Gambia. Compiled by A. A. Walker. Washington, [U.S. Govt. Print. Off.] 1963. 92 p.   Z3553.S5U5

GHANA
Formerly Gold Coast, a British colony; independence: 1957, united with former British Trusteeship Territory of Togoland.

The State Publishing Corporation (Distribution and Sales Division) occasionally issues *Government Publications Price List.* The *Ghana Gazette* includes lists of official publications at irregular intervals.
   The Research Library on African Affairs of the Ghana Library Board (formerly George Padmore Research Library on African Affairs) currently compiles the following two bibliographies, which list official publications in separate sections:

Ghana; a current bibliography. v. 1+ 1967+ Accra, Research Library on African
Affairs. bimonthly.   DLC

Ghana national bibliography. 1965+ Accra, Ghana Library Board. annual.   Z3785.G45

For retrospective publications, the following bibliographies will be of
assistance:

Bourret, F. M.   The Gold Coast; a Survey of the Gold Coast and British Togoland,
1919–1951. 2d ed. Stanford, Calif., Stanford University Press, 1952 [c1949] 248 p.
(The Hoover Library on War, Revolution, and Peace. Publication no. 23)
                                                                              DT511.B68   1952
     "Bibliography," p. 221–236, includes official documents.

Cardinall, Allan W.   A bibliography of the Gold Coast. Issued as a companion volume
to the Census report of 1931. Accra, Gold Coast Colony, Printed by the Government Printer [1932] xix, 384 p.   Z3785.C3
     Covers publications from the 16th century to 1931. "Parliamentary papers,
     etc." Section 10 (p. 241–258) ; "Maps," section 11 (p. 263–269). Reprinted in
     1970 by Negro Universities Press, Westport, Conn.

Gold Coast (Colony) Printing Dept.   Catalogue of government publications (official
and non-official) . Accra, 1939–?   Z3553.G6G6

Gt. Brit. Colonial Office.   Annual report on the Gold Coast. (1946–[54?]) London,
H.M. Stationery Off. (Its Colonial annual reports)   DT511.A323
     Includes official publications in its "reading list."

Johnson, Albert F.   A bibliography of Ghana, 1930–1961. [Evanston, Ill.] Published
for the Ghana Library Board by Northwestern University Press, 1964. 210 p.
                                                                              Z3785.J58
     A classified bibliography. "Government publications," p. [170]–193.

Witherell, Julian W., and Sharon B. Lockwood.   Ghana; a guide to official publications, 1872–1968. Washington, General Reference and Bibliography Division,
Library of Congress, 1969. 110 p   Z3785.W5

GUINEA

Formerly part of French West Africa; independence: 1958.

There is no national bibliography or list of official publications. The
quarterly catalog of recent acquisitions in the National Library lists
books or brochures published in or on Guinea.[10] A five-year bibliography
(from 28 September 1958 to 31 December 1963) was attached as an annex
to no. 1, 1964 of Recherches Africaines, issued by the Institut National
de Recherches et de Documentation of Guinea. (DT543.A3R4) For
other listings of official publications of Guinea, see also Africa, general
bibliographies.

---

[10] Bibliography, Documentation, Terminology (UNESCO), 9 (July 1969): 156.

IVORY COAST
Formerly part of French West Africa; independence: 1960.

The Bibliothèque nationale has issued a national bibliography since 1970, which includes official publications:

Bibliographie de la Côte d'Ivoire. 1970+ [Abidjan] Bibliothèque nationale.   DLC
    Published quarterly. Section two lists periodicals; section four, official pub-
    lications.

Organization for Economic Cooperation and Development. *Development Centre.* Essai
    d'une bibliographie sur la Côte d'Ivoire. Paris, 1964. 122 l. (*Its* CD/D/Bibl./1)
                                                     Z3689.O7

        Includes official publications, mainly under corporate entries (Côte d'Ivoire,
    etc.)

For retrospective listing of official publications, see Africa, general bibliographies.

KENYA
Formerly a British colony and protectorate; independence: 1963.

Currently, the Government Printer publishes the following catalog:

Kenya. Catalogue of government publications. 1st+ 1971+ Nairobi, Govt. Printer.
    annual.   Z3583.K4A3
        Earlier, the Government Printing and Stationery Dept. issued occasionally
    Publications on Sale at Government Printing and Stationery Department.

For retrospective listing of official publications, the following sources will be of help:

Gt. Brit. *Colonial Office.* Annual report on the Colony and Protectorate of Kenya.
    1946–[1962?] London, H.M. Stationery Off. (*Its* Colonial annual reports)
                                        DT434.E2A36
        Included in the "reading list" is a substantial listing of official publications.

Kenya Colony and Protectorate. The Kenya Gazette, Nairobi.   J8.B66
    ——— ——— Supplement. Proclamations, rules and regulations. 1914+ Nairobi.
    irregular.   J8.B66 Suppl.

U.S. *Library of Congress.* African Section. Official publications of British East Africa,
    compiled by Helen F. Conover. Washington, 1960–63. 4 v.   Z3582.U5
    Part 3. *Kenya and Zanzibar.*

Webster, John B., *and others.* A bibliography on Kenya. [Syracuse, N.Y.] Program of
    Eastern African Studies, Syracuse University [1967] xvii, 461 p. (Syracuse Univer-
    sity. Eastern African bibliographical series, no. 2, Kenya)   Z3583.K4W4

LESOTHO
Formerly Basutoland, a British dependency; independence: 1966.

No national bibliography or list of official publications issued currently. Official publications are listed in the following retrospective guides:

Balima, Mildred G. Botswana, Lesotho, and Swaziland: a guide to official publications, 1868–1968. Washington, General Reference and Bibliography Division, Library of Congress. [U.S. Govt. Print. Off.] 1971. xvi, 84 p.   Z3559.B3

Gordon, Loraine. Lesotho: a bibliography. Johannesburg, University of the Witwatersrand, Dept. of Bibliography, Librarianship and Typography, 1970. xvi 47 p.
                                                                      Z3558.G65

Gt. Brit. Colonial Office. Annual report on Basutoland. 1946–[1963?] London, H.M. Stationery Off. (Its Colonial annual reports)   DT781.A35
     The "reading list" includes official publications.

Groen, Juliette. Bibliography of Basutoland. [Cape Town] School of Librarianship, University of Cape Town, 1946. 30 p. ([Cape Town] University of Cape Town. School of Librarianship. Bibliographical series)   Z3558.G7

LIBERIA
Founded in 1822; republic, 1847.

No national bibliography or list of official publications issued. Official publications are listed in the following works:

Holsoe, Svend E. A bibliography of Liberian government documents. African studies bulletin (Stanford, California), v. 11, no. 1 (April 1968): 39–62 and v. 11, no. 2 (Sept. 1968): 149–194.   DT1.A2293 v. 11

——— A bibliography on Liberia. Newark, Published at the Dept. of Anthropology, Univ. of Delaware, by Liberian Studies Association in America, 1971+   Z3821.H6
     Contents: pt. 1. Books. —pt. 2. Publications concerning colonization. Official publications will be covered in subsequent parts. (Preface to v. 1)

Solomon, Marvin D., and Warren L. d'Azevedo. A general bibliography of the Republic of Liberia. Evanston, Ill., 1962. 68 p. (Northwestern University, Evanston, Ill. Working papers in social science, no. 1)   Z3821.N6 no. 1

U.S. Treaties, etc. 1933–1945 (Franklin D. Roosevelt) Exchange of official publications. Agreement between the United States of America and Liberia. [Jan. 1942] Washington, U.S. Govt. Print. Off., 1942. 6 p. ([U.S. Dept. of State. Publication 1758] Executive agreement series 239)   JX236 1929 no. 239
                                                                      Z690.U7L5
     Includes a list of Liberian official publications.

MALAGASY REPUBLIC

Formerly Madagascar; under French rule 1885–1960; independence: 1960.

There is no special bibliography or list of official publications. Currently, the national bibliography includes official publications under corporate entries:

Bibliographie annuelle de Madagascar. 1964+ Tananarive, Bibliothèque Universitaire et Bibliothèque Nationale.   Z3701.B5
    A classified bibliography of all publications issued during the year. An author index, including corporate authors, helps to locate official publications.

Retrospectively, official publications are listed in the following bibliographies:

Duignan, Peter. Madagascar (the Malagasy Republic), a list of materials in the African collections of Stanford University and the Hoover Institution on War, Revolution, and Peace. [Stanford, Calif.] Hoover Institution, Stanford University, 1962. 25 p. (Hoover Institution. Bibliographic series, 9)   Z3701.D8

Grandidier, Guillaume. Bibliographie de Madagascar. [1500–1955] Paris, Comité de Madagascar, 1906 [i.e. 1905]–57. 3 v. (1909 p.)   Z3701.G85
    A bibliography for the period 1956–63 was prepared under the direction of Jean Fontvieille, librarian-founder of the Bibliothèque Universitaire in Tananarive, to complete the above bibliography.[11]

U.S. Library of Congress. African Section. Madagascar and adjacent islands; a guide to official publications. Compiled by Julian W. Witherell. Washington, [U.S. Govt. Print. Off.] 1965. 58 p.   Z3702.U5

MALAWI

Formerly Nyasaland, a British protectorate; member of the Federation of Rhodesia and Nyasaland, 1953–1963; independence: 1964.

There is no national bibliography. The National Archives issues a list of publications deposited under the legal deposit act:

Malawi. National Archives. Material deposited under the printed publications act. Zomba. [1968?+]   DLC
    Issued monthly with annual cumulation.

Retrospectively, the following two works list official publications:

Gt. Brit. Colonial Office. Annual report on Nyasaland. 1946–[1962?] London, H.M. Stationery Off. (Its Colonial annual reports)   DT862.A55
    The "reading list" includes official publications.

---

[11] Bibliographie annuelle de Madagascar, 1964, Introduction, p. 5.

U.S. *Library of Congress. African Section.* The Rhodesias and Nyasaland; a guide to official publications, compiled by A. A. Walker. Washington, 1965. 285 p.
                                                                                        Z3573.R5U5
    "Publications of the Federation of Rhodesia and Nyasaland," p. 7–46; "Publications of Nyasaland," p. 194–228.

MALI

Formerly part of French West Africa, named French Sudan; 1958, Sudanese Republic; 1959–60, Federation of Mali (with Senegal); 1960, Republic of Mali.

There is no national bibliography or list of official publications. For listing of official publications, see Africa, general bibliographies, and:

Brasseur, Paule. Bibliographie générale du Mali (anciens Soudan français et Haut-Sénégal-Niger). Dakar, IFAN, 1964. 461 p. (Institut français d'Afrique noire. Catalogues et documents, 16)   Z3711.B7

Cutter, C. H. Mali: a bibliographic introduction. African studies bulletin, v. 9, no. 3 (Dec. 1966): 74–87.   DT1.A2293 v. 9

MAURITANIA

Formerly part of French West Africa; independence: 1960.

No national bibliography or list of official publications issued. For retrospective listing of official publications, see general bibliographies for French-speaking West Africa and other general bibliographic tools for Africa.

MAURITIUS

Under French administration, 1715–1810; British administration, 1810–1968; independence: 1968.

The Government Printer occasionally issues *Government Publications on Sale at the Government Printing Office.* The Mauritian official and semiofficial publications from the earliest times have been recorded in the following bibliography, supplemented currently in the publications of the Archives Department:

Mauritius. *Archives Dept.* Bibliography of Mauritius, 1502–1954, covering the printed record, manuscript, archivalia and cartographic material [by] A. Toussaint, chief archivist. Port Louis, Printed by Esclapon, 1956. xvii, 884 p.   Z3703.M3A5
    Divided into four groups, group C lists "government and semi-official publications, 1810–1954." The official publications of the earlier, French period are listed in group A, "early imprints and private publications." From 1955, the bibliography is continued by the Archives Department's *Report* (annual), and its quarterly *Memorandum of Books Printed in Mauritius . . .* (see below).

—— Memorandum of books printed in Mauritius and registered in the Archives Office. Port Louis. quarterly.   Z3553.M3A24

Published since 1893 in the *Government Gazette*, it lists in two parts: "official and semi-official publications"; "private publications." Issued also separately.

—— Report. 1950+ Port Louis, Govt. Printer. annual.   CD2355.M3A33

From 1955, the "List of publications printed in Mauritius in . . ." is numbered as Supplement 1, etc. The arrangement of the list in four groups (A–D), with occasional listing of maps (as group F), is the same as in Toussaint's bibliography, the group C being "Government and semi-official publications."

Other bibliographic tools, listing Mauritian official publications:

Gt. Brit. *Colonial Office*. Annual report on Mauritius. 1946–[1966?] London, H.M. Stationery Off. (*Its* Colonial annual reports)   DT469.M4A14

Includes official publications in its "reading list."

Hahn, Lorna, *and* Robert Edison. Mauritius: a study and annotated bibliography. Washington, American University, Center for Research in Social Systems, 1969. 44 p.   Z3553.M3H32

"Government publications," p. 16–24.

U.S. *Library of Congress. African Section.* Madagascar and adjacent islands; a guide to official publications. Compiled by Julian W. Witherell. Washington, 1965. 58 p. Mauritius, pp. 30–40.   Z3702.U5

NIGER

Formerly part of French West Africa; independence: 1960.

No national bibliography or list of official publications issued. For retrospective listing of official publications see general bibliographies on French-speaking West Africa and other general bibliographic tools for Africa.

NIGERIA

Formerly under British rule; independence: 1960.

The Printing Division of the Federal Ministry of Information occasionally publishes a *List of Government Publications.*

Official publications are currently listed in the following Nigerian national bibliography:

Nigerian publications [1st]+ 1950–52+ [Ibadan] Ibadan University Press. annual. Z3553.N5N5

From July 1970, issued by the National Library of Nigeria in Lagos. Documents of the federal government and regional governments are listed in a separate section. Kept up to date by quarterly and weekly supplements.

The following bibliographies cover retrospective or current official publications for Nigeria or its regions:

Ahmadu Bello University, *Zaria, Nigeria. Institute of Administration.* Publications of the Government of the Northern Region of Nigeria, [1960–62] Zaria.
                                                                           Z3553.N5A67

Gt. Brit. *Colonial Office.* Annual report on Nigeria. 1946–[1955?] London, H.M. Stationery Off. (*Its* Colonial annual reports)   DT515.A573
Includes official publications in its "reading list."

Ibadan, Nigeria. University. *Library.* Nigerian periodicals & newspapers, 1950–1955; a list of those received from April 1950 to June 1955 under the Publications ordinance, 1950. Ibadan, 1956. 23 p.   Z6960.N5I2
    Continued from 1955 in the Library's *Nigerian Publications* (see above). Includes official periodicals.

Nigeria. *National Archives.* A handlist of Nigerian official publications in the National Archives headquarters, Ibadan. Compiled by L. C. Gwam. Ibadan, 1964. 188 l.
                                                                           CD2423.A5
Nigeria. *National Archives. Kaduna Branch.* A provisional guide to official publications at the National Archives, Kaduna. Compiled by J. C. Enwere. [Kaduna] 1962. 78 l.   Z3553.N5A52

Northern Nigerian publications. [1966?+] Zaria, Nigeria, Ahmadu Bello University, Kashim Ibrahim Library, annual.   Z3553.N5N63
    Includes official publications.

U.S. *Library of Congress. African Section.* Nigeria; a guide to official publications. Compiled by Sharon B. Lockwood. Washington, 1966. 166 p.   Z3553.N5U48
    Lists official publications issued from 1861 to 1965 by both the British administrations and the Nigerian federal and regional governments. A revised edition of an earlier similar bibliography (*Nigerian Official Publications, 1869–1959.* Z3553.N5U5).

RHODESIA

Formerly, as Southern Rhodesia, under British rule; 1953–63, part of the Federation of Rhodesia and Nyasaland; 1963–65, self-governing colony within the British Commonwealth; unilateral declaration of independence, 1965; republic, 1970–.

Currently official publications are listed in:

Rhodesia national bibliography. 1967+ Salisbury, National Archives. annual.
                                                                           Z3573.R5R54
    "List of publications deposited in the Library of the National Archives." Superseded: National Archives of Rhodesia. *List of Publications Deposited in the Library of the National Archives* (1961–66. Z965.N37).

Official publications are also listed in the following retrospective bibliographies:

Rhodesia and Nyasaland. *Federal Information Dept.* Catalogue of official publications. Salisbury. [annual?]   Z3582.R5

U.S. *Library of Congress. African Section.* The Rhodesias and Nyasaland; a guide to official publications. Compiled by A. A. Walker. Washington, 1965. 285 p.
                                                                           Z3573.R5U5

The bibliography lists, in separate sections, official publications of the Central African Interterritorial Agencies before Federation, the Federation of Rhodesia and Nyasaland, Northern Rhodesia (now Zambia), Southern Rhodesia and Nyasaland (now Malawi). Also listed are British official publications relating to the Central African Territories.

Willson, Francis M. G., *and others*. Catalogue of the parliamentary papers of Southern Rhodesia, 1899–1953. Salisbury, Dept. of Government, University College of Rhodesia and Nyasaland, 1965. xxx, 484 p. (Salisbury, Rhodesia. University College of Rhodesia and Nyasaland. Dept. of Government. Source book series, 2)
JQ2921.A23 no. 2
Continued in Norman W. Wilding's *Catalogue of the Parliamentary Papers of Southern Rhodesia and Rhodesia, 1954–1970, and Federation of Rhodesia and Nyasaland, 1954–1963*, issued as Source Book no. 6, by the University College of Rhodesia, Salisbury, in 1970.

RWANDA

Part of German East Africa, 1890–1918; League of Nations Mandate and United Nations Trust Territory, administered by Belgium [Ruanda-Urundi], 1919–62; independence: 1962.

No national bibliography, or list of official publications issued. For retrospective bibliographies, see Belgium, and:

Clément, Joseph R. Essai de bibliographie du Ruanda-Urundi. [Usumbura, Service des A.I.M.O., 1959] 201, xxii l. Z3971.C5
Includes some official publications.

Université Nationale du Rwanda. *Bibliothèque*. Fichier topographique de la collection rwandaise. v. 1, no. 1+ juin, 1969+ [Butare] DLC
Includes official publications under corporate entries.

Webster, John B. The political development of Rwanda and Burundi. [Syracuse, N.Y., Maxwell Graduate School of Citizenship and Public Affairs, Syracuse University] 1966. 121 l. ([Syracuse University] Program of Eastern African Studies. Occasional paper no. [16]) DT1.S915 no. 16
"Bibliography" (l. 101–121) includes official publications.

SENEGAL

Formerly part of French West Africa; member of the Federation of Mali, 1959–60; independent republic, 1960–.

There is no national bibliography or special list of official publications. Official publications are currently listed in:

Archives nationales du Sénégal. *Centre de documentation*. Bulletin bibliographique des archives du Sénégal. no. 1+ jan. 1963+ Dakar. irregular. Z3711.A73a

For retrospective listing, the following bibliographies include official publications:

Archives nationales du Sénégal. *Centre de documentation.* Éléments de bibliographie sénégalaise, 1959–1963 [par] Laurence Porgès. Dakar, 1964. 141 l.   Z3711.A72
  Includes a considerable number of official publications.

Porgès, Laurence. Bibliographie des régions du Sénégal. Dakar, Ministère du Plan et du développement, 1967 [ᶜ1969] 705 p.   DLC

SIERRA LEONE
Former British colony and protectorate; independence: 1961.

There is no national bibliography. Publications, including government documents, are listed in:

Sierra Leone. *Library Board.* Sierra Leone publications. Freetown, [1962+]
                                                                         Z3553.S555
  "A list of books and pamphlets in English received by the Sierra Leone Library Board under the Publications (Amendment) Act, 1962."
  In two sections: "Official publications"; "Semi-official and other publications."

The *Sierra Leone Government Gazette* (J8.B74) frequently includes a list of "Government publications on sale at Government Bookshop." Retrospectively, official publications are listed in the following works:

Gt. Brit. *Colonial Office.* Annual report on Sierra Leone. 1946–[1958?] London, H.M. Stationery Off.   DT516.A15
  Official publications are included in its "reading list."

Luke, *Sir* Harry C. J. A bibliography of Sierra Leone. 2d enl. ed. New York, Negro Universities Press, [1969] 230 p.   Z3553.S5L8   1969
  Reprint of the 1925, ed. (Oxford University Press, London). "State and parliamentary papers," p. 192–209; "Maps," p. 210–214.

U.S. *Library of Congress. African Section.* Official publications of Sierra Leone and Gambia. Compiled by A. A. Walker. Washington, [U.S. Govt. Print. Off.] 1963. 92 p.
                                                                         Z3553.S5U5

Williams, Geoffrey J. A bibliography of Sierra Leone, 1925–1967. New York, Africans Pub. Corp. [1971] xxii, 209 p.   Z3553.S5W55
  A classified bibliography. Official publications can be identified through the "author index."

SOMALIA
Formerly under British (northern section) and Italian (southern section) rule; independence: 1960–.

No national bibliography or list of official publications issued. For retrospective listing, the following works include official publications:

Gt. Brit. *Colonial Office.* Report on the Somaliland Protectorate. 1948–[1958?] London, H.M. Stationary Off. (*Its* Colonial annual reports)   DT406.A14
  Its "reading list" includes official publications.

Somaliland, Italian. Camera di commercio, industria ed agricoltura. *Sezione fiere e mostre*. Bibliografia somala. Mogadiscio, Scuola tip. Missione cattolica, 1958. 135 p.
Z3796.S6
Includes some official publications and maps.

U.S. *Library of Congress. General Reference and Bibliography Division*. Official publications of Somaliland, 1941–1959; a guide, compiled by Helen F. Conover. Washington, 1960. 41 p.   Z3516.U5

SOUTH AFRICA

Union of South Africa, 1910–61, formed from the former self-governing colonies of Cape and Natal, and the Orange Free State and Transvaal, within the British Commonwealth; Republic of South Africa, 1961– .

Official publications are currently listed in the SANB, *South African National Bibliography. Suid-Afrikaanse Nasionale Bibliografie*, published by the State Library in Pretoria (Z3603.P7). It began publication as an alphabetical author list in 1933:

Pretoria. State Library. Publications received in terms of copyright act no. 9 of 1916. Apr. 1933+ Pretoria.   Z3603.P7
Published monthly, originally under the title *List of Copyright Additions*, with annual cumulation beginning in 1938. In 1959 it changed to a classified bibliography, published quarterly with annual cumulation under the new title *SANB, South African National Bibliography* . . . Currently, official publications are listed under individual classes. An author index is included.

The South African Public Library in Cape Town also published lists of official documents (since 1946), first in its *Quarterly Bulletin* (Z965.-S767), later in:

Africana nova. Sept. 1958–[1969] [Cape Town, South African Public Library] quarterly.
Z3603.A65
Separate lists of official publications of the central government and provincial authorities were included from March 1962.

South African Public Library, *Cape Town*. Quarterly bulletin. Kwartaalblad. v. 1+, Sept. 1946+ Cape Town.   Z965.S767
Lists of official publications included through December 1961. Continued in *Africana Nova*.

The Government Printer issues a monthly mimeographed list, *Official Publications Issued During . . .*, which is also reprinted in the *Government Gazette. Staatskoerant* (J8.B775).

There is no general retrospective bibliography of official publications. There are, however, several lists, covering certain periods or certain fields. In 1970, the first volume of a *Bibliography of South African Government Publications*, covering statistics 1910–68, was published by the Department of Cultural Affairs, Division of Library Services (see entry below).

Other works covering retrospective official publications are the following:

Isaacson, Isaac. The official publications of the Union of South Africa and the provinces of the Union of South Africa. [Capetown?] South African Library Association, 1949. 155–162, 31–36 1.   Z3605.I73
    Reprinted from *South African Libraries* v. 7, 1939/40 and v. 11, 1943 (Z671.-S69) .

────── A finding list of South African Commissions and committees of enquiry under names of chairmen. South African libraries, v. 20, 1952/53: 42–48; 84–86.
                                                                                    Z671.S69

London. University. *Institute of Advanced Legal Studies.* Union list of Commonwealth and South African law: a location guide to Commonwealth and South African legislation, law reports, and digests held by libraries in the United Kingdom at May 1963. 1963 ed. London [1963] 129 p.   DLC LL

Mendelssohn, Sidney. Mendelssohn's South African bibliography . . . London, K. Paul, Trench, Trübner, 1910. 2 v.   Z3518.M41
    Includes official publications under names of colonies (e.g. Cape Colony, etc.) and an appendix "South African imperial blue books" (v. 2, p. 653–710). A "revision project" is under way at the South African Library in Cape Town, to complete and extend Mendelssohn's bibliography to 1925. Reprinted, London, Holland Press, 1957–58, and 1968.

Musiker, Reuben. Guide to South African reference books. 4th rev. ed. Cape Town. A. A. Balkema, 1965. 110 p. (Balkema academic and technical publications)
                                                                            Z3601.M8   1965
    Fifth edition published in 1971 (136 p.)

────── South African bibliography; a survey of bibliographies and bibliographical work. Hamden, Conn., Archon Books, [1970] 105 p.   Z3601.A1M9
    Describes lists and bibliographies of government documents in section C: "official publications," p. [75]–79 [12]

Schutte, P. J. 'n Beredeneerde gesamentlike katalogus van die Zuid-Afrikaansche republiek. Pretoria, State Library, 1966. 170 p. (Pretoria. State Library. Bibliographies, no. 9)
    A catalog of "green books" of Transvaal, before the union (annual reports and certain other official documents) for 1881–1900. In three parts: classified list, chronological list, index.

South Africa. *Dept. of Cultural Affairs. Division of Library Services.* South African government publications: Department of Statistics, 1910–1968. [Pretoria, Government Printer] 1969. 123 p.   Z3605.S6
    Classified by broad subjects. The first volume of a proposed *Bibliography of South African Government Publications.*

South Africa. *Office of Census and Statistics.* Official yearbook [of the Union of South Africa] Pretoria, Government Printer, 1918+   DT752.A3
    Includes "Bibliography of the Union of South Africa," listing reports and other official documents from 1910.

─────────────────

[12] A bibliography entitled *Cape Official Publications 1854–1910,* compiled by Reuben Musiker and N. Musiker at the State Library, Pretoria, will be published by G. K. Hall, Boston.

South Africa. *Parliament. House of Assembly.* Index to the manuscript annexures and printed papers of the House of Assembly, including select committee reports and bills and also to principal motions and resolutions and commission reports. 1910/20+ Cape Town.   J705.M3
    Latest, 1910–61, issued in 1963. For the earlier (pre-Union) period, the (Cape of Good Hope. *Parliament. House.*) *Index to the Annexures and Printed Papers* . . . covers the periods 1854–97; 1898–1903; 1904–10, in three volumes (J707.M3)

South Africa. *Printing and Stationery Dept.* List of official publications issued by the Government Printing and Stationery Department. [1916–38?] Pretoria.   Z3605.S72
    Also issued in Afrikaans under the title *Lys van offisiëlle publikasies* . . . (Z3605.S722).

South African Public Library, *Cape Town.* Classified list of South African annual publications as at March 31st, 1951. Cape Town, 1951. 42 p. (Grey bibliographies, no. 4)
                                                   Z3518.S56
    Includes official annuals and annual reports.

Webb, Colin de B., *comp.* A guide to the official records of the colony of Natal. 2d rev. ed. [Pietermaritzburg] University of Natal, 1968. 318 p.   Z3592.W4   1968

SOUTH WEST AFRICA

German protectorate (colony) 1884–1915; South African occupation, 1915; League of Nations class C mandate, administered by South Africa 1920–; name changed in 1968 to Namibia by U.N. General Assembly.

De Jager, Theo. South West Africa. Suidwes-Afrika. Pretoria, State Library, 1964. 216 p. (Pretoria. State Library. Bibliographies, no. 7)   Z3771.D4
    An alphabetical author listing, which includes official publications.

Voigts, Barbara. South West African imprints, a bibliography. [Cape Town] University of Cape Town, School of Librarianship, 1963 [cover 1964] 58 p. (University of Cape Town, School of Librarianship. Bibliographical series)   Z3771.V6
    Official publications, p. 39–49.

Welch, Florette J. South West Africa: a bibliography. Cape Town, University of Cape Town, School of Librarianship, 1967. 41 p. (University of Cape Town. School of Librarianship. Bibliographical series)   Z3771.W4   1967
    Covers the years 1919–46.

SUDAN

Formerly under Anglo-Egyptian rule; independence: 1956.

There is no national bibliography and no list of official publications. Some official documents are listed in the following bibliographies:

Cairo. Dār al-Kutub al-Miṣrīyah. *Qism al-Irshād.* Qā'imah bi-al-kutub wa-al-marāji' 'an al-Sūdān. [A bibliography of works about Sudan] Cairo, 1961. 41, 67 p.
                                            Z3665.C35 Orien Arab
    Includes publications in Arabic and Western languages.

Dāghir, Yūsuf Asʿad. al-Uṣūl al-ʿArabīyah lil-dirāsāt al-Sūdānīyah. Beirut, 1968.
[Librairie orientale]   Z3665.D34 Orien Arab
    Sudanese bibliography, Arabic sources (1875–1967). Includes some govern-
    ment publications.

Hill, Richard L. A bibliography of Anglo-Egyptian Sudan, from the earliest times to
    1937. London, Oxford University Press, H. Milford, 1939. 213 p.   Z3711.H64
    Arranged by broad subjects, most official documents listed in sections "Law,"
    p. 162–163 and "Administration," p. 168.

Khartum. Jāmiʿat al-Khartūm. al-Maktabah. [al-Fihris al-musannaf li-majmūʿat al-
    Sūdān. Khartum] 1971. 1 v. (unpaged)   Z3665.K48
    Classified catalog of the Sudan collection, University of Khartoum. Includes
    section "directories and official government publications."

el Nasri, Abdel R. A bibliography of the Sudan, 1938–1958. London, New York, Pub-
    lished on behalf of the University of Khartoum by the Oxford University Press,
    1962. 171 p.   Z3711.N3
    Arranged by broad subjects, with official publications listed mainly in the
    section "government and politics," p. 74–97. Intended to supplement R. L.
    Hill's bibliography. (See above)

SWAZILAND

Formerly a British protectorate; independence: 1968.

No national bibliography or list of official publications issued.
Retrospectively, official publications are included in the following
works:

Arnheim, Johanna. Swaziland, a bibliography. [Capetown] University of Cape Town,
    School of Librarianship, 1963. 23 p. ([Cape Town] University of Cape Town.
    School of Librarianship. Bibliographical series)   Z3607.S9A7 1963
    First published in 1950. Arranged by broad subjects, it includes official docu-
    ments in various classes.
    "South African imperial blue books," p. 17–18.

Balima, Mildred G. Botswana, Lesotho, and Swaziland: a guide to official publica-
    tions, 1868–1968. Washington, General Reference and Bibliography Division,
    Library of Congress [U.S. Govt. Print. Off.] 1971. xvi, 84 p.   Z3559.B3

Gt. Brit. Colonial Office. Swaziland; report. 1946–[1966?] London, H. M. Stationery
    Off.   HC517.S9A35
    Includes official publications in its "reading list."

Wallace, Charles S. Swaziland; a bibliography. Johannesburg, University of the Wit-
    watersrand. Dept. of Bibliography, Librarianship and Typography, 1967. 87 p.
                                                                       Z3607.S9W34

Webster, John B, and Paulus Mohome. A bibliography on Swaziland. Syracuse, N.Y.,
    Bibliographic Section, Program of Eastern African Studies, Syracuse University,
    1968. 32 l. (The Program of Eastern African Studies. Occasional bibliography no.
    10)   Z7165.A42S9 no. 10

TANZANIA

Tanganyika: part of German East Africa, 1884–1916; British occupation, 1916; League of Nations Mandate and U. N. Trusteeship, 1919–61, under British administration; independent republic, 1962; merged with Zanzibar to form Tanzania, 1964–.

Zanzibar: Under British rule, 1890–1963; independence: 1963; merged with Tanganyika to form Tanzania, 1964– .

The Government Printer in Dar es Salaam occasionally issues a list of government publications, continuing the lists issued earlier by the Government Printer of Tanganyika (Z3516.T3). In 1970 an attempt at compiling a national bibliography resulted in the first issue of a list called *Printed in Tanzania 1969; a List of Publications Printed in Mainland Tanzania During 1969 and Deposited with the Tanganyika Library Service and the Library of the University of Dar es Salaam, Together with Some Publications Published in Tanzania but Printed Elsewhere* (Dar es Salaam, Printed by Printpak Tanzania Ltd. for the Tanganyika Library Service Board, 1970. DLC). The list is issued annually and includes mostly official publications.

Another publication listing Tanzanian official publications is the *Library Bulletin and Accessions List,* issued since 1956 by the Makerere University Library in Kampala, Uganda (see Uganda).

For retrospective listings, the following works will be of assistance:

Gt. Brit. *Colonial Office.* Annual report on Zanzibar. 1946–[1960?] London, H. M. Stationery Off. (*Its* Colonial annual reports)   DT434.Z3G7
    Includes official publications in its "reading list."

Handbook of Tanganyika. 2d ed. Edited by J. P. Moffett. [Dar es Salaam, Government Printer, 1958] 703 p.   DT438.H3 1958
    "Bibliography," p. 567–677 includes official publications.

U.S. *Library of Congress. African Section.* Official publications of British East Africa, compiled by Helen F. Conover. Washington, 1960–63. 4 v.   Z3582.U5
    Part 2: *Tanganyika;* part 3: *Kenya and Zanzibar.*

TOGO

Formerly German Protectorate of Togoland, 1894–1914; divided between France (eastern part) and Great Britain (western part), and administered under the League of Nations Mandate and the United Nations Trusteeship from 1922. Western part merged with Ghana in 1957, eastern part became independent republic of Togo, 1960.

No national bibliography or list of official publications issued. For retrospective listing of official publications, see Africa, General bibliographies.

UGANDA
Formerly a British protectorate; independence: 1962; republic, 1963–.

Official publications are listed currently in:

Library bulletin and accessions list. [no. 1+, 1956+] [Kampala] Makerere University
    College [Library] quarterly.   Z965.L5

Uganda. Printing Dept. Catalogue of government publications. Entebbe.   Z3583.U4A3
    The 1965 edition lists official documents "published prior to 1st Jan., 1965."

Other bibliographic works listing official publications of Uganda:

Gt. Brit. Colonial Office. Uganda; report for the year. 1946–[1961?] London, H. M.
    Stationery Off. (Its Colonial annual reports)   DT434.U2G57
    Official publications are included in the "reading list."

Marani, K. P. A bibliography on Uganda government publications, 1963–1969.
    [Kampala] 1971. 103 l.   Z3583.U4M3
    Carbon copy of a dissertation submitted to East African School of Librarian-
    ship, Makerere University. In two parts: Non-serial, and serial publications.

U.S. Library of Congress. African Section. Official publications of British East Africa,
    compiled by Helen F. Conover. Washington, 1960–63. 4 v.   Z3582.U5
    Part 4: Uganda.

UPPER VOLTA
Until 1960, part of French West Africa; independence: 1960.

No national bibliography or list of official publications issued. Retrospectively, official publications of Upper Volta are listed in general bibliographies of French-speaking West Africa (see Africa, General bibliographies), and also in:

African Bibliographic Center. French-speaking West Africa: Upper Volta today,
    1960–1967; a selected and introductory bibliographical guide. [Washington, 1969,
    c1968] 37 p. (Its Special bibliographic series, v. 6, no. 1)   Z3507.A45 vol. 6, no. 1

Izard, Françoise, Michèle d'Huart, and Philippe Bonnefond. Bibliographie générale
    de la Haute-Volta, 1956–1965. Paris, C. N. R. S.; Ouagadougou, C. V. R. S., 1967.
    300 p. (Recherches voltaïques, 7)   DT553.U7A26 no. 7

ZAIRE, REPUBLIC OF
Congo Free State, under sovereignty of the Belgian King Leopold II,
1884–1908; Belgian Congo, 1908–60; independence, 1960 as Democratic
Republic of Congo; renamed Zaïre in October 1971.

There is no bibliography or list of official publications. The Bibliothèque nationale began publication of a Bibliographie nationale in
April 1971. For retrospective bibliographies, see Africa, General bibliographies, and also Belgium.

The following bibliography includes official publications of Katanga:

Walraet, Marcel. Bibliographie du Katanga. [1824–1949] [Bruxelles, 1954–60] 3 v.
Z3693.K3W3

ZAMBIA

Formerly Northern Rhodesia, under British rule; 1953–63, part of the Federation of Rhodesia and Nyasaland; independence: 1964.

There is no national bibliography. The Government Printer in Lusaka issues an annual *List of Publications,* kept up to date with monthly lists, as a supplement to the *Zambia Government Gazette.*

Retrospectively, Zambian (Northern Rhodesian) official publications were listed in the following bibliographic tools:

Gt. Brit. *Colonial Office.* Annual report on Northern Rhodesia. 1946–[1962?] London, H. M. Stationery Off. *(Its* Colonial annual reports)   DT963.A3
 Official publications are included in the "reading list."

Rhodesia, Northern. List of publications. Lusaka, Govt. Printer. annual. Z3573.Z3R5
 Kept up to date by monthly supplements. Issued as supplement to *Northern Rhodesia Government Gazette.*

U.S. *Library of Congress. African Section.* The Rhodesias and Nyasaland; a guide to official publications, compiled by A. A. Walker. Washington, 1965. 285 p.
Z3573.R5U5
 "Publications of the Federation of Rhodesia and Nyasaland," p. 7–46; "Publications of Northern Rhodesia," p. 47–117.

NEAR EAST

Changes that have occurred in the Near East in modern times make the search for official documents difficult. Government and boundary changes create complicated problems for the librarian and especially for the cataloger, who must make entries for official publications reflect the changes. The cataloger, the reference librarian, and the researcher must, therefore, be well acquainted with the political history of the area and with the changing governmental structure in individual countries. Even the delimitation of what area constitutes the Near East, or the Middle East as it is often referred to, has undergone considerable changes.

There are many works dealing with the political history of the Near East. Works dealing with the governmental organization of individual countries are less numerous. The following general bibliographies include more or less comprehensive listing of official documents for Near Eastern countries; some also containing background information on political developments and information which may lead the researcher to further bibliographical sources:

American University of Beirut. *Economic Research Institute.* A selected and annotated bibliography of economic literature on the Arabic speaking countries of the Middle East, 1938–1952. Beirut, Gedeon Press, 1954. 199 p.   Z7164.E15A6
────── ────── Supplement. 1953+ Beirut, American Press. annual. Z7164.E15A62

────── A selected and annotated bibliography of economic literature on the Arab countries of the Middle East, 1953–1965. Beirut, 1967. xvii, 458 p.   Z7165.A67A56
"Consolidates the annual 'Supplements' to the bibliography which covered the years 1953 up to 1962 and includes materials appearing in the three following years."

Davison, Roderic H. The Near and Middle East: an introduction to history and bibliography. Washington, Service Center for Teachers of History [1959] 48 p. (Service Center for Teachers of History. Publication no. 24)   Z3013.D33

A Post-war bibliography of the Near Eastern mandates; a preliminary survey of publications on the social sciences dealing with Iraq, Palestine and Trans-Jordan, and the Syrian states, from Nov. 11, 1918 to Dec. 31, 1929 arranged in an alphabetical list by authors, with a limited index by subject matter. Presented in ... eight fascicles by languages . . . Stuart C. Dodd, Ph.D., general editor. Beirut, American Press, 1932–[36]   H31.A6 no. 1, etc.
                                                                  Z3451.P85

334

Stanford Research Institute. Area handbook for the Peripheral States of the Arabian
Peninsula. Prepared for the American University. [Washington, U.S. Govt. Print.
Off.] 1971. 201 p.   DS247.A14S78
"DA pam no. 550-92."
Includes bibliographical sources on Yemen Arab Republic, People's Republic
of Yemen, Kuwait, The Gulf States (United Arab Emirates) and Oman, for-
merly Muscat and Oman.

United Nations Educational, Scientific and Cultural Organization. *Middle East Science
Cooperation Office*. Middle East social science bibliography; books and articles
on the social sciences published in Arab countries of the Middle East in 1955–1960.
Cairo, 1961. 152 p.   Z7165.N35U5
"Jurisprudence," p. 107–132.

U.S. *Dept. of State. Library Division*. Point four, Near East and Africa; a selected
bibliography of studies on economically underdeveloped countries. New York,
Greenwood Press [1969] 136 p.   Z3013.U5 1969
Reprint of the 1951 edition.

U.S. *Foreign Service Institute. Center for Area and Country Studies*. Near East and
North Africa; a selected functional and country bibliography. [Washington, 1968]
43 p.   Z3013.U525

U.S. *Library of Congress. American Libraries Book Procurement Center, Cairo*. Accessions list, Middle East. v. 1+ Jan. 1963+ Cairo. monthly.   Z3013.U54
A cumulative author index is issued at the end of each year as a supplement,
and a cumulative list of serials appears annually in July.

EGYPT

From the 16th century until 1882 (nominally until World War I) under
Turkish rule; British occupation, 1882; British protectorate, 1914–22;
kingdom, 1922–53; republic, 1953– (United Arab Republic, 1958–71;
Arab Republic of Egypt, 1971–).

Official publications are currently included in:

Nashrat al-īdāʿ al-shahrīyah. Cairo, Dār al-Kutub al-Qawmīyah, Jan. 1969+ monthly.
monthly.   DLC Orien Arab
"Legal deposit monthly bulletin." Superseded *al-Nashrah al-Miṣrīyah lil-
matbūʿāt*, issued 1955–68? (see below).

U.S. *Library of Congress. American Libraries Book Procurement Center, Cairo*. Ac-
cessions list, Middle East. v. 1+ Jan. 1963+ Cairo. monthly.   Z3013.U54
Every July issue is an annual list of serials, including government publications.
A cumulative author index is issued at the end of each year.

The following publications list or include retrospective official documents in general, or for certain fields:

American University at Cairo. *Library*. Guide to U. A. R. Government publications
at the A. U. C. Library. [Cairo] Periodicals and Documents Dept., American Uni-

versity in Cairo Library, 1965. 20, 41 p.   Z3655.A5
Includes titles in Arabic and Western languages.

Cairo, Dār al-Kutub al-Miṣrīyah.   Egypt, subject catalogue. Cairo, Egyptian National
Library Press, 1957–63. 3 v. (1098 p.) (Egyptian National Library publications)
                                                                  Z3651.C27
Official publications are included in the classified arrangement, mostly under
corporate entries. Volume three is an author index.

—— Qā'imah bi-ba'ḍ al-maṭbū'āt al-ḥukūmīyah. Cairo, 1959. 30 p.
                                            Z3655.C35 Orien Arab
List of Egyptian government publications in Arabic and Western languages,
issued during 1952–58.

Cairo. Ma'had al-Takhṭīṭ al-Qawmī. List of publications issued by the Institute of
National Planning. Sept. 1960/July 1962+ Cairo.   Z7165.E4C29

Cairo. Markaz al-Wathā'iq al-Tarbawīyah lil-Jumhūrīyah al-'Arabīyah al-Muttaḥidah.
al-Dalīl al-bibliyūjrāfī. Cairo, [1961] 11, 114 p.   Z3655.A4 Orien Arab
A bibliographical directory for the publications of the Central Ministry of
Education and the Ministry of Education of the Southern Region (i.e. Egypt),
1950–60.

—— —— Cairo, 1962 [i.e. 1963] 10, 161 p.   Z5815.E3C28   1963 Orien Arab
Covers 1950–61.

Egypt. *Government Press*. Catalogue of publications in stores. 1909–?   Z3655.E35
Title and name of issuing agency varies.

Egypt. *Maṣlaḥat al-Misāḥah*. A list of maps, plans, and publications. Cairo, National
Print. Dept. [1903–?]   Z6027.E4E4
Title and name of the issuing agency varies.

Egypt. *Ministry of Agriculture*. List of publications in English issued by the ministry.
Cairo [1937. 16 p.]   Z5075.E3E4

al-Hay'ah al-'Āmmah li-Shu'ūn al-Maṭābi' al-Amīrīyah.   Qā'imat al-maṭbū'at al-
mawjūdah bi-Sālat Bay' al-Maṭbū'āt al-Ḥukūmiyah bi-Maydan al-Ūbirā, Cairo,
1960. 37 p.   DLC Orien Arab
List of publications in the Sales Hall of Government Publications in Opera
Square.

al-Nashrah al-Miṣrīyah lil-maṭbū'āt. [1955–68?] Cairo, Dār al-Kutub al-Miṣrīyah.
                                            Z3651.C3 Orien Arab
"Egyptian publications bulletin," issued by the National Library. Superseded
in 1969 by *Nashrat al-īdā' al-shahrīyah (Legal Deposit Monthly Bulletin)*.

Sulaymān, Salāḥ M. A. Dalīl al-maṣādir al-iḥṣā'īyah. Sirs al-Layyān, 1959. 45 p.
                                          Z7Z7554.E4S8 Orien Arab
A directory of statistical sources in the U.A.R.

United Arab Republic. *Wizārat al-Tarbiyah wa-al-Ta'līm*. Ta'rīf bi-maṭbū'āt Wizārat
al-Tarbiyah wa-al-Ta'līm. 1960–62. Cairo, 1962. 30 p.   Z5811.U28 Orien Arab
List of publications of the Ministry of Education, a selected list, 1960–62.

Iran
Absolute monarchy to 1906; constitutional monarchy, 1905–.

Official publications are currently included in the following bibliographies:

Afshār, Īraj. Kitābhā-yi Īrān. Teheran. annual.   Z3366.A6 Orien Pers
"Bibliography of Persia." Began with 1954/55 issue. Volumes for 1955/56 to
1963 issued also as a cumulative volume.

Teheran. Kitābkhānah-i Millī. Kitābshināsī-i millī. Teheran. annual
Z3366.T4 Orien Pers
"National bibliography, Iranian publications." Issued by the National Library
of Iran since 1963. A monthly edition also issued since March 1970.

Retrospective bibliographies, listing official publications:

Iran. *Sifārat-i Kubrā-yi Shāhanshāhi. U.S.* Bibliography on Iran. Washington, Embassy of Iran, 1958. 100, 36 p.   Z3366.A53
A reprint of U.S. Library of Congress, General Reference and Bibliography
Division's *Iran; a Selected and Annotated Bibliography* (Washington, 1951)
"Supplement, taken from 'The Danneshjoo,' vol. II-vol. V, compiled by Meer
Nasser Sharify." 36 p. at end.

Mushār, Khānbābā. Fihrist-i kitābhā-yi chāpī-i Fārsī. Teheran [1958–63] 2 v.
Z3366.M8 Orien Pers
"A bibliography of books printed in Persian," published by the Iranian Council of Philosophy and Humanistic Sciences. The first volume gives titles in alphabetical order, the second gives both titles and an index of authors.

———— Mu'allifīn-i kutub-i chāpī Fārsī va 'Arabī. Teheran [1961/62–65] 6 v.
PJ7521.M8 Orien Pers
A comprehensive Persian and Arabic bibliography, covering a wide field of
subjects, from the second half of the 19th century.

U.S. *Library of Congress. General Reference and Bibliography Division.* Iran; a selected and annotated bibliography, compiled by Hafez F. Farman. Washington,
1951. 100 p.   Z3366.U53 1951

Iraq
Under Turkish rule from the 16th century to World War I; a constitutional monarchy under the League of Nations Mandate, administered by Great Britain, 1925–32; independent monarchy, 1932–58; republic, 1958–.

There is no national bibliography and no list of official publications.
Since 1965 the National Library has annually issued a bulletin listing
publications received in accordance with the deposit law, and since
1971, has also issued a monthly depository bulletin. Official publications
are also included in:

Bagdad. Jāmi'at Baghdād. *al-Maktabah al-Markazīyah.* al-Nashrah al-'Irāqīyah lil-
maṭbū'āt. Baghdād.   Z3036.B35 Orien Arab

Published since January 1964 by the Central Library of the University of Bagdad, this semiannual bibliography is occasionally accompanied by supplements. Titles are arranged by subjects, and there is an author index.

Retrospective official publications are included in the following bibliographies:

Bagdad. Jāmiʿat Baghdād. *al-Maktabah al-Markazīyah. Qism al-Maṭbūʿāt al-Ḥukūmi-yah.* Fihris mawḍuʿī bi-al-maṭbūʿat al-ḥukūmīyah fī al-Maktabah al-Markazīyah li-Jāmiʿat Baghdād. Baghdād, al-Maktabah al-Markazīyah, 1969. 53, 14 p. in Arabic; 15, 3 p. in English.   DLC Orien Arab
"Classified catalog of government publications available in the Central Library, Baghdad University."

Bagdad. *al-Makṭabah al-Waṭanīyah.* al-Nashrah al-ʿIrāqīyah lil-maṭbūʿāt, tuṣdiruhā al-Maktabah al-Waṭanīyah. al-Nashrah al-ūlā li-ʿām 1965. Baghdād, 1967. 57 p. in Arabic; 2 p. in English.   DLC Orien Arab
Includes government publications.

U.S. *Treaties, etc. 1933–1945 (Franklin D. Roosevelt)* Exchange of official publications. Agreement between the United States of America and Iraq. (Feb. 1944) Washington, U.S. Govt. Print. Off., 1944. 20 p. ([U.S. Dept. of State. Publication 2194] Executive agreement series no. 403)   JX236 1929 no. 403
                                                                              Z690.U7I75
Includes a list of Iraq official publications.

ISRAEL

Independent republic, 1948–.

Currently official documents are listed or included in the following publications:

Hadashot ʿal pirsume ha-memshalah. [1953+] Tel Aviv, Government Printer.
                                                                              Z3477.H3 Hebr
"News about government publications." An informative circular describing selected official publications.

Israel. Government yearbook. 1950+ Jerusalem.   J693.P22213
The English edition includes a selected list of official publications, compiled by the State Archives.

Israel. *Ganzakh ha-medinah veha-sifriyah.* Reshimat pirsume ha-memshalah. 1+ 1965+ [Jerusalem]   Z3477.A3 Hebr
"Israel government publications," issued by the State Archives bimonthly (1956–60), later quarterly. The last quarterly number is an annual cumulation, with indexes in Hebrew and English.

——— Reshimah shel pirsume ha-memshalah. [Jerusalem] 1952+   Z3477.A562 Hebr
"List of government publications." A biennial publication, in Hebrew and English, issued by the Government Printer. Includes author, title, and subject indexes.

Israel. *Lishkat ha-ʿitonut.* Newspapers and periodicals appearing in Israel. [Jan. 1965+ Tel Aviv?] Government Press Office.   Z6958.I8A32
Includes government periodicals.

Madrikh li-tekufonim be-mada'e ha-teva, ha-teknologyah uve-khalkalah. 1+ 1963+
Tel Aviv.   Z6958.I8A3 Hebr.
"Directory of serials in pure and applied science and economics published
in Israel." Issued by ha-Merkaz le-informatsyah mada'it ve-tekhnologit (1963)
and later by ha-Merkaz le-meda' tekhnologi u-mada'i. Includes serials published
by government agencies.

U.S. *Library of Congress. American Libraries Book Procurement Center, Tel Aviv.*
Accessions list, Israel. v. 1+ Apr. 1964+ Tel Aviv. monthly.   Z3476.U5

—— Serial titles submitted; numerical (code number) list. Dec. 31, 1965+ Tel Aviv.
                                                                    Z6956.I75U5

For retrospective and specialized listing of official publications, the
following bibliographies and catalogs may be of assistance:

Israel. *Embassy. Gt. Brit.* Catalogue des publications scientifiques d'Israël, 1948–1955.
Paris, 1955. 164 p.   Z7409.I8
A catalog of scientific publications of Israel, collected by the Office of the
Science Attaché at the Embassy of Israel in London.

Israel. *Merkaz ha-hasbarah.* Katalog pirsumim. 1962. Jerusalem, Ha-madpis Ha-mem-
shalti [1962?]   DLC
A catalog of the publications and film strips of the Central Office of Information, through October 1962.

Israel. *Misrad ha-beri'ut. ha-Ma'badot ha-merkaziyot.* Publications, 1948–1968. Jerusalem, Government Central Laboratories, Ministry of Health, 1969. 24 p. Z6658.I85
Includes author and subject indexes.

JORDAN

Under Turkish rule from the 16th century to World War I; part of the
League of Nations Mandate of Palestine, under British administration,
called Transjordan, 1922–46; independent kingdom, 1946–.

There is no current bibliography or list of official publications. The
following publications list legal and some other official documents:

Isa, Ibrahim Khalil. al-Murshid li-'l-qawanin wa 'l-anzimat 'l-Urdunīya wa ta'dilatuha.
Amman, the author, 1966. 157 p.[13]
A Guide to Jordanian laws and regulations and their amendments.

—— al-Murshid li-'l-tashari' al-Urdunīya. Amman, the author, 1967. 177 p.[14]
Second edition of the guide to Jordanian legislation. Covers laws and regulations up to January 1967.

Patai, Raphael. Jordan, Lebanon and Syria; an annotated bibliography. New Haven,
HRAF Press, 1957. 289 p. (Behavior science bibliographies)   Z3013.P3
Issued by the Human Relations Area Files. Includes some official documents.

----

[13] Cited in *Bibliography, Documentation, Terminology* (UNESCO, Paris) 8 (Jan. 1968):
14.
[14] ibid. 9 (March 1969): 58.

KUWAIT
Under British protection, 1899–1961; independent monarchy, 1961–.

There is no known bibliography or list of official publications and no national bibliography. For the pre-1961 period the British Political Resident in the Persian Gulf (Bahrain), issued "a number of series headed 'Notice' which give details of rules, regulations and rules of Court which apply in the various Protected States. There is one series for Kuwait, one for Bahrain, one for Qatar, and two for the Trucial States. Each of these series is separately numbered, beginning afresh each year." [15]

LEBANON
Under Turkish rule from the 16th century to World War I; under French mandate until 1941; independent republic, 1941–.

There is no bibliography or list of official publications. The National Library (Dār al-Kutub al-Watanīyah) published in 1964 and 1965 two issues of a national bibliography entitled *al-Nashrah al-biblīyū-grafīyah al-lubnānīyah* ... and two issues of the *Bulletin bibliographique libanais des oeuvres intellectuelles et des imprimés au Liban*. Both ceased publication after 1965. The American University of Beirut occasionally issues bibliographies which include some official publications. Some Lebanese official documents are included in:

Patai, Raphael. Jordan, Lebanon and Syria; an annotated bibliography. New Haven, HRAF Press, 1957. 289 p. (Behavior science bibliographies)   Z3013.P3
    Issued by Human Relations Area Files. Includes some official documents.

SAUDI ARABIA
Under Turkish rule from the 18th century to 1913; monarchy, 1913– .

There is no national bibliography and no list of official publications. When available, official documents are occasionally listed in the *Accessions List, Middle East*, issued by the Library of Congress' American Libraries Book Procurement Center in Cairo.

SYRIA
Under Turkish rule from the 16th century to World War I; League of Nations Mandate, administered by France, 1920–41 [–46]; republic, 1941– (United Arab Republic. 1958–61).

There is no national bibliography and no separate listing of official

---

[15] International Committee for Social Sciences Documentation, *Étude des bibliographies courantes des publications officielles nationales. A Study of Current Bibliographies of National Official Publications*, ed. Jean Meyriat (Paris: UNESCO, 1958) , p. 243.

publications. Since 1971, the Ministry of Culture, Dept. of Libraries and Cultural Centers, has issued a bibliographical bulletin of books published in the Arab Syrian Republic, which includes official publications:

al-Nashrah al-maktabīyah bi-al-kutub al-ṣādirah fī al-Jumhūrīyah al-'Arabīyah al-Sūrīyah. Damascus, Mudīrīyat al-Marākiz al-Thaqāfīyah al-'Arabīyah wa-al-Maktabāt, 1971+   DLC Orien Arab

Other bibliographic tools which will be of assistance are the following:

Bent, Frederick T. Annotated bibliography of the government and administration of Syria. [Dec. 1954–Aug. 1955] Beirut. [American University of Beirut?] 20 p. "A listing of the available material on the Syrian government and its administration." [16]

Farès, Louis E. Répertoire général des publications périodiques de la République arabe syrienne, mis-à-jour en avril/mai 1968; avec une documentation complète concernant les moyens de publicité en Syrie. Damas [1968?] 101 l.   Z6958.S9F35 Includes official periodicals.

Maktab al-Dirāsāt al-'Arabīyah. Liste générale des publications du bureau. Damas, [1963]   Z3481.M3 Publications of the Bureau des documentations syriennes et arabes. In four parts, it lists: periodical publications, legislative documents and miscellaneous studies, documents concerning commerce, and international and local treaties concluded by Syria.

Patai, Raphael. Jordan, Lebanon and Syria; an annotated bibliography. New Haven, HRAF Press, 1957. 289 p. (Behavior science bibliographies)   Z3013.P3 Issued by the Human Relations Area Files. Includes some official documents.

TURKEY
Sultanate to 1923; republic, 1923– .

Official publications are currently listed in:

Türkiye bibliyografiası. 1934+ Ankara, Türk Tarih Kurumu Basımevi.   Z2835.T93 Frequency varies. Includes decennial cumulations for 1928–38 and 1939–48. Edited by the National Library (Millî Kütüphane, Bibliyografya Enstitüsü), it includes official publications in its classified arrangement, under corporate and other headings. Official publications are marked by an asterisk.

For retrospective listing, the following bibliographies include official publications, or may be of assistance in the search for official publications:

Başbuğoğlu, Filiz, Lâmia Acar and Necdet Ok. 1928–1965 [i.e. Bin dokuz yüz yirmi sekiz, bin dokuz yü altmış beş] yılları arasında Türkiye'de basılmış, bibliyografyaların bibliyografyası. Ankara, Ayyıldız Matbaası, 1966. 270 p. (UNESCO Türkiye Millî Komisyonu yayinları)   Z2831.A1B3 Orien Turk Bibliography of Turkish bibliographies, 1928–65.

İskit, Server R. Türkiyede neşriyat hareketleri tarihine bir bakış. İstanbul, Devlet basımevi, 1939. 484 p.   Z445.I82

[16] Middle East Institute, Washington, D.C., *Current Research on the Middle East* (1955), p. 54 (Z3013.M5).

A glance on the history of publication operations (including official publications) in Turkey. "Bibliyoğrafya," p. 341–440.

Koray, Enver. Türkiye tarih yayınları bibliyografyası, 1729–1955. 2. basım. Istanbul, Maarif Basımevi, 1959. 680 p.   Z2846.K6 1959 Orien Turk
Bibliography of historical publications in Turkey.

Thompson, Lawrence S.   Basic Turkish reference books. [Ankara, 1952] 11 p.
Z1035.8.T8T5

Turkey. İstatistik Genel Müdürlüğü.   İstatistik Genel Müdürlüğü yayınları. Ankara.
Z7554.T9A3 Orien Turk
Publications of the General Office of Statistics. Title varies. Earlier issued by İstatistik Umum Müdürlüğü; currently by Devlet İstatistik Enstitüsü.

Turkey. Laws, statutes, etc.   Evraki matbut baski ve yollama talimatnamesi. İstambul, Devlet matbaası, 1934, 14 [3] p.   Z232.T87T8
Regulations governing printing and dispatch of printed matter, including official publications.

Turkey. Millî Eğitim Bakanliği.   Maarif Vekâleti yayımlari kataloğu. 1942–? İstanbul, Maarif Basımevi.   Z232.T87T86
Catalog of the publications of the Ministry of Education. Title and the name of the issuing ministry varies.

U.S. Bureau of the Census.   Bibliography of social science periodicals and monograph series: Turkey, 1950–1962. [Washington, 1964] 88 p. (Its Foreign social science bibliographies. Series P–92, no. 14)   Z7161.U43 no. 14
An annotated classified bibliography. Includes a considerable number of official publications.

U.S. Library of Congress. General Reference and Bibliography Division. Turkey: a selected list of references. Comp. by Grace Hadley Fuller. Washington, 1944. 114 p.
Z2846.U5

YEMEN
Monarchy until 1962; republic, 1962– , named Yemen Arab Republic.

There is no current list of official publications and no national bibliography at the present time.

YEMEN, People's Democratic Republic
Under British rule until 1967, (Federation of South Arabia, 1959–67, including Aden); People's Republic of Southern Yemen, 1967– , name changed to People's Democratic Republic of Yemen in 1970.

There is no current list of official publications and no national bibliography. Some official publications of the former British administration were listed in:

Gt. Brit. Colonial Office.   Annual report on Aden and Aden Protectorate. 1946– [1957/58?] London, H. M. Stationery Off. (Its Colonial annual reports)
DS249.A2A35
Includes a list of official publications issued during the year.

ASIA AND THE PACIFIC AREA

The problem of the bibliographic control of official publications in countries of Asia and the Pacific area seems to follow the pattern observed in Western and other countries. Bibliographies of official publications are rare, although catalogs or lists issued by government printers or national libraries exist in a number of countries. Elsewhere, official publications are listed more or less consistently in national bibliographies, lists of publications registered under legal deposit acts, or in accessions lists, but usually without special distinction and consequently are difficult to identify.

Bibliographic tools of a general character which include official publications and bibliographies or lists of official publications covering a number of countries will be listed first, followed by individual countries in alphabetical order.

Bibliographie de l'Océanie. 1946+ Paris, Service du distribution du C. I. A. P. annual.
                 Z4001.B5
  Arranged by broad subject headings. Official publications are listed mainly under "Administration."

Boudet, Paul. Bibliographie de l'Indochine française. Hanoi, Imprimerie d'Extrême-Orient, 1929–[1967] 4 v.   Z3226.B68
  A classified bibliography, covering the period 1913–35. Official publications are included. Vol. 4 (Paris, A. Maisonneuve, 1967), published in two parts, part two being a subject index.

Cammack, Floyd M., *and* Shiro Saito. Pacific island bibliography. New York, Scarecrow Press, 1962. 421 p.   Z4001.C3
  "Based on a selection of materials in the Pacific collection at the University of Hawaii's Gregg M. Sinclair Library."
  Divided into four areas (Oceania, Melanesia, Micronesia, and Polynesia), it includes a considerable number of official publications.

Conference on Access to Southeast Asian Research Materials, Library of Congress, 1970. Proceedings. Edited by Cecil Hobbs. Washington, 1971. 235 p.
              Z688.S65C6 1970
  Includes numerous bibliographical references on official publications.

Cumulative bibliography of Asian studies, 1941–1965: author bibliography. Boston, Mass., G. K. Hall, 1969 [i.e. 1970] 4 v.   Z3001.C93
Official publications are listed under corporate entries, by countries, etc.

Cumulative bibliography of Asian studies, 1941–1965: subject bibliography. Boston, Mass., G. K. Hall, 1970. 4 v.   Z3001.C94
Arranged by areas and countries, with subdivisions by subjects. Official publications are included under various subject headings.

Embree, John F., and Lillian O. Dotson. Bibliography of the peoples and cultures of mainland Southeast Asia. New Haven, Yale University. Southeast Asia Studies, 1950. xxxiii, 821 p.   Z3001.E5
Official publications included under individual countries (Burma, Cambodia, Laos, Thailand, Vietnam), mainly under "social organization and law."

Garde, P. K. Directory of reference works published in Asia. Répertoire des ouvrages de référence publiés en Asie. [Paris] UNESCO [1956] xxvii, 139 p. (UNESCO bibliographical handbooks. Manuels bibliographiques de l'UNESCO, 5)   Z1035.G27
Bibliographies of official publications listed p. 12–13.

Gosling, Lee A. P. Maps, atlases and gazetteers for Asian studies: a critical guide. New York, State Education Dept., 1965. 27 p. (Foreign Area Materials Center, University of the State of New York. Occasional publication no. 2) Z1009.N54 no. 2

Harvard University. Library. Southern Asia: Afghanistan, Bhutan, Burma, Cambodia, Ceylon, India. Laos, Malaya, Nepal, Pakistan, Sikkim, Singapore, Thailand, Vietnam. Cambridge, Distributed by Harvard University Press, 1968. 543 p. (Its Widener Library shelflist, 19)   Z3185.H3
Official publications listed mainly under "government and administration," under individual countries.

Indochina, French. Direction des archives et des bibliothèques. Liste des imprimés déposés. Hanoi, Imprimerie d'Extrême-Orient [1922–44?]   Z3226.I42

Indochina, French. Laws, statutes, etc. Recueil général de la législation et de la réglementation de l'Indochine à jour au 31 décembre 1925. Hanoi-Haiphong, Service de législation et d'administration du gouvernement général, 1927–28. 7 v.   DLC LL
In four parts; pt. 4 includes indexes to parts one to three.

Indochina, French. Laws, statutes, etc. (Indexes) Recueil général de la législation et de la réglementation de l'Indochine. Répertoire chronologique et alphabétique des lois, décrets, ordonnances royales, arrêtés, décisions et circulaires publiés de 1931 à 1937, précédé d'un répertoire chronologique et alphabétique des textes antérieurs à 1931, promulgués, modifiés ou abrogés entre le 1er janvier 1931 et le 31 décembre 1936. Hanoi, Imprimerie d'Extrême-Orient, 1938–39. 4 v.   DLC LL

—— Répertoire chronologique et alphabétique des lois, décrets, arrêtés ministériels promulgués en Indochine du 1. janvier 1926 au 1. janvier 1935, par Raoul Nicolas. Hanoi, Impr. d'Extrême-Orient, 1935. 565 p.   DLC LL

—— Répertoire chronologique et alphabétique des lois, décrets, arrêtés ministériels promulgués en Indochine du 1er janvier 1935 au 1er janvier 1944, par Raoul Nicolas. Hanoi, Impr. d'Extrême-Orient, 1943.   DLC LL
Pt. 1, Partie chronologique.

—— Répertoire chronologique et alphabétique des lois, décrets, ordonnances, etc., promulgués ou appliqués en Indochine depuis l'occupation de la Cochinchine (1861) jusqu'au 31 décembre 1917, par H. Petitjean. Saigon, Impr. nouvelle A. Portail, 1918. 913 p.   DLC LL

Leeson, Ida. A bibliography of bibliographies of the South Pacific. Published under
the auspices of the South Pacific Commission. London, New York, Oxford University Press, 1954. 61 p.   Z4008.O2L4
    Includes a considerable number of bibliographies and lists of official publica-
    tions.

Nunn, Godfrey R.   East Asia; a bibliography of bibliographies. [Honolulu] East West
Center Library, 1967. 92 l. (Occasional papers of East West Center Library, no. 7)
                                                                      Z3001.A1N8
    Lists bibliographies of official publications for China, Japan and Korea.

—— South and Southeast Asia; a bibliography of bibliographies. [Honolulu] East
West Center Library, 1966. 59 l. (Occasional papers of East West Center Library,
no. 4)   Z3221.A1N8
    Bibliographies or lists of official publications are listed separately under each
    country.

Roth, H. O.   South Pacific government serials; a select list. [Auckland] University of
Auckland Library, 1967. 21 p. (University of Auckland Library. Bibliographical
bulletin, 4)   Z4001.R6

Southeast Asian periodicals & official publications. Canberra, National Library of Australia, 1970. 5 v.   Z6957.Z9S68
    "This list has been compiled in the first place as a convenient interim listing
    of the National Library's holdings of periodicals and official publications of the
    countries indicated above."
    Contents: Pt. 1, Brunei, Malaysia, Sabah, Sarawak and Singapore; pt. 2, Burma,
    Cambodia, Laos, Timor & Vietnam; pt. 3, Indonesia; pt. 4, Philippine Islands;
    pt. 5, Thailand.

United Nations. *Economic Commission for Asia and the Far East. Library.* Asian
bibliography. v. 1+ Jan./June 1952+ Bangkok. semiannual.   Z3008.E2U5
    Issued 1950–51 (quarterly) under the title *Supplement to the Consolidated
    List of Publications in the ECAFE Library.*

—— Bibliographies in the ECAFE Library. Bangkok, 1960. 34 p. (*Its* Bibliographical
bulletin no. 1)   Z3001.A1U5
    Bibliographies of official publications, p. 4–5.

U.S. *Dept. of State. Library Division.*   Point four, Far East; a selected bibliography of
studies on economically underdeveloped countries. Washington, 1951. 46 p. (*Its*
Bibliography no. 57)   Z3001.U5

—— Point four, Near East and Africa; a selected bibliography of studies on economically underdeveloped countries. Washington, 1951. 136 p. (*Its* Bibliography
no. 56)   Z3013.U5
    Includes Afghanistan, Ceylon, India, Nepal, Pakistan, and Portuguese India.
    Reprinted in 1969 by Greenwood Press, New York.

U.S. *Library of Congress.*   Far Eastern languages catalog. Boston, G. K. Hall, 1972. 22 v.
                                                                     Z3009.U56
    "... a dictionary catalog covering Chinese, Japanese, and Korean works proc-
    essed in the Library of Congress since 1958 ... providing—through a single
    catalog—access to a substantial part of the East Asian language collections of
    the Library of Congress."

U.S. *Library of Congress. Orientalia Division.*   Southeast Asia; an annotated bibliography of selected reference sources in Western languages. Comp. by Cecil Hobbs.

Rev. and enl. New York, Greenwood Press [1968] 180 p.   Z3221.U524 1968
Reprint of the 1964 ed. Arranged by countries and broad subject headings.

—— Southeast Asia subject catalog. Boston, G. K. Hall, 1972. 6 v.   Z3221.U525
Arranged by broad subjects under the following countries: Brunei, Burma,
Cambodia, Indonesia, Laos, Malaysia, Philippines, Portuguese Timor, Sabah,
Sarawak, Singapore, Thailand, Vietnam (North) and Vietnam (South). Vol.
6 contains listing of general bibliographies on Southeast Asia, and a "list of
periodicals cited."

—— Southern Asia accessions list, v. 1+ Jan. 1952+ Washington. monthly. Z3221.U52
Published quarterly 1952–56 under the title, Southern Asia Publications in
Western Languages.

U.S. Library of Congress. Reference Dept.   Indochina; a bibliography of the land and
people, compiled by Cecil C. Hobbs [and others] New York, Greenwood Press
[1969] 367 p.   Z3221.U53
Reprint of the 1956 ed. Covers Vietnam (Annam, Cochinchina, Tonkin), Laos
and Cambodia. Official publications are listed mainly under "Government and law,"
p. 114–133.

Yale University. Library. Southeast Asia Collection.   Checklist of Southeast Asia serials;
Southeast Asia Collection, Yale University Library. Boston, G. K. Hall, 1968.
xxiv, 320 p.   Z3009.Y34
Includes a considerable number of government serials.

Yunesuko Higashi Ajia Bunka Kenkyū Sentā, Tokyo.   A survey of bibliographies in
Western languages concerning East and Southeast Asian studies. Tokyo Centre
for East Asian Cultural Studies [c1966+] (Centre for East Asian Cultural Studies.
Bibliography no. 4+)   Z3001.Y84
Includes bibliographies and lists of official publications.

AFGHANISTAN
Constitutional monarchy.

No national bibliography or list of official publications issued. The
following works include some official publications:

Bibliographie der Afghanistan-Literatur 1945–1967 [von] Arbeitsgemeinschaft Afghanistan und Deutsches Orient-Institut (Deutsche Orient-Stiftung) in Zusammenar-
beit mit der Dokumentationsleitstelle für den Modernen Orient beim Deutschen
Orient-Institut Hamburg und dem Institut für Entwicklungsforschung und Ent-
wicklungspolitik der Ruhr-Universität Bochum. Hamburg, 1968–69. 2 v. Z3016.B5
First volume lists works in European languages, second volume, in oriental
languages and supplemental listings in European languages. Arranged by broad
subjects, it lists a considerable number of official documents.

U.S. Treaties, etc., 1933–1945 (Franklin D. Roosevelt)   Exchange of official publications. Agreement between the United States of America and Afghanistan. [Feb.
1944] Washington, U.S. Govt. Print. Off., 1944. 15 p. ([U.S. Dept. of State. Publication 2219] Executive agreement series 418)   JX236 1929 no. 418
                                                   Z690.U7A35 1944b
Includes a list of official publications of Afghanistan.

Wilber, Donald. Annotated bibliography of Afghanistan. 3d ed. New Haven, Human
Relations Area Files Press, 1968. 252 p. (Behavior science bibliographies)
                                          Z3016.W5   1968
    In its classified arrangement, it includes a number of Afghan official pub-
lications.

AUSTRALIA

A group of self-governing colonies until 1901; Commonwealth of Australia, within the British Commonwealth, 1901–.

Since 1965, the Commonwealth Government Printing Office (now,
Australian Government Publishing Service) has issued a monthly sales
list entitled *Australian Government Publications* (original title: *Commonwealth Publications*). A consolidated list, representing a cumulation
of monthly lists, appears at irregular intervals. It also lists parliamentary
documents, bills, acts, statutory rules, etc.

    Bibliographic control of the official publications of the Common-
wealth, the six States (New South Wales, Queensland, South Australia,
Tasmania, Victoria, Western Australia), the Northern Territory, the
Australian Capital Territory, Papua-New Guinea, and other territories,
is assured currently by the following publications of the National Library
of Australia:

Australian national bibliography. Jan. 1961+ Canberra, National Library of Australia.   Z4015.A96
    From 1961 to 1966 it was published monthly with annual cumulations. From
January 1967, it has appeared four times a month, with monthly and annual
cumulations. Official publications are included in a single alphabetical author-
title-subject arrangement. From January 1968, maps are no longer included
in the bibliography but listed in a quarterly list entitled *Australian Maps*.
Superseded its *Annual Catalogue of Australian Publications*.

Canberra, Australia. National Library. Australian government publications. 1961+
Canberra. annual.   Z4019.C33
    Superseded the Library's earlier publication (1952–60), with the same title,
and in part its *Annual Catalogue of Australian Publications* (1936–60). Arranged
alphabetically by corporate body, with author-title-subject index. Includes Commonwealth, territories, and states publications. From 1971 published quarterly
with annual cumulation.

Current Australian serials; a subject list. 1963+ Canberra, National Library of Australia. annual.   Z6961.C8
    "...a successor, enlarged in size, to the select list of Australian periodicals,
annuals and serials, which appeared in the *Annual Catalogue of Australian
Publications* (now *Australian National Bibliography*) until 1960." Official serials
are listed under subjects, and in the alphabetical index under their respective
issuing agencies. Volume for 1963 included in *Australian Public Affairs Information Service; Subject Index to Current Literature*, 1963. (Z7165.A8A8) .

Retrospective official publications of Australia are recorded or described in the following bibliographic tools:

Australia. *Parliament.* The records of the proceedings and the printed papers. 1st+
Parliament; 1901/02+ Canberra.   J905.L3
    General Index to the Papers Presented to Parliament has been published as
follows: 1901–09, Paper no. 55, session 1910, v. 2; 1910–19, Paper no. 153, session
1920–21, v. 2; 1920–29, Paper no. 59, session 1929–31, v. 2; 1929–37, Paper no. 71,
session 1937–40, v. 3; 1937–49, Paper no. 15, session 1954–55, v. 2; 1950–61, Paper
no. 375, session 1964–66, v. 13.
    A cumulative index called *First Consolidated Index to the Papers Presented to
Parliament, 1901–1949,* covering the 1st to 18th Parliaments, was published in
1955 as Paper no. 100, session 1954–55, v. 2.

Borchardt, Dietrich H.   Australian bibliography; a guide to printed sources of information. [2d ed.] Melbourne, Canberra . . . Cheshire [1966] 96 p.   Z4011.B65   1966
    A description of Australian official publications in chapter "government pub-
lications," p. 53–59.

Canberra, Australia. National Library.   Annual catalogue of Australian publications.
no. 1–25; 1936–60. Canberra. 25 v.   Z4011.C22
    Beginning with no. 2 (1937), it includes official publications in a separate
section, called "Official publications of the Commonwealth, Commonwealth
territories and States," except for the period 1941–44. Superseded in part by the
annual cumulation of *Australian National Bibliography,* and in part by the
annual volumes of *Australian Government Publications,* 1961+.

Canberra, Australia. National Library. *Australian Bibliographical Centre.* Australian
bibliography and bibliographical services. Canberra, Australian Advisory Council
on Bibliographical Services, 1960. 219 p.   Z4039.C3
    Includes bibliographies, catalogs, and lists of official publications and an
author-title index.

Ferguson, *Sir* John A.   Bibliography of Australia. Sydney, Angus and Robertson, 1941–
[69]   Z4011.F47
    In seven volumes, it covers the years 1784–1900 and includes official docu-
ments, mainly from New South Wales.

Foxcroft, Albert B.   The Australian catalogue; a reference index to the books and
periodicals published and still current in the Commonwealth of Australia. Melbourne, Whitcombe & Tombs Ltd., 1911. 118 p. 72, 4, 9 p.   Z4011.F69
    "The following special appendix includes only the works issued from the
Government Printing Offices of New South Wales, South Australia and Victoria,
similar publications of Queensland, Tasmania, and Western Australia being
incorporated in the main body of the catalogue." (Note preceding the "Special
Appendix.")

In 1965 the Library of the Parliament of New South Wales issued
*Government Documents in Australia: Papers on Their Production, Use
and Treatment* (Sydney, 73 1., Z4019.N4. See below, under Australian
States and Territories). A second edition, issued in 1970, is entitled
*Government Publications in Australia: Papers on Their Use and Under-
standing* (Sydney, The Library of Parliament, 1970, 110 p. Reference
monograph no. 8). It is a collection of articles by various authors, edited
by Russell L. Cope, librarian of the Parliamentary Library of New
South Wales, describing and listing official publications of the Australian
Commonwealth and of several Australian states.

Following are catalogs, lists, indexes, and specialized bibliographies, which may be of assistance to researchers in Australian official documents:

Australia. *Atomic Energy Commission. Research Establishment.* List of report publications. Lucas Heights, 1970. 90 p. Z5160.A9

Australia. *Bureau of Census and Statistics.* Publications. [Canberra] Z4019.A32
Issued monthly with annual cumulations by the Bureau under a variant name: Commonwealth Bureau of Census and Statistics.

Australia. *Bureau of Meteorology.* List of publications, 1945–1960. Melbourne, Director of Meteorology, 1960. 85 p. Z6684.A8A5

Australia. *Bureau of Mineral Resources, Geology and Geophysics.* Catalogue of publications. [Canberra] Z6034.A9A25

Australia. *Commonwealth Scientific and Industrial Research Organization.* List of publications. 1949+ Melbourne. Z7914.R5A8
The list also includes publications of the predecessors of the present organization (Advisory Council of Science and Industry, 1916–20; Institute of Science and Industry, 1920–26; Council for Scientific and Industrial Research, 1926–49).

Australia. *Dept. of National Development.* Index to Australian resources maps of 1940–59. Canberra, 1961 [i.e. 1962] 241 p. Z6027.A95A8
—— —— Supplement for 1960–64. Canberra, 1966. 250 p. Z6027.A95A8 Suppl.

Australia. *Dept. of the Navy.* Catalogue of Australian charts and admiralty charts of Australian waters. 1947+ Sydney. Z6027.A89A3
Issued by the Department's Hydrographic Service (formerly Hydrographic Branch).

Australia. *Laws, statutes, etc.* The acts of the Parliament of the Commonwealth of Australia, 1901–1950, to which is prefixed the Commonwealth of Australia constitution act, 63 and 64 Vict. ch. 12, as altered to 31st December, 1950. With notes of cases, tables and indexes. Sydney, Law Book Co. of Australasia, 1952–55. 6 v. (5908 p.) DLC LL
—— —— Cumulative supplement. 1951–56+ Sydney, Law Book Co. of Australasia. DLC LL Suppl.

—— Statutory rules made under Commonwealth acts from 1901 to 1956 and in force on 31st December, 1956. Also selected proclamations, orders, etc., with notes of cases, tables and index. Sydney, Butterworth, 1958–60. 5 v. DLC LL

Bignold, Hugh B. General index of Commonwealth statutes, in force on 1st January, 1920, with copious cross-references. Sydney, The Law Book Co. of Australasia, 1920. 312 p. DLC LL

Canberra, Australia. National Library. Index atlas to maps in series in the Map Collection, National Library of Australia. Canberra, 1966+ (loose-leaf) Z6027.A89C3
Kept up to date by amendment pages.

Finlayson, Jennifer A. S. Historical statistics of Australia; a select list of official sources. Canberra, Dept. of Economic History, Research School of Social Sciences, Australian National University, 55 p. Z7554.A8F54

Jackson (John) and Associates. Guide to Australian Tariff Board reports 1961–1966
& 1967 reports released to 31st March, 1968. Sydney [1968] 65 p.   Z7164.T2J3
Includes reports of the Special Advisory Authority.

Linge, G. J. R. Index of Australian tariff reports, 1901–1961. Canberra, Research
School of Pacific Studies, Australian National University, 1967. 96 p. (Research
School of Pacific Studies. Aids to research series, A/1 1964)   Z7164.T2L55
────── Supplement, 1961–67. Canberra, 1967. 38 p.   Z7164.T2L55 Suppl.

Palmer, George R. A guide to Australian economic statistics. [2d ed.] Melbourne,
Macmillan, 1966, xix, 324 p.   HA37.A94P3   1966
"A survey of Australian statistical publications," p. 15–37.

Australian states and territories

The government printing offices of several Australian states issue and
were issuing in the past sales lists of official state publications. Publications of individual States are also listed in National Library's *Australian
National Bibliography* and in its *Australian Government Publications*.
The government gazettes of several states also include lists of official
publications for sale.

A description of official documents of New South Wales, Queensland,
South Australia and Tasmania can be found in:

New South Wales. *Parliament. Library.* Government documents in Australia: papers
on their production, use and treatment. [Sydney] 1965. 73 l.   Z4019.N4
Issued by authority of the Joint Library Committee of the Parliament of New
South Wales, it contains a number of articles on state publications by various
authors. Particular references are made to parliamentary papers. A second
edition was issued in 1970, edited by Russell L. Cope, under the title: *Government Publications in Australia: Papers on Their Use and Understanding.*

The following bibliographies, indexes, and lists relate to official publications of individual states and territories:

New South Wales

New South Wales. *Government Printing Office.* Monthly list of New South Wales gov-
enment publications. [Sydney]   DLC
Similar lists were published in the past under titles *List of Printed Public
Documents on Sale* and *List of Public Documents on Sale* (Z4049.N55) .

New South Wales. *Laws, statutes, etc. (Indexes)* General index to the statutes of
New South Wales in force on 1st January, 1936. [By] J. B. Collier. Sydney, Bris-
bane, The Law Book Co. of Australasia Ltd. 1936. 296 p.   DLC LL

────── The statutes of New South Wales, with tables of statutes and index with cross
references. v. 0–15; 1894–1919. Sydney, Law Book Co. of Australasia. 16 v.   DLC LL
Volume 15 includes "Appendix containing historical table of acts 1824–1919,
showing all repeals and consolidations and the amendments affecting acts now
in force, chronologically arranged."
────── ────── Alphabetical and chronological tables of acts in force to end of
1915. Historical tables showing all repeals and amendments [1824] to end of 1915.

General index volumes 0 to xi inclusive. Sydney, Law Book Co. of Australasia, 1916. [305] p.   DLC LL

New South Wales. *Parliament.* Joint volumes of papers presented to the Legislative Council and Legislative Assembly. Sydney.   J911.L3
There are consolidated indexes for the periods 1880/81–91, 1904–24, and 1925–46/47

New South Wales. *Parliament. Legislative Council.* Journal of the Legislative Council. 1+ 1856/57+ Sydney, 1857+   J911.J3
Continuation of its *Votes and Proceedings.*
A *Consolidated Index to the Minutes of the Proceedings and Printed Papers* (v. 3–5, 1894–1954, published 1955–65). Each volume covers 20 years.

Sydney. Public Library of New South Wales. Catalogue of the Free Public Library, Sydney, for the years 1869–87. Reference Dept. Sydney, C. Potter, Govt. Printer, 1895. 833 p.   Z975.S98   1895
—— Supplementary catalogue of the Public Library of New South Wales, Sydney, for the years 1888–1910. Sydney, 1895–1912. 5 v.   Z975.S98   1895 Suppl.
Volumes for 1888–95 have title: *Supplement to the Catalogue.* Supplement for 1911–15 printed in galley slips for the use of the staff only.
—— Subject-index of the books in the author catalogues for the years 1869–95. Reference Dept. Sydney, Turner and Henderson, Printers, 1903. 908 p.
Z975.S98   1895 Index
Subject index for supplements 1896–1910 included in each volume. The catalog and its supplements include many documents from New South Wales, as well as from other Australian States and the Commonwealth.

—— Official publications. Jan. 1968?+ Sydney. monthly.   DLC
"This list will be published each month with the exception of December, the entries for which will be cumulated to appear in the January issue of each year. The latter issues will also have a list of all official serials, including annuals and series, received during the preceding year."

Queensland

Currently, Queensland official publications are recorded in the *Australian National Bibliography* and the *Australian Government Publications,* both issued by the National Library of Australia. Several retrospective bibliographies (e.g. National Library's *Annual Catalogue of Australian Publications,* 1936–60) list Queensland's official publications for earlier periods.

South Australia

South Australia. *Laws, statutes, etc. (Indexes)* Index to the statutes in force in South Australia and the regulations thereunder to the close of the parliamentary session of ... Adelaide.   DLC LL
Cover title: *Index to Acts of South Australia. From 1837 to the End of the Parliamentary Session of ...*

South Australia. *Parliament.* Proceedings, with copies of the documents ordered to be printed. 1st+ Parliament; 1857/58+ Adelaide.   J921.H3
Indexes to parliamentary papers: 1857–81 (no paper no. indicated) ; 1881–

1900, Paper no. 51, session 1901; 1901–15, Paper no. 43, session 1916; 1916–37, Paper no. 73, session 1938; 1938–61, Paper no. 36, session 1964.
   Indexes to the votes and proceedings: 1857–68; 1868–74; 1874–1900, Paper no. 51, session 1901; 1901–15, Paper no. 25, session 1917; 1916–62, Paper no. 92, session 1964.
   Included in the papers are also cumulative indexes to public and private bills.

South Australia. *Parliament. Legislative Council.* Index to the minutes of the proceedings and to the printed papers connected therewith [1857–1926] Adelaide.
                                                                    J921.J45 Index
   Includes cumulative indexes for 1857–74, 1875–84, 1885–1904, and annual indexes 1905–26. A cumulative index for 1905–15 is Paper no. 23, session 1917 (J921.H3).

Tasmania

Tasmania. *Parliament.* Journals and printed papers. v. 1+ 1884+ [Hobart]   J926.L3
   Indexes to papers: 1856–91; 1856–99; 1856–1921; 1856–1941.

Victoria

The Government Printing Office issues currently a monthly list of official publications and occasionally a *Consolidated List of Publications, Summary.* Earlier, from 1927, it issued a *List of Books, Pamphlets, etc. on Sale* (Z4379.V65). The following tools will also be of assistance:

Geary, W. R. C. Bibliography of publications, 1946–1965. [Armadale, Melbourne] State Rivers and Water Supply Commission, 1967. 84 p.   Z7935.G4

Victoria, *Australia. Parliament. Legislative Assembly.* Index to the parliamentary papers, reports of select committees and returns to orders, bills, etc. 1851–1909. Comp. by J. M. Worthington. Melbourne, J. Kemp. Govt. Printer, 1909. 323 p.
                                                                    J931.K3 Index

Western Australia

Crowley, Francis K. The records of Western Australia. Perth, 1953. 1 v. in 2 (1094 p.)
                                                                    Z4436.C7
   "Public records" p. 3–107.
   Includes "index of persons" and "general index."

Western Australia. *Parliament.* Minutes and votes and proceedings of the Parliament, with papers presented to both Houses. 1st+ Parliament; 1890/91+ Perth.
                                                                    J936.L3
   Superseded *Votes and Proceedings, with Papers of the Legislative Council.*
   General Index to the Printed Papers Presented to the Legislative Council 1870–1889 and to Parliament ... 1890–1946. Compiled by L. P. Hawley. (Perth, 1946. J936.L3 Index) .

Zalums, Elmar. Western Australian government publications, 1829–1959; a bibliography. 2d ed. Canberra, National Library of Australia, 1971. [4], 95 p.
                                                                    Z4435.Z34   1971

Territories

Australia. *Dept. of Territories.* Annotated bibliography of select government publications on Australian territories, 1951–1964. Canberra, 1965. 55 p.   Z4019.A87
"This bibliography is intended to present a reasonably comprehensive list of publications issued mainly by the Dept. of Territories and Territory administrations from 1951 to early 1964."

Government publications of Papua and New Guinea. no. 1/2+ Jan./June 1968+ Port Moresby, New Guinea, Administrative College. quarterly.   Z4812.G66
"List of titles received by the Library of the Administrative College of Papua and New Guinea."

BHUTAN

Absolute monarchy until 1969; democratic monarchy, 1969–.

There is no bibliography. Some official documents are included in the following publications:

American University, *Washington, D.C. Foreign Areas Studies Division.* Area handbook for Nepal (with Sikkim and Bhutan). Washington, 1964. 448 p.   DS485.N4A8
At head of title: U.S. Army. "Department of the Army pamphlet no. 550–35." Includes bibliographies.

Karan, Pradyumna P. Bhutan; a physical and cultural geography. Lexington, University of Kentucky Press, 1967. 103 p.   DS485.B503K28
Bibliography: p. 100–103.

BURMA

Under British control from 1824 (Lower Burma) and 1884 (Upper Burma) to 1948 (Japanese occupation, 1942–45); independence: 1948.

Catalogs or lists of official publications have been published under various titles since 1908. Currently the Government Book Depot issues lists of official publications printed in English and in Burmese. The following catalogs and lists have been published periodically, or occasionally:

Burma *(Union) Government Book Depot.* Catalogue of books. Rangoon, Supdt., Union Govt. Print. and Stationery. annual.   Z3217.A32
Published from 1954 when it superseded its *Catalogue of Books and Maps.* Title varies *(Catalogue of Publications in Stock;* currently called: *Catalogue of Books of the Revolutionary Government of the Union of Burma Book Depot).*

For retrospective listing, the following bibliographies, catalogs, and lists will be of assistance:

Burma. List of official publications (other than confidential) issued in Burma, which are exempted from registration. [1908–27] Rangoon [1909–28] annual. Z3217.A23
For publications previous to 1908, see India, *List of Nonconfidential Publications Exempted from Registration* (Z3205.I75).

Burma. *Government Book Depot.* Catalogue of books and maps. [1917?–54] Rangoon, Supdt., Govt. Print. and Stationery. semiannual.   Z3217.A3
    Superseded in 1954 by its *Catalogue of Books* (see above).

—— List of publications. [1927–? Rangoon, 1928–?]   Z3205.B91

New York University. *Burma Research Project.* Annotated bibliography of Burma. Frank N. Trager, director and editor; John N. Musgrave, Jr., Chief bibliographer; Janet Welsh, assistant. New Haven, Human Relations Area Files, 1956. 230 p. (Behavior science bibliographies)   Z3216.N38
    "Burma official, selected publications by the government of Burma," p. 164–174.

Whitbread, Kenneth. Catalogue of Burmese printed books in the India Office Library. London, H. M. Stationery Off., 1969. 231 p.   Z3216.W45
    An alphabetical catalog of titles, including official publications. Contains a subject index.

CAMBODIA

Kingdom under French control from 1863–1953 (Japanese occupation, 1941–45); independence: 1953– ; Khmer republic, 1970– .

There is no national bibliography and no lists of official publications. The following publications include some official documents:

Chicago. University. *Cambodia Research Project.* Bibliography of Cambodia. New Haven, Human Relations Area Files, 1956. 17 p. (Behavior science bibliographies)
                                                                                    DLC
Fisher, Mary L. Cambodia: an annotated bibliography of its history, geography, politics and economy since 1954. [Cambridge, Mass.] Center for International Studies, Massachusetts Institute of Technology, 1967. 66 p.   Z3228.C3F5
    Includes a substantial number of official publications.

Phnom-Penh, Cambodia. Bibliothèque royale. Liste des journaux, des bulletins, des revues et des livres en dépôt légal aux Archives nationales à Phnom-Penh et qui ont été partagés pour remettre au Gouvernement fédéral. Phnom-Penh, 1951. 1 v.[17]

CEYLON

Formerly under British control; independence: 1948–; Socialist Republic of Sri Lanka, 1972–.

For current listings see:

Ceylon. *Office of the Registrar of Books and Newspapers.* Catalogue of books; books printed in Ceylon and registered under the Printers and Publishers Ordinance (Cap. 137) as amended by the Printers and Publishers (Amendment) Act no. 38 of 1951. Colombo, Government Press, 1960+ quarterly.   DLC
    Official publications are included in its section two. It continues the list published in part five of the *Ceylon Government Gazette. Lankanduva gasat patraya* (J8.B53) .

---

[17] Godfrey R. Nunn, *South and Southeast Asia; a Bibliography of Bibliographies* (Honolulu: East West Center Library, 1966) , p. 33. (Z3221.A1N8) .

Ceylon national bibliography. Lanka jatika grantha namavaliya. Ilankait teciya nur-
patti. v. 1, no. 1+ Jan. 1963+ Colombo, National Bibliography Branch, Dept. of
National Archives.   DLC
> Issued monthly in Sinhalese, Tamil, and English. Includes an author-title-
> subject index and a classified subject section for English publications. Two
> issues published in Nov. and Dec. 1962 (no. 1, 2).

U.S. *Library of Congress. American Libraries Book Procurement Center, Delhi.* Accessions list, Ceylon. v. 1+ Mar. 1967+ New Delhi. quarterly.   Z3211.U5
> Government publications are marked by an asterisk and listed mostly under
> corporate entries. A cumulative list of serials and an author index are included
> once a year (December).

For retrospective listing, the following catalogs, indexes, etc., will be
of assistance:

Ceylon. *Government Record Office.* Catalogue of government publications dealing
with Ceylon. Colombo, 1926. 16 p.   Z3213.C42

Ceylon. *Parliament.* Ceylon sessional papers. Colombo, Govt. Press.   J611.H6
> "Index to papers and sessional papers laid before the Legislative Council of
> Ceylon from 1855 to July 1931, and before the State Council of Ceylon from
> July 1931 to end of 1933, compiled by S. Gunawardana (of the Government
> Record Office)." Published in 1934, reprinted in 1950, by the Ceylon Govern-
> ment Press (JQ657.5.G85).
> A cumulative index issued also for 1934–49.

Ceylon. *Registrar and Receiver of Books.* Register of books printed in Ceylon and
registered under ordinance no. 1 of 1885. Colombo, Government Printing Works,
1889–?   Z3211.C42
> "Reprinted from the quarterly statements published in the *Ceylon Govern-
> ment Gazette.*"

Ceylon. *Registrar General's Dept.* The Ceylon blue book. Colombo, 1892–[1938?]
                                                                         J611.R2
> Included regularly a list of official publications.

Goonetileke, H. A. I. A bibliography of Ceylon; a systematic guide to the literature
on the land, people, history, and culture published in Western languages from
the sixteenth century to the present day. Zug, Switzerland, Inter Documentation
Co. [c1970] 2 v. (lxxx, 865 p.) (Bibliotheca Asiatica, 5)   Z3211.G65
> Includes official publications, also an index of corporate authors.

CHINA
Empire until 1912; republic, 1912–49.

Official publications of the Chinese empire and the Chinese republic
before 1949 have been recorded in a great number of general and specialized bibliographies or catalogs. In the early 1930's there were several
catalogs issued by the National Library of China listing holdings of
government publications in some libraries. Also, the Bureau of International Exchange in Shanghai issued a list of official publications offered
for international exchange. It would be almost impossible to list here

all these bibliographic tools. Therefore, only those which list a substantial number of official publications or those which may lead the researcher to more detailed and more specialized sources of information concerning official documents are included. Following are catalogs or lists of official publications:

China. *Bureau of International Exchange.* List of Chinese government publications. [Shanghai] Pub. by Academia sinica. Bureau of International Exchange, 1930. 67 p.
Z3105.C53
In two parts: 1. Central Kuomintang publications. 2. Central government publications. List of publications, Academia sinica. Appendix: Publications of international interests.

Chung yang t'u shu kuan, *T'ai-pei.* Kuo li chung yang t'u shu kuan ts'ang kuan shu mu lu. Nanking, 1934. 10, 318 p.   Z3105.C56 Orien China
Catalog of Chinese official publications in the National Central Library at Nanking.

Kuo li Pei-p'ing t'u shu kuan hsien ts'ang kuan shu mu lu. [Peiping, 1932] 91 p. (Pt. 2)
Catalog of holdings of official publications in the National Library of Peiping. (Pt. 2) Lists publications of the central government, local governments, and publications of the Kuomintang (1924–32).[18]

Pei-ching t'u shu kuan hsien ts'ang Chung-kuo cheng fu ch'u pan p'in mu lu. [Peking, 1928] 86 p. (Pt. 1)
Catalog of Chinese government publications in the Metropolitan Library. Lists official publications from 1911 to the end of March 1928 and a few publications from the last years of the Ch'ing dynasty.[18]

The *Quarterly Bulletin of Chinese Bibliography,* published by the Chinese National Committee on Intellectual Cooperation in Shanghai from 1934 to 1937 (v. 1–4) and from 1940 to 1947 (New series v. 1–7), listed in its English edition, government publications separately in vol. 1 (1934), and in volumes 1–5 of the new series (1940–45. Z3103.Q23).

The following general bibliographies also include a substantial number of official publications:

Cordier, Henri. Bibliotheca Sinica. Dictionnaire bibliographique des ouvrages relatifs à l'Empire chinois. 2. éd. rev., corr., et considérablement augm. New York, B. Franklin [1968] 6 v. (Burt Franklin bibliography & reference series 250)
Z3106.C65   1968
Reprint edition. Volumes 1–5 originally published in Paris, 1904–24; volume 6 compiled by East Asiatic Library, Columbia University and originally published in New York, 1953. Part 1, chapter 8: "Gouvernement," p. 531–546; pt. 1, chapter 9: "Jurisprudence," p. 546–558. Vol. 5 is supplement and index, vol. 6 is "Author index."

---

[18] Têng, Ssŭ-yü., *An Annotated Bibliography of Selected Chinese Reference Works,* Rev. ed. (Cambridge: Harvard University Press, 1950), p. 80–81.

Têng, Ssŭ-yü, *and* Knight Biggerstaff. An annotated bibliography of selected Chinese reference works. Rev. ed. Cambridge, Harvard University Press, 1950. 326 p. (Harvard-Yenching Institute studies, v. 2)   Z1035.T32   1950
    "Maps and atlases," p. 72–73; "Gazetteers," p. 73–75; "Law," p. 80; "Official publications," p. 80–81.

Tsing Hua Political Science Association, *Peking.* Reader's guide to political literature in China. [Peiping, China, Ho Tsi Printing Co., 1929] 61, 154, [2] p.   Z3106.T88
    "Bibliography of China. Compiled under the direction of W. A. Slade, Chief, Division of Bibliography, Library of Congress", p. 13–26. Appended is a similar list in Chinese, with a section on government publications having titles also in English or French (154 p.) .

A considerable number of bibliographies, catalogs, etc., concerning certain areas or certain fields of government publishing, were issued in China and elsewhere. Of special interest are the "gazetteers", i.e., records "of all important facts pertaining to a limited geographical area and of all significant activities occurring in it," [19] such as changes in political boundaries, local government, local officials, population figures, economic conditions, etc. The gazetteers were compiled as early as the third century A.D., generally by local authorities or on the basis of local government documents.

Following are a few examples of such specialized bibliographies, catalogs, lists, etc. of official publications:

China. *Chung yang ti chih tiao ch'a so. T'u shu kuan.* Chung yang ti chih tiao ch'a so t'u shu kuan ts'ung shu mu lu. Catalogue of the Library of the National Geological Survey of China. Publication series. [Peking, Peking Leader Press] 1927. 44 p.
                                                          Z6035.C52

—— Publication list. [1928–1949?] Nanking, Library, National Geological Survey of China.   Z6034.C5C5

—— Ti chih tiao ch'a so t'u shu kuan. Catalogue of the Library of the National Geological Survey of China. Maps and atlas, series A. [Peiping] 1928. 89 p.
                                                    Z6027.C55A5

China. *Hai kuan tsung shui wu ssŭ shu.* Catalogue of customs publications. 6th issue. Shanghai, Statistical Dept. of the Inspectorate General of Customs, 1936. 13 p. (*Its* Maritime customs, 3. Miscellaneous series, no. 16)   Z7164.T2C4   1936

—— Catalogue of customs publications, with prices. 1st issue. Published by order of the Inspector General of Customs. Shanghai, Statistical Dept. of the Inspectorate General, 1887. 10 p. (*Its* Maritime customs, 3. Miscellaneous series, no. 16)   Z7164.T2C4

Chu, Shih-chia. Chung-kuo ti fang chih tsung lu. Shanghai, 1958. 318, [2] 105 p.
                                          Z3107.A2C45 Orien China
    A union catalog of holdings of the gazetteers in 50 different collections (42 in China, six in Japan, two in the United States) .

---

[19] Têng, Ssŭ-yü, *An Annotated Bibliography of Selected Chinese Reference Works,* Rev. ed. (Cambridge: Harvard University Press, 1950) , p. 73.

Lin, Fu-shun. Chinese law, past and present; a bibliography of enactments and commentaries in English text. New York, East Asian Institute, Columbia University [1966] xliii, 419 p.   DLC LL

Lowe, Joseph Dzen-Hsi. *comp.* A catalog of the official gazetteers of China in the University of Washington. Zug, Inter Documentation Co. A. G. [c1966] 72 p. (Bibliotheca Asiatica, no. 1)   Z3109.L68
    Catalog of collection in the University of Washington Library.

Padoux, Georges. List of English and French translations of modern Chinese laws and regulations. [Peking, 1936] [567]–644, 8 p.   DLC LL
    "Reprinted from the Chinese social and political science review, vol. xix, no. 4, Jan. 1936." "Additions" to March 1936, 8 p. at end.

Pei-ching t'u shu kuan. Kuo li Pei-p'ing t'u shu kuan Chung wên yü t'u mu lu. Catalog of Chinese maps in the National Library of Peiping. Peiping [1933] 2, 174 p.
                                                                    Z999.P38 Orien China

U.S. *Bureau of Foreign and Domestic Commerce.* "Finding list," bibliography of modern Chinese law in Library of Congress. Comp. and ed. July–Dec. 1944 by China Legal Section, Far Eastern Unit, Bureau of Foreign & Domestic Commerce, Dept. of Commerce. [Washington] Mimeographed by the China American Council of Commerce & Industry [1944?] 48 l.   DLC LL

U.S. *Library of Congress. Orientalia Division.* A catalog of Chinese local histories in the Library of Congress. By Chu Shih Chia. Washington, U.S. Govt. Print. Off., 1942. 552, 21 p.   Z3107.A2U57 1942 Orien China
    In Chinese, with foreword also in English. Chinese title: *Kuo hui t'u shu kuan ts'ang Chung-kuo fang chih mu lu.*

—— Official gazetteers of the provinces, prefectures, and districts of China in the Library of Congress. January 1934. Arranged in the official Chinese order. 3d ed. Prepared by B. A. Claytor in the Division of Orientalia. Washington, D.C., 1934. 61 l.   Z3107.A2U6 1934
    Photographic reproduction, reduced, of the manuscript catalog cards.

For retrospective listing of official publications of Manchuria (Manchukuo, under the Japanese occupation, 1932–45), lists of official publications in Chinese and Japanese have been published periodically as supplements to *Manshukoku Koho,* the official gazette of Manchukuo. The following sources will also be of assistance:

U.S. *Consulate. Mukden.* List of Manchukuo publications issued between August and December 1937, inclusive. [n.p., 1938] 9 l.   Z3107.M3U45
    Typescript. "Enclosure no. 1 to despatch no. 90 of Wm. R. Langdon, American Consul, Mukden, Manchuria, dated September 9, 1938." "Source: Manchukuo Government gazette no. 1255, June 16, 1938."

U.S. *Library of Congress. Reference Dept.* Manchuria; an annotated bibliography, compiled by Peter A. Berton, consultant in Manchurian bibliography, with the assistance of members of the Orientalia Division and the General Reference and bibliography Division. Washington, 1951. 187 p.   Z3107.M3U5

—— Manchuria; a selected list of bibliographies, compiled by Peter A. Berton, consultant in Manchurian bibliography, with the assistance of Helen Dudenbostel Jones, bibliographer, General Reference and Bibliography Division, Washington, 1951. 15 p.   Z3107.M3U47

In 1967 the following general reference tool describing some 2,200 works concerning the People's Republic of China (Mainland) and the Republic of China (Taiwan) and including a considerable number of government publications was issued:

Berton, Peter A. M., *and* Eugene Wu. Contemporary China; a research guide. Prepared for the Joint Committee on Contemporary China of the American Council of Learned Societies and the Social Science Research Council. Stanford, Calif., Hoover Institution on War, Revolution, and Peace, 1967. xxix, 695 p. (Hoover Institution bibliographical series, 31)   Z3106.B39
  Covers publications of the Republic of China from 1945 and those of the People's Republic of China from 1949.

CHINA, Republic of
Government transferred to Taipei, Taiwan, in 1949.

There is no special bibliography or list of government publications. These are partly recorded in the national bibliography, compiled by the National Central Library (Chung yang t'u shu kuan, T'ai-pei) and issued from 1956 to 1961 under the title *Chung-hua min kuo ch'u pan t'u shu mu lu,* covering the period 1949 to 1960 (Z3101.C5 Orien China). A cumulative edition, *Chung-hua min kuo ch'u pan t'u shu mu lu hui pien* (Z3101.C53 Orien China), was issued in 1964 covering 1961–63, which also included titles listed in previous volumes, thus covering the entire period 1948–63. In September 1960, the National Central Library began issuing The *Monthly List of Chinese Books* in English. Suspended in July 1967, it reappeared in July 1968 under the title *Hsin shu mu lu,* with added title *The Monthly List of Chinese Books* (Z3101.H76 Orien China).
  The following bibliographies also include official publications of the Republic of China:

Chung yang t'u shu kuan, *T'ai-pei.* A selected and annotated bibliography of the Republic of China, 1958–1959. Taipei, National Central Library, 1960. 127 p.
                        Z3108.A5C5

—— Selected bibliography of the Republic of China. Chung-hua min kuo ch'u pan t'u shu hsüan mu. Taipei, National Central Library, 1957. 59 p.
                   Z3307.F7C47 Orien China

U.S. *Bureau of the Census.* Bibliography of social science periodicals and monograph series: Republic of China, 1949–1961. [Washington, U.S. Govt. Print. Off., 1962] 24 p. (*Its* Foreign social science bibliographies. Series P–92, no. 4.)   Z7161.U43 no. 4
  Government publications can be identified through an "Index of issuing agencies."

CHINA, People's Republic of
Proclaimed in Peking in 1949.

There is no special bibliography or list of official publications. In 1950 a list appeared in the *Yenching Journal of Social Studies* (July 1950, p. 165–175) under the title "China (People's Republic, 1949–) official documents." A national bibliography which includes in its classified arrangement official documents, began publication in 1950 in Peking under the title *Ch'üan kuo hsin shu mu,* compiled by the Library of the Publishing Industry Supervisory Bureau, Ministry of Culture (Wên hua pu. Ch'u pan shih yeh kuan li chü. T'u shu kuan). Several issues of the *Ch'üan kuo hsin shu mu* were translated into English by the East-West Center, University of Hawaii:

National bibliography of new books; selected issues. [Honolulu] East-West Center, 1966. 2 v. (Occasional papers of Research Translations, Institute of Advanced Projects, East-West Center. Translation series, no. 17–18)   AS9.H38 no. 17–18
    Translation of no. 8–11, Apr. 16–June 15, 1965 (serial no. 256–259) of *Ch'üan kuo hsin shu mu.*

An annual cumulation of the national bibliography was begun in 1956, the first volume covering 1949–54, under the title *Ch'üan kuo tsung shu mu.* The following bibliographies cover selected legal and other official publications of the People's Republic of China:

Hsia, Tao-tai. Guide to selected legal sources of Mainland China; a listing of laws and regulations and periodical legal literature, with a brief survey of the administration of justice. Washington, Library of Congress [U.S. Govt. Print. Off.] 1967. 357 p.   DLC LL

U.S. *Bureau of the Census.* Bibliography of social science periodicals and monograph series: Mainland China, 1949–1960. [Washington, U.S. Govt. Print. Off., 1961] 32 p. (*Its* Foreign social science bibliographies. Series P–62, no. 3)   Z7161.U43 no. 3
    Includes some official publications which can be identified through an "index of issuing agencies."

For additional listing of Chinese official documents, see U.S. Joint Publications Research Service, under United States, Federal agencies.

FIJI
Under British control, 1874–1970; independence: 1970.

There is no current bibliography or list of official publications. The Central Archives of Fiji and the Western Pacific High Commission in Suva compiled a catalog of microfilmed archival and library materials, which includes government documents of Fiji. The catalog, in mimeographed form in two volumes (Archives series, Library series), was issued in a revised and enlarged edition with indexes in 1970. (CD2775.F5C44)

Other works which list or include official publications are the following:

Baksh, S. Serial publications of the Government of Fiji. Suva, Central Archives of Fiji and the Western Pacific High Commission, 1970. 16 l. (Central Archives of Fiji and W.P.H.C. Reference Library. Serial publications catalogue, no. 2)
Z4651.B3 1970
First edition of the catalog published in 1967.

Fiji. Fiji blue book. [1876–1940] Suva. F. W. Smith, Govt. Printer. annual   J961.R2
Includes a more or less extensive list of official publications.

Gt. Brit. *Colonial Office.* Annual report on Fiji. [1946–68?] London, H. M. Stationery Off. (*Its* Colonial annual reports)   DU600.A33
Official publications listed separately in its "reading list."

Snow, Philip A. A bibliography of Fiji, Tonga, and Rotuma. Preliminary working ed. Coral Gables, Fla., University of Miami Press, 1969, xliii, 418 p.
Z4651.S65 1969
Fiji government publications are listed mainly in the chapter "administration."

INDIA

Under British rule, 1774–1947; independent dominion, 1947–50; republic, 1950–.

Bibliographic control of the government publications of India has been one of the most consistent of any country since the second half of the 19th century, not only on the national level but also on the state and local levels.

Currently, official publications are listed in the following bibliographies and catalogs:

India (*Republic*) *Government of India Publication Branch.* Catalogue of civil publications relating to agriculture, forestry, civic, commerce, finance, legislation, industry, public health, railways, science, trade, etc. Delhi.   Z3205.I84P8
Issued irregularly since 1925 at intervals of several years, it is kept up to date with monthly supplements and annual cumulations.

Indian national bibliography. v. 1+ Jan./Mar. 1958+ [Calcutta] Central Reference Library.   Z3201.A2I5
Volume I. no. 1 of the national bibliography was preceded by an issue dated 1957 and called "experimental fascicule," issued by the National Library of India, and by another issue, dated Oct./Dec. 1957. Published quarterly to 1963 and monthly from January 1964. Part two of the bibliography is devoted to government publications, both national and state, in two sections, classified and alphabetical.

U.S. *Library of Congress. American Libraries Book Procurement Center, Delhi.* Accessions list, India. v. 1+ July 1962+ New Delhi. monthly.   Z3201.U54
Official publications are listed mostly under corporate entries and are marked with an asterisk. An annual supplement, "Cumulative list of serials" has been published since 1969 in July (Z3201.U542).

For retrospective listing and general description of official publications, the following bibliographies, catalogs, and guides will be of assistance to researchers:

Campbell, Francis B. F.   Index-catalogue of Indian official publications in the library, British Museum. London, Library Supply Co.; New York, G. E. Stechert, [1900] 6, 193, 314, 72 p.   Z3205.C18
  "Refers mainly to the more modern portion of the collection of Indian official publications issued in India subsequent to the Mutiny—so far as the documents have been deposited in the library of the British Museum."

——— Index catalogue of Indian official publications. (British Museum.) Accessions. no. 1. (Nov. 30, 1899) [London, 1900] 1 p. 1., 16 columns   Z3205.C18

Diehl, Katharine S., and Hemendra K. Sircar.   Early Indian imprints. New York, Scarecrow Press, 1964. 533 p.   Z3202.D5
  "Based on the William Carey Historical Library of Serampore College." Includes a considerable number of early official documents. See its subject index: "Government documents," p. 511.

Gt. Brit. India Office.   A classified list, in alphabetical order, of reports and other publications in the Record branch of the India Office. December 1892. London, Printed by Eyre and Spottiswoode, 1894. 230 p.   Z3206.G78

——— East India (Parliamentary papers).   Annual lists and general index of the Parliamentary papers relating to the East Indies published during the years 1801–1907 inclusive. London, Printed for H.M. Stationery Off., by Eyre and Spottiswoode, Lt. [1909] xlvii, 194 p.   Z3205.G74

——— A list of the principal Indian government publications on sale in this country and at the various government presses in India. August 1891. [London, Printed by Eyre and Spottiswoode, 1891] 37 p.   Z3205.G75

India. General catalogue of all publications of the government of India and local governments and administrations. Calcutta, Printed for the Government of India by the Superintendent, Government Printing, India.   Z3205.I8
  Published during the early decades of the 20th century, generally twice a year, it listed, in three parts: publications for sale, acts and regulations of the Imperial and Legislative Councils, and publications issued only under special orders and not for sale.

India. List of non-confidential publications exempted from registration, which were issued by the departments of the Government of India and by local governments and administrations. [Calcutta, 1892–1909]   Z3205.I75
  The list covers publications from the third quarter of 1892 to 1907. Issued quarterly 1892 to March 1900, annually, 1902–07. From 1908 it was continued by separate lists for the various departments of the government of India and for the provincial governments of Assam, Bengal, Bihar, and Orissa, Bombay, Burma, Central Provinces, Coorg, Madras, Northwest Frontier Province, Punjab, and the United Provinces of Agra and Oudh. Beginning with 1927, the separate lists for the various departments of the government of India were replaced by the following list:

India. Central Publication Branch.   List of official publications not included in the General catalogue of Government of India publications. 1927–[40?] New Delhi.
                                                                    Z3205.I822
  Issues for 1927–36 have title: List of Non-Confidential Publications ... Super-

sedes the *List of Publications* (*Other Than Confidential*) ... issued by the various departments of the Government of India.

India (*Republic*) *Government of India Publication Branch*. List of official publications not included in the general catalogue of Government of India publications, issued during the period 1-1-1940 to 31-12-1960. Delhi, Manager of Publications, 1967. 95 p. Z3205.I84P84

India (*Republic*) *High Commissioner in the United Kingdom*. List of publications received in the Publications Branch. London. Z3206.A46
  Title varies: to Nov. 1928, *Publications Received in the Record Branch*; Dec. 1928 to June 1935, *Official Publications Received in the Record Branch*. Issued earlier by Gt. Brit. India Office.

India (*Republic*) *High Commissioner in the United Kingdom. Library*. A short catalogue. London, Office of the High Commissioner for India, 1933. 533 p.
Z3209.I5
  A classified catalog. Official publications, mostly under corporate entries, can be identified through the "Combined alphabetical author and subject index." See "Government," p. 458-471.

India (*Republic*) *Parliament*. List of publications (periodical or ad hoc) issued by various ministries of the Government of India. New Delhi, Parliament Secretariat.
Z3205.I83P3
  Third edition issued in 1958 (282 p.)

India (*Republic*) *Parliament. House of the People*. Catalogue of parliamentary publications for sale. New Delhi, Lok Sabha Secretariat. [1957?+] DLC

Indian Documentation Service. Indian government publications in print: subject list. Corr. up to 31st December, 1959. Naisubzimandi [1971] 442 p. Z3205.I87

Scholberg, Henry. The district gazetteers of British India. A bibliography. Zug, Inter Documentation, (1970). 131 p. (Bibliotheca Asiatica, 3) Z3201.S36
  Includes bibliographical references.

Shukla, Champaklal P. A study on the publications of the government of India, with special reference to serial publications. Ann Arbor, Univ. Microfilms, 1953. 1751 l.
Microfilm AC-1 no. 5732
  Microfilm copy of a typewritten thesis, University of Michigan. (University Microfilms, Ann Arbor, Mich. Publication no. 5732)

Singh, Mohinder, *M.A.* Government publications of India; a survey of their nature, bibliographical control and distribution systems, including over 1500 titles. Assisted by J. F. Pandya; foreword by S. R. Ranganathan. [1st ed.] Delhi, Metropolitan Book Co. [1967] 270 p. Z3205.S63
  The book lists ministries in alphabetical order, giving a short historical description and listing their most important publications. It also lists catalogs of publications of individual government agencies.

Government agencies

Most government agencies issue from time to time lists of their official publications. These are described in Mohinder Singh's *Government*

Publications of India, listed above.[20] For the period 1908–26, after the
List of Non-Confidential Publications Exempted from Registration was
discontinued, various departments of the Government of India issued
separate annual lists, usually under the title *List of Publications (Other
Than Confidential) Issued by . . .* Some of the departments which issued
such lists are the following: Defence Dept. (Z3205.I83D4) , Dept. of Com-
merce (Z3205.I83C7), Dept. of Education, Health and Lands (Z3205.-
I83E4), Dept. of Industries and Labour (Z3205.I83I4), Dept. of Military
Supply (Z6724.S8I5) , Dept. of Revenue and Agriculture (Z3205.I83R4) ,
Finance Dept. (Z3205.I83F4) , Finance Dept., Military Finance (Z3205.-
I83F45), Foreign and Political Dept. (Z3205.I82F7), Home Dept. (Z3205.-
I83H7) , Legislative Dept. (Z3205.I83L5) , Munitions Board (Z3205.-
I83M9) , Public Works Dept. (Z3205.I83P9) , Railway Board (Z3205.-
I83R2) .

Other retrospective and current catalogs covering certain agencies or
fields, which may be of assistance to the researcher, are the following:

India. *Office of the Economic Adviser.* Guide to current official statistics. Prepared
by S. Subramanian. Delhi, Manager of Publications, 1943–49. 3 v. in 4.   HA37.I382
   Contents: v. 1. Production and prices Suppl.: Working class cost of living
   index numbers in India, a critical study.–v. 2. Trade, transport and communications, and finance, excluding public finance.–v. 3. Public finance, education,
   public health, census, labour, consumption of commodities and miscellaneous.

India. *Railway Board.* Catalogue of Technical papers issued by Technical Section of
Railway Board of India, 1925. Delhi, Government of India Press, 1925. 53 p.
                                                              Z7231.I39

India. *Survey of India Dept.* Map catalogue. Calcutta.   Z6027.I39A25
   From 1947, superseded by India (Republic) Survey of India, *Map Catalogue.*

India *(Republic) Council of Scientific and Industrial Research.* csir publications: a
catalogue. [Compiled by G. J. Narayana and others] New Delhi, 1964. 64 p.
                                                              Z7403.I43

India *(Republic) Geological Survey.* List of publications. 1946+ Delhi, Manager of
Publications. irregular.   Z6034.I3A3

India *(Republic) Laws, statutes, etc. (Indexes)* Index and chronological table of cen-
tral acts and ordinances, repealed and un-repealed from 1834 to June 1951, by
Jnanendra Nath Baksi. Calcutta, Bhowanipur Book Bureau [pref. 1951]   DLC LL
   "Supplement . . . from July, 1951 to December, 1952" (Calcutta, Eastern Law
   House, 1953 (20 p.) inserted.

——— Index to Central and State acts. Delhi, Manager of Publications, 1961. 432 p.
                                                              DLC LL

<hr>

[20] See also: *Seminar on Government of India Publications, Delhi, 1970. Papers
Presented* (New Delhi, 1970?) (Z689.S36 1970) , Appendix 1, "List of ministries, departments, etc. which sell or distribute their publications without the agency of Manager
of Publications," and Appendix 5, "Names of ministries, departments, etc., offices and
organizations of the Government of India, which issue lists or catalogues of their publications." (Issued by the Government of India Libraries Association.)

India *(Republic) Ministry of Education.* Catalogue of publications. 1962. [New Delhi]
                                                               Z3205.I84E4
    The catalog covers publications from 1937 through 1962, and is arranged by
broad subjects. A later edition (1965) covers publications from January 1963
to August 1965.

India *(Republic) Survey of India.* Map catalogue. Dehra Dun, Printed at the Map
    Publication Office, Survey of India. [1947+]   Z6027.I39A252
    Supersedes India. Survey of India Dept. *Map Catalogue.*

Inter-Documentation Company A. G., Zug, Switzerland. India: Census, 1872–1951.
    A checklist and index. Zug, 1966. 18 p. (Basic collections in microedition)   DLC

U.S. *Library of Congress. Census Library Project.* Census and vital statistics of India
    and Pakistan contained in official publications and famine documents, an an-
    notated bibliography by Henry J. Dubester. Washington, 1950. Microfilm 4685 Z

States and territories

Many Indian states occasionally issue catalogs or lists of their official
publications. There is no comprehensive checklist of Indian state publications, but the *Indian National Bibliography* (Calcutta, Central Reference Library, 1958+ Z3201.A2I5) does include a considerable number
of state publications in its classified arrangement. The Library of Congress' Book Procurement Center in Delhi includes in its monthly *Accessions List, India* a substantial number of Indian state publications. For
retrospective research, the identification of state documents is often difficult because of extensive changes in state boundaries, creation of new
states, mergers, etc. in the past. A thorough study of the historical developments in this respect is therefore indispensable for the research in the
official documentation of Indian states. *The Statesman's Yearbook* (London, JA51.S7) and other similar sources contain basic information on this
subject.
    Catalogs or lists of government publications of the following states
(as of 1970) have been published in recent years:

Andhra Pradesh
1953–, formerly part of Madras and Hyderabad States.

Andhra Pradesh, *India (State)* Government publications for sale. Hyderabad, Govt.
    Press.   DLC

Assam

Assam. *Government Book Depot.* Catalogue of books and publications. Shillong,
    Printed at the Govt. Central Press. semiannual. (irregular)   Z3207.A8A3

Bihar

Bihar, *India (State)*   Bihar government publications, catalogue of books. Patna.
Printed by the Superintendent, Govt. Press.   Z3207.B5A35

Gujarat
1960–, formerly north and west portion of Bombay State.

Gujarat, *India (State)*   Catalogue of Gujarat government publications. Rajkot, Printed
at the Govt. Press. irreg.   Z3207.G8A3

Jammu and Kashmir

Jammu and Kashmir.   Catalogue of books available in press stock for sale and issue
to departments. Jammu, Ranbir Govt. Press. annual.   Z3205.J3

Kerala
1956–, formerly greatest part of Travancore-Cochin.

Kerala, *India (State)*   Catalogue of publications for sale at the Government Press.
Trivandrum, Government Press.   DLC

Madhya Pradesh
1956–, formerly part of the previous state of same name, of the state of
Madhya Bharat, states of Bhopal and Vindhya Pradesh, etc. Before
1950, Central Provinces.

Madhya Pradesh, *India (State)*   Catalogue of publications, corrected up to ... Nagpur-
Bhopal, Govt. Press Book Depot.   DLC

———— List of publications. Monthly supplement. Nagpur-Bhopal, Govt. Press Book
Depot.   DLC

Maharashtra
1960–, formerly east and south portion of Bombay State.

Maharashtra, *India (State)*   Catalogue of books printed in the Maharashtra state.
Bombay. quarterly.   DLC

Mysore
1956–, formerly the old states of Mysore and Coorg and the Kannada-
language districts of other neighboring states.

Mysore. *Government Central Book Depot.* Catalogue of official publications in English
and Kannada available for sale. Bangalore, Govt. Press.   Z3205.M98

Orissa

Orissa, *India.* Catalogue of publications. Cuttack, Superintendent, Orissa Government Press.   Z3205.07
  Continues, in part, the *Catalogue of Bihar and Orissa Government Publications* (1929?–36) .

Punjab

In 1947 divided between India and Pakistan; 1956, merged with the state of Patiala and East Punjab States Union; 1966, southeastern portion divided between the new state of Haryana and the Union Territory of Himachal Pradesh; Chandigarh made Union Territory and joint capital of Haryana and Punjab.

Punjab, *India (State) Superintendent, Government Printing.* Punjab Government publications; general catalogue. Simla.   Z3205.P92
  Supersedes an earlier publication with the same title, issued to 1947.

Rajasthan (1948–)

Rajasthan, *India.* Catalogue of publications. Jaipur, Govt. Central Press. Z3207.R3A3

Tamil Nadu
Formerly, state of Madras; name changed in 1968.

Madras [Tamil Nadu] (State) Catalogue of government publications. Madras, Printed by the Director of Stationery and Printing. irregular.   Z3205.M26

Uttar Pradesh
Formerly United Provinces of Agra and Oudh; name changed to Uttar Pradesh in 1950.

Uttar Pradesh, *India. Printing and Stationery Dept.* Catalogue of publications issued by the government of Uttar Pradesh and obtainable from the book depot, Government Central Press, Allahabad. Allahabad, Superintendent, Print. and Stationery, Uttar Pradesh. annual.   Z3207.U5U53
  Accompanied by quarterly supplementary lists.

West Bengal
Formerly part of the Province of Bengal. In 1947, divided between India and Pakistan (East Pakistan); western portion constituted as the state of West Bengal.

West Bengal Government Press. *Publication Branch.* List of publications added during the year. Calcutta.   Z3205.W47

Following are retrospective bibliographies and catalogs of government publications of present and former Indian states and provinces:

Assam. List of publications (other than confidential) issued by the Assam administration during the year ... which are exempt from registration. Shillong [1909–1927]   Z3205.A84
>   Issued by the government of Eastern Bengal and Assam, 1908–1911. Continued from 1928 by the *Catalogue of Books and Publications* (Assam. Government Book Depot. Z3207.A8A3). For publications issued before 1908, see India. *List of Non-Confidential Publications Exempted from Registration* (Z3205.I75).

Bengal. List of publications (other than confidential) issued by the government of Bengal which are exempted from registration. Calcutta [1909–1927]   Z3205.B46
>   For publications issued before 1908, see India. *List of Non-Confidential Publications Exempted from Registration* (Z3205.I75).

Bengal. *Secretariat.* Catalogue of the publications of the government of Bengal available for sale at the Bengal Secretariat book depot. Calcutta [1926?+]   Z3205.B47

Bihar, *India (Province)* Catalogue of publications. Patna, Superintendent, Government Printing, Bihar [1937?+]   Z3205.B473
>   Continues in part the *Catalogue of Bihar and Orissa Government Publications.* (See below)

Bihar, *India (Province) Book Depot.* List of publications (other than confidential) issued by the Bihar Book Depot ... which are exempted from registration. 1937+ [Patna, 1938+]   Z3205.B475
>   Continues a similar list issued by the Bihar and Orissa government. (See below)

Bihar and Orissa. Catalogue of Bihar and Orissa government publications. Patna, Superintendent, Government Printing, Bihar and Orissa. [1929?–36]   Z3205.B48
>   Issued until 1936, then continued in part of Bihar, India (Province) *Catalogue of Publications* and Orissa, India. *Catalogue of Publications.*

Bihar and Orissa. *Book Depot.* List of publications (other than confidential) issued by the Bihar and Orissa Book depot ... which are exempted from registration. 1912–1935–36. [Patna, 1913–37]   Z3205.B5

Bombay *(Presidency)* General catalogue of all publications of the government of Bombay (including Sind) [1925?–?] Bombay, Superintendent, Govt. Printing and Stationery.   Z3205.B68

—— List of non-confidential publications issued by the departments of the government of Bombay (exclusive of publications appearing in the general catalogue) [Bombay, Gvt. Central Press, 1908–41]   Z3207.B7B74

Bombay *(State)* Catalogue of government publications. Bombay, Printed at the Govt. Central Press.   Z3207.B7B77
—— —— Supplementary catalogue. [Bombay]   Z3207.B7B772
>   Published occasionally between 1950 and 1960. In 1960 Bombay State was divided into states of Gujarat and Maharashtra.

Central Provinces, *India.* List of official publications (other than confidential) issued in the Central Provinces (including Berar) which are exempted from registration. [Nagpur, Govt. Press, 1908–26]   Z3205.C39

Central Provinces, *India. Government Press Book Depot, Nagpur.* List of publications for sale at the Central Provinces Government Press Book Depot ... publications relating to Central Provinces and Berar and imperial publications. Nagpur, Printed at the Government Press, 1927–[50] Z3205.C395
From 1935, title: *Catalogue of Publications Corrected up to* ... A monthly supplement also published (Z3205.C396). In 1950, Central Provinces became the state of Madhya Pradesh.

Coorg, *India.* List of official publications exempted from registration. [n.p. 1909–?] Z3207.C6A3
Title varies: *List of Non-Confidential Publications Exempted From Registration; List of Publications (Other Than Confidential) Which Are Exempted From Registration.* In 1956 Coorg merged with Mysore state.

Madras *(Presidency) Government Press.* Catalogue of government publications on sale at the Government Press. Madras, Govt. Press. [1901–49?] Z3205.M2
From 1950 continued by Madras *(State) Catalogue of Government Publications.* Name of the state changed to Tamil Nadu in 1968.

—— List of official publications (other than confidential) issued by the government of Madras. [Madras, Government Press, 1909–36?] Z3205.M18

Punjab. *Superintendent, Government Printing.* Punjab government publications; general catalogue. Lahore. Z3205.P9
Title, from 1908–16, *List of Official Publications (Other Than Confidential) Issued by Departments of the Government of India and Local Governments and Administrations; 1917–26, List of Publications (Other Than Confidential) Issued by the Punjab Government and the Heads of Departments in the Punjab.* Superseded by two publications with the same title in 1947, issued by Superintendent, Government Printing, Punjab, India, and by Superintendent, Government Printing, Punjab, Pakistan.
The following guide deals, in a classified arrangement, with Punjab government reports and statistics: Fazal, Cyril P. K. A guide to Punjab government reports and statistics. [Lahore, The Civil & Military Gazette, Ltd.] 1939. 256 p. (Board of Economic Inquiry, Punjab. Publication no. 10. General editor: J. W. Thomas) B3205.P93.

Travancore. *Government Press.* Government publications for sale at the Government Press. Trivandrum, Government Press. Z3205.T77
After 1956, see Kerala.

United Provinces of Agra and Oudh. *Government Book Depot.* Catalogue of books. Allahabad, 1923–[27?] Z3205.U5

United Provinces of Agra and Oudh. *Government Press.* Catalog of publications issued by the government of the United Provinces and obtainable from the Book Depot, Government Press, Allahabad. Allahabad, The Superintendent, Government Press, United Provinces, 1928–[38?] annual. Z3205.U51

—— List of publications (other than confidential) issued by the government of the United Provinces and officers subordinate to it ... which are exempted from registration. [Allahabad, 1909–?] Z3205.U6
Title, through 1916, *List of Non-Confidential Publications Exempted from Registration.*
After 1950, United Provinces became the state of Uttar Pradesh.

Union Territories

Current publications of the Union Territories of India are listed to a considerable extent in the *Accessions List, India,* issued by the U.S. Library of Congress, American Libraries Book Procurement Center, Delhi, and in its *Annual Supplement: Cumulative List of Serials* (Z3201.-U54).

Sikkim

The following works include official documents of the Protectorate of Sikkim.

American University, *Washington, D.C. Foreign Areas Studies Division.* Area handbook for Nepal (with Sikkim and Bhutan). Washington, 1964. xv, 448 p. DS485.N4A8

Schappert, Linda G. Sikkim, 1800–1968; an annotated bibliography. Honolulu East-West Center Library, East-West Center, 1968. 69 p. (Occasional papers of East-West Center Library, no. 10)   Z3207.S53S3

Indonesia

Formerly Dutch East Indies; Japanese occupation, 1942–45; independent republic, 1945–.

There is no current bibliography or list of official publications. These are, however, included in the following general bibliographies or lists:

Berita bibliografi. 1955+ Djakarta, Gunung Agung.   Z3273.B44
    Published bimonthly. (Monthly, up to 1963, quarterly, 1964–66. Publication suspended 1967–68.) Superseded *Catalogus dari buku-buku jang diterbitkan di Indonesia* (1870–1954). (Z3278.A5C3 Orien Indo). Monthly issues for 1955 issued as a section of *Buku kita; untuk buku dan pembatja* (Z3271.B8 Orien Indo). From January 1969 published by Jajasan Idayu. Cumulated annually. Government publications are listed in the general classified arrangement.

Indonesia. *Kantor Bibliografi Nasional.* Bibliografi nasional Indonesia. [Djakarta] Kantor Bibliografi Nasional, Departemen Pendidikan Dasar dan Kebudajaan. quarterly.   Z3261.A36 Orien Indo
    Published from 1963 as a continuation of Indonesia, Kantor Bibliografi Nasional, *Berita bulanan* (Z3271.A43 Orien Indo). Publication suspended from April 1965 to March 1970.

U.S. *Library of Congress. Library of Congress Office, Djakarta.* Accessions list, Indonesia, Malaysia, Singapore and Brunei. v. 1+ July 1964+ Djakarta.   Z3271.U5
—— —— Cumulative list of serials. Jan. 1964/Sept. 1966+ Djakarta. Z3271.U52
    Published monthly (quarterly, before April 1968), with the "Cumulative list of serials," issued once a year. A cumulative author index is included in the final issue of each volume. From Sept./Oct. 1970, includes publications of Malaysia, Singapore, and Brunei. Lists a substantial number of official publications.

Following are retrospective bibliographies of government publications:

Pusat Dokumentasi Ilmiah Nasional. Bibliografi penerbitan badan-badan Pemerintah Indonesia, 1950–1969. Djakarta [1971] 412 p.   Z3275.P86 Orien Indo
  Bibliography of Indonesian Government publications. Covers all agencies, except the Dept. of Agriculture. Parliamentary documents are not included.

Sjahrial-Pamuntjak, Rusina. Daftar penerbitan Pemerintah Republik Indonesia; suatu usaha pertjobaan. Djakarta, Perpustakaan Sedjarah Politik dan Sosial, 1964. 56 p.   Z3262.S4 Orien Indo
  List of government publications of Indonesia, covering the period 1945 to 1962.

Other bibliographies which may be of assistance to researchers for both the pre-1945 and the post-1945 period are the following:

Dutch East Indies. *Centraal Kantoor voor de Statistiek. Bibliotheek.* Catalogus der boekwerken betreffende Nederlandsch-Indië, aanwezig in de bibliotheek van het Centraal Kantoor voor de Statistiek (bijgewerkt tot 18 november 1938) Batavia, 1938. xviii, 309 p.   Z3276.D95
  Classified, with author index.

Echols, John M. Preliminary checklist of Indonesian imprints during the Japanese period (March 1942–August 1945) with annotations. Ithaca, N.Y., Modern Indonesia Project, Southeast Asia Program, Dept. of Asian Studies, Cornell University, 1963. 56 p. (Cornell University. Modern Indonesia Project. Bibliography series)   Z3278.A5E3

———— Preliminary checklist of Indonesian imprints, 1945–1949, with Cornell University holdings. Ithaca, N.Y., Modern Indonesia Project, Southeast Asia Program, Dept. of Asian Studies, Cornell University, 1965. 186 p. (Cornell University. Modern Indonesia Project. Bibliography series)   Z3261.E25
  Both checklists include a considerable number of official publications under corporate entries.

Excerpta Indonesica. 1+ Jan. 1970+ [Leyden, Centre for Documentation on Modern Indonesia, Royal Institute of Linguistics and Anthropology] quarterly. Z3273.E83
  In two parts: Pt. 1 contains abstracts of selected periodical articles on Indonesia; pt. 2 is a selected accessions list of Indonesian newspapers, periodicals, and books, including government publications, received in the Library of the Royal Institute of Linguistics and Anthropology in Leyden, Netherlands.

Hague. Koninklijke Bibliotheek. Bibliografie van in Nederland verschenen officiële en semiofficiële uitgaven. 1+ 1929+ 's-Gravenhage, Staatsdrukkerij. annual. Z2439.H18
  Title 1929–52, *Nederlandse overheidsuitgaven.* Official publications of Dutch East Indies listed to 1939.

Indonesia. *Departemen Penerangan.* List of publications issued by the Dept. of Information, Republic of Indonesia. [Djakarta] Directorate of Publicity and Home Information [1959?+]   Z3275.A5

Leigh, Michael B. Checklist of holdings on Borneo in the Cornell University Libraries. Ithaca, N.Y., Southeast Asia Program, Dept. of Asian Studies, Cornell University, 1966. 62 l. (Cornell University. Dept. of Asian Studies. Southeast Asia Program. Data paper no. 62)   Z3277.B6L4
  Includes official publications on Indonesian Borneo.

Lev, Daniel S. A bibliography of Indonesian government documents and selected Indonesian writings on government in the Cornell University Library. Ithaca, N.Y., Southeast Asia Program, Dept. of Far Eastern Studies, Cornell University,

1958. 58 1. (Cornell University. Southeast Asia Program. Data paper no. 31)
Z3275.L4

Thung, Yvonne, *and* John M. Echols. A guide to Indonesian serials, 1945–1965, in
the Cornell University Library. Ithaca, N.Y., Modern Indonesia Project, Southeast Asia Program, Dept. of Asian Studies, Cornell University, 1966. 151 p. (Cornell University. Modern Indonesia Project. Bibliography series)   Z6958.I45T5

U.S. *Library of Congress. Netherlands Studies Unit.* Netherlands East Indies, a
bibliography of books published after 1930, and periodical articles after 1932,
available in U.S. Libraries. Washington, Library of Congress, Reference Dept.,
1945. 208 p.   Z3276.U62
Government publications are included in its classified arrangement.

For additional listing of Indonesian official documents, see also U.S.
Joint Publications Research Service, under United States, Federal
agencies.

JAPAN

Currently, Japanese official publications are listed in the following
bibliographies and other periodical publications:

Biburosu, (Biblos; monthly magazine for branch libraries, executive and judicial, and
other special libraries.) Tokyo, National Diet Library. 1950+ monthly.
DLC Orien Japan
Includes a monthly report on official publications.

Nōhon shūhō. (Current publications) June 1955+ Tokyo. National Diet Library
weekly.   DLC Orien Japan
From 1961, divided into two parts: government publications and trade publications. This weekly national bibliography began as a monthly publication,
called *Nōhon geppō,* with issue no. 1, covering April–June 1948. It was superseded by *Kokunai shuppanbutsu mokuroku* (v. 1, no. 1, July-Aug. 1949, and
last issue, v. 7, no. 3, March-May 1955). *Nōhon shūhō* (Current publications) is
cumulated annually in *Zen Nihon shuppanbutsu sōmokuroku* (see below).

Seifu kankōbutsu geppō. v. 1+ Comp. by Seifu Kankōbutsu Fukyū Kyōgikai. Tokyo
[1957+] monthly.   Z3305.S4 Orien Japan
Monthly bulletin of government publications, issued by the Government
Printing Bureau. Title from 1957 to March 1961, *Seifu kankōbutsu mokuroku.*
The first issue listed official publications for 1956.

Seifu kankōbutsu shimbun. 1966+ Tokyo, Zenkoku Kampō Hambai Kyōdō Kumiai.
semimonthly.   DLC Orien Japan
Government publication newspaper. Reports on selected new government
publications and contains advance notices on new publications.

Seifu kankōbutsu tenji mokuroku. 1963+ Tokyo, National Diet Library. annual.
Z3305.K32 Orien Japan
Catalog of government publications. Superseded an earlier publication called
Kanchō shiryō tenji mokuroku (Z3305.K3)

Zen Nihon shuppanbutsu sōmokuroku. 1948+ Tokyo, National Diet Library. annual.
Z3301.Z4 Orien Japan
Japanese national bibliography. Annual cumulation of the weekly *Nōhon*

shūhō. In two parts: government publications and trade publications. Occasionally the two parts are published separately.

Before 1927 there were no separate bibliographies or lists of government publications. These were partly included in Japanese general bibliographies and in the catalogs of the Imperial Library.[21] Japanese official documents are also included in:

Wenckstern, Friedrich von. A bibliography of the Japanese empire; being a classified list of all books, essays and maps in European languages relating to Dai Nihon (Great Japan) published in Europe, America and in the East from 1859–93 A.D. ... To which is added a facsimile reprint of: Léon Pagès. Bibliographie japonaise depuis le XVe siècle jusqu'à 1859. Leiden, E. J. Brill, 1895 [1894] xiv, 338, 67 p. Z3301.W47

—— —— Volume II. Comprising the literature from 1894 to the middle of 1906 ... with additions and corrections to the first volume and a Supplement to Léon Pagès' Bibliographie japonaise ... Tokyo, The Maruzen Kakushiki Kaisha (Z. P. Maruya & Co. Ltd) 1907. xvi, 486, 28, 21 p. Z3301.W47

Wenckstern's bibliography is continued from 1906 to 1943 in Oskar Nachod's seven volume *Bibliographie von Japan, 1906–1926 [–1938–1943]* published by K. W. Hiersemann, Leipzig, 1918–[44?] (Z3301.-W472).

After 1927, the following catalogs or lists of government documents were published:

Kanchō kankō tosho geppō. [1927–42] Tokyo, Naikaku Insatsukyoku. DLC Orien Japan
 Monthly bulletin of government publications. From 1927 to 1937 published quarterly under the title *Kanchō kankō tosho mokuroku.* Arranged by government agencies and by subjects. It included not only publications of central agencies, but also those of government universities and schools, of the prefectures, Korea (Chosen), Kwantung, Sakhalin, South Sea islands, and Taiwan (Formosa).

Kokuritsu Kokkai Toshokan, Tokyo. Checklist of Japanese government official publications. [Tokyo] National Diet Library [1949] Z3305.K6

—— Kanchō kankōbutsu sōgō mokuroku. [v. 1–8, Sept. 1945/1950–1958] Tokyo, 1952–60. DLC Orien Japan
 Union catalog of government publications. A classified catalog of official publications of the central government. Continued after 1958 in *Zen Nihon shuppanbutsu sōmokuroku* (Japanese national bibliography).

—— Kanchō kankōbutsu tenjikai. Tokyo, 1958. 75 p.
 Exhibition of government publications. "Lists 1448 titles, including about 50 representative titles published by post–1868 Meiji government, catalogues of government publications with brief annotations, and representative postwar publications." [22]

---

[21] For a description of the development of Japanese bibliography, see U.S. Library of Congress, *Quarterly Journal* 26 (April 1969): 98–104.

—— Kankōchō chikuji kankōbutsu ichiran. Tokyo, 1960. 104 p.
    Directory of periodic government publications. Lists periodicals as of De-
    cember 1959.[22]

—— Obun ni yoru kanchō kankōbutsu ichiran. List of Japanese government publications in European languages, 1945–1958. Rev. and enl. ed. Tokyo, 1959. 91 p.
                                                              DLC Orien Japan
    First ed. published in 1956, for the period 1945–55. "Arranged in the order
    of organs as determined by the Japanese government statute in 1958." Ap-
    pendix includes a "list of publications of the Supreme Commander for the Al-
    lied Powers, 1946–52."

Kokuritsu Kokkai Toshokan, *Tokyo. Renrakubu.* Kuni (chūō kanchō, kōkyō kigyōtai,
    seifu kankei kikan, seifu kankei dantai) ga henshū kanshū shi, seifu kankei dantai
    shuppansha ga hakkō shita kankōbutsu ichiran. List of the publications compiled
    by or under supervision of the government of Japan (central government agencies;
    public corporations and extra-departmental organizations) and published by
    extra-departmental organizations (gaikaku-dantai) or commercial publishers. (Pre-
    liminary edition) Tokyo, 1969. 175 l.   Z3305.K69 Orien Japan
    Lists some 1,800 titles published by 235 agencies and organizations, as of
    February 1969.

Other bibliographical tools which will be of assistance to researchers
are the following:

Nihon no Sankō Tosho Henshū Iinkai. Guide to Japanese reference books. Chicago,
    American Library Association, 1966. 303 p.   Z3306.N5 1966
    Includes Sino-Japanese characters, their romanization, and English trans-
    lation of each title. Based on the revised Japanese edition, it includes bibliogra-
    phies and lists of official publications, p. 6; statistics, p. 125; law, p. 135.

Semmon Toshokan Kyōgikai. Nihon tōkei sōsakuin. Tokyo, National Diet Library,
    1959. xli, 1483 p.   HA1832.S4 Orien Japan
    General index of Japanese statistics.

Sōrifu Tōkeikyoku kankō shiryō sōmokuroku. Tokyo, 1966.
    Bureau of Statistics catalog. "A list of all the publications of the bureau during
    the period of 1871 to February 1966." [23]

U.S. *Bureau of the Census.* Bibliography of social science periodicals and monograph
    series: Japan, 1950–1963. [Washington, 1965] 346 p. (*Its* Foreign social science
    bibliographies. Series P–92, no. 20)   Z7161.U43 no. 20
    An annotated classified bibliography. Includes a considerable number of of-
    ficial publications.

KOREA

Independence until 1910; under Japanese rule, 1910–45; divided into
North Korea, under Soviet occupation, and South Korea, under Amer-

---

[22] Nihon no Sankō Tosho Henshū Iinkai, *Guide to Japanese Reference Books* (Chicago: American Library Association, 1966) , p. 6.
[23] *Bibliography, Documentation, Terminology,* (UNESCO, Paris) v. 8, (March 1968) :
59. (Z1007.B5775).

ican occupation, 1945–48; People's Democratic Republic of Korea, 1948– and Republic of Korea, 1948–.

The following bibliographies include retrospective listing of a substantial number of official publications of pre-1945 Korea, and of the two post-1945 Koreas:

Korea (*Government-General of Chosen, 1910–1945*). *Kambō. Bunshoka.* (Chōsen Sōtokufu oyobi shozoku kansho shuyō kankō tosho mokuroku) Keijo, Chōsen sōtokufu, Shōwa 5–? (1930–?)   Z3317.A3 Orien Japan
  Catalog of the principal publications of the Government-General of Korea and its subordinate agencies and offices.

Sŏyangbon Han'guk munhŏn mongnok, 1800–1963. Bibliography of Korea; publications in the western language [sic] 1800–1963 (in the Russian language) [Seoul, National Assembly Library, 1967] 227 p.   Z3316.S65 Orien Korea
  In two parts: 1. an abridged reprint of the first volume of Library of Congress' *Korea, an Annotated Bibliography* (Washington, 1950) and two continuations, compiled by Soon-Hi Lee (1950–58), and Yong-Sun Chung (1959–63); 2. reprint of the second volume of Library of Congress' *Korea, an Annotated Bibliography* ("Publications in the Russian language.")

U.S. *Library of Congress. Reference Dept.* Korea, an annotated bibligraphy . . . Washington, 1950. 3 v.   Z3316.U6   1950a
  A classified bibliography in three volumes: 1. publications in western languages, 2. publications in the Russian language, 3. Publications in Far Eastern languages.

KOREA, DEMOCRATIC PEOPLE'S REPUBLIC OF

U.S. *Bureau of the Census.* Bibliography of social science periodicals and monograph series: North Korea, 1945–1961. [Washington, 1962] 12 p. (*Its* Foreign social science bibliographies. Series P–92, no. 8)   Z7161.U43 no. 8
  A classified bibliography. Includes some official publications.

U.S. Dept. of the Army. Communist North Korea; a bibliographic survey. Washington, U.S. Govt. Print. Off. 1971. 130 p.   Z3321.U53

Yang, Key P. Ch'uryŏsŏ yŏkkŭn Miguk Kukhoe Tosŏgwan sojang pukkoe charyo mongnokchip. Seoul, Kukt'o T'ongirwon, 1970 755 p.   Z3321.Y35 Orien Korea
  "A classified list of North Korean materials selected from the Korean collection in the Library of Congress."
  In mimeographed form, issued by the National Unification Board, Republic of Korea.

For additional listing of North Korean documents, see also U.S. Joint Publications Research Service, under United States, Federal agencies.

KOREA, REPUBLIC OF

Currently, official publications are listed in the following bibliographies:

Chŏngbu kanhaengmul mongnok. 1948/65+ [Seoul] National Assembly Library.
                                                      Z3317.C44 Orien Korea

"Government publications in Korea." Issued annually since 1967. Entries are arranged by government agencies.

Taehan Min'guk ch'ulp'anmul ch'ongmongnok. 1945–62+ [Seoul] Central National Library. Z3316.T3 Orien Korea
"Korean national bibliography." Issued monthly with annual cumulations. Includes a section on government publications.

Other bibliographic tools which list or describe official publications are the following:

Korea (*Republic*) *Chŏngbu Kanhaengmul Chojŏng Simŭi Wiwŏnhoe.* Chŏngbu kan-haengmul hyŏnhwang. [Seoul, 1965?] 29 1. Z3317.A5 Orien Korea
"Current conditions in government publishing." Published by the Committee on Reappraisal of Government Publications.

Korea (*Republic*) *Kongbobu.* Chŏngbu kanhaengmul mongnok [1948–61. Seoul, 1961] 93 p. Z3317.A53 Orien Korea
Government publications in Korea, issued by the Ministry of Public Information. A supplement covering official publications for January-November 1962, was issued in 1962.

Surveys and Research Corporation, *Washington, D.C.* Statistical publications in Korea, an interim report to the Government of the Republic of Korea. Seoul, Statistical Advisory Group, Surveys and Research Corp., 1961. 38, 32 p. Z7554.K8S9
"Han'guk t'onggye kanhaengmul ŭi chŏngbich'aek."

U.S. *Bureau of the Census.* Bibliography of social science periodicals and monograph series: Republic of Korea, 1945–1961. Washington, 1962 48 p. (*Its* Foreign social science bibliographies. Series P–92, no. 9) Z7161.U43 no. 9
A classified bibliography. Includes official publications, which can be identified through an "index of issuing agencies."

Yang, Key P. Reference guide to Korean materials, 1945–1959. Washington, 1960. 131 1. Z3320.Y3
Typescript (carbon copy) of a thesis (M.S.) , Catholic University of America. Materials selected from the Korean collection of the Library of Congress.

LAOS

French protectorate, 1893–1949 (Japanese occupation, 1941–45); independent kingdom, 1949–.

There is no national bibliography and no list, current or retrospective, of official publications. Some official documents of Laos are listed in general bibliographies on Indochina (see Asia and Pacific area, General bibliographies) and in the following two bibliographies:

Kéne, Thao. Bibliographie du Laos. [Vientiane, Laos] Édition du Comité littéraire, 1958. 68, [7] 1. Z3238.L2K4
Includes an index to the special issue of *France-Asie* (v. 12, no. 118–119, 1956) on Laos and a list of Laotian serials.

Lafont, Pierre B. Bibliographie du Laos. Paris, École française d'Extrême-Orient; dépositaire: Adrien-Maisonneuve, 1964. 269 p. (Publications de l'École française d'Extrême-Orient, v. 50) Z3228.L3L3

MALAYSIA

Under British control, 1819–1957; 1826–1945, part of Straits Settlements (1942–45, under Japanese occupation); independent Federation of Malaya, 1957–63; Federation of Malaysia, including the Federation of Malaya, State of Singapore, North Borneo (Sabah) and Sarawak, 1963– ; Singapore seceded in 1965.

Currently Malaysian government publications are listed in:

Malaysia. Current list of publications. Kuala Lumpur, Government Printer. quarterly.
DLC
    Similar lists were published from 1939, first by Straits Settlements. Publications Bureau *(Publications Bureau Price List.* Z3249.G7S8) , later by the Government Printer of the Federation of Malaya *(Current List of Publications).*

The Government Printer of Sabah (formerly North Borneo) occasionally issues *Publications List,* which also includes the official publications of Sarawak.

The Malaysian national bibliography, *Bibliografi Negara Malaysia* (February 1967+, Kuala Lumpur, Z3261.B5) includes government publications in both of its two parts: 1. classified (Category 3: "government publications"); 2. alphabetical section. The U.S. Library of Congress, Library of Congress Office, Djakarta, *Accessions List, Indonesia, Malaysia, Singapore, and Brunei,* (Z3271.U5), lists official publications of Malaysia from Sept./Oct. 1970. The following works will also be of assistance to researchers:

Anuar, Hedwig. A guide to current government publications of the Federation of Malaya. *In* Library Association of Malaya and Singapore. News letter, v. 3, May 1959: 1–9. DLC

Cheeseman, Harold A. R. Bibliography of Malaya, being a classified list of books wholly or partly in English, relating to the Federation of Malaya and Singapore. London, New York, Published for the British Association of Malaya by Longmans, Green [1959] 234 p. Z3246.C5
    Includes a substantial number of official publications in its classified arrangement.

Gt. Brit. *Colonial Office.* Annual report on Sarawak. 1947–[62?] London, H. M. Stationery Off. DS646.36.G7
    Official publications listed in its "bibliography."

——— Colony of North Borneo; annual report. 1947–[62?] London, H. M. Stationery Off. DS646.33.G7
    Title 1947–51, *Report on North Borneo.* Official publications listed in its "reading list."

Hazra, Niranjan K. Malaysian serials; a check list of current official serials of the Malaysian governments. Singapore, Dept. of History, Center for South East Asia Studies in the Social Sciences, University of Singapore, 1963? 18 p.[24]

---

[24] Godfrey R. Nunn, *South and Southeast Asia; a Bibliography of Bibliographies* (Honolulu; East West Center Library, 1966), p. 44. (Z3221.A1N8).

Leigh, Michael B. *and* John M. Echols. Checklist of holdings on Borneo in the Cornell University Libraries. Ithaca, N.Y., Southeast Asia Program, Dept. of Asian Studies, Cornell University, 1960. 62 l. (Cornell University. Dept. of Asian Studies. Southeast Asia Program. Data paper no. 62)   Z3277.B6L4
    Includes official monographs and serials of East Malaysia and Brunei.

Mallal, Bashir A. Malayan legal bibliography. Majallah perpustakaan Singapura. Singapore library journal, v. 1, Oct. 1961: 55–75.   Z671.M32

U.S. *Library of Congress. Division of Bibliography.* British Malaya and British North Borneo: a bibliographical list. Comp. by Florence S. Hellman. Washington, 1943. 103 p.   Z3246.U67 1943

MALDIVE ISLANDS
British protectorate, 1887–1965; independence, 1965– ; republic, 1968–.

There is no current or retrospective bibliography of official publications. Some retrospective listings can be found in the Royal Commonwealth Society, Library, *Subject Catalogue of the Library of the Royal Empire Society* (London, 1967 Z7164.C7R82 1967).

MONGOLIA
Chinese province, 1691–1911; under Russian protection, 1912–19; Chinese province 1919–21; independent, 1921– ; People's Republic, 1924–.

Official publications are listed in general bibliographies published in Mongolia or abroad, without special distinction. No separate lists of government publications are known to be published.
    The following two recent publications in English give an outline of the governmental organization and list a number of official publications:

Murphy, George G. S. Soviet Mongolia; a study of the oldest political satellite. Berkeley, University of California Press, 1966. 224 p.   DS798.M78
    Includes "Bibliography," p. 207–217.

Sanders, Alan J. K. The People's Republic of Mongolia: a general reference guide. London, New York, Oxford U. P., 1968. 232 p.   DS798.S33

For additional listing of Mongolian documents, see also U.S. Joint Publications Research Service, under United States, Federal agencies.
    The following bibliographies in the Russian language cover Mongolian publications, including government documents:

Akademiiā nauk SSSR. *Biblioteka.* Bibliografiiā Mongol'skoĭ Narodnoĭ Respubliki, 1951–1961. Moskva, 1963. 118 p.   Z3107.M7A63
    A similar bibliography, covering the years 1935–50, was published by the Soviet Academy of Sciences in 1953.[25]

----
[25] *Bibliography, Documentation, Terminology,* (UNESCO), v. 4, no. 6, (Nov. 1964): 164. Z1007.B5775).

—— Ukazatel' bibliografiĭ po mongolovedeniĭu na russkom i͡azyke, 1824–1960. Leningrad, 1962. 88 p.   Z3107.M7A65

Ulan Bator, Mongolia. Gosudarstvennai͡a publichnai͡a biblioteka. Bibliografii͡a rabot po Mongolii. Ulan Bator, 1962+   Z3107.M7U4
    The bibliography lists books and other materials in Russian and other European languages concerning Mongolia, received at the State Public Library.

NAURU

German colony, 1888–1914; occupied by Australia in 1914; League of Nations Mandate, administered by Great Britain, 1920–47; U.N. Trusteeship, administered jointly by Australia, Great Britain and New Zealand, 1947–68; independent republic, 1968–.

No current list of official publications is known to exist. For the post-World War II period, there is the following Australian bibliography:

Australia. *Dept. of Territories.* Annotated bibliography of select government publications on Australian territories, 1951–1964. Canberra, 1965. 55 p.   Z4019.A87
    Nauru publications, p. 33.

NEPAL
Kingdom

There is no current or retrospective national bibliography or list of official publications. Currently, official publications are listed in:

U.S. *Library of Congress. American Libraries Book Procurement Center, Delhi.* Accessions list, Nepal. v. 1+ Apr. 1966+ New Delhi.
    Published three times a year.   Z3207.N4U5

The following bibliographic tools include some official publications:

American University, *Washington, D.C. Foreign Areas Studies Division.* Area handbook for Nepal (with Sikkim and Bhutan). Washington, 1964. 448 p.
        DS485.N4A8
    At head of title: U.S. Army. "Department of the Army pamphlet no. 550–35." Bibliographies on Nepal, p. 133–142; 229–234; 299–314; 359–362.

Bhasin, A. S. Documents on Nepal's relations with India and China, 1949–66. Bombay, Academic Books [1970] xxvi, 295 p.   DS485.N4B376

Fisher, Margaret W. A selected bibliography of source materials for Nepal. Berkeley, University of California, HRAF, 1956. 44 p.   DLC

Gupta, Anirudha. A critical study of source material on contemporary Nepal, 1950–1960. International studies, (Bombay, New York) v. 3, April, 1962: 451–474.
        JX18.I55

Nepal. *National Planning Commission. Library.* Nepal reports bibliography. Singha Durbar, Kathmandu, 1968. 24 l.   Z7165.N37A53
    A classified bibliography of Nepalese official and other reports in the library of the National Planning Commission.

U.S. *Dept. of State.* [Survey of publications in Kathmandu, by Le Roy Makepeace, Publications Procurement Officer] New Delhi, 1952. 1 v. (various pagings)
Z3207.K3U5   1952

Wood, Hugh B.   Nepal bibliography. Kathmandu, Bureau of Publications, College of Education, 1959. 108 p.   Z3207.N4W6   1959b

NEW ZEALAND

British colony, 1840–1907; dominion, 1907–47; complete autonomy within the British Commonwealth, 1947–.

Government publications are listed currently in:

New Zealand. *Government Printing Office.*   Government publications. 1953+ Wellington.   DLC
     Frequency varies. Currently published every two or three months. Sectional catalogs are occasionally issued for the following subjects: agriculture, botany, farming, education, history and the Maori, scientific and industrial research, statistics, miscellaneous.

New Zealand national bibliography. Wellington, National Library of New Zealand, 1967+   DLC
     Published monthly, with annual cumulations, in three sections: 1. books, pamphlets, art prints, music scores, and sound recordings; 2. maps; 3. periodicals. Section one includes government publications, including reports in the *Appendices to the Journals of the House of Representatives,* bills and acts. It replaced *Current National Bibliography,* published up to 1965 by the National Library Service, and the annual *Copyright Publications,* published by the General Assembly Library. First annual cumulation covers 1966.

Other current lists and indexes which include official publications:

Index to New Zealand periodicals, and current national bibliography of New Zealand books and pamphlets. 1940+ Wellington.   Z6962.N5I5
     Title, 1940–49 and 1966+, *Index to New Zealand Periodicals.* From 1950 to 1965, *Current National Bibliography.* Published as second part of the *Index.* Published 1940–55, by the New Zealand Library Association, 1956–65, by the National Library Service, currently by the National Library of New Zealand.

National Library of New Zealand. Union list of serials in New Zealand libraries. 3d ed. Wellington [1969+]   Z6945.N285
     First edition of the *Union List* issued by the National Library Service in 1953, with supplements 1953–61. Second edition issued 1964–68, in three looseleaf volumes.

The following bibliographies contain retrospective listing of government publications or list reference sources:

Bagnall, Austin G.   New Zealand national bibliography to the year 1960. Wellington, Government. Print. 1969 [i.e. 1970]+   Z4101.B28
     Includes official publications, except serials and parliamentary papers. To be published in five volumes, vol. 5 to be an index.

Davison, Beverley J. *comp.* New Zealand Oceanographic Institute list of publications as at March 1st, 1968. [Wellington] N. Z. Oceanographic Institute [1968] 20 p. (N. Z. Oceanographic Institute. Miscellaneous publication no. 40)   GC1.W4 no. 40

Harris, John. Guide to New Zealand reference material and other sources of information. 2d ed. [Wellington] New Zealand Library Association, 1950. 114 p.
Z4116.H3 1950
———— ———— Supplement. no. 1+ June 1951+ Wellington, New Zealand Library Association.   Z4116.H3 1950 Suppl.

New Zealand. *Dept. of Statistics.* Catalogue of New Zealand statistics. 1962+ Wellington.   Z7554.N5A25

———— Statistical publications. 1840–1960; mainly those produced by the Registrar-General 1853–1910 and the Government Statistician 1911–1960. Wellington, R. E. Owen, Govt. Printer, 1961. 66 p.   Z7554.N5A5

New Zealand. *General Assembly. House of Representatives.* Index to the Appendices to the Journals of the House of Representatives of New Zealand. 1854–1913+ Wellington.   J941.M33
Indexes issued as follows: 1854–1913, 1914–22, 1923–38, 1939–53, and 1954–63.

New Zealand. *General Assembly. Library.* Catalogue of the General Assembly Library of New Zealand. Comp. chiefly by E. Seymour Stocker and Edward Samuel. Wellington, J. Mackay, Govt. Printer, 1897. 2 v.   Z975.W4 1897
Includes in a dictionary arrangement concise statement of the official publications of both New Zealand and the provinces which were abolished in 1876.

———— Supplement to the Catalogue of the General Assembly Library of New Zealand. Wellington, J. Mackay, Govt. Printer, 1899. 109 [1] 2 p.   Z975.W4 1897 Supp.
Continued by lists of accessions 1899+ and by *Copyright Publications.*

———— Copyright publications. 1933/34–[65] Wellington. annual.   Z975.W42
From 1946 to 1954 there was a separate section for government publications, kept up to date by a mimeographed monthly list, still published. The annual edition was superseded from 1966 by the annual *New Zealand National Bibliography.*

———— A finding list of British parliamentary papers relating to New Zealand, 1817–1900, by J. O. Wilson. Wellington, General Assembly Library, 1960. 28 l.
Z4109.N53

New Zealand. *Government Stationery Office, Wellington.* Books on New Zealand. A list of publications on scientific and historical subjects, containing reliable information relative to the Dominion of New Zealand . . . Obtainable from the Government Printer, Wellington, N. Z. [Wellington, W. A. G. Skinner, Govt. Printer, 1929] 16 p.   Z4101.N53

———— Price-list of public acts, 1908–1938 and publications on sale at the Government Stationery Office, Wellington, N. Z. Wellington, E. V. Paul, Govt. Printer, 1939. 113 [2] p.   Z4109.N55 1939
———— ———— Amendment. Wellington, E. V. Paul, Govt. Printer, 1939–[44?]
Z4109.N55 Amend

New Zealand Library Association. A bibliography of New Zealand bibliographies. Prelim. ed. Wellington, 1967. 58 p.   Z4101.A1N4
Under broad subject headings, it lists 315 bibliographies concerned with various aspects of New Zealand history, government, literature, etc. Official publications, p. 10–11.

Scholefield, Guy. New Zealand official papers; finding your way through them. New
    Zealand libraries, v. 7, Oct. 1944: 161–164.   Z671.N45
    Describes mainly parliamentary publications, statutes, and the official gazette.

U.S. *Library of Congress. Division of Bibliography.* New Zealand: a selected list of
    references. Compiled by Helen F. Conover. [Washington] 1942. 68 p.   Z4101.U6

PAKISTAN

Under British rule, 1840–1947; independent dominion 1947–56; republic, 1956– ; East Pakistan became independent Bangladesh in 1971.

The Manager of Publications in Karachi issues from time to time
catalogs and other lists of official publications of Pakistan central government and also a monthly *Bulletin Regarding New Publications.* The
following bibliographies and catalogs list more or less currently the
official publications:

Pakistan. Catalogue of the government of Pakistan publications. [1962+] Karachi,
    Manager of Publications.   Z3195.A22
    Issued irregularly with occasional supplements.

The Pakistan national bibliography. 1962+ Karachi, Govt. of Pakistan, Directorate of
    Archives & Libraries, National Bibliographical Unit.   Z3191.P33
    In two parts. Part two lists government and semiofficial publications.

U.S. *Library of Congress. American Libraries Book Procurement Center, Karachi.*
    Accessions list, Pakistan. v. 1+ July/Dec. 1962+ Karachi, Dacca, American Libraries
    Book Procurement Centers. monthly.   Z3191.U53
    Official publications are indicated by an asterisk preceding the country desig-
    nation. A quinquennial author index 1962–66, was published in 1968.

——— ——— Annual supplement: cumulative list of serials. 1970+ Karachi,
    Dacca, American Libraries Book Procurement Centers.   Z3191.U53 Suppl.
    Issued 1967–70 as pt. 2 of July issue. Each volume cumulative from 1962.

——— Annual list of serials. 1966. Karachi, Dacca, American Libraries Book Procure-
    ment Centers. 1 v.   Z6958.P2U5
    "Serials acquired from 1962 to July 1, 1966."

A classified *Pakistan National Bibliography, 1947–1961* has been compiled by a Pakistan bibliographical working group and is to be published by the National Book Centre of Pakistan in seven volumes. It
includes official publications. Vol. 1 appeared in January 1973 (Z3191.
P32).

Other bibliographic tools for retrospective listing of official publications of Pakistan are the following:

Datta, Rajeshwari. Union catalogue of the Government of Pakistan publications held
    by libraries in London, Oxford and Cambridge. London, Mansell Information/
    Publishing, 1967. [64] p.   Z3195.D37

Ghani, A. R. *comp.* Pakistan; a select bibliography. Lahore, Pakistan Association for the Advancement of Science, University Institute of Chemistry, 1951. xxii, 339 p. Z3196.G5
Arranged by broad subjects. Includes official publications.

Moreland, George B., *and* Akhtar H. Siddiqui. Publications of the Government of Pakistan, 1947–1957. Karachi Institute of Public and Business Administration, University of Karachi, 1958. 187 p. Z3195.M6
Lists publications under government agencies, arranged in alphabetical order. It includes publications not listed in the *Catalogue of the Government of Pakistan Publications,* which are not for sale. It also covers publications of the National Assembly, the Supreme Court, acts and ordinances, president's orders, etc.

Pakistan. *Central Statistical Office.* Key to official statistics. [Karachi, 1962+] HA37.P253

Pakistan. *Stationery and Printing Dept.* Catalogue of the government of Pakistan publications. Karachi, Manager of Publications, 1952. 77 p. Z3195.A52
Supplements published in 1953 and 1957.

Siddiqui, Akhtar H. Reference sources on Pakistan; a bibliography. [1st ed.] Karachi, National Book Centre of Pakistan [1968] 32 p. Z1035.S55
A classified bibliography of bibliographies. "Public documents," p. 23.

U.S. *Library of Congress. Census Library Project.* Census and vital statistics of India and Pakistan contained in official publications and famine documents, an annotated bibliography by Henry J. Dubester. Washington, 1950. 1 v. Microfilm 4685 Z

Usmani, M. Adil. Status of bibliography in Pakistan. Karachi, Library Promotion Bureau, 1968. 106 p. (Library Promotion Bureau. Publication no. 4) Z3192.5.U8
"Government publications," p. 36–38, 83–86.

Provinces

Until 1971 when East Pakistan became the Republic of Bangladesh, provincial official publications were listed in the following catalogs:

East Pakistan. *Government Press.* Catalogue of publications. Tejgaon, Dacca. [irregular] Z3197.E2A3
Continued the pre-1947 East Bengal, Government Press, *Catalogue of publications.*

West Pakistan. West Pakistan Government publications; general catalogue. Lahore, Printed by the Superintendent, Govt. Printing, West Pakistan. [irregular] Z3195.A33
Supplemented by monthly lists.

For retrospective listing of provincial publications the following lists and catalogs will be of assistance:

North-West Frontier Province, *India.* List of non-confidential publications exempted from registration. Peshawar. [irregular] Z3205.N87
Issued from about 1908 to 1926.

Punjab, *Pakistan (Province) Superintendent, Government Printing.* Punjab Government publications; general catalogue. Lahore. [1949?+]   Z3195.A32
    Supersedes an earlier publication with the same title, issued by Superinten-
    dent, Government Printing, Punjab, to 1947.

The following bibliography of Punjab includes a substantial number
of government documents:

Malik, Ikram A.   A bibliography of the Punjab and its dependencies, 1849–1910.
    Lahore, Research Society of Pakistan, University of the Punjab, 1968. 309 p.
    (Research Society of Pakistan. Publication no. 8)   Z3197.P8M3
    Chapter two lists government reports, chapter three, selections from the
    printed records of the Office of the Financial Commissioner and of the Punjab
    Administration.

Official publications of the province of Sind were listed in the following catalogs:

Bombay *(Presidency)* General catalogue of all publications of the government of
    Bombay (including Sind). Bombay, Superintendent, Government Printing and
    Stationery [1925?—?]   Z3205.B68

Sind, *India. Government Book Depot and Record Office.* Catalogue of publications.
    Karachi.   Z3205.S6
    First published in 1939 and kept up to date by supplements to January 1st
    1942.

For the pre-1947 listing of official publications of East Pakistan, see
India, States and Territories, retrospective bibliographies for Assam and
Bengal.

PHILIPPINES
Under Spanish rule, 1565–1898; under United States rule, 1898–1946
(Japanese occupation, 1942–45); independent republic, 1946–.

There is no separate bibliography or list of official publications issued
currently, although the Philippine Bureau of Printing includes in its
annual pamphlet *Stock Forms* a "Price list of public documents for
sale." In the past, two attempts were made to issue a list of official publications. In 1958–59, the Bureau of Public Libraries issued a monthly
mimeographed list, *Philippine Government Publications,* and in 1964–
66 and 1967–68, the National Library, Public Documents, Exchange and
Gift Division, issued *Checklist of Philippine Government Publications.*
Currently, the government publications are listed in:

Philippine bibliography. 1963/64+ Diliman [Quezon] University of the Philippines
    Library. annual.   Z3291.P48
    In two parts: Part two is "government publications," listed in alphabetical
    order by author or title.

For retrospective listing, the bibliographic coverage of official publications is fairly complete. The following bibliographies and lists cover official publications from the earliest period of Philippine printing:

Bibliographical Society of the Philippines. Checklist of Philippine government documents, 1917–1949. Compiled by Consolación B. Rebadavia. Quezon City, University of the Philippines Library, 1960. xv, 817 p.   Z3295.B52

——— Checklist of Philippine government documents, 1950. Washington, Library of Congress, 1953. 62 p.   Z3295.B5

Chicago. University. *Philippine Studies Program.* Selected bibliography of the Philippines, topically arranged and annotated . . . Preliminary ed. New Haven, Human Relations Area Files, 1956. 138 p. (Behavior science bibliographies)   Z3291.C45
"Official general publications," p. 3–10.

Manila. National Library. *Legislative Reference Division.* Checklist of publications of the government of the Philippine Islands September 1, 1900 to December 31, 1917. Compiled by Emma Osterman Elmer. Manila, Bureau of Printing, 1918. 288 p.   Z3295.M27
Includes publications of the Philippine provinces.

Newberry Library, *Chicago.* A catalogue of printed materials relating to the Philippine Islands, 1519–1900, in the Newberry Library. Compiled by Doris V. Welsh. Chicago, 1959. 179 p.   Z3299.N4

Philippine Islands. *Bureau of Printing.* Price list of public documents for sale by the Bureau of Printing. Manila, Bureau of Printing (1909–23?)   Z3295.P45
In English and Spanish.

Quezon, Philippines. University of the Philippines. *Institute of Public Administration. Library.* List of Philippine government publications, 1945–1958. Compiled by Andrea C. Ponce and Jacinta C. Yatco. Manila, 1959–[1960] 2 v.   Z3295.Q5
Contents: Pt. 1. Publications of agencies under the Dept. of Agriculture and Natural Resources, Dept. of Commerce and Industry, Dept. of Education, and Dept. of Labor. —Pt. 2. Publications of agencies under the Depts. of Finance, Foreign Affairs, Health, and Justice. Pt. 2 compiled by Jacinta Y. Ingles and Ursula G. Picache.

U.S. *Army. Forces in the Pacific.* The Philippines during the Japanese regime, 1942–1945; an annotated list of the literature published in or about the Philippines during the Japanese occupation. Prepared by Office of the Chief of Counter-Intelligence, Philippine Research and Information Section, GHQ, AFPAC. [Manila] 1945. 44 p.   Z3296.U45

U.S. *Library of Congress.* Bibliography of the Philippine Islands. Published under the direction of the Library of Congress and the Bureau of Insular Affairs, War Department. Washington, U.S. Govt. Print. Off., 1903. xxi, 397, 439 p. (57th Cong., 2d sess. Senate. Doc. no. 74)   Z3291.U5
Contents: Pt. 1. A list of books (with references to periodicals) on the Philippine Islands in the Library of Congress, by A. P. C. Griffin . . . with chronological list of maps in the Library of Congress, by P. L. Phillips. —Pt. 2. Biblioteca filipina o sea catálogo razonado de todos los impresos, tanto insulares como extranjeros . . . por T. H. Pardo de Tavera.

Following are a few examples of specialized bibliographies in the field of legal literature and statistics:

Francisco, Vicente J.   Legal bibliography. Manila, East Pub., 1950. xvi, 346 p.   DLC LL
Companion volume to the author's *Legal Research* (DLC LL) .

Moreno, Federico B.   Official gazette desk book. 1956+ Quezon City, Philippines,
Index Pub. House.   DLC LL
Annual index of the Official gazette of the Philippines.

Pacis-Nebrida, Leticia, *and* Avelino P. Tendero.   An annotated Philippine legal bibliography. Manila, 1954. 37 p.   DLC LL
At head of title: Institute of Public Administration, University of the Philippines.

Philippines *(Republic)* *Office of Statistical Coordination and Standards.* An annotated bibliography of official statistical publications of the Philippine government. Manila, 1963. 25 l. *(Its* oscas monograph no. 1)   HA37.P545 no. 1

——— Statistical services of the Philippine government, July 1964. 3d ed. Manila
[1964] 115 p.   HA37.P55   1964

A number of government agencies and institutions issued in the past
and issue currently bibliographies, catalogs, or lists of their publications.

SINGAPORE

Under British rule, 1819–1959 (part of Straits Settlements, 1826–1945;
Japanese occupation, 1942–45); autonomous state within the British
Commonwealth, 1959–63; member of the Federation of Malaysia, 1963–
65; independent republic, 1965–.

Currently, Singapore official publications are listed in:

Singapore.   Catalogue of government publications. [Singapore, 1949?+]   Z3248.S5A25

Singapore national bibliography. 1967+ Singapore, National Library. annual.
Z3248.S5A3
Includes government publications in its classified arrangement.

For retrospective listing of Singapore official publications, the following works will be of assistance:

Singapore. Annual report. 1946–[59?] Singapore, Govt. Print. Off.   J618.T3S5
Includes official publications in its "bibliography."

Singapore year book. [1964 +] Singapore, Govt. Print. Off.   DS598.S7S6
Includes official publications in its "bibliography."

Srinivasagam, Elizabeth. Guide to Singapore government departments and serials, as
of 30th August, 1963. Majallah perpustakaan Singapura. Singapore library journal,
v. 3, April 1964: 70–90.   Z671.M32

Straits Settlements. Blue book for the year. Singapore, Printed at the Government
Printing Office. [1874–1938?]   J618.R2
Lists of official publications and newspapers included from 1904.

THAILAND

Kingdom, called Siam before June 1939.

There is no current bibliography or list of government publications.
For retrospective listing, the following lists will be of assistance:

Bangkok, Thailand. National Library. List of Thai government publications covering the years B. E. 2497 (1954), B. E. 2498 (1955), B. E. 2499 (1956) prepared by
National Library, Dept. of Fine Arts. Bangkok [1957] 32 l.   Z3237.B3

Bangkok, Thailand. Thammasat University. *Institute of Public Administration.* List
of Thai government publications, prepared by Research Division, Institute of
Public Administration, Thammasat University. Bangkok, 1958. 43 l.   Z3237.B33
Publications listed under ministries and their subordinate agencies. Covers
mostly post-World War II publications.

Bibliography of Thai government publications. v. 1, 1962. Bangkok, Thai Library
Association, 1962.[26]

Chiravadhana Chakrabandh, M. R. Thai government periodical directory. [Bangkok]
National Library, 1965. 16 p.   Z3237.C45

Thailand. *Laws, statutes, etc. (Indexes)* Laws, royal decrees, and ministerial regula-
tions relating to public administration in Thailand; a selective index to the law
directories, 1951–56, and Royal Thai government gazettes, 1957–58. Compiled by
Research Division, Institute of Public Administration, University of Thammasat.
[Bangkok, Institute of Public Administration, Thammasat University] 1958. 54 l.
DLC LL

Thailand. Samnakngān Sathiti hǣng Chāt. Statistical bibliography, 1966. [Bangkok]
National Statistical Office, Office of the Prime Minister [1969] 100 p.   Z7554.T5A3

The following general bibliographies which include government documents of Thailand will also be of assistance to researchers:

Amara Raksasataya. Bannānukrom thāng sāngkhomsāt khǭng Thai thāng phāsā
Thai lae tawantok. Thailand: social science materials in Thai & western languages.
Bangkok, National Institute of Development Administration, 1966. 378 p.
Z7165.T5A7
Official publications mainly under "Thailand."

Bangkok, Thailand. Chulālongkorn University. *Central Library.* Bibliography
of material about Thailand in Western languages. Bangkok, 1960. 325 p.   DLC

Bitz, Ira. A bibliography of English-language source materials on Thailand in the
humanities, social sciences, and physical sciences. Washington, Center for Research
in Social Systems, American University, 1968. 272 p.   Z3236.B56

Cornell University. *Thailand Project.* Bibliography of Thailand; a selected list of
books and articles with annotations by the staff of the Cornell Thailand Research
Project. Ithaca, N.Y., 1956. 64 l. (Cornell University. Southeast Asia Program.
Data paper, no. 20)   Z3236.C6
Includes official publications under broad subject headings.

---

[26] *Bibliographical Services Throughout the World, 1960–1964*, (UNESCO, 1969), p. 185.
(Z1008.U54).

Cornell University. *Libraries.* Catalogue of Thai language holdings in the Cornell University Libraries through 1964. Compiled by Frances A. Bernath. Ithaca, N.Y., Southeast Asia Program, Dept. of Asian Studies, Cornell University, 1964. 236 p. (Cornell University. Southeast Asia Program. Data paper, no. 54)   Z3240.C6
    Offset reprint of catalog cards. Official publications mostly under corporate entries (Thailand . . . , p. 170–202) .

Mason, John B., *and* H. Carroll Parish. Thailand bibliography. Gainesville, Fla., Dept. of Reference and Bibliography, University of Florida Libraries, 1958. 247 p. (University of Florida Libraries, Dept. of Reference and Bibliography. Bibliographic series, no. 4)   Z3236.M3
    "Books, pamphlets, theses and government documents," p. 3–[103].

TONGA
British protectorate, 1900–70; independent kingdom, 1970–.

There is no bibliography or list of official publications. Some official documents are included in the following works:

Gt. Brit. *Colonial Office.* Tonga; a report. 1946–[63?] London, H.M. Stationery Off.
                                                                    DU880.A15
    Some official documents included in its "reading list."

Snow, Philip A. A bibliography of Fiji, Tonga and Rotuma. Preliminary working ed. Coral Gables, Fla., University of Miami Press, 1969. xliii, 418 p. Z4651.S65   1969
    "Tonga: Administration," items 9091–9114.

VIETNAM
Under French control, 1858/1884–1945 (Japanese occupation, 1940–45); divided by the Geneva cease-fire agreement of 1954 into a northern zone (Democratic Republic of Vietnam) and a southern zone (Republic of Vietnam.

For the period ending in 1954, official publications of the French administration and local authorities are included in general bibliographies of Indochina (see Asia, General bibliographies). The following bibliographies also include some retrospective listing of official publications:

Jumper, Roy. Bibliography on the political and administrative history of Vietnam, 1802–1962, selected and annotated . . . [Saigon] Michigan State University, Vietnam Advisory Group [1964] 115 p.   Z3228.V5J8   1964

Nguyên-thê-Anh. Bibliographie critique sur les relations entre le Viet-Nam et l'Occident (Ouvrages et articles en langues occidentales) . Paris, Maisonneuve & Larose, 1967. 311 p.   Z3228.V5N45   1967

VIETNAM, Democratic Republic of
There is no current or retrospective bibliography or list of official publications. Some official publications are listed in:

Keyes, Jane G.   A bibliography of North Vietnamese publications in the Cornell University Library. Ithaca, N.Y., Southeast Asia Program, Dept. of Asian Studies, Cornell University. 1962. 116 p. (Cornell University. Southeast Asia Program. Data paper, no. 47)   Z3228.V5K4
—— —— A bibliography of Western-language publications concerning North Vietnam in the Cornell University Library; supplement of Data paper 47. Ithaca, N.Y., Southeast Asia Program, Dept. of Asian Studies, Cornell University, 1966. 280 p. (Cornell University. Southeast Asia Program. Data paper, no. 63)
Z3228.V5K4 Suppl.

For additional listing of North Vietnamese documents, see also U.S. Joint Publications Research Service, under United States, Federal agencies.

VIETNAM, Republic of

"Official publications and government documents . . . figure in the quarterly lists of non-periodical publications submitted to the Copyright Department; there are no separate lists for such publications." [27] The quarterly lists, prepared by the Directorate of Archives and National Libraries, have been included earlier in the *Journal officiel* of the Republic of Vietnam (*Công-báo Việt-Nam Cộng-Hòa*).

Retrospectively, official publications are listed in the following bibliography:

Vietnam. Nha Văn-Khộ và Thư'-viện Quốc-gia. Thư'-tịch về ấn-phẩm-công Việt-Nam. Bibliography on Vietnamese official publications, (1960–1969). Saigon, Directorate of National Archives and Libraries. [1969] 134 l.   Z3227.V53
Arranged by ministries and various services within ministries. Listed are Vietnamese-, French-, and English-language materials. An updated 2d ed. (1960-71) published in 1972.

Official publications are also listed in the following general bibliographies:

Cornell University. Libraries.   A checklist of the Vietnamese holdings of the Wason Collection, Cornell University Libraries, as of June 1971. Compiled by Giok Po Oey, with the assistance of Nguyen Hoa. Ithaca, N.Y., Southeast Asia Program, Dept. of Asian Studies, Cornell University, 1971. 377 p. (Cornell University. Southeast Asia Program. Data paper, no. 84)   Z3228.V5C67

Michigan. State University, *East Lansing. Vietnam Project.* What to read on Vietnam; a selected annotated bibliography. 2d ed., with a supplement covering the period Nov. 1958 to Oct. 1959. New York, Institute of Pacific Relations, 1960. 73 l.
Z3228.V5M5   1960

Trần Thị Kim Sa. Bibliography on Vietnam, 1954–1964. Thư'-tịch về Việt-Nam, 1954–1964. Saigon, National Institute of Administration [1965] 255 p.   DLC Orien

[27] *Bibliographical Services Throughout the World, 1960–1964*, (UNESCO, 1969), no. 224. (Z1008.U54).

Vietnam. Bộ Thông Tin và Thanh Nieên. Văn Khố và Thu'Viện. Thu' mục. Catalogue
   of books. Saigon [1965+]   DLC Orien
      Issued by the Ministry of Information, Archives and Libraries Service.

WESTERN SAMOA

German protectorate, 1900–14; New Zealand occupation, 1914–20;
League of Nations Mandate, 1920–46 and U.N. Trusteeship, 1946–61,
both administered by New Zealand; independent kingdom, 1962–.

The following publications include bibliographic notes citing official
publications:

Davidson, James W.   Samoa mo Samoa; the emergence of the independent state of
   Western Samoa. Melbourne, New York, Oxford University Press, 1967. 467 p.
                                                                 DU819.A2D3

Western Samoa. Handbook of Western Samoa. Wellington, N.Z., W. A. G. Skinner,
   Government Printer, 1925. 174 p.   DU819.A2A5   1925
      Bibliography, p. 140–174.

INDEX

The index includes selected personal and corporate authors, titles of works, names of geographical areas—countries provinces, states, etc.—and names of international governmental organizations. Corporate authors are listed mostly under names of individual countries.

Dubester, Henry J., 42, 87, 271, 310, 311, 365, 383
Dublin, National Library of Ireland, 274
Duignan, Peter, 321
Dullard, John P., 119
Dumbarton Oaks, 157
Duncombe, Herbert S., 144
Dunn, H. H., 213
Dunne, J. C., 185
Durón, Jorge F., 230
Dutch East Indies, 370, 371
Duvivier, Ulrick, 212
Dzherova, Liŭba, 288

ECA; *see* United Nations, Economic Commission for Africa
ECAFE; *see* United Nations, Economic Commission for Asia and the Far East
ECE; *see* United Nations, Economic Commission for Europe
ECE, the First Ten Yeaars, 165
ECLA; *see* United Nations, Economic Commission for Latin America
ECSC; *see* European Coal and Steel Community
EEC; *see* European Economic Community
EFTA; *see* European Free Trade Association
EFTA Bulletin, 176
EFTA Reporter, 176
ELDO; *see* European Space Vehicle Launcher Development Organization
ENEA; *see* European Nuclear Energy Agency
EPTA (Expanded Program of Technical Assistance) , 177
EPU; *see* European Payments Union
ERIC; *see* U.S. Educational Research Information Center
ESRO; *see* European Space Research Organization
ESRO/ELDO Bulletin, 177
ESSA; *see* U.S. Environmental Science Services Administration
EURATOM; *see* European Atomic Energy Community
Early Indian Imprints, 362
Early Printing in California, 92; *Colorado,* 93; *Michigan,* 112
East Africa: a Guide to Official Publications of Kenya, Tanzania and Uganda, 310
East Africa High Commission and Other Regional Documents, 310
East African Common Services Organization, 308
East African Community, 309
East Asia; a Bibliography of Bibliographies, 345
East Bengal, Government Press, 383
East Central Europe, 285–300
East Central Europe; a Guide to Basic Publications, 286
East European Accessions Index, 286
East Germany, a Selected Bibliography, 292
East India (Parliamentary Papers) , 362
East Pakistan, 382, 383, 384
East Punjab States Union, 367
Eastern Europe Education: a Bibliography of English Language Materials, 286
Eastern Marketing and Nutrition Research Division (U.S.) , 33
Eastern Utilization Research and Development Division (U.S.) , 33
Eastin, Ray B., 11, 21, 32
Echols, John M., 371, 372, 378
Ecology (U.S.) , 18.88
Economic and Social Committee of the EEC and Euratom, 172
Ecuador, 227
Ecuador, 215, 217
Eddy, Henry H., 125
Eder, Phanor J., 226
Edison, Robert, 323

Kletke, Karl, 256
Knizhnaĩa letopis', 301, 304
Knizhnyĩ front, 302
Knudson, William, 136
Kokunai shuppanbutsu mokuroku, 372
Kongl, placater, resolutioner, förordningar och påbud, samt andre allmänne hand-lingar, 283
Koray, Enver, 342
Korea, 373, 374–375
Korea (Democratic People's Republic), 375
Korea (Republic), 375–376
Korea, an Annotated Bibliography, 375
Koren, John, 196
Korshunov, Oleg P., 239, 286, 302
Kraus, Joe W., 133
Krivokapić, Radovan V., 299
Krueger, Ruth C., 129
Kuhlman, A. F., 82, 83
Kulazhnikov, Mikhail N., 302
Kuo hui t'u shu kuan ts'ang Chung-kuo fang chih mu lu, 358
Kuo li chung yang t'u shu kuan ts'ang kuan shu mu lu, 356
Kuo li Pei-p'ing t'u shu kuan Chung wên yü t'u mu lu, 358
Kuo li Pei-p'ing t'u shu kuan hsien ts'ang kuan shu mu lu, 356
Kuri, Salme, 305
Kuwait, 335, 340
Kwantung, 373
Kypriakē Bibliographia, 245
Kyriak, Theodore E., 63

LASL (Los Alamos Scientific Laboratory), 35
Labor (U.S.), 17.33, 50
Labour (Canada), 199
Lafont, Pierre, B., 376
Lambert, Fred L. Jr., 121
Lambert, Sheila, 266
Lancaster, Henry O., 196
Lane, Margaret T., 83, 84, 106
Laos, 344, 345, 346, 376
La Peyrie, 249
Lapp, J. A., 102
Larcier, Ferdinand, 243
Larwood, James, 98
Latin America, 165–166; *see also* Caribbean Area; and Central and South America
Latin America, 1935–1949; a Selected Bibliography, 215
Latin American Institute for Economic and Social Planning, 184
Latin American Serial Documents; a Holdings List, 215
Latin American Treaty Collections, 215
Latvia, 306
Law Library Journal, 86, 92
Lawrence, Mary M., 170
Laws, Rules and Regulations (U.S.), 17.10
Leafloor, Lorne B., 202
League of Arab States, 184
League of Nations, 167–168
League of Nations and Disarmament, 168
Lebanon, 340
Lee, Charles E., 127
Lee, John W. M., 109
Lee, Soon-Hi, 375

ence Services, 162; Office of Legal Affairs, 159; Office of Public Information, 160; Relief and Rehabilitation Administration, 166; Secretariat, 160; Technical Assistance Administration, 166

United Nations and Disarmament, 160

United Nations Conference on International Organization, 162

United Nations Documents Index, 154, 157, 158, 161, 164, 178, 179, 180, 183, 184, 190

United Nations Educational, Scientific and Cultural Organization (UNESCO), 5, 181, 189–191; Middle East Science Cooperation Office, 335

United Nations Industrial Development Organization (UNIDO), 191

United Nations Institute for Training and Research (UNITAR), 154, 191

United Nations Juridical Yearbook, 160

United Nations Official Records, 162

United Nations Publications, 162, 180

United Nations Relief and Rehabilitation Administration (UNRRA), 166

United Nations Security Council Index, 163

United Provinces of Agra and Oudh, 367, 369

United States: Administration on Aging, 32; Advisory Commission on Intergovernmental Relations, 32; Aeronautical Chart and Information Center, 33; Aeronautics, National Advisory Committee for, 65; Agency for International Development, 33; Aging, Administration on, 32; Aging, Office of, 32, 87; Agricultural Chemistry and Engineering, Bureau of, 36; Agricultural Experiment Stations, 46; Agricultural Marketing Service, 45, 46; Agricultural Research Administration, 33; Agricultural Research Service, 33; Agriculture, Dept. of, 47–48; Air Force, Dept. of the, 52–53; Alaska Forest Research Center, 59; Allegheny Forest Experiment Station, 60; American Ethnology, Bureau of, 36; Appalachian Forest Experiment Station, 61; Arms Control and Disarmament Agency, 34; Army, Dept. of the, 53–54; Army, Forces in the Pacific, 385; Army Material Command, 53; Army Supply and Maintenance Command, 53; Atomic Energy Commission, 34–35; Atomic Energy Commission, Laboratory, Ames, Iowa, 35;

Board of Governors of the Federal Reserve System, 35; Board on Geographic Names, 36; Budget, Bureau of the, 80;

Bureau of: Agricultural Chemistry and Engineering, 36; American Ethnology, 36; Chemistry and Soils, 36; Commercial Fisheries, 36; Education, 71; Employment Security, 36–37; Fisheries, 37, 57; Foreign and Domestic Commerce, 37, 358; Foreign Commerce, 37; Forestry, 58; International Business Operations, 37; International Commerce, 38; International Programs, 37; Labor, 38, 87; Labor Standards, 38; Labor Statistics, 38–39; Land Management, 39; Mines, 40; Plant Industry, Soils and Agricultural Engineering, 40; Public Roads, 40–41, 56; Reclamation, 41; Sport Fisheries and Wildlife, 41; the Budget, 80; the Census, 42, 80, 87, 146, 197–198, 246, 247, 272, 273, 279, 283, 287, 289, 290, 292, 296, 297, 299, 302, 304, 342, 359, 360, 374, 375, 376; Yards and Docks, 42, 70;

Business and Defense Services Administration, 42;

California Forest and Range Experiment Station, 60; Cambridge Research Laboratories, U.S. Air Force, 52; Census, *see* Bureau of the Census; Central States Forest Experiment Station, 59; Chemistry and Soils, Bureau of, 36; Child Development, Office of, 42; Children's Bureau, 42; Civil Aeronautics Administration, 55–56; Civil Aeronautics Authority, 55; Civil Aeronautics Board, 43; Civil and Defense Mobilization, Office of, 71; Civil Defense, Office of, 71; Civil Rights, Commission on, 45; Civil Service Commission, 43; Coast and Geodetic Survey, 43–44; Coast Guard, 44–45; Coast Survey, 43; Commerce, Dept. of, 48; Commercial Fisheries, Bureau of, 36; Commission on Civil Rights, 45; Commission on Intergovernmental Relations, 45;

Congress, 21–30; Joint Committee on Atomic Energy, 28; Joint Economic Committee, 28; House, 22, 26, 27; House, Committee on Banking and Currency, 28; House, Committee on Science and Astronautics, 29; House, Committee on the Judiciary, Subcommittee no. 5, 29; House, Committee on Un-American Activities, 29; House, Library, 27; House, Select Committee on Small Business, 29; Senate, 22, 23, 26, 27; Senate, Committee on Banking and Currency, 29; Committee on Government Operations, 14, 28; Senate, Committee on Small Business, 29; Senate, Committee on the Judiciary, 29; Senate, Committee on the Judiciary, Subcommittee to Investigate

☆ U.S. GOVERNMENT PRINTING OFFICE : 1976 O — 548–430